About Island Press

Since 1984, the nonprofit organization Island Press has been stimulating, shaping, and communicating ideas that are essential for solving environmental problems worldwide. With more than 1,000 titles in print and some 30 new releases each year, we are the nation's leading publisher on environmental issues. We identify innovative thinkers and emerging trends in the environmental field. We work with world-renowned experts and authors to develop cross-disciplinary solutions to environmental challenges.

Island Press designs and executes educational campaigns, in conjunction with our authors, to communicate their critical messages in print, in person, and online using the latest technologies, innovative programs, and the media. Our goal is to reach targeted audiences—scientists, policy makers, environmental advocates, urban planners, the media, and concerned citizens—with information that can be used to create the framework for long-term ecological health and human well-being.

Island Press gratefully acknowledges major support from The Bobolink Foundation, Caldera Foundation, The Curtis and Edith Munson Foundation, The Forrest C. and Frances H. Lattner Foundation, The JPB Foundation, The Kresge Foundation, The Summit Charitable Foundation, Inc., and many other generous organizations and individuals.

This publication is made possible in part with support from the Richard H. Driehaus Foundation.

The opinions expressed in this book are those of the author(s) and do not necessarily reflect the views of our supporters.

MAKING HEALTHY PLACES

MAKING HEALTHY PLACES

DESIGNING AND BUILDING FOR WELL-BEING, EQUITY, AND SUSTAINABILITY

SECOND EDITION

EDITED BY NISHA BOTCHWEY,
ANDREW L. DANNENBERG,
AND HOWARD FRUMKIN

ISLANDPRESS | Washington | Covelo

DOI: http://doi.org/10.5822/978-1-64283-158-0

Library of Congress Control Number: 2021945377

All Island Press books are printed on environmentally responsible materials.

Manufactured in the United States of America
10 9 8 7 6 5 4 3 2 1

Keywords: air quality, biophilic design, built environment, climate change, community design, community engagement, community resilience, COVID-19, equity, food access, gentrification, health care, health policy, healthy home, healthy school, land use, mental health, nature, nutrition, physical activity, research, social capital, technology, transportation, urban health, vulnerable populations, water quality, well-being, workplace

We dedicate this book to our students and the practicing professionals
who design and build healthy places in the United States and around the globe.

To our teachers, mentors, and colleagues,
who challenge and enrich our perspectives on healthy places.

To our families, who inspire us to advance healthy places every day.

To those, now and in the future, who make healthy places
for well-being, equity, and sustainability.

CONTENTS

PART IV: LOOKING FORWARD, TAKING ACTION

FOREWORD

Richard J. Jackson

In 1999, I was serving as the director of the National Center for Environmental Health at the US Centers for Disease Control and Prevention (CDC) in Atlanta. We focused on the environmental health of the United States, including human disease from air and water pollution, food contamination, environmental microbes and chemicals, radiation, global climate threats, and chronic disease epidemics with environmental origins such as inactivity, obesity, and depression. These challenges consumed my thinking.

Five years earlier my little family had moved to suburban Atlanta from Berkeley, California, where our sons had walked or bicycled to school and I had commuted to work by public transit. Parks and trails were readily accessible and well used. In Atlanta, our sons could not walk to school because there were no sidewalks within blocks of their schools. We drove them by car to participate in their sports and other activities. Half of the parks in Atlanta were primarily only accessible by car, implying that pedestrians were unwelcome. Not surprisingly, roadways were packed with cars and dangerous for bicyclists.

On a hot, humid day while driving on the seven-lane Buford Highway near my CDC office, I saw an older woman bent over with osteoporosis as she walked in the worn dirt patch next to the busy traffic lanes. She likely lived in one of the homes of the working poor nearby and was struggling to get her groceries home. An hour later during our CDC staff meeting, my thoughts kept returning to that elderly woman. I thought, if she collapsed and died next to that road, the cause of death would be listed as "Heatstroke," but the real causes of death were air pollution, lack of tree cover, and few transportation options. If she were killed by a truck on that busy road, the cause of death would be "Motor Vehicle Trauma," rather than the true causes: lack of sidewalks and inadequate public transportation. These underlying causes of death were amplified by poverty and discrimination, as well as the cultural indifference to the needs of the poor reflected in the dominance of the automobile in modern society.

Not long thereafter, I wrote a thought piece with my urban planner colleague, the late Christopher Kochtitzky, in which we speculated on the health impacts of urban sprawl, focusing on how the design of suburbs that center on the use of automobiles and discourage walking and bicycling for transportation may contribute to obesity and associated chronic diseases. We received fierce criticism accusing us of "junk science" from the homebuilder industry as well as from some members of Congress. We recognized they were correct to the extent that we had little evidence for our ideas because of the paucity of scientific research on the relationship of the built environment and health. In fact, some health leaders believed that the health harms from poor housing in crowded cities had been remedied by the automobile's takeover of the early twentieth century.

Working with public health friends and many new colleagues over the next several years, we reached out to federal agencies and national organizations that focus on urban planning, architecture, and transportation. We sought to learn how they view their missions and to convey our concerns about the potential health impacts of the decisions made by the professionals in those fields. We invited visits by individual researchers and policy leaders who were investigating related topics. We asked these new colleagues to present at our national public health meetings, and in turn, we were invited to present the public health viewpoint at their national planning, architecture, and transportation conferences.

In September 2003, we assembled the now widely cited full issue of the *American Journal of Public Health* on "Built Environment and Health," which included important contributions from these built environment fields. In 2004, we published *Urban Sprawl and Public Health*, the predecessor of the current book, summarizing what was then known about health impacts of urban sprawl. Subsequently in 2011, we published the first edition of the current book, *Making Healthy Places*, broadening the content to cover many aspects of health and the built environment beyond urban sprawl. The first edition of *Making Healthy Places* has been widely used for teaching public health and planning students in graduate-level health and built environment courses in the United States, Australia, and elsewhere, but the literature in the field has continued to grow exponentially. For example, a PubMed search of the public health and medical literature using the keywords "built environment" and "health" identifies 90 articles published in 2001–2005, 400 articles in 2006–2010, 1,138 articles in 2011–2015, and 2,741 articles in 2016–2020.

Today, the United States and most of the world are facing three major crises: the COVID-19 pandemic, health inequities and racism, and climate change. All these crises have health implications that can be addressed at least in part by built environment solutions.

The COVID-19 pandemic has highlighted numerous challenges, including how to maintain public transit systems at a time when social distancing is needed, widespread limitations in physical space and internet access for workers and their families spending more of their days at home, protection of essential workers in health care facilities and grocery stores, and the provision of places (often closed streets) for walking and biking to help maintain mental health. It is our hope that widespread vaccination will bring the pandemic under control in the United States by the time this book is published, and work is currently underway to improve the design of transit systems, offices, stores, medical facilities, and other components of the built environment so that our communities will be better prepared for future pandemics. Major governmental investments to replace decayed infrastructure and obsolete buildings and eliminate community-destroying urban roadways are being proposed, with associated invigoration of employment and the economy.

Throughout human existence, families and tribes have learned to be cautious and fearful of those who are newly arrived, who look different, and who have different customs and cultures. In some societies, one response has been to create a racist culture that discriminates against those not in the majority population and leads to substantial economic and health disparities. When these behaviors became illegal in the United States, they became hidden in processes designed to discriminate against persons of color, such as Jim Crow laws, poll taxes, and the redlining of mortgage availability. The disenfranchisement from education, employment, and the ability to create wealth for oneself and an economic legacy for family has perpetuated negative beliefs and marginalization. Substantial societal resources are regularly invested in the development and redevelopment of the built environment for schools, housing, parks, health care facilities, transportation systems, and other built structures. Political decisions that actively opt for more equitable investment of these societal resources for improving the built environment can begin to compensate for the years of underinvestment and disinvestment in disadvantaged communities.

The third major crisis, climate change, will prove to have the most severe and long-term impacts on the health of people throughout the world. Sea level rise, driven by melting glaciers and polar ice sheets and by thermal expansion of the oceans, threatens millions of coastal inhabitants who will be forced to migrate. As urban areas become unbearably hot, populations will move toward cooler regions and demand new housing, transportation, and commercial infrastructure. Atmospheric disruptions are leading to more heat waves, hurricanes, blizzards, floods, droughts, and wildfires with attendant losses of property and lives. Increased crowding and population movements will accelerate infectious disease threats as well as anti-immigrant backlash. Improvements in the design of buildings, transportation systems, energy systems, water systems, and communities can help promote healthy density and mitigate the contribution of the built environment to climate change, as well as help adapt the physical environment to be more resilient and sustainable in relation to the inevitable adverse impacts of climate change on health and society. A long-term view that recognizes the value of the triple bottom line—people, planet, prosperity—will yield global benefits.

The built environment is culture—and social policy—set in concrete both figuratively and literally. Just as the making of concrete requires large inputs of materials and energy and lasts decades or centuries, the built environment shapes behavior and the future culture of those who live and work within it. In medicine and public health, we work to optimize options because every intervention brings risks and benefits; so too should we seek to optimize the design and construction of our built environments. There is no better place to start than with knowledge, such as that offered in this second edition of *Making Healthy Places*.

For many years, I taught a course titled "Built Environment and Health" at the UCLA Fielding School of Public Health in a classroom that had operable windows. During a class break, I directed the students to go to the windows and describe the hilly campus street below. The students remarked on the speed of the vehicles going down the hill, the lack of bicycle lanes, and the bicyclists using the sidewalk to go up the hill. At that point I instructed the students to repeat after me, first in class and then loudly through the open window: "Just because it is this way doesn't mean it has to be this way."

We hope the readers of *Making Healthy Places* will absorb the knowledge and develop the skills needed to design and build healthy communities and to confront pandemics, inequities, and climate change. In doing so, our readers will become leaders in fulfilling the vision of "just because it is this way doesn't mean it has to be this way."

DISCLOSURE OF COMPETING INTERESTS
Richard J. Jackson discloses no competing interests.

PREFACE

Nisha Botchwey, Andrew L. Dannenberg, and Howard Frumkin

Since the first edition of *Making Healthy Places* was published in 2011, the field of healthy community design has evolved substantially. Further research has linked many community and building design features to specific health outcomes. Built environment approaches have become more prominent in addressing major societal problems, including health disparities, obesity, and climate change. Younger people are increasingly gravitating to walkable and livable communities, attracted by opportunity and vibrant lifestyles and reluctant to drive long distances to school, work, and amenities. Major professional associations in planning, transportation, and architecture have formed committees or working groups that focus on the links between those disciplines and health. Similar to prior efforts to certify green and sustainable buildings, and in response to consumer demand, healthy building and neighborhood certification schemes have emerged.

More students and professionals are now learning about and using the principles of healthy community design in their work. Universities are offering more graduate-level courses on health and the built environment, and some now offer concurrent degree programs in public health and urban planning. Planning agencies, health departments, and planning and design firms are hiring staff knowledgeable about the links between health and design. The increased availability of broadband internet services and smartphones has led to the growth of new industries—for example, e-bike and e-scooter shared micromobility programs; transportation network companies and rideshare, such as Uber and Lyft; and shared lodging options, from couch surfing to Airbnb and Vrbo—all of which influence land use, housing, community and economic development, and transportation planning. Autonomous and electric vehicles are being developed and may become common in the next decade or so (predictions vary widely), with substantial implications for transportation infrastructure, community design, traffic congestion, and air pollution. Wider use of new technologies such as sensors, GIS mapping capabilities, Google Street View, and drones is increasing the types and amounts of information available to built environment and public health professionals, as well as influencing how, when, and where people live, work, play, learn, and travel.

Also in this time, the rapidly intensifying climate crisis has focused attention on disaster vulnerability in the built environment, on the contributions of the built environment to greenhouse gas emissions, and on the need to build resilience. Increasing recognition of racism in the United States and globally has highlighted how historical patterns such as redlining manifest in contemporary environmental inequities; zip codes are stronger predictors of health than genetic codes. Most recently, the COVID-19 pandemic has upended work, shopping, education, and recreation—and therefore the form of workplaces, homes, streets, and transportation systems. In short, the built environment—and its effects on health, well-being, and sustainability—is a tremendously dynamic and consequential area of research and practice.

In developing this edition of *Making Healthy Places*, we sought to increase the diversity of voices of contributors by gender, race, and geography. The contributors include scholars and practitioners from across the globe in fields ranging from public health, planning, architecture, industrial design, and urban design to sustainability, social work, emergency medicine, and public policy. The new lead editor, Dr. Nisha Botchwey, is a planning and public health scholar and dean of the Hubert H. Humphrey School of Public Affairs. Her expertise in city planning, social justice, and community engagement complements the expertise of Drs. Andrew L. Dannenberg and Howard Frumkin in public and environmental health, medicine, and climate science.

In revising this book, we reviewed chapter-specific comments from more than two hundred students, primarily from urban planning and public health, who used *Making Healthy Places* as their textbook in Dr. Dannenberg's public health and built environment class at the University of Washington. The students' required "reading reflections" highlighted strengths (which we tried to retain) and weaknesses (which we tried to remedy), as well as the need for an updated edition.

For this second edition, we have updated the references throughout the book. Although most of the key messages in the first edition still hold true, we expanded the treatment of some topics that received less attention in 2011. We have integrated a more global perspective and added content on sustainability to most chapters. We added new chapters on the relation of the built environment to equity and health disparities, issues across the life span, climate change, resilience, new technology developments, and the evolving impacts of the COVID-19 pandemic.

The book's website, https://islandpress.org/makinghealthyplaces, has been updated to include chapter discussion questions, the glossary, and research opportunities from the text, as well as a discussion of the importance of disclosing competing interests. The website also includes a link to the Built Environment and Public Health Clearinghouse, bephc.org, which includes numerous resources for this field.

Consistent with best practices in peer-reviewed scientific journals, the editors asked all chapter contributors to indicate their competing interests (conflicts of interests). These have been defined as "financial and non-financial interests that could directly undermine, or be perceived to undermine the objectivity, integrity and value of a publication, through a potential influence on the judgements and actions of authors with regard to objective data presentation, analysis and interpretation."[1] We believe that disclosure of competing interests, real or perceived, is especially important in textbooks, as our authors select and curate large amounts of information—a process susceptible to bias—and many of our readers are students who are still developing their critical thinking skills. The importance of declaring competing interests is discussed more fully on this book's website, https://islandpress.org/makinghealthyplaces. The editors provide the following information for the period beginning three years prior to starting work on this book and while doing the editing:

- Nisha Botchwey reports serving as an unpaid board member or advisory committee member of the East Lake Family YMCA, Arthur M. Blank Family YMCA, Thriving Cities Project (Duke University), Center for Design and Health (University of Virginia), Stuart Weitzman School of Design Dean's Council (University of Pennsylvania), Voices for Healthy Kids Strategic Advisory Committee (American Heart Association); serving as a paid member of the AARP Livability Index Technical Committee; grant funding from the National Science Foundation, Robert Wood Johnson Foundation, and Enterprise Community Partners Southeast; and receipt of the William R. and June Dale Prize for Excellence in Urban and Regional Planning (California State Polytechnic University, Pomona).

- Andrew Dannenberg reports serving as an unpaid board or advisory committee member for the Seattle Bicycle Advisory Board, the Washington State Transportation Commission Autonomous Vehicle Work Group Health and Equity Subcommittee, the Transportation Research Board Transportation and Public Health Committee, the Center for Active Design Fitwel Advisory Council, and the Rails to Trails Conservancy Futures Council.
- Howard Frumkin reports serving as an unpaid board or advisory committee member for the Bullitt Foundation, the Seattle Parks Foundation, the Washington State Academy of Sciences, the Global Consortium on Climate and Health Education (Columbia University), EcoAmerica, the Harvard Center for Climate, Health, and the Global Environment, the Planetary Health Alliance (Harvard University), the Yale Center on Climate Change and Health, the University of Virginia School of Architecture Center for Design + Health, the Health Environment Research Agenda for Europe (Institut National de la Santé et de la Recherche Médicale and Instituto de Salud Global Barcelona), the European Centre on Environment and Human Health (University of Exeter), and the Medical Society Consortium on Climate and Health (George Mason University). As the preparation of this book neared completion, he began employment with the Trust for Public Land, a nonprofit organization that promotes parks, green space, and land conservation.

We hope these disclosures help ensure the integrity of every chapter in this book and become more common in textbooks in coming years.

We believe that "design matters" and that good design can lead to healthier and happier people. We hope that the readers of this book, especially students and practicing professionals in public health, planning, architecture, civil engineering, and transportation, will find the content to be useful as they consider the role of the built environment in advancing major societal goals such as health and well-being, equity, sustainability, and resilience.

REFERENCE

1. Nature Portfolio. Competing interests. No date. Accessed October 27, 2021. https://www.nature.com/nature-research/editorial-policies/competing-interests

ACKNOWLEDGMENTS

The process of planning, curating, writing, and editing this second edition of *Making Healthy Places* has deepened our commitment to healthy, equitable, and sustainable built environments. It has also filled us with gratitude for the many people who contribute to and support this important work. In particular, we thank the chapter authors. This edition has sixty-four chapter contributors, eighteen more than the first edition in 2011. These are global all-stars, expert in their fields and passionate about applying the insights in their chapters to the actual production and maintenance of healthy places. The contributors also share the editors' values of well-being, equity, and sustainability in both wealthy and low- and middle-income countries. They dedicated valuable time to writing during the difficult days of the COVID-19 pandemic, submitted informative chapters, responded to revision recommendations, and together made this book possible.

We also thank the many people who assisted us in the creation of the book. Our intelligent, dependable, and hard-working "book sherpa," Olivia Chatman, was an urban planning graduate student at the outset of the book project and is now a built environment professional. She managed files, coordinated contributor contributions, set up conference calls, tracked down image permissions, reformatted references, updated the accompanying website, and consistently kept us on track throughout the writing and production. Her project management skills, organization, and patience were phenomenal; every time we needed something, she readily directed us to it, created it, or sourced it. Yicong Yang and Meaghan McSorley read and provided helpful comments on many draft chapters. Madison Douglas assisted in the literature review for chapter 22. Bon Woo Koo readily redrew and adapted figures, created maps, and reformatted tables to provide a consistent presentation or high-quality images. Last but not least, we thank Heather Boyer, Annie Byrnes, and Sharis Simonian at Island Press for assisting us through the many stages of publishing this second edition.

We also recognize the hundreds of scholars, thought leaders, and doers whose research and practice are the building blocks of this field and this book. When the built environment–health connection was gaining attention at the start of this century, very few research studies addressed it. Today, a PubMed search on "built environment" and "health" yields more than four thousand hits. Communities have been transformed, students inspired, and careers redirected. The people who continue to lay this foundation are public health researchers and practitioners, architects, planners, landscape architects, public affairs scholars, elected and appointed officials, community leaders, academics, developers, and advocates. They are our colleagues and friends from all corners of the world. We stand on their shoulders, inspired by their curiosity and passion for healthy places.

Two colleagues deserve special mention. Dick Jackson, co-editor of the first edition of this book, was an early champion and thought leader regarding the links between health and the built environment. One of the founders of this field, he continues to inspire. Chris Kochtitzky, a planner with a long career in public health at the Centers for Disease Control and Prevention, was also a leader in the field, until his untimely death in 2020. We mourn his loss.

Each of us editors would like to thank the others. Co-editing a book is an intense process, with countless decisions to debate and settle. In working on this book, we juggled busy schedules, mismatched time zones, thousands of miles of geographic separation, and sometimes different instincts about how to present our material, yet we always enjoyed our time together and never stopped respecting and valuing one another's perspectives. In the end, we are closer than when we started. We are grateful for this collaboration and friendship.

Finally, we thank our families: Edward, Niara, Andrew, and Nicolas (Nisha); Kate, Ned and Jennifer, and Alice and Mike (Andy); and Joanne, Gabe, and Amara (Howie). We appreciate their inspiration, support, and love more than we can say.

CHAPTER 1

AN INTRODUCTION TO HEALTHY, EQUITABLE, AND SUSTAINABLE PLACES

Howard Frumkin, Andrew L. Dannenberg, and Nisha Botchwey

KEY POINTS

- The *environment* consists of the external (or nongenetic) factors—physical, nutritional, social, behavioral, and others—that act on humans, and the *built environment* is made up of the many aspects of their surroundings created by humans, such as buildings, neighborhoods, and cities.
- *Health* is conventionally defined as complete physical, mental, and social well-being. This definition extends beyond the absence of disease to include many dimensions of comfort and well-being.
- Clinicians care for individual patients. Public health professionals aim to improve health at the level of populations.
- The design professions include urban planning, architecture, landscape architecture, interior design, and transportation planning. Each focuses on an aspect of the built environment.
- Both the public health profession and the design professions took modern form during the nineteenth century in response to rapid population growth, industrialization and urbanization, and the resulting problems of the urban environment.
- Public health practice is evidence-based, relying heavily on assessment, surveillance, and data collection.

- Leading causes of suffering and death include heart disease, cancer, diabetes, stroke, injuries, and mental illness. Many of these causes are related to community design and associated behavioral choices.
- Even though public health has evolved as a distinct field from planning and architecture, these domains have numerous opportunities to collaborate, and this collaboration can lead to improved health, well-being, and sustainability in many ways.

INTRODUCTION

The citizens of Bay City were fed up. Getting across town to go to work or shopping had become an ordeal; the streets seemed perpetually clogged, and it was impossible to find parking. For people who had bought homes in the suburbs, life seemed to take place more and more in their cars—chauffeuring children to school and soccer games, driving long distances to stores, and worst of all, commuting to work. Meanwhile, the *Bay City Courier* reported a steady drumbeat of bad news: air quality was worsening, the health department reported a growing epidemic of obesity, and nearly every day there was a tragic car crash that killed or injured somebody.

The mayor, the city council, and the transportation department teamed up to address some of the quality-of-life problems. They envisioned an ambitious program of road building. Key components included a six-lane arterial highway along the bay shore, two new arterials crossing the city, and thousands of new parking spaces. Although this plan would destroy historic and beautiful bay views, sever a few older neighborhoods, and remove half of a prized city park, it would move traffic more effectively.

But the roads were never built. The local health department, urban planners, architects, physicians and nurses, park officials, historic preservationists, environmentalists, and neighborhood associations all came together in a remarkable display of unity. The coalition they formed proposed an alternative plan, one that centered on extensive pedestrian and bicycle infrastructure, investments in bus and light-rail transit and a bike-share program, mixed-use development along the bay shore, and investments in parks throughout the city. The plan emphasized equity and included policies to avoid displacing established communities and to ensure a mix of housing types. The cost of this alternative plan would be slightly less than that of the combined road projects, and it would create a similar number of construction jobs.

The alternative plan won the day. It took more than twenty years to implement, and it required considerable political leadership to stick with it during the inevitable cost overruns and budget crises. But after twenty years, a remarkable series of changes had ensued. The proportion of people walking or biking to work had risen from 3 percent to 14 percent, and the proportion of students walking or biking to school had risen from 5 percent to 21 percent. Transit ridership had increased more than fourfold. Traffic volume had actually decreased, air quality had improved marginally, and the epidemic of obesity had stabilized and was showing signs of reversing. Because many young families had moved into the city, the public schools had improved considerably and were now among the best in the state. And Bay City had become a destination city, attracting several prized high-tech and biotech firms because of its well-recognized commitment to environmental sustainability, health, equity, and quality of life.

This is a book about healthy places—places in which people can grow up, live, work, play, study, pray, and age in ways that allow them to be safe and healthy, to thrive, and to reach their full potential. It is also a book about environmentally sustainable places, because in the long run, there can be no healthy people without a healthy, intact planet.

A healthy place can be very small, such as an ergonomically designed chair that reduces strain on the back, shoulders, and arms. A healthy place can be immense, such as a planet with a relatively stable climate that allows ecosystems, forests, waterways, and farms to remain balanced and productive, in turn allowing humans to pursue their lives in relative safety, security, and predictability. The healthy places we explore in this book are intermediate in scale, ranging from buildings to metropolitan areas. Nearly all these places are designed and created by people—hence the term **built environment**.

In this chapter, we define some basic concepts in environment, health, planning, and design. While many of these concepts have their roots in early history, the modern health and design professions took shape during the last two centuries.

In *Merriam-Webster's Collegiate Dictionary*, the first definition for *environment* is straightforward: "the circumstances, objects, or conditions by which one is surrounded." The second definition is more intriguing: "the complex of physical, chemical, and biotic factors (as climate, soil, and living things) that act upon an organism or an ecological community and ultimately determine its form and survival." From a human health perspective, the environment includes all the external (or nongenetic) factors—physical, nutritional, social, behavioral, and others—that act on humans. The built environment consists of those settings designed, created, and maintained by human efforts—buildings, neighborhoods, food stores, public plazas, playgrounds, roadways, and more. Even seemingly natural settings, such as parks, are often part of the built environment because they have been sited, designed, and constructed by people. The built environment depends on supporting infrastructure systems for such necessities as energy, food, water, housing, and transportation, so these systems are also considered part of the built environment.

A frequently cited definition of **health** comes from the 1948 constitution of the World Health Organization: "A state of complete physical, mental, and social well-being and not merely the absence of disease or infirmity."[1] This broad definition goes well beyond a narrowly biomedical view to include many dimensions of thriving, including comfort, happiness, and well-being. However, some people who have adapted to disabilities or limitations (such as a chronic disease or a mobility limitation) object to this definition because they consider themselves to be healthy.

There are many health professions. Some are clinical and focus on providing **health care** (and preventive services) to individuals; examples include medicine, nursing, dentistry, physical therapy, and occupational therapy. Other health professions operate at the community level, focusing on populations. These professions collectively make up the **public health** field. Public health is dedicated to fulfilling society's interest in assuring conditions in which people can be healthy, conditions that range from effective health care systems to healthy environments. Public health professionals pursue this mission by assessing and monitoring community health to identify problems, developing public policies to solve these problems, and working to ensure access to appropriate and cost-effective care, including preventive care. These functions have been codified as the "ten essential public health services" (figure 1.1), a common framework for health departments and other service providers.

Although complementary, health care and public health are quite distinct. Health care delivers clinical services to individuals; public health focuses on entire populations.

Environmental health, a subfield of public health, focuses on the relationships between people and their environments. It aims to promote healthy environments and to control environmental hazards. Traditional environmental health focused on **sanitation** issues, such as clean water, sewage, waste management, food safety, and rodent control. Beginning during the Industrial Revolution, and accelerating in the 1970s (following publication of Rachel Carson's *Silent Spring*), environmental health expanded its scope to address chemical and radiological hazards, such as pesticides and air pollution. And most recently, beginning at about the turn of the century, environmental health has addressed cross-cutting issues, including the built environment, climate change, and sustainability—topics that are addressed in this book.

An important national framework for public health in the United States is *Healthy People*, a report issued every ten years by the Department of Health and Human Services (healthypeople.gov). Healthy People sets goals and objectives for health and well-being, along with indicators and measures. The latest version, *Healthy People 2030*, includes a section on Environmental Health, which addresses several toxins and heat, and another on Neighborhood and Built Environment, which addresses a range of issues, including air and water quality, housing, noise, toxic pollutants, healthy transportation, and motor vehicle safety.

The **design** professions are those that focus on the form, function, and operation of things and spaces. There are many design professions, ranging from industrial design (consumer products) to graphic design (visual images). In this book, we focus on several design professions whose work relates to the built environment. Each has specific training

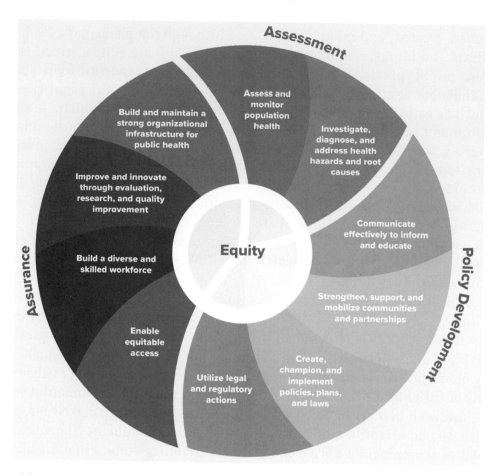

Figure 1.1. Public health professionals focus on providing ten essential public health services designed to maintain and improve health in communities.
Source: CDC, Public Health Professionals Gateway, 2020. https://www.cdc.gov/publichealthgateway/publichealthservices/essentialhealthservices.html. Reference to specific commercial products, manufacturers, companies, or trademarks does not constitute its endorsement or recommendation by the U.S. Government, Department of Health and Human Services, or Centers for Disease Control and Prevention.

pathways, professional organizations, and areas of specialization (table 1.1). Design professionals may work in many settings, including government (especially planners), the private sector (such as in real estate development), the nonprofit sector, and academia.

Architecture is the design profession that operates at the scale of buildings. Architects may specialize in a certain class of buildings, such as commercial or residential structures, or even more specifically, hospitals or laboratories. Many architects now incorporate **green building** principles, such as energy efficiency and the use of renewable resources.

Urban planning (also known as town planning, city planning, or city and regional planning) is dedicated to envisioning, planning, designing, and monitoring the layout and function of cities—sometimes referred to as **citymaking**. Planners may use the tools of **urban design** at the scale of projects within a larger community plan.

Transportation planning (along with the closely related field of transportation engineering) focuses on transportation infrastructure—not only streets and highways, but also mass transit and the infrastructure for nonmotorized travel, such as sidewalks and bike paths.

Civil engineering is the field of engineering focused on the design, construction, and maintenance of infrastructure such as bridges, roads, canals, and dams. A related field, **environmental engineering**, empha-

Table 1.1. Key subjects taught to students and common credentials in public health, planning, architecture, and landscape architecture.

Profession	Topics Studied	Common Credentials (US)
Public health	Biostatistics Environmental health sciences Epidemiology Health policy and management Social and behavioral sciences	Master's degree in public health such as MPH or MSPH; doctoral degree such as PhD or DrPH
Planning (including transportation planning)	History of city planning Planning theory Planning and zoning law Urban spatial structure Transportation and land use Environmental considerations at the regional and municipal scales Tools and methods, such as statistical analysis, geographical information systems, demographics, participatory planning	Master's degree in planning, such as MCP, MUP, MSP, or MCRP Certification by the American Institute of Certified Planners (AICP)
Architecture	History of architecture Design process Construction materials and methods Design of cities Materials and energy in buildings Ergonomics Universal design at the site, building, and interior space scales	Bachelor's or master's degree in architecture Registered architect (requirements vary by state)
Landscape architecture	History of landscape architecture Design process City planning Construction materials and methods Environmental best practice Ecological systems Graphic communication Design of public spaces Universal design at the site scale	Bachelor's or master's degree in landscape architecture Registered landscape architect (requirements vary by state)
Civil and environmental engineering	Surveying Transport engineering, road and rail design Hydrology, fluid mechanics, drainage, and sewer design Solid mechanics and structural engineering Geotechnical engineering Environmental engineering Building materials and construction engineering	Bachelor's or master's degree in civil and environmental engineering Professional engineer (license requirements vary by state)

Note: Each of these professions has a body of knowledge specific to its discipline. Students in each discipline are increasingly encouraged to take courses in the allied professions.

sizes environmental performance. Civil and environmental engineers might collaborate in designing stormwater systems and working to prevent erosion, conserve water, and reduce contamination of rivers and streams—all goals that directly or indirectly promote human health.

Landscape architecture focuses on the arrangement of natural and built elements on the land, from the design of parks to plans for large-scale watershed management.

These professions are all related. The health professions, in promoting health, may consider features of the built environment such as **land use** or transportation strategies. The design professions may identify health as a key goal of their work. In this book, we explore why and how these professions need to collaborate to achieve safe, healthy settings for all people.

HEALTH AND THE BUILT ENVIRONMENT: ANCIENT ORIGINS

Designing and building safe and healthy places must have been a goal for our earliest ancestors (even if they didn't phrase it quite that way). The elements can be harsh, and we know that our forebears sought protection in caves or built crude shelters.

The greatest of ancient civilizations were built according to complex plans, from the scale of buildings to the scale of vast cities. In ancient city remains across the world, there is evidence of grid-like, hierarchical street arrangements, of monuments and public spaces, of terraces and aqueducts carefully built to manage water flow, and of sophisticated building designs. In the ruins of past civilizations from India to Rome and from Greece to Egypt to South America, archaeologists have found the remains of water pipes, toilets, and sewage lines, some dating back more than four thousand years.[2] Many of these achievements reflected efforts to protect health.

Modern health challenges in the built environment often have ancient origins. Indoor air quality has been a long-standing challenge;

there is evidence in the sinus cavities of ancient cave dwellers of high levels of smoke in their caves.[3] Mold was apparently a scourge in some ancient buildings, described in vivid detail in the Old Testament as a greenish or reddish "plague" on walls (Leviticus 14:33–45). European history was changed forever when rats spread bubonic plague (the "Black Death") in fourteenth-century cities.[4,5] Modern cities continue to struggle with water and sewage management (see chapter 6), with indoor air quality and mold (see chapter 4), and with infestations of rats and other pests,[6] whose control depends in large part on modifications to and treatment of the built environment.

BIRTH OF MODERN PUBLIC HEALTH

Modern public health took form largely during the age of industrialization, with the rapid growth of cities in the seventeenth and eighteenth centuries. "The urban environment," wrote one historian,

> fostered the spread of diseases with crowded, dark, unventilated housing; unpaved streets mired in horse manure and littered with refuse; inadequate or non-existing water supplies; privy vaults unemptied from one year to the next; stagnant pools of water; ill-functioning open sewers; stench beyond the twentieth-century imagination; and noises from clacking horse hooves, wooden wagon wheels, street railways, and unmuffled industrial machinery.[7(p22)]

Epidemics of cholera, typhoid, yellow fever, and diphtheria erupted with regularity. Social reformers, scientists and engineers, physicians, and public officials responded to these conditions in various ways across the industrializing nations.[2,8-10]

Many interventions by early public health leaders focused on the built environment. For example, regular outbreaks of cholera and other diarrheal diseases in the eighteenth and nineteenth centuries[11] highlighted the need for water systems with clean source water, treatment including filtration, and distribution through pipes. Similarly, sewage management became a necessity, especially after the provision of piped water and the use of toilets created large volumes of contaminated liquid waste.[8,10]

Another important impetus to public health action was the workplace—a unique and often exceedingly dangerous built environment (see chapter 13). Although the air, water, and soil near industrial sites could become badly contaminated in ways that would be familiar to modern environmental professionals,[9,12] some of the most dire conditions were found within the factories, memorably called "dark Satanic mills" by poet William Blake.

Charles Turner Thackrah (1795–1833), an English physician, became interested in the diseases he observed among the poor in the city of Leeds. In 1831, he described many work-related hazards in a short book with a long title: *The Effects of the Principal Arts, Trades and Professions, and of Civic States and Habits of Living, on Health and Longevity, with Suggestions for the Removal of Many of the Agents which Produce Disease and Shorten the Duration of Life*. The notion that people's physical circumstances can determine their health and that some groups of people are disproportionately sickened sounds obvious today, but in Thackrah's time it was revolutionary. Public outcry and the efforts of reformers such as Thackrah led England to promulgate the Factory Act in 1833 and the Mines Act in 1842, which began to improve working conditions. In the United States, the pioneering physician Alice Hamilton (1869–1970) documented links between workplace conditions and illness among miners, tradesmen, and factory workers, first in Illinois (where she directed that state's Occupational Disease Commission from 1910 to 1919) and later from an academic position at Harvard. Her work helped establish that workplaces could be dangerous places.

A key development in the seventeenth through nineteenth centuries was the quantitative observation of population health—the beginnings of **epidemiology**. With the tools of epidemiology, observers could systematically attribute certain disease outcomes to specific environmental exposures. John Graunt (1620–1674), an English merchant and haberdasher, analyzed London's weekly death records and published his *Natural and Political Observations upon the Bills of Mortality* in 1662. Graunt's work was one of the first formal analyses of vital statistics and a pioneering example of demography. Almost two centuries later, when the British Parliament created the Registrar-General's Office (now the Office of Population Censuses and Surveys) and William Farr (1807–1883) became its compiler of abstracts, the link between vital statistics and environmental health was forged. Farr described fertility and mortality patterns, identifying rural-urban differences, variations between acute and chronic illnesses, and seasonal trends and implicating certain environmental conditions in illness and death. Farr's 1843 analysis of mortality in Liverpool led Parliament to pass the Liverpool Sanitary Act of 1846, which created a sanitary code for Liverpool and a public health infrastructure to enforce it.

Farr's contemporary Edwin Chadwick (1800–1890) was a pioneer in combining social epidemiology with environmental health. At the age of thirty-two, Chadwick was appointed to a royal commission that helped to reform Britain's Poor Laws. Five years later, following epidemics of typhoid fever and influenza, the British government asked him to investigate sanitation. His classic report, *Sanitary Conditions of the Labouring Population*, published in 1842, drew a clear link between living conditions—in particular overcrowded, filthy homes, open cesspools and privies, impure water, and miasmas—and health and made a strong case for public health reform. In 1848, the Public Health Act created the Central Board of Health, with power to impanel local boards that would oversee street cleaning, trash collection, and water and sewer systems. Public health and urban planning were at this point inseparable. As sanitation commissioner, Chadwick advocated such innovations as urban water systems, toilets in every house, and transfer of sewage to outlying farms where it could be used as fertilizer.[13] Chadwick's work helped to establish the role of public works—sanitary engineering projects—in protecting public health. It also presaged a theme that would be forcefully argued 150 years later with the rise of the **environmental justice** movement: that disenfranchised groups, usually low-income and racial and ethnic minority and Indigenous communities, are disproportionately exposed to harmful environmental conditions (see chapter 9).

The physician John Snow (1813–1858) was, like William Farr, a founding member of the London Epidemiological Society. Snow gained immortality in the history of public health for what was essentially an environmental epidemiology study. During an 1854 outbreak of cholera in London, he observed a far higher incidence of disease among people who lived near or drank from the Broad Street pump than among people with other sources of water (figure 1.2). He persuaded local authorities to remove the pump handle, and the epidemic in that part of the city soon abated. (There is some evidence that it may have been ending anyway, but this does not diminish the soundness of Snow's approach.)

An important development in public health was the formation of departments of health (often originally called boards of health) at the municipal and state levels, a trend that blossomed during the late nineteenth century. The US Congress formed a National Board of Health in 1879 to regulate quarantines at US borders and to advise states. These government agencies reflected the view among both elected leaders and the public that government had a legitimate and crucial role in protecting public health. The American Public Health Association was formed in 1872 and marked growing professionalization in the public health field. To this day, primary responsibility for public health in the United States defaults to state and local authorities,

consistent with the Tenth Amendment to the US Constitution. The federal public health apparatus—consisting of the Centers for Disease Control and Prevention (CDC), the National Institutes of Health (NIH), the Food and Drug Administration (FDA), the Environmental Protection Agency (EPA), and other agencies—performs national functions such as disease surveillance, research, and regulation and supports state and local counterparts. This fragmentation has long been identified as a barrier to effective public health functioning,[14] as exemplified by the COVID-19 response. In other countries, public health responsibility is substantially more centralized and coordinated.

More than a century after outbreaks of infectious disease motivated the formation of public health agencies, public health threats have evolved, and so have the roles of these agencies. Sanitary reform and other advances have been remarkably successful; of the nearly thirty years of increased life span the United States had achieved by the late twentieth century, only five were due to medical interventions, and the remainder reflected public health interventions, many of them environmental.[15,16] Persistent, emerging, and reemerging infectious diseases such as flu, HIV-AIDS, and COVID-19 continue to be a challenge, despite the predictions of some optimists in the early days of antibiotics that infections would soon be conquered. We humans share the planet with microbes and will always confront infections. But chronic diseases, including heart disease, cancer, and stroke, have overtaken infectious diseases as leading causes of death (table 1.2)[17,18] and suffering. Injuries, especially in relation to motor vehicle crashes, are recognized as a major public health burden. Ailments such as diabetes, depression, arthritis, and asthma take a huge toll. Risk factors such as sedentary lifestyles and obesity—products of a complex web of genetic, behavioral, and environmental factors—are key targets of public health interventions. These developments have all

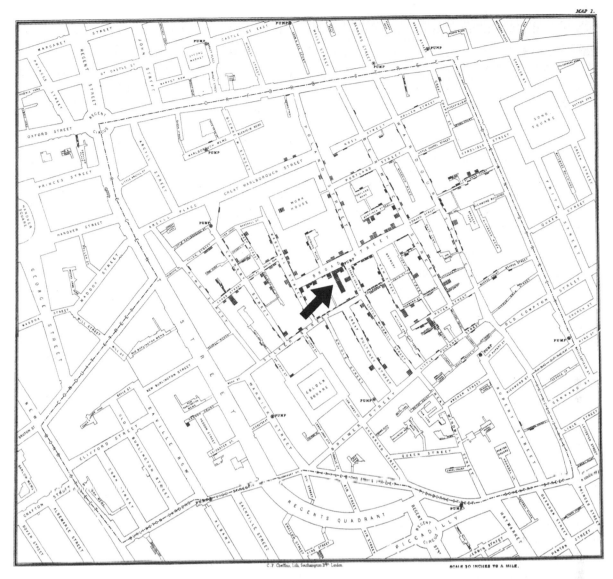

Figure 1.2. In a classic epidemiological investigation of a cholera outbreak in London in 1854, physician John Snow implicated a specific source of disease by documenting that cholera cases (indicated by black dots) clustered around the water pump on Broad Street (arrow).
Source: Public domain. Obtained from Wikimedia Commons via https://commons.wikimedia.org/wiki /File:Snow-cholera-map-1.jpg.

contributed to the increasing public health focus on the built environment.

This brief history of public health helps highlight several essential concepts at the interface of health and the built environment:

- Government has a key role in ensuring healthy conditions, including a healthy built environment.
- Eliminating socioeconomic inequities is fundamental to achieving public health.
- A primary role for public health is collecting and analyzing population health data and basing public health interventions on those data.
- Science has a central place in advancing public health; this includes developing empirical evidence of the effectiveness of interventions.
- A healthy built environment—together with multilevel approaches such as education and regulation—can address a range of health threats, including some of those most prevalent in today's societies.

Table 1.2. Leading causes of death in the United States, 1900, 1950, and 2019.[a-c]

Ranking	1900	1950	2019
1	Pneumonia and influenza	**Diseases of the heart**	**Diseases of the heart**
2	**Tuberculosis**	**Cancer**	**Malignant neoplasms**
3	Diarrhea, enteritis, and ulceration of the intestines	**Stroke**	**Unintentional injuries**
4	**Diseases of the heart**	**Unintentional injuries**	**Chronic lower respiratory diseases**
5	**Stroke**	Certain diseases of early infancy	**Stroke**
6	Nephritis, all forms	Influenza and pneumonia, except pneumonia of newborn	Alzheimer's disease
7	**Unintentional injuries**	**Tuberculosis**	**Diabetes**
8	**Cancer**	**General arteriosclerosis**	Nephritis, nephrotic syndrome, and nephrosis
9	Senility	Chronic and unspecified nephritis and other renal sclerosis	Influenza and pneumonia
10	Diphtheria	**Diabetes mellitus**	Suicide

Note: Causes in boldface may be related to the built environment.

a. Anderson R. Deaths: leading causes for 2000. In: *National Vital Statistics Reports*. Centers for Disease Control and Prevention; 2002:52(9).

b. Centers for Disease Control and Prevention, National Center for Health Statistics. Leading causes of death, 1900–1998. No date. Accessed October 26, 2021. https://www.cdc.gov/nchs/data/dvs/lead1900_98.pdf

c. Kochanek KD, Xu J, Arias E. Mortality in the United States, 2019. National Center for Health Statistics, December 2020. NCHS data brief 395. Accessed October 26, 2021. https://www.cdc.gov/nchs/products/databriefs/db395.htm

CONTEMPORARY PRACTICE OF PUBLIC HEALTH

Several concepts are central to understanding contemporary public health (as well as health care). The first is **evidence-based practice**—the idea that empirical evidence should be systematically collected, evaluated, and used as the basis for decisions. Whether the issue is a clinician's advice to take a particular blood pressure medication or a health commissioner's advice to invest in bicycle trails, the ideal evidence base should demonstrate **efficacy** (does it work?), **safety** (is it reasonably free from adverse effects?), and **cost-effectiveness** (does it deliver value for money?).

Sometimes available evidence does not permit strong, unambiguous conclusions. In such cases, health professionals invoke the **precautionary principle**, a policy of protecting the public from harm even when full scientific understanding of a hazard is not available. For example, many health professionals support the removal of bisphenol A from polycarbonate plastic food containers owing to concerns about reproductive toxicity and cancer, even though the evidence base is not yet complete.

A core activity in public health is surveillance. Public health **surveillance** is defined as the ongoing systematic collection, analysis, and interpretation of data essential to the planning, implementation, and evaluation of public health practice. Federal, state, and local public health agencies routinely collect information on births and deaths (vital statistics), health behaviors (such as smoking and diet), exposures (such as air pollution), and the occurrence of illnesses and injuries. They then disseminate these data to those responsible for prevention and disease control so that the information can be applied in a timely manner.[19] Traditionally, surveillance includes **mortality** information—causes of and age at death—which allows health officials to identify top killers, follow trends, and target preventive efforts. Surveillance also includes information about **morbidity**, the occurrence of illness and injury in a community—an important parameter given that many ailments, from arthritis to depression to hypertension, cause considerable suffering without necessarily causing death. **Incidence** refers to the rate of onset of new cases of a disease per unit of time, whereas **prevalence** refers to the proportion of a population suffering from a disease at a given point in time. Surveillance often extends to aspects of the built environment outside of traditional public health but highly relevant to health, such as levels of walking and cycling, quality of housing, and density of neighborhood green space.

A challenge for health officials is comparing the burdens of different diseases. Just measuring mortality, as shown in table 1.2, does not capture the full extent of suffering and disability caused by a disease. For example, anxiety, arthritis, and asthma rarely kill people, but they cause considerable suffering. And a young man dying in a car crash at age twenty-one is different than an elderly man dying of heart disease at age ninety-one, in that more potential years of life are lost. One metric used to address this challenge is the **disability-adjusted life year** (DALY), a measure of overall disease burden. One DALY is one year of healthy life lost due to either disability or premature death. Metrics such as this can help with setting public health priorities when, for example, deciding whether to allocate scarce resources to fighting a rare but fatal disease or a common but mild disease.

The science base of public health relies heavily on **epidemiology**—the study of the distribution and causes of health outcomes in specified populations and the application of this study to control health problems. Surveillance is an integral component of epidemiology, but the practice of epidemiology goes beyond surveillance to identify associations among risk factors, disease, and preventive strategies. For example, epidemiological research revealed the linkages between smoking and cancer, lead paint and cognitive and behavioral deficits, and seat belt use and injury prevention.

A range of epidemiological studies exists, each with its own strengths and weaknesses. The most definitive study design is the **randomized controlled trial (RCT)**—a true scientific experiment in which investigators manipulate variables. For example, Group A might receive a certain medication and Group B a placebo to determine whether the medication outperforms the placebo in preventing or treating a disease. Such RCTs are rarely possible with regard to the built environment. However, randomization sometimes occurs unintentionally—a situation called a **natural experiment**—and alert investigators can take advantage of it. For example, residents in a Chicago public housing project were randomly assigned to apartments, some near trees and some not, and researchers used this circumstance to evaluate the effect of trees on residents' health and well-being[20] (see chapter 16).

Most epidemiological studies of environmental factors are *descriptive*, relying on observational data. When such a study uses group data instead of data on individual people, it is called an **ecological study** (not to be confused with the scientific discipline of ecology). For example, one ecological study correlated the extent of sprawl in different cities with rates of motor vehicle fatalities.[21] More definitive are studies that use data on individuals. Another kind of descriptive study is the **cross-sectional study**, in which data on exposures and health outcomes are collected at the same time within a defined population. Cross-sectional studies can be carried out rapidly and can provide useful clues, but they cannot determine whether the outcome came before or after the exposure—a barrier to concluding that an association is causal. For example, a city might survey residents to determine whether they have sidewalks in front of their house (exposure) and their levels of physical activity (health outcome). If the study showed residents with sidewalks to be more physically active, it would be unclear whether sidewalks caused more physical activity or whether physically active people chose to live in places with sidewalks.

Analytical studies provide stronger support for causal associations. A **case-control study** compares people with and without a certain *condition* to assess whether certain exposures are associated with the condition. A **cohort study** takes the reverse approach, comparing people with and without a certain *exposure*, to assess whether the exposure is associated with particular health outcomes. In both of these study designs, a crucial feature is comparing different groups to each other to look for associations between exposures and health outcomes.

Accurate comparisons can be derailed by **bias**. Bias occurs, for example, when participants in a study do not represent the larger population of interest or when data collected about exposures or outcomes are systematically skewed. Epidemiological results may also be invalid due to **confounding**, which occurs when a third factor, something other than the exposure and outcome, distorts the observed association between exposure and outcome. For example, in a study on lung cancer and commuting travel mode, if drivers smoke more than other commuters, smoking could act as a confounder, giving the appearance that driving is linked to lung cancer. Epidemiologists use various analytical methods to minimize bias and confounding.

Public health professionals assess epidemiological data for evidence of **causation**. In 1965, the British epidemiologist Sir Austin Bradford Hill proposed criteria that are often referenced in this assessment.[22] Under the Hill criteria, causation is supported if the association between exposure and outcome has been found consistently in different places and by different investigators, if the association is strong, and if there is a **dose-response relationship**—meaning that more exposure leads to more of the health outcome. A clear temporal relationship, demonstrating that the exposure preceded the health outcome, needs to be established. Finally, the association should be biologically plausible. These factors, considered together, help researchers assess the likelihood that an association is causal.

In public health as in many scientific fields, single studies are informative, but when many studies converge on a conclusion, the evidence is far more compelling, underlining the importance of **evidence synthesis**. A **systematic review** takes a structured approach to identifying and combining available studies; one such method, the **meta-analysis,** statistically combines individual studies to quantify the overall effect found in the literature. These methods are invaluable; by attempting systematically to reduce bias, they distill rigorous conclusions from available data. Different groups exist that systematically collect and evaluate available evidence. One leading example is the Cochrane Collaboration, a global network of thousands of researchers based in the United Kingdom that synthesizes medical and public health evidence (cochrane.org). Another is the *Guide to Community Preventive Services* (or *Community Guide*), based at the CDC (thecommunityguide.org), and still another, with an environmental focus, is the Collaboration for Environment Evidence (environmentalevidence.org). These sources offer authoritative summaries of interventions such as urban design principles and walk-to-school programs. Choosing interventions that have consistent evidence of success affords decision-makers and communities a degree of confidence that an intervention will work.

The public health goal of generating such data is prevention. Three types of prevention exist. Most public health prevention efforts are **primary prevention**, stopping illness and injury from occurring. Traffic calming near schools is an example of primary prevention of pedestrian injuries, while social distancing is a primary prevention strategy for airborne infections. **Secondary prevention** consists of detecting and treating disease early to avoid progression (by using Pap smears, for example), and **tertiary prevention** reduces the impact of an existing disease (through rehabilitation after an injury, for example); these efforts are performed mainly by health care providers. Public health prevention activities include modifying environmental exposures, offering education and community outreach, developing policies that promote health, enforcing laws, providing links to clinical care, and maintaining a competent public health workforce. These strategies can be combined to increase effectiveness. For example, in an effort to increase physical activity, public health, transportation, and law enforcement officials might work together to construct sidewalks and safe crossings, begin a physical activity education campaign, and enforce traffic laws. Health professionals conduct **program evaluations** of health programs and policies to determine if they achieve their goals and if program modification, expansion, or discontinuation is warranted.

Health disparities are a central concept in public health. Health disparities exist when populations differ in their exposure to risk factors; in their level of disease, injury, or disability; or in their access to health care. Factors associated with health disparities include race, ethnicity, and social class. Health disparities often reflect entrenched injustices, long-standing discriminatory practices, and racism—often expressed through features of the built environment. One example is historical **redlining**—the discriminatory practice, from the 1930s through passage of the 1968 Fair Housing Act and the 1977 Community Reinvestment Act, of grading minority neighborhoods as "red" or high risk for mortgage lenders. Research has linked redlining to increased risks of asthma, cancer, violence, COVID-19, and poor general health in affected neighborhoods two or three generations later. Many of these redlined neighborhoods remain segregated, and they often sustain disproportionate exposure to multiple environmental risks such as substandard housing, poor air quality, poor transit service, absence of parks and green space, and toxic chemicals.[23] Health disparities are explored in detail in chapter 9.

ORIGINS OF MODERN CITY PLANNING

Although cities have been planned and buildings designed and built for millennia, modern city planning was forged in the same urban crucibles that gave rise to modern public health. The cities of the eighteenth and nineteenth centuries, growing rapidly and chaotically, triggered a range of responses that set the stage for modern planning. Full histories of planning are available elsewhere;[24,25] here we present a brief summary to highlight some important roots.

One response to chaotic urban growth was recognition of the need for sanitary engineering for water, sewage, and waste management in cities. The concept of an urban sewage system—requiring a water supply, an engineered network of pipes, and carefully designed street surfaces to achieve drainage—required, as one historian wrote, "the coordinated reconstruction of urban places on a citywide scale."[26(p86)] The engineering approach—the analysis of complex systems; the forecasting of future needs; the parallel planning of utilities, land use, transportation, and commerce—was a natural precursor to multifaceted (if not comprehensive) city plans.[27]

As large-scale engineering projects unfolded, civil engineers consolidated their professional standing, forming professional organizations and networks. This corresponded to a more general growth of professionalization and bureaucratization of government during the Progressive Era, from the 1890s to the 1920s. In the United States, reformers hoped that these trends would replace graft with efficiency and deliver more effective services to the public. In the United Kingdom, the Town and Country Planning Association was founded in 1899; ten years later, the Housing and Town Planning Act required municipalities to undertake town planning. City manager forms of government sprang up around the United States, promising administrative skill and discipline. These developments, too, paved the way for modern planning, but they were not entirely positive in their effects. A technocratic, top-down approach based on the authority of experts could impede community involvement and often discriminated against ethnic and racial minorities.[28]

A contrasting movement with a very different spirit also set the stage for urban planning: the work of social reformers who reacted against the injustices of urban life.[29] These were exemplified by the *settlement house movement*, best remembered through Hull House in Chicago.[30] Educated, idealistic volunteers, almost all women, chose to live in slums where they worked to improve living conditions for their neighbors by providing teaching, child care, food, public baths, playgrounds, kitchens, and other resources. Many of the settlement houses also documented conditions in their communities, from Alice Hamilton's focus on workplaces, started while she lived at Hull House, to careful surveys of neighborhoods and especially of tenement housing. Hull House founder Jane Addams (1860–1935) provided a typical set of observations in her memoir: "The streets are inexpressibly dirty, the number of schools inadequate, sanitary legislation unenforced, the street lighting bad, the paving miserable and altogether lacking in the alleys and smaller streets, and the stables beyond description. Hundreds of houses are unconnected with the street sewer."[30(p98)] Such documentation, along with the more quantitative surveys undertaken by some settlement houses, foreshadowed the assessments city planners would carry out years later.

The settlement house movement had its counterparts in the emerging urban planning profession. In 1909, Benjamin Clark Marsh (1878–1952), author of *An Introduction to City Planning: Democracy's Challenge in the American City*, placed social justice at the center of his agenda, arguing that city planning—including strict regulation of private land development—was necessary for the amelioration of urban poverty and misery.

Another nineteenth-century precursor to modern city planning sprang from the 1893 Chicago World's Fair. The fairgrounds design, by Daniel Burnham (1846–1912) and Frederick Law Olmsted (1822–1903), embodied neoclassical and Beaux Arts design principles: grandeur, monumentalism, symmetry, order, and balance. Burnham's ambition did not apply only to buildings: "Make no little plans," he famously declared, "they have no magic to stir men's blood. Make big plans; aim high in hope and work. Remember that our sons and grand-sons are going to do things that would stagger us. Let your watchword be order and your beacon beauty."[24(p188)]

Thus a legacy of the Chicago World's Fair was the **City Beautiful movement**, which influenced city design for several decades in Chicago, Washington, DC, Detroit, and elsewhere. Driven less by engineering necessity than by a vision of elite culture and monumental grandeur as civic virtue, it was a movement dedicated to a "White City" aesthetic[31] that would "win hegemony over the emerging national culture."[32] In approaching the city as a canvas on which good form could be brushed, the City Beautiful movement helped set planning on a path to marginalizing low-income and non-White communities.

Olmsted pioneered the field now known as landscape architecture with work that began before the Civil War and continued through the end of the nineteenth century.[33,34] Some of his most famous creations were urban parks (including New York's Central Park and

Montreal's Mount Royal Park), but he also designed parklike settings such as college campuses (Stanford, Berkeley, Cornell, Smith, Bryn Mawr, and Mount Holyoke), estates (Asheville's Biltmore Estate), and hospitals (Maclean Hospital in Belmont, Massachusetts). He designed systems of green space and roadways such as Boston's Emerald Necklace, landscaping near the US Capitol, and the park systems of Buffalo and Milwaukee. He designed one of the first planned communities in the United States: Riverside, Illinois. This remarkable body of work left a legacy of urban form, conceived on a large scale and executed with the support of municipal governments, that combined topography, vegetation, water, transportation, and other elements.

With these developments, urban planning came into its own as a profession in the early years of the twentieth century. The First National Conference on City Planning and the Problems of Congestion was held in Washington, DC, in 1909. At these early conferences, the social agenda, including public housing, development regulations, and tax policy designed to reduce poverty, collided with a more technical approach whose goals were efficiency and economic performance. The latter approach prevailed; for the second conference, in 1910, "the Problems of Congestion" was dropped from the title, and the fifth conference, titled "The City Scientific," cemented the professional momentum toward the technical.[28] The American City Planning Institute (a forerunner of today's American Planning Association) was founded in 1917.[35]

In the early twentieth century, zoning emerged as a key tool for urban planners that would have major impacts on health. Private landowners wanted noxious land uses such as slaughterhouses and factories to be banned from residential and commercial land in which they had invested. This gave rise to the concept of separation of land uses, with distinct zones established for residential, commercial, industrial, recreational, and other uses. In addition to supporting land values, public health was an explicit goal of zoning. For example, when the city of Euclid, Ohio, adopted a zoning scheme that prevented Ambler Realty from developing land for industrial purposes, Ambler sued, claiming that the ordinance amounted to an unjustifiable government **taking**. The case went to the US Supreme Court. An amicus curiae brief from the National Conference on City Planning and other groups argued for zoning based on public health considerations: "the man who seeks to place the home for his children in an orderly neighborhood, with some open space and light and fresh air and quiet, is not motivated so much by considerations of taste or beauty as by the assumption that his children are likely to grow mentally, physically and morally more healthful in such a neighborhood than in a disorderly, noisy, slovenly, blighted and slum-like district.[36(P545)] The Supreme Court ruled in favor of Euclid in 1926, establishing zoning as a central technique of US city planning.

An important development was the growth of the **regional plan**. This represented not only an expanded scale from that of the city but also an appreciation of the ecosystem context of human activities. Inspired by Scottish biologist Patrick Geddes (1854–1932), regional planners looked at topography, hydrology, flora, industrial development, and human settlement as a system. Lewis Mumford (1895–1990), for example, defined a *region* as "any geographic area that possesses a certain unity of climate, soil, vegetation, industry, and culture." He advocated planning on a regional scale "so that all its sites and resources, from forest to city, from highland to water level, may be soundly developed, … [considering] people, industry and the land as a single unit."[37(P151)] Mumford was a founder of the Regional Planning Association of America in 1923, together with architects, developers, and financiers. Early regional planners held an optimistic view of the automobile; they viewed it as a breakthrough technology that would distribute population rationally and help balance land uses over broad areas.

Another pioneer of landscape architecture was Ian McHarg (1920–2001). Born in the gritty industrial city of Glasgow, McHarg cherished the surrounding Scottish countryside. As a longtime professor at the University of Pennsylvania, he applied ecological thinking to human placemaking, calling for integration of watersheds, forests, soil, and other elements of the natural world into the design of human habitat. His highly influential 1969 book, *Design with Nature*, fused urban planning, landscape architecture, and environmentalism.

Grand schemes were to become a signature product of planners and architects, echoing Burnham's injunction. One of the best known examples was the **Garden City movement**, launched in the United Kingdom by Sir Ebenezer Howard (1850–1928) in the final years of the nineteenth century. This movement was inspired by utopian literature of the time; Howard envisioned highly idealized garden cities on concentric circular footprints, each housing 32,000 people on 9,000 acres (about 3,600 hectares), combining residential and commercial buildings, open spaces, public parks, and broad radial boulevards and achieving economic self-sufficiency. Few places ever implemented this model exactly, but the ideas of planning and of combining urban and natural elements became highly influential worldwide. The Swiss architect Le Corbusier (1885–1965) was perhaps the best known of the urban grand schemers. His **Radiant City** design consisted of a geometric assembly of commercial skyscrapers and high-rise residences, mass produced, uniform, and filled with uniform furniture. His plan for Paris, remarkably, called for the demolition of much of the historic city. This plan evoked passionate public opposition, but Le Corbusier and his supporters insisted that "the design of cities was too important to be left to citizens."[38(p190)] The New York "master builder" and power broker Robert Moses (1888–1981) also exemplified the grand scheme, building a mammoth network of highways, bridges, and other public works and in the process trampling local preferences and razing numerous neighborhoods.

Opposing such excesses was the writer and urbanist Jane Jacobs (1916–2006), whose classic *Death and Life of Great American Cities* (1961) was an eloquent plea for grounding urbanism in the daily rhythms of ordinary people's lives—carefully observed and scrupulously respected. This tension between the "fairy city" fantasy[39] and a more granular, populist approach would become a recurring motif in planning—and one that echoes in public health as well.

Beginning in the 1920s with the widespread market penetration of automobiles and accelerating rapidly after World War II, urban populations began to disperse from cities in a pattern known as **urban sprawl** or suburban sprawl. Many forces drove urban sprawl—*push* factors such as inner-city poverty and crime, *pull* factors such as access to green space and better schools in the suburbs, policy instruments such as mortgage policies that favored new construction over renovation, and massive investment in highways.[40] Planning policies in suburban communities—both policies that permitted rapid, relatively chaotic growth and zoning and subdivision policies with requirements such as large lots—also contributed. Early critics recognized that sprawl could undermine urban life and have negative health consequences,[41] many of which are discussed in this book.

An important development in planning and one that indirectly affected public health policy was the development of transportation planning. In the years following World War II, as US federal funding propelled construction of the Interstate Highway system, more and more cities confronted the need to plan for highway construction. The Federal-Aid Highway Act of 1962 required, as a condition of federal highway funding, that all urbanized areas with at least fifty thousand people undertake "continuing, comprehensive, and cooperative" planning. The result was **metropolitan planning organizations** (**MPOs**), assemblies of local elected officials and transportation agency representatives.[42] More than four hundred MPOs now operate across the United States. They are responsible for planning the use of transportation funds in their metropolitan areas, work that has direct implications for land use and economic development and, ultimately, for health. A pervasive barrier to the smooth functioning of MPOs is the very large number of political jurisdictions that an MPO typically comprises—often many dozens of towns, cities, counties, law enforcement agencies, school systems, utility districts, and other entities, each with its own interests.

Urban planner Emily Talen[43(p1)] writes of planning's "multiple traditions that, though inter-related, often comprise opposing ideals: the quest for urban diversity within a system of order, control that does not impinge freedom, an appreciation of smallness and fine-grained complexity that can coexist with civic prominence, a comprehensive perspective that does not ignore detail." To these traditions might be added the recurring tension between private property rights and the public good; the pressing need to focus on the rights of disenfranchised populations; the tension between grand plans imposed from above and participatory, democratic processes; and the vexing difficulty of planning across countless political jurisdictions. Many of these characteristic themes of planning are highly applicable to public health as well.

CONTEMPORARY PRACTICE IN THE DESIGN PROFESSIONS

Since the early 1900s, planning has evolved to encompass a broad range of specialties and to become more focused on process and livability issues. From the early emphasis on separating incompatible uses and defining distinct zones within cities, the field progressed to an emphasis on grand plans and then to an emphasis on **growth management**, through compact, mixed-use urbanism, often motivated explicitly by considerations of health and environmental sustainability.[44,45]

Local government participates in the process of urban development in three ways.[46] First, it influences the location and intensity of development with **zoning** ordinances, which use the police power of the city to regulate development. Second, it provides urban infrastructure, such as roads and parks, and it receives taxes and fees. Third, it initiates specific development projects.

These efforts often reflect the priorities laid out in a municipal **land use plan**. Land use and environmental planning is a local responsibility, usually delegated to a citizen-led **planning commission**. Planning involves problem identification and goal setting, information gathering and analysis, the design of alternatives, and synthesis. Physical plans lay out the current and future land uses of the city or larger region, including transportation and public facilities. Planning generally incorporates public input, using methods such as surveys, newsletters and websites, and community meetings or design workshops known as **charrettes** (figure 1.3). The final choice of plans is a political decision, and decision-makers may or may not choose the plan most favorable to promoting health. Often the politics involve balancing near-term needs and long-term outcomes, special interests, and the ideological leanings of the politicians and the communities they represent.

Contemporary comprehensive plans usually devote considerable attention to land use, transportation and circulation, community facilities, parks, and recreation. They often address additional elements of open space and conservation, environmental hazards and safety, noise, housing, economic development, urban design, and historic preservation. Such plans can be crafted for urban, suburban, metropolitan, and rural areas. They may include detailed specific provisions for such elements as housing, schools, public transit, parks and open space, streets and vehicle circulation, bicycle and pedestrian access and circulation, and health and emergency services.[47]

Figure 1.3. Charrettes—intensive, hands-on workshops—are an important component of public input on community design, bringing people from different disciplines and backgrounds together to explore options for development of a site, as depicted at the Map Room Project in Savannah, Georgia.
Source: Photo courtesy of Yanni Alexander Loukissas

Modern planners use a range of tools to advance planning goals. These tools may include **subdivision regulations**, **special or conditional use permits**, and **planned unit development**. The most important implementation tool is zoning, which regulates private property by specifying uses such as residential or commercial, **density** limits, and other features of land use. **Conservation zoning** aims to preserve green space within or at the edge of cities, and **inclusionary zoning** ensures the availability of some **affordable housing** in the urban neighborhoods. A recent planning tool, **form-based zoning**, represents a new approach to development regulation. Traditional zoning aims to separate different land uses, such as residential, commercial, and industrial, by proscribing certain uses in certain places and to control development intensity by defining permissible density, height limits, and so on. Form-based zoning aims to help communities achieve a desired urban form and **land use mix**. It does so by prescribing the desired urban form in terms of building type (for example, height, configuration, and coverage), the relationship of building types to the street (in terms of **setbacks**, for example), and desirable streetscapes and landscapes. Because allowable activities are related to building type, buildings with more than one use are permitted. As described in chapter 11, **mixed-use** communities, in which homes, schools, stores, offices, recreational facilities, and other uses are proximate to each other or even co-located, offer substantial health benefits. Proponents of form-based zoning argue that compared to traditional zoning, this approach can more easily promote sustainable and healthy development patterns.[48] In some places, planners are combining the best features of traditional and form-based zoning.

New Urbanism is one of the more recent developments in planning. This framework and others closely related to it—such as **traditional neighborhood design** and **smart growth**—advocate principles that were common before automobiles came to dominate urban form. These principles include providing alternatives to travel by automobile, specifically pedestrian and bicycle infrastructure and public transit, as well as designing for mixed land use, connectivity, and vibrant activity centers. These ideas are enunciated in the Ahwahnee Principles.[49] Another related planning approach is **transit-oriented development**, which clusters residential, commercial, and recreational space around transit nodes—typically featuring high-density, mixed-use development and limited parking within walking distance of a subway, light rail, or bus stop and decreasing density at greater distances from the stop. Two other planning concepts deserve mention: **infill development**, which locates construction in the interstices of areas that are less dense than desired, and **brownfield** development, which remediates and redevelops properties with industrial or other contamination.

Urban planning is inherently political because local public officials must ultimately approve policies, plans, ordinances, and development projects. Private real estate developers propose **site plans** for projects that build or rebuild the city. Successful developments incorporate local regulations and public goals into project plans. Many development projects confront opposition from local residents, a phenomenon known by the acronym **NIMBY**, or "not in my backyard." Although residents may oppose many kinds of projects, from cannabis dispensaries to cell phone towers, a particularly troubling situation is resistance to high-density or affordable housing, which can perpetuate both housing shortages and the effects of discrimination.[50,51] Planners work within a matrix of competing interests, including economic development, social equity, environmental preservation, and aesthetics—and, increasingly, health.

These many advances in planning have parallels in architecture. In recent years, technological innovation, market demand, and regulations have shifted building design toward incorporating environmental sustainability and health. There were many drivers. Beginning in the 1960s, the environmental movement provided fertile ground for innovative, environmentally conscious architectural design. The 1973 oil crisis focused attention on energy prices and emphasized the need for energy efficiency in buildings. In the United States, the American Institute of Architects formed a Committee on the Environment in 1989, and the US Green Building Council (USGBC) launched in 1993. In the United Kingdom, the Building Research Establishment Environmental Assessment Method, or BREEAM system, the world's first system for assessing the environmental performance of buildings, was launched in 1990, and in the United States, USGBC debuted its **Leadership in Energy and Environmental Design**, or **LEED**, system in 1998.[52] Around the world, architects began designing for energy efficiency, water reclamation, daylighting, and related attributes. The concept of green building is now well established. A foundational principle is **life cycle assessment**—consideration of the entire life of a building, from the sourcing of the components used to make it, to the "metabolism" of the building while in use, to demolition and disposal at the end of its useful life. Key elements of green buildings include energy, materials, and water efficiency; the use of renewable energy sources and sustainably sourced materials; and pollution and waste minimization. The use of natural elements such as daylighting, vegetation, and materials such as wood and stone exemplifies **biophilic design**. Green buildings are discussed in chapters 12 through 15, in the context of housing, workplaces, health care facilities, and schools, respectively, and rating systems used for green buildings are discussed in chapter 22.

Are green buildings also healthy? At a high level, the answer is yes, because environmental stewardship contributes to a planet on which humans can thrive. Many features of green buildings also directly promote health: daylighting, irresistible staircases that encourage physical activity, and avoidance of materials that off-gas toxins.[53] But sometimes environmental and health goals collide.

One such collision occurred following the 1973 oil crisis, when architects began designing **tight buildings**—buildings that reduced heating and air-conditioning demand (and therefore energy use) by limiting outside air circulation. The reduced supply of fresh air, sometimes accompanied by moisture buildup and mold growth inside buildings, was associated with discomfort and mental and physical symptom complaints and labeled as the **sick building syndrome** (or building-related illness).[54,55] This exemplified the problem of unintended consequences and the need to balance energy conservation with indoor air quality in building design (see chapter 4).

Another design profession whose work has advanced in recent years is landscape architecture. The traditional domains of this profession—hardscape, waterscape, and greenscape—are now routinely envisioned as including people and communities, plants and animals, and abiotic features such as rock and water—all interacting. According to the American Society of Landscape Architects (asla.org), sustainable landscapes are "responsive to the environment, re-generative, and can actively contribute to the development of healthy communities. Sustainable landscapes sequester carbon, clean the air and water, increase energy efficiency, restore habitats, and create value through significant economic, social and, environmental benefits."[56]

This broad, ecologically grounded approach builds on the legacy of Olmsted and McHarg and extends it to human health. Landscape architecture has increasingly relied on health evidence, incorporating opportunities for physical activity, stress reduction, social interaction, and other benefits into the design of outdoor spaces.[57,58] In addition, landscape ar-chitects are at the forefront of climate change adaptation (see chapter 17), helping, for example, to select climate-tolerant vegetation, maintain soil health, upgrade stormwater management, and utilize tree canopies to reduce the urban heat island effect[59]—efforts that often protect human health. Some of this work is carried out with **green infrastructure** such as bioswales and retention ponds, which utilize natural processes to deliver needed benefits such as flood control and carbon sequestration (see chapter 16).

EQUITY

A central theme in both public health and the design professions is equity. Health disparities are a pervasive reality in most societies. People who are poor, members of ethnic and racial minorities, or in any way disenfranchised or marginalized typically suffer worse health than those who are more privileged. They have higher rates of diseases and injuries, they recover more slowly when ill and endure more disability, and they die earlier. Achieving **health equity** is a profound moral challenge for health and design professionals, and indeed for all of society.

Many mechanisms operate to create and maintain health disparities—the stress of living with racism and discrimination, adverse childhood experiences that manifest across the entire life span, lack of access to health care, and others.[60] An important set of mechanisms relates to the built environment. These are explored in depth in chapter 9 and discussed individually in the chapters shown in table 1.3, which summarizes the mechanisms.

Growing evidence of how the built environment contributes to health disparities and activism by members of affected communities and their allies has increased awareness in recent years. A seminal moment for the US environmental justice movement came in 1982, when a hazardous waste landfill set to accept soil contaminated with polychlorinated biphenyls (PCBs) was sited in a predominately African American community in Warren

Table 1.3. Ways in which the built environment can affect health disparities.

Circumstance That Could Deepen Health Disparities	Circumstance That Could Rectify Health Disparities	Chapters in Which Discussed
Toxic environmental exposures such as polluted air and hazardous waste sites	Strict regulation of air pollution emissions; cleanup of hazardous waste sites	4
Poor housing quality	Ample affordable, healthy, sustainable housing	12
Poor school quality	Identify and correct deficiencies in school buildings, especially in deprived areas	15
Disproportionate exposure to workplace hazards	Industrial hygiene and other primary preventive measures to ensure safe workplaces, especially those with workforces drawn from ethnic and racial minority populations	13
Racism	Eliminate systems that rank human value based on the color of people's skin	9
Disordered, unsafe neighborhoods	Public investments, public-private partnerships, and community initiatives to maintain neighborhoods	9
Lack of access to reliable transportation	Provision of good pedestrian/bicycle infrastructure and transit service, focusing on underserved areas	11
Lack of access to greenspace	Provision and maintenance of parks, and park programming, in underserved areas	16
Lack of nearby, accessible, affordable health care	Provision of accessible health facilities in underserved areas	14
Lack of access to healthy, affordable food	Provision of grocery stores selling fresh, healthy food in underserved areas	3
Excess vulnerability to disasters such as floods and storms	Vulnerability mapping and disaster planning focused on most vulnerable areas	17, 18
Lack of political voice and power in planning the built environment	Inclusive, transparent, responsive government	20, 21

County, North Carolina.[61,62] The community rose in protest, attracted national attention, and inspired many other communities to identify and resist such exposures. The themes of environmental justice have since been amplified and applied to many specific domains with relevance to the built environment: transportation justice,[63] food justice,[64] housing justice,[65] climate justice.[66] With more than one billion people—a fourth of the world's urban population—living in **slums**, inequity is a central reality of contemporary cities. A global environmental justice movement has emerged,[67] with important impetus from Indigenous peoples, whose shared histories include the expropriation of traditional places.

The killing of George Floyd in May 2020 triggered a boiling over of pleas for social justice worldwide. This coincided with Isabel Wilkerson's[68] description of racism in the United States as a caste system that has long excluded and disenfranchised those at the bottom of the hierarchy, leading to grossly inequitable health outcomes, premature deaths, and poorer quality of life. Questions of equity and justice are central to the pursuit of healthy, sustainable built environments and are woven throughout the chapters of this book.

The health impact pyramid (chapter 19) highlights the magnitude of the impacts of interventions to improve health and reduce disparities. Built environment interventions have substantial impacts on health and equity by changing the context in which decisions are made. Although a full discussion is beyond the scope of this book, even larger impacts in improving health and reducing disparities can be made by improving the socioeconomic factors that influence health, such as investing disproportionately larger of shares of societal resources for disadvantaged populations in child care, education, jobs, health services, and other necessities of life.

SUSTAINABILITY

This chapter has set the stage for the remainder of the book by exploring the foundations of both public health and the design professions. A third foundation relates closely to these two: environmental sustainability. Growing awareness of the need for planetary stewardship and growing professional efforts to respond have greatly influenced the interface of human health and the built environment.

Environmental stewardship has been part of indigenous wisdom for millennia, and in modern times, writers from Henry David Thoreau (1817–1862) to John Muir (1838–1914), from Aldo Leopold (1887–1948) to Rachel Carson (1907–1964), called attention to humanity's place in the context of larger ecosystems. A landmark in modern recognition of these issues was the 1987 publication of *Our Common Future* by the World Commission on Environment and Development (WCED, also known as the Brundtland Commission).[69] This report introduced the concept of **sustainable development**, defined as "development that meets the needs of the present without compromising the ability of future generations to meet their own needs." This report set the stage for the United Nations Conference on Environment and Development (UNCED, also known as the Earth Summit) five years later, in Rio de Janeiro. The Earth Summit crystalized growing global concerns about changes that threatened the very stability of the planet and therefore of the prospects for human health and well-being.

Those planetary changes are far-reaching. They stem from the vast exploitation of energy—predominantly from the fossil fuels coal, petroleum, and later natural gas—beginning on a large scale in the nineteenth century and accelerating rapidly in the second half of the twentieth century. No longer dependent just on muscle, wind, and gravity, societies developed a dizzying array of technologies. The human enterprise ramped up exponentially, as reflected by population growth, economic growth, growth in resource use, growth of cities—in fact, by almost any and every indicator of human activity. This historical shift has been called the **Great Acceleration**. It led to significant improvements in human circumstances, such as poverty reduction, improved child survival, and longer life expectancy (albeit unequally distributed). But these advances came at a cost: the pillaging of many of the planet's systems.

Our species—a mere fraction of 1 percent of Earth's biomass—has triggered substantial changes in the chemistry of the atmosphere and the oceans; an increase in the planet's surface temperature; a rapid mass extinction of species unrivalled in the last sixty-five million years; alterations in biogeochemical cycles including those of phosphorus, nitrogen, and water; appropriation and reconfiguration of more than half the planet's land surface; and pervasive contamination of the biosphere by persistent toxic chemicals. These planetary changes are so far-reaching that scientists have recognized the dawn of a new geological epoch, the **Anthropocene**.[70] These changes are accelerating, leading scientists to warn that we risk transgressing **planetary boundaries** that could have catastrophic results.[71]

These planetary changes have profound impacts on human health and well-being. In coming years, those impacts will only increase. The emerging field of **planetary health** studies these impacts and how to limit the threats to human health and well-being, both by slowing and even reversing dangerous planetary trends and by adapting to inevitable changes—"avoiding the unmanageable, and managing the unavoidable."[72,73]

This takes us back to the UNCED in 1992. That conference was followed by a portfolio of international activities, such as the UN Framework Convention on Climate Change (UNFCCC, ratified 1994) and the UN Convention on Biological Diversity (CBD, ratified 1993), all aiming to advance sustainability. In addition, existing international efforts were reoriented to align with UNCED goals; for example, the UN Human Settlements Programme (UN-Habitat, established 1978) embraced the goal of sustainable urban development. Importantly, the Rio Declaration on Environment and Development that emerged from the Earth Summit made it clear that sustainability has much to do with health: "Human beings are at the center of concerns for sustainable development. They are entitled to a healthy and productive life in harmony with nature."[74]

The international framework for much of this work was codified in 2000, when the United Nations issued its Millennium Development Goals (MDGs). These were intended to guide global efforts through 2015. There were eight goals, related to poverty reduction, education, gender equality, health, and environmental sustainability. In 2015, the MDGs were supplanted by the **Sustainable Development Goals (SDGs)** (figure 1.4). The SDG framework is substantially more complex than the MDGs. It includes 17 individual goals, each with a set of targets (169 in all), each in turn with indicators (230 in all). The SDGs provide a shared reference point for most countries and a framework for public and private investments to achieve a wide range of social goals.

The SDGs, and more broadly the concept of sustainability, map in complex ways to health, to the built environment, and to the intersection of the two. An example of these relationships is shown in figure 1.5, which shows the major sources of greenhouse gas (GHG) emissions by economic sector. The most obvious links to the built environment are in buildings and transportation, which together account for 20 percent of GHG emissions.

Figure 1.4. The Sustainable Development Goals. Two of the goals map directly to the subject of this book: SDG3, on health, and SDG11, on cities and communities. Not only do they interact with each other, but many other goals, such as SDG 6, on water and sanitation, SDG7, on energy, and SDG13, on climate, are strongly connected as well.
Source: United Nations, 2020. https://www.un.org/sustainabledevelopment/. The content of this publication has not been approved by the United Nations and does not reflect the views of the United Nations or its officials or Member States.

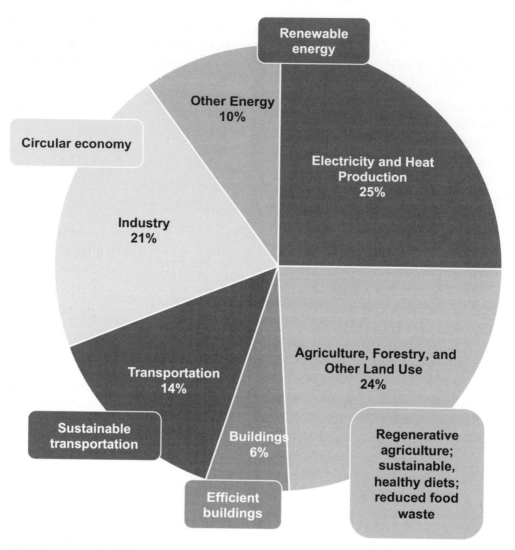

Figure 1.5. Global sources of greenhouse gas emissions and system-level strategies for reducing them. Source: Adapted from US EPA 2015. https://www.epa.gov/ghgemissions/global-greenhouse-gas-emissions-data

Because climate change threatens health, reducing these emissions through efficient buildings and transportation—achieving **net zero emissions** through **decarbonization**—represents a set of public health strategies. Not only that, emissions reductions offer additional direct, immediate health benefits, as explored in chapter 17.

But those transportation and building slices of the pie are not the only ways in which the built environment figures in sustainability efforts. Electricity and heat production are relevant, because much of that production goes to buildings. (In fact, some calculations suggest that buildings account not for 6 percent but for as much as 40 percent of GHG emissions.) Industry relates to the built environment, both in the way components of buildings and other infrastructure are manufactured and in the consumption patterns of urban residents. Even the "agriculture, forestry and other land use" category relates to the built environment. For example, as cities expand their footprint, they convert peri-urban land use from forest and grassland to urban surfaces, diminishing an important carbon sink. Throughout this book, we will continue to encounter complex and fascinating links among health, the built environment, and sustainability.

THE MODERN INTERSECTION OF PUBLIC HEALTH, DESIGN, EQUITY, AND SUSTAINABILITY

Planning and public health, as described in this chapter, both sprang from the excesses, inequities, and perils of nineteenth-century cities. And the same historical forces that gave rise to these cities—industrialization and rampant exploitation of the natural world—also gave rise to today's climate crisis and other planetary emergencies. Are there examples of planning and public health deliberately converging toward the design of healthy, equitable, and sustainable places?

More than a century after the birth, and later estrangement, of modern planning and public health, they are again finding common ground.[75][78] There are textbooks (including this one), a rich research literature, joint courses, graduate certificates and degree programs, cross-fertilization at professional meetings, and jointly trained professionals working in government, the private sector, and civil society (see chapter 23). Comprehensive plans and building policies increasingly address public health (albeit not as much as they might).[77][79]

An important example of implementing these ideas in practice is the **Healthy Cities movement**. Leonard Duhl, a professor of public health, city planning, and psychiatry at the University of California, Berkeley, and Trevor Hancock, a Canadian public health physician,[80] contributed much to this movement. Beginning in the 1980s, they proposed an approach to urban health that combined health care delivery with "upstream" factors such as built environment design, emphasized prevention, focused on community-based coalitions and participatory governance, and aimed for sustainability and equity in addition to health.[81] This helped spark the Healthy Cities program at the European office of the World Health Organization, focused initially on eleven European cities but later expanding to more than four thousand cities and towns worldwide, including many in low-

and middle-income countries.[82][83] Although evidence that the Healthy Cities model works remains elusive,[84][85] the movement continues to the present and provides a comprehensive, far-reaching example of efforts to achieve healthy places.

The remainder of this book explores the intersection of public health, design, and sustainability. Part I (chapters 2 through 10) considers the major health issues that relate to the built environment. For example, community design can play an important role in promoting or discouraging physical activity (chapter 2). Other health issues include the food we eat (chapter 3), the air we breathe (chapter 4), the risk of injuries (chapter 5), the water we drink (chapter 6), our mental health (chapter 7), and the ways in which we form social bonds (chapter 8). These health issues do not affect everybody equally, and crucial cross-cutting concerns are equity and fairness, especially for vulnerable populations (chapter 9). Chapter 10 addresses life span issues—the needs of the very young, the very old, and people across the life span with special needs.

Part II (chapters 11 through 18) is organized by specific aspects of the built environment. It begins by considering transportation and land use at the scale of entire cities and regions (chapter 11) and then examines the smaller scale of homes (chapter 12), workplaces (chapter 13), health care settings (chapter 14), and schools (chapter 15), considering how health can be designed into each of these settings. A cross-cutting issue is how contact with nature can benefit people (chapter 16). Chapters 17 and 18 address, respectively, the immense challenges of climate change and how places can be designed to be resilient to disasters.

Part III (chapters 19 through 22) focuses on how to make change. Chapter 19 reminds us that environmental design is only part of the story; behavioral choices are an essential focus as well. Chapter 20 discusses policymaking, chapter 21 discusses community engagement, and chapter 22 describes some technical tools, such as health impact assessment and certification schemes. Together, these chapters constitute a toolbox for achieving healthy places.

Finally, part IV (chapters 23 through 27) takes a long view of making healthy, sustainable places. Chapter 23 discusses training the next generation of professionals, who will need to lead at the interface of design and health. Chapter 24 explores emerging technologies, from the Internet of Things to artificial intelligence, that are changing the way people interact with their built environment, and potentially the health consequences of those interactions. Chapter 25 discusses research needs, recognizing that healthy places depend in large part on a firm base of science. Chapter 26 addresses the topic that exploded on the scene as we were preparing this edition of the book: the COVID-19 pandemic. Finally, chapter 27 looks to the future and considers the intersection of the large themes of urbanism, health, and environmental sustainability through the eyes of a diverse panel of experts.

The journey from specific professional paradigms to the quest for healthy, equitable built environments and from there to cross-cutting, holistic solutions is one that invites us to think across disciplines, across **spatial scales**, and from the historical past to a long-term future—all unusual and sometimes uncomfortable efforts. The editors and authors of this volume are inspired by a vision of healthy places for all people and by our conviction that dedication, open minds, rigorous science, a commitment to justice and equity for all, political will, and aspirational thinking can lead to success. We invite you, the reader, to join us in this journey.

DISCUSSION QUESTIONS

1. Give three examples of the tensions between public goods (such as parks and roads) and private entitlements (such as freedom to use one's land for any desired purpose) that may arise in public health and urban planning decisions.

2. What types of information might a community collect when conducting surveillance related to the health effects of the built environment and community design? From what sources could such information be obtained?

3. Because financial profitability plays a major role in most private-sector decisions, how might health concerns be made a part of the bottom line for private developers and for lenders that finance developments?

4. Consider a study that evaluates the health of people in two communities, one with sidewalks and one without. The study authors find that the rate of lung cancer is higher in the community without sidewalks and conclude that sidewalks protect against lung cancer. What concerns would you have about accepting this conclusion? What alternative explanations might you propose for this study finding?

5. What information about the health implications of their work should land use and transportation planners be taught during their initial or subsequent training?

6. Give two examples of sustainability initiatives that also deliver improved health and two examples of sustainability initiatives that might undermine health.

7. Suppose that in each of two cities—one in western Europe and one in sub-Saharan Africa—urban planners and public health officials decide to work together to advance health through the built environment. What priorities do you think might emerge for the groups in each city, how would they differ, and what would be the implications for their work?

8. "Urban planners and public health officials should routinely engage with the communities they serve before and while implementing any programs." Please agree or disagree and explain your reasoning.

ACKNOWLEDGMENTS

This chapter draws on the introductory chapter from the first edition of this book, which was co-authored by Arthur Wendel, Robin Fran Abrams, and Emil Malizia.

DISCLOSURE OF COMPETING INTERESTS

Howard Frumkin, Andrew L. Dannenberg, and Nisha Botchwey's declarations appear in the preface.

REFERENCES

1. World Health Organization. Constitution. Accessed October 16, 2021. https://www.who.int/about/governance/constitution

2. Rosen G. *A History of Public Health.* Johns Hopkins University Press; 1993. Originally published 1958.

3. Brimblecombe P. *The Big Smoke: A History of Air Pollution in London since Medieval Times.* Methuen; 1988.

4. Cantor NF. *In the Wake of the Plague: The Black Death and the World It Made.* HarperCollins; 2001.

5. Kelly J. *The Great Mortality: An Intimate History of the Black Death, the Most Devastating Plague of All Time.* HarperCollins; 2006.

6. Sullivan R. *Rats: Observations on the History and Habitat of the City's Most Unwanted Inhabitants.* Bloomsbury; 2004.

7. Leavitt JW. *The Healthiest City: Milwaukee and the Politics of Health Reform.* Princeton University Press; 1982.

8. Duffy J. *The Sanitarians: A History of American Public Health.* University of Illinois Press; 1990.

9. Tarr JA. *The Search for the Ultimate Sink: Urban Pollution in Historical Perspective.* University of Akron Press; 1996.

10. Melosi M. *The Sanitary City: Urban Infrastructure in America from Colonial Times to the Present.* Johns Hopkins University Press; 2000.

11. Rosenberg R. *The Cholera Years: The United States in 1832, 1849, and 1866.* University of Chicago Press; 1962.

12. Tarr JA. Industrial waste disposal in the United States as a historical problem. *Ambix.* 2002;49(1):4-20.

13. Hamlin C. *Public Health and Social Justice in the Age of Chadwick: Britain, 1800–1854.* Cambridge University Press; 1998.

14. IOM Committee on Assuring the Health of the Public in the 21st Century. *The Future of the Public's Health in the 21st Century.* National Academies Press; 2002.

15. McKeown T. *The Role of Medicine: Dream, Mirage, or Nemesis?* Princeton University Press; 1979.

16. Bunker JP, Frazier HS, Mosteller F. Improving health: measuring effects of medical care. *Milbank Quarterly.* 1994:225-258.

17. Kochanek KD, Xu J, Arias E. Mortality in the United States, 2019. NCHS Data Brief 395, December 2020. Accessed October 16, 2021. https://www.cdc.gov/nchs/products/databriefs/db395.htm

18. CDC (Centers for Disease Control and Prevention) NCfHS. Leading Causes of Death, 1900–1998. No date.

19. Lee LM, Teutsch SM, Thacker SB, St. Louis ME. *Principles and Practice of Public Health Surveillance.* 3rd ed. Oxford University Press; 2010.

20. Taylor AF, Kuo FE, Sullivan WC. Views of nature and self-discipline: evidence from inner city children. *Journal of Environmental Psychology.* 2002;22:49-63.

21. Ewing R, Schieber RA, Zegeer CV. Urban sprawl as a risk factor in motor vehicle occupant and pedestrian fatalities. *American Journal of Public Health.* 2003;93(9):1541-1545.

22. Hill AB. The environment and disease: association or causation? *Proceedings of the Royal Society of Medicine.* 1965;58:295-300.

23. Nardone A, Chiang J, Corburn J. Historic redlining and urban health today in U.S. cities. *Environmental Justice.* 2020;13:109-119. doi:10.1089/env.2020.0011

24. Hall P. *Cities of Tomorrow: An Intellectual History of Urban Planning and Design in the Twentieth Century.* 3rd ed. Wiley-Blackwell; 2002.

25. Peterson J. *The Birth of City Planning in the United States.* Johns Hopkins University Press; 2003.

26. Peterson J. The impact of sanitary reform upon American urban planning, 1840–1890. *Journal of Social History.* 1979;13:83-103.

27. Schultz SK, McShane C. To engineer the metropolis: sewers, sanitation, and city planning in late-nineteenth-century America. *Journal of American History.* 1978;65(2):389-411.

28. Corburn J. *Toward the Healthy City: People, Places, and the Politics of Urban Planning.* MIT Press; 2009.

29. Fairfield JD. The scientific management of urban space: professional city planning and the legacy of progressive reform. *Journal of Urban History.* 1994;20(2):179-204.

30. Addams J. *Twenty Years at Hull-House, with Autobiographical Notes.* MacMillan; 1912.

31. Rydell RW. *All the World's a Fair: Visions of Empire at American International Expositions, 1876–1916.* University of Chicago Press; 1984.

32. Trachtenberg A. *The Incorporation of America: Culture and Society in the Gilded Age.* Hill and Wang; 1982.

33. Fisher ID. *Frederick Law Olmsted and the City Planning Movement in the United States.* UMI Research Press; 1986.

34. Rybczynski W. *A Clearing in the Distance: Frederick Law Olmsted and America in the 19th Century.* Simon and Schuster; 1999.

35. Legates R, Stout F. Modernism and early urban planning, 1870–1940. In: Legates R, Stout F, eds. *The City Reader.* Routledge; 2000:299-313.

36. McCormack MJ. Applying the basic principles of cognitive science to the Standard State Zoning Enabling Act. *Boston College Environmental Affairs Law Review.* 1999;27(3):519-566.

37. Mumford L. Regions—to live in. In: *The Survey Geographic.* 1925;54:151-152.

38. Fishman R. *Urban Utopias in the Twentieth Century: Ebenezer Howard, Frank Lloyd Wright, and Le Corbusier.* Basic Books; 1977.

39. Cronon W. *Nature's Metropolis: Chicago and the Great West.* Norton; 1991.

40. Jackson K. *Crabgrass Frontier: The Suburbanization of the United States.* Oxford University Press; 1987.

41. Frumkin H, Frank L, Frank LD, Jackson RJ. *Urban Sprawl and Public Health: Designing, Planning, and Building for Healthy Communities.* Island Press; 2004.

42. Sciara G-C. Metropolitan transportation planning: lessons from the past, institutions for the future. *Journal of the American Planning Association.* 2017;83(3):262-276. doi:10.1080/01944363.2017.1322526

43. Talen E. *New Urbanism and American Planning: The Conflict of Cultures.* Routledge; 2005.

44. Greenberg M, Mayer H, Miller KT, Hordon R, Knee D. Reestablishing public health and land use planning to protect public water supplies. *American Journal of Public Health.* 2003;93(9):1522-1526.

45. Sloane DC. Longer view: from congestion to sprawl: planning and health in historical context. *Journal of the American Planning Association.* 2006;72(1):10-18.

46. Malizia EE. City and regional planning: a primer for public health officials. *American Journal of Health Promotion.* 2005;19(5).

47. Berke PR, Godschalk DR, Kaiser EJ, Rodriguez DA. *Urban Land Use Planning.* 5th ed. University of Illinois Press; 2006.

48. Baird-Zars B, Sclar E, Fischer LA, Stahl V, eds. *Zoning: A Guide for 21st-Century Planning.* Routledge; 2020.

49. Local Government Commission. Ahwahnee Principles for Resource-Efficient Communities. Local Government Commission. Published 1991. Accessed October 16, 2021. https://www.lgc.org/who-we-are/ahwahnee/principles/

50. Scally CP, Tighe JR. Democracy in action? NIMBY as impediment to equitable affordable housing siting. *Housing Studies.* 2015;30(5):749-769. doi:10.1080/02673037.2015.1013093

51. Nguyen MT, Basolo V, Tiwari A. Opposition to affordable housing in the USA: debate framing and the responses of local actors. *Housing, Theory and Society.* 2013;30:107-130. doi:10.1080/14036096.2012.667833

52. Building Design + Construction. White Paper on Sustainability. Published 2003. Accessed October 16, 2021. https://www.bdcnetwork.com/2003-white-paper-sustainability-report-green-building-movement

53. MacNaughton P, Cao X, Buonocore J, et al. Energy savings, emission reductions, and health co-benefits of the green building movement. *Journal of Exposure Science and Environmental Epidemiology*. 2018;28(4):307-318. doi:10.1038/s41370-017-0014-9

54. Abdul-Wahab SA, ed. *Sick Building Syndrome in Public Buildings and Workplaces*. 2011 ed. Springer; 2011.

55. Tran VV, Park D, Lee Y-C. Indoor air pollution, related human diseases, and recent trends in the control and improvement of indoor air quality. *International Journal of Environmental Research and Public Health*. 2020;17(8):2927. doi:10.3390/ijerph17082927

56. American Society of Landscape Architects. What are sustainable landscapes? 2017. Accessed October 16, 2021. https://www.asla.org/sustainablelandscapes/about.html

57. Landscape Institute. Public health and landscape: creating healthy places. Landscape Institute. No date. Accessed October 16, 2021. https://www.landscapeinstitute.org/policy/health/

58. Brown RD, Corry RC. Evidence-based landscape architecture for human health and well-being. *Sustainability*. 2020;12(4):1360.

59. Klemm W, Lenzholzer S, Van Den Brink A. Developing green infrastructure design guidelines for urban climate adaptation. *Journal of Landscape Architecture*. 2017;12(7):60-71.

60. Marmot M. The *Health Gap: The Challenge of an Unequal World*. Bloomsbury Press; 2015.

61. Mohai P, Pellow D, Roberts, JT. Environmental justice. *Annual Review of Environment and Resources*. 2009;34(1):405-430. doi:10.1146/annurev-environ-082508-094348

62. Perez AC, Grafton B, Mohai P, Hardin R, Hintzen K, Orvis S. Evolution of the environmental justice movement: activism, formalization and differentiation. *Environmental Research Letters*. 2015;10(105002). doi:10.1088/1748-9326/10/10/105002

63. Bullard R, Johnson G. *Just Transportation: Dismantling Race and Class Barriers to Mobility*. New Society Publishing; 1997.

64. Alkon A, Agyeman J, eds. *Cultivating Food Justice: Race, Class, and Sustainability*. MIT Press; 2011.

65. Dawkins C. Realizing housing justice through comprehensive housing policy reform. *International Journal of Urban Sciences*. 2021;25(Suppl 1):266-281.

66. Schlosberg D, Collins LB. From environmental to climate justice: climate change and the discourse of environmental justice. *Wiley Interdisciplinary Reviews: Climate Change*. 2014;5(3):359-374. doi:10.1002/wcc.275

67. Martinez-Alier J, Temper L, Del Bene D, Scheidel A. Is there a global environmental justice movement? *Journal of Peasant Studies*. 2016;43(3):731-755. doi:10.1080/03066150.2016.1141198

68. Wilkerson I. *Caste: The Origins of Our Discontent*. Random House; 2020.

69. World Commission on Environment and Development. *Our Common Future*. Oxford University Press; 1987.

70. Steffen W, Crutzen PJ, McNeill JR. The Anthropocene: are humans now overwhelming the great forces of nature? *Ambio*. 2007;36(8):614-621. doi:10.1579/0044-7447(2007)36[614:TAAHNO]2.0.CO;2

71. Steffen W, Richardson K, Rockström J, et al. Planetary boundaries: guiding human development on a changing planet. *Science*. 2015;347(6223):1259855.

72. Myers S, Frumkin H, eds. *Planetary Health: Protecting Nature to Protect Ourselves*. Island Press; 2020.

73. Haines A, Frumkin H. *Planetary Health: Safeguarding Human Health and the Environment in the Anthropocene.* Cambridge University Press; 2021.

74. UNEP (United Nations Environmental Programme). Rio Declaration on Environment and Development. In: Report of the United Nations Conference on Environment and Development. August 12, 1992. https://www.un.org/en/development/desa/population/migration/generalassembly/docs/globalcompact/A_CONF.151_26_Vol.I_Declaration.pdf

75. Northridge ME, Sclar ED, Biswas P. Sorting out the connections between the built environment and health: a conceptual framework for navigating pathways and planning healthy cities. *Journal of Urban Health.* 2003;80(4):556-568.

76. Frank LD, Kavage S. Urban planning and public health: a story of separation and reconnection. *Journal of Public Health Management and Practice.* 2008;14(3):214-220.

77. Carmichael L, Townshend TG, Fischer TB, et al. Urban planning as an enabler of urban health: challenges and good practice in England following the 2012 planning and public health reforms. *Land Use Policy.* 2019;84:154-162. https://doi.org/10.1016/j.landusepol.2019.02.043

78. McKinnon G, Pineo H, Chang M, Taylor-Green L, Strategy AJ, Toms R. Strengthening the links between planning and health in England. *BMJ.* 2020;369. doi:10.1136/bmj.m795

79. Azzopardi-Muscat N, Brambilla A, Caracci F, Capolongo S. Synergies in design and health. The role of architects and urban health planners in tackling key contemporary public health challenges. *Acta Biomedica.* 2020;91(3-S):9-20.

80. Duhl L, ed. *The Urban Condition: People and Policy in the Metropolis.* Simon and Schuster; 1963.

81. Hancock T, Duhl L. *Healthy Cities: Promoting Health in the Urban Context.* WHO Europe; 1986.

82. Hancock T. The evolution, impact and significance of the health cities/healthy communities movement. *Journal of Public Health Policy.* 1993;14(1):5-18.

83. Tsouros AD. Twenty-seven years of the WHO European Healthy Cities movement: a sustainable movement for change and innovation at the local level. *Health Promotion International.* 2015;30(Suppl 1):i3-i7. doi:10.1093/heapro/dav046

84. de Leeuw E, Green G, Tsouros A, et al. Healthy Cities Phase V evaluation: further synthesizing realism. *Health Promotion International.* 2015;30:i118-i125. doi:10.1093/heapro/dav047

85. Kegler MC, Painter JE, Twiss JM, Aronson R, Norton BL. Evaluation findings on community participation in the California Healthy Cities and Communities program. *Health Promotion International.* 2009;24(4):300-310.

PART I

HEALTH IMPACTS OF THE BUILT ENVIRONMENT

CHAPTER 2

PHYSICAL ACTIVITY AND THE BUILT ENVIRONMENT

Nisha Botchwey, Meaghan McSorley, and M. Renée Umstattd Meyer

KEY POINTS

- Physical activity can help prevent numerous physical and mental health conditions, yet most people around the globe do not meet recommended physical activity levels.
- Some built environment attributes are associated with higher levels of physical activity. For example, people living in *mixed-use* communities with walkable destinations and accessible transit do more total physical activity than their counterparts living in residential-only neighborhoods.
- Promoting physical activity through the built environment is essential to public health and is also a sustainable climate change solution.
- Adding or improving recreation facilities is not enough to increase their use. Comprehensive interventions that include environmental changes, activity programs and marketing, and education have increased walking and biking to school and throughout cities.
- Living close to parks, trails, and recreation centers is related to greater use of facilities and more recreational physical activity.
- Access to recreation facilities, quality and safety of pedestrian facilities, and aesthetics are typically insufficient in areas with mostly low-income and racial/ethnic minority populations.

INTRODUCTION

When the COVID-19 pandemic hit Reynaldo's community in Oakland, California, at first he was sad that he would no longer be able to take the bus to school and play with his friends during recess. For the first several weeks, he played video games with his brothers and attended school remotely, which meant a lot of screen time. When the City of Oakland implemented its **Slow Streets** program a few months into the pandemic, Reynaldo was excited. Instead of playing video games, he and his brothers waited anxiously for remote classes to be over so that they could go outside and play soccer in the street near their house. The Slow Streets program closed select roads to through traffic that were redundant with other streets or had low traffic volumes and speeds. Only local residents and emergency vehicles could drive on these streets. The program's purpose was to create more space for physical activity, places for people like Reynaldo and his brothers to walk, bike, run, and play. Reynaldo loved having a safe place close to his home to play outside—before the pandemic, he would wait for his mother to finish work to drive them to a park. Reynaldo's mother was an essential worker and still had to drive to work during the pandemic, so the Slow Streets were a bit of an impediment for her, but worth it. She was happy that her boys were able to safely play soccer close to home during the scheduled Slow Street programs. Postpandemic, it is uncertain whether Slow Streets will remain.

Many of the conveniences of our modern world have contributed to increasingly sedentary lives. Many people live far from their jobs and drive cars long distances to reach them; others work or participate in school remotely due to advances in remote learning technologies that involve many hours of sitting at a desk each day. In many urban, suburban, and rural communities worldwide, children spend more time in front of screens than playing outside. There are many reasons that free outdoor play has given way to more screen time—parental restrictions that are intended to ensure children's safety[1] are part of larger, cultural changes. These changes include a diminished sense of community and changing societal norms, suggesting that heightened parental surveillance of children is preferred.[2] The neighborhood and physical environment also have important impacts on free outdoor play for children. As discussed below (and in chapter 9), parks, trails, and other facilities tend to be inequitably distributed and maintained.[2]

This chapter summarizes the research linking built environments to physical activity. It focuses on total physical activity, which is strongly related to health outcomes. This approach complements the focus of chapter 11 on transportation and land use, especially as it relates to walking and bicycling. It is widely understood that **physical activity** is good for health and well-being, but globally, one-fourth of adults and 80 percent of adolescents do not meet physical activity guidelines.[3]

Physical activity can lengthen and improve quality of life and reduce the risk for dozens of physical and mental health conditions, including most **chronic diseases** that are the most common causes of death, disability, and suffering among Americans[4] and people worldwide.[3]

Physical activity reduces the risk of being overweight or obese; of suffering from cardiovascular diseases such as high blood pressure, heart attacks, and stroke; and of developing type 2 diabetes. Physical activity also reduces the risk of many cancers, including colon and breast cancers. It reduces the risk of osteoporosis and of fall-related injuries and also helps improve mental health, with beneficial effects on anxiety, depression, and Alzheimer's disease. Physical activity is also associated with improved sleep. Few if any other health interventions are this broadly beneficial and have so few unwanted side effects—key reasons health professionals enthusiastically promote physical activity. Physical activity does pose potential risks, including injury and inhaling polluted air, but studies in a variety of settings consistently find that the benefits outweigh the risks.

Current guidelines are for young people to accumulate at least 60 minutes of **moderate-to-vigorous physical activity** (**MVPA**) daily and for adults to accumulate at least 150 minutes of MVPA or 75 minutes of vigorous physical activity, or a combination of these two, every week.[3,4] The World Health Organization estimates that up to five million deaths each year could be prevented by adequate physical activity.[3]

Understanding the factors that influence physical activity can lead to interventions based on evidence. The **social-ecological model** and the health impact pyramid[5] can help us understand the ways in which individual behaviors such as physical activity are also influenced by social and cultural, organizational, environmental, and policy factors (see chapter 1). The most effective interventions are likely to create changes at multiple levels. Building a park or sidewalk may not be sufficient to get people to use these facilities. A comprehensive approach would create supportive policies, systems, and environments that motivate people to take advantage of the opportunities. Policy, systems, and environment changes can affect whole communities on a relatively permanent basis.[1] As described below, Oakland's Slow Streets program and Bogotá's combination of *ciclovía* and *cicloruta* are examples of multilevel interventions.

Physical activity has traditionally been divided into utilitarian and recreational categories. **Utilitarian physical activity**, such as walking to the grocery store, mowing the lawn, or shoveling snow, has a primary purpose other than the activity itself (transportation is a central component of utilitarian physical activity). **Recreational physical activity**, such as playing basketball or taking a walk around the block, is performed for its own sake, for enjoyment, or for exercise. The distinction is important in the context of the built environment since design strategies and funding that promote each of these two kinds of physical activity may differ. For example, a trail that connects two points can be built by a department of transportation. A walking loop in a park is not considered useful for transportation, so it requires parks and recreation funding, not department of transportation allocations.

This chapter also considers another related distinction between two domains or purposes of physical activity: **active transportation** and **active recreation**. Active transportation is defined as walking or biking to reach a specific destination and may include the use of public transportation such as buses or trains. Active recreation means choosing leisure-time activities that are physically active (such as playing basketball in the park) versus sedentary (such as knitting or reading). Although walking is the most common type of activity done for both transportation and recreation

purposes, the environmental conditions that promote walking for transportation differ slightly from those that promote walking for recreation. In one study, trip distances for utilitarian walking were generally shorter and occurred in higher density, **mixed land use** areas, whereas recreational walking occurred more in residential areas and with longer trip distances.[6] In general, utilitarian physical activity, of which active transportation (such as walking) is a subset, makes up a greater proportion of a person's walking trips than recreational physical activity or active recreation.

Finally, it is also important to note that increasing walking, rolling, and general public transportation usage not only promotes health, but also has important environmental impacts. Many of the built environment attributes discussed in this chapter can also help reduce reliance on automobiles. According to the US Environmental Protection Agency, the transportation sector represents 28 percent of US greenhouse gas emissions and 14 percent of global emissions (these numbers include emissions associated with both private vehicles and commercial transportation). Encouraging people to walk more and drive less means fewer cars on the road, which in turn reduces noise and car crashes, as well as emissions, which in turn improves air quality.[7] **Vehicle miles traveled (VMT)** is a key measure from the field of transportation used to help understand how reliant particular communities are on private vehicles. Reduced VMT has been linked to greater residential density and mixed-use development, both of which will be discussed in the next section.[7] Encouraging people to drive less and walk more is an important long-term strategy to combat climate change and build more sustainable communities.

INCREASING ACTIVE TRANSPORTATION

Walkable communities, or neighborhoods, are those in which residents can walk to nearby destinations (box 2.1 and figure 2.1). Public transportation can help augment walkability because people typically walk or bike to reach

BOX 2.1 WHAT DO HIGHLY WALKABLE PLACES LOOK LIKE?

It is easy to picture walkability in large cities like New York, Copenhagen, and Hong Kong. They all have high residential density and mixed land use patterns that mix shops and homes, as well as ample sidewalks and bike lanes within well-connected street grids. There always seem to be people walking or biking around these cities. Such cities typically have excellent public transportation systems that encourage walking and biking to and from transit stops.

Suburbs have been much maligned for their sprawling development. Sprawl is a term often used to describe low-walkable communities with low density, disconnected streets, and separated land uses. Sprawl as a type of urban design accelerated during the mid-twentieth century in the United States, made possible by large numbers of people having automobiles and being able to drive long distances to destinations. However, many suburbs are trying to "retrofit" their sprawling development to include more of the elements typically found in larger cities. They do so by adding shops to residential areas, building multifamily housing, and creating walking and cycling paths among destinations.

In rural areas, walkability may take the form of compact town centers where people can park and do their shopping on foot when they arrive. Nature trails can be added to open spaces that may adjoin these town centers, and many rural areas have the strength of natural resources as potential attractions and places for physical activity. Streets can also be designed to safely accommodate walking and cycling by lowering speed limits and creating visual (for example, striping) or physical (for example, off-road paths) separation between people and cars. However, creative solutions are needed to address commonly occurring challenges in rural communities like consolidated school districts, which can leave behind vacant school buildings and "zombie" sidewalks that were designed with good intention but lead to nowhere.

---

their bus or train. Across eleven countries on five continents, walkable neighborhoods have consistently been linked to higher levels of physical activity.[8]

Land Use, Street Connectivity, and Residential Density

Mixed land use, street **connectivity**, and **residential density** are the built environment attributes most consistently related to total physical activity. Street connectivity refers to the directness of connections among streets. This can be contrasted to cul-de-sacs and "hierarchical" street networks, where a busy main road will feed into smaller streets that do not connect to one another—both of which are common suburban street patterns (see "Connectivity" in the Victoria Transportation Policy Institute Online Encyclopedia). Residential density refers to the number of households in a particular area—a city has a high residential density because many people live in apartments or condominiums that take up a small geographic area. Rural areas are typically low

residential density because most people live in single-family homes built on large lots. Additional built environment attributes that have been linked with increased active transportation include intersection density, distance to transit, and the number of destinations within walking distance.[9]

Measures of land use, street connectivity, and residential density have been combined to create a **walkability** index. Walk Score is a well-known and freely available example of a walkability index, although it does not measure these specific constructs and instead uses a more complex patented algorithm to calculate its walkability metrics. Walk Score has been shown to be a reliable indicator of access to amenities, and a higher Walk Score has also been associated with higher levels of physical activity among adults.[10] For more information about measures, see chapter 22. Compared to low-walkability neighborhoods, adults living in high-walkability neighborhoods were far more likely to meet the 150-minute weekly physical activity guidelines.[8]

Figure 2.1. People are more likely to choose to walk for transportation and for recreation when there is safe pedestrian infrastructure, as shown here in a Copenhagen neighborhood that includes both homes and shops, thus enabling people to walk or bike to complete many errands. Here, roads are primarily for people and bicycles, rather than cars, and it is safe for children to play or bicycle.
Source: www.pedbikeimages.org/Ryan Snyder

Many walkability indices measure the **macroscale pedestrian environment** at the level of administrative boundaries (for example, census tracts). The macroscale pedestrian environment is considered easier to measure because the data (for example, land use) are readily available; however, these elements are more difficult to modify because they cover a larger geographic area. The **microscale pedestrian environment** is measured at the level of the street segment, and it too has increasingly been studied and correlated with increased physical activity in children and adults.[11] The microscale consists of elements of street design, including transit stops, sidewalks, and crossing infrastructure, as well as other aesthetic elements like street trees, lighting, and building design.[11] These elements are much easier to modify, which makes under-standing them attractive to researchers and practitioners. The microscale pedestrian environment is more difficult to measure and has not been incorporated into many walkability measures.

The environmental attributes related to physical activity may be somewhat different for youth and seniors. Mixed-use development and recreation areas near one's residence are associated with greater levels of walking among youth.[12] The relationship between youth walking and residential density, intersection density, and the presence of at least one commercial land use were only significant among White youth, and there were other differences found between groups by race/ethnicity, gender, and high- versus low-income households, as well.[12] For older adults, walkability, perceived safety from crime, accessibility to destinations and recreational facilities, and aesthetically pleasing scenery all positively impact physical activity.[13] Additionally, Barnett et al.[13] note that the magnitude of impact may be underestimated by the current literature because so much of the research has been conducted in Western countries where low-density cities are the norm. Perceived safety from crime may play a particularly important role in influencing physical activity levels for vulnerable seniors.[1]

Activity-Supportive Social Environments

Social environment attributes include aesthetics, social support, crime, racism, and **incivilities** (such as litter or graffiti). These attributes can encourage or discourage physical activity, independent of whether the infrastructure such as sidewalks is ample. Features of the social environment are measured through observational audits or self-report. Although perception-based and objectively assessed measures of the built environment are separate constructs, both play important roles in encouraging physical activity.

In a study with older adults in racial and ethnic minority groups in Texas, perceived community racism appeared to moderate the association between opportunities for physical activity and self-reported physical activity.[14] Although opportunities for physical activity are typically associated with greater levels of physical activity,[9] Edwards and Cunningham found that subjects who perceived higher levels of community racism also perceived fewer opportunities for physical activity and were less physically active.[14]

For youth, the perceptions that they have friends nearby to play with and that their neighborhood is safe and welcoming have both been associated with less screen time and greater levels of physical activity.[15] For adults, the relationship between physical activity and perception-based measures of crime and aesthetics has been mixed.[9] Undesirable neighborhood aesthetics and incivilities, including litter, graffiti, and stray dogs, are more likely to be present in lower-income neighborhoods and may act as deterrents to recreational physical activity or walking,[16] but these findings are not universal.[17] Overall community design (for example, mixed-use and street connectivity) may override crime, graffiti, and incivilities in shaping active transportation in otherwise high-walkability neighborhoods. The relation of crime to physical activity remains unclear because research to date has used simple measures with minimal collaborations with criminologists.

Environmental Disparities

Low-income and racial or ethnic minority groups have some of the highest rates of obesity and obesity-related diseases in the United States. Although little research has examined the differential impacts of built environment interventions on low-income and racial or ethnic minority groups, there is some evidence that these infrastructure improvements disproportionately occur in neighborhoods with high-income and well-educated populations,[18] who then receive greater benefits from these investments. Additionally, public infrastructure improvements are increasingly linked with rising property values and may lead to the displacement of the communities that these investments seek to benefit.

People of color are more likely than White people to reside in neighborhoods with mixed land use and high street connectivity, both elements of good walkability.[19] However, they are also more likely than White people to report their neighborhoods as being aesthetically unpleasant, high in crime, heavy in traffic, and low in social cohesion.[19] Two studies highlighted environmental disparities. Neckerman et al.[20] compared poor and more affluent neighborhoods in New York City, using geographic information system technology and field observation, and found that low-income census tracts had significantly fewer trees, landmark buildings, clean streets, and sidewalk cafés and significantly higher rates of felony complaints, narcotics arrests, and vehicular crashes. Zhu and Lee[21] found that areas in Austin, Texas, with higher poverty or with greater percentages of Hispanics had higher neighborhood-level walkability and more sidewalks. However, these areas also had higher motor vehicle crash and crime rates and poorer pedestrian infrastructure, visual qualities, physical amenities, maintenance, and perceived safety.

Environmental Interventions

There is now strong evidence that the addition of walking and cycling paths, as well as of public transportation infrastructure, such as rail stops, contributes to increases in total physical activity.[9] **Complete streets** is a popular notion that streets should be designed to accommodate the mobility needs of drivers, cyclists, walkers, transit riders, and people with disabilities rather than primarily favoring motor vehicle users. Complete streets policies often mandate that all new road construction projects include bike and pedestrian facilities and can be adopted by local and state governments.[22] These policies help to create a network of bike and pedestrian facilities and encourage physical activity. Although complete streets approaches in rural communities might look different, there are rural communities working to make these types of changes (for example, see the Small Town and Rural Design Guide: https://ruraldesignguide.com).

Local, state, and federal programs are pursuing environmental changes that promote walking and bicycling. For example, Safe Routes to School programs promote the installation or improvement of sidewalks, bicycle lanes, crosswalks, and sidewalk curb ramps and lower posted speed. Examples of interventions to reduce traffic speeds include lowering speed limits, speed cameras, and street design elements such as speed humps and traffic-calming bump-outs called chicanes.[23] A longitudinal evaluation over five years and across 801 schools in Florida, Texas, Oregon, and Washington, DC, found that road engineering improvements alone resulted in an 18 percent increase in children walking or bicycling to school.[24] The same study also found that over five years, the educational and empowerment campaigns resulted in a 25 percent increase in children walking or biking to school, noting that the effects of the campaigns are cumulative.[24] Additionally, data from Bogotá, Colombia, and elsewhere document a substantial increase in bicycle trips as miles of new bikeways were built over two decades (figure 2.2). In Bogotá, these bikeways were also paired with programming such as ciclovía and cicloruta[25,26] as part of a multilevel intervention. Ciclovía is a program that closes streets to cars and allows people to play, walk, and bike in the streets. It was the precursor to Open Streets programming in the United States and around the world. Cicloruta is the largest network of cycling-only paths in Latin America.[25]

Building design may also play a role in encouraging physical activity. Making stairways more accessible within buildings encourages people to walk rather than take the elevator. For example, the Center for Active Design's guidelines suggest, among other design recommendations, including "grand staircases," which should be visible and attractive, and also indicate that stairs should be located near main entrances. King et al.[27] found that posting signage to encourage people to take the stairs resulted in up to a 35 percent increase in stair usage reported. Providing bike parking and showers on-site can also encourage active transportation, especially when paired with the removal of free parking (see chapter 13 for more information).

Some rural communities have incorporated creative solutions to promote physical activity, such as creating temporary bike lanes for a bike to school day, integrating drop-off areas for a walking school bus in which children walk together to school, or holding bike rodeos. Evidence suggests that more permanent approaches applied in urban and suburban areas, such as Safe Routes to Schools, could work in rural communities that have a

Figure 2.2. Some of the best evidence for "if you build it, they will come" is found in Bogotá, Colombia, where a substantial increase of the number of bikeway miles, along with programmatic interventions like ciclovías, led to commute mode share growth from 0.58 percent in 1996 to an estimated value of 9.1 percent in 2017. Source: Wikimedia commons, courtesy Felipe Restrepo Acosta. https://creativecommons.org/licenses/by-sa /3.0/deed.en

downtown where most destinations, including schools, are located. For rural communities with consolidated school districts or without a downtown area, other solutions are needed. For example, Whitefish, Montana, has held open streets events and bike rodeos and developed pop-up bike lanes using construction cones and signs.

INCREASING ACTIVE RECREATION

Recreational physical activity (also called active recreation or **leisure-time physical activity**) is undertaken for enjoyment, exercise, or health and well-being purposes. The environmental correlates of recreational physical activity are less well studied than those for active trans-

portation.[9] Some places are designed for recreational physical activity, including parks, trails, community centers, physical activity facilities (such as gyms, tracks, and courts), school grounds, and playgrounds (figure 2.3). Active recreation can also be carried out in settings designed for multiple functions, such as homes, sidewalks, and streets.[9] The image on the cover of this book of Minneapolis, Minnesota, shows people of all ages engaging in playful active recreation in a multifunctional park space. In this case, they appear to be doing tai chi, but the space can be used in a variety of ways.

The accessibility and quality of recreation facilities can be measured through direct

Figure 2.3. Well-designed playgrounds encourage children to be physically active and can help to reduce childhood obesity by offering an attractive alternative to watching television and playing video games.
Source: Photo courtesy of Nisha Botchwey

observation audits, GIS mapping, and self-reports.[17] Differences in measurement methods can make it difficult to compare results across studies.[17] This section summarizes evidence on the relation of built and social environment variables to recreational physical activity and walking, which is the most common type because it is readily available and inexpensive.

Access to Recreation Facilities

Living in proximity to parks, trails, and private recreation facilities is related to use and recreational physical activity.[9,27,28] Having accessible recreation, exercise, or sports facilities in neighborhoods tends to be associated with overall physical activity in most but not all studies.[9,17]

In one study of park users, for example, people living within one-fourth of a mile of a park were the biggest group of frequent users (43 percent); those who lived more than one mile away made up just 13 percent of the frequent users.[16] This information has been used by 10 Minute Walk, a nonprofit park advocacy group, to set a goal of everyone in the United States living within a ten-minute walk of a park by 2050.

For children and teenagers, proximity to recreation facilities in neighborhoods and school grounds may play a particularly strong role in physical activity and social connections, although not all studies have shown significant associations.[15] Having many places for physical activity in a neighborhood was associated with higher recreational activity and less screen time.[15] In a natural longitudinal experiment on adolescents who had a parent in the military, moves to places with greater objectively assessed accessibility to recreation facilities were associated with significant increases in physical activity.[29] Because military families typically relocate based on factors outside of their control, studies like this can help combat **self-selection** bias.[29] Self-selection here refers to the phenomenon that active people may move into highly walkable areas, so some of the correlation between walkable built environments and high levels of physical activity may be due to this self-selection effect. However, survey studies assessing preferences for physical activity and high- versus low-walkability neighborhoods suggest that active people do self-select into high-walkability neighborhoods, but self-selection alone does not explain the associations between neighborhood walkability and physical activity.[30]

Quality of Recreation Facilities

The quality and aesthetics of recreation facilities are important contributors to physical activity. Parks and trails that are well maintained, safe, clean, and well lit and that have facilities such as restrooms, drinking fountains, exercise equipment, open play spaces, playgrounds, and courts and fields are used more and contribute to higher physical activity levels among users than those without these features.[18] Although parks provide a suitable space for sedentary behaviors such as relaxing and picnicking and for contact with nature (see chapter 16), it is important that they also contain facilities that provide ample opportunities for physical activity.

Additionally, combining park improvements with programming—for example, free classes at the park or a public education campaign about available facilities—appears to be promising for increasing physical activity.[28] However, these programs and improvements should be guided by engagement with the communities they intend to serve.[31] Park space and programming needs of low-income and racial and ethnic minority groups may be different, and it is important for park planners to be attentive to the needs of their specific communities.[31]

For example, the Minneapolis Parks and Recreation Board (MPRB) engaged in a master planning process between 2016 and 2019. The goal of these plans was to prioritize park improvements, which were determined in partnership with communities and included ensuring that the facilities at each park matched the community's preferences. The MPRB's approach to the master planning process was locally hailed for its innovative and equitable approach to community engagement. The funding that supports this effort was provided through a joint agreement between the MPRB and the City of Minneapolis and was explicitly intended to "help address racial and economic equity across 160 neighborhoods" in the city by targeting maintenance and repairs first and then replacing outdated parks equipment based on community priorities. Park projects were ranked and prioritized based on seven equity criteria, which determined what was funded and when. These criteria included racially concentrated areas of poverty, population density, youth population, neighborhood safety, conditions and age of park assets, and historic investment (https://www.minneapolisparks.org/about_us/budget_financial/20-year_neighborhood_park_plan/).

Intervention Studies

Research on built environment interventions for recreational physical activity is somewhat mixed.[28] For example, although there is agreement that access to recreational facilities such as parks, trails, and gyms is generally associated with higher levels of physical activity,[27] individual studies may fail to find significant associations[28] when other factors eclipse the role of the facilities. For example, perceived community racism may override the importance of opportunities for physical activity.[14]

Creating opportunities for physical activity through temporary programs such as open streets, which close roads to cars to allow for walking and cycling, may positively impact leisure-time physical activity.[25,27] *Tactical urbanism* or demonstration projects that leverage fast, affordable, and lightweight modifications to the built environment offer opportunities to try out new configurations and have been used widely throughout the United States. Play Streets, a program of temporary closure of streets or activation of other publicly accessible spaces (for example, parking lots, fields, playgrounds, school grounds, or parks) for a set number of hours (recurring or episodic) with loose active play equipment (such as hula hoops and jump ropes) and supervision, engages both rural and urban children and youth in physical activity.[32]

In many rural areas, active recreation takes on a different meaning than in urban or suburban areas. In rural areas, the idea of active recreation is the ability to drive to a place where physical activity can more readily occur rather than walking, biking, or otherwise rolling from an origin to a destination or without one in mind.[33] One approach, promoted by the Rails-to-Trails Conservancy, is to create a comprehensive network of trails throughout the United States along unused rail corridors to help suburban and rural areas become more interconnected. More than 20,000 miles of rail trails have been built in the United States. Outside of the United States, rail trails are relatively rare because rail corridors are seldom abandoned. In the United Kingdom, Sustrans has created an extensive National Cycle Network of trails using a variety of rights-of-way.

Social and Economic Factors Related to Active Recreation

One of the critical challenges in this field is how to encourage physical activity among economically disadvantaged populations who bear a disproportionate burden of chronic disease in the United States (as discussed in chapter 9). The quality of recreation facilities and access to these facilities both tend to be poor in low-income communities.[31] A national study showed that low-income areas had less access to all types of public and private recreation facilities, and lack of access partially explained disparities in adolescent physical activity.[34]

Additionally, although adding programming in existing parks can increase parks usage, it is likely not enough to overcome the social barriers to physical activity in low-income communities.[35] In a randomized controlled trial on free parks programming, perceived safety and crime in neighborhoods and recreational spaces appeared to negatively influence participation in the programming.[35]

CONCLUSION

There is strong, international evidence that built environments play an important role in shaping physical activity[8] (table 2.1) and that physical activity has major impacts on health.[4] Creating community environments that support active transportation and recreation could have widespread and long-lasting effects, but the research indicates that numerous changes are needed in the macro- and microlevel built environments and social environments in the United States to make it easier for people to be physically active.

To support active transportation and more total physical activity among people of all ages, neighborhood walkability needs to be improved. To achieve this goal, changes in zoning and real estate practices are needed in some places to allow denser, mixed-use developments. Practices in the real estate development industry need to be changed so that, for example, financing encourages more mixed-use development (some current banking practices make it more difficult to finance mixed-use than single-use developments). Environmental changes, supported by education, programming, and policies, have been successful in increasing bicycling in general and active transportation to school. Policy changes that mandate connected streets and sidewalks and bicycle facilities that can support activity for both transportation and recreation purposes will be required for some communities (figure 2.4). Advocacy is a strategy that can be used to engage community

Table 2.1. Summary of built environment associations with physical activity (+ indicates a positive association, − a negative association, and o no association or insufficient studies to summarize).

	Active Transportation	Active Recreation
Macroscale		
Mixed land use	+	+
Street connectivity	+	o
Residential density	+	o
Access to destinations	+	o
Microscale		
Pedestrian infrastructure	+	+
Cycling infrastructure	+	+
Public transportation infrastructure	+	o
Access/proximity to parks and recreation facilities	o	+
Quality of parks and recreation facilities	o	+
Aesthetics (benches, lighting, public art, natural environment)	o	+
Social Environment		
Street activity (people on the street)	+	+
Crime	−	−
Incivilities	−	−
Social capital	o	+

Figure 2.4. When the Arthur Ravenel Jr. Bridge crossing the Cooper River in Charleston, South Carolina, was designed (to replace an old bridge), community leaders successfully argued for adding a pedestrian and bicycle path to the span, despite the extra costs; use of the path for both recreation and transportation has far exceeded expectations.
Source: Google Maps 2021

members to help environmental and policy changes through low-cost, grassroots efforts. For example, the Physical Activity Research Center completed Youth Engagement and Action for Health! (YEAH!) programming, research, and evaluation, and results indicate that youth advocacy is a promising intervention technique for improving physical activity environments.[36]

Different approaches to support physical activity are required for urban, suburban, and rural environments (box 2.2). Retrofit-ting existing low-walkable neighborhoods is a much more challenging task than building new because it often involves more than adding sidewalks; major redevelopments and costly changes to roads and other infrastructure are likely to be needed. Often, the best strategy is to lobby for more activity-friendly design elements—for sidewalks, lighting, and such—in development or redevelopment projects that occur for other reasons. To support active recreation, people need access to public parks, trails, and private recreation

---

BOX 2.2 PHYSICAL ACTIVITY AS AMENITY DURING CRISIS

Paradoxically, the COVID-19 pandemic beginning in 2020 saw both an increased demand on walking and cycling infrastructure—leading to overcrowding in many parks and trails—and increased sedentary behavior because people were no longer commuting to work or school and so typically moved less throughout the day. The increased demand on walking and cycling infrastructure was both due to fears about public transit usage—and the potential for the virus to spread in close quarters—and an increased time available for recreational physical activity due to much-reduced commuting behaviors.

As a result, the pandemic also highlighted the inequity of access to public open spaces. Walking and cycling infrastructure, parks, and other types of recreational facilities are often amenities that tend to be built and better maintained in wealthier neighborhoods. Wealthy people were thus able to be physically active in nearby parks as well as in their private backyards or able to access a private vehicle to drive to recreational spaces. Many people in low-income communities did not have the same opportunities for physical activity. Although not true everywhere, public transportation infrastructure in the United States is generally not robust enough to enable transit-dependent people to access a diversity of recreational facilities. And in many rural areas, parks and trails were at least temporarily closed during the pandemic, which prevented people from being physically active, despite having an abundance of space.

To respond to this increased demand, many cities—such as Oakland, Minneapolis, Boston, New York, and Los Angeles—began closing streets to cars to create more opportunities for physical activity. Other cities—such as Milan, Italy; Bogotá, Colombia; and Lima, Peru—installed demonstration projects and expanded bike lanes during the crisis, seizing the opportunity to show people the future of the city.

The City of Oakland, in particular, was attentive to the inequity of access to recreation opportunities and began closing streets in lower-income neighborhoods first as a part of its Slow Streets program. However, the city quickly found out from community members that many people in these neighborhoods preferred not to have their street closed because they still needed to get to work or have access other critical services. In response, Oakland stopped adding new Slow Streets to these communities and instead began to install simple traffic calming and pedestrian safety measures at "Essential Places": grocery stores, COVID-19 testing sites, and other food distribution sites. This story illustrates the necessity to effectively engage the community to identify high-priority local needs. For more details about its Slow Streets program, see the City of Oakland's website (https://www.oaklandca.gov/projects/oakland-slow-streets).

facilities. New research is documenting how parks can be designed to stimulate more physical activity. The strong link between aesthetics and active recreation suggests that well-designed places can attract people to be active.

Access to recreation facilities, quality and safety of pedestrian facilities, and aesthetics are generally poorer in areas with mostly low-income and racial or ethnic minority populations.[31] A high priority for community leaders should be to reduce disparities in the built environment so that disadvantaged communities have the infrastructure to support both active transportation and active recreation. However, this must be coupled with attention to the forces of gentrification, particularly "green gentrification," as infrastructure improvements are increasingly coupled with the displacement of these vulnerable populations (see chapter 9).

Further research is required to strengthen future interventions to promote physical activity through the built environment. First, it is important to understand how aspects of the built environment may differentially impact subgroups within the population. Youth, older adults, people in low-income groups, and racial and ethnic minorities all have unique experiences of the built environment that must be studied and understood so as to build better places for everyone. In particular, studying the relationship between infrastructure investments and displacement is an important area for future research. Additionally, the relationship between crime and physical activity requires collaboration with criminologists to improve measures and study design. Finally, larger and better-controlled studies of interventions on recreational environments specifically, with concurrent measures of programs and promotional efforts, are needed.

Physical activity plays a critical role in health and disease[4]; thus, it is imperative to mobilize efforts to create communities that facilitate physical activity as part of comprehensive health promotion strategies. Cities around the world are investing in various built and social physical activity interventions following examples of successful approaches for improving built environments that can be adopted by others.[9]

DISCUSSION QUESTIONS

1. Describe the differences between physical activity for transportation and physical activity for recreation. How do features of the built environment affect these types of physical activity differently?

2. Identify five key findings from research on the relationship between the built environment and physical activity. How could you use these key findings to design active communities in rural, in suburban, and in urban settings?

3. What programs can you implement or changes could you make to the built environment to increase physical activity in urban, suburban, and rural communities? Which attributes of the built environment could you target to support long-term increases in physical activity?

4. What changes to the built environment could you make to promote physical activity in low- to middle-income countries? What outcome would you expect from such changes, and how might your strategies in these areas need to be different from high-income countries?

5. Using table 2.1, for each of the environmental attributes at the macroscale, microscale, and social environment documented to be related to physical activity, identify the decision-maker groups with authority to make changes. For each type of decision-maker, identify some of the scientific, community, advocacy, and business groups that could be involved in educating and influencing these decision-makers.

ACKNOWLEDGMENTS

Preparation of this chapter was supported by the Physical Activity Research Center, a national program of the Robert Wood Johnson Foundation. Portions of this chapter are adapted from chapter 2, "Community Design for Physical Activity," by James F. Sallis, Rachel A. Millstein, and Jordan A. Carlson in the first edition of *Making Healthy Places* (2011).

DISCLOSURE OF COMPETING INTERESTS

Nisha Botchwey's declarations appear in the preface.

M. Renée Umstattd Meyer and Meaghan McSorley disclose no competing interests.

REFERENCES

1. Botchwey ND, Trowbridge M, Fisher T. Green health: urban planning and the development of healthy and sustainable neighborhoods and schools. *Journal of Planning Education and Research*. 2014;34(2):113-122. https://doi.org/10.1177/0739456X14531830

2. Lee H, Tamminen KA, Clark AM, Slater L, Spence JC, Holt NL. A meta-study of qualitative research examining determinants of children's independent active free play. *International Journal of Behavioral Nutrition and Physical Activity*. 2015;12(1):1-12.

3. World Health Organization. Physical activity fact sheet. Published November 26, 2020. Accessed November 15, 2021. https://www.who.int/news-room/fact-sheets/detail/physical-activity

4. US Department of Health and Human Services (USDHHS). *Physical Activity Guidelines for Americans*. 2nd ed. US Department of Health and Human Services; 2018. https://health.gov/sites/default/files/2019-09/Physical_Activity_Guidelines_2nd_edition.pdf

5. Frieden TR. A framework for public health action: the health impact pyramid. *American Journal of Public Health*. 2010;100(4),590-595. https://doi.org/10.2105/AJPH.2009.185652

6. Kang B, Moudon AV, Hurvitz PM, Saelens BE. Differences in behavior, time, location, and built environment between objectively measured utilitarian and recreational walking. *Transportation Research Part D: Transport and Environment*. 2017;57,185-194. https://doi.org/10.1016/j.trd.2017.09.026

7. Gomez-Ibanez JA, Humphrey NP. TRB special report: driving and the built environment: the effects of compact development on motorized travel, energy use, and CO_2 emissions. *TR News*. 2010;(268).

8. Adams MA, Ding D, Sallis JF, et al. Patterns of neighborhood environment attributes related to physical activity across 11 countries: a latent class analysis. *International Journal of Behavioral Nutrition and Physical Activity*. 2013;10(1):34.

9. Kärmeniemi M, Lankila T, Ikäheimo T, et al. The built environment as a determinant of physical activity: a systematic review of longitudinal studies and natural experiments. *Annals of Behavioral Medicine*. 2018;52(3):239-251.

10. Carr LJ, Dunsiger SI, Marcus BH. Walk Score™ as a global estimate of neighborhood walkability. *American Journal of Preventive Medicine*. 2010;39(5):460-463. doi:10.1016/j.amepre.2010.07.007

11. Cain KL, Millstein RA, Sallis JF, et al. Contribution of streetscape audits to explanation of physical activity in four age groups based on the Microscale Audit of Pedestrian Streetscapes (MAPS). *Social Science & Medicine*. 2014;116,82-92.

12. Kerr J, Frank L, Sallis J F, Chapman J. Urban form correlates of pedestrian travel in youth: differences by gender, race-ethnicity and household attributes. *Transportation Research Part D: Transport and Environment*. 2007;12(3):177-182. https://doi.org/10.1016/j.trd.2007.01.006

13. Barnett DW, Barnett A, Nathan A, Van Cauwenberg J, Cerin, E. Built environmental correlates of older adults' total physical activity and walking: a systematic review and meta-analysis. *International Journal of Behavioral Nutrition and Physical Activity*. 2017;14(1):1-24.

14. Edwards MB, Cunningham G. Examining the associations of perceived community racism with self-reported physical activity levels and health among older racial minority adults. *Journal of Physical Activity and Health*. 2013;10(7):932-939.

15. Kopcakova J, Veselska ZD, Geckova AM. Is a perceived activity-friendly environment associated with more physical activity and fewer screen-based activities in adolescents? *International Journal of Environmental Research and Public Health*. 2017;14(1):39.

16. Cohen DA, Han B, Derose KP, et al. Promoting physical activity in high-poverty neighborhood parks: a cluster randomized controlled trial. *Social Science & Medicine*. 2017;186,130-138.

17. Bancroft C, Joshi S, Rundle A, et al. Association of proximity and density of parks and objectively measured physical activity in the United States: a systematic review. *Social Science & Medicine*. 2015;138,22-30.

18. Smith M, Hosking J, Woodward A, et al. Systematic literature review of built environment effects on physical activity and active transport—an update and new findings on health equity. *International Journal of Behavioral Nutrition and Physical Activity*. 2017;14(1):158.

19. Cutts BB, Darby KJ, Boone CJ, Brewis A. City structure, obesity, and environmental justice: an integrated analysis of physical and social barriers to walkable streets and park access. *Social Science & Medicine*. 2009;69:1314-1322.

20. Neckerman KM, Lovasi GS, Davies S, et al. Disparities in urban neighborhood conditions: evidence from GIS measures and field observation in New York City. *Journal of Public Health Policy*. 2009;30:264-285.

21. Zhu X, C Lee. Walkability and safety around elementary schools: economic and ethnic disparities. *American Journal of Preventive Medicine*. 2008;34:282-290.

22. Trowbridge MJ, Schmid TL. Built environment and physical activity promotion: place-based obesity prevention strategies. *Journal of Law, Medicine & Ethics*. 2013;41(Suppl 2):46-51.

23. Elvik R, Vadeby A, Hels T, van Schagen I. Updated estimates of the relationship between speed and road safety at the aggregate and individual levels. *Accident Analysis & Prevention*. 2019;123,114-122.

24. McDonald NC, Steiner RL, Lee C, Rhoulac Smith T, Zhu X, Yang Y. Impact of the safe routes to school program on walking and bicycling. *Journal of the American Planning Association*. 2014;80(2):153-167.

25. Torres A, Sarmiento OL, Stauber C, Zarama R. The Ciclovía and Cicloruta programs: promising interventions to promote physical activity and social capital in Bogotá, Colombia. *American Journal of Public Health*. 2013;103(2):e23-e30.

26. Rosas-Satizábal D, Rodriguez-Valencia A. Factors and policies explaining the emergence of the bicycle commuter in Bogotá. *Case Studies on Transport Policy*. 2019;7(1):138-149.

27. King AC, Whitt-Glover MC, Marquez DX, et al. Physical activity promotion: highlights from the 2018 physical activity guidelines advisory committee systematic review. *Medicine & Science in Sports & Exercise*. 2019;51(6):1340-1353.

28. Hunter RF, Christian H, Veitch J, Astell-Burt T, Hipp JA, Schipperijn J. The impact of interventions to promote physical activity in urban green space: a systematic review and recommendations for future research. *Social Science & Medicine*. 2015;124,246-256.

29. Nicosia N, Datar A. Neighborhood environments and physical activity: a longitudinal study of adolescents in a natural experiment. *American Journal of Preventive Medicine*. 2018;54(5):671-678.

30. McCormack GR, Shiell A. In search of causality: a systematic review of the relationship between the built environment and physical activity among adults. *International Journal of Behavioral Nutrition and Physical Activity*. 2011;8(1):1-11.

31. Floyd MF, Taylor WC, Whitt-Glover M. Measurement of park and recreation environments that support physical activity in low-income communities of color: highlights of challenges and recommendations. *American Journal of Preventive Medicine*. 2009;36(4):S156-S160.

32. Umstattd Meyer MR, Bridges CN, Prochnow T, et al. Come together, play, be active: physical activity engagement of school-age children at Play Streets in four diverse rural communities in the U.S. *Preventive Medicine*. 2019;129:105869. doi:https://doi.org/10.1016/j.ypmed.2019.105869

33. Umstattd Meyer MR., Moore JB, Abildso C, Edwards MB, Gamble A, Baskin ML. Rural active living: a call to action. *Journal of Public Health Management and Practice*. 2016;22(5):E11-E20. doi:10.1097/PHH.0000000000000333

34. Gordon-Larsen P, Nelson MC, Page P, Popkin BM. Inequality in the built environment underlies key health disparities in physical activity and obesity. *Pediatrics*. 2006;117:417-424.

35. Cohen DA, Mckenzie TL, Sehgal A, Williamson S, Golinelli D, Lurie N. Contribution of public parks to physical activity. *American Journal of Public Health*. 2007;97:509-514.

36. Botchwey N, Jones-Bynes J, O'Connell K, Millstein RA, Kim A, Conway TL. Impact of a youth advocacy policy, systems and environmental change program for physical activity on perceptions and beliefs. *Preventive Medicine*. 2020;136. https://doi.org/10.1016/j.ypmed.2020.106077

CHAPTER 3

FOOD, NUTRITION, AND COMMUNITY DESIGN

Roxanne Dupuis, Karen Glanz, and Carolyn Cannuscio

KEY POINTS

- Individual-level interventions aimed at restricting calories and improving diet quality (and increasing activity levels) have failed to slow the obesity epidemic, leading researchers and practitioners to search for explanations and solutions in the food environment.
- Food environments—comprising food production, distribution, and marketing—vary dramatically within and across cities and from urban to rural areas.
- The toll of obesity is most evident in disadvantaged neighborhoods, which tend to lack supermarkets and fresh food yet have ample access to foods that are relatively inexpensive and calorie-dense but have little nutritional value.
- Various policy solutions are being launched on the local, regional, and national levels, with the promise of improved health as a rallying point for improvements in environments that include school food programs, changes in food marketing and nutrition labeling, and increased numbers of supermarkets and farmers' markets.
- The health effects of these policy changes are often difficult to measure, and benefits may become evident only after extensive and sustained environmental changes. Recent data suggest that the steep rise in obesity witnessed in the late twentieth and early twenty-first centuries in the United States may finally be slowing among children and adolescents, perhaps in part because of changes to the food environment. The COVID-19 pandemic may undermine this public health progress.[1]

INTRODUCTION

On Saturday, November 7, 2020, the streets of Philadelphia filled with drum lines and dance parties, cars honking, and both revelers and protesters reacting to the results of the Trump versus Biden presidential election. The streets, many blocked to traffic, were also filled with dinner tables and makeshift shelters, a reminder that the city and its food environment had shifted quickly and radically in response to the COVID-19 pandemic. Indoor dining had been constrained and supplanted with outdoor dining, grocery delivery and takeout had increased, and local shops posted signs limiting the number of customers inside and requiring masks. Although the overall mood of the largely Democratic city was buoyant, economic and health insecurity loomed.

Still, Center City's food economy is vibrant and diverse, unlike that in Philadelphia's disadvantaged neighborhoods. There the food landscape is marked by a limited range of outlets, dominated by corner stores with few

Figure 3.1. Many urban food landscapes are characterized by small stores, including corner stores with limited healthy options and quick-service take-out restaurants. A majority of Philadelphia schoolchildren visit corner stores daily as they travel to and from school.
Source: Google Maps 2021

healthful food options and by quick-service take-out restaurants. Prepandemic, the majority of schoolchildren in Philadelphia visited corner stores every day, often en route to or from school, procuring a ready supply of inexpensive and low-nutrition food—an average 475 to 650 calories per visit, at a cost of more than two dollars (figure 3.1).[2] As a resident of one of Philadelphia's high-poverty neighborhoods noted, "I don't know if that's like that in other places, too. But I know in Philadelphia if it's not there at the corner store then you're not going to get it."[3]

NUTRITION AND POPULATION HEALTH

The rate of obesity is rising globally and is highest in the United States. After a decades-long climb, the prevalence of obesity in the United States has remained relatively unchanged among children in recent years and, as of 2015–2016, stood at 18.5 percent.[4-6] Among adults, however, prevalence of **obesity (body mass index [BMI]** between 30 and 40) continues to increase, reaching approxi-mately 40 percent in 2015–2016.[7] These trends are projected to continue, with 50 percent of American adults expected to be obese by 2030 and 25 percent expected to be severely obese (BMI 40 and above).[8] Racial and ethnic disparities in obesity prevalence exist, with the highest burden among Black and Hispanic individuals.[6] Disparities by level of education and socioeconomic status are also marked, with high obesity rates among people with less than a high school education and those with incomes under the poverty line.[9] Obesity carries a social stigma, adverse economic costs (including employment discrimination), and a range of negative health consequences, including increased risk of cardiovascular disease, depression, pulmonary disease, musculoskeletal complaints, and impaired functional status.

Obesity occurs when energy (calories) consumed from food exceeds energy expended through physical activity. Chapter 2 focuses on physical activity and energy expenditure. This chapter focuses on the *consumption* side of the equation. A unique public health paradox exists alongside the obesity epidemic in that people can be overweight or obese (that is, *overnourished* due to caloric excess) yet still be lacking in the necessary nutrients for good health (*undernourished* due to micronutrient deficiencies). This is particularly noted among individuals with low socioeconomic status given that the high-fat and high-sugar foods implicated in weight gain are typically cheap and widely available but often fail to deliver adequate nutrients, whereas fresh, whole foods are can be expensive and difficult to obtain.

In low- and middle-income countries, the dual burden of undernutrition (in the form of wasting and stunting) and overnutrition (in the form of overweight and obesity) is particularly salient, with the burden falling primarily among the poorest.[10] These trends are similarly driven by changes to the food environment, with increased availability of high-fat and high-sugar foods, as well as urbanization, trade liberalization, and changes in food retail practices.[10]

Research has shown that *food insecurity*—the limited or uncertain availability of nutritionally sound, safe food—is common in the United States and is positively associated with being overweight.[11] Food insecurity is related to, but differs, from *hunger*, which refers to a physical feeling of discomfort.[12] Food-insecure youths may be particularly vulnerable to inhospitable food environments, as they turn to *fast food* more frequently and eat fewer meals at home with family.[13,14] Our food environments warrant a closer look as we tackle the companion ills of overnutrition and undernutrition.

Research on eating and physical activity has been guided until recently by biological and psychological models and theories that focus on individuals, families, and small social groups such as friends and co-workers. The rise of the obesity epidemic and the findings that most individual-level interventions to change eating behaviors have mixed effects have revealed the limitations of the dominant, individually focused models of behav-

ior.[15] More recently, *ecological models* of health behavior, which embrace the role of environments and policies, have gained attention.[16] A central tenet of ecological models is that, because behavior is influenced at multiple levels, the most effective interventions should operate at multiple levels. Diet and physical activity interventions that build knowledge, motivation, and behavioral change skills in individuals without changing food and built environments—and without attention to the effects of climate change on those environments and vice versa—are unlikely to be effective. A better understanding of individuals' food environments is essential to reducing the burden of obesity and improving public health.

OVERVIEW OF FOOD ENVIRONMENTS

Several conceptual models have been proposed to describe **food environments** and their range of potential health effects.[17] These models vary in their complexity and emphasis on different parts of the food environment. Here, we present a model that focuses attention on community or neighborhood food environments while also illustrating how these environments may be influenced by and interact with government and industry policies, the information or marketing environment, and an individual's characteristics (figure 3.2).

The food environment comprises different domains. The *community environment* defines the places where food can be obtained, including grocery stores, convenience stores, specialty stores, restaurants, and farmers' markets that are generally open to the public. Microenvironments accessible to various groups include homes, workplace and school cafeterias, and churches. The *consumer environment* describes what a person is exposed to once inside these food sources, especially in relation to availability of different types of foods, promotions, and price.[18] The marketing of unhealthy foods, in particular, shapes the consumer environment. The following sections of this chapter expand on what is known about the community and

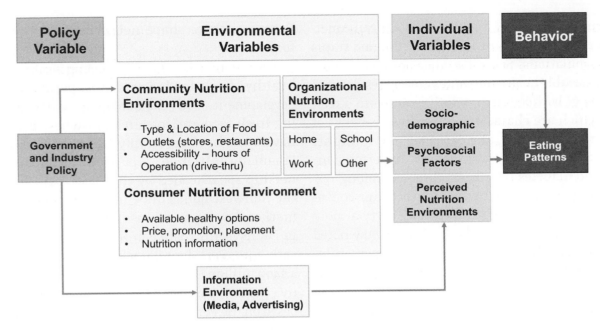

Policy Variable	Environmental Variables	Individual Variables	Behavior

Figure 3.2. As illustrated in this logic model of community nutrition environments, eating patterns are influenced by many variables, including government and industry policies, food availability, advertising, and personal beliefs. Source: Glanz K, Sallis JF, Saelens BE, Frank LD. Healthy nutrition environments: concepts and measures. *American Journal of Health Promotion.* 2005;19(5):330-333,ii.

consumer food environments of food stores and of restaurants.

Policies, defined as formal and informal rules, laws, and regulations, are important mechanisms for creating environmental changes. Both government and industry policies control food environments. Zoning decisions influence the preservation or loss of the agricultural land that is at the foundation of our food systems. School and employer policies dictate the resources, incentives, or deterrents to healthy eating in settings where children and adults spend most of their days. Family food rules and customs are policies that control food within homes.[19] Across these levels, behavioral economics principles (for example, behavioral cues or nudges) can be applied to facilitate behavior change.[20]

Food Stores: Distribution, Correlates, and Associations with Health Problems

Many researchers have studied how food environments vary across communities and have documented unequal distribution of food resources, as measured by the proximity of retail food outlets for various communities.[21]

Many studies have documented that supermarkets and fresh foods are limited in low-income, African American urban neighborhoods and many rural areas, but efforts at the state and federal levels have reversed this trend. Although the term **food deserts** and areas of **food apartheid**[22] are used to describe areas marked by a dearth of food options, researchers note that disadvantaged neighborhoods are often replete with calorie-dense, low-quality food options (that is, fast food), rather than devoid of food altogether. In other words, they can be described as **food swamps. Fresh food access** may serve as a more useful term for conceptualizing the availability of health-enhancing nutritional options in communities.

Low-income communities often have limited access to fresh foods, but the link between health and fresh food access as measured by proximity to supermarkets is less clear. This uncertainty may be driven in part by measurement challenges, including error in the assessment of both health and fresh food access. In 2009, Lovasi and colleagues reviewed twenty-two studies that examined the relationships between food environments and obesity risk in vulnerable African American, Hispanic, or low socioeconomic status populations. Several studies pointed to more favorable health outcomes among residents of neighborhoods in proximity to supermarkets, which are characterized by diverse stocks of fresh, prepared, and packaged foods.[9] Higher rates of obesity, overweight, hypertension, and diabetes have been observed among residents living near smaller grocery or convenience stores, which typically carry a more limited range of foods. Lovasi's review noted evidence that local food store mix may influence the health (and especially the BMI) of adolescents—particularly African American and Hispanic adolescents. In addition, the review included evidence of higher fruit and vegetable intake among residents with supermarkets nearby.[9] This finding extended to low-income participants in the **Supplemental Nutrition Assistance Program (SNAP)**. Adherence to dietary guidelines, as measured by the Alternate Healthy Eating Index (AHEI), was markedly worse in areas characterized by poorer objective (supermarket density) or subjective (resident-reported) measures of neighborhood food environment. Additionally, studies have found that SNAP recipients have a low diet quality.[23,24] These findings are salient to health; low AHEI scores have been linked to a range of chronic conditions, especially cardiovascular disease.[25]

Supermarkets within walking distance may foster access to and consumption of fresh, healthful foods while simultaneously serving as destinations that encourage physical activity—thereby favorably influencing both the caloric intake and energy expenditure sides of the physical activity and consumption equation. In addition to supermarkets, corner stores, farmers' markets, and online grocery programs make up the food retail environment. Although corner and convenience stores tend to be numerous, they offer limited healthy food options. On the other hand, farmers' markets are often less readily available, but offer fresh fruits and vegetables.

Together, these shape neighborhood retail food access.

Several approaches to increasing access to healthy, fresh foods focus on supermarket development, with the dual goals of delivering fresh food and jobs in areas where both have been in short supply. The Fresh Food Financing Initiative, a public-private partnership spearheaded by the Food Trust and the Reinvestment Fund, invested in supermarket development in underserved areas in Pennsylvania between 2004 and 2010.[26] In early 2010, President Barack Obama proposed a $400 million Healthy Food Financing Initiative (HFFI)—passed in the 2014 Farm Bill[27]—based on the Pennsylvania model, to be implemented across the country. These efforts have markedly increased access to supermarkets in low-income neighborhoods.[28,29] In addition to increasing access to food retailers, several strategies have focused on in-store food marketing to reshape the food environment by promoting healthy food purchases and restricting unhealthy ones.[30] Evidence suggests that placement strategies (for example, placing products at eye level)[31] and promotion strategies (for example, shelf labeling)[32] are effective at promoting the purchase of healthy foods and beverages.

Other interventions have targeted the healthfulness of foods sold at existing food retailers, including corner stores. These interventions generally incentivize store owners to stock healthier foods, including fresh produce, and to display these foods prominently—a behavioral economics strategy known as "choice architecture."[33] Farmers' markets are an increasingly common mechanism for delivering food to communities, with more than 8,000 in operation nationwide.[34] Such interventions are often paired with discount or voucher programs that make fresh fruits and vegetables more affordable.[35] Both corner store and farmers' market interventions have had moderate success in increasing the purchase and consumption of healthy foods.[33,35]

More recently, online food purchasing and delivery programs have become more commonplace. Such programs have the potential to increase access to healthy foods in neighborhoods with limited options. A review by Pitts and colleagues[36] found that online shopping may be both time-saving and convenient. Additionally, it may improve the food environment by reducing impulse purchases of unhealthy foods. Although online grocery shopping may make healthy foods more accessible, this can only be achieved if retail stores allow for the use of benefits such as SNAP online, which was not permitted up to early 2020.[36]

In the retail realm, another policy solution gaining momentum is the taxation of sugar-sweetened beverages (SSBs) through an excise tax, which increases the cost of SSBs for consumers. Such taxes have been successfully implemented locally in the United States—including in Berkeley, California, and Philadelphia—as well as in other countries. In Mexico, for example, SSB consumption fell by 7.3 percent after implementation of a one peso per liter tax,[37] while in Philadelphia, there was a 38 percent reduction in volume sales of taxed beverages.[38]

Restaurants: Distribution, Correlates, and Associations with Health Problems

In the United States, both children and adults increasingly eat meals prepared outside the home.[39] A greater reliance on restaurant meals has potential negative nutritional and health consequences because, compared with individuals who eat home-cooked meals, individuals who frequently eat restaurant food have a higher average caloric and fat intake and lower fruit, vegetable, and fiber consumption. Frequency of eating restaurant meals is associated with higher weights and increases in weight, perhaps because of the many unhealthy choices available in restaurants, large portion sizes, and the resultant higher calorie intake.[21,40]

Fast-food restaurants, in particular, have been identified as potential contributors to higher obesity prevalence.[41] Some fast-food chains have begun to respond by adding healthier food options, such as salads, to their menus, although fast-food operators perceive a limited demand for these options.[42] Proximity to fast-food restaurants in poorer neighborhoods and less healthful options within fast-food restaurants may partially explain the higher obesity prevalence among economically disadvantaged populations.[43] Findings are mixed about whether the proximity of fast-food restaurants is related to higher rates of obesity in children or adults, but it is clear that most meals from full-service restaurants and fast-food outlets do not currently contribute to a healthful food environment,[44] despite certain efforts to do so, including the "Kids LiveWell" initiative launched by the National Restaurant Association to offer healthier options for children.[45]

To improve the nutrition environment at restaurants, the 2010 Patient Protection and Affordable Care Act mandated calorie labeling at all chains across the United States. A meta-analysis of menu labeling studies found that these led to a reduction of approximately 18 calories per meal,[46] although more recent data suggests this could be higher at 60 calories per transaction.[47] To date, however, there is limited evidence that calorie labeling has led to healthier product reformulation.[47]

Measuring Changes to the Food Environment

To understand how interventions affect population health, we need to understand the process by which they change the food environment and measure such changes to the food environment. Measures have varied from simple counts of food stores and types, often analyzed with geographic information system methods, to assessments of the foods available in stores and restaurants.[40,48] One such measure of the food environment is the Nutrition Environment Measures Survey (NEMS), which has been widely used and adapted to multiple food environments, including food stores (NEMS-S) and restaurants (NEMS-R). The NEMS quantifies the availability of healthy food options, their price and quality, and other factors that promote the consumption of healthy foods, such as marketing.[40,48]

AGRICULTURE AND FOOD SYSTEMS

Agricultural systems undergird the food environments visible in locales across the United States. They are at the beginning of the *food system chain*, which also involves food processing and production, food marketing and distribution, and ultimately food choice by institutions and consumers. As it stands, the US food system is "largely unhealthy, inequitable, environmentally damaging, and insufficiently resilient to endure the impacts of climate change, resource depletion, and population increases, and is therefore unsustainable."[49(p151)]

Agricultural systems are shaped by legislation known as the Farm Bill, which was first enacted during the Great Depression to ensure the nation's food supply and protect farmers from the vicissitudes of economic cycles and unpredictable growing conditions. Congress revisits the Farm Bill at approximately five-year intervals, defining and redefining commodity, trade, marketing, and conservation programs, as well as national food assistance programs such as SNAP, the program for Women, Infants and Children, the School Breakfast Program, and the National School Lunch Program. The Farm Bill influences both the food and built environments by shaping nutrition programs and the use and preservation (or loss) of agricultural land. For example, the most recent (2018) Farm Bill made funding for farmers' markets permanent and expanded funding for fruit and vegetable prescription programs.[50] The 2008 Farm Bill included $4 billion in additional funding for conservation through mechanisms such as the Conservation Stewardship Program, which assists farmers in protecting the natural resources on their property. The program fosters adoption of activities such as organic farming, as well as reduced use of synthetic pesticides, fertilizing practices that decrease pollution, and crop rotation that controls erosion and improves soil quality.

The Farm Bill evolves through a federal legislative process and is influenced by agriculture, food industry, and public health advocates, but there is now an increasing movement throughout the United States to promote development of local and sustainable food systems. Much of this movement is spearheaded by grassroots and nonprofit groups, often with the support of philanthropic foundations. This work is not directly focused on disease prevention. Rather, it taps into the dual motivations of improving human and environmental well-being, defined broadly. It acknowledges the environmental and health costs of large-scale agribusiness, including water and soil contamination through heavy pesticide use, erosion and loss of biodiversity due to overemphasis on single-crop agriculture, and development of antibiotic-resistant organisms because of overreliance on antibiotics in animal feed. The current agribusiness model centralizes food production, necessitating transport of the food supply over large distances. This practice exacts a toll in terms of fuel consumption and emissions.[51] It also demands a high degree of food processing (such as freezing or canning), thereby potentially compromising the nutrient content of produce.

Examples of *local food* programs abound— from the Boston-based Food Project (http://thefoodproject.org), which engages youths in urban and suburban farming and food distribution, to the A Garden in Every School program in California (https://garden.org/learn/articles/view/744/), championed as a way to green both schoolyards and children's diets. Across the United States there is resurgent interest in the **community garden** as a way to augment the local food supply (figure 3.3). Preliminary evidence suggests that involvement in community gardening may be associated with higher fruit and vegetable intake.[52] Cautious optimism about the role of community gardens in improved health is warranted. The American Community Gardening Association[53] reports that home values may increase and crime rates may decrease in areas surrounding community gardens, although research is nascent in this arena. In low- and middle-income countries, urban gardens and farms are increasingly important to food systems and have been proposed as a strategy for improving food security.[52] However, little is known about the human health effects of consuming foods produced through urban and peri-urban agriculture, especially in areas where surface water is polluted with domestic and industrial waste and soil is contaminated with hard metals, such as lead.

Many of the issues discussed here have already been impacted by climate change and are expected to worsen. The increase in greenhouse gas emissions from human activity affects multiple components of the food system, including flora and fauna, and, ultimately, the nutritional status of populations.[54]

CLIMATE AND SOCIAL JUSTICE IMPLICATIONS OF FOOD ACCESS

Policy interventions to improve the food environment will have the most impact on health of humans and the planet when they simultaneously attend to issues of climate and social justice. Across the globe, women, people living in poverty, and racial/ethnic minorities are at greatest risk of the negative consequences of climate change on the food supply and food security.[54] In the US context, the impacts of climate change and environmental degradation

Figure 3.3. (*top*) Nearby residents work their plots in community gardens. In the Historic Hartnet Community Garden supported by the West Atlanta Watershed Alliance, residents spend a weekend morning clearing the ground for the upcoming planting. (*bottom*) In the North Dekalb Community Garden, a two-acre community garden in Atlanta, Georgia, sponsored by the nearby mall and auto dealership in partnership with the International Rescue Committee, Atlanta Community Food Bank, and the Global Grower's Network, local refugee families who farm the land are permitted to keep the food they grow or sell it, providing income to their families. Source: (*top*) Photo courtesy of Janelle Wright, West Atlanta Watershed Alliance. (*bottom*) Photo courtesy of Nisha Botchwey.

BOX 3.2 FOOD ENVIRONMENT AND FOOD SYSTEM SUSTAINABILITY

Sustainability refers to the creation and maintenance of "the conditions under which humans and nature can exist in productive harmony to support present and future generations."[a] Although typically associated with a nation's agricultural system, Downs and colleagues[b] argue that sustainability efforts should also focus on the food environment (including the "built food environment" as described in this chapter) because it "contains the total scope of options within which consumers make decisions about which foods to acquire and consume."[b(p3)] Many of the elements of the food environment that influence food choices—including product, price, place, and promotion—have a negative downstream effect on the environment.[b] Such elements include the type and amount of packaging, number of miles foods travel between production and consumption, and the carbon footprint of certain food items such as beef. In fact, a move toward more sustainable diets, defined as "a pattern of eating that promotes health and well-being and provides food security for the present population while sustaining human and natural resources for future generations,"[c(p283)] is an important strategy to address climate change and environmental degradation.[d,e]

REFERENCES

a. US Environmental Protection Agency. Learn about Sustainability. No date. Accessed February 15, 2021. https://www.epa.gov/sustainability/learn-about-sustainability.

b. Downs SM, Ahmed S, Fanzo J, Herforth A. Food environment typology: advancing an expanded definition, framework, and methodological approach for improved characterization of wild, cultivated, and built food environments toward sustainable diets. *Foods*. 2020;9(4).

c. Dietary Guidelines Advisory Committee. *Scientific Report of the 2015 Dietary Guidelines Advisory Committee: Advisory Report to the Secretary of Health and Human Services and the Secretary of Agriculture*. US Department of Agriculture, Agricultural Research Service; 2015.

d. Rose D, Heller MC, Roberto CA. Position of the Society for Nutrition Education and Behavior: the importance of including environmental sustainability in dietary guidance. *Journal of Nutrition Education and Behavior*. 2019;51(1):3-15.e11.

e. El Bilali H, Callenius C, Strassner C, Probst L. Food and nutrition security and sustainability transitions in food systems. *Food and Energy Security*. 2019;8(2):e00154-n/a.

on food access have been disproportionately felt among low-income communities and communities of color.[49] Attending to this problem requires acknowledgment of the historical legacy of colonialism and slavery and the continued oppression of Indigenous communities and communities of color.[55]

CONCLUSION

Eating patterns that include increasingly large portion sizes and calorie- and fat-laden foods have contributed to the fast growing obesity epidemic in the United States. At the same time, the food systems and food environments in US cities and towns provide a bounty of food yet often a dearth of healthful choices. In communities, the food stores, restaurants, and institutional food services in schools and worksites play a role in what we eat, and studies have revealed socioeconomic and racial disparities in the distribution of healthful foods. Agricultural policies at the base of the food chain have been developed in past decades with little attention to the health of people and the health of the environment.

In recent years, a variety of strategies to create more health-promoting food environments have been designed and implemented. They include policies to incentivize development of supermarkets and farmers' markets, as well as efforts to protect the nation's farmland from development. These activities complement approaches that require nutrition information on menus at restaurants, tax sugar-sweetened beverages,[56] and change food assistance program requirements. Going forward, these approaches should be evaluated and the most successful approaches widely implemented.

BOX 3.3 FOOD ACCESS DURING EMERGENCIES: A COVID-19 CASE STUDY

The COVID-19 pandemic has had far-reaching effects on food access for low-income families, with many having lost their jobs as a result of widespread illness and resulting effects on businesses. This burden has been disproportionally borne by Black and Hispanic households.[a] Low-income children, who rely on the School Breakfast Program and National School Lunch Program for up to two-thirds of their daily meals, have been particularly affected by school closures.[b]

Bouts of food insecurity can have life-long consequences. To remedy this issue, schools have sought creative solutions for delivering meals to their students, including by setting up pickup stations that allow for the acquisition of multiple days' worth of meals and by delivering meals along school bus routes.[a,b]

At a policy level, the Families First Coronavirus Response Act has expanded the scope of food assistance programs such as the Supplemental Nutrition Assistance Program. Under the Pandemic Electronic Benefit Transfer (P-EBT) program, additional funds are made available to families to account for the cost of meals usually served at school.[a,b]

Although this case study highlights the impact of COVID-19 on food access, the implications are not limited to pandemics. Food supply is part of the critical infrastructure and should be included in disaster preparedness plans for all emergencies and natural disasters—hurricanes, floods, heat waves, earthquakes, snow emergencies, and riots.[c]

REFERENCES

a. Kinsey EW, Hecht AA, Dunn CG, et al. School closures during COVID-19: opportunities for innovation in meal service. *American Journal of Public Health*. 2020:e1-e9.
b. Dunn CG, Kenney E, Fleischhacker SE, Bleich SN. Feeding low-income children during the Covid-19 pandemic. *New England Journal of Medicine*. 2020;382(18):e40.
c. Kinsey EW, Hammer J, Dupuis R, Feuerstein-Simon R, Cannuscio CC. Planning for food access during emergencies: missed meals in Philadelphia. *American Journal of Public Health*. 2019;109(5):781-783.

The health effects of these policy changes are often difficult to measure, and benefits may become evident only after extensive and sustained environmental changes. Recent data suggest that the steep rise in obesity witnessed since the early 1990s may finally be slowing in children,[7] perhaps in part because of changes to the food environment. More work needs to be done to ensure the benefits of these interventions reach all segments of the population, particularly the most vulnerable.

DISCUSSION QUESTIONS

1. How does the food environment either support health or contribute to adverse health consequences and health disparities?

2. How can the production, distribution, and marketing of food contribute to risk of obesity and other chronic diseases?

3. What considerations related to social justice and racial equity affect food environments?

4. What strategies have been tried and found promising for improving the food environment to support the health of communities?

5. How do health emergencies and natural disasters affect food insecurity?

COMPETING INTERESTS DISCLOSURE

Carolyn Cannuscio, Karen Glanz, and Roxanne Dupuis disclose no competing interests.

REFERENCES

1. Browne NT, Snethen JA, Greenberg CS, et al. When pandemics collide: the impact of COVID-19 on childhood obesity. *Journal of Pediatric Nursing*. 2021;56:90-98.

2. Lent MR, Vander Veur S, Mallya G, et al. Corner store purchases made by adults, adolescents and children: items, nutritional characteristics and amount spent. *Public Health Nutrition*. 2015;18(9):1706-1712.

3. Cannuscio CC, Weiss EE, Asch DA. The contribution of urban foodways to health disparities. *Journal of Urban Health*. 2010;87(3):381-393.

4. Hales CM, Fryar CD, Carroll MD, Freedman DS, Ogden CL. Trends in obesity and severe obesity prevalence in US youth and adults by sex and age, 2007–2008 to 2015–2016. *JAMA*. 2018;319(16):1723-1725.

5. Ogden CL, Carroll MD, Lawman HG, et al. Trends in obesity prevalence among children and adolescents in the United States, 1988–1994 through 2013–2014. *JAMA*. 2016;315(21):2292-2299.

6. Hales CM, Carroll MD, Fryar CD, Ogden CL. Prevalence of obesity among adults and youth: United States, 2015–2016. National Center for Health Statistics Data Brief. 2017(288):1-8.

7. Flegal KM, Kruszon-Moran D, Carroll MD, Fryar CD, Ogden CL. Trends in obesity among adults in the United States, 2005 to 2014. *JAMA*. 2016;315(21):2284-2291.

8. Ward ZJ, Bleich SN, Cradock AL, et al. Projected U.S. state-level prevalence of adult obesity and severe obesity. *New England Journal of Medicine*. 2019;381(25):2440-2450.

9. Lovasi GS, Hutson MA, Guerra M, Neckerman KM. Built environments and obesity in disadvantaged populations. *Epidemiologic Review*. 2009;31(1):7-20.

10. Popkin BM, Corvalan C, Grummer-Strawn LM. Dynamics of the double burden of malnutrition and the changing nutrition reality. *The Lancet*. 2020;395(10217):65-74.

11. Adams EJ, Grummer-Strawn L, Chavez G. Food insecurity is associated with increased risk of obesity in California women. *Journal of Nutrition*. 2003;133(4):1070-1074.

12. Feeding America. What Is Food Insecurity? No date. Accessed February 13, 2021. https://hungerandhealth.feedingamerica.org/understand-food-insecurity/

13. Au LE, Zhu SM, Nhan LA, et al. Household food insecurity is associated with higher adiposity among us schoolchildren ages 10–15 years: the Healthy Communities Study. *Journal of Nutrition*. 2019;149(9):1642-1650.

14. Larson N, Laska MN, Neumark-Sztainer D. Food insecurity, diet quality, home food availability, and health risk behaviors among emerging adults: findings from the EAT 2010-2018 Study. *American Journal of Public Health*. 2020;110(9):1422-1428.

15. Timlin D, McCormack JM, Kerr M, Keaver L, Simpson EEA. Are dietary interventions with a behaviour change theoretical framework effective in changing dietary patterns? A systematic review. *BMC Public Health*. 2020;20(1):1857.

16. Glanz K, Rimer BK, Viswanath K, eds. *Health Behavior: Theory, Research, and Practice*. 5th ed. Jossey-Bass/Wiley; 2015.

17. Story M, Kaphingst KM, Robinson-O'Brien R, Glanz K. Creating healthy food and eating environments: policy and environmental approaches. *Annual Review of Public Health*. 2008;29:253-272.

18. Glanz K, Sallis JF, Saelens BE, Frank LD. Healthy nutrition environments: concepts and measures. *American Journal of Health Promotion*. 2005;19(5):330-333,ii.

19. Sallis JF, Glanz K. Physical activity and food environments: solutions to the obesity epidemic. *Milbank Quarterly*. 2009;87(1):123-154.

20. Roberto CA, Kawachi I. Use of psychology and behavioral economics to promote healthy eating. *American Journal of Preventive Medicine*. 2014;47(6):832-837.

21. Larson NI, Story MT, Nelson MC. Neighborhood environments: disparities in access to healthy foods in the U.S. *American Journal of Preventive Medicine.* 2009;36(1):74-81.

22. Reese AM. Black food geographies: race, self-reliance, and food access in Washington, DC. UNC Press Books; 2019.

23. Fang Zhang F, Liu J, Rehm CD, Wilde P, Mande JR, Mozaffarian D. Trends and disparities in diet quality among us adults by Supplemental Nutrition Assistance Program participation status. *JAMA Network Open.* 2018;1(2):e180237.

24. Andreyeva T, Tripp AS, Schwartz MB. Dietary quality of Americans by Supplemental Nutrition Assistance Program participation status: a systematic review. *American Journal of Preventive Medicine.* 2015;49(4):594-604.

25. Chiuve SE, Fung TT, Rimm EB, et al. Alternative dietary indices both strongly predict risk of chronic disease. *Journal of Nutrition.* 2012;142(6):1009-1018.

26. The Food Trust. About PA *FFFI.* Published 2012. Accessed February 13, 2021. http://thefoodtrust.org/pafffi/about

27. America's Healthy Food Financing Initiative. About America's Healthy Food Financing Initiative. Published 2021. Accessed February 13, 2021. https://www.investinginfood.com/about-hffi/

28. Glanz K, Johnson L, Yaroch AL, Phillips M, Ayala GX, Davis EL. Measures of retail food store environments and sales: review and Implications for healthy eating initiatives. *Journal of Nutrition Education and Behavior.* 2016;48(4):280-288.e281.

29. Harries C, Koprak J, Young C, Weiss S, Parker KM, Karpyn A. Moving from policy to implementation: a methodology and lessons learned to determine eligibility for healthy food financing projects. *Journal of Public Health Management and Practice.* 2014;20(5):498-505.

30. Glanz K, Bader MD, Iyer S. Retail grocery store marketing strategies and obesity: an integrative review. *American Journal of Preventive Medicine.* 2012;42(5):503-512.

31. Foster GD, Karpyn A, Wojtanowski AC, et al. Placement and promotion strategies to increase sales of healthier products in supermarkets in low-income, ethnically diverse neighborhoods: a randomized controlled trial. *American Journal of Clinical Nutrition.* 2014;99(6):1359-1368.

32. Karpyn A, McCallops K, Wolgast H, Glanz K. Improving consumption and purchases of healthier foods in retail environments: a systematic review. *International Journal of Environmental Research and Public Health.* 2020;17(20).

33. Thorndike AN, Bright OJM, Dimond MA, Fishman R, Levy DE. Choice architecture to promote fruit and vegetable purchases by families participating in the Special Supplemental Program for Women, Infants, and Children (WIC): randomized corner store pilot study. *Public Health Nutrition.* 2017;20(7):1297-1305.

34. USDA National Agricultural Statistics Service. National Farmers Market Managers. 2020.

35. Bowen DJ, Barrington WE, Beresford SA. Identifying the effects of environmental and policy change interventions on healthy eating. *Annual Review of Public Health.* 2015;36:289-306.

36. Pitts SBJ, Ng SW, Blitstein JL, Gustafson A, Niculescu M. Online grocery shopping: promise and pitfalls for healthier food and beverage purchases. *Public Health Nutrition.* 2018;21(18):3360-3376.

37. Colchero MA, Guerrero-López CM, Molina M, Rivera JA. Beverages sales in Mexico before and after Implementation of a sugar sweetened beverage tax. *PLOS ONE.* 2016;11(9):e0163463.

38. Roberto CA, Lawman HG, LeVasseur MT, et al. Association of a beverage tax on sugar-sweetened and artificially sweetened beverages with changes in beverage prices and sales at chain retailers in a large urban setting. *JAMA.* 2019;321(18):1799-1810.

39. USDA Economic Research Service. U.S. food-away-from-home spending continued to outpace food-at-home spending in 2019. Published 2020. Accessed November 8, 2020. https://www.ers.usda.gov/data-products/chart-gallery/gallery/chart-detail/?chartId=58364

40. Saelens BE, Glanz K, Sallis JF, Frank LD. Nutrition Environment Measures Study in restaurants (NEMS-R): development and evaluation. *American Journal of Preventive Medicine*. 2007;32(4):273-281.

41. Cobb LK, Appel LJ, Franco M, Jones-Smith JC, Nur A, Anderson CA. The relationship of the local food environment with obesity: a systematic review of methods, study quality, and results. *Obesity (Silver Spring)*. 2015;23(7):1331-1344.

42. Glanz K, Resnicow K, Seymour J, et al. How major restaurant chains plan their menus: the role of profit, demand, and health. *American Journal of Preventive Medicine*. 2007;32(5):383-388.

43. Han J, Schwartz AE, Elbel B. Does proximity to fast food cause childhood obesity? Evidence from public housing. *Regional Science and Urban Economics*. 2020;84.

44. Powell LM, Nguyen BT. Fast-food and full-service restaurant consumption among children and adolescents: effect on energy, beverage, and nutrient intake. *JAMA Pediatrics*. 2013;167(1):14-20.

45. Moran AJ, Block JP, Goshev SG, Bleich SN, Roberto CA. Trends in nutrient content of children's menu items in U.S. chain restaurants. *American Journal of Preventive Medicine*. 2017;52(3):284-291.

46. Long MW, Tobias DK, Cradock AL, Batchelder H, Gortmaker SL. Systematic review and meta-analysis of the impact of restaurant menu calorie labeling. *American Journal of Public Health*. 2015;105(5):e11-24.

47. Petimar J, Zhang F, Cleveland LP, et al. Estimating the effect of calorie menu labeling on calories purchased in a large restaurant franchise in the southern United States: quasi-experimental study. *BMJ*. 2019;367:l5837.

48. Glanz K, Sallis JF, Saelens BE, Frank LD. Nutrition Environment Measures Survey in stores (NEMS-S): development and evaluation. *American Journal of Preventive Medicine*. 2007;32(4):282-289.

49. Shannon KL, Kim BF, McKenzie SE, Lawrence RS. Food system policy, public health, and human rights in the United States. *Annual Review of Public Health*. 2015;36:151-173.

50. Bleich SN, Moran AJ, Vercammen KA, et al. Strengthening the public health impacts of the Supplemental Nutrition Assistance Program through policy. *Annual Review of Public Health*. 2020;41:453-480.

51. Haines A, McMichael AJ, Smith KR, et al. Public health benefits of strategies to reduce greenhouse-gas emissions: overview and implications for policy makers. *The Lancet*. 2009;347(9707):2104-2114.

52. Al-Delaimy WK, Webb M. Community gardens as environmental health interventions: benefits versus potential risks. *Current Environmental Health Reports*. 2017;4(2):252-265.

53. American Community Gardening Association. Research. No date. http://www.communitygarden.org/learn/resources/research.php

54. Myers SS, Smith MR, Guth S, et al. Climate change and global food systems: potential impacts on food security and undernutrition. *Annual Review of Public Health*. 2017;38:259-277.

55. Kumanyika SK. A framework for increasing equity impact in obesity prevention. *American Journal of Public Health*. 2019: e1-e8.

56. Brownell KD, Farley T, Willett WC, et al. The public health and economic benefits of taxing sugar-sweetened beverages. *New England Journal of Medicine*. 2009;361(16):1599-1605.

CHAPTER 4

THE BUILT ENVIRONMENT AND AIR QUALITY

Patrick Lott Kinney and Priyanka Nadia deSouza

KEY POINTS

- Air pollution remains a major health challenge facing cities throughout the world.
- Although ambient (outdoor) air pollution is the dominant concern, household (indoor) air pollution remains a significant global health burden as well.
- The health effects of air pollution are well established and depend on exposure levels.
- The spatial orientation of human activities and noxious sources within cities plays a key role in determining air pollution exposures that people and communities encounter.
- Air quality solutions are being successfully implemented by cities, many of which bring both health and climate benefits.
- Equitable access to clean air is an essential feature of a healthy city.

INTRODUCTION

Ella Kissi-Debrah was born and raised in Lewisham, a neighborhood in southeast London. Her family's home was just 25 meters (82 feet) from the South Circular Road, a busy traffic route that girdles London's south side. Ella was an active child who enjoyed gymnastics, dancing, and swimming, played several musical instruments, and dreamed of being a pilot.

However, as a young girl she developed severe asthma. By the time she reached school age, she was being hospitalized every month or two for severe asthma attacks. On a winter day in February 2013, when Ella was nine years old, one of these attacks ended her life.

Air pollution was a particular threat for Ella. Her walking route to school took her along the South Circular Road, where levels of two pollutants—nitrogen dioxide and particulate matter—routinely exceeded legal limits. In the winter, when air quality worsened, her attacks came more frequently. In the two days preceding her death, local air pollution levels had spiked.

Beginning in the 1990s, the automobile fleet in the United Kingdom and across Europe had shifted dramatically from gasoline to diesel engines, propelled by government incentives and extensive public messaging, in an effort to reduce transportation-related carbon dioxide (CO_2) emissions. In the United Kingdom between 1995 and 2012 (the period encompassing Ella's brief life), the diesel share of private automobiles rose from less than 10 percent to more than 50 percent; for buses, taxis, and trucks, the diesel share approached 100 percent. But the shift to diesel engines greatly increased emissions of particulate matter and oxides of nitrogen.[1,2] Ambient levels of these pollutants rose, especially along busy roads such as the South Circular Road. Epidemiologic data documented large numbers of associated excess deaths.[3-5]

Grief-stricken, Ella's mother worked with prominent British physicians and epidemiologists to determine whether air pollution had contributed to her daughter's death. In December 2020, following an extensive inquest, the Southwark Coroner's Court ruled that air pollution "made a material contribution" to Ella's death, and air pollution—for the first time in the United Kingdom—was listed as a cause of death on a death certificate.[6] This tragic episode exemplified how transportation choices—in this case, motor vehicle technology—as well as community design—the proximity of roadways to residential areas—can directly affect health, especially of vulnerable people. Both transportation choices and the community design affected health through their effects on air quality (as well as through other pathways, as discussed in other chapters).

CLEAN AIR: A BASIC NEED

Healthy places provide equitable access to clean air for all citizens to breathe, an essential ingredient of a healthy life. Many parts of the world fall short of this ideal. Most **air pollution** is place based, deriving from the juxtaposition of noxious emissions and human activities in specific geographic patterns. This has been true since the dawn of human history, when cooking in caves exposed our ancestors to high levels of combustion products. In recent centuries, following the Industrial Revolution, it has been true in the cities of high-income countries (HICs), from London to Pittsburgh—the result of concentrated industrial and commercial activity in cities. Although HICs have seen dramatic improvements in air quality since the 1970s, cities in low- and middle-income countries (LMICs) have manifested dramatically high levels of air pollutants—the result of a combination of factors, including industry, burning solid fuels in households, and highly polluting motor vehicles. This chapter explores the sources of air pollution in cities, its health effects, and strategies for achieving clean, healthy air.

According to the World Health Organization (WHO), air pollution occurs when the environment is contaminated by any chemical, physical, or biological agent that modifies the natural characteristics of the atmosphere.[7] The vast majority of air pollution we breathe is produced by human activities that take place at home, in transit, at work, or by the range of industrial and energy systems that support human societies, especially when those activities involve burning of fuels. Dust blown from roadways or deserts can also degrade air quality, as can pollen, fire smoke, and microorganisms. With increasing industrialization and modernization of our lifestyles, the menu of air pollutants we encounter has become more complex. There are thousands of potentially dangerous substances that end up in the air and in our bodies. However, for practical purposes, we usually define "air quality" based on the concentrations of a handful of key pollutants that tend to be present where people settle in communities and that have well-established health impacts (table 4.1).

We determine air quality by comparing the measured concentrations of one or more of these key pollutants to health-based benchmarks. A concentration is usually expressed in units of micrograms of a pollutant per cubic meter of air. For gases, another common measure is the volume of pollutant gas per volume of air, expressed in parts per million or sometimes parts per billion. Health-based standards are defined as average concentrations over a defined period, ranging from several hours (for example, ozone: O_3), one day (for example, sulfur dioxide: SO_2, nitrogen dioxide: NO_2, carbon monoxide: CO, coarse particulate matter: PM_{10}), or a year (for example, fine particulate matter: $PM_{2.5}$). Official air pollution measurements are usually made at fixed locations in or around a city. This provides a general view of air quality in a city but says little about the nature of air quality in specific neighborhoods

Table 4.1. Major urban air pollutants and their sources and health effects.

	Health Effects	Sources and Trends
Particulate matter ($PM_{2.5}$; PM_{10}; others)	Causes both short-term and long-term damage to the cardiovascular and respiratory systems, including outcomes such as symptoms, hospital visits, and premature death. Recent studies also show neurological effects.	Combustion of fuels, leading to direct emissions of PM and gases (SO_2, NO_x, VOCs) that can convert to PM in the atmosphere. Smaller particles (i.e., less that 2.5 micrometers in aerodynamic diameter) are most harmful, both because of the toxins they contain and their ability to get into and cause harm in the body. Trending downward in the United States and China, but steady or rising in many other countries.
Tropospheric ozone (O_3)	Causes short-term lung function declines and irritation and inflammation of the respiratory system. Also associated with both acute and chronic mortality.	Formed through reactions in the air involving nitrogen oxides and volatile organic compounds along with sunlight. Concentrations are usually higher downwind of cities. Trends show persistent challenges in many parts of the world.
Nitrogen oxides (NO_x)	Causes short-term lung function decline and increased risk of respiratory infections.	High temperature combustion, especially by motor vehicles. Undergoes reactions in air that can result in ozone and/or $PM_{2.5}$ formation. Nitrate particles contribute to acid precipitation. Trends vary depending largely on motor vehicle fuel and emission control choices.
Volatile organic compounds (VOCs)	Associated with a range of effects (depending on the compound) such as eye and nose irritation, nausea, and cancer.	Outdoor sources include motor vehicle fuels and evergreen trees; consumer products and building materials emit large amounts indoors. Indoor concentrations higher than outdoors in HICs. Not routinely monitored.
Sulfur dioxide (SO_2)	Irritates the lungs, causing respiratory symptoms, especially among asthmatics.	Emitted by burning of coal or petroleum products containing sulfur (e.g., diesel fuel). Undergoes reactions in the atmosphere to form sulfate $PM_{2.5}$, with effects on health and acid precipitation. Has been decreasing due to reduced fuel sulfur content and emission controls on coal plants.
Carbon monoxide (CO)	Interferes with delivery of oxygen; can cause fatigue, headache, neurological damage, and death.	Combustion of fuels. Motor vehicles are the principal source in cities. Has declined rapidly in HICs due to motor vehicle controls.
Lead (Pb)	Accumulates in organs and tissues; causes learning disabilities and damage to the nervous system.	Emitted by motor vehicles burning fuels containing lead. As of 2020, lead had been eliminated from gasoline in every country but Algeria, and that country had plans for elimination.
Biological pollutants (such as pollen, mold, mildew)	Associated with allergic reactions, respiratory symptoms, fatigue, and asthma.	Trees, grasses, and weeds release pollen in spring through summer. Indoor allergens and molds can be a problem, especially when there is excess moisture.

Source: Adapted from Samet JM. Community Design and Air Quality, Table 4.2. In: Dannenberg AL, Frumkin H, Jackson RJ, eds. *Making Healthy Places*. Island Press; 2011. https://doi.org/10.5822/978-1-61091-036-1_4

within the city. Human exposures to air pollution, and resulting health impacts, are determined by the sequence of concentrations each person encounters over time—at home, along roads, in stores, at work, at school, and so on—weighted by the amount of time spent in each of those settings. Particularly important are exposures that occur close to emission sources, such as motor vehicles on roadways. The term *inhaled dose* also incorporates breathing rates, which differ depending on activity level, as well as age and preexisting respiratory disease. A person riding a bicycle in traffic for thirty minutes will breathe more heavily and sustain a higher dose of pollution than a person sitting in a car for the same thirty minutes. However, this difference will be reduced or eliminated if the cyclist gets to her destination in fifteen minutes and it takes the car an hour because of traffic congestion.

AIR POLLUTION AND HUMAN HEALTH

Modern recognition of air pollution as a human health threat began with a series of pollution disasters in the twentieth century. For example, twenty people died over a few days in the small town of Donora, Pennsylvania, in October 1948, when a temperature inversion enabled noxious fumes from factories to build up to deadly levels. In December 1952, a more severe air pollution disaster occurred over five days in London, again brought on by a temperature inversion. Here the culprit was coal burning, used to heat homes and buildings. Based on an analysis of death records in London before, during, and after the episode, epidemiologists estimated that more than ten thousand people may have died prematurely from exposure to air pollution.[8]

These air pollution disasters led in time to regulations, such as the US Clean Air Act of 1970, which set air quality standards to control air pollution to avoid future health effects. Regulations led to the need for evidence on what levels could be considered safe, which led in turn to research studies to quantify the relationships between various air pollutants

and adverse health effects. Starting in the 1970s and continuing until the present, both epidemiologic and experimental approaches have been used to generate the needed evidence. Epidemiology studies collect data in populations to quantify associations between air pollution and adverse health outcomes over time or across locations. Experimental studies set up controlled exposures to air pollutants in the laboratory and then analyze health outcomes in human volunteers, animals, or cell tissue samples. Epidemiology and experimental studies offer complementary advantages and limitations and together have provided a solid framework to support health-based air pollution regulations.[9] An example of the output from one important health study is shown in figure 4.1. This displays the concentration-response-function between long term average concentrations of $PM_{2.5}$ and fractional increases in mortality rates across six US cities.[10] Subsequent, larger studies have reinforced these early findings.[11,12] The health effects of common air pollutants are summarized in table 4.1, along with information about sources and trends.

Although all the pollutants in table 4.1 have the potential to cause adverse impacts on human health, two of them, $PM_{2.5}$ and ozone, are thought to be associated with the largest global burden of disease and death.[13] **Particulate matter (PM)** refers to small solid or liquid particles (also called aerosols), formed via combustion or friction, that remain suspended in the air long enough to affect air quality. PM comes in many sizes, measured by diameter, which influences how long it stays airborne and how deeply it penetrates into our lungs. $PM_{2.5}$ refers specifically to PM having aerodynamic diameters smaller than 2.5 micrometers (for comparison, human hair has a diameter of about 60 micrometers). The special health relevance of $PM_{2.5}$ relates in part to its small size, which enables the particles to penetrate deep into our lungs and potentially distribute elsewhere in the body, and also to its composition, which includes toxic substances such as

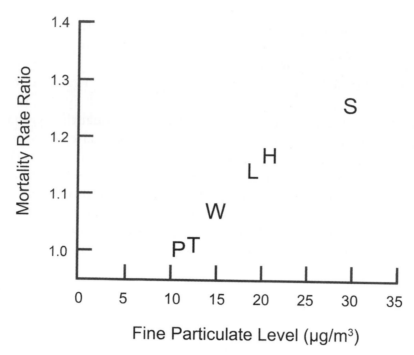

Figure 4.1. Estimated adjusted mortality and mean fine particulate ($PM_{2.5}$) levels in the classic Six Cities study of air pollution. (P denotes Portage, Wisconsin; T Topeka, Kansas; W Watertown, Massachusetts; L St. Louis, Missouri; H Harriman, Tennessee; and S Steubenville Ohio.)
Source: From Dockery DW, Pope CAI, Xu X, et al. An association between air pollution and mortality in six U.S. cities. *New England Journal of Medicine.* 1993;329(24):1753-1759. Copyright © 1993 Massachusetts Medical Society. Reprinted with permission from Massachusetts Medical Society.

trace metals, acids, and organic carbon compounds. **Nitrogen oxides (NO_x)** are formed by high temperature combustion and are emitted by motor vehicles, power plants, and other combustion sources. Diesel vehicles, even modern "clean" diesels, emit large amounts of NO_x and have contributed to a worsening NO_2 air quality problem in Europe in recent years, as exemplified in the account that opens this chapter.[14] **Ozone** in the troposphere (that is, near Earth's surface) is formed by reactions of NO_x and volatile organic compounds (VOCs) in the presence of sunlight. VOCs are emitted from a variety of sources, including motor vehicles and vegetation. When inhaled, ozone irritates the linings of our respiratory system, causing constriction of the airways and inflammatory reactions that can lead to long-term damage to the lungs. Both $PM_{2.5}$ and ozone have been associated with a wide range of adverse health effects, including impacts on respiratory symptoms, hospital visits, and premature death.[14-16] See box 4.1.

GLOBAL PATTERNS AND SOURCES OF AIR POLLUTION

Although progress has been made in improving air quality in many cities, air pollution remains a health challenge throughout the world. The challenge has been especially great in LMIC cities. In the 1990s, WHO declared Mexico City the most polluted megalopolis in the world.[17] As recently as 2013, Beijing recorded daily mean $PM_{2.5}$ concentrations approaching 600 µg/m³, sixty times higher than the WHO guideline.[18] In 2019, Delhi held the distinction of being the most polluted capital city in the world.[19] Although pollution levels are much lower in HIC cities, they still pose health risks at current levels.

Table 4.2 shows annual mean levels of $PM_{2.5}$ in 2019 for a selection of world cities that span the range of observed urban air quality. Also shown are the **air quality index (AQI)** rankings, as defined by the US Environmental Protection Agency (EPA). Although still quite polluted, Beijing and Mexico City have made

BOX 4.1 OZONE: A COMPLICATED POLLUTANT

Although ozone is a simple molecule composed of three oxygen atoms, its story is rather complicated. Ozone is not emitted from smokestacks or tailpipes as are other pollutants; instead, it is a "secondary pollutant" that forms in the air from precursors, such as nitrogen oxides (NO_x) and volatile organic compounds (VOCs). From a health standpoint, ozone can be either good or bad, depending on where it is found. Ozone in the stratosphere protects our health by blocking incoming solar ultraviolet energy that can cause skin cancer. But ozone in the troposphere, where we live and breathe, is unhealthy because it is a strong oxidant that burns our eyes, nose, and lungs and can cause respiratory problems that may lead to hospitalization or death. Air quality standards for ozone represent levels above which scientific evidence demonstrates adverse health effects. The World Health Organization ozone standard is 100 μg/m³ for an eight-hour average. Interestingly, ozone usually reaches its highest levels in places far downwind from where the precursor pollutants were emitted. This is partly because it takes time for ozone-forming reactions to occur and partly because NO_x reacts with and destroys ozone in the areas where NO_x is emitted—that is, cities. A final complication is that because the chemistry of ozone formation is nonlinear, policies to reduce concentrations of NO_x or VOCs may actually increase ozone concentrations. This phenomenon may explain the recent upward trend in ozone concentrations in China during a period in which NO_x emissions have been declining.

Table 4.2. Air quality index (AQI) ranges and observed 2019 annual mean $PM_{2.5}$ concentrations in major world cities.

AQI	$PM_{2.5}$ Range (μg/m³)	City	Observed $PM_{2.5}$ (μg/m³)
Unhealthy	55.5–150.4	Delhi, India	98.6
		Dhaka, Bangladesh	83.3
Unhealthy for sensitive groups	35.5–55.4	Beijing, China	42.1
Moderate	12.1–35.4	Accra, Ghana	30.3
		Santiago, Chile	27.7
		Seoul, S. Korea	24.8
		Athens, Greece	22.3
		Mexico City, Mexico	20.5
		Paris, France	14.7
		Rome, Italy	12.9
Good	0–12.0	London, UK	11.4
		Moscow, Russia	10.0
		Berlin, Germany	9.7
		Madrid, Spain	9.2
		New York City, USA	8.6
		Stockholm, Sweden	6.1

Data Source: IQAir website.

substantial progress in improving air quality. Delhi, Dhaka, and many other LMIC cities in South Asia dominate the list of "unhealthy" cities worldwide.[19] The cleanest cities are in HICs with robust air quality regulations that impose strict limits on emissions from most urban and nonurban sources. Several world cities, including Moscow, London, Rome, and New York City, report "good" air quality and in some cases meet the stringent WHO guideline of 10 ug/m³.

Figure 4.2 shows a global map of estimated $PM_{2.5}$ concentrations in 2019, taken from the 2020 *State of Global Air* report.[20] Regions with the highest levels are in Africa, the Middle East, and South and East Asia. High $PM_{2.5}$ in the northern half of Africa is dominated by dust from the Sahara Desert. Figure 4.3, from the 2019 *State of Global Air* report, shows that average $PM_{2.5}$, but not ozone, concentrations are lower in regions with higher levels of socioeconomic development.[21]

Air pollution concentrations are usually higher (typically by about a factor of two) in cities than in surrounding areas, due largely to the high density of human activities concentrated there—for example, driving, cooking, manufacturing, waste burning, construction—most of which result in emissions of air pollution. In addition to bearing the impacts of these local sources, urban residents also breathe pollutants that have been transported over long distances from upwind sources. Regional sources may include pollution from agriculture, land clearing, indus-

try, power plants, upwind cities, wildfires, and dust storms. For example, in Delhi and other cities in the Indo-Gangetic plain of North India, air pollution in winter is dominated by smoke (aerosols) from the burning of stubble from paddy fields as farmers prepare to grow wheat. Similar regional impacts are observed through much of South Asia and Africa.

Table 4.3 lists important sources of urban air pollution and the spatial scale of the impacts. Some sources are ubiquitous, such as motor vehicles. Others remain problematic mainly in LMIC cities. Responsible sources include poorly tuned motor vehicles powered by low-quality fuels emitting dense black plumes of organic and elemental carbon particles along with multiple gaseous pollutants. Outdoor burning of waste generates these same pollutants, as well as an array of toxic compounds derived from the materials being burned. Indoor heating or power generation using coal or low-grade oil spews a toxic mix of particles and sulfur oxides. Domestic cooking and heating with solid fuels such as wood, dung, and charcoal

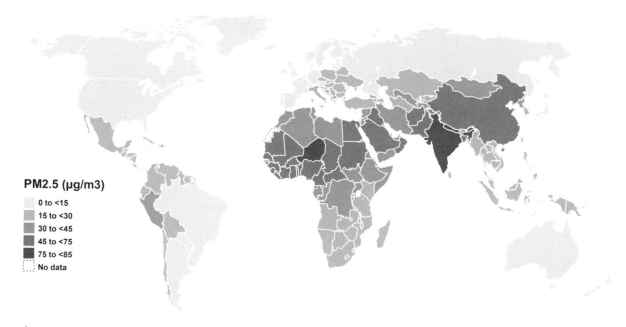

PM2.5 (µg/m3)
- 0 to <15
- 15 to <30
- 30 to <45
- 45 to <75
- 75 to <85
- No data

Figure 4.2. Annual average population-weighted $PM_{2.5}$ concentrations in 2019. The World Health Organization guideline is 10 micrograms per cubic meter (µg/m³). Low- and middle-income countries have substantially higher air pollution levels than wealthy countries.
Source: Health Effects Institute. *State of Global Air 2020: A Special Report on Global Exposure to Air Pollution and Its Health Effects*. Health Effects Institute; 2020.

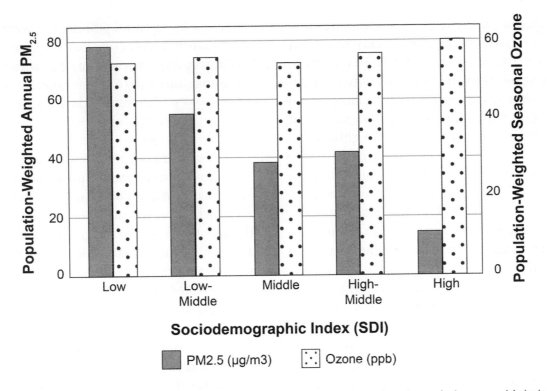

Figure 4.3. Trends in population weighted mean PM₂.₅ and ozone concentrations by sociodemographic index. As explained in the text, particulate matter levels track with sociodemographic development, whereas ozone does not.
Source: Health Effects Institute. *State of Global Air 2019. Special Report.* Health Effects Institute; 2019.

Table 4.3. Important sources of pollutants observed in cities (text in bold italic font indicates sources that are especially relevant in cities in low- and middle-income countries).

Pollution Source	Pollutants of Concern	Spatial Scale
Domestic cooking	NO_x (gas stoves); $PM_{2.5}$, CO (biomass stoves)	Household/Local/Urban/Regional
Waste burning	$PM_{2.5}$, air toxins	Local/Urban
Industrial processes	$PM_{2.5}$, VOCs, many others	Local/Urban/Regional
Transportation	NO_x, CO, $PM_{2.5}$, SO_2, Ozone	Local/Urban
Heating buildings	NO_x, CO, VOCs, $PM_{2.5}$	Local/Urban
Commercial food preparation	VOCs, $PM_{2.5}$, CO	Local
Power generation	SO_2, $PM_{2.5}$	Urban to Regional
Green space (trees, grasses, and weeds)	Pollen; VOCs	Urban to Regional
Agriculture (from fertilizer; crop burning; dust)	VOCs, $PM_{2.5}$	Regional
Wildfire	$PM_{2.5}$, VOCs, NO_x, Ozone	Regional
Dust from open land	$PM_{2.5}$, PM_{10}	Regional

Note: Urban air quality can be affected both by emissions within the city, as well as by upwind, regional sources.

are a significant source of indoor pollution and an important source of outdoor pollution in many urban areas of the developing world.

Air pollution in cities can vary substantially over space and time, depending on the pollutant, spatial scale of its impacts, and weather patterns. In general, neighborhoods that are closer to emission sources face consistently higher air pollution concentrations than other places. Likewise, activity patterns that bring individuals into close proximity to urban pollution sources for extended periods promote higher personal exposures. For example, pedestrians, vendors, and those engaged in a range of commercial activities are often concentrated along busy roadways in African cities, where pollution from motor vehicles leads to unhealthy pollution hot spots. Concentrations of regional pollutants such as ozone, or PM originating from distant upwind sources, tend to be more uniformly distributed throughout a city. However, for both local and regional pollutants, weather has a profound impact on the time course of air pollution experienced in a city, with concentrations varying by a factor of ten or more over different weather conditions.

Household Air Pollution

Air pollution is not only a problem outdoors. Indeed, most people spend upward of 80 percent of their time indoors, where they can be exposed to a wide range of pollutants of both indoor and outdoor origin. Cooking and heating at home are particularly significant sources of pollution in and around households, especially in LMICs, where nearly three billion people still rely on solid fuels (for example, wood, dung, crop residues, charcoal, coal)[22] (figure 4.4). Women and children are disproportionately exposed since women often carry the burden of both cooking and child rearing. Gathering solid fuel for daily use can be a significant time burden for women and

Figure 4.4. Solid fuels are used for cooking and heating by nearly three billion people. As shown in this photo, women and children are disproportionately exposed to the dangerous combustion products.
Source: Photo courtesy of Ashden/Jo Walton

children in LMICs and a risk factor for sexual assault, as well as an important contributor to forest and habitat destruction. Because solid fuel combustion affects pollutant levels both indoors and outdoors, the term *household air pollution (HAP)* is often now used for this phenomenon. HAP not only affects pollution within the home, but is also a substantial contributor to outdoor air pollution.[23] Solid fuel combustion generates a complex mix of toxic particles and gases, including $PM_{2.5}$, black carbon, carbon monoxide, and methane.[24] The global burden of premature deaths due to household air pollution was estimated to be 2.31 million in 2019,[13] reflecting the impacts both indoors and outdoors of $PM_{2.5}$ on a range of health outcomes, including pneumonia among children and heart disease among adults. Although still substantial, impacts appear to be on a downward trend today compared with the about 4.36 million premature deaths in 1990[13] as people shift to cleaner fuels. Other important health risks of solid fuels include burns related to exposed flames.[22]

The problem of indoor air pollution is not limited to LMICs. Modern homes and offices can emit and trap a wide range of pollutants indoors where people spend the vast majority of their time. In HICs, important indoor air pollution sources include cooking with gas (a key source of NO_x), cigarette smoking ($PM_{2.5}$), and other indoor behaviors involving combustion, including unvented heating appliances, candles, and incense. These can be important sources of NO_x, $PM_{2.5}$, and other pollutants. Indoor materials and furnishings, including particle board, furniture, and paints, as well as personal care products such as fragrances, can emit substantial levels of volatile organic compounds, yielding indoor concentrations far higher than outdoors. This is exacerbated by lack of ventilation with fresh, outdoor air that is typical of modern, tight, energy-efficient buildings that trap indoor pollutants, as well as moisture and CO_2, and can lead to mold growth and respiratory problems (moisture) and cognitive/attention deficits (CO_2).

Although the health significance of elevated indoor VOC exposures remains uncertain, exposures to a complex mix of VOCs, lack of fresh air, and high CO_2 levels may contribute to "sick building syndrome," which is associated with fatigue, headaches, and other symptoms among building occupants.[25] Pollutants of outdoor origin such as $PM_{2.5}$ can penetrate indoors, adding to the exposure and health burden encountered indoors.

To reduce impacts from indoor cooking and heating with solid fuels, proactive governments are implementing programs to provide their citizens with clean household fuels. China, for example, is rapidly developing natural gas infrastructure to replace coal as a heating fuel in many cities. The Indian government has launched the ambitious *Pradhman Mantri Ujjwala Yojana* program, which has made liquefied petroleum gas (LPG) accessible as a cooking fuel to more than eighty million rural households that previously lacked an LPG connection. Research has been underway to study the factors that promote the sustained use of such fuels to guide future policies. In the interim, researchers have examined how clean cookstoves can mitigate indoor air pollution. However, the uptake and sustained use of cleaner burning cookstoves has proven very challenging. Researchers have identified household- and community-level factors that affect the adoption of such stoves, such as local cooking practices, occupation, income, and education level.[24,26] Source elimination or reduction is the primary strategy to address indoor air quality problems in HICs, where energy savings and carbon emission reduction goals are leading to ever tighter, more energy efficient buildings.

AIR POLLUTION AND EQUITY

Evidence shows that air pollution exposures vary as a function of income and race, both between and within countries and cities. Deep racial disparities have been documented in exposure to air pollutants in the United States, and these disparities have increased over time.[27-30] Moreover, disparities exist in the health consequences of air pollution across race, ethnicity, and income, and there is evidence of disparities along the urban-rural gradient.[31,32]

There are many reasons for these higher exposures and associated elevated risks. Historic racial discrimination and segregation in the United States, for example, and policies such as **redlining** (the systematic discriminatory denial of services such as mortgages, insurance, and loans to minority neighborhoods, widely practiced by government and private firms in US cities beginning in the 1930s) led to the concentration of poverty in inner-city neighborhoods, resulting in poorer housing quality, more air pollution sources, and therefore higher exposure to pollution in these areas, as well as disparities in access to health care and poorer overall health.[33] Research has also demonstrated that the disproportionate siting of industrial facilities in neighborhoods with high proportions of minority residents has contributed to persistent racial inequalities in pollution in the United States.[34] Chapter 9 explores these issues in more detail.

Zooming out to a global perspective, there are transnational inequalities in exposure to air pollution, as noted earlier in this chapter. Part of this reflects differences in economic and political capacity for developing and implementing air quality regulations. In addition, some firms based in HICs site polluting factories in LMICs, where regulations are less stringent. However, even though most global premature deaths due to air pollution occur in LMICs, few cities in these nations have air quality monitors, and when they do, air quality data are rarely made publicly available.[35] There is also a dearth of funding for air pollution science in much of the Global South, even though there is an urgent need to do more work to recenter the experiences of the Global South in the field of air pollution science. For example, although cities such as Delhi have now become the quintessential examples in the media of highly polluted cities, which has inspired some political action, other highly polluted cities and towns such as the Raipur-Dhanbad industrial area in India have escaped attention.

For cities in the Global South, environmental justice concerns are equally important and operate in different ways. Nairobi, which was built from the ground up by British colonial settlers, was designed for the White population to live in the green leafy highlands in the north of the city, and Black Kenyans were forced to live in the cramped plains to the east of the city. Divisions in the city persist to the current day. A recent air monitoring study reported remarkably high concentrations of PM$_{2.5}$ and respirable soot particles along sidewalks in Nairobi's congested central business district, where local residents work and shop.[36,37] The city is segregated on the basis of class instead of race. Cities must therefore work to ensure that their policies are equitable.

CLEAN AIR SOLUTIONS

Although air pollution remains a serious challenge worldwide, progress has been evident in some of the most polluted cities. Successful control programs have incorporated innovation across three dimensions: information, incentives, and institutions.[18] First, information to document levels and trends in air pollution is critical. This helps regulators identify key sources, provides data for research on health effects, and increases public awareness and support for action. Data on PM$_{2.5}$ levels measured at the US embassy in Beijing, for example, raised public awareness and political pressure for action in China. Air pollution data in Mexico City were used to carry out early epidemiology studies documenting impacts on child health, providing strong incentives for action. Data can also be used to calibrate air quality models, which are necessary to determine which sources to control by how much so as to reduce levels. Measurements of emission levels from large sources, such as power plants and factories, are another type of critical data.

Such data support accountability and evaluation of changes over time.

It is also important to provide incentives for the implementation of regulations, without which regulations are likely to fail to achieve progress in cleaning the air. For example, the US Clean Air Act provides both penalties and financial incentives for states to implement clean air plans. In Mexico City, subsidies to reduce the cost of conversion to clean technologies have proven effective in encouraging retirement of old taxis. China's air quality programs include financial incentives for progress at the local level.

From an institutional perspective, because air pollution does not respect administrative boundaries, sustained progress requires a coordinated approach across different jurisdictions. Also, because sources can derive from many different urban activities, success is more likely when there is engagement with public and private actors across multiple sectors, including transport, energy, agriculture, domestic fuels, and industry. In the remainder of this section, we describe some of the approaches that have proven successful in improving air quality in global cities.

Motor vehicles often represent the largest single source sector responsible for poor air quality in cities, especially for $PM_{2.5}$ and NO_x.[14] A range of options is available to tackle air pollution from motor vehicles, including changes to fuels, engine technology and performance, restrictions in vehicle density (for example, low-emission zones and alternate-day driving), increasing public transit availability, creating infrastructure to promote walking and biking, and changing land use patterns to ensure buffer zones between people and transportation corridors. As discussed in box 4.2, a **low-emission zone** (**LEZ**) is a defined area, usually in a city center, where access by some polluting vehicles is restricted or deterred with the aim of improving air quality.

Initial programs to address motor vehicle pollution have usually focused on technology solutions. Mexico City's first air pollution control plan in the 1990s targeted vehicle fuels, technology, and performance, including eliminating lead in gas, reducing the sulfur of diesel fuels (which reduces PM emissions), adding oxygenates to gas to promote more efficient combustion, and mandating catalytic converters and other clean-burning technologies on vehicles. Another successful switch to a cleaner fuel was seen in Delhi after the Supreme Court of India issued an injunction of 2006 that mandated that all public service vehicles in the city transition to liquified natural gas. More recently, electric vehicles (EVs) have been viewed as potentially attractive alternatives for cities because they eliminate tailpipe emissions, which often occur in street canyons and near the breathing zones of urban residents. However, if the energy generated to power EVs comes from fossil fuel sources such as coal, regional pollution can increase. This can be avoided if adoption of EVs occurs alongside a simultaneous shift to cleaner energy. However, even fully renewably charged EVs are not a complete panacea because they still can generate some pollution via brake and tire wear and resuspension of road dust.[38] EV adoption can be encouraged by decreasing taxes on these vehicles, providing subsidies for EV purchases, providing widely available and affordable charging infrastructure, and restricting purchases of internal combustion vehicles.

Land use and zoning changes can reduce the number of vehicle trips by locating residential areas close to jobs and shopping districts or with easy access using public transport (see chapter 11). Increased commuting by public transportation results in lower congestion, lower emissions per person, and thus overall lower emissions from the transport sector. Although potentially very effective and sustainable, such changes take time to be implemented. In the shorter term, cities can implement strategies to restrict access of polluting vehicles to dense urban areas. For example, HIC cities such as London have instituted congestion charging to reduce vehicle numbers and have designated low-emission zones to limit access to low-emission vehicle types (box 4.2). Other cities, such as Jakarta, have implemented programs to prohibit the use of vehicles on certain days, based on whether the license number ends in an odd or an even number.

Programs to enable switching from motorized to active transport (walking and cycling) can reduce air pollution and provide substantial cardiovascular health benefits to the individuals who take part, helping counteract the epidemic of chronic diseases in cities. The design of bike- and pedestrian-friendly streets, such as ensuring the presence of bicycle lanes and footpaths, is crucial to encourage use of active transport and is an important lever for city managers. Some have questioned whether air pollution encountered while walking or biking may offset the benefits (box 4.3).

Regulating land use to separate noxious sources from residential areas has been a successful strategy for reducing pollution exposure; in fact, this was an early motivation for urban zoning (see chapter 1). For example, Mexico City closed or relocated heavy industries such as refineries, cement factories, and metal smelters that contributed to its severe pollution problem. China relocated nearly two thousand large industrial sources that contributed to Beijing's air pollution as part of the 2013 national clean air action plan. Where relocating sources is not practical, regulators can mandate the use of cleaner production methods and fuels and enhanced emissions controls on existing industries. Cities can also build green buffers between residents and sources of air pollution such as congested roadways. In addition to helping to alleviate air pollution exposures, green space has been shown to provide a wide range of ancillary health benefits (see chapter 16) via improved mental health, access to physical activity and social interactions, and other pathways.

Coal burning for energy production, industrial processes, and household uses was a key source of air pollution in the Beijing region that was targeted in China's 2013 Clean Air Action Plan. Coal burning was both a local and a regional issue, demanding a regional strategy to ensure success. China shut down four coal-burning power plants in Beijing and reduced coal combustion by more than 75 percent in the broader region surround-

BOX 4.3 CYCLING IN CITIES: GOOD OR BAD FOR HEALTH?

Efforts to promote bicycling opportunities in cities have expanded rapidly recently. Bike lanes are being created and bike-sharing systems expanded. The COVID-19 pandemic reinforced the trend of increased biking. As explored in chapter 11, cycling is effective in reducing greenhouse gas and air pollution emissions and also promotes more physical activity, which reduces morbidity and mortality from cardiovascular diseases. Cycling is also very popular; in many cities, it is the fastest and most economical way to get around. But congested cities are often polluted cities, especially along busy roadways. In addition, cycling exposes users to potential injury risks via collisions with other cyclists or motorists. Thoughtful citizens who want to help improve both their own health and the health of the planet ask a simple question: what is the trade-off between health and environmental benefits of cycling and the health risks from exposure to air pollution and injury risks while cycling? This question has been the subject of an increasing number of studies, and the news is generally good.[a,b] In a landmark 2016 study, Tainio et al. described a sliding scale of trade-offs between physical activity health benefits and air pollution health harms, using all-cause mortality as the common metric of health. Their analysis showed that for any city with annual average $PM_{2.5}$ levels under 95 $\mu g/m^3$ (a level exceeded by only 1 percent of global cities), health benefits are maximized for thirty minutes a day of cycling.[a] Even with longer durations of cycling, up to one hundred minutes/day, the health benefits of cycling outweigh air pollution–related harms. Above that point, the balance tips, and the harm from inhaling pollutants outweighs the benefits of physical activity. In cities with cleaner air—say, the global average urban $PM_{2.5}$ levels (22 $\mu g/m^3$)—people can cycle for as long as seven hours a day and still enjoy net health benefits. Although these findings do not account for road traffic fatalities, other studies have suggested these harms are far lower than the benefits of cycling (see, for example, Mueller et al.[c]).

REFERENCES

a. Tainio M, de Nazelle AJ, Götschi T, et al. Can air pollution negate the health benefits of cycling and walking? *Preventive Medicine.* 2016;87:233-236.
b. Woodcock J, Tainio M, Cheshire J, O'Brien O, Goodman A. Health effects of the London bicycle sharing system: health impact modelling study. *BMJ.* 2014;348.
c. Mueller N, Rojas-Rueda D, Cole-Hunter T, et al. Health impact assessment of active transportation: a systematic review. *Preventive Medicine.* 2015;76:103-114.

ing Beijing. Subsidies were provided to offset increased costs of installing and operating emission control equipment on coal-burning industrial sources in China. These measures have contributed significantly to recent improvements in Beijing's air quality.

Although cities have many levers to tackle air pollution, care must be taken to ensure that solutions help to alleviate persistent inequities in access to clean air. Fine-scale maps of existing air pollution levels across a city can be developed using citizen science–driven low-cost sensor studies, supported by freely available satellite remote sensing data. These in turn can identify existing hot spots and inequities and can assist in targeting solutions that reduce or eliminate them.

AIR QUALITY AND CLIMATE CHANGE

Air pollution emitted by human activities in and around cities has significant negative implications for human health, as well as for the climate. Some of the same pollutants that directly harm our health, such as ozone and black carbon particles, also promote climate change. Other emitted gases such as CO_2 and methane, although not directly harmful to health at levels typically encountered, come from sources that also emit health-relevant pollutants, such as motor vehicles and power plants. As a result, mitigating air pollution in cities is closely linked to mitigation of climate change. But addressing one problem does not necessarily solve the other—as evidenced by the significant improvements in air quality witnessed in the United States since 1970 while greenhouse gas emissions continued to rise into the twenty-first century. Smart solutions to the twin challenges of air pollution and climate change should be designed and implemented in a coordinated way. HIC cities such as New York and London have set ambitious greenhouse gas emission reduction goals that, if carefully designed, can also bring further local health benefits via improved air quality, reduced traffic accidents, more green space, improved biking and walking infrastructure, and other pathways. LMIC cities such as Delhi and Mexico City have prioritized air quality goals, but have the potential to also make progress on low-carbon economic development. The challenge of climate change is explored in chapter 17.

CONCLUSION

Healthy places should provide equitable access to clean air for all citizens to breathe, an essential component of a healthy life. However, although progress has been made in many cities to improve air quality over recent decades, substantial challenges remain on the pathway to ensuring healthy air for all urban residents. Most air pollution is place-based, deriving from the juxtaposition of noxious emissions and human activities in specific geographic patterns. Cities can contain a range of air pollution sources, including those related to transportation, cooking, manufacturing, power generation, waste burning, and construction. In general, neighborhoods that are closer to emission sources face consistently higher air pollution concentrations than other places. Likewise, activity patterns that bring individuals into close proximity to urban pollution sources for extended periods lead to higher personal exposures and resulting health risks. Air quality in cities can also be influenced by activities occurring in the larger region upwind, including agriculture, land clearing, industry, power plants, upwind cities, wildfires, and dust storms. Clean-air solutions seek to separate people from polluting sources, where possible, while also reducing the volume of pollution emitted from the sources via tech-nology improvements. Solutions are likely to be most successful when implemented in a context that includes reliable information on sources and levels of pollution, effective incentives, and inclusive institutional arrangements.

DISCUSSION QUESTIONS

1. What are the primary sources of air pollution in your community?
2. What are the links between air pollution and climate change?
3. Motor vehicles are a major source of air pollution in many cities. Identify three transportation strategies for reducing air pollution and explain how they would function.
4. Access air pollution monitoring data for your city (usually available from the health department or the environment department—or at https://www.iqair.com/us/). Can you find any inequitable patterns? Are poorer neighborhoods disproportionately located near emissions sources such as major roadways or incinerators?
5. "Tight buildings" save energy by reducing air exchange between the inside and the outside, but doing so can result in a buildup of indoor pollutants. How might this problem be addressed to optimize both the building's energy performance and the quality of indoor air?
6. Climate change is increasing the risk of wildfires, which generate large quantities of smoke. Investigate a recent wildfire season, describe its impacts on air quality in affected areas, and discuss built environment strategies to reduce harm.
7. Read up on recent efforts to introduce clean cookstoves in a particular region in the Global South, discuss the challenges that arose, and discuss how these might be overcome in future efforts.

DISCLOSURE OF COMPETING INTERESTS

Patrick Lott Kinney and Priyanka Nadia deSouza disclose no competing interests.

REFERENCES

1. Plumer B. Europe's love affair with diesel cars has been a disaster. *Vox*. October 16, 2015. https://www.vox.com/2015/10/15/9541789/volkswagen-europe-diesel-pollution

2. Vidal, John. The rise of diesel in Europe: the impact on health and pollution. *The Guardian*. September 22, 2015. https://www.theguardian.com/environment/2015/sep/22/the-rise-diesel-in-europe-impact-on-health-pollution

3. Atkinson RW, Analitis A, Samoli E, et al. Short-term exposure to traffic-related air pollution and daily mortality in London, UK. *Journal of Exposure Science and Environmental Epidemiology*. 2016;26(2):125-132.

4. Anenberg SC, Miller J, Minjares R, et al. Impacts and mitigation of excess diesel-related NO_x emissions in 11 major vehicle markets. *Nature*. 2017;545(7655):467-471.

5. Liu NM, Grigg J. Diesel, children and respiratory disease. *BMJ Paediatrics Open*. 2018;2(1).

6. BBC. Ella Adoo-Kissi-Debrah: Air pollution a factor in girl's death, inquest finds. *BBC News*. December 16, 2020. https://www.bbc.com/news/uk-england-london-55330945

7. WHO. Air pollution. Published 2021. Accessed October 23, 2021. https://www.who.int/health-topics/air-pollution/

8. Bell ML, Davis DL, Fletcher T. A retrospective assessment of mortality from the London smog episode of 1952: the role of influenza and pollution. *Environmental Health Perspectives*. 2004;112(1):6-8.

9. Schraufnagel DE, Balmes JR, Cowl CT, et al. Air pollution and noncommunicable diseases: a review by the Forum of International Respiratory Societies' Environmental Committee, Part 2: Air pollution and organ systems. *Chest*. 2019;155(2):417-426.

10. Dockery DW, Pope CA, Xu X, et al. An association between air pollution and mortality in six US cities. *New England Journal of Medicine*. 1993;329(24):1753-1759.

11. Pope III CA, Burnett RT, Thun MJ, et al. Lung cancer, cardiopulmonary mortality, and long-term exposure to fine particulate air pollution. *JAMA*. 2002;287(9):1132-1141.

12. Di Q, Wang Y, Zanobetti A, et al. Air pollution and mortality in the Medicare population. *New England Journal of Medicine*. 2017;376(26):2513-2522.

13. Murray CJ, Aravkin AY, Zheng P, et al. Global burden of 87 risk factors in 204 countries and territories, 1990–2019: a systematic analysis for the Global Burden of Disease Study 2019. *The Lancet*. 2020;396(10258):1223-1249.

14. Kelly FJ, Zhu T. Transport solutions for cleaner air. *Science*. 2016;352(6288):934-936.

15. US EPA. Integrated Science Assessment for Ozone and Related Photochemical Oxidants. February 2013.

16. US EPA. Integrated Science Assessment for Particulate Matter, EPA/600/R-08/139F. December 2009.

17. WHO-UNEP. Urban Air Pollution in the Mega Cities of the World. World Health Organization, United Nations Environment Programme, 1992.

18. World Bank. *Clearing the Air: A Tale of Three Cities*. World Health Organization; 2020.

19. IQAir. World Air Quality Report: Region & City PM2.5 Ranking. *Secondary World Air Quality Report: Region & City PM2.5 Ranking*. 2019. https://www.iqair.com/us/world-most-polluted-cities

20. Health Effects Institute. *State of Global Air 2020: A Special Report on Global Exposure to Air Pollution and Its Health Effects*. Health Effects Institute, 2020.

21. Health Effects Institute. *State of Global Air 2019; Special Report*. Health Effects Institute, 2019.

22. WHO. WHO indoor air quality guidelines: household fuel combustion. Secondary WHO indoor air quality guidelines: household fuel combustion. World Health Organization; 2014. https://www.who.int/airpollution/publications/household-fuel-combustion/en/

23. Smith KR, Bruce N, Balakrishnan K, et al. Millions dead: how do we know and what does it mean? Methods used in the comparative risk assessment of household air pollution. *Annual Review of Public Health*. 2014;35:185-206.

24. Quinn AK, Bruce N, Puzzolo E, et al. An analysis of efforts to scale up clean household energy for cooking around the world. *Energy for Sustainable Development*. 2018;46:1-10.

25. Abdul-Wahab SA. *Sick Building Syndrome*. Springer-Verlag. 2011;10:978-973.

26. Quansah R, Semple S, Ochieng CA, et al. Effectiveness of interventions to reduce household air pollution and/or improve health in homes using solid fuel in low- and-middle income countries: a systematic review and meta-analysis. *Environment International*. 2017;103:73-90.

27. Bell ML, Ebisu K. Environmental inequality in exposures to airborne particulate matter components in the United States. *Environmental Health Perspectives*. 2012;120(12):1699-1704.

28. Colmer J, Hardman I, Shimshack J, Voorheis J. Disparities in PM2.5 air pollution in the United States. *Science*. 2020;369(6503):5755-78.

29. Miranda ML, Edwards SE, Keating MH, Paul CJ. Making the environmental justice grade: the relative burden of air pollution exposure in the United States. *International Journal of Environmental Research and Public Health*. 2011;8(6):1755-1771.

30. Tessum CW, Apte JS, Goodkind AL, et al. Inequity in consumption of goods and services adds to racial-ethnic disparities in air pollution exposure. *Proceedings of the National Academy of Sciences*. 2019;116(13):6001-6006.

31. Hajat A, Hsia C, O'Neill MS. Socioeconomic disparities and air pollution exposure: a global review. *Current Environmental Health Reports*. 2015;2(4):440-450.

32. Bell ML, O'Neill MS, Cifuentes LA, et al. Challenges and recommendations for the study of socioeconomic factors and air pollution health effects. *Environmental Science and Policy*. 2005;8(5):525-533.

33. Nardone A, Casey JA, Morello-Frosch R, Mujahid M, Balmes JR, Thakur N. Associations between historical residential redlining and current age-adjusted rates of emergency department visits due to asthma across eight cities in California: an ecological study. *The Lancet Planetary Health*. 2020;4(1):e24-e31.

34. Corburn J. Concepts for studying urban environmental justice. *Current Environmental Health Reports* 2017;4(1):61-67.

35. deSouza P. Air pollution in Kenya: a review. *Air Quality, Atmosphere & Health*. 2020;13(12):1487-1495.

36. Kinney PL, Gichuru MG, Volavka-Close N, et al. Traffic impacts on PM2.5 air quality in Nairobi, Kenya. *Environmental Science and Policy*. 2011;14(4):369-378.

37. Gatari MJ, Kinney PL, Yan B, et al. High airborne black carbon concentrations measured near roadways in Nairobi, Kenya. *Transportation Research Part D: Transport and Environment*. 2019;68:99-109.

38. Holmatov B, Hoekstra AY. The environmental footprint of transport by car using renewable energy. *Earth's Future*. 2020;8(2).

CHAPTER 5

INJURY, VIOLENCE, AND THE BUILT ENVIRONMENT

Corinne Peek-Asa and Christopher N. Morrison

KEY POINTS

- Injuries and violence are two of the leading causes of premature life lost and disability globally.
- As described in the Haddon matrix, the public health approach to reducing the overall burden due to injuries involves preventing injury events, reducing injury severity, and supporting physical and psychological recovery.
- Modifying the built environment, including making physical changes to roadways, homes, workplaces, and public spaces, is a critical component of any comprehensive approach to injury prevention, especially for injuries related to transportation, falls, fire, drowning, and violence.
- Modifying the built environment is among the most effective, low-cost, and long-lasting prevention approaches available to prevent injuries.

INTRODUCTION

In April 2017, Peter, age ten, and his sister Anika, age eight, were walking home from their elementary school in a small town in eastern Europe and were hit by a car. Peter's arm was broken, and Anika had a traumatic brain injury. With no sidewalk available, the children had been walking on the dirt on the side of the road and were about to enter a nar-row road bridge when a speeding car veered into them to avoid an oncoming car that was crossing the bridge. Both children recovered, but their family had considerable medical care costs and days away from work and school.

Although behaviors of the individuals involved—such as the driver's speeding—contributed to this crash, features of the roadway were perhaps the major cause. Roadway features that contributed to the crash include the narrow bridge width, not having a protected place for pedestrians to walk, and not having any signage to remind drivers to watch out for pedestrians or to beware of the narrow roadway. In such environments, the onus to avoid injury rests with drivers and pedestrians. By contrast, environments designed to protect all roadway users integrate safety into the design.

Injuries are a leading cause of death and disability worldwide, and they disproportionately impact children and seniors and people living in lower-resource environments. In part, this inequitable burden arises because inequity exists at many levels in the built environment. At the individual and family levels, those with more resources can afford to buy safer cars, live in safer neighborhoods, and purchase safety devices such as smoke alarms. At the community level, investments to promote safety such as road improvements are not always distributed equitably (figure 5.1).

Figure 5.1. This view of a family walking along a road in Costa Rica illustrates the dangers that a lack of infrastructure poses to pedestrian safety. The Make Roads Safe campaign has called on the international community to improve road safety for both pedestrians and motor vehicle occupants.
Source: Make Roads Safe: The Campaign for Global Road Safety, Commission for Global Road Safety, FIA Foundation

Nearly five million people around the world die from injuries every year, and nearly one hundred million require some type of health care due to an injury. Injuries are the leading cause of death for youth and have a higher incidence in low and low-middle income countries.[1] In the United States, injuries lead to more than 240,000 deaths each year, and injuries are the leading cause of death for those aged one through forty-four. Figure 5.2 shows that the leading mechanisms of injury death are poisoning (for example, opioid overdose), transportation, and falls. The design of the built environment can have considerable impact on the likelihood of injury for most of these mechanisms, especially motor vehicle–related injuries, falls, fire, and drowning. Globally, most types of injuries decreased from 1990 to 2013, especially in high- and middle-income countries.[1] Many of these decreases are due to changes in the built environment.

In this chapter, we describe some conceptual approaches to injury prevention that are helpful when thinking about how the built environment interacts with other prevention approaches. We explore the many ways the built environment influences injury and violence risk, including for both intentional injuries and unintentional injuries. We conclude with examples of successful built environment prevention approaches.

THE BUILT ENVIRONMENT WITHIN INJURY PREVENTION THEORY

The word *accident* is defined as an unforeseen and unplanned event or circumstance. Although commonly used as a synonym, injuries are not "accidents" because injuries are highly predictable events with well-documented risk and protective factors. Almost all injuries are potentially preventable. It is challenging to think of an example of an

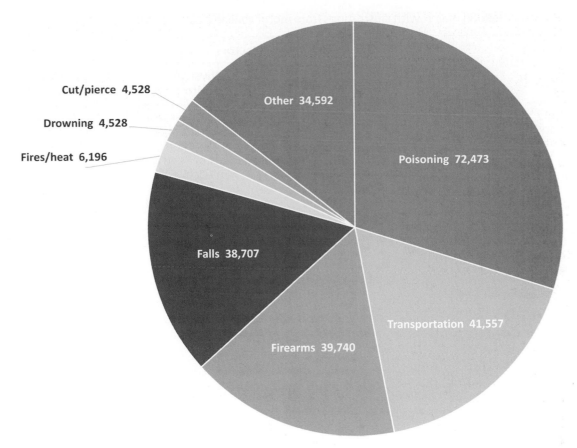

Figure 5.2. Injury deaths by mechanism, United States, 2018.
Source: Adapted from WISQARS (https://www.cdc.gov/injury/wisqars/index.html). Reference to specific commercial products, manufacturers, companies, or trademarks does not constitute its endorsement or recommendation by the U.S. Government, Department of Health and Human Services, or Centers for Disease Control and Prevention.

injury for which environmental interventions (such as changing policy or altering the physical features) or individual-level interventions (such as education) would not have reduced the probability of its occurrence. Given the predictability of injuries, many types of approaches can intervene in the injury causal pathway.[2] Injuries are categorized into two main groups: **unintentional injuries**, which include those from most road traffic crashes, falls, fires, and drownings; and **intentional injuries**, which include homicide/assault and suicide/self-harm.

The Haddon Matrix: A Framework for Injury Prevention

The **Haddon matrix** is a framework that helps identify approaches to injury prevention by identifying components that can be modified

to reduce injury risk and aligning these components with strategies that address different phases of injury (see the example using road traffic injuries in table 5.1).[3] The causal model of injuries includes host, vehicle, and vector components, each of which can be modified to reduce the risk of injury. The "host" is the individual at risk of injury. Factors such as age and gender and behaviors such as substance use and risk-taking are characteristics that can increase risk for injury. Objects, inanimate or animate, can contribute to a host being injured. Inanimate objects, called vehicles, include motor vehicles or firearms; animate objects, called vectors, include other individuals, or animals, that can increase a host's risk of injury. Examples of vectors are a drunk driver, a homicide perpetrator, and an aggressive dog.

Table 5.1. The Haddon matrix with illustrations from motor vehicle crash prevention.

| Phases | Factors | | | |
	Human Host	Vehicle/Vector	Physical Environment	Sociocultural Environment
Preinjury (Primary Prevention)	Reduce alcohol intoxication; programs to teach driving safety	Vehicle features that prevent crashing, such as improved vehicle stability, handling, and visibility	Improvements in road structure; traffic controls, traffic calming measures	Policies that reduce crash rates, such as graduated driver licensure and driving under the influence laws; strong safety culture
Injury (Secondary Prevention)	Use of seat belts; child safety seats, including proper placement and use by age of child	Increase energy absorbed by the vehicle frame; safety features such as airbags, headrests, shatterproof windshields; collapsible steering columns	Energy-absorbing guard rails	Policies requiring use of seat belts and car seats; programs to provide car seats; educational programs about car seat installation and placement
Postinjury (Tertiary Prevention)	Stabilize serious injuries; reduce bleeding and other complications; provide physical and psychological rehabilitation services	Vehicle design for easier extrication; vehicle systems that inform emergency services when and where a crash occurs	Enhanced emergency medical systems and field care	Support for infrastructure of trauma care, including 911 system, emergency and trauma care, and rehabilitation services

The environment is a critical component of the injury causal model, and the Haddon matrix divides the environment into the built and socio/cultural/political components. The built environment includes the physical space in which we live, work, study, travel, and play, whereas the sociocultural component includes the policies and social influences that influence injury risk. These two facets of the environment are intertwined. For example, many elements of the built environment, such as crosswalks and highway guard rails, are in place because of policies that require them.

The Haddon matrix divides these causal components, found in the columns of the matrix, into three phases of injury prevention: preinjury, injury, and postinjury. Preinjury interventions, called primary prevention, aim to prevent the injury event from occurring. Stop signs to prevent car crashes, swimming pool fences to prevent drowning, firearm storage safes to prevent firearm injuries in children, and safety caps on pill bottles to prevent ingestion by children are all examples of primary prevention related to the built environment. Primary prevention is often the most cost-effective approach because it prevents the injury and all the financial, physical, and psychological sequelae that impact individuals, families, and communities.[4]

Injury-phase interventions, called secondary prevention, aim to reduce injury severity once a potential injury-producing exposure has occurred. Motorcycle and bicycle helmets, seat belts, life vests, and bulletproof vests are examples of secondary prevention. Some of the most effective secondary prevention strategies do not eliminate all injuries. For example, a motorcycle helmet is effective in reducing head injury in motorcycle crashes, but it is not effective in preventing injury to other body regions. Similarly, seat belts do not prevent all injuries in vehicle crashes, but they do reduce overall severity.

Postinjury interventions, called tertiary prevention, are designed to reduce the consequences of the injury after it has occurred. These efforts can include emergency response, trauma care, and rehabilitation services. Many lives have been saved, for example, with the development of organized trauma care systems.

Specific injury prevention strategies can be divided into two broad groups based on need for host actions. **Passive intervention** requires no input or action by the host, and many prevention approaches that integrate the built environment are passive. For example, modifications in a roadway to reduce sharp curves or to manage traffic flow reduce the risk of crashing. **Active intervention** requires that the host take some type of action for the intervention to work. Seat belts and helmets are examples, as the host must actively engage the prevention strategy each time they drive. Passive intervention strategies are usually considered more effective, especially when compared to active interventions that require frequent or time-consuming action. Airbags, which require no driver action, will deploy in any crash, whereas a seat belt can only be effective if the rider remembers to fasten it.

EXAMPLES OF BUILT ENVIRONMENT APPROACHES IN REDUCING INJURY RISK

In addition to the conceptual framework embodied in the Haddon matrix, built environment approaches to reducing injury risk have a strong empirical base. The following sections provide examples of preventive interventions applied to specific mechanisms of injury.

Roadway Safety

The mechanism that places the greatest burden on global public health is transportation injury. A total of 63.9 million people were injured in crashes worldwide in 2017,[5] and around 1.3 million people die every year.[6] Transportation injuries have such immense human and economic costs that the United Nations' 2030 Agenda for Sustainable Development includes the goal of halving deaths and injuries in road traffic crashes. The Haddon matrix suggests that essential steps to achieving that goal include reducing crash incidence (primary prevention), reducing the severity of crashes when they occur (secondary prevention), and improving access to health care for people injured in crashes (tertiary prevention).

Although most transportation globally is by motor vehicles—such as passenger cars, buses, and trucks—more than half of injuries and deaths occur among vulnerable roadway users, including bicyclists, pedestrians, and motorcyclists. This proportion varies from country to country. In the United States, vulnerable road users, which include persons of color disproportionately, account for about one-third of roadway fatalities.[7,8] The incidence is considerably higher in low- and middle-income countries, where these transportation modes are used more commonly. Despite these regional differences, empirical studies from around the world provide strong evidence regarding roadway designs that are effective preventive interventions to protect these groups.[9] For example, protected bicycle lanes wholly separate bicyclists from motor vehicle traffic and substantially reduce the likelihood of bicycle versus motor vehicle crash occurrence. Traffic-calming measures, such as speed bumps, reduce both the likelihood and severity of motor vehicle versus pedestrian crashes.[10] Dedicated taxi hailing sites (for example, "taxi ranks") limit the risks that distracted pedestrians will collide with a motor vehicle while signaling for a ride. A key goal for such strategies designed to protect vulnerable roadway users is to reduce the speed difference between users, which reduces problems associated with visibility, increases reaction time, and limits the severity of initial impacts.

In addition to protecting vulnerable road users, modifying the built environment can also reduce the injury burden for motorists. The occurrence and severity of single-vehicle crashes (for example, a collision with a tree) and of crashes involving multiple vehicles can be reduced by altering many aspects of the built environment, including roadway configurations, signage, lighting, rules, and enforcement. For example, placing speed cameras at strategic locations is a low-cost primary prevention strategy that can reduce crash incidence. Although it is not possible to wholly eliminate risks for road users, careful attention to roadway designs can have considerable public health benefits. The Vision Zero movement highlights many of these improved roadway designs to prevent traffic-related injuries and deaths.[11]

Interpersonal Violence

Acts of violence—which occur when a person intentionally inflicts injury upon another person—can be categorized according to the relations between the victim(s) and the perpetrator(s).[12] **Interpersonal violence** includes acts of aggression and assault against children, elders, intimate partners, acquaintances, and strangers. Approximately 22.9 million incidents of nonfatal interpersonal violence occurred globally in 2017.[5] Interpersonal violence is a separate, albeit closely related, problem to **structural violence**, which refers to acts of neglect or harm by formal or informal institutions, including racism, police violence, and other biases.

Altering the built environment can reduce interpersonal violence. This strategy is based on theories of crime opportunities, which assume that perpetrators are rational actors and that their decision to commit violence can be altered.[13] For example, **routine activities theory** suggests that crime and violence occur due to the convergence in space and time of motivated offenders, suitable targets, and absence of capable guardians.[14] According to this theory, limiting interactions between offenders and potential victims and increasing real or perceived guardianship will reduce the likelihood that violence will occur. Public spaces can be designed with these goals in mind, and empirical studies provide strong evidence to support these theoretical mechanisms. For example, improved lighting reduces crime in small geographic areas. Removing blight and providing visible cues that a space is monitored and well attended, such as cleaning and greening vacant lots, decrease gun violence. Limiting retail alcohol outlet density and reducing interactions between intoxicated people who might become offenders or victims can reduce alcohol-related assault, intimate partner violence, and child maltreatment.

Violence in the Workplace

People spend considerable time in their workplaces, and occupational hazards are a leading cause of injury (see chapter 13). Workplace violence is a leading cause of occupational death and provides a good example of how environmental modifications can reduce risk.[15] In 1999, nearly half of the 651 workplace homicides in the United States were in the retail industry, with most concentrated in convenience stores; by 2018, the number of workplace homicides decreased to 453, with only 20 percent in the retail industry.[16]

The decrease in workplace homicide overall and retail homicide is largely attributable to an environmentally based prevention approach that originated in the 1970s called **crime prevention through environmental design (CPTED)**. CPTED aims to modify the work environment to decrease vulnerability to crime, allowing businesses direct control of the environment rather than relying on indirect control of criminal behavior.[15,17] In a retail store, CPTED principles include measures that influence lighting, visibility, entry and egress, and cash handling, which together create a positive work environment attractive to customers but not potential robbers (figure 5.3).

(a)

(b)

Figure 5.3. (a) Consistent with the principles of crime prevention through environmental design, good lighting, good internal and external visibility, and an orderly appearance may decrease the risk of robbery in this convenience store. (b) Poor internal visibility and a disorderly appearance may increase the risk of robbery in this store. Source: Photographs courtesy of the Workplace Violence Prevention Program, Dr. Corinne Peek-Asa and Dr. Carri Casteel, University of Iowa Injury Prevention Research Center

Published evaluations of the CPTED approach indicate that it is successful in reducing robberies, as well as assaults and homicides to employees. Businesses that introduced the CTPED approach experienced robbery decreases between 30 percent and 84 percent compared to control stores.[15,18] Many CPTED approaches, such as improved lighting and visibility, are relatively low cost compared with more expensive approaches such as surveillance cameras. Policies that require CPTED elements, introduced in some states such as Florida, as well as professional organizations that provide information to retail business owners, help increase the prevalence of CPTED components found in stores. CPTED principles have also been applied in school settings to reduce violence-related behaviors.[19]

Home Modification to Prevent Fall Injuries

Falls are a common injury, with many fall injuries occurring at home and in the workplace. Rates of fatal falls in the United States among all age groups are increasing, with fatality rates nearly doubling from 5.0 per 100,000 in 2000 to 11.8 per 100,000 in 2018. Falls are particularly problematic for older people because of the potential for serious consequences that include death, disability, and loss of independence. In the United States in 2018, the overall fall-related death rate was 11.8 per 100,000 population; for individuals aged seventy-five to seventy-nine, the comparable rate was 45.1, and for those aged eighty-five and over, it was 271.0.

A large proportion of injuries occur in the home. Risk for falling is multifaceted, including biologic risk factors such as poor vision, muscle weakness, or chronic conditions; behavioral factors such as inactivity or alcohol use; and environmental risk factors. Homes in which elderly people live often have at least one, and sometimes more, environmental hazards, which can include obstructed pathways, loose throw rugs and other trip hazards, poor maintenance of stairways, poor lighting and visibility, hard surfaces on which to fall, and lack of safety devices such as grab bars.[20,21]

These different risk factors interact to create fall risk. A Cochrane review of elderly fall prevention programs concluded that interventions addressing multiple risk factors specific to an individual may reduce the rate of falls compared with usual care or attention control (interventions not designed to prevent falls, such as social visits). But the evidence is weak for impacts of such multifactorial interventions on other fall-related outcomes such as fractures. Multiple component interventions designed for a group, usually including exercise, may reduce the rate of falls and the risk of falling compared with usual care or attention control.[22]

The Centers for Disease Control and Prevention's National Center for Injury Prevention and Control also emphasizes the importance of multifaceted, community interventions as highlighted in a compendium of fall prevention programs accompanied by an intervention guide.[23] The compendium identifies three programs focused only on home modification and twelve programs focused on multifaceted interventions, of which eleven included a home safety component.[23] The home safety components most frequently included a home hazard checklist or a home assessment to identify modifiable factors to increase home safety. Occupational therapists usually have the expertise to deliver this component, as they are trained to make recommendations such as moving throw rugs and installing grab bars and other safety devices. Disseminating elderly fall prevention programs on a large scale and ensuring that participants can achieve the program goals are public health challenges.

Drowning Prevention

Except for installation of swimming pool fencing, tailoring the built environment to decrease water-related injury has not been a major public health focus. Each year in the United States, more than forty-five hundred people die from drowning, of which approximately six hundred are children between the ages of one and nine years.[24] Creating effective environmental strategies for addressing water-related injuries is particularly challenging because these injuries occur in a variety of settings, such as homes, swimming pools, open water, and irrigation ditches. In addition, platform diving, coming into contact with motorboat propellers or moving sailboat booms, and fishing from docks that are situated near overhead power lines all increase the risk of water-related injuries.

Installing pool fencing is one of the most effective environmental strategies for protecting children from unintentional drowning. Fencing is most effective when it surrounds a pool on all four sides, is of sufficient height and design to resist climbing attempts, and has a secure, self-closing, and self-latching gate.[25] Although this built environment solution prevents at least three-fourths of all childhood pool drownings, implementing appropriate fencing regulations and laws has proven difficult because legislation for pool fencing is largely promulgated at the county level.

Globally, many children drown in open bodies of water. Bangladesh, for example, has one of the highest childhood drowning rates in the world, in part because parents who work in the large open bodies of water used for rice farming are unable to provide adequate supervision of their children while they work. One built environment prevention approach has been to create safe, enclosed spaces to keep children away from the water.[26] Further research is needed to evaluate many of the interventions intended to reduce water-related injuries by altering the built environment, as well as other approaches such as addressing alcohol use in water settings.

Residential Fire Injuries

Globally, nearly nine million injuries and more than 120,000 deaths occur annually from fire and sources of heat.[27] Fire and burn-related injury rates are disproportionately high in low- and middle-income countries. Seven of the eight countries (India, China, Russia, United States, Nigeria, Pakistan, Democratic Republic of the Congo, and Ethiopia) that accounted for half of the world's fire- and burn-related deaths in 2017 were low- and middle-income countries. Although death rates are highest among young children and the elderly, the highest injury rate is among those aged five to thirty; injuries related to fire and sources of heat have equal or higher rates among women than men.

Fire and hot substance-related injuries occur most frequently in the home, and the most common causes are residential fires, cooking, and smoking. Residential fire injuries have higher death and injury rates among women than men and have a disproportionate impact on children. Fire deaths and disabilities are heavily concentrated in countries that have a high prevalence of indoor cook stoves that expose residents to open flames, often on the floor and in the central portion of the home. An estimated three billion people live in homes with open cook stoves. Design improvements to reduce open cooking in homes can both increase safety and reduce indoor air contaminants from the cooking process. Approaches have included alternate sources of heat, such as through solar panels; adding covers that reduce flame exposure and can move smoke outside the home; and implementing larger communal cook stoves outside of homes.

Residential fire injuries have been reduced in the United States through home modifications such as the installation of smoke alarms, sprinkler systems, fire extinguishers, and devices such as rope ladders to enable escape. Functioning smoke detectors cut the risk of dying in a home fire by about 40 percent, and 75 to 80 percent of the fires that would have grown large enough to be reported in the absence of alarms are not reported when alarms are present because individuals do not need fire department aid. In the United States, approximately 88 percent of homes have at least one installed smoke alarm, largely due to ordinances that require their presence. However, approximately 25 to 35 percent of alarms are not functional because the battery has expired or been removed. Hard wiring smoke alarms to the residence's electric system has helped prolong smoke alarm functionality. Studies have shown that communities can increase smoke alarm presence and promote smoke alarm maintenance through ordinances requiring their presence and educational campaigns.[28]

Smoke alarms are a good example of the interplay between built environment approaches, policy, and education. Other contributors to reducing residential fire deaths in the United States have involved building codes and regulations, including policies such as residential sprinkler systems and those that modify the fire resistance of materials in the home (for example, fire-retardant materials, fire-resistant cigarettes).

Implementation of these regulations varies by state and country, but generally regulations on the built environment are concentrated in high-resource and high-infrastructure countries. The absence of resources to improve the home environment and safety cultures to regulate their use contributes to disparity in injury rates among various populations.

CONSIDERATIONS WHEN IMPLEMENTING BUILT ENVIRONMENT INTERVENTIONS

We now turn to practical considerations for implementing evidence-based strategies in real-world settings. The availability and suitability of injury intervention strategies to address a given problem in a particular setting are often influenced by social, political, and financial considerations.

Balance between Exposure-Limiting Approaches and Risk-Limiting Approaches

Injury prevention approaches can reduce the risk of injuries through several mechanisms. Consistent with the Haddon matrix, one consideration in prioritizing an intervention approach is whether the risk reduction occurs through reducing exposure to the activity causing injury or in reducing risk for being injured when doing the activity. For exam-

ple, one approach to reducing playground injuries is to reduce exposure to playground equipment. But playgrounds provide substantial benefits as a dedicated environment for children to interact and engage in physical activity. Built environment interventions can encourage play on playgrounds—thereby increasing exposure—and concomitantly decrease risks for injury while playing. These approaches include impact-absorbing surfaces, height-appropriate equipment, well-designed hand grabs, and placement to avoid overcrowding of equipment. Integrating safe design to encourage activity is one advantage of built environment approaches.

Cost Effectiveness and Implementation

Built environments that reduce injury and violence incidence can have considerable public health benefits, including large reductions in the costs of treating injuries. However, the benefits from prevention are often hidden because they result in treatment and disability costs that are not paid (because the injury was prevented), whereas the costs for implementation are paid directly. Thus, it can be difficult to convince decision-makers to incorporate injury prevention into environmental design when the public health imperative conflicts with economic and amenity considerations. Pedestrian safety barriers are a costly addition to roadways. Sprinkler systems to prevent fires can be expensive to install and maintain in multiunit housing developments. Entrance and exit control of retail space might require cumbersome renovations. The individuals or entities that must invest in the prevention, such as the property owner who purchases a sprinkler system or the city that installs bike lanes, will often not be the same entity that covers the costs of injuries that occur should these approaches not be implemented. Such obstacles are common in prevention science, where public health practitioners are challenged to demonstrate benefit based on *averted potential events* that are yet to occur. Unlike treatment, where practitioners can provide concrete examples of individuals or groups that have benefited from an intervention, prevention must rely on empirical research to demonstrate that interventions produce net benefits.

One approach to encourage decision-makers to incorporate injury prevention into environmental designs is cost-effectiveness research, which compares the financial costs and health benefits for the interventions. This method requires that researchers calculate the public health impact of an intervention (measured as events averted, lives saved, years of life saved, or disability adjusted life years saved). The estimated financial cost per health outcome is then calculated based on the costs for treatment, lost productivity, and other relevant factors, and the total costs of the intervention are compared to the estimated savings. For example, smoke detectors are a low-cost prevention strategy to reduce risks of injury from house fires. A review in Dallas, Texas, calculated that each $1 spent on smoke detectors saved approximately $3.21 in total costs, which equated to a total of $3.8 million saved between 2001 and 2011.[29] Administrators and health officials can use such information to compare available interventions and decide where and whether to allocate resources to preventive interventions, although a **cost-effectiveness analysis** should not be the sole criterion for assessing the public health value of an intervention.

Integration of Multiple Approaches

Given that injury prevention is rarely the only consideration when designing physical environments, public health practitioners must partner with other professionals to ensure that public health thinking is embedded in the design of physical space. Equipped with compelling empirical evidence, including the results of cost-effectiveness studies, public health has contributed to the design and installation of public and private spaces in many ways that are now taken for granted. For example, building codes regulate the size, materials, and dimensions of new and reno-vated buildings; minimum design standards apply to new roadway construction; and liquor licensing authorities limit concentrations of retail alcohol outlets within some geographic areas. More heavily regulated industries typically provide greater opportunities to accommodate injury prevention, often because the public authorities who provide the regulatory oversight also bear the financial costs of injuries that occur. For instance, people injured on public roads may place a burden on nearby publicly funded health services. However, other industries, from toy manufacturers to construction firms to insurance companies, may incorporate injury prevention into built environments to reduce insurance premiums, mitigate liability, and attract customers.

SUMMARY

Features of the built environment affect injury occurrence, injury severity, and injury recovery. Safe physical spaces can take many forms. We often assume that investment in infrastructure is the most important component for a safe built environment, and although investment is essential, it requires leadership that prioritizes safety in infrastructure development. Thus, perhaps the most important factor is the strength of the safety culture—meaning the extent to which leaders and decision makers prioritize safety in their design decisions. Future public health leaders need to be knowledgeable about built environment approaches and serve as advocates for these strategies.

DISCUSSION QUESTIONS

1. Select an injury type and fill in the cells for the Haddon matrix to identify built environment approaches to prevent that type of injury.
2. Research provides critical evidence to support built environmental approaches to prevent injuries. In most cases, it is not feasible or ethical to test the impact of built environment interventions using an experimental study design in which the

researchers select research participants, groups, or places to receive the intervention; select others to receive a control condition; and then compare injuries for the intervention versus control groups. What alternatives approaches are available? What are the strengths and weaknesses of these approaches?

3. A strong conceptual framework and clear empirical evidence are necessary but insufficient conditions to implement a built environment approach to prevent injury. What obstacles might public health practitioners face when attempting to implement a preventive intervention to reduce injury? How could they overcome these obstacles?

4. Based on your results for question 1, select one cell from the Haddon matrix and investigate the theory and empirical evidence supporting the intervention you proposed. How strong is the theoretical foundation? How robust is the scientific evidence? How successful have public health practitioners been at implementing this approach?

DISCLOSURE OF COMPETING INTERESTS

Corinne Peek-Asa discloses no competing interests.

Christopher N. Morrison discloses no competing interests.

REFERENCES

1. Haagsma JA, Graetz N, Bolliger I, et al. The global burden of injury: incidence, mortality, disability-adjusted life years and time trends from the Global Burden of Disease study 2013. *Injury Prevention*. 2016;22(1):3-18.

2. Institute of Medicine. *Reducing the Burden of Injury: Advancing Prevention and Treatment*. Bonney RJ, Fulco CE, Liverman CT, eds. National Academies Press; 1999.

3. Haddon W. Advances in the epidemiology of injuries as a basis for public policy. *Public Health Reports*. 1980;95(5):411-421.

4. Hemenway D. *While We Were Sleeping: Success Stories in Injury and Violence Prevention*. University of California Press; 2009.

5. Disease and Injury Incidence and Prevalence Collaborators. Global, regional, and national incidence, prevalence, and years lived with disability for 354 diseases and injuries for 195 countries and territories, 1990–2017: a systematic analysis for the Global Burden of Disease Study 2017. *The Lancet*. 2018;392(10159):1789-1858.

6. Global Status Report on Road Safety 2018: Summary. (WHO/NMH/NVI/18.20). World Health Organization; 2018.

7. NHTSA. 2018 fatal motor vehicle crashes: overview. National Center for Statistics and Analysis No. DOT HS 812 826; 2019.

8. Schmitt A. *Right of Way: Race, Class, and the Silent Epidemic of Pedestrian Deaths in America*. Island Press; 2020.

9. Federal Highway Administration. Making Our Roads Safer One Countermeasure at a Time. FHWA-SA-18-029. US Department of Transportation; 2018.

10. Teft BC. Impact speed and a pedestrian's risk of severe injury or death. *Accident Analysis and Prevention*. 2013;50:871-878.

11. Vision Zero Network. What Is Vision Zero? 2021. https://visionzeronetwork.org /about/what-is-vision-zero/

12. World Report on Violence and Health: Summary. World Health Organization. 2002. https://www.who.int/violence _injury_prevention/violence/world_report /en/summary_en.pdf

13. Cornish DB, Clarke RV. Understanding crime displacement: an application of rational choice theory. *Criminology*. 1987;25(4):933-948.

14. Clarke RVG, Felson M. *Routine Activity and Rational Choice: Advances in Criminological Theory*. Transaction Press; 1993.

15. Casteel CH, Peek-Asa C. The effectiveness of crime prevention through environmental design (CPTED) concepts in reducing robberies. *Journal of Preventive Medicine*. 2000;18(4S):99-115.

16. Bureau of Labor Statistics. Census of Fatal Occupational Injuries. https://www.bls .gov/iif/oshcfoi1.htm

17. Jeffery CR. *Crime Prevention through Environmental Design*. SAGE Publications; 1971.

18. Peek-Asa C, Casteel CH. Documenting the need for translational research: an example from workplace violence prevention. *Injury Prevention*. 2010;16:50-52.

19. Vagi KJ, Stevens MR, Simon TR, Basile KC, Carter SP, Carter SL. Crime Prevention Through Environmental Design (CPTED) characteristics associated with violence and safety in middle schools. *Journal of School Health*. 2018;88(4):296-305.

20. Gill TM, Williams CS, Robison JT, Tinetti ME. A population-based study of environmental hazards in the homes of older persons. *American Journal of Public Health*. 1999;89:553-556.

21. Gitlin LN, Mann W, Tomit M, Marcus SM. Factors associated with home environmental problems among community-living older people. *Disability Rehabilitation*. 2001;23(17):777-787.

22. Hopewell S, Adedire O, Copsey BJ, et al. Multifactorial and multiple component interventions for preventing falls in older people living in the community. *Cochrane Database of Systematic Reviews*. 2018;7(7):CD012221 http://doi.org/10.1002 /14651858.CD012221.pub2

23. Stevens J, Burns E. *A CDC Compendium of Effective Fall Interventions: What Works for Community-Dwelling Older Adults.* 3rd ed. Centers for Disease Control and Prevention, National Center for Injury Prevention and Control. 2015. https://www.cdc.gov/homeandrecreationalsafety/falls/compendium.html

24. Web-based Injury Statistics Query and Reporting System (WISQARS). Published 2019. Accessed October 11, 2021. https://www.cdc.gov/injury/wisqars/index.html

25. Quan L, Bennett E, Branche C. Interventions to Prevent Drowning. In: Doll LS, Bonzo SE, Mercy JA, Sleet DE, eds. *Handbook of Injury and Violence Prevention.* Springer; 2007:81-96.

26. Gupta M, Rahman A, Dutta NC, et al. Implementing a crèche-based community drowning programme in rural Bangladesh: a process evaluation. *Injury Prevention.* 2021. http://doi.org/10.1136/injuryprev-2020-044066

27. James SL, Lucchesi LR, Bisignano C, et al. Epidemiology of injuries from fire, heat and hot substances: global, regional and national morbidity and mortality estimates from the Global Burden of Disease 2017 study. *Injury Prevention.* 2020;26(Supp 1):i36-i45. http://doi.org/10.1136/injuryprev-2019-043299

28. Harvey LA, Poulos RG, Sherker S. The impact of recent changes in smoke alarm legislation on residential fire injuries and smoke alarm ownership in New South Wales, Australia. *Journal of Burn Care and Research.* 2013;34(3):e168-175. http://doi.org/10.1097/BCR.0b013e318257d827

29. Yellman MA, Peterson C, McCoy MA, et al. Preventing deaths and injuries from house fires: a cost-benefit analysis of a community-based smoke alarm installation programme. *Injury Prevention.* 2018;24(1):12-18.

CHAPTER 6

WATER, HEALTH, AND THE BUILT ENVIRONMENT

Charisma S. Acey and Emmanuel Frimpong Boamah

KEY POINTS

- The design of the built environment can impact the availability of water and management of wastewater and stormwater in a community.
- Climate change and land use planning can aggravate or relieve the challenges of too little water, too much water, or poor water quality.
- Social inequality and vulnerability threaten the sustainability and resilience of water systems around the world.
- Innovative approaches to ensuring water quantity and quality involve cross-sector collaboration, community participation, and greater attention to natural ecosystems.

INTRODUCTION

In January 2018, officials in Cape Town, South Africa, announced that the city only had ninety days' worth of water left at then-current supply and usage levels. They declared April 12, 2018, to be Day Zero, the day that supplies were predicted to run out. The crisis was many years in the making. In addition to galvanizing public action with the stark messaging, officials put into place many measures to decrease water usage, such as diverting water from agriculture; allowing people to collect a small amount of household water per person per day at designated centers; increasing fees for high levels of water consumption; forbidding the use of municipal water for pools, lawns, and other nonessential services; and reducing water pressure. These conservation measures sufficiently extended water availability until winter rains in June 2018 restored water levels in the local dam and led authorities to postpone Day Zero indefinitely. However, there is still a long way to go for Cape Town to have a sustainable and resilient water system. The township areas, populated by poor, mostly Black, residents, still experience regular water shortages.

Providing safe water is perhaps the most ancient challenge of built environments. Eight billion of us—half living in urban areas—depend on water supply, wastewater treatment, and stormwater management to support healthy communities. Although it may seem that water and sanitation issues were solved a century ago in highly industrialized countries, in high- and low- to middle-income countries (LMICs) water access is not universal, clean, affordable, or governed fairly and consistently.[1] Urbanization has stretched the capacity of networked infrastructure to its limits. Climate change affects the availability and quality of freshwater while intensifying the risk of flooding and damaged infrastructure.[2] One-fifth of the world's people reside in river basins where water demand exceeds natural groundwater recharge from rain, snowmelt, and streamflow (figure 6.1). Among the five

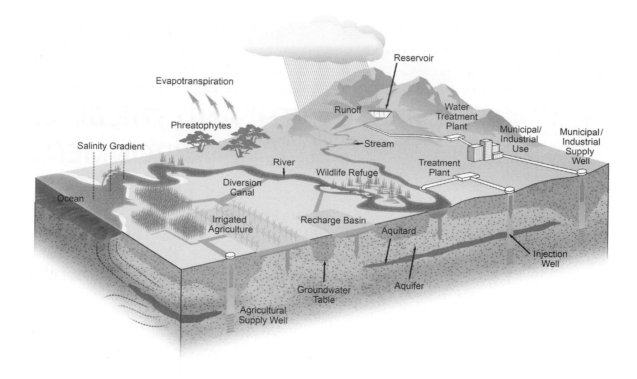

Figure 6.1. Water flows through the hydrological cycle, contaminated at some stages by surface runoff, industry, agriculture, and sewage and cleansed in other stages by water and wastewater treatment plants and ground filtration, when demand does not exceed recharge.
Source: California Water Plan Update 2013. California Department of Water Resources, 2014.

hundred largest cities in the world, one quarter are currently **water stressed**.[3] One in three people lacks access to *safely managed drinking water services* free from microbial or chemical contamination, and more than half do not have *safely managed sanitation services* such as hygienic toilets that treat and dispose of human wastes.[4] Persistent threats from global infectious diseases such as cholera have shined a glaring light on these disparities in LMICs and the need to guarantee universal access to water and sanitation. At the same time, fiscal crises have led to deregulation and the privatization of networked infrastructure, making piped water unaffordable for the most vulnerable.[5] More than 80 percent of **wastewater** globally is discharged untreated into rivers or the sea. The cascading effects on water supplies affect drinking water, as well as water for industry, agriculture, and aquatic life.

This chapter provides an overview of the issues affecting **potable water** supply, the built environment, and community health and considers interventions that center sustainability, resilience, equity, and community in addressing these challenges.

WATER SUPPLY AND THE BUILT ENVIRONMENT

Communities rely on multiple sources of water such as fresh surface waters and groundwater aquifers for drinking and other purposes. In the United States, households are primarily served by **public water systems (PWS)**, which are municipal water systems that provide year-round water supply to the population within a geographic area. In 2017, around 310 million people (more than 90 percent) relied on PWS, with 13 million households reliant on private wells for their drinking water.[6] Water and wastewater services are affordable for the majority of Americans, yet nearly 12 percent find water bills unaffordable. Increasing inequality and poverty along with higher water rates are expected to potentially triple that rate in the short term. The fact that water utility customers face shutoff for nonpayment in the United States has emerged as a *human rights* issue[7] (box 6.1). The presence of legacy contaminants such as lead in the water supply in places like Flint, Michigan, and Newark, New Jersey, has made national headlines. This **environmental justice** issue disproportionately affects racial minorities and Indigenous communities due to unequal enforcement of laws protecting water quality and failure to build and maintain adequate infrastructure.

The UN General Assembly has recognized the human right to water, acknowledging that everyone, without discrimination, is entitled to adequate, safe, accessible, and affordable water. Despite this, significant inequalities persist in access to water within and between countries, and especially between rural and urban settings.

The World Health Organization and UNICEF Joint Monitoring Program (JMP) estimates that, in 2017, only 275 million (about 27 percent) of households in sub-Saharan Africa had access to safe drinking water. The JMP defines safe water as improved water sources (by design and construction such as piped water or protected wells) that are located on premises, available when needed, and free from priority chemical and fecal contaminants. Estimated levels of access to improved water sources are higher in Latin America and Caribbean countries (around 480 million or 74 percent households) and Central and Southern Asian countries (1.2 billion or 60 percent households). A majority of households in LMICs drink from unimproved water sources (for example, rainwater, unprotected spring, or dug well) or travel distances (about thirty minutes or more) to queue in accessing water (for example, community handpump boreholes). Some rural households are able to access water through a stream, pond, lake, or river, exercising the **prior appropriation doctrine** due to first in claims or **riparian rights** based on ownership of land that contacts a waterway. Some urban households, especially in informal settlements, pay vendors or water trucks to fill storage tanks or resort to a mix of state-sanctioned and unsanctioned modes of water services (see figure 6.2).[8,9] As communities struggle to access water, many are increasingly turning to bottled water with emerging markets (for example, countries in Asia, sub-Saharan Africa, and the Middle East) driving the $65 billion bottled water industry.[10,11]

Water supply is also central to daily hygiene practices such as hand washing, washing of

BOX 6.1 THE HUMAN RIGHT TO WATER AND SANITATION

In 2010, all 193 member-states of the United Nations passed a historic resolution (64/292) recognizing the human right to water and sanitation. It was the culmination of four decades of global activism for the hundreds of millions who lack access to safe drinking water and sanitation. The right to water and sanitation encompasses nations taking steps to prevent threats to health from using unsafe and toxic water. The resolution also specifies that water should be treated as a social and cultural good first, not as an economic good. This was a reversal of the Dublin Principles, established in 1992 leading up to the Rio Earth Summit, which called for treating water as an economic good in all its uses given growing concerns from utilities over cost recovery, as well as water scarcity and sustainability. In 2014, residents of Detroit, Michigan, engaged in highly publicized protests against water shutoffs for those who could not afford to pay. The UN Special Rapporteur on the Human Right to Water and Sanitation declared at the time that failing to restore access to water for citizens unable to pay their bills would put the United States in violation of international human rights law. California has been the only US state to pass a human right to water law. Passed in 2012, California Assembly Bill 685 specifies that every human being has the right to safe, clean, affordable, and accessible water. Globally, South Africa and Slovenia are among a handful of countries that constitutionally guarantee the right to water. Other countries are working to establish the right to water through a variety of social policies.

(a)

(b)

(c)

Figure 6.2. Images of water supply in African Countries: (a) a woman carrying water sachets in Ghana, (b) a young boy using a ground pump in Nigeria, and (c) a woman in South Africa dispensing clean water from a PureMadi Ceramic Filter.
Source: (a) Photo courtesy of Nisha Botchwey. (b) Wikimedia Commons courtesy Effsamuel3. https://creativecommons.org/licenses/by-sa/4.0/deed.en. (c) Photo courtesy of James Smith, PureMadi.

clothes and utensils, and bathing that can prevent infectious bacterial, parasitic, and viral diseases. For instance, the 2020 SARS-COV-2 pandemic elevated the role of water in personal and community hygiene. In slowing down infection, individuals were advised, among other actions, to wash their hands for at least twenty seconds. However, about 75 percent of households in low-income countries either do not have access to handwashing facilities or have the facility but lack access to water and soap.[4]

The built environment presents anthropogenic pressures on water supply involving water withdrawals, dam diversions, and industrial development (box 6.2). Globally, about 92 percent of our **water footprint** is in the agricultural sector.[12] Every pound of food produced requires water, hence, the idea of **virtual water or embodied water** with water-stressed LMICs (for example, Pakistan, India, Uzbekistan, China, and Turkey) leading virtual water exports.[13] Cape Town's "Day Zero" crisis was partly due to increased water consumption by fruit and wine farmers in the Western Cape.[14] Hydroelectric dam construction is on the rise in LMICs (for example, India and Ethiopia) as part of exploring avenues to meet their increasing energy demand.

Additional anthropogenic pressures expose water to pollutants from **point-source pollution** and **nonpoint-source pollution**. Point source pollutants involve the discharge of contaminants from easily identifiable and confined places, such as effluent discharge from factories and hospitals, oil refineries, concentrated animal feeding operations (CAFOs), sewage, and municipal sewage treatment plants. Nonpoint source pollutants result from the runoff or infiltration of contaminants from diffused sources such as agricultural, residential, and commercial/industrial land uses.

Meeting these challenges will require periodic testing of PWS and private wells, establishing a baseline of water quantity and quality levels and frequent monitoring, and, more importantly, investing in water and wastewa-ter infrastructure, especially in low-income communities in high-, middle- and low-income countries.

WASTEWATER DISPOSAL

The disposal of water is as important as its supply. Left untreated or improperly disposed of, wastewater can serve as pollutants (*nonpoint sources*) for surface and groundwater drinking sources, which threatens public health. Access to sewage disposal methods for households and industries becomes vital in the collection, transportation, treatment, and disposal of wastewater.

The main methods of sewage disposal in the United States are public sewers (82 percent of households), septic tanks or cesspools (18 percent of households), and others (< 1 percent of households). Public sewers or **sanitary sewer systems**, often known as the *centralized approach*, involve collecting and transporting domestic and industrial sewage to a municipal sewage treatment facility for treatment and final disposal into a water body. In sub-Saharan Africa, households and industries have limited access to public sewer systems. For instance, a municipal wastewater treatment facility (Kaliti Treatment Plant) in Addis Ababa, the capital of Ethiopia, only serves 13,000 households in a city of more than four million people; similarly, the Bugolobi Sewage Treatment Works in Uganda covers only 55 percent of sewage generated within its catchment area while the remaining drains into wetlands without treatment.[15]

The intermittent overflows of untreated sewage from sanitary sewer systems, or **sanitary sewer overflows**, are a key environmental challenge for municipalities. The United States Environmental Protection Agency[16] estimates at least 23,000 to 75,000 sanitary sewer overflows annually. These overflows are often the results of improper sewer design, vandalism, sewer defects that allow stormwater and groundwater to overload the system, blockages in the sewer systems, and a lack of proper maintenance of public sewer systems. These

BOX 6.2 CASE STUDIES ON WATER SUPPLY AND BUILT ENVIRONMENT

Case 1: Flint Water Crisis

In April 2014, officials in Flint, Michigan, northwest of Detroit, tried to save money by switching the city's water source from Detroit Water and Sewerage to the Flint River. Flint is a city of about 99,000 residents that is majority Black and has a 40 percent poverty rate. The water was harder (high in dissolved minerals) than water used by Detroit. Although residents repeatedly reported problems with the smell and color of their water and new skin rashes in children immediately after the switch, city officials regularly ignored them and denied that there was anything wrong. The city had neglected to put anticorrosion treatment in the water, which led to leaching of lead from old pipes prevalent throughout the water distribution system. Lead is a neurotoxin that can cause lifelong disability. There is no safe level of lead in the human body, and exposure is especially harmful to children and pregnant women. Other water-quality problems from the switch led to an outbreak of Legionnaire's disease and three boil water advisories due to *Escherichia coli* (*E. coli*) and total coliform water-quality violations. It required intervention from the federal Environmental Protection Agency and the American Civil Liberties Union for officials to take any action. There have been a number of lawsuits related to official inaction. By 2020, the city had replaced 85 percent of the water service lines, but many residents still do not have access to clean water. Residents, activists, and academics cite the racial and class makeup of Flint to explain why this ongoing public health crisis has still not been resolved.

Case 2: Lagos Water Supply

Lagos, Nigeria, one of two megacities in Africa, is home to an estimated fourteen million people. Water supply in Lagos has been a constant game of catch-up, with priority always for industry and residential areas. The vast majority of people do not have access on their premises to safely managed water sources and rely on a mix of wells, water vendors, and boreholes. Less than 1 percent of the metropolitan area has sewers. The Lagos Water Corporation has recently sought to attract private investment to enhance the financial viability of the utility. High-profile protests in 2018 by activists such as Environmental Rights Action/Friends of the Earth, Nigeria, have decried the water utility's prioritization of revenue over equity. They argue many large companies profit off of the dire situation by setting up private treatment plants and selling water to the public at high prices.

Case 3: Arsenic Contamination of Water Supplies in Bangladesh

In Bangladesh, arsenic contamination of shallow aquifers is a natural phenomenon. Up until the early 1970s, poor drinking water infrastructure and wastewater treatment systems strained by regular monsoons and flooding led to the country experiencing among the highest levels of infant mortality in the world from cholera and other diarrheal diseases. Aid programs successfully helped control diseases by constructing millions of tube wells by driving a tube into the earth that tapped into groundwater. Infant mortality fell by 50 percent. However, these projects did not test for arsenic, which led to the unexpected outcome of exposing the population to excessive levels of the poisonous and potentially lethal compound. Thirty-four million people in West Bengal still live in areas with groundwater concentrations above the government standard, with one million having to use arsenic-contaminated water. Geologists and engineers have found that the problem could be solved by digging large wells deeper than five hundred feet. Filtering and the more costly solution of piped water provision would also work, along with regular monitoring and maintenance of drinking water sources and regular monitoring of the population.

overflows are prevalent in older municipalities with **combined sewer systems** (CSSs). These systems combine sanitary sewer with stormwater systems, ensuring the collection of sewage (domestic and industrial) and stormwater runoff into one pipe for treatment at a municipal wastewater treatment facility and discharge into a water body. There are about 860 municipalities in the United States with CSSs.[17] During heavy precipitation (for example, rainfall or snowmelt), these CSSs experience **combined sewer overflows,** leading to the discharge of untreated or partially treated domestic and industrial sewage into water bodies.

The use of **on-site wastewater treatment systems (OWTSs)**, also known as the *decentralized approach*, within rural and suburban areas settlements also poses challenges for wastewater treatment. Developing public sewer systems, with their costly networks of pipes, pump stations, and treatment plants, involves signifi-

cant investments. Households and industries in rural and suburban areas often have no or limited access to public sewers, making them rely on OWTSs, such as septic systems, which are mainly underground wastewater collection and treatment structures made from concrete, plastic, or fiberglass (for example, septic tanks). Some urban and suburban areas, mostly informal or slum communities in the Global South, also resort to other sewage disposal methods, including disposing of feces through pit latrines or the Kumasi Ventilated Improved Pit latrine and disposing of other forms of domestic and industrial wastewater into open spaces, such as beaches, backyards, or nearby water bodies. Not managed carefully, these decentralized approaches often contaminate the aquifer (and private wells), especially when a septic tank fails (leaks or breaks) (figure 6.3).

Some measures are employed to address contamination challenges from OWTS. For

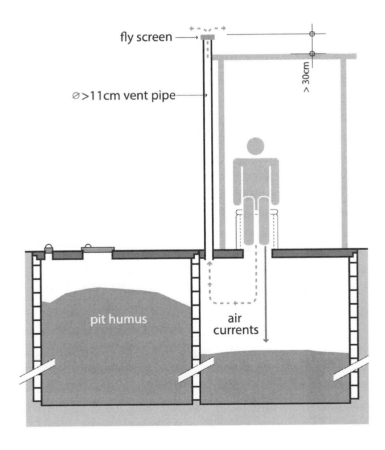

Figure 6.3. The Kumasi Ventilated Improved Pit Latrine (KVIP) was developed in Ghana in the 1970s. It is a twin-pit VIP latrine, allowing the contents of one pit to compost while the other pit is in use. Once fully composted, content can be removed manually and spread on fields without health risks. Although KVIPs were first developed as a technology for public toilets, they have become a preferred mode of sanitation for households in Ghana given that they require little maintenance and no water. Source: Tilley E, Ulrich L, Lüthi C, Reymond P, Zurbrügg C. Compendium of Sanitation Systems and Technologies. 2nd rev. ed. Swiss Federal Institute of Aquatic Science and Technology (Eawag); 2014:64.

example, some OWTSs have leaching beds that gradually release partially treated water from septic tanks into the soil. Others involve paying vacuum trucks to collect and dispose of wastewater (mostly fecal sludge) from the septic tank or pit latrines to a treatment facility. Some countries in the Global South, such as Zambia, Ghana, Bangladesh, and Sri Lanka, are managing wastewater from OWTSs using innovative, nature-based approaches to, for instance, recover energy (biofuels) from wastewater or treat wastewater for use in aquaculture.

CLIMATE CHANGE, (STORM)WATER MANAGEMENT, AND HEALTH

The impacts of climate change on water are already being felt within communities. From drought conditions (too little water) to flooding (too much water), climate change presents a **water paradox**: residents in some communities, especially low-income residents, suffer from flood events and lack access to clean drinking water. The health and human rights implications from this paradox are enormous, including the loss of human lives from thirst or floods, outbreak of diseases, such as cholera, after flood events, and contamination of drinking water sources from flood events.

Too Little Water

Water stress is increasingly a threat in many communities in the Global North and Global South (box 6.3). It is estimated that thirty-seven countries face high water stress levels, meaning they withdraw more than 80 percent of the water available to domestic, agricultural, and industrial users.[18] Some of these countries face water stress because they are located in arid environments (for example, countries in the Middle East and North Africa), and others (for example, South Africa, India, and Botswana) are due to local climate, hydrology and anthropogenic processes. Since 2000, more than 79 metropolitan areas have experienced urban drought or temporary water stress due to excess water demand over the available supply, with large cities such as Beijing, Chennai, Houston, Mexico City, Lagos, Los Angeles, Sydney, and Rio Janeiro facing higher risks of urban droughts and disasters.[19] By 2050, approximately 233 million residents in more than 27 percent of cities globally will have exhausted their water resources.[20] For instance, around 65 percent of India's reservoirs were running dry as of June 2019, which severely affected areas within Maharashtra's west-central state.[21] The Rio Grande, serving more than five million people in the United States (Colorado, New

---

BOX 6.3 CASE STUDY ON CLIMATE CHANGE AND TOO LITTLE WATER

Climate change is already having a profound impact on California's water resources. By 2050, scientists project a loss of at least 25 percent of the snowpack in the Sierra Mountains, an important source of urban, agricultural, and environmental water. Warmer temperatures mean more precipitation as rain instead of snow, increasing the risk of flooding. With less snow and heavier rainfall, more surface runoff (for example, sediment, nutrients, pollutants, and trash) flows into rivers and lakes. At the same time, drought can make coastal waters more saline. And as the sea rises, saltwater intrudes into freshwater. Increased weather variability may also result in increased dryness in the southern regions of the state. The sea level has risen about seven inches at the Golden Gate Bridge in the last century. Continued sea level rise could threaten many coastal communities, as well as the sustainability of the agriculturally important Sacramento–San Joaquin Delta. California's Department of Water Resources (DWR) is beginning to address these impacts through mitigation and adaptation measures to ensure an adequate water supply in the present and future. In 2006, DWR formed a Climate Change Matrix Team with representatives from every area of the department. The team is tasked with staying abreast of current research, coordinating on all climate change issues affecting DWR. This work has guided the development of the DWR Climate Action Plan.

Mexico, Texas) and Mexico, experienced seasonal droughts for more than a decade with severe water impacts on farming and water supply for urban households.[22,23]

Measures to address water stress include both household and municipal-level efforts. Household efforts include installing water-efficient toilets, water-saving showers, and low-flow faucet aerators and checking for leaks from faucets and pipes. In Global South countries, rainwater collection, or **rain harvesting**, in barrels is often employed by households, especially in rural areas. However, households' rainwater harvesting is prohibited by places such as Colorado in the United States because it takes away water supply from agriculture and other water-rights holders. Some municipal-level measures include repairing broken pipes and other infrastructural damages and providing regular system maintenance. Harvesting wastewater, or what some consider as the new black gold, for irrigation, drinking, and heating and cooling remains a priority in several countries and municipalities. Investment in **desalination** methods may also remain essential, especially in municipalities (for example, California) facing excess salinity in their drinking water. However, high investment costs and energy consumption, and the production of hypersaline concentrate (brine) and iodine-depleted water, make desalination less attractive.[24,25]

Too Much Water

Flood events, such as the March 2019 flooding (after Cyclone Idai) that killed more than 750 people in Mozambique, Malawi, and Zimbabwe, remind us that water excess is as much a health hazard as water scarcity (box 6.4). Climate change drives more frequent and severe heavy rain events and sea level rise, leading to flood events. Extreme rain events are expected in many parts of the world as the hydrological cycle intensifies, which will lead to increases in future flood events.[26] Although climate change plays a part in flood events, the built environment either exacerbates or mitigates the impacts of flood events. Increases in impervious surfaces (for example, paved roads and parking lots) contribute to human-induced global warming through urban heat island effects, which drive the frequency and intensity of extreme weather events (for example, precipitation, hurricanes, and cyclones) and snowfield/glacial melting. These extreme events often lead to flood events. Building within flood-prone zones, poorly managed stormwater runoff especially due to a lack of stormwater infrastructure or maintenance of existing infrastructure, and unsanitary conditions such as poor management of solid waste and sewage also exacerbate the impacts of flood events. In sub-Saharan Africa, rapid urbanization and growth in informal communities have outpaced land use planning, solid waste management, and stormwater and sewer infrastructure planning.[27,28] Some suggest that the impacts from the Hurricane Harvey floods in Texas could have been minimized if city planning measures, such as zoning, were in place to control increases in impervious surfaces, such as paving over coastal prairie wetlands.[29,30]

The public health effects of such flood events have been enormous. These include increasing human risk to waterborne diseases (for example, cholera, rotavirus, and typhoid), chemicals, and pathogens as floodwaters inundate private wells and public water systems. For instance, the aftermath of *El Niño* rains and floods is linked to outbreaks and deaths from waterborne diseases (for example, cholera and typhoid) and vector-borne diseases (for example, malaria and dengue). About 68 percent of waterborne disease outbreaks in the United States between 1948 and 1994 were attributed to extreme precipitation and flood events.[31] In municipalities that use untreated water sources, gastrointestinal illness rates in children are higher during weeks with more precipitation than during other weeks.[32,33]

Some efforts can be in place to minimize the extent to which the built environment can exacerbate the climate-flood nexus and

BOX 6.4 CASE STUDIES ON TOO MUCH WATER

Case 1: Case Study on Climate Change and Too Much Water: Indonesia and Sea Level Rise

Jakarta, Indonesia's capital and home to more than ten million people, is known as the fastest sinking city in the world. In Jakarta, known for its low-lying, swampy coastal topography alongside the Java Sea with thirteen rivers coursing through it, some parts of the metropolitan area, especially near the coast, are sinking by as much as five inches or more annually. Rising sea levels and lack of infrastructure have led to excessive groundwater withdrawals and subsidence. Sixty percent of residents depend on groundwater. Recent extreme flood events have killed and displaced thousands, mostly the urban poor. The severity of floods is compounded by the politics of infrastructure development in Jakarta, itself the legacy of centuries of Dutch colonialism.[a] Nearly half of the city's land area now sits below sea level. Some estimates predict parts of Jakarta will be fully submerged by 2050. Indonesia's president announced a $33 billion plan in 2019 to move its capital inland on the island of Borneo away from Jakarta due to challenges of sea level rise. The plan is controversial as environmentalists worry about the protected habitat of endangered species in the new location.

Case 2: Philadelphia Stormwater Infrastructure Planning and Design

Greenworks Philadelphia, launched in 2009, is the city's comprehensive sustainability plan. The plan uses green infrastructure—parks, trees, vegetation, waterfronts, wetlands, urban agriculture, community gardens, and soils—to capture and manage stormwater at the source.[b] In addition to recharging groundwater and improving ecosystem quality, this approach also creates additional opportunities for recreation, fresh food production, energy efficiency, economic development, and productive uses of vacant land.[c] The plan is complemented by the Philadelphia Water Department's Green City Clean Water Plan, which uses green stormwater infrastructure to diminish the amount of combined sewer overflows. The city estimates that these investments could result in a $2.2 billion return on $1.01 billion spent over a forty-year period.

REFERENCES

a. Goh K. Urban waterscapes: the hydro-politics of flooding in a sinking city. *International Journal of Urban and Regional Research*. 2019;43(2):250-272.
b. Greenworks: A Vision for a Sustainable Philadelphia. Philadelphia: Office of the Mayor; 2016. https://beta.phila.gov/documents/greenworks-a-vision-for-a-sustainable-philadelphia/
c. Rouse D, Bunster-Ossa I. *Green Infrastructure: A Landscape Approach*. American Planning Association; 2013.

its public health effects. Flood-responsive and well-designed and enforced land use controls (for example, zoning regulations) can prevent development in flood-prone areas; ensure the right balance between pervious and impervious surfaces; install the needed stormwater infrastructure; and protect wetlands, which serve as natural sponges to slow water runoffs and trap contaminants. In terms of storm surges and coastal flooding, a mix of local coastal zone management strategies, both hard (for example, riprap revetments, groins, and gabions) and soft approaches (for example, beach nourishing, sand dune regeneration, marshland), with the involvement of residents, can prevent shoreline retreat from storm surges and protect against flooding in coastal communities, especially island nations.

Finally, stormwater management, specifically *water-sensitive urban design*, such as the city of Philadelphia's *green stormwater infrastructure*, remains vital to planning and designing the built environment. Green infrastructure involves a range and network of small- and large-scale planned and unplanned green spaces to ensure infiltration, evapotranspiration, storage, and re-use of stormwater to maximize a range of ecosystem services and benefits.[34,35] The terms *green infrastructure* and *low-impact development (LID)* are sometimes used interchangeably. Both are alternative nature-based approaches to enhancing infiltration, evaporation, and storage of stormwater runoff compared to traditional stormwater management or *gray infrastructure*, but the scale of implementation differentiates green infrastructure from LID. LID projects are implemented at the site scale, while green infrastructure projects are implemented at larger city, county, basin, or watershed scales, often involving a network of LID projects managed as an integrated system to maximize social, economic, and environmental benefits.[36] Some examples of projects at the site or larger scales include bioretention or bioinfiltration cells or rain gardens, planter boxes, bioswales, permeable pavements, rainwater harvesting, green roofs/parking/streets, urban tree canopy, and stormwater wetlands.[37] For instance, the City of Atlanta's Rodney Cook Sr. Park includes bioretention or rain gardens to filter stormwater flows from pipes, stormwater planters to capture runoff from streets, rainwater-harvesting cisterns to capture rainwater, and a constructed stormwater wetland with installed aeration foundation and native plant buffers to improve water quality. The network of small-scale designs (for example, rain gardens, stormwater planters, aeration fountain) and large-scale design (wetland) are planned, designed, and managed as an integrated system, allowing the park to provide diverse benefits, including diversion of stormwater runoffs into the park (capable of storing 10 million gallons of stormwater) and park amenities, including a playground, a plaza, and an amphitheater. These examples of green infrastructure leverage surface runoff to meet community needs (stormwater services, especially for low-income populations) while also minimizing the harms caused by too much water (figure 6.4).

REGULATORY, COMMUNITY, AND NATURE-BASED APPROACHES TO CLEAN AND AFFORDABLE WATER

A range of approaches are needed to address the impact of the built environment on water supply and quality and deal with water scarcity and the impacts of a changing climate on water resources. These can be divided into categories such as regulation, governance (for example, integrated water resources management), regional and watershed approaches, ecological or water sensitive design, technology and engineering to better manage supply and demand, behavior change, and equitable policies such as subsidies and lifelines to increase affordability.[38,39] For instance, regulatory approaches in the US include the **Clean Water Act (CWA)**, which ensures that *water-quality standards (WQS)* meet the required *total maximum daily load* or the accepted threshold of pollutants that a water body can receive while maintaining its WQS. The CWA achieves this through, for instance, the *National Pollutant Discharge Elimination System* permit program to regulate point-source pollution and to provide Section 319 funding for state governments to address nonpoint sources such as farming and forestry operations. The *National Primary Drinking Water Regulations*, as part of enforcing the *Safe Drinking Water Act*, also regulate the drinking water standards by expecting public water supplies to test for microbial, chemical, and radiological contaminants to meet prescribed levels or the *maximum contaminant levels*.

Although regulatory approaches have had a significant, positive impact on water quality in the United States since the 1970s, the focus on specific pollutants and polluters is also a limited approach given the diffuse threats to drinking water and water resources described in this chapter. Around the world, new approaches to the challenges of water supply and quality integrate nature and community to solve complex challenges. For example, the RISE (Revitalising Informal Settlements and their Environments) program, based out of Monash University in Melbourne, Australia,

Figure 6.4. Examples of green stormwater infrastructure found along the Atlanta Beltline. The images depict both small-scale and large-scale approaches to directing, slowing, filtering, and storing water.
Source: Photos courtesy of Atlanta BeltLine

is a five-year program that aims to bring nature-based water improvements to informal settlements. The project uses a "water sensitive cities" approach to address the health of residents and their environments. This approach integrates nature-based solutions such as constructed wetlands, biofiltration gardens, stormwater harvesting, and local sanitation systems into buildings and landscapes, a strategy that requires less maintenance than big pipes approaches. Similarly, as more of Europe experiences challenges related to water scarcity and quality, many local authorities are using an *ecosystems services (ESS)* approach. Ecosystems services, broadly defined, refer to the ways in which humans benefit from healthy natural ecosystems. In 2014, the European Commission funded the DESSIN (Demonstrate Ecosystem Services Enabling Innovation in the Water Sector) group, consisting of twenty partner organizations, including nongovernmental organizations, technology development companies, and research institutes, to develop a framework to evaluate ESS innovations. The complex relationship between water, wastewater, and stormwater and the built environment amid older and emerging threats is causing communities around the world to look for more integrated frameworks that combine these various approaches.

CONCLUSION

The complexity of designing and managing interrelated potable water, wastewater, and stormwater systems for community health is daunting. Many problems cannot easily be regulated, such as nonpoint-source pollution from urban runoff. Moreover, decision-makers must manage the problems of too little and too much water associated with the increasing frequency of droughts and extreme flooding events tied to climate change. Sometimes, resolving one problem creates another, making water management a "wicked" problem requiring more input from vulnerable communities most affected. As demonstrated in the examples in this chapter, such problems require interdisciplinary, collaborative, and integrated approaches across scale and sector to improve community health. This includes decentralized, polycentric governance models that prioritize water equity, where everyone benefits according to their need and pays according to their ability.[3] Creative and equitable approaches to finance and maintain water infrastructure that empower community members are needed to meet the human right to water and the UN Sustainable Development Goals.[40] Increasingly, communities are exploring alternatives to the "big pipes in, big pipes out" approach to community water management, embracing water-sensitive design, green infrastructure, and other nature-based approaches in the built environment that simultaneously protect natural ecosystems and human health and are resilient to global environmental change.

DISCUSSION QUESTIONS

1. Thinking about where you live, how might greater community involvement in water decision-making help address the challenges of water, wastewater, and stormwater management?

2. How can nature-based approaches help address the problems of too much and too little water in cities? What can make these approaches more effective?

3. What regulations protect water quality in the United States? How effective are they? What are their limitations, and why?

4. What are the similarities and differences facing countries with differing levels of economic development in the Global North and Global South when it comes to water, wastewater, and stormwater?

5. Describe the challenges of water affordability. In your community, are there specific households that disproportionately face some of these affordability challenges? If so, why? What factors make potable water unaffordable to households? What kinds of interventions could help make water more affordable?

6. Do onsite sewerage systems offer a solution to the large percentage of the world's population lacking safely managed sanitation services? What are the benefits? What are the challenges?

7. List the challenges communities face in meeting the human right to water expressed in Goal 6 of the UN Sustainable Development Goals. What are the barriers in realizing the human right to water? What would you advise decision-makers to prioritize in meeting this challenge?

ACKNOWLEDGMENTS

The authors wish to thank Jamon Franklin for research assistance with several case studies included in the chapter.

DISCLOSURE OF COMPETING INTERESTS

Charisma S. Acey reports serving as an unpaid board member or advisory committee member of the Research and Academic and Partner Constituency Group (RAPCG) of the General Assembly of Partners to UN-Habitat, Sanitation and Water for All Research & Learning Group, Lancet Commission Working Group on WASH in High-Income Countries, and faculty affiliate to the Berkeley Water Center (University of California, Berkeley), serving as a paid member of the National Socio-Environmental Synthesis Center Scientific Review Committee (University of Maryland), paid consultancy for Water and Sanitation for the Urban Poor and Aquaya Institute, and grant funding from the Foundation for Food and Agricultural Research and NSF-funded Innovations at the Nexus of Food, Energy, and Water Systems program at the University of California, Berkeley.

Emmanuel Frimpong Boamah reports serving as an unpaid board member of the Buffalo Niagara Waterkeeper.

REFERENCES

1. Meehan K, Jepson W, Harris LM, et al. Exposing the myths of household water insecurity in the global north: a critical review. *Wiley Interdisciplinary Reviews: Water.* 2020;7(6), e1486.

2. Rotzoll K, Fletcher CH. Assessment of groundwater inundation as a consequence of sea-level rise. *Nature Climate Change.* 2013;3(5),477-481.

3. Frimpong Boamah, E. Governing to deliver safe and affordable water: perspectives from urban planning and public policy. In: Smith K, Ram P, eds. *Transforming Global Health.* Springer; 2020:1-18.

4. The WHO and UNICEF. *Progress on Household Drinking Water, Sanitation and Hygiene 2000–2017. Special Focus on Inequalities.* United Nations Children's Fund (UNICEF) and World Health Organization (WHO) Joint Monitoring Programme for Water Supply and Sanitation; 2019.

5. Graham S, Marvin S. *Splintering Urbanism: Networked Infrastructures, Technological Mobilities and the Urban Condition.* Routledge; 2002.

6. EPA. Report on the Environment. United States Environmental Protection Agency. 2018. https://cfpub.epa.gov/roe/indicator.cfm?i=45

7. Mack EA, Wrase S. A burgeoning crisis? A nationwide assessment of the geography of water affordability in the United States. *PLOS ONE.* 2017;12(1), e0169488.

8. Acey CS. Silence and voice in Nigeria's hybrid urban water markets: implications for local governance of public goods. *International Journal of Urban and Regional Research* 2018;43(2):313-336.

9. Post A, Ray I. *Hybrid Modes of Urban Water Delivery in Low- and Middle-Income Countries.* Oxford University Press; 2020.

10. Jaffee D, Newman S. A bottle half empty: bottled water, commodification, and contestation. *Organization & Environment.* 2013;26(3):318-335.

11. Bakker KJ. *Privatizing Water: Governance Failure and the World's Urban Water Crisis.* Cornell University Press; 2010.

12. Hoekstra AY, Mekonnen MM. The water footprint of humanity. *Proceedings of the National Academy of Sciences.* 2012;109(9):3232-3237.

13. Dalin C, Konar M, Hanasaki N, Rinaldo A, Rodriguez-Iturbe I. Evolution of the global virtual water trade network. *Proceedings of the National Academy of Sciences.* 2012;109(16):5989-5994.

14. LaVanchy GT, Kerwin MW, Adamson JK. Beyond "Day Zero": Insights and lessons from Cape Town (South Africa). *Hydrogeology Journal.* 2019;27(5):1537-1540.

15. Wang H, Wang T, Zhang B, et al. Water and wastewater treatment in Africa—current practices and challenges. *CLEAN–Soil, Air, Water.* 2014;42(8):1029-1035.

16. EPA. National Pollutant Discharge Elimination System (NPDES): Sanitary Sewer Overflows (SSOs). 2020. https://www.epa.gov/npdes/sanitary-sewer-overflows-ssos

17. EPA. National Pollutant Discharge Elimination System (NPDES): Combined Sewer Overflows (CSOs). 2020. https://www.epa.gov/npdes/combined-sewer-overflows-csos

18. Gassert F, Reig P, Luo T, Maddocks A. *Aqueduct Country and River Basin Rankings: A Weighted Aggregation of Spatially Distinct Hydrological Indicators.* World Resources Institute; 2013.

19. Zhang X, Chen N, Sheng H, et al. Urban drought challenge to 2030 sustainable development goals. *Science of the Total Environment.* 2019;693:133536.

20. Flörke M, Schneider C, McDonald RI. Water competition between cities and agriculture driven by climate change and urban growth. *Nature Sustainability.* 2018;1(1):51-58.

21. Patel K. Water shortages in India. Earth Observatory of NASA. Published 2019. Accessed May 20, 2020. https://earthobservatory.nasa.gov/images/145242/water-shortages-in-india

22. Guido Z. Drought on the Rio Grande. National Oceanic and Atmospheric Administration. Published 2012. Accessed May 20, 2020. https://www.climate.gov/news-features/features/drought-rio-grande

23. Blythe TL, Schmidt JC. Estimating the natural flow regime of rivers with long-standing development: the northern branch of the Rio Grande. *Water Resources Research*. 2018;54(2):1212-1236.

24. Jones E, Qadir M, van Vliet MT, Smakhtin V, Kang S-M. The state of desalination and brine production: a global outlook. *Science of the Total Environment*. 2019;657:1343-1356.

25. Ovadia YS, Gefel D, Aharoni D, Turkot S, Fytlovich S, Troen AM. Can desalinated seawater contribute to iodine-deficiency disorders? An observation and hypothesis. *Public Health Nutrition*. 2016;19(15):2808-2817.

26. Taylor CM, Belušić D, Guichard F, et al. Frequency of extreme Sahelian storms tripled since 1982 in satellite observations. *Nature*. 2017;544(7651):475-478.

27. Amoako C, Frimpong Boamah E. The three-dimensional causes of flooding in Accra, Ghana. *International Journal of Urban Sustainable Development*. 2015;7(1):109-129.

28. Douglas I, Alam K, Maghenda M, Mcdonnell Y, McLean L, Campbell J. Unjust waters: climate change, flooding and the urban poor in Africa. *Environment and Urbanization*. 2008;20(1):187-205.

29. Zhang W, Villarini G, Vecchi GA, Smith JA. Urbanization exacerbated the rainfall and flooding caused by Hurricane Harvey in Houston. *Nature*. 2018;563(7731):384-388.

30. Jacob J, Pandian K, Lopez R, Biggs H. Houston-Area Freshwater Wetland Loss, 1992–2010. Texas A&M University System; 2012.

31. Curriero FC, Patz JA, Rose JB, Lele S. The association between extreme precipitation and waterborne disease outbreaks in the United States, 1948–1994 *American Journal of Public Health*. 2001;91(8):1194-1199.

32. Uejio CK, Yale SH, Malecki K, Borchardt MA, Anderson HA, Patz JA. Drinking water systems, hydrology, and childhood gastrointestinal illness in central and northern Wisconsin. *American Journal of Public Health*. 2014;104(4):639-646.

33. Trtanj J, Jantarasami L, Brunkard J, et al. Ch. 6: Climate impacts on water-related illness. In: Crimmins A, Balbus J, Gamble J, et al., eds. *The Impacts of Climate Change on Human Health in the United States: A Scientific Assessment*. US Global Change Research Program; 2016:157-188.

34. Norton BA, Coutts AM, Livesley SJ, Harris RJ, Hunter AM, Williams NS. Planning for cooler cities: a framework to prioritise green infrastructure to mitigate high temperatures in urban landscapes. *Landscape and Urban Planning*. 2015;134:127-138.

35. EPA. What Is Green Infrastructure. EPA. 2020. https://www.epa.gov/green-infrastructure/what-green-infrastructure

36. Vogel JR, Moore TL, Coffman RR, et al. Critical review of technical questions facing low impact development and green infrastructure: a perspective from the Great Plains. *Water Environment Research*. 2015;87(9):849-862.

37. Frumkin H, Das MB, Bertollini R, Desai S, Rogers B. Protecting health in dry cities: considerations for policy makers. *BMJ*. 2020;371:m2936. http://dx.doi.org/10.1136/bmj.m2936

38. Newman P. Sustainable urban water systems in rich and poor cities-steps towards a new approach. *Water Science and Technology*. 2001;43(4), 93-99.

39. Acey C. The human right to water: the role of the private sector in urban water sector reform (Lagos, Nigeria). In: Hoey L, Rumbach A, Shake, J. eds. *International*

Planning Case Studies Project. University of Michigan and Texas A&M; 2016. https://planningcasestudies.org /casestudylibraryprotected

40. Acey C. Hybrid governance and the human right to water. *Berkeley Planning Journal*. 2017;28(1):10-39. https://escholarship.org /uc/item/33n9744k

CHAPTER 7

BUILT ENVIRONMENTS, MENTAL HEALTH, AND WELL-BEING

Xiangrong Jiang, Chia-Ching Wu, Chun-Yen Chang, and William C. Sullivan

KEY POINTS

- Built environments can promote or hinder mental health.
- Urbanization is often associated with poor mental health. It is not urbanization per se, however, but specific features of urban life that influence mental health. Good design, based on evidence, can promote mental health.
- Although urban settings with noise and traffic can increase stress, incorporating natural elements and beauty into the built environment can help people cope with stress.
- The conditions of modern life place great demands on—and often exhaust—our ability to pay attention. We can design settings to alleviate mental fatigue and restore people's capacity to pay attention.
- Dilapidated, dangerous, and polluted places have a variety of negative impacts on people and their psychological states.
- Environmental injustice and inequity impact the mental health and well-being of individuals across the world. Planners, designers, and community leaders should work together to improve physical settings for everyone, but especially the most vulnerable among us.

INTRODUCTION

When Anita found a studio apartment at a reasonable cost close to her urban university campus, she thought hard about renting it. On the one hand, if she moved into this apartment, she could better manage her budget and her commute would be considerably reduced. She also appreciated that the neighborhood felt lively. On the other hand, the apartment was near a highway and a train line, and she wondered about all the late-night activity and noise in the neighborhood. Given that Anita relies on a small stipend as a graduate research assistant and that she had early morning classes, she decided to rent the apartment.

But a year after the move, Anita noticed that she was not on top of her game. Whereas last year Anita was efficient in studying and work, this year she is significantly less productive. She has trouble submitting homework on time, and her mind wanders a great deal in class. Because of the noise and late-night activity in her neighborhood, Anita does not sleep as well in her new place as she has in the past. She is also more likely to be annoyed by mistakes she makes, and she has been feeling impatient and irritable with others. In a recent meeting with her office mate and study partner, Anita lost her temper and made a cutting remark. Her friend has not spoken to her since and now leaves the office when Anita arrives.

Anita now wonders if the change in her well-being has something to do with the conditions she faces every day in her apartment and neighborhood—the constant noise, feelings of being crowded, and the sense that she can't get away from it all. She is right to be concerned. The quality and characteristics of the settings we inhabit—the places where we live, work, and play—can support or undermine our mental health. This chapter examines the extent to which built environments promote mental health and well-being, improve happiness, alleviate stress, facilitate recovery from mental fatigue, affect anxiety and depression, and contribute to (or mitigate) aggression and violence.

Each of us requires certain essentials of life from our surroundings, and sometimes these requirements can conflict with one another. For example, when we want to focus on challenging work, we likely require a quiet place without distractions. When we crave engagement, we might want lively public spaces that encourage social interactions. The extent to which a setting supports mental health, well-being, and happiness is dependent on the match between a person's needs and the characteristics of the setting. The more successful the match, the greater the likelihood that the person will experience higher levels of mental health and well-being; the greater the mismatch, the more likely it is that the person will experience psychological distress.

Mental health, well-being, and happiness are complex, layered concepts that are related but not identical. **Mental health** is a state of emotional, psychological, and social well-being in which people realize their own abilities, can cope with the normal stresses of life, work productively, and make contributions to their community.[1] **Subjective well-being** is a multifaceted construct that includes affective (emotional) and cognitive (evaluative) components.[2] It is usually assessed through people's self-evaluations of their own satisfaction in work, family, and social relations, their interest and engagement, and their general fulfillment. **Happiness** may be conceptualized at three levels.[3] The first level is a momentary feeling of happiness, such as the emotional high people experience when listening to music or scoring a point in a game. This level of happiness, although certainly pleasurable, is typically short-lived. The second level of happiness is a subjective assessment of how people feel about their lives. Someone might ask, "How are you?" to which you might respond, "I'm feeling good." People generally feel happy when their emotions are tipped more toward satisfaction, contentment, or curiosity than frustration, anger, or boredom. The third level of happiness is an assessment of one's quality of life—how well one is flourishing or fulfilling one's potential. It is less directly emotional and more cognitive. When people describe this level of happiness, they might say that they are more in harmony with their true selves and consequently have few inner conflicts.

Place attachment is an aspect of well-being that relates to the built or natural environment. It is the emotional bond between people (an individual or a group) and a place. Researchers who explore place attachment consider the affective, cognitive, and behavioral components of people's attachment, as well as the social and physical characteristics of the place. Disrupting place attachment—say, through uprooting people from their neighborhood or through the destruction brought by climate change or natural disaster—can undermine well-being and threaten mental health.

An important dimension of mental health is **cognitive functioning**. This is the ability to learn, reason, make decisions, solve problems, remember, and, importantly, pay attention. Cognitive functioning is essential to being productive, managing our lives, achieving goals, and having rewarding social relationships.

Several conditions may threaten mental health, well-being, and happiness. **Stress** is the feeling of not having the resources to meet the demands of the moment. People experience stress over big life changes, such as a divorce or loss of a job, as well as everyday challenges. Stress triggers a fight-or-flight response that increases heart rate and blood pressure and makes people more alert. These physiological changes can help people respond more effectively to a threat.[4] But when a person is in constant fight-or-flight mode, long-term damage can result. Chronic stress increases the risk of cancer, cardiovascular disease, high blood pressure, and mental disorders such as depression.[4] **Anxiety** is a feeling of nervousness or fear in response to an upcoming event or potential danger. It is associated with a host of symptoms: restlessness, panic, fatigue, increase in heart rate, and trouble sleeping.[5] Occasional anxiety is a normal part of life, not a disorder. But if the anxious feelings are intense, persistent, and disruptive of everyday life, people are said to have an anxiety disorder. Stress and anxiety often happen simultaneously and have similar symptoms, but there is a key difference. Although stress is often caused by external events, anxiety is usually caused by the fear or worry of events that have not yet happened.[6]

Depression is a common illness that negatively affects how people feel. Most people experience short periods of depression, but depression is considered a mood disorder if it persists for more than two weeks. The symptoms of depression include anger, sadness, sleep disturbance, low energy, feelings of worthlessness, and loss of interest in things.[7] Depression negatively impacts cognition and work performance and is associated with fatal diseases such as cancer and cardiovascular disease.[8]

PROMOTING MENTAL HEALTH, WELL-BEING, AND HAPPINESS

The impact of built environments on people's mental health is well established. Even though some people look for opportunities in lively places such as New York City, noisy and crowded places often cause stress and can even lead to aggression. Places of natural tranquility and serenity, order, and beauty, on the other hand, can help people recover from stress and restore one's capacity to pay attention. Walkable neighborhoods help prevent depression by encouraging social interaction and physical activity. And having secure housing, safe places, opportunities to mingle with others, and adequate heating, ventilation, water, light, and access to nature has a positive impact on well-being.[9,10,11]

Psychologists have shown that subjective well-being contributes positively to many dimensions of life. People who have high levels of subjective well-being have better relationships, higher incomes, better job performance, more creativity and productivity, better physical health and longevity, better mental health, and in general more fulfilling and happier lives than do people with low levels of subjective well-being. Well-being is not only a by-product of such positive factors in a person's life, but it can also be a cause of them. The positive emotions associated with high subjective well-being allow people to build their mental resources in a chain of successful behaviors.[12]

Although great effort is dedicated to finding psychological interventions (for example, prescription drugs or therapies) to promote well-being and especially to remove impediments to well-being (for example, negative moods or depression), the built environment is too often overlooked as a source of well-being. Some features of built environments are associated with the levels of happiness that people experience. These features include neighborhood population density (not feeling too crowded), access to nearby nature, and a relatively short distance to public facilities and amenities (for example, transit stations, commercial districts, sport facilities, squares, libraries, and banks).[13,14]

The built environment can also indirectly impact happiness by creating the conditions that promote social support, a critical factor underlying happiness. Urban settings that attract people and provide comfortable places to interact support the development of social ties among neighbors. And places that support physical activity such as walking or playing support both the development of social ties and happiness.[15] In a case study of Dubai, for instance, a number of features of the built environment were associated with higher levels of happiness. Those features included the availability of play and recreation areas such as a gym or pool and public spaces that support participation in community events.[16] In another study in Berlin, Paris, London, New York, and Toronto, the perceived quality of schools and health care facilities was associated with residents' levels of happiness.[14]

A variety of other features of built settings impact happiness and well-being. In suburban settings, as density increases, perceived environmental quality can decrease, which, in turn, decreases the sense of well-being in many residents.[17] The presence of water in urban and suburban settings is also positively related to well-being.[18,19] Affordable housing of good quality, with good energy efficiency and adequate ventilation, has also been linked to higher levels of well-being.[11]

Easy access to personally meaningful places and daily services contributes to higher perceived environmental quality, which, in turn, is positively associated with well-being.[17] People who live in settings with greater amounts of green space have greater life satisfaction,[20] as do those who perceive their neighborhood to be aesthetically pleasing and cohesive.[21]

People who feel an emotional bond with the places in their community report higher levels of well-being[22] and are less likely to move away than individuals who feel less connected.[23] There is no simple formula that designers and planners can use to create place attachment. Still, designers and planners can increase the likelihood that such ties develop by creating places that are attractive, support social interactions, are relatively quiet, and invite people to linger. Being sure that such spaces are a part of every neighborhood, campus, and business district will have important consequences.

COUNTERACTING STRESS AND DEPRESSION

Particular features of the built environment can promote or reduce feelings of annoyance, distress, anxiety, and in some cases, depression. For example, exposure to high levels of traffic, noise, and air pollution is associated with depression. And poor neighborhood design—the absence of pedestrian ways, public open spaces, or retail stores—or low levels of maintenance in public spaces can contribute to distress and depression in nearby residents.[8,24,25]

People who live in dilapidated neighborhoods, where, for instance, housing units have nonfunctioning kitchen facilities and heating breakdowns and where people are exposed to negative aesthetics such as trash, broken glass, and deserted buildings, are more likely to suffer from depressed moods or clinical depression than people in better maintained neighborhoods.[24]

When facing uncontrollable environmental factors (for example, noise, traffic, distractions, or air pollution), people often experience greater stress levels than when not facing these same circumstances. In urban environments, traffic and noise are inevitable characteristics of daily life. But such factors become stressors when they exceed the amount an individual can tolerate. Urban dwellers have little power to control the sources of these environmental stressors. Noise is a particular problem: noise generated from traffic is associated with high levels of stress.[26] Noisy sources such as housing renovation, construction, and airports are all associated with elevated levels of stress.[8,27] Besides noise, air pollution is another stressor for urban residents, which may lead to depression, autism and psychotic disorders.[28-30]

As discussed in chapter 16, access to green space has been shown to mitigate stress. Tree canopy density is positively and linearly related to recovery from stress.[31] Access to parks provides not only opportunities for aesthetic experiences, but also a chance to get away from stressful stimuli.

Walkable environments—spaces that promote a significant amount of walking for transportation or exercise—can reduce depressive symptoms. To produce walkable environments, designers and planners should create moderate to high levels of building density; ensure there are a variety of desirable, nearby destinations; and include blocks that are relatively short in length to increase the number of intersections (figure 7.1). A recent study found that the higher the walkability of a neighborhood, the fewer depressive symptoms elderly women reported.[32]

For many individuals who experience seasonal depression, living or working in buildings with large windows that allow exposure to daylight may reduce the intensity and duration of their symptoms. But what about the millions of people who work on a daily basis without exposure to sunlight because they work in windowless areas of large buildings? Designers and planners should work to ensure that these people gain exposure to daylight during work hours.

In sum, the design of buildings and neighborhoods can have systematic impacts on psychological stress and depression. Designers and planners can promote psychological health by creating places that are not noisy or crowded; that promote access to daylight; that encourage social interaction; and that invite people to walk, run, play, ride bicycles, and engage in other forms of physical activity.

IMPROVING ATTENTION

Cognitive functioning is also a dimension of mental health. Healthy cognitive functioning—the ability to learn, reason, make decisions, solve problems, remember, and pay attention—is essential to being productive, managing our lives, achieving goals, and having rewarding social relationships. All the indicators of well-being and happiness depend on healthy cognitive functioning.

A central but often unappreciated component of human effectiveness and well-being is our capacity to pay attention. Paying attention

Figure 7.1. Walkable environments result from pedestrian-friendly designs, a high density of buildings, and a variety of nearby destinations (for example, eating, parks, shopping). Walkable settings promote not only physical exercise, but also mental health.
Source: www.pedbikeimages.org/Dan Burden

is necessary for everything we want to accomplish in life. It is fundamental to learning, problem solving, planning, and persevering. It is necessary to maintain an ongoing train of thought, set goals, initiate and carry out tasks, monitor and regulate one's behavior, and function effectively in social situations.

Our capacity to pay attention has become an increasingly taxed resource in modern society. The explosion of information and the ubiquity of digital communications and digital media have placed unprecedented cognitive demands on humans. And everyday life—dealing with traffic, unexpected or delicate social interactions, problems at work, and complex decisions—all take additional tolls on this resource.

Unfortunately, our capacity to pay attention is also a fragile resource that gets depleted with use. We often run out of this capacity before our work is complete. Although we all have experienced this mental fatigue, we may not be aware of the price it exacts in terms of our effectiveness. When we are mentally fatigued, we have difficulty focusing and concentrating, our memory suffers, we miss subtle social cues, we are more likely to be impulsive, and we are more likely to jump to conclusions than when we are not as fatigued.[33]

Some configurations of the built environment have the capacity to alleviate mental fatigue and help restore a person's capacity to pay attention. Other configurations delay or inhibit this restorative process.

Particular features of built environments, such as natural elements, can alleviate mental fatigue and restore attention. An environment is restorative when it places few demands on you to pay attention. Places that gently hold attention allow people to recover from mental fatigue. As discussed further in chapter 16, there is considerable evidence of the attention-restoring effects of natural settings, even natural places within cities. For instance, classrooms with views of trees can significantly improve students' attentional performance.[34] Looking at natural views has been shown to improve older adults' executive functioning—that is, their ability to plan, evaluate, and regulate their emotions and behaviors.[35]

Built and natural environments that include water are associated with higher perceived restoration of attention capacity than those without water.[36] Besides natural views, natural sounds have been found restorative, too. People who were exposed to natural sounds before performing cognitive tasks outperformed those exposed to no sound or to a control condition.[37] Previous research has demonstrated links between contact with nature and effective attentional functioning in a variety of populations: AIDS caregivers, cancer patients, students, children with attention deficit/hyperactivity disorders, prairie restoration volunteers, participants in a wilderness program, and employees of large organizations.

In sum, we live in an information-intensive world that requires us to engage our attention and focus on a great number of things during our waking hours. Such requirements put great demands on our attention and result in many of us feeling mentally fatigued a good deal of our adult lives. The good news is that we can design cities, neighborhoods, workplaces, and homes in ways that help us recover from this fatigue. Such settings should have low levels of noise, present few distractions, and provide a sense of "being away" from the hustle and bustle of life.

REDUCING ANGER, AGGRESSION, AND VIOLENCE

Under certain conditions, humans—especially younger males—have a propensity for aggression and violence. Some portion of this propensity is associated with the places that we design, build, and inhabit.[38] Designers and planners can reduce aggressive tendencies through the places they create.

Crowding is linked to aggressive behavior. The number of people per room (social density) rather than the number of people per acre (spatial density), is the critical factor affecting the perception of crowding. High social density subjects individuals to unwanted interactions with others. These unwanted interactions can become a source of frustration that sometimes leads to aggressive behavior. For instance, when social density in prisons increases, so does the frequency of aggression.

High social densities also affect children. When preschoolers are crowded, their level of cooperation decreases and aggressive behaviors increase. The same pattern holds for elementary school children and for adolescents in the Global North[39] and the Global South.[40] These findings beg the question: how crowded is too crowded? Although there is no specific recommended number of people per room that can be generalized across situations, the key factors appear to be people's level of choice regarding social interactions with others and their capacity to coordinate activities (for example, when to study, watch television, or entertain). It is difficult to reduce the impacts of crowding in public transportation or other public settings where choice and coordination are extremely limited.

Recent studies have focused on the relationship between aggressive and violent behaviors and the natural environment. For example, adolescents who reside in urban environments surrounded by a large number of green spaces, such as parks, fields, and golf courses, were shown to have fewer aggressive behaviors than those who resided in environments with little green space. Increasing urban vegetation beyond the current standard, studies found, had an impact equivalent to about 2 to 2.5 years of age-related behavioral maturation.[41]

Environments having plenty of green spaces and trees, large sizes of trees, and greenery-treated vacant lots are associated with a significant reduction in violent crimes and assault activities.[42] The conditions that predict crimes are diverse and include a complex mix of economic, social, governmental, and physical environmental factors.[43] Here, we focus on the role of the built environment

in reducing crime. As discussed in chapter 5, **crime prevention through environmental design** (CPTED) is a widely used concept employed to reduce aggressive and criminal behavior by adjusting the characteristics of the built environment. The basic concepts include creating opportunities for informal surveillance of neighborhood spaces, reducing access to some neighborhood spaces, sending signals that people care about the nearby environment, and promoting a sense of ownership of nearby outdoor spaces.[43]

Improving walkability in cities is another factor that can enhance public safety. Greater walkability leads to more pedestrian activity, thus creating higher levels of informal surveillance, which impedes criminal behaviors. Although increasing intersection density strengthens the connectivity of streets, it is also correlated with crime. A greater number of intersections makes street networks more permeable and enhances the numbers of strangers on streets.[44]

Improving infrastructure in urban settings may also reduce crime. Such improvements include enhancing the design of public transportation stations and stops, upgrading buildings and lighting, and reducing the physical signs of disorganization. Each of these improvements is associated with reducing adolescent violent behaviors and criminal activities.[45]

Cities can also reduce violent crime by making spaces cooler in the summer. The two most common ways of reducing summer heat in cities are to add trees and to employ light-colored surfaces. A fourteen-year study conducted in 436 US counties found that higher temperatures were associated with increased risk of violence.[46]

A recent review examining the impacts of the built environment on crime concluded that the strongest evidence concerns the physical conditions of housing. In Hong Kong, for example, the number of floors in residential buildings is associated with antisocial behaviors such as harassing neighbors, creating graffiti, and engaging in vandalism.[47] In the United States, after public housing authorities began demolishing high-rise public housing and provided opportunities for families and individuals to live in affordable, scattered-site housing, researchers found that rates of homicide, assault, and violent crime decreased in nearby and surrounding areas.[48] They argue, however, that reducing crime does not require demolishing buildings. Investments to rehabilitate existing homes and install secure doors and windows on abandoned homes were associated with significant reductions in total crimes, assaults, and gun assaults. Indeed, urban renewal efforts that displaced people have also been associated with mental health burdens, probably related to the severing of long-standing community bonds.[49,50]

One familiar form of aggression is road rage. Road rage refers to an acute event or act motivated by anger within the context of driving. It is an act of aggression on the part of one driver directed toward another driver, passenger, or pedestrian. This aggression may be expressed verbally, through an obscene gesture, or with an action involving the vehicle itself (such as flashing lights, blasting the horn, tailgating, braking aggressively, or purposefully colliding with another vehicle). Road rage can spill out of the car and result in altercations involving fists, feet, clubs, and even knives and guns.

The causes of road rage are not well understood. Road rage is likely due to some combination of the anonymity provided by being in a vehicle, the stress of modern life, and the increasing length of typical automobile commutes. In some cases, aggressive driving may be exacerbated by the driver's use of alcohol or drugs, the number of miles driven per day, high traffic density, and even aggressive environmental stimuli in the form of billboards and building signs.[51]

Most suggestions for preventing road rage relate to changes in social policy and education.[52] But the built environment can also play a role in reducing the incidence of aggressive

behavior on the road. Perhaps the best strategy would be to build communities that make it possible for people to walk or ride their bikes to work, that substantially reduce automobile commute times, and that provide reliable, safe public transportation. As evidence throughout this book makes clear, reducing our reliance on automobiles will have a range of positive impacts on health, including reductions in road rage.

Creating places in which there is less aggression and violence depends in part on providing people with walkable neighborhoods, a basic level of functioning in their housing, a minimal level of management of vacant buildings, and a level of green infrastructure that sends a message that people care about the neighborhood. By responding to the information described above and by working together, planners, designers, policymakers, and community members can create settings that reduce aggressive and violent tendencies in people.

WAYFINDING

Being lost is almost always painful. Whether you become lost while listening to a lecture, using a computer program, or making your way to someplace, feeling disoriented and confused can be an agonizing experience. In contrast, knowing where you are, or at least feeling confident that you will find your way, can increase the quality of your experience.

Scholars have studied the characteristics of the built environment that help people find their way. They have noted that people are more likely to stay oriented—thus avoiding the anxiety and frustration of being lost—when a setting has distinct elements. The elements can be objects such as buildings, districts such as the soccer field zone in a large park, or regions within a city. These elements serve as landmarks, cues to where people are in relation to the larger setting. A successful wayfinding system should have settings that are cognitively comprehensible, with adequate information along navigating paths.[53]

Many years ago, urban planner Kevin Lynch suggested these distinct qualities contribute to a city's **legibility**.[54] He argued that a legible city provides an important sense of emotional security as well as an invitation to explore. Places with distinct landmarks and districts, clear edges and pathways, and appropriate signage increase legibility, help people stay oriented, and promote less stressful interactions with the built environment.

INEQUITY

Inequitable distribution of public amenities and the burden of disproportionate exposure to hazardous conditions among particular socio-economic and ethnic groups have considerable implications for mental health and well-being. Public amenities such as parks and green space, transportation infrastructure, and healthy food availability are inequitably distributed (see chapter 9). Disparities in access to resources in the built environment increase the likelihood that vulnerable individuals will suffer mental health consequences. For children and low-income adults, living in high-rise, multifamily housing is linked to anxiety and depression.[55] These symptoms are likely a response to general stresses of poverty, as well as to the noise and crowding often experienced in low-income, high-rise housing. People who have little social standing, economic clout, or political power disproportionately confront noise and crowding, which, as seen above, can have strikingly negative implications for mental health. Many poor people and people of color lack the resources to escape their daily living environments. Planners and designers have a special obligation to create living environments that protect people from undue levels of noise and crowding.

Communities that include large numbers of vulnerable people often shoulder a disproportionate burden of pollution. Some examples are well known—the lead-poisoned water in Flint, Michigan, and the poisoned portions of Louisiana known as Cancer Alley, for example—and there are hundreds more examples.[56]

Such environmental exposures amplify the stresses of poverty; the **cumulative exposures** have corrosive impacts on mental health. Poor people and people of color are also disproportionately likely to be exposed to polluted air, which is a risk factor for depression[57-59] and other common mental health disorders[60] and possibly for autism, impaired neuropsychological development in children,[61,62] and even psychotic disorders.[63]

Environmental justice and inequity and their impacts on mental health and well-being are global issues (figure 7.2). In central and eastern Europe, for instance, hazardous sites and activities are disproportionately located in communities with high concentrations of ethnic or national minorities.[64] A study in Shenzhen, China, reported significant social inequalities in park accessibility and park quality at the community level.[65]

The inequities described above result from social processes.[66] Fortunately, we can learn from work that addresses these injustices. Greening initiatives, such as turning vacant lots into small green spaces, can improve mental health and sense of safety in urban environments.[67] The Baltimore Green Network, for example, is a city-led effort that uses sustainable, innovative, and cost-effective practices for stabilizing and holding land for redevelopment and reusing vacant land to green neighborhoods, reduce stormwater runoff, grow food, and create public spaces. The reused vacant lots strengthen the social connection of neighborhoods, increase the city's tree canopy, and create jobs, which all help promote mental health of local residents.

Policymakers, designers, and planners should create policies and settings that eliminate disparities in access to healthy places and healthy conditions. Access to health-promoting conditions—sunlight; fresh air; clean water; safe, walkable neighborhoods; parks—is a human right that, when violated, leads to a range of negative, long-term, and often intergenerational outcomes.

Figure 7.2. Aerial view of a northern section of Johannesburg, South Africa. An impoverished neighborhood (on the left) is separated from a more affluent neighborhood (on the right). In such resource-limited neighborhoods, lack of access to safe housing, parks, green space, transportation infrastructure, and other amenities has impacts on the mental health of residents.
Source: Google Earth (2021), https://t.ly/g9hV

COVID-19

One role of built environments is to create a safe, attractive context for people to have social interactions and build healthy lifestyles. Excellent built spaces are designed to encourage people to come together and promote social engagement.[68] Urban planners and designers strive to generate a sense of place attachment in residents. Cities provide diversity and density, which stimulate exchanges of ideas and support social interactions. But with the eruption of COVID-19 in 2020, as discussed in chapter 26, built spaces needed to enable people to distance from one another.

To fight infectious diseases such as COVID-19, which spreads through aerosol transmission, cities need well-ventilated indoor spaces and plenty of opportunities for people to maintain social distance outdoors (see chapter 1). Close contact between people accelerates the transmission of infectious disease. Some public venues, such as outdoor cafés and public parks, support social distancing.

Social distancing during the COVID-19 pandemic changed the way people use public spaces and the extent to which they feel supported by their living environments. Many of the settings in which people typically encounter others—at work, restaurants, religious services, taverns, entertainment venues, and athletic facilities, for example—were closed or had their capacity dramatically reduced. The result was a profound reduction in social encounters that surely reduced some people's sense of belonging. This, in turn, likely contributed to observed increases in anxiety and depression,[69,70] but surprisingly not in loneliness, at least initially.[71,72] Other factors, such as economic hardship, also played a role increased feelings of anxiety and depression.[73]

The discrepancy between one's need to belong and one's satisfaction with ongoing personal relationships predicts loneliness.[74] Unmet needs for social connections lead to loneliness, which, in turn, often leads to reductions in well-being.[75]

The pandemic demonstrated the power of public spaces and especially parks and recreational spaces in partially alleviating some of these mental health challenges. Such public spaces were one of the few settings in which people could reduce stress and anxiety; they could be distant from one another and still experience social connections. The pandemic seems to have strengthened people's recognition of the power of public outdoor spaces to promote mental health. Can designers and planners leverage this recognition to create places that will enhance mental health for coming generations?

CONCLUSION

The design of built environments has important consequences for mental health. Crowded, noisy, dilapidated, and unsafe places and places that lack green space are associated with a range of negative outcomes, from slowing our capacity to recover from mental fatigue to increasing psychological distress and depression. These conditions have also been linked to increases in mild aggression, violence, and severe violence.

The good news is that several features of the built environment promote mental health and well-being. Settings that provide opportunities for people to recover from stress and mental fatigue, lessen depression, and reduce violence and crime promote happiness and well-being. To promote psychological health, designers and planners should create places that are not noisy or crowded, are awash in daylight and have easy access to natural element such as trees and water, support social interactions, and encourage people to engage in a great variety of physical activities.

With our growing understanding of the pervasive impacts of the built environment on mental health and well-being comes the responsibility to use this knowledge to create places in which individuals, families, and communities thrive. Well-designed places can increase the resilience people have in the face of challenges, threats, and unprecedented situations. We need to improve access to well-designed places to dramatically reduce disparities in healthy outcomes. It is a high calling to create healthy places.

DISCUSSION QUESTIONS

1. Can you identify a place or places that make you feel more comfortable, peaceful, happy, or calm? What features do you think most contribute to those feelings?
2. If there is a place that makes you feel happy, is that a short-lived, momentary response? Or does that place contribute to your long-term sense of well-being?
3. Social isolation and loneliness are bad for mental health, and crowding is bad for mental health. What features of the built environment do you think promote a "just right" amount of social interaction?
4. Why do you think road rage is so well recognized relative to "sidewalk rage"? What policy implications would you draw from a comparison of the two?
5. A key public health strategy during the COVID-19 pandemic was "social distancing." What do you think were the mental health consequences? Can you think of built environment strategies that would have minimized any adverse consequences while minimizing the risk of infection?
6. Displacement—say, by being evicted from a home or being priced out of a neighborhood—is a frightening and anxiety-provoking experience. What strategies can you think of to minimize these adverse outcomes?

DISCLOSURE OF COMPETING INTERESTS

Xiangrong Jiang, Chia-Ching Wu, Chun-Yen Chang, and William C. Sullivan disclose no competing interests.

REFERENCES

1. World Health Organization. Mental health: strengthening our response. March 30, 2018. https://www.who.int /news-room/fact-sheets/detail/mental -health-strengthening-our-response

2. Yap SC, Anusic I, Lucas RE. Does happiness change? Evidence from longitudinal studies. In: Sheldon KM, Lucas RE, eds. *Stability of Happiness*. Elsevier; 2014:127-145.

3. Nettle D. Happiness: The science behind your smile. Oxford University Press; 2006.

4. Russell G, Lightman S. The human stress response. *Nature Reviews Endocrinology*. 2019;15(9):525-534.

5. Mayo Clinic. Anxiety Disorders Overview. May 4, 2018. https://www.mayoclinic .org/diseases-conditions/anxiety /symptoms-causes/syc-20350961

6. American Psychological Association. What's the difference between stress and anxiety? September 21, 2020. https://www .apa.org/topics/stress/anxiety-difference

7. World Health Organization. "Depression: let's 'talk'" says WHO, as depression tops list of causes of ill health. March 30, 2017. https://www.who.int/news/item/30-03 -2017--depression-let-s-talk-says-who-as -depression-tops-list-of-causes-of-ill -health

8. Bosch Mvd, Meyer-Lindenberg A. Environmental exposures and depression: biological mechanisms and epidemiological evidence. *Annual Review of Public Health*. 2019;40(1):239-259.

9. Bratman GN, Hamilton JP, Daily GC. The impacts of nature experience on human cognitive function and mental health. *Annals of the New York Academy of Sciences*. 2012;1249(1):118-136.

10. Bratman GN, Daily GC, Levy BJ, Gross JJ The benefits of nature experience: improved affect and cognition. *Landscape and Urban Planning*. 2015;138:41-50.

11. Ige J, Pilkington P, Orme J, et al. The relationship between buildings and health: a systematic review. *Journal of Public Health*. 2019;41(2):e121-e132.

12. Diener E, Ryan K. Subjective well-being: a general overview. *South African Journal of Psychology*. 2009;39(4):391-406.

13. Yin C, Shao C, Dong C, Wang X. Happiness in urbanizing China: the role of commuting and multiscale built environment across urban regions. *Transportation Research Part D: Transport and Environment*. 2019;74:306-317.

14. Hogan MJ, Leyden KM, Conway R, Goldberg A, Walsh D, McKenna-Plumley PE. Happiness and health across the lifespan in five major cities: the impact of place and government performance. *Social Science & Medicine*. 2016;162:168-176.

15. Al Zaabi M, Shah SM, Sheek-Hussein M, Abdulle A, Al Junaibi A, Loney T. Results from the United Arab Emirates' 2016 report card on physical activity for children and youth. *Journal of Physical Activity and Health*. 2016;13(s2):S299-S306.

16. Reeder A, Lambert L, Pasha-Zaidi N. Happiness and the built environment. In Lambert L, Pasha-Zaidi N, eds. *Positive Psychology in the Middle East/North Africa*. Springer; 2019:71-90.

17. Kyttä M, Broberg A, Haybatollahi M, Schmidt-Thomé K. Urban happiness: context-sensitive study of the social sustainability of urban settings. *Environment and Planning B: Planning and Design*. 2016;43(1):34-57.

18. Foley R, Kistemann T. Blue space geographies: enabling health in place. *Health & Place*. 2015;35:157-165.

19. Gascon M, Zijlema W, Vert C, White MP, Nieuwenhuijsen MJ. Outdoor blue spaces, human health and well-being: a systematic review of quantitative studies. *International Journal of Hygiene and Environmental Health*. 2017;220(8): 1207-1221.

20. White MP, Alcock I, Wheeler BW, Depledge MH. Would you be happier living in a greener urban area? A fixed-effects analysis of panel data. *Psychological Science*. 2013;24(6):920-928.

21. Kent JL, Ma L, Mulley C. The objective and perceived built environment: what matters for happiness? *Cities & Health*. 2017;1(1):59-71.

22. Scannell L, Gifford R. The experienced psychological benefits of place attachment. *Journal of Environmental Psychology*. 2017;51:256-269.

23. Clark WAV, Duque-Calvache R, Palomares-Linares I. Place attachment and the decision to stay in the neighbourhood. *Population, Space and Place*. 2017;23(2):e2001.

24. Rautio N, Filatova S, Lehtiniemi H, Miettunen J. Living environment and its relationship to depressive mood: a systematic review. *International Journal of Social Psychiatry*. 2017;64(1):92-103.

25. Generaal E, Timmermans EJ, Dekkers JEC, Smit JH, Penninx BWJH. Not urbanization level but socioeconomic, physical and social neighbourhood characteristics are associated with presence and severity of depressive and anxiety disorders. *Psychological Medicine*. 2019;49(1):149-161.

26. Wagner J, Cik M, Marth E, et al. Feasibility of testing three salivary stress biomarkers in relation to naturalistic traffic noise exposure. *International Journal of Hygiene and Environmental Health*. 2010;213(2):153-155.

27. Ventimiglia I, Seedat S. Current evidence on urbanicity and the impact of neighbourhoods on anxiety and stress-related disorders. *Current Opinion in Psychiatry*. 2019;32(3).

28. Gu X, Liu Q, Deng F, et al. Association between particulate matter air pollution and risk of depression and suicide: systematic review and meta-analysis. *British Journal of Psychiatry*. 2019;215(2):456-467.

29. Suades-González E, Gascon M, Guxens M, Sunyer J. Air pollution and neuropsychological development: a review of the latest evidence. *Endocrinology*. 2015;156(10):3473-3482.

30. Newbury JB, Arseneault L, Beevers S, et al. Association of air pollution exposure with psychotic experiences during adolescence. *JAMA Psychiatry*. 2019;76(6):614-623.

31. Jiang B, Li D, Larsen L, Sullivan WC. A dose-response curve describing the relationship between urban tree cover density and self-reported stress recovery. *Environment and Behavior*. 2016;48(4):607-629.

32. Koohsari MJ, McCormack GR, Nakaya T, et al. Urban design and Japanese older adults' depressive symptoms. *Cities*. 2019;87:166-173.

33. Sullivan WC, Li, D. (2021). Nature and attention. In: Schutte AR, Taurquati J, Stevens JR, eds. *Nature and Psychology: Biological, Cognitive, Developmental, and Social Pathways to Well-Being*. Springer Nature Switzerland; 2021.

34. Li D, Sullivan WC. Impact of views to school landscapes on recovery from stress and mental fatigue. *Landscape and Urban Planning*. 2016;148:149-158.

35. Gamble KR, Howard Jr JH, Howard DV. Not just scenery: viewing nature pictures improves executive attention in older adults. *Experimental Aging Research*. 2014;40(5):513-530.

36. White M, Smith A, Humphryes K, Pahl S, Snelling D, Depledge M. Blue space: the importance of water for preference, affect, and restorativeness ratings of natural and built scenes. *Journal of Environmental Psychology*. 2010;30(4):482-493.

37. Abbott LC, Taff D, Newman P, Benfield JA, Mowen AJ. The influence of natural sounds on attention restoration. *Journal of Park and Recreation Administration*. 2016;34(3):5-15.

38. Krahé B. *The Social Psychology of Aggression*. Routledge, 2020.

39. Evans GW. Child development and the physical environment. *Annual Review of Psychology*. 2006;57(1):423-451.

40. Ferguson KT, Cassells RC, MacAllister JW, Evans GW. The physical environment and child development: an international review. *International Journal of Psychology*. 2013;48(4):437-468.

41. Younan D, Tuvblad C, Li L, et al. Environmental determinants of aggression in adolescents: role of urban neighborhood green space. *Journal of the American Academy of Child & Adolescent Psychiatry*. 2016;55(7):591-601.

42. Bogar S, Beyer KM. Green space, violence, and crime: a systematic review. *Trauma, Violence, & Abuse*. 2015;17(2):160-171.

43. Cozens P, Love T. A review and current status of crime prevention through environmental design (CPTED). *Journal of Planning Literature*. 2015;30(4):393-412.

44. Sohn D-W. Residential crimes and neighbourhood built environment: assessing the effectiveness of crime prevention through environmental design (CPTED). *Cities*. 2016;52:86-93.

45. Cassidy T, Inglis G, Wiysonge C, Matzopoulos R. A systematic review of the effects of poverty deconcentration and urban upgrading on youth violence. *Health & Place*. 2014;26:78-87.

46. Berman J, Bayham J, Burkhardt J. Hot under the collar: a 14-year association between temperature and violent behavior across 436 US counties. *Environmental Research*. 2020;191:110181.

47. Yau Y. Does high-rise residential building design shape antisocial behaviour? *Property Management*. 2018;36(4):483-503.

48. Kondo MC, South EC, Branas CC, Richmond TS, Wiebe DJ. The association between urban tree cover and gun assault: a case-control and case-crossover study. *American Journal of Epidemiology*. 2017;186(3):289-296.

49. Fullilove MT. Psychiatric implications of displacement: contributions from the psychology of place. *American Journal of Psychiatry*. 1996;153:12.

50. Mehdipanah R, Schulz AJ, Israel BA, et al. Neighborhood context, homeownership and home value: an ecological analysis of implications for health. *International Journal of Environmental Research and Public Health*. 2017;14(10):1098.

51. Sansone RA, Sansone LA. Road rage: what's driving It? *Psychiatry (Edgmont)*. 2010;7(7):14-18.

52. Asbridge M, Smart RG, Mann RE. Can we prevent road rage? *Trauma, Violence, & Abuse*. 2006;7(2):109-121. doi:10.1177/1524838006286689

53. Ulrich RS, Berry LL, Quan X, Parish JT. A conceptual framework for the domain of evidence-based design. *HERD: Health Environments Research & Design Journal*. 2010;4(1):95-114.

54. Lynch K. *The Image of the City*. MIT Press; 1960.

55. Evans GW, Wells NM, Moch A. Housing and Mental Health: a review of the evidence and a methodological and conceptual critique. *Journal of Social Issues*. 2003;59(3):475-500.

56. Villarosa L. The refinery next door. *New York Times Magazine*. August 2, 2020.

57. Fan SJ, Heinrich J, Bloom MS, et al. Ambient air pollution and depression: a systematic review with meta-analysis up to 2019. *Science of the Total Environment*. 2020;701:134721.

58. Wang R, Liu Y, Xue D, Yao Y, Liu P, Helbich M. Cross-sectional associations between long-term exposure to particulate matter and depression in China: the mediating effects of sunlight, physical activity, and neighborly reciprocity. *Journal of Affective Disorders*. 2019;249:8-14.

59. Gu X, Liu Q, Deng F, et al. Association between particulate matter air pollution and risk of depression and suicide: systematic review and meta-analysis. *British Journal of Psychiatry*. 2019;1-12.

60. Bakolis I, Hammoud R, Stewart R, et al. Mental health consequences of urban air pollution: prospective population-based longitudinal survey. *Social Psychiatry and Psychiatric Epidemiology*. 2020.

61. Suades-Gonzalez E, Gascon M, Guxens M, Sunyer J. Air pollution and neuropsychological development: a review of the latest evidence. *Endocrinology*. 2015;156(10):3473-3482.

62. Alvarez-Pedrerol M, Rivas I, Lopez-Vicente M, et al. Impact of commuting exposure to traffic-related air pollution on cognitive development in children walking to school. *Environmental Pollution*. 2017;231(Pt 1):837-844.

63. Newbury JB, Arseneault L, Beevers S, et al. Association of air pollution exposure with psychotic experiences during adolescence. *JAMA Psychiatry*. 2019;76:614-623.

64. Varga C, Kiss I, Ember I. The lack of environmental justice in Central and Eastern Europe. *Environmental Health Perspectives*. 2002;110(11):A662-A663.

65. Xu M, Xin J, Su S, Weng M, Cai Z. Social inequalities of park accessibility in Shenzhen, China: the role of park quality, transport modes, and hierarchical socioeconomic characteristics. *Journal of Transport Geography*. 2017;62:38-50.

66. Martuzzi M, Mitis F, Forastiere F. Inequalities, inequities, environmental justice in waste management and health. *European Journal of Public Health*. 2010;20(1):21-26.

67. Kondo MC, South EC, Branas CC. Nature-based strategies for improving urban health and safety. *Journal of Urban Health*. 2015;92(5):800-814.

68. Zakariya K, Harun NZ, Mansor M. Spatial Characteristics of urban square and sociability: a review of the city square, Melbourne. *Procedia—Social and Behavioral Sciences*. 2014;153:678-688.

69. Hossain MM, Tasnim S, Sultana A, et al. Epidemiology of mental health problems in COVID-19: a review. *F1000Research*. 2020;9:636.

70. Loades ME, Chatburn E, Higson-Sweeney N, et al. Rapid systematic review: the impact of social isolation and loneliness on the mental health of children and adolescents in the context of COVID-19. *Journal of the American Academy of Child and Adolescent Psychiatry*. 2020;59(11):1218-1239. e1213.

71. Luchetti M, Lee JH, Aschwanden D, et al. The trajectory of loneliness in response to COVID-19. *American Psychologist*. 2020;75(7):897-908.

72. Niedzwiedz CL, Green MJ, Benzeval M, et al. Mental health and health behaviours before and during the initial phase of the COVID-19 lockdown: longitudinal analyses of the UK Household Longitudinal Study. *Journal of Epidemiology and Community Health*. 2020:jech-2020-215060.

73. Witteveen D, Velthorst E. Economic hardship and mental health complaints during COVID-19. *Proceedings of the National Academy of Sciences*. 2020;117(44):27277-27284.

74. Baumeister RF, Leary MR. The need to belong: desire for interpersonal attachments as a fundamental human motivation. *Psychological Bulletin*. 1995;117(3):497.

75. Mellor D, Stokes M, Firth L, Hayashi Y, Cummins R. Need for belonging, relationship satisfaction, loneliness, and life satisfaction. *Personality and Individual Differences*. 2008;45(3):213-218.

CHAPTER 8

SOCIAL CAPITAL AND COMMUNITY DESIGN

Kasley Killam and Ichiro Kawachi

KEY POINTS

- Social capital is broadly defined as the resources that individuals and groups can access through their social networks.
- Social capital affects health through the exchange of social support, collective action, and the maintenance of social norms to promote healthy behaviors.
- The built environment can affect social capital by providing opportunities for formal and informal social interactions, promoting investment and collaboration in a shared space, and conferring a sense of belonging.
- Examples from around the world support the notion that social capital can be fostered by thoughtful design decisions and modifications to the built environment.
- Opportunities for future research and application include more studies demonstrating causality and rapid responses to how the built environment can respond to evolving needs for social capital due to the loneliness epidemic and the COVID-19 pandemic.

INTRODUCTION

In 2017, the *New York Times* published a haunting article about an apartment complex in Tokiwadaira, Japan, where a sixty-nine-year-old man passed away without being noticed by his neighbors.[1] Because he also lacked family and close friends, his corpse went undiscovered for three years. Lonely deaths like his have become so common recently that the Japanese coined a term, *kodokushi*, to describe them.

One factor that may have contributed to the man's isolation was the monolithic structure and design of the apartment complex in which he lived, with its sprawling buildings and 4,800 single-family apartments. Given that US surgeon general Dr. Vivek Murthy declared loneliness an "epidemic," it is important to consider how our surroundings may help or hinder our relationships.[2]

Social isolation (the objective experience of being alone) and **loneliness** (the subjective experience of feeling disconnected from other people) can result from a lack of social capital. When they persist for too long, isolation and loneliness are linked to a host of long-term negative outcomes, including low life satisfaction, depression, suicidal ideation, cognitive decline, low immunity, high blood pressure, inflammation, heart disease, and stroke.[3-7] Moreover, the mortality risk associated with lacking close relationships is comparable to the risk from smoking or consuming alcohol and higher than the risk from being obese or physically inactive.[8] Evidently, social connection and the resources that come from it are vital to our well-being. In this chapter, we explore how the built environment can influence people's social ties and, in turn, their health.

WHAT IS SOCIAL CAPITAL?

Social capital comprises the resources that individuals and groups can access through their social networks. At the microlevel, individuals who are connected to a social network routinely engage in the exchange of social support, whether instrumental (for example, a neighbor drives you to the airport), informational (for example, a friend lets you know about a job opportunity), or emotional (for example, a family member comforts you). At the group level, the resources derived from social networks manifest as norms of **reciprocity**, wherein community members routinely help each other (for example, your elderly neighbor babysits for you while you go to the dentist and, in return, you shop for their groceries); **collective efficacy**, wherein community members self-organize to take action (for example, neighbors gather signatures to support a local ordinance); or a **sense of belonging**, wherein community members feel solidarity, trust, and attachment toward one another (for example, co-workers gather for a monthly potluck). Social capital may be derived from a variety of social networks, such as neighborhoods, schools, churches, or workplaces.

Building on the work of sociologists Pierre Bourdieu and James Coleman, the concept of social capital was later popularized by the political scientist Robert Putnam.[9-11] According to Putnam, social capital can be both a "private good" (that is, benefiting the individual) and a "public good" (that is, benefiting the community).[12] The nature of a public good is that it is nonexcludable—that is, individuals cannot be excluded from its use and can benefit from it without "paying" for it. For example, people who belong to a community with high social capital are more likely to cooperate with guidelines to wear protective face masks during a pandemic. As a result, the reduced risk of viral transmission will benefit even those few individuals who do not wear face masks and who prioritize individual freedom above the collective good. In this chapter, we will primarily focus on community-level social capital or social capital as a public good.

An important distinction is often drawn between bonding and bridging. **Bonding social capital** refers to ties between community members who are similar to each other with respect to socioeconomic status, race and ethnicity, religious affiliation, or other dimensions of social identity. **Bridging social capital** refers to ties between community members that cut across these dimensions. In some instances, groups can have strong bonding capital, but lack bridging social capital; for example, White supremacists are racially homogeneous and maintain strong social connections to one another via social media and participation in rallies. However, their views are disconnected from the mainstream, and their actions actively contribute to the erosion of trust, solidarity, and harmony in society.

MECHANISMS THROUGH WHICH SOCIAL CAPITAL AFFECTS HEALTH

Four key pathways are involved in linking social capital to health outcomes. The first is network-based resources, as mentioned above. One such resource is information channels through which new ideas are introduced and then spread and become adopted within a community. The diffusion of information can sometimes occur through weakly connected but widely dispersed social ties; in the influential paper on "the strength of weak ties," Mark Granovetter introduced the notion that information often spreads from distant network members.[13] For instance, he found that job seekers were more likely to learn about employment opportunities from friends of friends than from other sources. Another form of network-based resources takes the form of tangible aid. In a qualitative study, participants in a low-income neighborhood in Oakland, California, pointed to the importance of social capital for securing a new supermarket and other amenities in their community.[14] In turn, improved access to healthy foods and other amenities that support healthy living could improve their health.

Second, social capital has been linked to health outcomes via the positive psychosocial and physiological effects of social cohesion. **Social cohesion** can be viewed as the cognitive and emotional aspect of social capital—that is, the perception of trust and feelings of solidarity associated with belonging to a group. Consider the "stress-buffering effect." Persistent stress can lead to inflammation, a weakened immune system, and ultimately illness and disease. Social cohesion can buffer against these deleterious outcomes. For instance, when those living in a community are familiar with their neighbors, an overall sense of security can mitigate fear of local crime.

The third pathway is the ability of residents to mobilize to undertake collaborative action, also known as *collective efficacy*. Examples relevant to health promotion include a community coming together to protest the closure of a local hospital, support zoning restrictions against fast-food outlets, or advocate for the passage of local ordinances related to smoking in public places. Another type of community action is *informal social control*, which refers to the ability of residents to maintain social order, such as cleaning up litter on the streets, fixing vandalism, and addressing other types of incivilities. The **broken windows theory** posits that features of the built environment such as litter and vandalism are demoralizing to residents and can adversely affect their mental health and overall health.[15] A community that is rich in social capital is better equipped to intervene to stop the spread of physical disorder in the built environment.

The final mechanism through which social capital may affect health is through the maintenance of social norms and social pressure. For instance, if your peers exercise on a daily basis, you may be more inclined to exercise regularly as well. In the case of a pandemic, the maintenance of social norms around wearing face masks and practicing physical distancing relies on the community for enforcement.

There are not enough police to issue citations to every person breaking the rules; instead, community members must step in to maintain these norms through the threat of sanctions (for example, expressing disapproval toward noncompliers, although doing so may occasionally lead to conflict).

HEALTH OUTCOMES ASSOCIATED WITH SOCIAL CAPITAL

Research on the relationship between social capital and health has grown exponentially in recent decades. Early studies examined ecological associations between social capital at the US state level and mortality rates, finding that states with the highest social capital—assessed by survey-based measures of trust between citizens—exhibited the lowest age-adjusted mortality rates.[16]

A 2019 systematic review found that 88 percent of studies reported at least partial support for a positive association between social capital and physical health. The studies primarily examined overall self-reported health, but also more specific indicators such as cardiovascular disease, obesity, diabetes, infectious disease, and cancer. However, only 28 percent of studies found exclusively positive findings, whereas 59 percent showed mixed results. This suggests a more nuanced relationship between social capital and health (to which we return below).[17] In another 2019 review, investigators included mental health outcomes such as depression and anxiety and similarly concluded that considerable research supports the link between social capital and health.[18]

Social capital can also have "dark sides," such as the **social contagion** of unhealthy behaviors.[19] Researchers have modeled how behaviors can transfer from person to person in a manner similar to infectious disease.[20] For instance, youth may be influenced in one social network (for example, a community club) to develop maladaptive smoking or drinking habits and then pass those on to peers in another social network (for example, at school). Social networks can also cause quite literal contagion, as observed with the spread of COVID-19 in 2020. Networks may promote advantageous or disadvantageous health behaviors; they are outcome-agnostic. Another dark side is that the benefits of social capital are not necessarily evenly distributed within a given population. For example, highly trusting individuals who live in low-trust communities have worse health than those in high-trust communities. By contrast, low-trusting individuals who live in high-trust communities have worse health than those in low-trust communities, indicating a cross-level interaction between social cohesion and individual characteristics.[21]

A final consideration is the role of social media. People can leverage social media and other online platforms to maintain or grow their social capital, such as by staying connected with professional acquaintances on LinkedIn or meeting people who share a rare illness through a virtual patient support group on Facebook. The research on the health effects of social media is still nascent and thus far mixed. Some evidence suggests that the way people use social media and their emotional attachment to it are more predictive of mental health and overall health than how much time they spend on it.[22] For instance, using social media to stay in touch or schedule plans to meet in person can be beneficial, whereas using it as a substitute for meaningful interactions can be detrimental. Additionally, misinformation may spread through social media; consider people who passed away after ingesting harmful substances that they believed would prevent or cure COVID-19 based on false claims online.

MECHANISMS THROUGH WHICH THE BUILT ENVIRONMENT AFFECTS SOCIAL CAPITAL

How might the built environment play a role in cultivating—or inhibiting—social capital? To answer this question, consider the links that exist between people's physical surroundings and their social lives. Specific features of the built environment may enable or impede various kinds of social interactions. Formal, planned interactions such as town meetings or team sport practices can only happen when there is a place for them to occur. In this way, the built environment can help build both bonding and bridging social capital by strengthening ties among people who are already bound by a common thread or encouraging contact between people who might otherwise remain disparate or isolated.

Most encounters that people have on a daily basis are informal and spontaneous in nature, such as bumping into a friend while running an errand or seeing a "regular" at the coffee shop. These interactions are also important for facilitating social capital, as they can spark conversations between neighbors and new acquaintances.[23] In the 1961 classic *The Death and Life of Great American Cities*—one of the first works to use the term *social capital* in its contemporary sense—Jane Jacobs pointed out that casual interactions depend on structural elements such as the layout of streets (for example, the width of sidewalks) and building features (for example, entrance stoops).

In particular, the built environment can facilitate both formal and informal interaction, and thereby the development of social capital, through "third places" and "social infrastructure." First described by Ray Oldenberg in *The Great Good Place*, examples of third places include cafés, restaurants, barbershops, playgrounds, and parks. These are distinct from first places (the home) and second places (the workplace) and provide ways for people to use their neighborhoods beyond private living and working. In *Palaces for the People*, Eric Klinenberg took this notion a step further by introducing **social infrastructure** as not only the physical places, but also the institutions and facilities such as schools, libraries, and churches that shape the ways people interact. Also consider public transportation, the absence of which can isolate residents in remote areas and therefore prevent them from accessing social capital.

Moreover, the built environment may confer a sense of shared ownership, identity, belonging, and collaboration that, in turn, can contribute to social capital. For instance, consider a neighborhood association that recruits residents to participate in a street cleanup; when residents are invested in spaces beyond their private home, a bond emerges with others who are similarly invested. In turn, it can enhance neighborhood stability.[24] Conversely, the more time people spend at home away from the public eye, the less community social capital there is. Taken together, the built environment may influence social capital through "activity-based" (that is, facilitating interaction) or "meaning-based" (that is, engendering belonging) mechanisms.[25]

RELATIONSHIP BETWEEN THE BUILT ENVIRONMENT AND SOCIAL CAPITAL

In 2018, researchers conducted a systematic review of the literature, examining data from more than ninety thousand participants in seven countries.[26] Overall, they found a significant relationship between features of the built environment and social capital. For instance, better access to destinations such as retail shops and health clinics through close proximity or walkability contributed to more familiarity with neighbors and higher social engagement. Greater diversity of land use was an important factor, with residential, commercial, and recreational properties intermingled. Mixed land use provides opportunities for daily interactions among community members, leading to more trust, a greater sense of connection, and collective efficacy. Design further played a role; the New Urbanist approach that prioritizes walkable neighborhoods, housing and amenities within close proximity, and accessible public spaces showed mixed but overall positive results.

Density tends to have a complex, inverted U-shaped association with social capital. Perhaps counterintuitively, high population concentration and urbanization have been linked with fewer social interactions and a decreased sense of community (figure 8.1). Presumably, that is because dense settings may invite people to withdraw into their private spaces. Urban sprawl tends to be associated with built environment characteristics that make interactions between neighbors less frequent and reliance on vehicles for transport almost unavoidable.[27] Car reliance has a detrimental effect on civic life, in part due to decreased opportunities for chance encounters while walking, but also because of the amount of time people spend in cars. Community involvement plummets as peoples' commute times lengthen.[12] On balance, middensity places appear to be optimal for interaction with neighbors and participation in groups, even though neighborhood pride and attachment may be highest at lower densities and use of neighborhood facilities may peak at higher densities.[28]

REAL-WORLD EXAMPLES AND STRATEGIES

In the early 1980s, a New Urbanist community in Florida called Seaside was designed with the specific intention of promoting a sense of community. It features a pedestrian orientation with footpaths, large porches on houses set close to the street, and a central retail area within walking distance. As a result, residents who were interviewed reported a high degree of social interaction and sense of community.[29] Seaside was an early example of a conscious effort not only to create social capital, but also to evaluate whether urban design was successful in doing so. Many more followed. Kentlands is a residential community in Gaithersburg, Maryland, with New Urbanist design features intended to promote connection. These include a mix of housing types, connected streets described by one resident as "rich and pleasant for walking," and clusters of ten to twenty houses surrounding a shared green space. These features contrast sharply with Orchard Village, a neighboring residential community characterized by classic suburban design features: no common greens or landmark structures, homes with

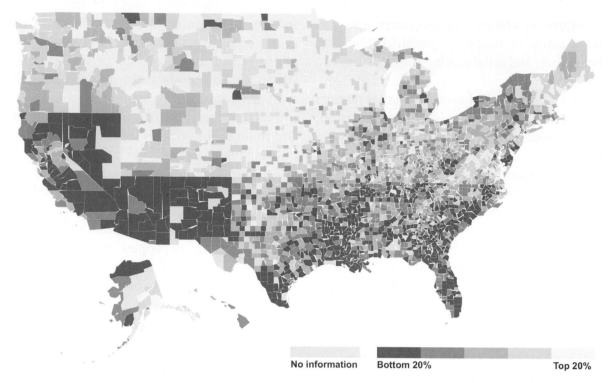

No information   Bottom 20%   Top 20%

Figure 8.1. Social capital at county levels. Darker color indicates weaker social capital, whereas lighter color indicates stronger social capital. At a bird's-eye view, it appears that rural regions may have stronger social capital than dense urban regions.
Source: United States Joint Economic Committee. The Geography of Social Capital in America. *The Social Capital Project*. April 2018. https://www.jec.senate.gov/public/index.cfm/republicans/2018/4/the-geography-of-social -capital-in-america

garages more prominent than porches, and sidewalks that are narrow or nonexistent. Compared with residents of Orchard Village, Kentlands residents report a greater sense of community.[25] Although some such communities have received criticism—being built on previously undeveloped land with consequent environmental impacts, not being integrated with transit systems, catering to more affluent households—they do provide good examples of design for social connectedness.

There are two key approaches to changing the built environment to increase social capital. One approach, exemplified by Seaside, is at the community level: designing new neighborhoods from the ground up to optimize for social connection; modifying existing neighborhoods in small but meaningful ways, such as installing more benches in parks or planting shrubs in vacant lots; refurbishing isolated or underserved communities through increased

access to public transportation or other systemic neighborhood improvement projects; and investing in public amenities such as libraries and community centers. Iconic projects such as New York City's High Line become popular community gathering spots (box 8.1). During the COVID-19 pandemic in 2020, there was a rise in community-level interventions to enable people to be socially engaged from a safe distance. For instance, Portland, Oregon, and other cities closed streets to vehicle traffic so that residents could more easily walk six feet apart; Dallas, Texas, launched a "parklet" pilot program to extend sidewalks and provide open-air seating in front of restaurants; San Francisco, California, painted circles on park grass to designate physical distancing; Vilnius, Lithuania, dedicated its plazas and squares for cafés to continue serving patrons outdoors; and from Bogotá, Colombia, to Berlin, Germany, countless neighborhoods

BOX 8.1 REPURPOSING PHYSICAL SPACES TO SERVE SOCIAL PURPOSES

Not only the form of the built environment matters, but also the function. Repurposing physical spaces to serve social purposes is a promising strategy. The High Line in New York City and the Promenade Plantée in Paris (figure 8.2) are elevated railways that were transformed into pedestrian parks.

Figure 8.2. The Promenade Plantée in Paris: a repurposed railway for recreational and social use.
Source: Hemis/Alamy Stock Photo

expanded their bike lanes, some intending the changes to be permanent. Research has previously shown that efforts such as these can increase social cohesion.[30]

Community-level approaches do not need to be dramatic to be effective. A bench, for instance, is not a radical innovation, but it is essential for older adults who need to rest when out walking or doing errands; 69 percent of older adults feel that benches are vital.[31] The idea for "friendship benches" began in Zimbabwe and has since spread around the world, heralded as an effective, low-cost mental health intervention.[32] Originally meant for trained counselors and patients to sit and discuss depression or other troubles in a relaxed way, friendship benches have been installed in schools across Canada to promote peer-to-peer support. Another example is "men's sheds"

or communal workshops where men come together to do woodwork and other projects and, in the process, develop camaraderie and friendships. Men's sheds originated in Australia, spread throughout the United Kingdom and other countries, and have been shown to enhance health and well-being.[33]

A second approach focuses on the building interior. Offices, residential buildings, assisted living facilities, hospitals, and other structures can incorporate design features that facilitate interaction and belonging within their walls. To be sure, space is limited, and there is a trade-off between downsizing functional spaces for living or working and increasing public areas for gathering. Nonetheless, many tech companies have seen the value of shared space and incorporated cafés, cafeterias, game rooms, lounges, and other leisure venues into their offices to promote connection and bonding social capital between employees. The Google Community Space and Salesforce Ohana Floor in San Francisco dedicated building space for local nonprofit organizations and other community members to use for free, thereby enhancing opportunities for bridging social capital.

Communal living offers another way to prevent loneliness and build social capital at the interior level. The proportion of people in the United States who live alone, rather than with roommates or family members, nearly doubled from the 1960s to the second decade of the twenty-first century,[34] yet there is a countermovement of "intentional communities" around the globe: intergenerational residences in Singapore, kibbutzim in Israel, co-housing in Denmark, and co-living memberships for "digital nomads" who travel the world while working remotely. Similar to student dorm rooms with shared spaces and activities, communal living may be an appealing option for people who want social capital to be a key feature of their home life; it may also combat loneliness.[35]

A notable example that incorporates both community- and interior-level approaches is Gallaudet University in Washington, DC, which is designed for students who are deaf or hard of hearing. Gallaudet developed "Deaf-Space" guidelines with more than 150 recommendations to improve five key elements: space and proximity, sensory reach, mobility and proximity, light and color, and acoustics. For instance, desks in classrooms and seating in common areas are positioned in circles instead of rows to facilitate lipreading, and pathways outdoors are wider to allow more room to gesture sign language. Challenges posed by aging, physical disability (such as immobility or blindness), mental illness (such as depression or social anxiety), and other conditions can be isolating and lonely and may inhibit people from building social capital. But as Gallaudet demonstrates, thoughtful adjustments to the built environment can improve accessibility and, in turn, opportunities for social capital for all; consider a ramp that not only benefits people in wheelchairs, but also parents pushing strollers, older adults with reduced agility, and anyone with an injury.

In line with the DeafSpace guidelines, the architecture firm HKS came up with six core design principles specifically to help urban planners, community connectors, and policymakers build third spaces that foster social health: accessibility (for example, wide sidewalks, stationary seating along main paths, mixed land use zoning codes), activation (for example, repurposed streets and plazas for events, art to inspire conversation, streamlined permit processes), choice (for example, adaptable seating and configurations, community engagement in the design process), comfort (for example, enclosure through overhangs or front porches, incentivization for developers to dedicate a percentage of space to the public), nature (for example, community gardens, windows optimized for sunlight, zoning policies for green space), and uniqueness (for example, decor from local artists, co-creation of spaces and programming).[36] The consultancy firm Happy City demonstrated these tactics when working in the Bloemhof neighbourhood of the Netherlands to improve mobility and public spaces for marginalized groups, including by engaging youth and vulnerable residents in a co-design process.[37] Happy City published a set of guidelines like those above for building sociability in multifamily housing (table 8.1).

Many of these efforts are congruent with the global movement to make cities "age-friendly" to accommodate the growing population of people over the age of sixty-five (see chapter 10). The US Census Bureau estimates that by 2030, older adults will make up 21 percent of the population, up from 15 percent in 2016.[38] Other countries, including Japan and Germany, are also facing aging populations. As a result, the World Health Organization

Table 8.1. Happy City guidelines for designing for sociability in multifamily housing.

Culture and values	People feel a stronger sense of belonging and attachment to places that reflect their culture, values, and sense of self.
Doing things together	Residents who have opportunities to do meaningful or enjoyable things together are more likely to develop a sense of trust and connection.
Exposure	People who live in spaces that give them a greater sense of control over their exposure to others are more likely to build positive social connections.
Tenure	The longer people can stay in their community, the greater the bonds of trust and local social connection.
Social group size	Social group size has a direct influence on the quality and intensity of trusting relationships that people develop.
Feeling safe	People are more likely to build trusting and meaningful relationships in environments that feel safe.
Participation	Residents who are involved in project design and site management processes are more likely to develop a sense of belonging and contribute to their community.
Walkability	Mixed-use neighborhoods that encourage walking are most likely to be associated with positive social encounters and a strong sense of community.
Nature	Access to nature is strongly linked to positive neighborhood relationships and trust among community members.
Comfort	People are more likely to engage with others in environments that feel pleasant and comfortable.

Source: Adapted from Rios, P. Architecture helped me heal. So I helped create a new guide to fight loneliness. Happy Cities Digest (blog). March 5, 2019. https://medium.com/happy-cities/happy-homes-b6d269a4cbe4

(WHO) galvanized efforts to prepare communities and foster healthy aging, and one of the eight domains WHO identified is encouraging social participation and reducing isolation and loneliness. Indeed, 86 percent of older adults in the United States think it is important to have places within the community to meet and socialize with friends and neighbors.[39]

Making improvements to the built environment is not without challenges. Certain development efforts that are welcomed by some communities may be protested by others. A park might be seen as an asset in a safe neighborhood but a liability in a high-crime area. In Oakland, for example, a cleanup group mobilized to restore part of a creek in a low-income area, but residents protested out of fear that it would attract crime.[40] Furthermore, efforts to revitalize underserved neighborhoods may backfire; by improving streets and sidewalks for residents, a neighborhood may gentrify and become unaffordable for those

residents, thereby displacing them and exacerbating inequities (see chapter 9). It is important to consider such ramifications and design or revamp built environments in a way that is inclusive of people from all backgrounds; doing so helps promote bridging social capital. Finally, a challenge is demonstrating cause and effect. While there is ample documentation of the association between built environment decisions and community social capital, more research is needed to shore up causal inference, including the study of natural experiments and interventions.

SUMMARY

The built environment is a promising avenue for building social capital. Characteristics of the built environment that warrant particular attention by urban planners include mixed land use, street walkability, and the presence and upkeep of public gathering spaces (see table 8.2 for more). Even modest environmental

Table 8.2. Summary of influential design elements related to social capital.

Positive aspects of the built environment for social capital
Mixed-use zoning and development
Green space, including parks, foliage, and community gardens
Walkability and features such as benches, front porches, and courtyards
Third places and social infrastructure, including libraries, community centers, and cafés
Access to public transportation

Negative aspects of the built environment for social capital
Urbanization and urban sprawl
High density
Barriers such as industrial areas and highways
Vehicle-oriented instead of pedestrian-oriented streets
Absence of communal gathering spaces

changes in existing public spaces hold the potential to enhance community social capital and create a corresponding improvement in health.

This area is ripe for innovation, both in research and application. More studies of targeted interventions that meet the unique needs of a given population and demonstrate causality are needed. Another opportunity is greater partnership between urban planners, real estate developers, public health experts, and community leaders to prioritize social capital in their work. A great example of cross-disciplinary collaboration is the work of the urbanist Charles Montgomery in partnership with psychologists, neuroeconomists, and happiness researchers to build immersive urban experiences and spaces that connect people (as described in chapter 27),[41] and more integrated efforts like his hold tremendous promise. A final suggestion for innovation is policy at the city or state level to designate a portion of new construction budgets toward shared community spaces. Many cities already require that 1 percent of new construction budgets be spent on public art; this requirement could be substituted or expanded to encourage investments into the development of places that facilitate social capital.

Two cultural trends make this topic especially relevant. The first is the high prevalence of loneliness in the United States and other countries, as described at the start of this chapter. A national survey conducted in 2019 reported that 61 percent of Americans felt lonely on a regular basis, and both the United Kingdom and Japan have appointed ministers for loneliness because the issue is so common.[42] Particularly among younger generations, men, and people in individualistic countries, there is hunger for greater connection and need for stronger social capital.[43] The second trend is the 2020 COVID-19 pandemic, which may not only exacerbate levels of loneliness in society due to quarantines and physical distancing, but also may spur significant changes to the built environment. At the community level, more people may leave cities to work remotely in less-dense neighborhoods. At the interior level, open-floor offices may be converted into more private workspaces, and restaurants may push tables farther apart. Some of these changes will be long lasting, and there will be more pandemics in the future for which we need to prepare. Consequently, there is value in reimagining where people live and how the physical spaces they occupy influence their interactions. A new design question may be how we can more safely gather to prevent the transmission of infectious diseases while still facilitating social capital. One approach may be recrafting the digital built environment and online places.

Finally, physical spaces for people to connect and gain a sense of belonging are necessary but not sufficient; the built environment can only support social capital to a certain extent. A gathering space will go unused if there are no community builders who organize markets, street fairs, and other activities and programming in which residents engage; if neighborhood crime is so high that people do not feel safe leaving their homes; or if inadequate funding leaves public restrooms, parks, and transportation in disrepair. The built environment serves as a literal and figurative foundation, but many cultural and societal factors must converge to strengthen social capital.

DISCUSSION QUESTIONS

1. What lessons can be learned from the design of previous planned communities to influence social capital?

2. What cost-effective strategies might enhance social interactions in an urban area? What about in a rural area?

3. Reflect on the shared spaces in your community. What elements contribute to social capital, and what elements inhibit it?

4. Imagine that you are responsible for overseeing new development in your city. What efforts would you take to incorporate insights about social capital into your plan? What stakeholders would you engage?

5. How do you think cultural influences, such as individualism and collectivism, might affect the connections between the built environment, social capital, and health in different countries?

6. What design strategies can you envision to promote social capital while reducing the risk of infection during a pandemic?

DISCLOSURE OF COMPETING INTERESTS

Kasley Killam and Ichiro Kawachi disclose no competing interests.

REFERENCES

1. Onishi N. A generation in Japan faces a lonely death. *New York Times*. November 30, 2017. https://www.nytimes.com/2017/11/30/world/asia/japan-lonely-deaths-the-end.html.

2. Murthy V. Work and the loneliness epidemic. *Harvard Business Review*. Published September 26, 2017. Accessed October 27, 2021. https://hbr.org/2017/09/work-and-the-loneliness-epidemic

3. O'Rourke HM, Collins L, Sidani S. Interventions to address social connectedness and loneliness for older adults: a scoping review. *BMC Geriatrics*. 2018;18(1):1-13.

4. LeRoy AS, Murdock KW, Jaremka LM, Loya A, Fagundes CP. Loneliness predicts self-reported cold symptoms after a viral challenge. *Health Psychology*. 2017;36(5):512.

5. Cacioppo JT, Hawkley LC, Thisted RA. Perceived social isolation makes me sad: 5-year cross-lagged analyses of loneliness and depressive symptomatology in the Chicago Health, Aging, and Social Relations Study. *Psychology and Aging*. 2010;25(2):453.

6. Valtorta NK, Kanaan M, Gilbody S, Ronzi S, Hanratty B. Loneliness and social isolation as risk factors for coronary heart disease and stroke: systematic review and meta-analysis of longitudinal observational studies. *Heart*. 2016;102(13):1009-1016.

7. Cacioppo JT, Cacioppo S. Older adults reporting social isolation or loneliness show poorer cognitive function 4 years later. *Evidence-Based Nursing*. 2014;17(2):59-60.

8. Holt-Lunstad J, Smith TB, Layton JB. Social relationships and mortality risk: a meta-analytic review. *PLOS Medicine*. 2010;7(7):e1000316.

9. Bourdieu P. The forms of social capital. In: Richardson JG, ed. *The Handbook of Theory: Research for the Sociology of Education*. Greenwood Press; 1986:241-258.

10. Coleman JS. *Foundations of Social Theory*. Harvard University Press; 1990.

11. Putnam RD. *Making Democracy Work: Civic Traditions in Modern Italy*. Princeton University Press; 1993.

12. Putnam RD. *Bowling Alone: The Collapse and Revival of American Community*. Simon and Schuster; 2000.

13. Granovetter MS. The strength of weak ties. *American Journal of Sociology*. 1973;78(6):1360-1380.

14. Altschuler A, Somkin CP, Adler NE. Local services and amenities, neighborhood social capital, and health. *Social Science & Medicine*. 2004;59(6):1219-1229.

15. O'Brien DT, Farrell C, Welsh BC. Broken (windows) theory: a meta-analysis of the evidence for the pathways from neighborhood disorder to resident health outcomes and behaviors. *Social Science & Medicine*. 2019;228:272-292.

16. Kawachi I, Kennedy BP, Lochner K, Prothrow-Stith D. Social capital, income inequality, and mortality. *American Journal of Public Health*. 1997;87(9):1491-1498.

17. Rodgers J, Valuev AV, Hswen Y, Subramanian S. Social capital and physical health: an updated review of the literature for 2007–2018. *Social Science & Medicine*. 2019;236:112360.

18. Ehsan A, Klaas HS, Bastianen A, Spini D. Social capital and health: a systematic review of systematic reviews. *SSM—Population Health*. 2019;8:100425.

19. Villalonga-Olives E, Kawachi I. The dark side of social capital: a systematic review of the negative health effects of social capital. *Social Science & Medicine*. 2017;194:105-127.

20. Hill AL, Rand DG, Nowak MA, Christakis NA. Infectious disease modeling of social contagion in networks. *PLOS Computational Biology*. 2010;6(11):e1000968.

21. Subramanian SV, Kim DJ, Kawachi I. Social trust and self-rated health in US communities: a multilevel analysis. *Journal of Urban Health*. 2002;79(1):S21-S34.

22. Bekalu MA, McCloud RF, Viswanath K. Association of social media use with social well-being, positive mental health, and self-rated health: disentangling routine use from emotional connection to use. *Health Education & Behavior*. 2019;46(2_suppl):69S-80S.

23. Altschuler A, Somkin CP, Adler NE. Local services and amenities, neighborhood social capital, and health. *Social Science & Medicine*. 2004;59(6):1219-1229.

24. Temkin K, Rohe WM. Social capital and neighborhood stability: an empirical investigation. *Housing Policy Debate*. 1998;9(1):61-88.

25. Kim J, Kaplan R. Physical and psychological factors in sense of community: new urbanist Kentlands and nearby Orchard Village. *Environment and Behavior*. 2004;36(3):313-340.

26. Mazumdar S, Learnihan V, Cochrane T, Davey R. The built environment and social capital: a systematic review. *Environment and Behavior*. 2018;50(2):119-158.

27. Frumkin H, Frank L, Frank LD, Jackson RJ. *Urban Sprawl and Public Health: Designing, Planning, and Building for Healthy Communities*. Island Press; 2004.

28. Bramley G, Dempsey N, Power S, Brown C, Watkins D. Social sustainability and urban form: evidence from five British cities. *Environment and Planning A*. 2009;41(9):2125-2142.

29. Plas JM, Lewis SE. Environmental factors and sense of community in a planned town. *American Journal of Community Psychology*. 1996;24(1):109-143.

30. Robert Wood Johnson Foundation. Open Streets. County Healthy Rankings and Roadmaps. Published 2016. Accessed November 9, 2021. https://www.countyhealthrankings.org/take-action-to-improve-health/what-works-for-health/strategies/open-streets

31. AARP. Creating Meaningful Public Spaces. 2019. https://www.aarp.org/content/dam/aarp/research/surveys_statistics/liv-com/2019/home-community-preferences-survey-meaningful-public-spaces-infographic.doi.10.26419-2Fres.00231.009.pdf

32. Chibanda D, Weiss HA, Verhey R, et al. Effect of a primary care–based psychological intervention on symptoms of common mental disorders in Zimbabwe: a randomized clinical trial. *JAMA*. 2016;316(24):2618-2626.

33. Ballinger ML, Talbot LA, Verrinder GK. More than a place to do woodwork: a case study of a community-based men's shed. *Journal of Men's Health*. 2009;6(1):20-27.

34. Ortiz-Ospina E. The rise of living alone: How one-person households are becoming increasingly common around the world. *Our World in Data*. Published 2019. Accessed October 26, 2021. https://ourworldindata.org/living-alone

35. Kim G. How cohousing can make us happier (and live longer). TED talk. Published 2017. Accessed October 26, 2021. https://www.ted.com/talks/grace_kim_how_cohousing_can_make_us_happier_and_live_longer#t-618828

36. Peavey E. How the built environment can foster social health. HKS, Inc. Published 2020. Accessed November 9, 2021. https://www.hksinc.com/how-we-think/research/connecting-irl-how-the-built-environment-can-foster-social-health/

37. Happy City. Walkable Rotterdam: Bloemhof. Happy City. Published 2020. Accessed November 9, 2021. https://thehappycity.com/project/walkable-rotterdam/

38. US Census Bureau. The Graying of America: More Older Adults Than Kids by 2035. US Census Bureau. Published 2018. Accessed. https://www.census.gov/library/stories/2018/03/graying-america.html

39. AARP. Home and Community Preferences Survey: Forming Strong Community Connections. 2018. doi:https://doi.org/10.26419/res.00231.008

40. Altschuler A, Somkin CP, Adler NE. Local services and amenities, neighborhood social capital, and health. *Social Science & Medicine*. 2004;59(6):1219-1229.

41. Montgomery C. The Happy City Experiment (YouTube Video). TedxVancouver. Published 2014. Accessed November 9, 2021. https://www.youtube.com/watch?v=7WiQUzOnA5w

42. Cigna. Loneliness is at epidemic levels in America. Cigna. Published 2020. Accessed November 9, 2021. https://www.cigna.com/about-us/newsroom/studies-and-reports/combatting-loneliness/

43. Barreto M, Victor C, Hammond C, Eccles A, Richins MT, Qualter P. Loneliness around the world: age, gender, and cultural differences in loneliness. *Personality and Individual Differences*. 2021;169:110066.

INEQUITY, GENTRIFICATION, AND URBAN HEALTH

Helen V. S. Cole and Isabelle Anguelovski

No city is [healthier] than the highest death rates in any ward or block.

—Benjamin Marsh,
an early city planning leader, 1909

KEY POINTS

- Urban environmental inequalities are often compounded and multifaceted.
- Deep, enduring histories of segregation and unequal urban development have structured and shaped urban inequalities.
- Neighborhood gentrification processes deepen existing urban inequities and lead to new patterns of spatial disinvestment with implications for health inequity.
- Environmental justice groups are increasingly facing a paradox whereby environmental improvements in historically marginalized neighborhoods contribute to displacement pressures, thereby complicating community activism and strategies for creating healthy urban places.
- Civic resistance, activism-driven neighborhood transformation, and policy and planning tools are all essential to achieve healthy urban places for all.

INTRODUCTION

East Boston, the former shipbuilding and heavily industrial Latino and Italian neighborhood next to Logan International Airport, faces multiple and overlapping environmental risks and inequities despite three decades of civic mobilization for **environmental justice** (**EJ**) and recent cleanup. For the majority of the twentieth century, East Boston's working-class and immigrant residents were exposed to air, water, and noise contamination from industrial activities along the Boston Harbor, Chelsea Creek, and Logan International Airport.[1] From 1995 onward, community organizing work spurred the development of new green spaces such as Piers Park, the East Boston Greenway, Bremen Street Park, Lopresti Park, and Bayswater Street Park in addition to initial water cleanup and brownfield redevelopment efforts. At the beginning of the 2020s, East Boston boasted a healthier environment, but residents are still exposed to enduring air and water pollution, face new climate risk from sea level rise and intense flooding, and are now facing pressures related to **gentrification** and displacement in the context of large-scale urban greening and fast-paced luxury waterfront redevelopment.[2] Those tensions prompt the inevitable question: who will benefit from a rebranded and greener neighborhood in the near future? Will it become yet another enclave of green privilege for a few in a historically segregated city?

In the United States, early 1980s and 1990s EJ mobilization targeted urban environmental contamination from waste or industrial facilities and their unequal and inequitable impacts on the health of socially marginalized residents. These impacts—many of them attributed to **environmental racism**—have burdened historically marginalized groups more than upper-income and White residents, and they are also a source of inequity—that is, injustice. At the same time, many activists began mobilizing for long-term neighborhood transformation and environmental improvements by advocating for new green spaces, playgrounds, gardens and farmers' markets, adequate, affordable and good-quality housing, and affordable and efficient transit systems. Yet neighborhoods that are transformed into healthy and equitable urban places face challenges. As residents receive new environmental amenities and traditionally **locally unwanted land uses** (known as **LULUs** in the planning community) such as toxic waste sites or contaminating industries close down or are remediated, developers re-"discover" those neighborhoods and invest in new high-end housing for wealthier residents. As a result, working-class and minority residents often become displaced to the often-grayer neighborhoods they can afford. This process of cleanup and greening, land revalorization, selective profit accumulation, and displacement illustrates what is increasingly known as environmental **gentrification**.[3]

In many instances, under seemingly technical and forward-looking visions for urban "sustainability" that incorporate concepts such as compactness, sustainable transport, smart growth, increased density, mixed land uses, resilience, and greening, planners and elected officials might plan interventions that conceal or overlook **equity** issues and create **environmental privilege**.[4] Thus, new amenities in the name of environmentalism face

the risk of becoming a new form of LULUs: a greenLULU.[5]

In this chapter, we ask: why do historically marginalized neighborhoods disproportionately face environmental health risks? What solutions can help address these urban health inequities? Here we discuss the origins of urban inequities using an environmental justice framework. We relate how these origins and specific inequities have led to the emergence of new forms of inequalities via gentrification and their implications for **health equity**. Although urban social and environmental inequities are major determinants of health inequity worldwide, we focus on the specific context of the Global North, drawing primarily on examples from the United States to give greater context to the problems we discuss. Finally, we present several potential solutions for creating and maintaining healthy and equitable cities.

POLICY AND PLANNING ORIGINS OF INEQUITIES IN THE BUILT ENVIRONMENT

Inequitable conditions within and between cities are created and maintained by long histories of injustices. For example, in the United States, neighborhoods are segregated by race, class, and more broadly by privilege, resulting from a history of racist policies and practices. These have included the more subtle recent practices hidden beneath **urban renewal** rhetoric, as well as the overt separate-but-equal mantra of the Jim Crow era of extensive racial segregation, all growing out of the country's colonialist origins and the importance of slavery in producing lucrative profits for White slave owners. The very idea of race, in fact, has its origins in the need to enforce a concept of "otherness" by which slave owners could justify keeping Black people in poor conditions and holding them as property. Although legal slavery ended more than 150 years ago, inequitable conditions persist. In many cities around the United States, often centrally located neighborhoods known as "Freedman's towns" (those settled by recently freed slaves with few resources in the late 1800s, who were still excluded economically and socially despite their relative freedom) now represent inner-city areas of disinvestment and marginalization in different ways since their establishment.

Marginalization of Black communities became entwined with urban planning policies and practices to enforce Jim Crow–era segregation laws. Restrictive covenants, which openly declared by race who was allowed to live in an area, and **redlining** practices, which used race-based "risk" calculations to segregate neighborhoods via mortgage lending practices, severely limited the economic growth and ability to improve the built and natural environments of many inner-city areas,[6] leading to poor-quality housing and unhealthy environments in addition to concentrated poverty and crime. Although many of these overtly racist housing practices were made illegal by the 1968 Fair Housing Act, their legacy persists in the form of neighborhood decay, devaluation, and disinvestment.

Racial segregation resulting from these policies became further entrenched as US cities grew and developed new infrastructure. In the transportation domain, many highways were expanded to make suburban living more convenient for wealthy, White residents fleeing decaying urban centers in the 1960s and 1970s (a trend often referred to as "White flight"), while already marginalized neighborhoods were dissected and demolished through urban renewal policies. Highways also created new physical boundaries reinforcing segregation patterns and exclusion from access to resources. Zoning changes and decisions, those policies guiding urban land use in cities, also played a part in such decisions.

Examples abound throughout the United States. In Dallas, the 10th Street neighborhood, a former Freedman's town and once-vibrant middle-class Black community just south of downtown, has been physically severed from wealthier parts of its district since the construction of Interstate 35 in 1955. In addition, the physical separation of this neighborhood led to the decision by the city to zone 10th Street as industrial. In turn, this zoning distinction has prevented homeowners from keeping up their historic homes, as they are consistently denied permits due to their presence as residents being considered "nonconforming use" of the land. Meanwhile, in the predominantly Black neighborhood of Pittsburgh in South Central Atlanta, residents are physically bound to their area by a combination of highways and railway tracks. Residents are unable to reach other parts of Atlanta by any means if a train is stalled on a crossing (a common occurrence), which residents report has substantial impact on their employment possibilities and abilities to reach resources outside of the neighborhood (figure 9.1).

ENDURING INEQUITIES IN THE BUILT ENVIRONMENT AND THEIR EFFECTS ON HEALTH

Due to these histories of unequal urban development shaped by racist policies and practices, significant inequities in the built environment in cities endure. Here we describe four specific embodiments of urban injustices and their implications for the health of residents.

Disproportionate Exposure to Hazards

In communities of color and low income neighborhoods, residents have traditionally received less protection from contamination and other environmental risks than those in majority White and higher-income neighborhoods. Governmental regulating capacity and oversight ability of contaminating industries are traditionally weak, with historically marginalized communities suffering from an unequal enforcement of environmental protection laws and other regulatory policies such as the Clean Air Act or the Clean Water Act.[7,8] These same communities also face procedural obstacles, lower capacity and political power, and weaker recognition of their own understandings of risks, which together prevent them from participating meaningfully in land

Figure 9.1. Aerial view of the Pittsburgh neighborhood a few miles south of downtown Atlanta, Georgia. This historically Black neighborhood is surrounded by rail lines and a highway, limiting egress to other parts of the city when a train is traversing or stalled on a crossing.
Source: Google Earth 2021

use decisions and policy measures that affect risk distribution.[9]

Although such procedural injustices are rampant and shape much environmental risk exposure, zoning has also been a strong contributor to spatial environmental inequalities through the segregation of urban communities by race and class, as described above, and the concentration of noxious facilities in communities of color and low-income neighborhoods.[8,10] For instance, in New York City, the 1961 Zoning Resolution divided the city into residential, commercial, and manufacturing areas, introducing incentive zoning and encouraging the creation of public plazas in development. However, regulations passed during the following years and decades that did not require buffer zones between industrial uses and residential areas eventually allowed for the expansion of manufacturing into lower-income and Black neighborhoods. Such decisions exemplified environmental racism

and often revealed that, even when residents of color hold a higher socioeconomic status, they still, on average, tend to face disproportionate exposure to contaminating facilities—in New York City and throughout the United States.[8]

Seminal studies such as those by the US Government Accountability Office in 1983[11] and the United Church of Christ Commission for Racial Justice in 1987[12] and later research in environmental epidemiology and sociology revealed that minorities and low-income populations suffer from greater environmental harm from waste sites, disposal facilities, transfer storage, incinerators, refineries, and other contaminating industries—those traditionally referred to as LULUs—than White and rich communities.[13,14] Communities such as the Manchester neighborhood in Houston located right next to oil refineries exemplify those risks (figure 9.2).

Decades later, despite some substantial and emblematic local victories and changes

Figure 9.2. Oil refinery in the vicinity of homes in the Manchester community of Houston, Texas. The residents who live in these homes, adjacent to heavy industry, are predominantly Hispanic and low income and are at greater risk of environmental harm than people who live elsewhere.
Source: Google Maps 2021

in federal policies with the passing of the landmark 1994 environmental justice-centered executive order signed by President Bill Clinton (rewritten several times) to prevent **environmental injustices** in federal policies and programs, these inequities persist. In 2007, on the twentieth anniversary of the landmark United Church of Christ study, the widely used report "Toxic Waste and Race at Twenty" demonstrated that minority communities still disproportionately faced environmental contamination.[15] More recent studies, such as one in Charleston, South Carolina, in 2012 by Sacoby M. Wilson et al., reveal that race and ethnicity remain significant predictors of inequalities in the distribution of Toxic Release Inventory facilities, an inventory of contaminating industries and sites required by the Environmental Protection Agency.[16]

Results pointing to similar trends are found for health *risks*—not only *exposure* to toxics. Although isolating single environmental exposures in epidemiological research is difficult, existing evidence has demonstrated that living near environmental hazards is associated with adverse birth outcomes, childhood cancer, asthma hospitalization rates, and even chronic diseases such as diabetes and chronic respiratory diseases; for example, residential proximity to highways was associated with preterm birth.[10] In the South Park and Georgetown neighborhoods of Seattle, which hosts the heavily polluted Duwamish River, residents experience a shorter life expectancy—up to twelve years shorter—than residents of wealthier, safer neighborhoods.[17]

Disproportionate Vulnerability to Disasters

Patterns of urban development also shape inequalities in exposure to climate change risks and impacts. Working-class, minority, and immigrant residents are often forced to live in informal settlements, public housing, or hazardous and high-risk locations such as floodplains, urban heat islands, and communities with limited vegetated spaces. They also suffer from preexisting health conditions[18] and have fewer resources to prepare for, cope with, and recover from climate impacts and shocks. We refer here both to material and financial resources to evaluate areas threatened by an extreme event, weatherize or repair homes, economically recover, and influence political decisions. For example, following climate disasters, disadvantaged communities—whether in the Rockaways, Queens (New York City), Tremé (New Orleans), or La Prosperitat (Barcelona)—are more likely to face displacement, ensuing loss of social and political networks, and a lack of power over decisions about where, what, and how to rebuild (figure 9.3). In the case of the COVID-19 pandemic, minorities and working-class residents tend to live in more crowded and smaller homes and work in essential jobs required to maintain critical infrastructure operations, where they are more exposed to contagion than other residents (see chapter 26).

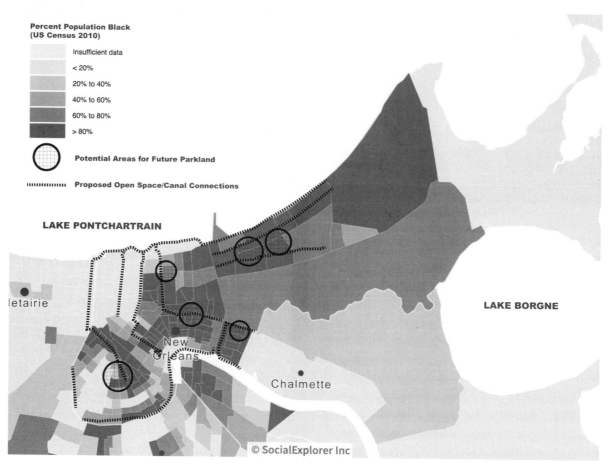

Figure 9.3. The infamous "green dot map." In January 2006, six months after Hurricane Katrina hit New Orleans, Louisiana, the first plan, *Action Plan for New Orleans: The New American City*, outlined proposed principles of rebuilding and presented a map that showed low-income and majority Black neighborhoods designated as potential green space (green dot neighborhoods, represented by black circles in the above map) in plans for reducing the rebuilt city's footprint. Sparking strong controversy among residents and concerns about erasure of past Black neighborhoods, the plan was not successful, and residents continued to rebuild in the green dot areas.
Source: Map by Olivia E. Chatman. Adapted from "Parks and Open Space Plan." *Action Plan for New Orleans: The New American City*. Bring New Orleans Back Commission, Urban Planning Committee, City of New Orleans. 2006. https://nolaplans.com/plans/BNOB/Urban%20Planning%20Action%20Plan%20Final%20Report.pdf
Base Map: Black or African American Alone, 2000. Social Explorer (based on data from US Census Bureau & Social Explorer; accessed July 23, 2021).

Inequitable Access to Services and Environmental Amenities

In addition to being exposed to greater environmental toxins and worse conditions, as described above, residents of disinvested neighborhoods have also been unjustly excluded from many essential and health-promoting goods and services. For example, unequal access to healthy, fresh, local, and affordable food in working-class and minority communities has permeated the urban landscapes of many underserved neighborhoods.[19] Even as more neighborhoods of color now benefit from new supermarkets or fresh food markets thanks to years of food justice mobilization, their residents often face financial obstacles and sociocultural constraints to purchase food. Historic spaces of environmental refuge such as community gardens or urban farms are also now increasingly "practiced" and "captured" by gentrifiers.[20] Inaccessibility of healthy food may lead to poor diets and ultimately poor health (see chapter 3).

Similar patterns are seen in access to basic environmental amenities, which make neighborhoods more livable and healthy. In Baltimore, for instance, from the early 1900s to at least the early 1970s, segregation ordinances, racial covenants, home improvement associations, and the Home Owners Loan Corporation together with the Parks and Recreation Board all contributed to segregating Black neighborhoods; these places then received fewer trees, as well as smaller parks, and became both more congested and less maintained over time[21] (figure 9.4). Urban reforestation programs also

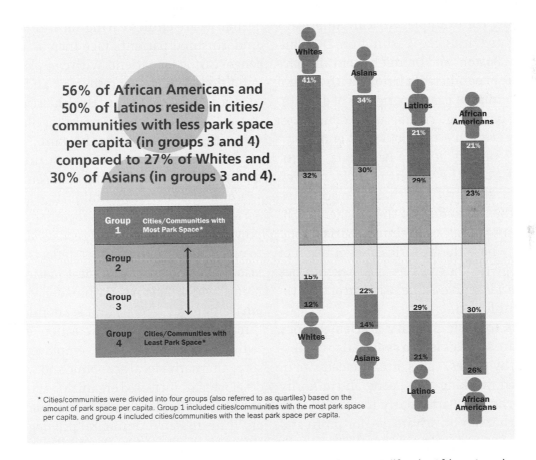

Figure 9.4. Race/ethnicity and park space per capita in Los Angeles County, California. African Americans and Latinos were more likely to reside in cities/communities with less park space per capita (56 percent and 50 percent, respectively, resided in cities/communities in quartiles 3 and 4) compared with White and Asian residents (27 percent and 36 percent, respectively, resided in cities/communities in quartiles 3 and 4). Source. Los Angeles County Department of Public Health. Parks and Public Health in Los Angeles County: A Cities and Communities Report; May 2016.

tend to benefit neighborhoods with a higher percentage of owner-occupied (that is, higher-income) homes, often prompted by active neighborhood associations advocating for tree planting.[22] Lack of access to green space means that residents of these neighborhoods also lose the health benefits of exposure to green space and other environmental amenities,[23] whose physical and emotional restorative effects seem particularly important for residents exposed to chronic stress.[24]

Even when working-class communities and communities of color receive an ample provision of new green amenities and spaces, those are not always integrated, welcoming, and perceived as safe, with minority and immigrant residents often exposed to exclusionary and controlling discourses and practices about urban nature and what activities can take place in it. For example, African Americans in segregated cities like Washington, DC, Philadelphia, Boston, and Detroit historically have traumatic or conflicted relations with natural spaces because of past experiences of discrimination, lynching, crime, and exclusion in nature.[25] Even in a multicultural and seemingly welcoming city like Barcelona, Spain, the creation of the Passeig Sant Joan green corridor in the early 2010s has been accompanied by the rebranding of the broader neighborhood into a high-end White expatriate community, where the historic concentration of Chinese-owned businesses and presence has become undesirable as the redesign of the avenue has unfolded.

Access to basic primary and emergency health care services is also essential to achieving healthy places, yet is often inadequate in segregated, working-class, poor, and minority neighborhoods. Particularly for health care systems that rely on private not-for-profit and for-profit entities to provide health care, such as the case in the United States, access is further hindered by health care gentrification, the process by which health care facilities are increasingly catering to wealthy residents with private insurance to the exclusion of publicly insured or uninsured residents. The commercialization and privatization of health care in the United States has led distribution patterns based on profit rather than ensuring equitable access to quality care. For example, in Garland, Texas, a suburb of Dallas with a population 250,000, the city's only hospital closed in 2017 when its new owners, a large health care organization, saw no way for it to make a profit.[26] One recent analysis showed that between 2000 and 2014, predominantly minority neighborhoods were more likely than predominantly White neighborhoods to lose health care facilities.[27] Meanwhile, urgent care centers and stand-alone emergency rooms are strategically located in wealthier neighborhoods where they can ensure profit from private insurance holders or those who can afford to pay out of pocket. In addition, not-for-profit primary care clinics caring for uninsured or underinsured patients face increasing challenges caring for patients with complex health conditions, with fewer resources, and who are at risk for displacement. Health crises, such as the COVID-19 pandemic, further illuminate inequities in accessing health care.

This diversity of amenities ensuring a high quality of life and well-being has been the subject of much environmental justice activism. Socioeconomic well-being, together with the provision of environmental goods and services to underserved communities, reflects the philosophy of the environmental justice movement, which advances a broader vision for environmental, social, and economic justice through community wealth creation, equitable redistribution of resources, employee ownership, alternative local economic and workforce development, increased organizing at the union or neighborhood level, and overall questioning of White and environmental privilege.[4,28] For example, in places like the Dudley neighborhood in Boston, Massachusetts, the activism of neighborhood groups such as Alternatives for Community and Environment–Environmental Justice (ACE-EJ), the Dudley Street Neighborhood Initiative (DSNI), and the Food Project has led to comprehensive transformation through new parks, community farms, local health care clinics, workforce development and training, and minority business ownerships, making many of those spaces "safe havens" for residents (figure 9.5).

The Problem of Housing Quality and Accessibility

Another injustice faced by residents of disinvested neighborhoods is the struggle to secure housing—specifically housing that is accessible, affordable, and of good quality—due to lack of resources and concentrated poverty. Housing insecurity is an important determinant of poor population health.[29] Although housing may exist in many urban neighborhoods, some—as in the case of Barry Farms in Washington, DC, or Cabrini Green in Chicago—was in such disrepair that it became uninhabitable and was ultimately torn down. In addition, families whose property was inherited through generations, as is common among many low-income communities and communities of color, may also face bureaucratic problems when property titles become entangled or lost, creating barriers for repairing or selling a home.

Public housing, which is intended for families unable to pay for market-rate rental or privately owned housing, has historically been sited in segregated, impoverished neighborhoods.[30] However, in the 1990s, the Department of Housing and Urban Development (HUD) began a process of dismantling housing facilities under the pretense of transition toward a voucher-based system that would allow families to choose where to live. But many facilities in the HUD network had long since been in poor condition. For example, by 1985, in the largest HUD facility in the nation once located in West Dallas, years of maintenance neglect left thirteen hundred of the original thirty-five hundred units vacant and uninhabitable. These homes were also located across the street from a lead smelting plant in an area prone to flooding from the nearby Trinity River and near many other heavily polluting industries. Thus, residents faced overlapping exposures placing them at greater risk of poor health.

Another barrier to accessing housing has to do with real estate speculation and landlord abuses. In the case of public housing voucher programs, even families holding vouchers may have difficulty finding landlords willing to rent to them in states and cities with no antidiscrimination housing policies. Disinvested neighborhoods often have poor-quality market-rate rental housing that may not be adequately maintained by owners, who have little incentive to do so. If such properties have low rents and are accessible to low-income renters, such as those holding vouchers, the owners may decide to "flip" the rental properties into new more profitable luxury housing. Even in cities with protective policies, low-income renters are at risk for abuse and exclusion from healthy and affordable housing.

THE PROBLEM OF GENTRIFICATION

Many areas formerly targeted for massive urban renewal and demolition, such as those experiencing the unjust conditions described above, have been some of the first areas to experience urban revival and land redevelopment. They are being rebranded from "abandoned, blighted ghettos" to "up-and-coming neighborhoods" with much "cultural vitality," from which new economic value can be extracted through condominium developments or conversions.[31]

Contextualizing and Defining Gentrification

Gentrification is characterized by changes in social and demographic indicators, with the arrival of new, mostly White, upper-income residents and the progressive displacement and replacement of socially vulnerable groups. It can be driven by new commercial development, real estate construction, tourism, or art districts and is associated with more expensive costs of living.[32] Precisely due to the conditions described in the policy and planning

Figure 9.5. Comprehensive environmental improvements in the Dudley neighborhood of Boston, Massachusetts. Activism of neighborhood groups led to numerous local investments, among them new parks, fresh food stands, and community farms.
Source: Photos courtesy of Isabelle Anguelovski

origins of inequities in the built environment discussed above, many disinvested neighborhoods, where land has been relatively inexpensive due to environmental degradation or lack of resources and amenities, are thus at risk for being gentrified. The causes and drivers of gentrification can generally be classified as either demand side (that is, relating to the preferences of incoming, wealthier, more privileged populations) or supply side (that is, referring to the supply of new luxury goods or services that may attract more privileged populations). Characteristics such as being in a convenient, central location and the availability of affordable land may attract investors and new residents.

As neighborhoods are gentrified, long-term residents, often marginalized communities of ethnic or racial minorities, and low-income residents are at risk for displacement as the cost of housing and other costs of living rises. Even if they are not physically displaced, long-term residents also may face social or cultural exclusion from neighborhood resources, events, or social life. Social networks and support may be ruptured for staying residents, and changes to the types of and cost of services may exclude lower-income residents.[33] Emerging research shows that although gentrification processes may be beneficial for the mental and physical health of the residents still living in a neighborhood at large, often the health of lower-income or minority residents, those likely to be long-term residents of the neighborhood, either does not benefit or is harmed by this process.[2,34,35]

The Special Case of Green Gentrification

Recently, the dynamics leading to gentrification—combining capitalist investments, governmental decisions and programs, classism and racism, and continued resident exclusion—have also come to include another process: neighborhood greening. Beyond the United States and across the globe, creating new environmentally friendly neighborhoods is at the center of many urban sustainability agendas.[36] Cities like Vancouver, Austin, Copenhagen, Amsterdam, Bristol, and Barcelona have integrated nature-based interventions as part of their urban brand, and all compete in the race to be the most livable city.[37] Those cities and others are embedded in a logic of green growth, competitive urbanism, resource attraction, and even **racialized capitalism**.[38] In an effort to attract wealthy residents and investors to support local economies, cities sell new urban futures of restored ecologies and a new revitalized urban landscape while erasing minority and immigrant identities, places, and practices. This racialized capitalism financially penalizes minority, Black, and Indigenous people of color and excludes them from the various benefits resulting from the restoration of the very environments they were previously rooted in. Here, new real estate projects go hand in hand with greening, which adds monetary value and profits to White and wealthy individuals without considering the subsequent negative social impacts on people who are Black and low income. In many ways, sustainability eludes core urban questions at the intersection of racial inequalities, social hierarchies, and environmental privilege.

Social and racial environmental inequalities can also materialize over time, often upon the announcement of construction of green spaces and green infrastructure such as parks, gardens, greenbelts and greenways, rain gardens and bioswales, green roofs and walls, green streets and alleys, or restored waterways (see chapter 6). In the United States, projects such the Atlanta Beltline, the Boston Rose Kennedy Greenway and the East Boston Greenway, the 606 trail in Chicago, the Trinity River Corridor redevelopment in Dallas, and the smaller but citywide green stormwater infrastructure interventions Green City Clean Waters program in Philadelphia have led to inequalities and displacement of low-wealth and minority residents.

One core social limitation of such interventions is that few begin with an equity lens and include concrete measures for ensuring that greening benefit all residents, in particular communities and residents who are historically vulnerable to environmental racism and displacement. Many projects include an implicit assumption of "green" trickle-down effects spreading to benefit all. However, such effects are increasingly associated with green exclusion and privilege and **green gentrification** and displacement.[3] Green gentrification, for example, refers to the adoption of urban green agendas that lead or contribute to the displacement of the most socially marginalized residents despite being sold as providing universal benefits.

Although gentrification is often eventually produced by other urban economic and social dynamics, spatial and quantitative studies of green gentrification are able to parse out the role greening (in the sense of nature-centered interventions) itself plays, at the very least, in accelerating or increasing gentrification.[39,40] In Atlanta, housing values spiked by 18 percent and 27 percent between 2011 and 2015 for homes located within 0.8 kilometer (0.5 mile) of the Atlanta Beltline greenbelt.[41] As property values increase, working-class residents are faced with increased rental prices, as well as property tax or maintenance cost spikes, associated with living in greener, higher-valued neighborhoods. Similar exclusionary dynamics are found with climate-resilient infrastructure, as the siting of green infrastructure tends to overlook the socioenvironmental vulnerability and potential displacement of lower-income and minority neighborhoods and overall privileging investments in higher-income but less marginalized neighborhoods.[42]

This siting is found to amplify what is known as **climate gentrification**, as poorer residents might become displaced to less protected and more socially and ecologically vulnerable neighborhoods.[43] In Boston, for instance, the so-called resilient greening of East Boston and the 2018 Boston Harbor Plan "activate" formerly no-go industrial zones through new visions of a green and resilient Boston. Contaminated waterfronts thus become transformed into green resilient parks and attract luxury condo developments, from which long-term Latino and Italian residents are culturally and financially excluded.

In sum, environmental, or green, gentrification shows that high-income residents are those able to afford high-quality houses in green neighborhoods while shifting environmental burdens and LULUs to the most marginalized—often more contaminated, poorly connected, and with substandard access to healthy and affordable food—neighborhoods to which working-class residents are forced to move due to lack of affordability elsewhere. Environmental gentrification is thus the flipside (or follow-up) of what critical health scholar Mindy Fullilove called "Negro Removal" because "green and white arrival" accompanies displacement.[44] Here the racial aspect of Whiteness becomes hidden by the word *green*, thus transforming these greening initiatives into a new type of LULUs that residents increasingly view with an eye of concern: GreenLULUs. Thus, in considering the overall health impacts of new green amenities, these complex social and economic impacts, including gentrification, displacement, or exclusion from benefits, must also be evaluated.[45]

SOLUTIONS

Today, one of the key challenges for land use planning and sustainability planning depends greatly on how the planning profession and policymakers are able to address the conflicts and controversies that emerge as part of sustainable development and livability initiatives. This challenge illuminates the need to think carefully about the interaction between the social and physical environments of neighborhoods and cities and to design interventions to create healthy cities accordingly.[45] Here we focus on potential solutions implemented on the local level, both municipal-led and citizen-led.

Civic Mobilization

Today, justice groups have organized to improve housing access for marginalized groups together with more environmentally friendly and green neighborhoods. Here, acknowledging the need for overall economic security and for access to safe and well-maintained homes, demands often combine healthy homes with an economic demand. This demand includes funding for jobs, training for energy efficiency and renewable energy projects, or revenue redistribution from utility companies for weatherizing buildings.[28] Many of those mobilizations are connected to the Green New Deal, a political agenda focused on constructing a more just, sustainable, green economy. Such demands are accompanied by improved transit systems so that working-class residents and others can have improved commuting options to jobs and services. Greening public housing or building green affordable housing, however, entails complex challenges such as aligning project goals and financial components with community priorities, preventing long-term displacement, and creating an affordable housing or mixed use development stock that can be resident-owned.

Another target of environmental justice activism is the implementation of greening or sustainability agendas. Many municipal interventions have prompted community resistance against projects or amenities associated with environmental gentrification.[46] Resistance has also occurred to complete streets planning policies, which municipalities use to make neighborhoods more walkable and livable and to bring the streets back to pedestrians and bikers. Here, civic mobilization is a fundamental tool against unequal green investments or sustainability. For instance, in Portland, Oregon, and Minneapolis, Minnesota, city plans to enhance *biking* safety and improve bike infrastructure have been met with the resistance of some locals who resent bike lanes and perceive that safety and "sustainable mobility" seem only to have become a concern because White, young residents are moving to the neighborhood or riding through—signs of pending threats of displacement.[47] *Food* justice activists also protest the opening of so-called healthy food stores (that is, Whole Foods), contesting food privilege and food gentrification in their neighborhood while defending the preservation of culturally based practices and venues around food such as historic, locally owned stores or markets, community-driven coops, and resident farmed and managed gardens.[19]

Alternative Redevelopment Strategies

Residents and activists have also articulated alternative redevelopment strategies known as *Just Green Enough* through which environmental cleanup is combined with demands for affordable homes and place identity and against new green amenities at any price. In Brooklyn, New York, longtime residents of Newtown Creek together with local business owners have defended such ideas by embracing the neighborhood industrial base, advocating for more affordable housing and greater state control of real estate development, and building partnerships with middle-class residents who support their vision.[48] Other groups ask for new spatial and land arrangements and equitable development plans that can guarantee more *liberating*, *emancipatory*, and *secure territories* and address deep histories of segregation, erasure, and land dispossessions. Civic groups like Building Bridges Across the River, which is leading the construction of the 11th Street Bridge Park in Washington, DC's Anacostia neighborhood, are working with local and national financial entities to secure new land and affordable homes for long-term Black residents while supporting Black-owned businesses and other Black venues.

Inclusive Decision-Making and Accountable Governance

Planning for more environmentally just cities also requires renewed participatory mechanisms,[49] mutual trust, recognition of residents' diverse and legitimate knowledge and needs, and inclusive decision-making. Because city planning is generally dominated by private interests and unequal power relations over who gets to discuss and decide interventions,[50] prioritizing traditionally unheard and invisible voices and repairing experiences of trauma and mistrust are essential (see chapter 21). Such practices are particularly needed for the planning and use of green and public spaces to ensure that outsiders will not police, coerce, or surveil minority or immigrant bodies[51] and will allow for their users to practice recreational activities and sports in ways that will fulfill the restorative health opportunities offered by green and public space. Inclusive green planning and design require both resident-led placemaking (rather than architect-driven design) and the noncriminalization of practices and livelihoods, as the Black Lives Matter movement denounces. In Barcelona, children's "relational well-being" in the Parc Central de Nou Barris has been enabled by the municipality's and by residents' vision to integrate the park's design and infrastructure within the existing urban and social fabric of the working-class neighborhood. Over time, the preservation of this fabric and of a vision of a neighborhood-centered park has allowed for the creation of informal networks of support that enable children's free play.[52] Green spaces where historically (racially, ethnically, socioeconomically, or gender) opposed groups could also come together and interact through a language of caring, creating spaces for interaction that can help overcome stereotypes can be promising (both material and immaterial) grounds for achieving restorative or reparative justice in urban greening.

Antidisplacement Policies

Last, *antidisplacement* policies are also much needed and have become the center of greater state and municipal attention. Antidisplacement policies are often the result of community activism and contestation and can take the form of city, regional, or national policies; financial tools; or community-led initiatives. For instance, community land trusts such as the Dudley Land Trust in Boston's immigrant and minority neighborhoods of Roxbury and North Dorchester have been guaranteeing residents' land ownership and control while laying out new sociospatial practices of well-being and political freedom. In the neighborhood of La Bajada in West Dallas, residents came together to create and enact a Neighborhood Overlay Stabilization plan that limits development in the neighborhood to small, single-family homes or to resources that are meant to benefit the community, which must be approved by residents. Financial tools use taxation or subsidies to encourage or discourage certain types of development and are often used by cities to encourage the development of affordable homes or to prevent the eviction of lower-income residents. Finally, policy tools such as rent control and inclusionary zoning are being implemented by cities in an attempt to limit pressures on low-income and minority neighborhoods and residents. Table 9.1 summarizes several (although not an exhaustive list) antidisplacement tools currently in use. Additional antidisplacement approaches have been suggested in several reviews.[53-55]

Although many of these policies have direct or indirect impacts on health and health equity, particularly in considering a "health in all policies" approach, a more intentional strategy of considering the health equity impacts of proposed policies is via a health impact assessment. Health impact assessments use existing published data or newly collected data to estimate the future health impacts of proposed policies or laws and thus can be used to weigh the potential benefits and risks of proposals (chapter 22). To improve health equity, such assessment tools should intentionally include dimensions of justice such as those described throughout this chapter and particularly the impacts of the unintended consequences that may arise when histories of racial and class segregation, environmental racism, and gentrification are not purposefully included in analyses.

CONCLUSION

Aristotle, in describing the ideal city-state, asserted that the best form of government is

Table 9.1. Examples of policy, planning, and financial tools and community-driven initiatives designed to fight displacement.

Tool	Definition	Strengths	Limitations	Example
Policy or planning tool				
Rent control	Regulations that support renters in obtaining, maintaining, and keeping affordable housing. Traditionally a government regulation that places a ceiling on rent for designated units.	Reduces burden from housing costs on renters, allowing them to remain in their homes and gain benefit from economic development in their neighborhood. Supports mixed-income communities.	Some real estate economists warn that limiting rent to below market rates will cause overconsumption of controlled apartments or reduce incentives to rent and therefore create counterproductive results by constraining housing supply.	In Vienna, Austria, limited-profit housing associations are subsidized housing indirectly controlled by the municipality. These units are developed by private developers through a city-regulated process and protected by the Limited-Profit Housing Act, which sets parameters for setting fair rent prices and managing repairs and quality.
Inclusionary zoning	Planning ordinance in which developers set aside a given share of new housing to be affordable for people with low to moderate incomes. Tends to range from 8% to 12% of units set aside in US cities to 30% or more in Europe (up to 56% in the city of Nantes in France)	Creates mixed-income communities. Utilizes private developer funds.	Difficult to enforce with complex requirements and a lack of uniform oversight for developers. Reliance on the private market makes inclusionary zoning policies more suitable to cities with a high demand for housing; they may be less successful in cities with less competitive real estate markets.	In 2005, the City of Atlanta, Georgia, began construction of the Atlanta BeltLine. To mitigate dramatic rises in housing prices around the BeltLine, the city developed the BeltLine Overlay District (roughly one-half mile on either side of the BeltLine corridor), where stand-alone or mixed-used multiunit buildings with at least ten units must include 15% affordable units.
Defense of single-family homes	"Single-family home" is the housing typology of a detached unit intended for a single household. Single-family home land use policies, such as single-family home zoning designations, prevent communities from building any type of housing in a given area aside from a single-family home.	Creates less-dense cities and therefore facilitates a different feel of urban life. Preserves smaller, more affordable homes that in many cases hold cultural significance to communities. Deters the conversion of smaller homes into multihousing condo complexes, which tend to be built for gentrifying residents.	Single-family zoning means *less* housing, and less housing supply may lead to more expensive housing.	When land in the La Bajada neighborhood of West Dallas, Texas, began attracting real estate investment, neighborhood organizations became concerned that the character of the neighborhood, a largely Hispanic neighborhood of small, single-family cottage-style homes, would be lost to development. Residents organized to approve a neighborhood stabilization overlay plan, meaning that the only types of development that can be built within the area are single-family homes that are no taller than 27 feet and facilities that support the community.

Table 9.1. Continued

Tool	Definition	Strengths	Limitations	Example
Financial tools				
Limitations or freezes to property tax	Taxes are usually calculated by a local government based on the value of the property. A limitation or freeze to property tax prevents property tax increases for eligible taxpayers.	Property taxes, especially in economically growing and gentrifying US cities, represent a large expense for most homeowners and remain when a mortgage is paid off, making property tax freezes and limitations a robust tool in places with high levels of home ownership but lower incomes.	Because many property tax limitation and freeze programs require residents to prove length of homeownership, eligible residents may be prevented from benefiting from these exemptions if they do not have access to clean titles. If not created specifically to support long-time homeowners, property tax reduction can become an incentive to developers and end up benefiting builders rather than homeowners.	Since 2014, Philadelphia, Pennsylvania, longtime homeowners (ten or more years of ownership) who have seen their property tax rate triple within a tax year and who make below 150% of the median income adjusted for family size can apply for real estate tax relief through the Longtime Owner Occupants Program (LOOP). Effectively, once approved, LOOP works by limiting the home's assessment increase to 50% and locking in that assessment for as long as the owners remain eligible.
Tax on vacant housing units	A tax on vacant housing is a citywide, or in some cases countywide, tax policy that requires property owners to pay a fee for unoccupied housing units. The objective of the tax is to ensure available housing in a city is utilized.	Encourages landowners to make more units of housing available to renters, which would then increase the overall housing stock. Increases housing supply without development.	Difficult to measure success when vacancy rates rely on self-reporting. Does not distinguish between different types of vacancy.	As a part of a larger policy initiative to address housing affordability, Vancouver, Canada, currently taxes vacant housing units through an Empty Houses Tax. The goal of the tax is to return empty or underutilized properties to the long-term rental market for Vancouver residents.
Rent subsidy or voucher	Rental subsidies or vouchers are a method to aid struggling and qualified households with affording rental units, either through a people-based program through the private market or a project-based program.	Reduces rent burden for recipients. Tenant-based vouchers do not limit recipients to certain (usually disinvested in) neighborhoods.	Because of how the value of the subsidy is calculated, many recipients continue to be rent burdened. Research shows that many recipients continue to stay in "disadvantaged" neighborhoods, mostly because landlords in wealthier neighborhoods do not show much trust in housing vouchers and their holders.	In Philadelphia , the Philadelphia Redevelopment Authority merged with nonprofit Philadelphia Housing Development Corporation to create a $2 million city-funded program to provide $300 monthly rent vouchers for tenants who are rent burdened (spending more than 30% of their income on rent) and live in income restricted properties. A second phase will specifically target aiding households that are also receiving federal tenant-based vouchers.

Table 9.1. Continued

Tool	Definition	Strengths	Limitations	Example
Community-driven initiatives				
Formal recognition of right to stay or return	Policies instigated by campaigns led by community activists to formally recognize the right to stay or right to return have been designed to ensure that the original residents and those with long-term connections to gentrifying neighborhoods are able to receive affordable housing within their communities. These strategies include assistance to renters, home buyers, and existing homeowners provided by municipal agencies.	Formally recognize the importance of honoring generational and emotional connection to place and the social impact of urban renewal policies on historically vulnerable groups.	Does not address the challenge residents will face as they continue to live in their changing neighborhoods.	The N/NE Neighborhood Housing Strategy in Portland, Oregon, includes loan assistance for home repair, down payment assistance for first-time homebuyers, and the creation of new affordable housing for Black residents who have been impacted by redlining, racial zoning, and eminent domain.
Community land trusts	Community land trusts are nonprofit, community-based organizations designed to ensure community control and ownership of land.	Guarantees affordable units to members of the trust for generations thanks to the purchase or construction of such units by local nonprofit organizations and socially oriented developers. Trusts typically aid tenants to avoid foreclosure by providing technical and real estate assistance.	Some groups voiced concern that residents of community land trusts units are limited for addressing intergenerational wealth gaps (especially between White residents and residents of color) due to the inability to sell their homes for full equity.	Dudley Square, Boston, residents were exposed to more than 1,500 vacant and contaminated lots in the 1980s. The Dudley Street Neighborhood Initiative (DSNI) began to hold meetings with residents and developing plans, which included sections on business development, affordable housing, social services and programs, education, and public spaces. In a rare circumstance, through means of eminent domain granted by the Boston Redevelopment Authority, the DSNI was able to acquire tax-delinquent properties and vacant private land known as the Dudley Triangle, which encompasses 30 acres. The Dudley Land Trust now includes 225 affordable housing units in addition to a playground, a community garden and greenhouse, and commercial and office space.

Source: Prepared by Ariella Levitch and Erin Monroe.

one in which inequities are absent and everyone can live happily. Scenarios of environmental injustice and subsequent urban renewal and green gentrification as described in this chapter illuminate a complex array of overlapping social and environmental determinants of health that must be considered together when determining whether a neighborhood is "healthy." They span from redlining and other racist zoning practices that have led to segregated cities and unequal urban development to poor diet due to lack of adequate access to food that is both healthy and affordable. It is within this paradox of inequality that the burden and benefits of urban environments for health must be considered.

Many working-class, minority, and immigrant communities face complex, compounded, and overlapping environmental and health injustices: eliminating sources of contamination, fighting climate risks, and attracting new environmental amenities while addressing neighborhood rebranding and dispossession, high-end centered investments, green gentrification, and displacement. Progressive community mobilization and policy initiatives can help remediate those injustices, but only if they combine greater investments in and *real* access to greening, nature-driven programs, and climate-protective infrastructure for marginalized groups with antidisplacement and prohousing rights policies. Only these bold and radical measures can help address deep historic inequalities, **structural inequality**, and structural racism and build sustainable, green, and healthy cities for all.

DISCUSSION QUESTIONS

1. How does environmental racism take place in cities, and what are its drivers and manifestations?
2. What role does urban greening play in producing environmental inequalities and health injustices?
3. How do the different types of environmental justice manifest in urban examples you are familiar with?
4. What urban policies and interventions can mitigate the impacts of gentrification on socially marginalized residents' lives, and how?
5. What land use planning tools and changes allow just and equitable urban greening?

DISCLOSURE OF COMPETING INTERESTS

Helen V. S. Cole reports serving as an unpaid advisory board member for the Safer Childbirth Cities project of Cities Challenge and Ariadne Labs (USA). She also served as an unpaid member of the workgroup to incorporate health criteria into the evaluation of urban planning initiatives of the Department of Infrastructure and Natural Space of the Barcelona Region (Diputació de Barcelona, Spain) and the Nature and Health roundtable of the Nature Conservation Network (Xarxa per a la Conservació de la Natura, Spain). During the time she was writing this chapter, her work was funded by a Juan de la Cierva incorporation fellowship (IJC2018-035322-I) from the Spanish Ministry of Science and Innovation. Her research also supports the María de Maeztu Programme for Units of Excellence of the Spanish Ministry of Science and Innovation (CEX2019-000940-M) at the Institute for Environmental Science and Technology (ICTA) from the Universitat Autònoma de Barcelona (UAB).

Isabelle Anguelovski reports serving as an unpaid advisory board member of the Science Plan and of the Barcelona Pact of the Ajuntament de Barcelona. During the time she was writing this chapter, her work was funded by an ERC Starting Grant GreenLulus (GA678034) and the H2020 collaborative project Naturvation (730243) from the European Union. Her research also supports the María de Maeztu Programme for Units of Excellence of the Spanish Ministry of Science and Innovation (CEX2019-000940-M) at the Institute for Environmental Science and Technology (ICTA) from the Universitat Autònoma de Barcelona (UAB).

REFERENCES

1. Douglas EM, Kirshen PH, Paolisso M, et al. Coastal flooding, climate change and environmental justice: identifying obstacles and incentives for adaptation in two metropolitan Boston Massachusetts communities. *Mitigation and Adaptation Strategies for Global Change*. 2012;17(5):537-562. doi:10.1007/s11027-011-9340-8

2. Anguelovski I, Triguero-Mas M, Connolly JJT, et al. Gentrification and health in two global cities: a call to identify impacts for socially-vulnerable residents. *Cities & Health*. Published online 2019:1-10.

3. Gould KA, Lewis TL. *Green Gentrification: Urban Sustainability and the Struggle for Environmental Justice*. Routledge; 2017.

4. Park L, Pellow D. *The Slums of Aspen: Immigrants vs. the Environment in America's Eden*. New York University Press; 2011.

5. Anguelovski I. From toxic sites to parks as (green) LULUs? New challenges of inequity, privilege, gentrification, and exclusion for urban environmental justice. *Journal of Planning Literature*. 2016;31(1):23-36. doi:10.1177/0885412215610491

6. Sugrue TJ. *The Origins of the Urban Crisis: Race and Inequality in Postwar Detroit*. Princeton University Press; 2005.

7. Checker M. *Polluted Promises: Environmental Racism and the Search for Justice in a Southern Town*. New York University Press; 2005.

8. Taylor D. *Toxic Communities: Environmental Racism, Industrial Pollution, and Residential Mobility*. New York University Press; 2014.

9. Freudenberg N, Pastor M, Israel B. Strengthening community capacity to participate in making decisions to reduce disproportionate environmental exposures. *American Journal of Public Health*. 2011;101(Suppl 1). doi:10.2105/AJPH.2011.300265

10. Brender JD, Maantay JA, Chakraborty J. Residential proximity to environmental hazards and adverse health outcomes. *American Journal of Public Health*. 2011;101(Suppl 1):S37-52. doi:10.2105/AJPH.2011.300183

11. US General Accounting Office. Siting of Hazardous Waste: Demographics of People Near Waste Facilities; 1983. https://www.gao.gov/assets/rced-83-168.pdf

12. United Church of Christ Commission for Racial Justice. Toxic Wastes and Race in the United States: A National Report on the Racial and Socio-Economic Characteristics of Communities Surrounding Hazardous Waste Sites; 1987.

13. Bullard RD. Ecological inequities and the New South: Black communities under siege. *Journal of Ethnic Studies*. 1990;17(4):101-115.

14. Mohai P, Saha R. Which came first, people or pollution? Assessing the disparate siting and post-siting demographic change hypotheses of environmental justice. *Environmental Research Letters*. 2015;10(11). doi:10.1088/1748-9326/10/11/115008

15. Bullard RD, Mohai P, Saha R, Wright B. *Toxic Wastes and Race at Twenty: 1987–2007*. United Church of Christ Justice and Witness Ministries; 2007.

16. Wilson SM, Fraser-Rahim H, Williams E, et al. Assessment of the distribution of toxic release inventory facilities in metropolitan Charleston: an environmental justice case study. *American Journal of Public Health*. 2012;102(10):1974-1980. doi:10.2105/AJPH.2012.300700

17. Gould L, Cummings B. Duwamish Valley Cumulative Health Impacts Analysis; 2013.

18. Watts N, Adger WN, Agnolucci P. Health and climate change: policy responses to protect public health. *Environnement, Risques et Sante*. 2015;14(6):466-468. doi:10.1016/S0140-6736(15)60854-6

19. Alkon A, Guthman J. *The New Food Activism: Opposition, Cooperation, and Collective Action*. University of California Press; 2017.

20. Joassart-Marcelli P, Bosco F. Alternative food and gentrification: farmers markets, community gardens and the transformation of urban neighborhoods. In: Curran W, Hamilton T, eds. *Just Green Enough*. Routledge; 2018.

21. Grove M, Ogden L, Pickett S, et al. The legacy effect: understanding how segregation and environmental injustice unfold over time in Baltimore. *Annals of the American Association of Geographers*. 2018;108(2):524-537. doi:10.1080/24694452.2017.1365585

22. Watkins SL, Mincey SK, Vogt J, Sweeney SP. Is planting equitable? An examination of the spatial distribution of nonprofit urban tree-planting programs by canopy cover, income, race, and ethnicity. *Environment and Behavior*. 2017;49(4):452-482. doi:10.1177/0013916516636423

23. Triguero-Mas M, Dadvand P, Cirach M, et al. Natural outdoor environments and mental and physical health: relationships and mechanisms. *Environment International*. 2015;77:35-41. doi:10.1016/j.envint.2015.01.012

24. Grahn P, Stigsdotter UK. The relation between perceived sensory dimensions of urban green space and stress restoration. *Landscape and Urban Planning*. 2010;94(3-4):264-275. doi:10.1016/j.landurbplan.2009.10.012

25. Finney C. Black Faces, *White Spaces: Reimagining the Relationship of African Americans to the Great Outdoors*. University of North Carolina Press; 2014.

26. Franzosa E, Cole H. The gentrification of American healthcare. Barcelona Lab for Urban Environmental Justice and Sustainability. Published 2018. Accessed November 25, 2020. http://www.bcnuej.org/2018/06/21/the-gentrification-of-american-healthcare/

27. Tsui J, Hirsch JA, Bayer FJ, et al. Patterns in geographic access to health care facilities across neighborhoods in the United States based on data from the national establishment time-series between 2000 and 2014. *JAMA Network Open*. 2020;3(5):e205105. doi:10.1001/jamanetworkopen.2020.5105

28. Agyeman J, Schlosberg D, Craven L, Matthews C. Trends and directions in environmental justice: from inequity to everyday life, community, and just sustainabilities. *Annual Review of Environment and Resources*. 2016;41(1):321-340. doi:10.1146/annurev-environ-110615-090052

29. Vásquez-Vera H, Palència L, Magna I, Mena C, Neira J, Borrell C. The threat of home eviction and its effects on health through the equity lens: a systematic review. *Social Science and Medicine*. 2017;175:199-208. doi:10.1016/j.socscimed.2017.01.010

30. Vale LJ. *Purging the Poorest: Public Housing and the Design Politics of Twice-Cleared Communities*. University of Chicago Press; 2013.

31. Summers BT. *Black in Place: The Spatial Aesthetics of Race in a Post-Chocolate City*. University of North Carolina Press; 2019.

32. Lees L; Slater T; Wyly EK. *The Gentrification Reader*. Routledge; 2010.

33. Oscilowicz E, Honey-Rosés J, Anguelovski I, Triguero-Mas M, Cole H. Young families and children in gentrifying neighbourhoods: how gentrification reshapes use and perception of green play spaces. *Local Environment*. 2020;25(10):765-786. doi:10.1080/13549839.2020.1835849

34. Gibbons J, Barton MS. The association of minority self-rated health with black versus white gentrification. *Journal of Urban Health*. 2016;93(6):909-922.

35. Dragan KL, Ellen IG, Glied SA. Gentrification and the health of low-income children in New York City. *Health Affairs*. 2019;38(9):1425-1432.

36. Connolly JJT. From Jacobs to the just city: a foundation for challenging the green planning orthodoxy. *Cities*. 2019;91:64-70. doi:10.1016/j.cities.2018.05.011

37. Garcia-Lamarca M, Anguelovski I, Cole H, et al. Urban green boosterism and city affordability: for whom is the "branded" green city? *Urban Studies*. Published December 11, 2019. doi:10.1177/0042098019885330

38. Pulido L. Geographies of race and ethnicity II. *Progress in Human Geography*. 2017;41(4):524-533. doi:10.1177/0309132516646495

39. Rigolon A, Németh J. Green gentrification or "just green enough": do park location, size and function affect whether a place gentrifies or not? *Urban Studies*. 2020;57(2):402-420. doi:10.1177/0042098019849380

40. Anguelovski I, Connolly JJT, Masip L, Pearsall H. Assessing green gentrification in historically disenfranchised neighborhoods: a longitudinal and spatial analysis of Barcelona. *Urban Geography*. 2018;39(3):458-491. doi:10.1080/02723638.2017.1349987

41. Immergluck D, Balan T. Sustainable for whom? Green urban development, environmental gentrification, and the Atlanta Beltline. *Urban Geography*. 2018;39(4):546-562. doi:10.1080/02723638.2017.1360041

42. Shokry G, Connolly JJ, Anguelovski I. Understanding climate gentrification and shifting landscapes of protection and vulnerability in green resilient Philadelphia. *Urban Climate*. 2020;31:100539. doi:10.1016/j.uclim.2019.100539

43. Anguelovski I, Connolly JJT, Pearsall H, et al. Why green "climate gentrification" threatens poor and vulnerable populations. *Proceedings of the National Academy of Sciences of the United States of America*. 2019;116(52):26139-26143. doi:10.1073/pnas.1920490117

44. Fullilove MT. Root shock: the consequences of African American dispossession. *Journal of Urban Health*. 2001;78(1):72-80. doi:10.1093/jurban/78.1.72

45. Cole HVS, Lamarca MG, Connolly JJT, Anguelovski I. Are green cities healthy and equitable? Unpacking the relationship between health, green space and gentrification. *Journal of Epidemiology and Community Health*. 2017;71(11). doi:10.1136/jech-2017-209201

46. Pearsall H, Anguelovski I. Contesting and resisting environmental gentrification: responses to new paradoxes and challenges for urban environmental justice. *Sociological Research Online*. 2016;21(3):121-127. doi:10.5153/sro.3979

47. Hoffmann ML. *Bike Lanes Are White Lanes: Bicycle Advocacy and Urban Planning*. University of Nebraska Press; 2016.

48. Curran W, Hamilton T. *Just Green Enough: Urban Development and Environmental Gentrification*. Routledge; 2017.

49. Schlosberg D. Theorising environmental justice: the expanding sphere of a discourse. *Environmental Politics*. 2013;22(1):37-55. doi:10.1080/09644016.2013.755387

50. Fainstein S. *The Just City*. Cornell University Press; 2010.

51. Pellow DN. Toward a critical environmental justice studies: Black Lives Matter as an environmental justice challenge. *Du Bois Review*. 2016;13(2):221-236. doi:10.1017/S1742058X1600014X

52. Pérez del Pulgar C, Anguelovski I, Connolly J. Toward a green and playful city: understanding the social and political production of children's relational wellbeing in Barcelona. *Cities*. 2020;96:102438. doi:10.1016/j.cities.2019.102438

53. Aboelata M, Bennett R, Yanez E, Bonilla A, Akhavan N. Healthy development without displacement: realizing the vision of healthy communities for all. Prevention Institute. July 2017 https://www.preventioninstitute.org/publications/healthy-development-without-displacement-realizing-vision-healthy-communities-all

54. Allbee A, Johnson R, Lubell J. Preserving, protecting, and expanding affordable housing: a policy toolkit for public health. 2015. http://www.changelabsolutions.org/sites/default/files/Preserving_Affordable_Housing-POLICY-TOOLKIT_FINAL_20150401.pdf

55. Causa Justa|Just Cause. Development without displacement: resisting gentrification in the Bay Area. April 2014. https://ncg.org/resources/development-without-displacement-resisting-gentrification-bay-area

CHAPTER 10

HEALTHY PLACES ACROSS THE LIFE SPAN

Nisha Botchwey, Nsedu Obot Witherspoon, Jordana L. Maisel, and Howard Frumkin

KEY POINTS

- The built environment "fits" different people differently. The concept of "person-environment fit" focuses on the need for built environments to accommodate people across a range of personal characteristics.
- Certain life circumstances require particular attention to ensure that the built environment promotes safety, health, and thriving. These include childhood, old age, and disabilities such as reduced mobility, vision, hearing, or cognition. Everybody experiences one or more of these circumstances at some point in their life.
- Many design strategies serve the needs of all these populations and therefore offer multiple benefits. Accordingly, "universal design" aims to make buildings, products, and environments accessible to all people, regardless of age, disability, or other factors.
- The key to optimizing health and development via the built environment for children, seniors, and people with functional disabilities is through understanding the nature and vulnerabilities of these population(s) and the environments that they live within. Solutions to vulnerabilities must be identified and implemented collaboratively with all the populations impacted.

INTRODUCTION

In Central City, a multigenerational family moves into a "livable neighborhood" with a range of housing choices and a ten-minute walk to everything that they need—a grocery store, shops and restaurants, parks, playgrounds, libraries, recreation centers, schools, medical and dental offices, and places of worship. Everybody in the family, from the grandparents to the children, can easily walk, ride a bike or scooter, or take public transit to get to work, school, a hospital, theater and arts venues, and natural areas within thirty minutes. The sidewalks, crosswalks, and curb cuts are all maintained and allow for safe passage. Grandma is delighted that she can get to the nearby YMCA in her wheelchair. The kids love the freedom of walking to and from school on their own as their friends along the route join them. Despite Grandpa's failing eyesight, every afternoon he walks to the neighborhood market, with help from the auditory cues at each street crossing, letting him know that it is safe to cross. Mom or Dad usually meets him there on their way home from the train to pick up any needed dinner ingredients before a relaxing walk home.

The vulnerabilities faced by seniors, children, and people with disabilities and low-income populations are due to personal characteristics and conditions in the social and built environments. The idea that community design impacts health, especially the vulnerable populations covered in this chapter, has long been recognized.

This chapter presents an overview of "person-environment fit" and ways the built environment can reduce vulnerabilities, with a particular focus across the life course (children and older adults) and on people with disabilities. We explore universal design as a systematic strategy to reduce vulnerabilities. Finally, we close with a reminder of the ethical codes from public health and built environment professions that require inclusive and nondiscriminatory practice, which implies accommodating all three populations discussed in this chapter.

HEALTHY PLACES ACROSS THE LIFE SPAN: CONCEPTS AND THEORIES

The **person-environment fit theory** explains how a person's individual characteristics influence and are influenced by the social and built environment in which the person lives, works, and plays. The environment fit across the life course and the levels of support or lack of support for health-promoting outcomes, from the individual level to social and economic policies within the environment, impact the person's overall well-being and resilience to future challenges. The goal of a healthy place across the life span is alignment of the development stage and ability status with the environment (homes, schools, workplaces, and other settings) to optimize safe and appropriate growth opportunities for individuals. When the person-environment fit is not aligned, **maladaptive behavior** (sedentary lifestyle; withdrawal or isolation; self-medication with tobacco, alcohol, and drugs) and greater vulnerabilities across populations may result. However, when the built environment accommodates people, whatever their abilities and circumstances, rather than compelling them to cope with unsuitable design, buildings, parks, and neighborhoods, the resulting **adaptive behavior** (aging in place, proactive coping, social engagement) enhances well-being for all individuals.

VULNERABLE POPULATIONS: CHILDREN, OLDER ADULTS, AND PEOPLE WITH DISABILITIES

A person can become **vulnerable** by the presence of a risk factor (such as poverty, underlying disease, or a child's inexperience), the absence of a needed resource in the environment (such as **zero-step entrances**), or both. Populations may be made vulnerable by their age, such as children and older adults; their disability and health status, such as people with mobility, vision, hearing, and cognitive impairments or chronic health conditions; their socioeconomic status, such as persons with low income or little education (discussed in chapter 9); and their isolation, such as people segregated by race, ethnicity, age, or geography (as in a rural area) (discussed in chapters 2, 7, 8, and 9). Multiple vulnerabilities can overlap—for example, disability and old age—and vulnerabilities may be superimposed on one another and on poverty, racism, or social isolation (figure 10.1). The following sections explore three populations—children, older adults, and people with disabilities—considering for each their demographics, their vulnerabilities (micro to macro neighborhood scales), and built environment solutions to assure their health and well-being.

Children

According to the US Health and Human Service's Office of Disease Prevention and Health Promotion, there are five stages of childhood, from pregnancy to young adulthood, with overlapping start and end years for each stage.[1] The prenatal period extends through pregnancy to birth and is the time of in utero development. Early childhood is usually defined as birth to year eight and is a time of tremendous physical, cognitive, socioemotional, and language development. At birth, the nervous, respiratory, reproductive, and immune systems are not yet fully developed. Young children breathe more rapidly and take in more air in proportion to their body weight than adults. They also have higher metabolic

Figure 10.1. A wheelchair-enabled swing in the Taupo Domain, New Zealand.
Source: Public domain courtesy Ingolfson

ceptible to environmental hazards, making the places where they spend the most time during this stage, such as homes, child care facilities, and schools (chapter 15), critical built environments to address. Contact with nature stimulates creativity and problem-solving skills that are key to executive function development. Evidence shows that children who spend time in nature manifest reduced attention deficit hyperactivity disorder symptoms and increased cognition, concentration, and academic performance (chapter 16).[4-6] Time spent outdoors, however, entails risks that must be managed. For example, drowning is the leading cause of death from injury among one- to four-year-old children in the United States.[7] It is critical that an adult supervise children while they are near and in pools, lakes, and other bodies of water. Children should also learn to swim and have access to a flotation device when in water to help prevent drowning.

Middle childhood extends from ages six to twelve. In this stage, children develop foundational skills for building healthy social relationships and learn roles that will prepare them for adolescence and adulthood. During this stage, children begin to face physical and emotional challenges as they approach their teenage years. Puberty can start at any age from eight to twelve for girls and nine to fourteen for boys; the variable age of onset and variable rates of maturation can pose challenges for children. Early childhood exposures to hormone disruptors such as phthalates and bisphenol A or to neurotoxins such as lead can disrupt normal growth and development. Middle childhood is also when the ability to go outside and play and navigate the neighborhood safely is critical. In addition to water- and road-related injuries, there is an increased risk for bike crashes, injury from running and playing on playgrounds, and ingesting poisonous products. Effective public health solutions to these risks include using booster seats, wearing seat belts, using bike helmets, taking caution on playground equipment, wearing

rates and a higher proportionate intake of food and liquid than do adults. Children have different behavior patterns than adults that place them at increased risk for harmful exposures, such as hand-to-mouth behavior as part of their learning and development. Children also benefit significantly through connecting with and spending time in nature. This interaction is an essential part of their development and growing appreciation for the environment.

The need to keep all children safe is a global issue. Annually, close to one million children die from preventable injuries, with the majority in low-wealth communities.[2] Injuries account for the majority of deaths and disabilities in children under age nineteen, with motor vehicle crashes the leading cause.[3] Injury prevention, as discussed in chapter 5, is realistic and achievable.

Cognitive, socioemotional, physical, and language development all happen in this critical early childhood stage. All children are sus-

swimming float aids, learning to swim, and keeping cleaning agents and other toxic products away from children.

Adolescents are ages ten to seventeen, another important time of biological changes when they experience puberty, explore, learn, and grow in their abilities to be independent. During adolescence, the body usually experiences a growth spurt, which is a time of very rapid increases in height, weight, and changes in the brain.[8] Puberty, which also happens during adolescence, is the time when sexual organs mature. These physical and psychological changes often occur at different rates. Again, early life exposures to harmful chemicals can cause serious challenges that may alter the onset and course of puberty. Several environmental endocrine disruptors (chemicals that interfere with the development of the hormonal systems) that significantly influence the normal course of puberty have been identified.[9] Many everyday products contain endocrine disruptors, including some plastic bottles and containers, liners of metal food cans, detergents, flame retardants, food, toys, cosmetics, and pesticides. In addition to injury concerns during childhood, adolescents are at risk as new drivers through higher exposures to alcohol and other drugs, increased suicide, and crime victimization concerns.

Finally, young adults, ages eighteen to twenty-five, are at a stage of transition when they face significant social and economic challenges with little organizational support at a time when society expects them to take on adult responsibilities and obligations, often with limited support. Racial health disparities in obesity, teen and unintended pregnancy, tooth decay, and educational achievement persist in this population, especially those living in poverty. Globally and in the United States among this age group, suicide is the second leading cause of death, and homicide is the fourth leading cause of death globally.[10,11] Homicides involving firearms have been the leading cause of death for young African American males since 1969.[12,13] Adverse childhood experiences contribute to these morbidity and mortality outcomes and can be behaviorally mediated[14] through family, school, neighborhoods, media exposure, intentional cultural responsiveness in health care, attention to disparate health, academic and economic outcomes, and positive youth development interventions.[15]

The environment children live in today is vastly different than previous generations. Dramatic expansions in technology, information, population, and material goods marked the end of the twentieth century. Some of these changes, especially manufactured chemicals, can impact not only the environment around us, but also our physical and mental health and that of our children. Adults and children are exposed to environmental health issues through the built, biological, and chemical environments.

Children in particular are especially vulnerable to environmental health issues and injury because they are constantly in a dynamic state of growth. This period spans the fetal stage and continues through adolescence, a dynamic state of growth when cells are multiplying and organ systems are developing rapidly. During this time, physiologically, children are very different from adults. Children are curious, exploring, and increasing mobility and activities, all of which provide opportunities for falls, burns, sports injuries, and poisonings.

Globally, environmental exposures contribute to the five major causes of death and illness among children under five years of age: perinatal illness, respiratory disease, diarrheal diseases, vector-borne diseases, and physical injuries. Air pollution is one of the most significant environmental risks to children, with more than half a million annually losing their lives to respiratory diseases due to indoor and outdoor air pollution and secondhand smoke (see chapter 4).[16] Poverty and lack of nutrition are the common risk factors linking to all these diseases. In the United States, one in forty children has a blood lead level considered unsafe, whereas 50 percent of the two million pesticide poisoning incidents each year involve children under the age of six and usually at home.[17,18] Both exposures can cause neurotoxicity during brain development, and pesticides are linked to certain forms of childhood cancer incidence.

Reducing or preventing injury is important to overall health and safety risks in early childhood. Use of baby gates and rails to prevent falls; preventing lead and pesticide exposures; promoting high-quality indoor air to reduce asthma incidence and severity in child care, schools, and home; safe streets and community designs to promote wellness and connection to nature; and protection from abuse all hold health and safety implications for children.

Children of color continue to experience disparities when it comes to the health and safety provisions available to them. African American and Latino children experience higher rates of traumatic injury and mortality.[19] Equity in health is an ethical and social justice issue.[20] Adequately addressing the obvious inequities that children of racial and ethnic groups endure will improve the health care and health status of all children.[21] Having youth play an active role in advocating for these improvements is critical to building their **agency** and well-being. The Youth Engagement and Action for Health program (box 10.1) is an excellent tool that communities can use with youth to help them build their abilities to create healthy change in their own communities. Overall, we cannot successfully address children's environmental health concerns without addressing the underlying determinants of health (chapter 1) that are at the root of childhood injuries.[21]

Older Adults

Adults age sixty-five or older generally face a gradual decline in physical and mental capacity, putting them at greater risk of disease and death. This is also typically the life

---

BOX 10.1 YOUTH ENGAGEMENT AND ACTION FOR HEALTH (YEAH!) YOUTH RENOVATE THEIR PARK IN LIHUE, HAWAII

Youth Engagement and Action for Health (YEAH!) is a fourteen-week curriculum to engage youth participants in planning and implementing projects designed to create healthier neighborhoods. Youth are trained to conduct neighborhood assessments, select a meaningful project, and advocate for change with local policy and decision makers. YEAH! helps youth understand how the design and function of their school or community impact their health, develop an action plan that can lead to changes, and advocate for these changes with decision-makers in their own community.

The Lihue, Hawaii, YEAH! club focused on a park renovation in 2018. Members noted that their neighborhood park was underutilized despite its prime location near Lihue's business district. They surveyed people utilizing the park—including a nearby fire department, as well as homeless men and women—to envision a park inclusive for all residents. The ten students presented their ideas to the county council, and a month later the mayor and council unanimously agreed to grant $80,000 to the redevelopment of Kalena Park. A new action group was also formed, the Kalena Park Community Action Group, comprising residents ranging from middle school youth to senior citizens. "Young people are key to effective community decision-making and positive outcomes for local residents," said Bev Brody, director of Get Fit Kauai. "The YEAH! project taught a group of our young people to become agents of change as they learned how to create better places for themselves and others to live."[a] Since the presentation, the park hosted a movie night for community members and their families using a large inflatable movie screen. More than one hundred people attended the event, and park renovations have progressed.

REFERENCE

a. Brody, B. Personal interview. March 9, 2019.

---

stage when people face numerous transitions, such as moving from full-time work to retirement, moving homes to somewhere more **age-friendly**, and facing an increased number of deaths of close loved ones.[22] The vulnerabilities that older adults confront include sensory and balance deficits, trip and fall risks, mobility restrictions, cognitive impairment, isolation, and risk of depression. Therefore, older adults may be particularly vulnerable to environmental hazards such as unsafe pedestrian infrastructure, air pollution and extreme weather events, and settings that impede social connections (see chapters 2, 4, and 8).

From 2010 to 2060, the over-sixty-five US population is projected to grow from forty million to ninety-four million, and the over-eighty-five population is projected to grow from six million to nineteen million. It is estimated that there will be more than half a million centenarians in the United States in 2060.[23] According to World Population Prospects 2019,[24] by 2050, one in six people in the world will be over the age of sixty-five, up from one in eleven in 2019.

Loss of Cognitive Ability

Although dementia and mild cognitive impairment are both common with aging, even those who do not experience these conditions may experience subtle cognitive changes.[25] Some features of the built environment may affect cognitive decline. Surprisingly, cognitive function in older adults is less in cities than in rural areas, despite exposures to noise, air pollution, and other factors associated with cognitive loss.[26] Attributes of the built environment that seem to support cognitive function include land use mix (which facilitates physical activity and social interaction), access to services and recreational facilities, and natural settings[27,28] (although the benefits of natural settings seem to vary from city to city, suggesting that other factors also play a role[29]). Conversely, poor quality microenvironments disorderly and poorly maintained spaces—may hasten cognitive decline.[30]

Some features of the built environment support function in people with cognitive decline.[31] These include ready visual access to frequently used rooms, clear navigational aids such as signs and landmarks, opportunities for both privacy and social interaction, support for movement and engagement in activities, and presence of familiar objects and furniture.

Loss of Hearing, Balance, Vision

As aging continues, the way that senses pass along information changes. A certain amount of stimulation is needed to be aware of a sensation. Aging demands more stimulation to be aware of the sensation.[32] Individual-level devices such as glasses, hearing aids, walkers, and other assistive devices, along with lifestyle changes and built environment interventions, are generally needed to address challenges many in this age group face.

- Hearing loss: According to the World Health Organization, hearing loss or difficulty impacts quality of life for more than 5 percent of the world's population, 466 million people.[33] Among seniors, it negatively impacts communication and can lead to social isolation and loneliness (chapters 7 and 8). Improving acoustics and reducing background noise to support clearer hearing, and both installing quality lighting and providing helpful signage to optimize use of visual cues reduce barriers for this population. During the COVID-19 pandemic, manufacturers produced transparent face masks to promote lipreading and easier interpretation of facial expressions to promote communication.

- Balance: Approximately one-third of people sixty-five and older experience falls every year. Multifactorial interventions that combine individual interventions like exercise, environment modifications, or medication review based on individual risk assessments are proven to reduce the rate of falls compared with usual care or attention control—a rebalancing of

the vigilance and arousal subsystems.[34] Interventions are recommended at multiple levels and can involve assistive technology, education on fall risk, home modifications, and community modifications. Place-based interventions include nonslip strips on stairs and slopes, automatic wayfinding lights after dark and at entrances, clutter removal, handrails, sloped walkways, and street corners with brightly colored paint, truncated domes, and zero-step entries[35] (figure 10.2).

- Vision challenges: Across the globe, 2.2 billion people have a vision impairment.[36] The comorbidities "depression, anxiety, low self-esteem and insecurity, social isolation, stress, mental fatigue, cognitive decline and dementia, reduced mobility, [and] falls" all contribute to reduced quality of life and early death. In addition to interventions noted for balance concerns, those built environment strategies

helpful for low vision or blindness include technology innovations with "GPS units, ultrasonic detectors, and smartphone applications ... accessible pedestrian signals, smart paint, talking signs, autonomous vehicles, integrated travel systems and devices that communicate between the pedestrian and the built environment."[37(p320)] See figure 10.3.

Housing and Aging

Many older adults live in unsafe or inadequate dwellings for their physical needs, and this will likely only get worse as the population ages. As of 2010, 3.6 percent of individuals age sixty-five and older resided in group quarters or nursing facilities.[38,39] As of 2018, according to the US Department of Health and Human Services Administration for Community Living and Administration on Aging's "Profile of Older Americans," 28 percent of individuals age sixty-five and older who live in households

Figure 10.2. Curb ramps support safe transitions for populations, especially children, seniors, and people with disabilities, as they cross the street. Features such as brightly colored paint and truncated domes provide detectable warnings for people with visual impairments of their exit from or entrance to a sidewalk.
Source: www.ped-bikeimages .org/Dan Burden

Figure 10.3. A Braille street sign at a pedestrian crossing in Brisbane for people with vision impairments that Australia implemented as an initiative of the city council.
Source: Wikimedia Commons courtesy John Robert McPherson. https://creativecommons.org/licenses/by-sa/4.0/deed.en

(not group facilities) live alone and remain in their homes and age in place. Many of them live in **naturally occurring retirement communities (NORCs)** where most of their neighbors are seniors. Most of the residents are women because they live longer than men and have less support and fewer financial resources to move to an alternative residence. In many low- and middle-income countries, older adults reside with their extended family rather than on their own or in a group facility. In the United States, the homeownership rate for individuals age sixty-five and older is 80 percent, comprising primarily older housing stock in the suburbs.

Fifty percent of households with residents age fifty and older in the United States live in suburban and exurban areas.[10] The geography of these environments requires personal vehicles to meet mobility needs like shopping, running errands, visiting family and friends, going out for dinner and entertainment, and accessing medical and public services. However, many older adults have physical and cognitive limitations. Ninety percent of trips by people age sixty-five and older are by private vehicles. Only 2.2 percent of trips by people over age sixty-five were on public transit in 2009, and 9 percent of trips by people age sixty-five and older are by foot (walking). Almost all older adults who do not drive are women.[41]

Thus, the design of the built environment plays an integral role in addressing the health and safety implications of housing and mobility for older adults in the United States and around the world. Given the state of housing and older adults, it is recommended that communities institute policies and designs that promote accessibility and allow for safe and flexible housing options (like accessory dwelling units and shared housing). Additionally, to address the acute health challenges that occur in households where seniors live alone, the linkage between health care, housing, and community- and home-based arrangements should be improved by modifying zoning and building codes and other local regulatory or institutional barriers to promote **aging in place** (building scale) and **aging in community** (neighborhood scale). To increase the survivability of older drivers and passengers, road conditions, signage, lighting, signalization, and the availability, accessibility, and safety of public transit should be improved. Additionally, safety, wayfinding, lighting, and siting facilities near streets with lower traffic volumes and better pedestrian facilities and roads are important interventions to encourage walking, especially among older women.[42,43]

People with Disabilities

Unlike age, **disability** is not an intrinsic feature of a person; it is a matter of person-environment fit. The International Classification of Function, Disability and Health defines disablement, or the act of becoming disabled, using a biomedical understanding of impairment and the social conception of disability.[43] Disability results from a mismatch between the goals and abilities of an individual and the demands of both the social and physical environment. This definition suggests that all people, at one time or another, are "disabled" by the demands of the environment, such as when they are sick, injured, tired, in an unfamiliar place, carrying a heavy item, dealing with adverse conditions, homeless, or victims of disasters. Thus, everyone will have a disability at some point in their lives, even if that means ordinary childhood and old age development stages and functions.

According to the World Health Organization's World Report on Disability, "about 15 percent of the world's population lives with some form of disability, of whom 2 to 4 percent experience significant difficulties in functioning."[44] Within the United States, about 40.1 million of the civilian noninstitutionalized population (12.6 percent) report a severe disability.[45] Among the total population, approximately 20.8 million (7.0 percent) have difficulty with ambulation, 15.1 million (5.1 percent) with cognitive functioning, 11.4 million (3.6 percent) with hearing, and 7.4 million (2.3 percent) with vision.[45] About 5.5 million adults use a wheelchair, and another 18.4 million use walking aids.[44] Adults age sixty-five and older use a wheelchair about four times the rate of adults between eighteen and sixty-four years, and they use walking aids about five times as often.[46] According to the US Centers for Disease Control and Prevention (CDC) Disability and Health System, there were a variety of disparities in the prevalence of disability across various races and ethnicities: the proportion of American Indians/Alaska Natives, Black non-Hispanic, Hispanic, Asian, Native Hawaiian/Pacific Islander, and White non-Hispanic with a disability are 30 percent, 25 percent, 17 percent, 10 percent, 17 percent, and 20 percent, respectively.[47] Many of these racial and ethnic demographic driven sources of vulnerability are only likely to increase in the near future as the prevalence of disability continues to rise. The rapid increase in the older population is increasing the prevalence of disability and driving demand for access to healthy built environments and safer transportation options.[48]

Millions of Americans experience barriers in the built environment and mobility throughout their communities[49,50]; these barriers are worse for individuals with disabilities who more frequently need health care, require greater accessibility to transportation, and have lower incomes than the general population.[51] Without access to housing, employment, transportation, or community activities, individuals with disabilities are more likely to be dependent on others, excluded from services and social contact, and become stuck in a disability-poverty cycle,[52] which in turn can lead to social isolation, depression, and health deterioration.[53,54] The COVID-19 pandemic highlighted and exacerbated these disparities (box 10.2).[55]

The current state of the built environment and public transportation systems in many communities is a major barrier to social participation, especially employment, for many individuals with disabilities. Commercial and public buildings are key sites of employment, civic engagement, and social activities. People with disabilities report being employed less than half as much as their nondisabled counterparts[56] and socializing, eating out, and attending religious services less often than their nondisabled counterparts.[57] Access to health care facilities and services is critical for people with disabilities to manage their health conditions.[58] There are also important design challenges in streetscape environments associated with public rights-of-way, including excessive cross-slopes, rough and slippery surface materials, irregular pavement, and lack of curb ramps. Many injuries among wheelchair users are related to the poor condition of outdoor ramps.[59] Any barrier to outdoor mobility further impedes the ability for individuals with disabilities to function independently

BOX 10.2 VULNERABLE POPULATIONS AND COVID-19

When COVID-19 forced people around the world to stay home, work remotely, and learn online, children, older adults, and people with disabilities realized different challenges. Children went from having the opportunity to leave home for school and other places to socially engage with friends and experience different environments to being in just one environment. This further restriction of their home range exposed them to greater exposure to toxins and risks in their home environments. For some children, internet access or an appropriate study space was not available, creating a cascade of academic setbacks for already disadvantaged populations.

Older adults realized greater social isolation, and existing technology barriers further kept them separated from their community. Some children and older adults experienced food insecurity, not receiving the regular meals previously available at school or at a senior center or other community institutions. Institutions like the YMCA of Metro Atlanta stepped in, providing child care for children of frontline workers, food distribution, and assistance with schoolwork.

and participate in the community.[60] A lack of "first/last mile" connectivity—poor pedestrian access to and from fixed transit route stops—is a key barrier along the travel chain.[61] Approximately 3.6 million people with disabilities cannot leave their homes because of transportation difficulties.[62] In 2020, a United Nations conference on COVID-19 emphasized the importance of community mobility and the need for affordable, accessible, and safe public transport to save lives and livelihoods.[63]

Improving housing is also a critical issue since the existing housing stock in the United States lacks basic accessibility features and close to 80 percent of persons ages fifty and older prefer to age in place[64]; only one-third of housing units are potentially modifiable, and less than 1 percent are wheelchair accessible.[65] Many houses have steps at all entrances and hallways and doorways that are too narrow for users of wheelchairs or walkers. In addition, many people with intellectual disabilities lack safe, affordable, accessible, and integrated housing.[66] These are not insignificant challenges. Researchers project that the number of households in the United States with at least one resident with a disability will almost double by 2050, rising from 17.1 million to 33.2 million.[67]

Most highly developed countries, and many less developed countries, have laws that ensure some level of physical access to the built environment for people with disabilities. For example, in the United States, the Americans with Disabilities Act (ADA; 1990, 2008) requires accessibility to all types of buildings with the exception of privately financed housing, and the Fair Housing Act and its amendments (1968, 1988) requires accessibility to multi-family housing. These accessibility laws have related guidelines that commonly cover the design of entries, corridors, restrooms, and other spaces, particularly for people using wheeled mobility devices, such as wheelchairs. Despite this limited scope, accessibility codes, generally speaking, are a positive result of the disability rights movement. Access to civic buildings, workplaces, public spaces, housing, and commercial spaces has improved for people with disabilities living in the United States and Canada, Scandinavia, Korea, Japan, the United Kingdom, and other regions.

Accessibility, or removing barriers to access and use of resources in buildings, was the initial paradigm of physical access for people with disabilities. One unintended consequence of accessibility codes, such as "Part M" in England and the ADA Standards for Accessible Design in the United States, was a two-class system of design: one set of solutions for people without disabilities and another for people with disabilities—for example, ceremonial stairs for the former and (nonceremonial) secondary ramps for the other. Accessibility regulations ultimately focus on giving people access to buildings and facilities, but not on other issues that support social integration, remove stigma, promote health, or increase employment opportunities.

UNIVERSAL DESIGN: A KEY STRATEGY TO ADDRESS HEALTHY PLACES ACROSS THE LIFE SPAN

The concept of **universal design** (UD), also known as inclusive design and design for all, emerged in the mid-1980s as a new paradigm for physical access. UD was initially defined as "the design of products and environments to be usable by all people, to the greatest extent possible, without the need for adaptation or specialized design."[68] UD does not eliminate the need for standards that define the legal baseline for minimum accessibility. Instead, UD seeks to raise the bar on accessibility, address issues not yet covered by government regulations, make access an integral part of good design, and expand the benefits beyond individuals with disabilities to any potentially vulnerable population. UD acknowledges that the facilitators of healthy living for one population (such as a **Safe Routes to School** policy) can benefit many populations.

Since its inception, the application of UD has expanded beyond building and product design and is now reflected in policies and practices in urban design, town planning, transportation, and even in education.[69,70] To support this expanded scope, and in keeping with the revisions to the World Health Organization's International Classification of Diseases evolving conception of disablement, UD has evolved from initially focusing solely on supporting independent function to addressing additional goals.[71] Embracing these new ideas, Steinfeld and Maisel offered a new definition: "Universal design is a process that enables and empowers a diverse population by improving human performance, health and wellness, and social participation."[72(p29)] The primary challenge for inclusive designers, then, is to build environments that meet people's evolving needs over the course of their entire lives. Given that building practices often meet only the needs of able-bodied adults, the reward for inclusive designers is the expansion of standard practices and the populations they serve.

Although the intentions are noble, there are several challenges. For example:

- Inclusive environments move beyond ergonomic standards. Persuading those who produce and those who use built environments to exceed accessibility standards can be challenging.
- Knowledge gaps still exist regarding an understanding of environmental barriers to socialization and the built features that encourage human bonding. Additional research is needed to determine relationships between design and socialization.
- Establishing safe, inclusive spaces that promote stable social connections is especially challenging in some lower-socioeconomic contexts.
- In many situations, social media is replacing physical, space-based socialization and therefore reduces physical human contact. The increasing reliance on technology for social participation poses risks to people without advanced technologies of being excluded from accessing social opportunities.
- Persuading people about the economic benefits of inclusive design is a difficult proposition because many think that it is more expensive. Although that is the case at times, inclusive design can often cost the same as typical projects and even save people money.

Despite the challenges, there are many tangible rewards:

- In home design, UD approaches make it easier to welcome visitors—parents with babies in strollers, travelers with luggage, those with mobility difficulties, and children who need safe play spaces. For example, **visitability** is an affordable, sustainable, and inclusive design approach for integrating basic accessibility features as a routine construction practice into all newly built homes. Visitability includes a few basic accessibility features. In the United States, they are one zero-step entrance at the front, side, or rear of the home; thirty-two-inch-wide clearances at doorways and hallways with at least thirty-six inches of clear width; and a bathroom with at least a sink and a toilet on the main floor.[73]

- Inclusive home design facilitates caregiving in the home, which delays the need for institutional living.
- Inclusive workplace design and business practices enable more people to be employed.
- Public buildings with inclusive components, such as multisensory wayfinding cues, intuitive floorplans, and grouped vertical circulation, promote ease of use for all people.
- Workplace design and business practices that follow inclusive principles reduce injuries resulting from repetitive motion, slips and falls, and overexertion.
- Inclusive commercial and retail spaces provide access to a wider range of clients and customers than do noninclusive spaces.
- Inclusively designed public spaces allow more people to enjoy public squares, parks, beaches, and other community venues and encourage a more active lifestyle and social participation than do areas without such spaces.
- Complete streets programs encourage rights-of-way to be designed for the safety and comfort of all users, regardless of age and ability, and promote changes to planning efforts that balance the needs of pedestrians, bicyclists, public transportation users, and motorists irrespective of age, ability, income, ethnicity, or mode of travel.[74]
- Technology, which is increasingly being embedded into physical environments, empowers people to become active in communities at all scales.
- If buildings are usable by everyone from the initial design and construction, fewer renovations are necessary in the future, thus saving money for the property owner.
- Businesses, organizations, and governments that incorporate inclusive design approaches contribute to the betterment of society; as a result, they are establishing reputations as entities that embrace social responsibility.

Mandatory regulations and standards are a vehicle for evidence-based building design. Experts across a variety of fields and disciplines (for example, architecture and engineering) usually develop them to translate research and practical knowledge to guidelines for practice. Architects, product designers, and other design professionals rely on these guidelines rather than directly consult the research literature.[75] Mandatory regulations and standards, however, are time-consuming to develop, cannot be changed easily, and are politically contentious. Thus, the knowledge embodied in typical regulations and standards often lags behind the growth of scientific evidence and practical experience, especially in the early stages of a field of knowledge.

UD can be implemented more quickly by using expert opinion to identify guidelines, updating them regularly, and creating incentives for adopting solutions, rather than applying punishments for failing to adopt. To this end, the Center for Inclusive Design and Environmental Access developed *innovative solutions for Universal Design*, or isUD (https:// www.thisisud.com). The isUD business model is based on the success of the US Green Building Council and the Green Building Initiative; both developed standards (that is, LEED and Green Globes, respectively) and provide services like certifying buildings that recognize competency in sustainable design practices. isUD is designed to offer similar resources and services to support and recognize UD adopters.

It facilitates UD at all stages of a project—from the design process to policies and practices—that enable people of all abilities to contribute. The program provides efficient access to practical UD knowledge and provides a step-by-step checklist for project teams to use to improve inclusivity. The adoption of isUD continues to grow as the need for more inclusive work environments gains attention; the prevalence of disability and older adults in the workforce increases; and work organizations increasingly strive to remove barriers to full participation of traditionally excluded groups such as racial, ethnic, and religious minorities, women, and members of gender and sexual orientation minorities.[76] With growing diversity in work organizations, organizational leaders have increasingly become aware of the importance of creating inclusive environments. As of 2021, a children's museum, a Fortune 500 company, a shared-workspace environment, a hotel, and a place of worship had all implemented UD.

Similarly, the concept of 8-80 Cities suggests that environments that support older adults also benefit children. "People who are 8 and 80 are the *indicator species* for good places to live. Redesign our cities to keep them safe, healthy and happy, and we'll have a place that works well for everyone."[77]

SOLUTIONS TO BUILT ENVIRONMENT CHALLENGES FOR CHILDREN, OLDER ADULTS, AND PEOPLE WITH DISABILITIES

The following topics offer evidence-based solutions to prevailing challenges for children, older adults, and people with disabilities at the building and neighborhood scales. Each solution discusses the population(s) impacted, a description of the solution, and why it is appropriate (table 10.1).

- School siting to limit environmental exposures (children). School siting can reduce adverse environmental exposures, which is important because negative environmental exposures are a major challenge for children's health. The US Environmental Protection Agency has developed guidelines for school siting (chapter 15).
- Safe Routes to School programs (children). The Safe Routes to School National Partnership (SRTSNP) has developed guidelines for local program implementation and technical support (chapter 15).
- Complete streets programs with enhanced visual crossings and audible signals (children, older adults, all disability statuses). Smart Growth America is a nonprofit organization that provides materials to support complete streets policies and implementation (chapter 11).
- Robust, accessible public transit and paratransit (older adults and all disability statuses). The Federal Transit Authority offers guidance about ADA compliance around transit and paratransit.
- Integrate *assistive housing* into walkable communities (older adults, all disability statuses). The American Association of People with Disabilities (AAPD) advocates for policy change and offers resources around this solution.
- Zoning for community integration of the cognitively impaired and other subpopulations. While no specific organization is considered the authority on this subject, the American Bar Association has released guidance on zoning for group homes. AAPD also advocates for related policy changes and provides resources for local governments.
- Improved access to healthy food sources (children, older adults, all disability statuses). The US Department of Agriculture tracks food deserts, and the CDC has additional resources on healthy food access (chapter 3).
- Housing policies that promote visitability (robust, accessible public transit systems) and aging in place and communities (older adults) (chapter 12). The US Department of Housing and Urban Development supports visitability and aging in place as they facilitate choice and independence.

Table 10.1. Examples of subpopulations, their health vulnerabilities, and possible built environment solutions.

Subpopulation	Population Health Vulnerability	Possible Built Environment Solution
Age		
Children	Susceptibility to environmental pollutants	School siting to limit environmental exposures
	Pedestrian and cyclist injury risk	Safe Routes to School programs
	Overweight and obesity	Complete streets programs
		Integrate inclusive design in buildings
Older adults	Pedestrian injury risk	Complete streets programs
	Reduced ability to drive	Policies supporting visitability and aging in place Integrate inclusive design in buildings
	Social isolation	
Disability status		
Cognitive impairment	Injury risk	Zoning for community integration of the cognitively impaired
	Social isolation	Enhanced signage and infrastructure
		Integrate assistive housing into walkable communities
		Integrate inclusive design in buildings
Mobility impairment	Nutritional deficits	Robust, accessible public transit and paratransit
	Physical inactivity	Complete streets programs
	Social isolation	Improved access to healthy food sources
		Housing policies that promote visitability and aging in place
		Integrate inclusive design in buildings
Vision impairment	Injury risk	Complete streets programs with enhanced visual crossings and audible signals
	Physical inactivity	Integrate inclusive design in buildings
Hearing impairment	Injury risk	Complete streets programs with enhanced visual crossings and audible signals
	Social isolation	Integrate inclusive design in buildings

- Local policymaking and implementation on aging in place and communities. The American Association of Retired Persons provides materials to support efforts on a local level.
- Integrate inclusive design in buildings (children, older adults, all disability statuses). The Center for Inclusive Design and Environmental Access at the University of Buffalo (http://idea.ap.buffalo.edu) has recently developed a certification program for inclusive building design.

CONCLUSION

To realize the potential for positive outcomes at the individual level (for example, optimal child development, social participation, active coping) and community level (community resilience, social capital, lower health care costs, better community health status) for vulnerable populations, health and built environment professionals should use the tools available to engage all populations in shaping the physical and social environments where children, seniors, and people with disabilities spend the majority of their time.

The ethics code endorsed by the American Public Health Association, for instance, states: "Public health should advocate and work for the empowerment of disenfranchised community members, aiming to ensure that the basic resources and conditions necessary for health are accessible to all."[78(p7)] The American Planning Association's Institute of Certified Planners code states: "We shall seek social justice by working to expand choice and opportunity for all persons."[79] In addition to their codes, associations such as the Institute of Transportation Engineers, American Society of Landscape Architects, and American Institute of Architects have established universal design, ensuring that built environments are usable by all without specialized design and that decisions are made with active input from those affected by them.

The aforementioned built environment, policy, and UD interventions can reduce vulnerabilities experienced by children, older adults, and people with disabilities. For sustained well-being across the life span, these populations require the inclusive and nondiscriminatory practice advanced by the built environment and public health professions, in coordination with one another.

DISCUSSION QUESTIONS

1. Name three vulnerable populations. For each group, explain why it is vulnerable and describe the specific health implications that people in that group face as a result of community design choices.
2. What issues would you need to consider before approaching individuals in a vulnerable population about design features in a new project that might have positive or negative impacts on them?
3. What are examples of (a) vulnerabilities that can be avoided through community design and (b) strategies that mitigate unavoidable vulnerabilities?
4. Identify universal design strategies that have improved health outcomes for children, older adults, or people with disabilities in low- and middle-income countries or have the potential to do so. Describe the social and policy environments in which these strategies were integrated into the design process or as a retrofit.
5. What applications of the 8-80 Cities concept could provide solutions to healthy places for vulnerable populations in your community?

ACKNOWLEDGMENT

The authors would like to acknowledge the late Christopher Kochtitzky, a built environment and public health champion, for his inspiration and early contributions to this chapter. We thank him for his unwavering support of healthy places for vulnerable populations throughout his life and career.

DISCLOSURE OF COMPETING INTERESTS

Nisha Botchwey's declarations appear in the preface.

Nsedu Obot Witherspoon discloses no competing interests.

Jordana L. Maisel reports grant funding from the National Institute on Disability, Independent Living, and Rehabilitation Research; National Highway Traffic Safety Administration; and Department of Transportation and serves as an unpaid board member or advisory committee member of the Amherst Senior Center, Self-Advocacy Network of Western New York, Main Street Smart Corridor Steering Committee, Shared Mobility Steering Committee, and Accessible Subcommittee for the Whole Building Design Guide.

Howard Frumkin's declarations appear in the preface.

REFERENCES

1. US Department of Health and Human Services (USHHS). 2020 Topics and objectives: early and middle childhood. *Healthy People*. 2020. Accessed July 20, 2021. https://www.healthypeople.gov/2020/topics-objectives/topic/early-and-middle-childhood

2. Tupetz A, Friedman K, Zhao D, et al. Prevention of childhood unintentional injuries in low- and middle-income countries: a systematic review. *PLOS ONE*. 2020;15(12): e0243464. https://doi.org/10.1371/journal.pone.0243464

3. Centers for Disease Control and Prevention (CDC), National Center for Injury Prevention and Control. *Protecting the Ones You Love: Child Injuries Are Preventable*. CDC; 2019. Accessed July 20, 2021. https://www.cdc.gov/safechild/index.html

4. Browning MHEM, Rigolon A. School green space and its impact on academic performance: a systematic literature review. *International Journal of Environmental Research and Public Health*. 2019;16(3):429. Published February 1, 2019. doi:10.3390/ijerph16030429

5. Norwood MF, Lakhani A, Fullagar S, et al. A narrative and systematic review of the behavioural, cognitive and emotional effects of passive nature exposure on young people: evidence for prescribing change. *Landscape and Urban Planning*. 2019;189:71-79.

6. McCormick R. Does access to green space impact the mental well-being of children: a systematic review. *Journal of Pediatric Nursing*. 2017;37:3-7. doi:10.1016/j.pedn.2017.08.027

7. CDC, National Center for Injury Prevention and Control. Web-Based Injury Statistics Query and Reporting System (WISQARS). CDC; 2020. Accessed July 15, 2021. http://www.cdc.gov/injury/wisqars

8. Youth.gov. Adolescent Development. Youth.gov. Accessed July 20, 2021. https://youth.gov/youth-topics/adolescent-health/adolescent-development

9. Özen S, Darcan Ş. Effects of environmental endocrine disruptors on pubertal development. *Journal of Clinical Research in Pediatric Endocrinology*. 2011;3(1):1-6. doi:10.4274/jcrpe.v3i1.01

10. National Institute of Mental Health (NIH). *Suicide*. NIH; 2021. Accessed July 20, 2021. https://www.nimh.nih.gov/health/statistics/suicide

11. World Health Organization (WHO). *Suicide in the World: Global Health Estimates*. WHO; 2019. License: CC BY-NC-SA 3.0 IGO. https://www.who.int/publications/i/item/suicide-in-the-world

12. WHO. *Youth Violence*. WHO; 2020. Accessed July 20, 2021. https://www.who.int/news-room/fact-sheets/detail/youth-violence

13. Bilchik S. Section I: gun violence in the United States. In: *Promising Strategies to Reduce Gun Violence*. US Department of Justice Office of Justice Programs Office of Juvenile Justice and Delinquency; 1999. https://ojjdp.ojp.gov/sites/g/files/xyckuh176/files/pubs/gun_violence/sect01.html

14. Viner RM, Ozer EM, Denny S, et al. Adolescence and the social determinants of health. *The Lancet*. 2012;379:1641-1652. doi:10.1016/S0140-6736(12)60149-4

15. Bernat DH, Resnick MD. Healthy youth development: science and strategies. *Journal of Public Health Management and Practice*. 2006;12(suppl 6):S10-S16.

16. WHO. *Inheriting a Sustainable World? Atlas on Children's Health and the Environment*. WHO; 2017. https://apps.who.int/iris/bitstream/handle/10665/254677/9789241511773-eng.pdf.

17. CDC. *Blood Lead Levels among US children*. CDC; 2017. Accessed July 20, 2021. https://www.cdc.gov/nceh/lead/docs/CBLS-National-Table-Update-042619-508.pdf

18. US Environmental Protection Agency (US EPA). *Pesticides and Their Impact on Children: Key Facts and Talking Points.* US EPA; 2017. https://19january2017snapshot.epa.gov/sites/production/files/2015-12/documents/pest-impact-hsstaff.pdf

19. Heerman WJ, Perrin EM, Sanders LM, et al. Racial and ethnic differences in injury prevention behaviors among caregivers of infants. *American Journal of Preventive Medicine.* 2016;51(4):411-418. doi:10.1016/j.amepre.2016.04.020

20. Witherspoon NO. Are we really addressing the core of children's environmental health? *Environmental Health Perspectives.* 2009;117(10):A428-A429.

21. Horn IB, Beal AC. Child health disparities: framing a research agenda. *Ambulatory Pediatrics.* 2004;4(4):269-275.

22. *Healthy People 2020.* USHHS; 2020. https://www.healthypeople.gov/2020

23. Vespa J, Armstrong DM, Medina L. *Demographic Turning Points for the United States: Population Projections for 2020 to 2060.* US Department of Commerce, Economics and Statistics Administration, US Census Bureau; 2018. https://www.census.gov/content/dam/Census/library/publications/2020/demo/p25-1144.pdf

24. United Nations, Department of Economic and Social Affairs, Population Division. World Population Ageing 2019: Highlights. United Nations (ST/ESA/SER.A/430). 2019. https://www.un.org/en/development/desa/population/publications/pdf/ageing/WorldPopulationAgeing2019-Highlights.pdf

25. Harada CN, Natelson Love MC, Triebel KL. Normal cognitive aging. *Clinics in Geriatric Medicine.* 2013;29(4):737-752. doi:10.1016/j.cger.2013.07.002

26. Robbins RN, Scott T, Joska JA, Gouse H. Impact of urbanization on cognitive disorders. *Current Opinion in Psychiatry.* 2019;32(3):210-217.

27. Wu Y-T, Prina AM, Jones A, et al. The built environment and cognitive disorders: results from the Cognitive Function and Ageing Study II. *American Journal of Preventive Medicine.* 2017;53(1):25-32.

28. Besser L. Outdoor green space exposure and brain health measures related to Alzheimer's disease: a rapid review. *BMJ Open.* 2021;11(5):e043456.

29. Besser LM, Hirsch J, Galvin JE, et al. Associations between neighborhood park space and cognition in older adults vary by US location: the multi-ethnic study of atherosclerosis. *Health Place.* November 2020;66:102459.

30. Wu YT, Prina AM, Jones A, et al. Micro-scale environment and mental health in later life: results from the Cognitive Function and Ageing Study II (CFAS II). *Journal of Affective Disorders.* 2017;218:359-364.

31. Alzheimer's Society. *Building Dementia-Friendly Communities: A Priority for Everyone.* Alzheimer's Society; 2013.

32. US National Library of Medicine. Aging changes in the senses. *MedlinePlus Medical Encyclopedia.* Accessed July 20, 2021. https://medlineplus.gov/ency/article/004013.htm

33. WHO. Deafness and hearing loss. WHO; 2021. Accessed July 20, 2021. https://www.who.int/health-topics/hearing-loss#tab=tab_1

34. Hopewell S, Adedire O, Copsey BJ, et al. Multifactorial and multiple component interventions for preventing falls in older people living in the community. *Cochrane Database of Systematic Reviews.* 2018;7(7):CD012221.

35. Clemson L, Stark S, Pighills AC, Torgerson DJ, Sherrington C, Lamb SE. Environmental interventions for preventing falls in older people living in the community. *Cochrane Database of Systematic Reviews.* 2019;2019(2):CD013258. Published February 6, 2019. doi:10.1002/14651858.CD013258

36. WHO. Blindness and vision impairment. WHO. 2021. Accessed July 20, 2021. https://www.who.int/news-room/fact-sheets/detail/blindness-and-visual-impairment

37. Emerson RW. Outdoor wayfinding and navigation for people who are blind: accessing the built environment. In: Antona M., Stephanidis C, eds. *Universal Access in Human–Computer Interaction. Human and Technological Environments*. Lecture Notes in Computer Science, vol 10279. Springer; 2017. https://doi.org/10.1007/978-3-319-58700-4_27

38. Joint Center for Housing Studies at Harvard University (JCHS). *Housing America's Older Adults: Meeting the Needs of an Aging Population*. JCHS; 2014. https://www.jchs.harvard.edu/sites/default/files/jchs_housing_americas_older_adults_2014_key_facts_1.pdf

39. Winick BH, Jaffee M. Planning aging-supportive communities. American Planning Association; 2015. https://www.planning.org/publications/report/9026902/

40. Hermann A. More older adults are living in lower density neighborhoods. Joint Center for Housing Studies; 2019. Accessed July 20, 2021. https://www.jchs.harvard.edu/blog/more-older-adults-are-living-in-lower-density-neighborhoods

41. US Department of Transportation (USDOT). National household travel survey. USDOT; 2009. https://nhts.ornl.gov/2009/pub/stt.pdf

42. Kan HY, Forsyth A, Molinsky J. Measuring the built environment for aging in place: a review of neighborhood audit tools. *Journal of Planning Literature*. 2020;35(2):180-194. doi:10.1177/0885412220903497

43. Palmer M, Harley D. Models and measurement in disability: an international review. *Health Policy and Planning*. 2011;27(5):357-364. https://doi.org/10.1093/heapol/czr047

44. WHO. The World Report on Disability 2011. WHO; 2011. https://www.who.int/teams/noncommunicable-diseases/sensory-functions-disability-and-rehabilitation/world-report-on-disability

45. US Census Bureau. Disability Characteristics, 2014–2018 American Community Survey 5-Year Estimates. US Census Bureau; 2019. https://data.census.gov/cedsci/table?q=disability&hidePreview=false&tid=ACSST5Y2018.S1810&t=Disability&vintage=2018

46. Taylor DM. *Americans with Disabilities: 2014*. US Census Bureau; 2014. Accessed July 20, 2021. https://www.census.gov/library/publications/2018/demo/p70-152.html

47. Courtney-Long EA, Romano SD, Carroll DD, Fox MH. Socioeconomic factors at the intersection of race and ethnicity influencing health risks for people with disabilities. *Journal of Racial and Ethnic Health Disparities*. 2017;4(2):213-222. doi:10.1007/s40615-016-0220-5

48. Dickerson AE, Molnar L, Bedard M, Eby DW, Classen S, Polgar J. Transportation and aging: an updated research agenda for advancing safe mobility. *Journal of Applied Gerontology*. 2019;38(12):1643-1660. doi:10.1177/0733464817739154

49. Rosso AL, Auchincloss AH, Michael YL. The urban built environment and mobility in older adults: a comprehensive review. *Journal of Aging Research*. 2011;2011:816106. https://doi.org/10.4061/2011/816106

50. National Council on Disability. (2015). *Transportation Update: Where We've Gone and What We've Learned*. National Council on Disability; 2015. https://ncd.gov/publications/2015/05042015

51. Syed ST, Gerber BS, Sharp LK. Traveling towards disease: transportation barriers to health care access. *Journal of Community Health*. 2013;38(5):976-993. doi:10.1007/s10900-013-9681-1

52. Mithen J, Aitken Z, Ziersch A, Kavanagh AM. Inequalities in social capital and health between people with and without disabilities. *Social Science & Medicine*. 2015;126:26-35. doi:10.1016/j.socscimed.2014.12.009

53. Cornwell EY, Waite LJ. Social disconnectedness, perceived isolation, and health among older adults. *Journal of Health and Social Behavior*. 2009;50(1):31-48. doi:10.1177/002214650905000103.

54. Steptoe A, Shankar A, Demakakos P, Wardle J. Social isolation, loneliness, and all-cause mortality in older men and women. *Proceedings of the National Academy of Sciences*. 2013;110(15):5797-5801. doi:10.1073/pnas.1219686110

55. Armitage R, Nellums LB. The COVID-19 response must be disability inclusive. *The Lancet Public Health*. 2020;5(5):e257. doi:10.1016/S2468-2667(20)30076-1

56. Houtenville A, Boege S. *Annual Report on People with Disabilities in America: 2018*. University of New Hampshire, Institute on Disability/UCED; 2019. https://disabilitycompendium.org/sites/default/files/user-uploads/Annual_Report_2018_Accessible_AdobeReaderFriendly.pdf

57. Rak EC, Spencer L. Community participation of persons with disabilities: volunteering, donations and involvement in groups and organisations. *Disability and Rehabilitation*. 2016;38(17):1705-1715. doi:10.3109/09638288.2015.1107643

58. Krahn GL, Walker DK, Correa-De-Araujo R. Persons with disabilities as an unrecognized health disparity population. *American Journal of Public Health*. 2015;105 Suppl 2(Suppl 2):S198-S206. doi:10.2105/AJPH.2014.302182

59. Edlich RF, Kelley AR, Morton K, et al. A case report of a severe musculoskeletal injury in a wheelchair user caused by an incorrect wheelchair ramp design. *Journal of Emergency Medicine*. 2010;38(2):150-154. doi:10.1016/j.jemermed.2007.07.067

60. Clarke P, Ailshire JA, Lantz P. Urban built environments and trajectories of mobility disability: findings from a national sample of community-dwelling American adults (1986-2001). *Social Science & Medicine*. 2009;69(6):964-970. doi:10.1016/j.socscimed.2009.06.041

61. Chandra S, Bari M, Devarasetty PC, Vadali S. Accessibility evaluations of feeder transit services. *Transportation Research Part A: Policy and Practice*. 2013;52:47-63.

62. Brumbaugh S. Travel Patterns of American Adults with Disabilities. Bureau of Transportation Statistics, US Department of Transportation; 2018. https://www.bts.gov/sites/bts.dot.gov/files/docs/explore-topics-and-geography/topics/passenger-travel/222466/travel-patterns-american-adults-disabilities-11-26-19.pdf

63. Environews Nigeria. COVID-19: Urban mobility tagged cornerstone of public services. *EnviroNewsNigeria*; 2020. Retrieved from https://www.environewsnigeria.com/covid-19-urban-mobility-tagged-cornerstone-of-public-services/

64. Binette J, Vasold K. 2018 Home and Community Preferences: A National Survey of Adults Age 18-Plus. AARP Research; 2018. https://www.aarp.org/research/topics/community/info-2018/2018-home-community-preference.html

65. Bo'sher L, Chan S, Ellen IG, Karfunkel B, Liao HL. Accessibility of America's housing stock: analysis of the 2011 American Housing Survey (AHS). US Department of Housing and Urban Development; 2015. https://www.huduser.gov/portal/sites/default/files/pdf/accessibility-america-housingStock.pdf

66. American Association on Intellectual and Developmental Disabilities (AAID). Housing—Joint Position Statement of AAIDD and The Arc. AAID; 2012. https://www.aaidd.org/news-policy/policy/position-statements/housing

67. Smith SK, Rayer S, Smith EA. Aging and Disability: implications for the housing industry and housing policy in the United States. *Journal of the American Planning Association*. 2008;74:3, 289-306, doi:10.1080/01944360802197132

68. Mace R. *Universal Design, Barrier Free Environments for Everyone*. Designers West; 1985.

69. Bringa OR. Making universal design work in zoning and regional planning: a Scandinavian approach. In: Nasar J, Evans-Cowley J, eds. *Universal Design and Visitability: From Accessibility to Zoning*. John Glenn School of Public Affairs/NEA; 2007:97.

70. Meyer A, Rose DH, Gordon D. *Universal Design for Learning: Theory and Practice*. CAST Professional Publishing; 2014.

71. Watchorn V, Larkin H, Hitch D, Ang S. Promoting participation through the universal design of built environments: making it happen. *Journal of Social Inclusion*. 2014;5(2), 65–88. doi:http://doi.org/10.36251/josi.77

72. Steinfeld E, Maisel J. *Universal Design: Creating Inclusive Environments*. Wiley; 2012.

73. Maisel, JL, Smith E, Steinfeld E. *Increasing Home Access: Design for Visitability*. AARP Public Policy Institute; 2008.

74. National Complete Streets Coalition. *Complete Streets Policy Inventory and Evaluation*. National Complete Streets Coalition; 2010.

75. Vaughan E, Turner J. The Value and Impact of Building Codes. Environmental and Energy Study Institute White Paper; 2013.

76. Barak, MEM. *Managing Diversity: Toward a Globally Inclusive Workplace*. SAGE Publications; 2016.

77. Walljasper J. "5 Questions for Gil Penalosa." AARP Livable Communities: Livability in Action; 2015. https://www.aarp.org/livable-communities/livable-in-action/info-2015/5-questions-for-gil-penalosa.html

78. Public Health Leadership Society. *Principles of the Ethical Practice of Public Health*. Public Health Leadership Society; 2002. https://www.apha.org/-/media/files/pdf/membergroups/ethics/ethics_brochure.ashx

79. American Planning Association. AICP Code of Ethics and Professional Conduct. APA; 2016. https://www.planning.org/ethics/ethicscode/

PART II

DESIGNING PLACES FOR WELL-BEING, EQUITY, AND SUSTAINABILITY

CHAPTER 11

TRANSPORTATION, LAND USE, AND HEALTH

Susan Handy

KEY POINTS

- Transportation and land use affect health through impacts on physical activity, air quality, injuries, social capital, mental health, and social equity.
- Transportation and land use are inextricably linked. Areas with good transportation access are more attractive for development, and developments with higher densities, a mix of land uses, and better street connectivity facilitate higher levels of walking, bicycling, and transit use, thereby promoting sustainability.
- Land use and transportation policies that can promote health and reduce automobile dependence include urban growth boundaries to promote compact development, upzoning to increase housing densities, incentives for transit-oriented development, elimination of minimum parking requirements, adoption of complete streets policies, and prioritization of funding for transit, bicycle, and pedestrian facilities.
- Planning for a "fifteen-minute city" or "twenty-minute neighborhood" promotes health by providing residents with access to goods and services within walking or bicycling distance of home.

INTRODUCTION

When my family and I moved to Davis, California from Austin, Texas, some years ago, besides the drier weather and closer proximity to family, we especially liked the opportunity to bike rather than drive everywhere. We promptly bought a bike trailer so that my husband and I could commute by bike to the University of California, Davis campus with our two preschoolers in tow. Our children were on their own bikes by kindergarten and biking themselves to school by fifth or sixth grade. Over the years, we did not always bike to campus, and we sometimes let our children drive to school once they had their licenses. But in that time we averaged less than five thousand miles a year on our primary car, and we met daily recommended levels of physical activity from commuting alone. With just two of us home now, we have seven bicycles in the garage, including a folding bike and our new electric-assist bike, which means that we have no excuse for driving anywhere within the city.

A car-light lifestyle is possible in Davis because of the ways it differs from the typical US suburb.[1] Every neighborhood in the city has at least one commercial center within easy walking and biking distance of housing. Apartments serving the large population of university students are found throughout the city and account for more than half of its housing units. Downtown Davis continues to function as the commercial center of the city thanks to public investments in downtown streets as well as policies that limit big-box stores. The city is relatively compact owing to strong growth management policies that limit outward expansion and protect surrounding agricultural land. A network of more than fifty miles of off-street paths with numerous tunnels and bridges over major streets encourage walking as well as bicycling. These paths are a key feature of a greenbelt system that provides access to schools, parks, and playgrounds throughout the city. A local transit system provides another easy way to get around, and the city is linked to Sacramento and the San Francisco Bay area by commuter rail. These and other qualities of the transportation system combined with the city's compact land use patterns make it possible for Davis residents to be less dependent on their cars.

The result is a healthier way of life. Driving is a sedentary activity, contributing to obesity and other health problems.[2,3] California counties with the highest amount of driving per capita tend to have the highest mean obesity rates.[4] Commuting by car is also stressful.[5] Long driving commutes are associated with poor mental health outcomes and related consequences, including negative mood, poor concentration, driver error, and traffic collisions.[6] Living in more car-dependent areas can contribute to increased blood pressure, headaches, and social isolation,[7] as well as depression.[8] Driving, whether passenger cars or freight trucks, also affects the health of drivers and nondrivers alike more indirectly through its contribution to air and water pollution, ambient noise levels, and the risk of injuries and fatalities.

Conversely, places that are built in a way that encourages active travel—walking, biking, skateboarding, scootering, and others— improve health (chapter 2). Active modes increase daily physical activity, leading to a broad range of health benefits.[9,10] Commuting by foot or by bicycle is less stressful and more satisfying than driving,[11] with benefits for mental health. Places that encourage the use of public transit also improve health given that transit riders often use active modes to get to or from bus stops or rail stations[12] and given that transit, if well used, produces less pollution per person.[13] When the use of transit or active modes replaces driving, the benefits compound: a decrease in the negative impacts of driving adds to the increase in the positive benefits of active travel. Places that promote active travel while discouraging driving produce health benefits for those who make the switch and for the community as a whole.[14]

Such places are not only healthier but are inherently more equitable. Not everyone is able to drive, owing to physical, mental, or financial limitations. Cities that make it possible to get to destinations by walking, bicycling, and transit help ensure that people unable to drive have access to jobs and services, as well as social and recreational activities that are important for health. Such places are also more environmentally sustainable, helping to reduce energy use, preserve natural habitat and working lands, save water, and reduce carbon footprints. This last benefit is especially important: transportation is one of the major contributors of greenhouse gas emissions, primarily owing to gasoline-powered vehicles. These places are also more fiscally viable in that they reduce infrastructure costs for local government by reducing maintenance needs and requiring less capacity to begin with. In these ways, they address all three "Es" of sustainability—equity (chapter 9), environment, and economics—with substantial benefits for health.

Understanding how cities are built is thus important for public health officials. The two components that most affect daily travel are land use patterns and the transportation system. Public policy shapes both components and can either foster car dependence, as is typical in the United States but also in some other parts of the world, or foster communities that are more people-oriented and that support active travel and improve public health. Many cities are aiming to reduce or avert car dependence, motivated in large part by concerns over climate change but with important benefits—direct and indirect—for health. This chapter introduces these themes by addressing the following questions:

- What are land use and transportation?
- Who makes decisions about land use and transportation?
- How can cities make healthier design choices about land use and transportation?
- What is the outlook for the design of cities?

WHAT ARE LAND USE AND TRANSPORTATION?

Land use patterns together with the transportation system determine the ease with which individuals can get to the places they need or want to be and are thus critical to understanding daily travel, including choices about driving versus riding transit, walking, or bicycling.[15] Land use patterns also shape the movement of goods in and around cities and the impact of these movements on residents, including noise, air pollutants, and traffic dangers.

Land use patterns are defined as the spatial distribution of different activities. Activities such as housing, retail, agriculture, industry, and parks fall into different land use classifications, which may be more or less specific depending on the purpose of the classification (such as a comprehensive plan or a zoning ordinance, as discussed below). A key characteristic of land use patterns is the intensity of the activity. Intensity for housing is often measured as population density (for example, persons per square mile), whereas intensity for retail, commercial, and industrial activities is measured as employment density (for example, jobs per square mile). The mix of different land uses within a given area is another important characteristic and is measured based on the percentages of different land uses within the area. The form and design of the buildings that contain activities are also important aspects of the built environment, and sometimes land uses are differentiated in part based on building type, such as single-family versus multifamily housing.

The role of the transportation system is to link one place to another. Transportation has numerous positive and negative impacts on health.[16] For people, transportation provides access to activities by linking home to work, for example, or the store to home. For goods, its purpose is to move resources and products from sources to end users. The transportation system consists of physical infrastructure such as roads, rails, airports, ports, and pipelines, as well as the public and private vehicles and services that make use of that infrastructure. The road network can be characterized in terms of its connectivity, meaning the number and directness of routes from one point to another. The **level of service** of the network (chapter 22) has traditionally been measured with respect to the actual time it takes to get from one point to another relative to the travel time in the absence of congestion, an approach that has tended to encourage capacity expansion.[17] Transit systems, most of which make use of the road network at least in part, are typically characterized in terms of the frequency of service and the coverage, meaning the share of the population living within a given distance of a bus stop or rail station, as well as qualities such as the accessibility of transit stops and the need for transfers. With limited budgets, transit agencies must find an effective balance between frequency and coverage.

Land use and transportation are inextricably linked in multiple ways.[15] First, the transportation system shapes land use patterns (figure 11.1). Expanding a freeway, for example, encourages development in the area served by the freeway because it speeds travel from that area to others. By increasing

Figure 11.1. The initiation of fast passenger ferry service across Puget Sound in Washington between downtown Seattle and the Kitsap County communities of Bremerton, Southworth, and Kingston influences land use and development choices being made in those communities.
Source: Photo courtesy of Puget Sound Regional Council

speeds, freeway building tends to encourage lower-density development, particularly when it serves the peripheral areas of cities as it often does. Building a new rail system can encourage higher-density development around its stations. With rail service, the area can continue to function with more people living and working there than when served by the road network alone. Second, land use patterns shape daily travel by determining proximity to potential destinations. Having stores and services close by makes walking and bicycling a possibility, whereas driving is often a necessity for shopping at large regional centers and big-box stores that draw people away from smaller local stores. Density is important for transit in that transit will only draw a financially sufficient number of riders if enough people live or work within close proximity to stations.[18]

Third, transportation is itself a land use in that roadways and railways account for a considerable portion of the land within an urban area. The strip of land set aside for a highway, known as the right-of-way, can be far wider than the highway itself. Parking lots and garages also consume a substantial share of land; in Los Angeles alone, parking takes up an area equivalent to nearly fourteen hundred soccer fields.[19] Although devoting land to transportation is necessary for connecting people to activities, the transportation facilities that occupy that land are often also an impediment to travel. Freeways and railways are barriers to movement that may sever communities. Low-income communities and communities of color have been especially impacted in this way by freeway building in the United States.[20] Parking lots add to the separation of activities and reduce population and employment densities while contributing to the **urban heat island effect**. These effects are problematic for pedestrians and bicyclists who are more sensitive to distances than drivers.

These relationships between transportation and land use are self-reinforcing,[15] which can be both good and bad from a health standpoint. Although the lower-density development that highway building encourages can have some benefits for health through better access to green spaces, better air quality, and less noise (although none of these is guaranteed), it increases the distances between activities and thus adds to car dependence and its negative impacts on health. Increased car dependence adds to the political pressure to build more freeways to reduce congestion (despite the well-established fact that building more freeways induces more driving[21]), thus reinforcing the cycle of car dependence. Conversely, improvements to transit systems, particularly investments in rail, enable higher-density development. Although higher-density development can have some negative effects for health stemming from more crowding and noise, it helps to ensure that more activities are within walking and bicycling distance and that the area has enough concentration of residents and jobs to justify further investment in transit, thereby reducing car dependence and improving health in a virtuous cycle. The challenge for cities is to coordinate their policies toward the self-reinforcing cycle of reduced car dependence.

WHO MAKES DECISIONS ABOUT LAND USE AND TRANSPORTATION?

Although land use and transportation are inextricably linked, land use and transportation planning are largely separate, at least in the US context. Although some of the planning practices described below, such as zoning, are used throughout the world, the governance structures and allocations of responsibilities vary widely from country to country and, in some cases, from state to state within the United States.

Land use patterns in the United States are shaped primarily by local policy. Most states have delegated the authority to regulate land use to local governments, usually cities and counties (some states have other kinds of local entities). Cities and, in some states, counties start with a **comprehensive plan** (also called a *general plan*) for their jurisdiction that looks ahead twenty or thirty years to lay out future land use patterns as well as public facilities such as schools and parks, infrastructure such as streets and stormwater systems, and other aspects of the city's built environment. Health is often an explicit consideration in these plans.[22] A city's plan provides the basis for the local ordinances that regulate land development, most notably **zoning ordinances** and **subdivision ordinances**. The zoning code dictates what land uses are allowed for each parcel of land in the city, as well as the intensity of development allowed. The subdivision ordinance comes into play when developers propose to divide a large parcel of land into multiple individual parcels to be sold to individual buyers. This is the process by which much of the residential development in the United States now occurs. The subdivision ordinance specifies rules about the spatial configuration of the proposed development, including the layout of the street network and the inclusion of sidewalks and bicycle paths.

Separation of uses has been the dominant approach to land use planning in the United States since as early as the 1920s. Conventional zoning practices separate land uses, keeping residential areas away from commercial and industrial areas, thereby protecting residents from potentially noxious neighbors but at the same time reducing their proximity to the places they may need to go. Zoning in the United States has also contributed to segregation by class and race through the widespread use of "single-family zoning" that prohibits anything but a single home on a single parcel (zoning was one of many public and private policies that contributed to racial segregation[23]; see chapter 9). Zoning also tends to limit population and employment densities by setting maximum building height and **floor area ratio** (**FAR**) (that is, the ratio of the area of the floor space of the building to the area of the parcel), thereby dispersing activities across a larger area. Also helping to lower densities are standards that require a minimum number of parking spaces for every development. Such practices give little thought to the implications for car dependence, to neither the longer travel distances they engender nor the difficulty of providing good transit service in the low-density areas they produce.

Although local governments have the power to plan for and regulate land development, the process is largely driven by private land developers who typically propose projects they expect to be profitable. Local government can encourage development projects that are health promoting and environmentally sustainable with incentives such as tax breaks, variances to zoning regulations, and favorable permitting processes. If developers see an unmet market demand for sustainably designed projects, they will build accordingly. For example, the Culdesac Tempe project near Phoenix is being built as a seventeen-acre community where one thousand residents will live without parking spaces; it is scheduled to open in 2022.[24]

Local governments also have responsibility for the local transportation system, meaning the streets within their jurisdiction and sometimes also local transit service. In addition to regulating the design of streets in new subdivisions, local governments own, maintain, and operate the street network. They determine how street space will be divided between cars, bicyclists, and pedestrians. They install stop signs and signals and set signal timing, including phases for pedestrians and bicyclists. They may invest in off-street paths for pedestrians and bicyclists, separated from car traffic. They maintain streets, including filling potholes, restriping bike lanes, and fixing sidewalks (although many cities put the onus for sidewalk maintenance on adjacent property owners). At the local level, transportation planning is often coordinated with land use planning through the comprehensive plan by the staff of the planning department, but day-to-day maintenance and operation of the street network is usually the responsibility of traffic engineers in the department of public works.

The highway system, from two-lane, undivided, rural highways to multilane, divided, urban freeways, is the responsibility of higher levels of government. The state departments of transportation design, build, own, maintain, and operate these facilities, but within urban areas, decisions about which highway projects to fund are largely the responsibility of **metropolitan planning organizations** (**MPOs**). MPOs are required by federal law in urbanized areas with populations of fifty thousand or more and have two primary responsibilities: the selection of projects that will receive federal transportation funding and the development of long-range transportation plans for the region. MPOs, at least in theory, provide a mechanism for coordinating transportation planning at a regional scale, which tends to coincide with daily patterns of commuting.[25] The federal government influences this by providing substantial funding for specified kinds of projects and by attaching planning requirements to this funding; it does not, with a few exceptions, make decisions about which projects to fund. Although it would seem logical to coordinate land use planning with long-range regional transportation plans given the relationships discussed in the previous section, MPOs, except for Portland (Oregon) Metro, have no responsibility for or power over land use planning.

Transit systems range from local systems run by cities or counties to regional systems usually run by specially created transit agencies. These agencies have their own governing boards and their own funding sources, such as fares and local sales or property taxes, but they also depend on federal funding, especially for capital projects such as purchasing buses or building a rail line. Transit agencies participate in the regional planning process led by the MPOs, and some of their funding may come through the MPO, but they have a substantial degree of autonomy. What they do not have is power over land development except for the land that the agency itself owns. Many transit agencies have been able to increase densities around transit stations by developing their own land, often in partnership with private developers and sometimes with the assistance of funding incentives offered by the MPO.

The complexity of the governance structures for land use and the transportation system helps explain why changing the built environment in ways that would improve health is so challenging. Moving the entire system in a new direction requires a coordinated effort among many entities, each with its own objectives. Nevertheless, many cities are making progress, especially where there is political leadership for such improvements.

HOW CAN CITIES MAKE HEALTHIER DESIGN CHOICES ABOUT LAND USE AND TRANSPORTATION?

The recipe for making cities healthier is the same as the recipe for making cities more environmentally sustainable, equitable, and fiscally sound, and its adoption is motivated by these potential benefits to varying degrees depending on the city. Well supported by research although not without controversy, the recipe includes (1) promoting compact development that ensures densities sufficient to support high-quality transit and that reduces the separation between activities and (2) prioritizing transit, walking, and bicycling over driving in transportation policies and investments.

The idea of compact development emerged from concerns over suburban sprawl and was at the core of the growth management movement that started in the United States in the 1970s. At a regional scale, the idea is to prevent the outward spread of urban development while using land within the urban boundaries more efficiently. Oregon adopted the most comprehensive growth management policy in the United States in 1973. This policy requires all urban areas in the state to establish an **urban growth boundary**, beyond which urban development is not allowed. The impetus for the policy was to protect both agricultural lands and natural resources, a concern that has motivated many cities to adopt similar growth boundaries even without a state mandate. The benefits for cities are both higher densities and closer proximity among activi-

ties, which together increase the viability of regional transit systems and help reduce automobile dependence. Compact development combined with regional transit investments helps improve accessibility to destinations at the regional scale.[15]

Changes to land use policies at the local scale are also essential. The number of cities in the United States and elsewhere in the world embracing the idea of a "**fifteen-minute city**" grew substantially during 2020 at least in part in response to the COVID-19 pandemic. This idea is a variation on the European concept of a "city of short distances" ("der Stadt de kürzen Wege" in German and "ville du quart d'heure" in French) in which residents have access to the goods and services they need on a regular basis within a short distance of home, close enough for walking or bicycling (figure 11.2).[26] Good connectivity among destinations is an essential component of the concept (figure 11.3). In conjunction with its comprehensive plan, Melbourne adopted a twenty-minute neighborhood policy and launched a pilot program in 2018 to enable residents to "live locally." Portland, Oregon, has also adopted the twenty-minute neighborhood concept, and other cities in the United States may follow. These ideas represent a new way of promoting the concept of local accessibility,[15] also embodied in earlier planning movements in the United States such as **traditional neighborhood design**, **smart growth**, and **New Urbanism**.

One way that cities, especially those in the United States, can foster the higher densities necessary for improved local and regional transit is through **up-zoning** that enables a greater intensity of development than allowed under a city's existing zoning ordinance. In 2018, Minneapolis, Minnesota, was the first city in the United States to adopt an up-zoning policy, which allows up to four housing units on parcels zoned for single-family housing. This enables landowners to replace a single-family home with a four-unit building or to add **accessory dwelling units (ADUs)**, also known as granny flats, in-law units, casitas,

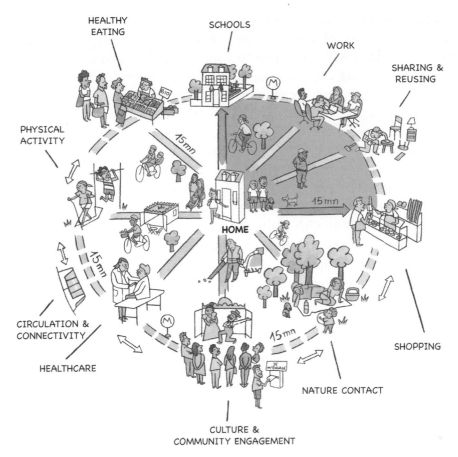

Figure 11.2. Activities of daily living potentially reachable in a fifteen-minute city.
Source: Micaël Dessin, Paris en Commun (translated from original)

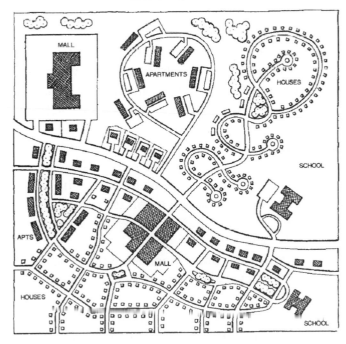

Suburban Sprawl

Traditional Neighborhood

Figure 11.3. A fifteen-minute city requires connectivity among destinations. This schematic shows how traditional neighborhood design (TND) offers substantially better connectivity than a suburban sprawl pattern. Destinations such as a school or a shopping mall are accessible by walking or cycling in the TND, but are neither safe nor convenient to reach by foot or bicycle in the sprawl design.
Source: Image courtesy of © DPZ CoDESIGN

and other names, while keeping the original home.[27] California has adopted several policies that enable and encourage ADUs as a way to address a significant housing shortage and to increase affordable housing. Oregon adopted an up-zoning policy in 2020, the first state to do so. Up-zoning is an important tool for promoting **infill development**, in which previously developed land is redeveloped at higher intensities, and for implementing **transit-oriented development**, or **TOD**, consisting of higher-density development with a mix of land uses in the vicinity of transit stations. These strategies often raise the specter of gentrification, necessitating additional measures to prevent the displacement of current residents especially in low-income communities and communities of color (chapter 9).

Ideas about transportation at the local level are also changing. One silver lining to the COVID-19 pandemic of 2020–2021 was a reuse of street space for purposes other than moving or storing cars. Cities throughout the world created slow streets by restricting access to residents and delivery vehicles only.[28,29] Some cities shut streets to traffic altogether, at least for periods of time. Many allowed restaurants to use parking areas for outdoor dining. These changes may in some cases become permanent, especially when they build on initiatives that began before the pandemic. Inspired by cities in Europe, Seattle, Portland (Oregon), and other US cities have reduced speed limits on residential streets, a change that reduces speeds for the fastest drivers.[30] Cities across the United States have adopted **complete streets** policies that mandate the accommodation of modes other than driving in the design of the public right-of-way, with the goal of ensuring safe travel by all users of the street.[31] A related idea is the use of **road diets** (figure 11.4) in which traffic lanes are reduced to create more space for bicycle lanes, turn lanes, and pedestrian refuge islands. Safe Routes to School programs focus on improvements that enhance safety for children walking and bicycling to schools. All these ideas build on the concept of traffic

calming, a set of well-established approaches to slowing vehicle traffic and improving safety for pedestrians and bicyclists.

Another recent change at the local level is the advent of **micromobility**, otherwise known as bike-sharing and scooter-sharing. These systems rent out bikes or scooters on an hourly basis, either through subscriptions or through trip-based fees. The first bike-sharing services involved partnerships between cities and private operators (for example, New York City's Citi Bike), but more recent services are privately owned and operated under agreements with cities. The new systems are usually dockless, meaning that the bikes can be parked anywhere that meets local rules (for example, in proximity to a bike rack), and in some cities, the systems offer electric-assist bicycles. Electric scooter-sharing systems first opened in 2017 and quickly proliferated in major US cities and elsewhere. The health effects of micromobility trips depend on whether they substitute for other modes of travel. Most bike-share trips do not replace driving trips, and many replace trips by active modes.[32] Riding an electric scooter does little to increase physical activity while exposing riders to considerable risk.[33]

European cities are arguably more people-oriented and measurably less car-dependent than US cities.[34] These cities have generally had the advantage of never having reached US levels of car dependence, although many were trending that way before adopting policies to stave it off. Amsterdam, for example, was headed toward car dependence in the early 1970s until the city reversed course to become the renowned bicycling city that it is today. Not all the inspiration comes from Europe, however. Notable examples from elsewhere include:

- Curitiba, Brazil, pioneered the concept of **bus rapid transit (BRT)** in 1974. Rather than investing in a metro rail system, the city chose the most cost-effective approach of upgrading its bus system to provide service comparable to a rail

(a)

(b)

Figure 11.4. (a) This four-lane road in San Antonio, Texas, is difficult for pedestrians to cross. (b) A conception of how the four-lane road would look if a road diet were built, converting the road to three lanes with bicycle lanes and pedestrian-crossing islands.
Source: Photos courtesy of Michael Ronkin & Marcel Schmaedick

system.[35] Innovations include BRT-only lanes down the center of boulevards and stations that resemble train stations with protection from weather, raised platforms, and other amenities. Bogotá, Colombia, inaugurated its TransMilenio BRT system in 2000; the system now carries two and a half million passengers a day in a region of more than ten million people (figure 11.5). Cities throughout the world have added BRT lines to their transit systems, but Curitiba and Bogotá are unique in the extent to which their systems depend on BRT.

Figure 11.5. The high-capacity Transmilenio bus rapid transit system in Bogotá moves large numbers of local residents daily and has led to a substantial reduction in air pollution and in road traffic fatalities.
Source: Wikimedia Commons, courtesy Josegacel29. https://creativecommons.org/licenses/by-sa/3.0/deed.en

- Bogotá has also made a major commitment to bicycling as another strategy for addressing worsening congestion and air quality. The city was the birthplace of Ciclovia in 1974, a weekly event in which major roads throughout the city are closed to cars and opened to active travel of all forms. As many as a million and a half residents participate each week. Since 2000, the city has invested in 550 kilometers (342 miles) of bicycle lanes and paths. The share of trips by bicycle increased from 0.6 percent in 1996 to more than 9 percent in 2017.[36] During the COVID-19 pandemic, the city opened an 84-kilometer (52-mile) emergency bike network. Plans include an additional 280 kilometers (174 miles) of bike lanes, aiming toward a goal of 50 percent of trips by bicycle or other forms of micromobility.

- Seoul, South Korea, lessened its car orientation when it removed the Cheonggye Freeway in 2003. This elevated freeway, built in 1968, covered Cheonggye Creek, which ran through the heart of Seoul and brought traffic, noise, and pollution to what became a shabby industrial area. After removing the freeway, the city created a linear park around the restored creek that promotes walking for recreation and transportation. It has become one of the most popular tourist attractions in the city. Following the success of this project, the city has demolished more than a dozen other expressways[37] and is planning to add bike lanes and restore a tram system.

WHAT IS THE OUTLOOK FOR THE DESIGN OF CITIES?

Automobile-oriented cities face numerous challenges in shifting toward healthier land use patterns and transportation systems. As discussed earlier, in the United States, local governments have the power to plan and regulate land development, but whether development occurs depends on private-sector initiatives, although public incentives can help (chapter 20). Local governments also have responsibility for the local street network, but not for the state or federal highways that pass through their boundaries. MPOs are the lead on long-range transportation plans, but they have no power over land use patterns, even though some use their funding to encourage transit-supportive land use policies. The lack of affordable housing in job-rich areas within many regions, leading to long commutes for low- and middle-income workers, stems from a lack of regionally minded action on the part of local governments. Coordinating land use and transportation planning at the regional scale is thus the first challenge to overcome.

The COVID-19 pandemic created opportunities such as those described earlier, but it also added to the challenges for cities. Plummeting transit ridership initially plunged these systems into financial crisis, mitigated in part by federal assistance. On the other hand, the pandemic forced transit agencies to rethink their approach and could lead to more efficient and effective transit systems. The shift to remote working for a sizable share of the workforce presents another opportunity, as both employers and employees consider a permanent shift to at least part-time telecommuting. But even part-time telecommuting—working from home a couple of days per week, for example—could enable workers to live farther from their workplaces, leading to longer trips on the days they do commute. The net benefit of remote working is uncertain for sustainability—and for health.

The implications of vehicle automation are also uncertain (chapter 24). Predictions of the advent of fully automated vehicles vary widely, but many experts are skeptical about widespread adoption anytime soon. The impacts are likely to be mixed.[38] The ability to ride in a vehicle without having to drive it may increase driving by making it more attractive, with negative implications for health. On the other hand, the use of such vehicles may reduce the land area needed for roads or parking, creating opportunities for the reuse of space for other modes, housing, parks, or other needed land uses. Automation also has the potential to reduce crashes due to driver error and to reduce driving stress, with benefits for public health. The most favorable scenario would be a shift from personal ownership of cars to a fleet of publicly available, electrically powered cars that operate like an on-demand transit system with multiple passengers in each vehicle.[39]

When concerns over health are coupled with concerns over climate change and **mobility justice**, the motivation for reducing car dependence and supporting active travel becomes more potent. Greenhouse gas emissions in the transportation sector can be reduced through technological innovations, such as electric vehicles, but reducing greenhouse gas emissions enough to meet the necessary targets means reducing the amount of driving, too. California's Senate Bill 375 of 2008 requires MPOs to develop plans that reduce driving through changes in land use patterns and the transportation system. Progress has been slower than hoped, owing in large part to the strength of local control over land use, but policies to encourage transit-supportive development have been adopted in recent years at the local and state levels in California.[40]

Mobility justice concerns in the United States arise from more than a century of residential segregation coupled with both underinvestment in local facilities and overinvestment in freeways through low-income Black and Latinx neighborhoods. Residents of these neighborhoods disproportionately experience the negative effects of the transportation system while having relatively poor access to jobs and other activities. Federal policy requires MPOs to consider the equity impacts of its plans, and some MPOs have begun to adopt processes that will help to ensure that past injustices are at least in part rectified with new investments in these neighborhoods, particularly in transit and active travel. Doing so without fueling gentrification and displacing current residents is another challenge for cities (chapter 9).

Building people-centered rather than car-dependent communities is good for health, as well as for environmental sustainability, economic vitality, and social equity. Compact land development combined with investments in walking, bicycling, and transit provide good accessibility to activities at the local level and good accessibility to regional opportunities via modes other than driving. In such places, residents could replace driving with active travel, generating benefits to themselves and the community. Achieving this vision requires close coordination between land use and transportation planning, as cities across the United States and around the world are adopting new strategies that will help them become more equitable and sustainable places to live, work, and play.

DISCUSSION QUESTIONS

1. What features of the built environment encourage and discourage physical activity and active transportation?
2. How do transportation systems and land use patterns impact environmental quality and climate change?
3. What policies facilitate development that promotes health and is equitable and sustainable? Of these, which are most feasible for your city or region, and why?
4. Why might some land use and transportation planners be reluctant to incorporate health considerations into their decisions?
5. How can more interactions between public health departments and planning departments be encouraged?

DISCLOSURE OF COMPETING INTERESTS

Susan Handy discloses no competing interests.

REFERENCES

1. Handy S. Accessibility-oriented urban design. In: T Banerjee, A Loukaitou-Sideris, eds. *The New Companion to Urban Design*. Routledge; 2019:585-598.

2. Behzad B, King DM, Jacobson SH. Quantifying the association between obesity, automobile travel, and caloric intake. *Preventive Medicine*. 2013;56(2):103-106.

3. Jacobson SH, King DM. Measuring the potential for automobile fuel savings in the US: the impact of obesity. *Transportation Research Part D: Transport and Environment*. 2009;14(1):6-13.

4. Lopez-Zetina J, Lee H, Friis R. The link between obesity and the built environment. Evidence from an ecological analysis of obesity and vehicle miles of travel in California. *Health & Place*. 2006;12(4):656-664.

5. Novaco RW, Gonzalez OI. Commuting and well-being. In: Hamburger YA, ed., *Technology and Psychological Well-Being*. Cambridge University Press; 2009:174-205.

6. Hennessy DA. The impact of commuter stress on workplace aggression. *Journal of Applied Social Psychology*. 2008;38(9):2315-2335.

7. Poharika M, Fitzgerald S. Urban sprawl and you: how sprawl adversely affects worker health. *AAOHN Journal*. 2004;52(6):242-246.

8. Gee GC, Takeuchi DT. Traffic stress, vehicular burden and well-being: a multilevel analysis. *Social Science & Medicine*. 2004;59(2):405-414. https://doi.org/10.1016/j.socscimed.2003.10.027

9. Cavill N, Kahlmeier S, Rutter H, Racioppi F, Oja P. Economic analyses of transport infrastructure and policies including health effects related to cycling and walking: a systematic review. *Transport Policy*. 2008;15(5):291-304.

10. Oja P, Titze S, Bauman A, et al. Health benefits of cycling: a systematic review. *Scandinavian Journal of Medicine & Science in Sports*. 2011;21(4):496-509.

11. Gatersleben B, Uzzell D. Affective appraisals of the daily commute: comparing perceptions of drivers, cyclists, walkers, and users of public transport. *Environment and Behavior*. 2007;39(3):416-431. https://doi.org/10.1177%2F0013916506294032

12. Le VT, Dannenberg AL. Moving toward physical activity targets by walking to transit: National Household Transportation Survey, 2001–2017. *American Journal of Preventive Medicine*. 2020;59(3):e115-e123.

13. Lowe M, Aytekin B, Gereffi G. "Public transit buses: a green choice gets greener." In: *Manufacturing Climate Solutions: Carbon-Reducing Technologies and U.S. Jobs*. Duke University Center on Globalization Governance & Competitiveness; 2009:chap 12.

14. Handy, S. What California gains from reducing car dependence. Institute of Transportation Studies, University of California, Davis. 2020. https://escholarship.org/uc/item/0hk0h610

15. Handy S. Why sustainable transport cannot ignore land use. In: Curtis C, ed. *Handbook of Sustainable Transport*. Edward Elgar; 2020:220-229.

16. Glazener A, Sanchez K, Ramani T, et al. Fourteen pathways between urban transportation and health: a conceptual model and literature review. *Journal of Transport & Health*. 2021;21:101070. https://doi.org/10.1016/j.jth.2021.101070

17. Volker JM, Lee AE, Fitch DT. Streamlining the development approval process in a post–level of service Los Angeles. *Journal of the American Planning Association*. 2019;85(2):114-132.

18. Santasieri C. Planning for Transit-Supportive Development: A Practitioner's Guide—Section 5: Local Planning and Transit-Supportive Development. FTA

Report No. 0057. Federal Transit Administration; 2014.

19. Peters A. See just how much of a city's land is used for parking spaces. Fast Company. 2017. https://www.fastcompany.com/40441392/see-just-how-much-of-a-citys-land-is-used-for-parking-spaces

20. Brinkman J, King D, Jacobson S. Freeway Revolts! Working Papers 19-29, Federal Reserve Bank of Philadelphia. 2019. https://www.philadelphiafed.org/the-economy/regional-economics/freeway-revolts

21. Handy S. Increasing highway capacity unlikely to relieve traffic congestion. Policy Brief. National Center for Sustainable Transportation, University of California, Davis. 2015. https://escholarship.org/uc/item/58x8436d

22. Ricklin A, Kushner N. *Integrating Health into the Comprehensive Planning Process: An Analysis of Seven Case Studies and Recommendations for Change.* American Planning Association; 2013.

23. Rothstein R. *The Color of Law: A Forgotten History of How Our Government Segregated America.* Liveright Publishing; 2017.

24. Culdesac Blog. Welcome to Culdesac Tempe. 2021. https://culdesac.com/

25. Sciara G-C, Handy S. Regional transportation planning. In: Giuliano G, Hanson S, eds. *The Geography of Urban Transportation.* Guilford Press; 2017:139-163.

26. Pozoukidou G, Chatziyiannaki Z. 15-minute city: decomposing the new urban planning eutopia. *Sustainability.* 2021;13(2):928. https://doi.org/10.3390/su13020928

27. AARP (formerly American Association of Retired Persons). All about accessory dwelling units. 2020. http://aarp.org/adu

28. Steckler B, Swift T, Pardo C. How are communities reallocating the street right-of-way to safely accommodate recreational and social activities during the COVID-19 pandemic? COVID Mobility Works. 2020. https://www.covidmobilityworks.org/insights/how-are-communities-reallocating-the-street-right-of-way-to-safely-accommodate-recreational-and-social-activities-during-the-covid-19-pandemic

29. Firth CL, Baquero B, Berney R, Hoerster KD, Mooney SJ, Winters M. Not quite a block party: COVID-19 street reallocation programs in Seattle, WA and Vancouver, BC. *SSM—Population Health.* 2021;14:100769-100769. https://doi.org/10.1016/j.ssmph.2021.100769

30. Anderson JC, Monsere C, Kothuri S. Effect of residential street speed limit reduction from 25 to 20 mi/hr on driving speeds in Portland, Oregon. Department of Civil and Environmental Engineering, Portland State University; 2020. https://www.portland.gov/sites/default/files/2020/pbot-20-mph-speed-study-finalv5.pdf

31. Carlson SA, Paul P, Kumar G, Watson KB, Atherton E, Fulton JE. Prevalence of complete streets policies in US municipalities. *Journal of Transport & Health.* 2017;5:142-150. https://doi.org/10.1016/j.jth.2016.11.003

32. McQueen M, Abou-Zeid G, MacArthur J, Clifton K. Transportation transformation: is micromobility making a macro impact on sustainability? *Journal of Planning Literature.* 2021;36(1):46-61.

33. Badeau A, Carman C, Newman M, Steenblik J, Carlson M, Madsen T. Emergency department visits for electric scooter-related injuries after introduction of an urban rental program. *American Journal of Emergency Medicine.* 2019;37(8):1531-1533.

34. Buehler R, Pucher J, Gerike R, Götschi T. Reducing car dependence in the heart of Europe: lessons from Germany, Austria, and Switzerland. *Transport Reviews.* 2017;37(1):4-28. http://doi.org/10.1080/01441647.2016.1177799

35. Duarte F, Rojas F. Intermodal connectivity to BRT: a comparative analysis of Bogotá and Curitiba. *Journal of Public Transportation.* 2012;15(2):1. http://doi.org/10.5038/2375-0901.15.2.1

36. Rosas-Satizábal D, Rodriguez-Valencia A. Factors and policies explaining the emergence of the bicycle commuter in Bogotá. *Case Studies on Transport Policy.* 2019;7(1):138-149.

37. Congress for New Urbanism. Model Cities: Seoul—Cheonggye Freeway. No date. Accessed October 20, 2021. https://www.cnu.org/highways-boulevards/model-cities/seoul

38. Rodier CJ. Travel effects and associated greenhouse gas emissions of automated vehicles. National Center for Sustainable Transportation, University of California, Davis. April 2018. https://escholarship.org/uc/item/9g12v6r0

39. Sperling D. *Three Revolutions: Steering Automated, Shared, and Electric Vehicles to a Better Future.* Island Press; 2018.

40. Barbour E, Grover S, Lamoureaux Y, Chaudhary G, Handy S. Planning and policymaking for transit-oriented development, transit, and active transport in California cities. National Center for Sustainable Transportation, University of California, Davis. March 2020. https://escholarship.org/content/qt7j37k8ms/qt7j37k8ms.pdf

CHAPTER 12

HEALTHY HOMES

David E. Jacobs and Amanda Reddy

KEY POINTS

- A major social determinant of health, housing is both a physical place where we spend most of our time, and a home is an expression of who we are individually and as a people. Housing and homes can support good physical and mental health and overall societal well-being or can contribute to disease and injury.
- Green healthy housing standards support sustainability by reducing energy and material use.
- Hazards in homes can include lead, allergens, mold, environmental tobacco smoke, carbon monoxide, asbestos, radon, volatile organic compounds, excessive heat and cold, crowding, barriers to accessibility, and conditions associated with falls and other injuries. These are linked to adverse health outcomes, including asthma, allergies, lung cancer, injuries, poor mental health, poisoning, fatalities, and neurodevelopmental disorders.
- Certain historic housing policies have contributed to inequities in health, wealth, opportunity, and community vitality through segregation, unaffordability, substandard housing quality, and shortages. Past and current racist and discriminatory housing practices have prevented communities of color and low-income households from building wealth and accessing healthy housing, worsening disparities in health and other outcomes.

- Examples of effective healthy housing interventions include improving ventilation and moisture control, diverting radon gas, controlling pests through integrated pest management, eliminating lead hazards, and installing smoke and carbon monoxide alarms.
- Strategies to promote healthy housing include implementation of healthy and green housing guidelines for new and existing construction, enhancement and enforcement of proactive housing code inspections, improved integration of healthy housing principles into disaster recovery/emergency preparedness and other home improvement programs, greater access to multicomponent home visit programs, increased public and private investment and policies that promote smoke-free homes, accessibility, and affordability.
- Healthy housing saves lives, reduces disease and injury, increases quality of life, reduces poverty, helps mitigate climate change, and contributes to the achievement of the United Nations' Sustainable Development Goals.

INTRODUCTION

Abang Ojullu remembers vividly the day she put her daughter Ananaya on a small ambulance jet bound for Sioux Falls, South Dakota. Her child's asthma attack was too severe for doctors in rural Worthington, Minnesota, to treat. Soon thereafter, they moved into an apartment renovated using green and healthy housing principles. Unlike the family's previous residences, this three-bedroom unit included air conditioning, plenty of fresh air, exhaust fans in the kitchen and bathrooms, and no mold anywhere. Since moving in, Ananaya has not been sick once. "Now she's perfect," brags Abang. "It's amazing." Ananaya recently scored noticeably better on a breathing test used to measure asthma control. This story vividly demonstrates the direct impact of the home environment on health.[1]

Housing occupies a special place among built environments. Houses and other living quarters are structures that serve as shelters, providing protection from weather and potentially hostile environments. Admonitions to "stay home" during the COVID-19 pandemic underscored the importance of healthy housing. In housing that has hazards, increased time at home may exacerbate other health problems.

Homes are places laden with meaning for the people who live in them, objects of aspirations, sources of personal and cultural identity, safe and secure havens, and the settings for family life.[2,3] Accordingly, good housing promotes health and well-being, whereas substandard housing conditions have far-reaching consequences (figures 12.1 and 12.2).

Healthy homes are sited, designed, built, and maintained to promote the health of their occupants by creating indoor spaces, exterior building envelopes, and outdoor yards that are healthy and by linking occupants to

Figure 12.1. An easy-to-build healthy home designed for Haiti with natural light and ventilation, clean water, and renewable energy. At least a prototype of this design was subsequently built in Haiti. Source: Archive Global, image produced by reCOVER team from UVA as winning entry for Kay e Sante nan Haiti competition

Figure 12.2. Large numbers of people in low- and middle-income countries lack clean water, basic sanitation, and adequate housing, as in this Jakarta, Indonesia, slum. Source: Wikimedia Commons, courtesy of Jonathan McIntosh. https://creativecommons.org /licenses/by/2.0/deed.en

healthy neighborhoods.[4] Housing is generally divided into single-family and multifamily categories, the latter often sharing common spaces, ventilation, plumbing, electrical, and other building systems. Housing can be either owner-occupied or rental. Some areas especially in low-income countries have informal housing settlements, where ownership of both land and the structure is poorly documented and where basic services such as water, power, and sanitation are lacking, which has important implications for community investment and sustainability.

The connection between housing and health has been recognized since the Code of Hammurabi (Section 229), circa 1750 BC.[5] The public health and healthy housing movements have common roots in the efforts over a century ago to address slum housing. The first modern housing laws were established to respond to infectious disease threats to public health.[6] For example, the provision of indoor plumbing improved sanitation and led to the control of cholera and other waterborne illnesses. Recently, there has been increased understanding of the relationship between housing and chronic diseases such as asthma, allergy, depression, cardiovascular disease, and lead poisoning. Housing may pose risk factors for injuries from falls and electrocutions (chapter 5). Inadequate housing also contributes to social inequalities (chapter 9); for example, housing instability, scarcity, and inadequate investment can be tied to increased homelessness, crime, stress, abuse, violence, and other antisocial behavior.

The World Health Organization (WHO) published international housing and health guidelines in 2018,[7] with specific recommendations on crowding, indoor thermal conditions, injury prevention, accessibility, and other healthy housing issues, based on systematic evidence reviews. These guidelines apply to both existing housing and newly constructed dwellings in high- and low-income countries. Housing will become increasingly important to health as the world's urban population and the population of persons over age sixty are expected to double by 2050. By providing protection from cold, heat, and other extreme weather conditions, housing also plays an important role in adapting to the impacts of climate change.

The growing awareness of the housing and health nexus led the US Department of Housing and Urban Development (US HUD) and the Centers for Disease Control and Prevention (CDC) to launch the nation's healthy homes initiative in 1999.[8] Ten years later, the US Surgeon General issued "A Call to Action to Promote Healthy Homes."[4] These reports and others reflect the emerging consensus that healthy housing adheres to ten key principles (box 12.1). Additional features of a healthy home include adequate lighting, security, sufficient space for each occupant (although there is no consensus definition of sufficient space), housing sustainability, and housing equity. Adequate housing also provides important psychosocial benefits, such as providing a safe haven from a world that may be stressful and violent.

Several reviews have examined how housing influences health.[9-11] WHO conducted systematic literature reviews for crowding, accessibility, and thermal conditions and also quantified the large burden of disease associated with inadequate housing.[12]

Substantial disparities in housing quality and location lead to health inequities.[13] Other broad social dynamics such as homelessness, lack of affordable housing, residential segregation, and inadequate residential development planning are intertwined and result in negative health outcomes.[14,15] For example, high housing cost burdens are inversely associated with physical and mental well-being. Families with severe housing cost burdens spend 75 percent less on health care and 40 percent less on food, and low-income seniors with severe housing cost burdens spend 62 percent less on health care.[16] These households forgo healthy food or delay health care or medications to pay the rent. Rents have risen faster than incomes since 2000 in the United States. More low-income people are renting their homes than ever before, and the supply of affordable housing and rental assistance has not kept pace.[16]

As a result, more households cannot afford a decent home, especially those economically stressed by the recent pandemic. Strategies to overcome homelessness and housing disparities are complex and include new housing production, preservation of existing housing, increased subsidies, more and better jobs, expansion of housing trust funds, equitable access to finance, and equitable disaster recovery efforts. These issues are discussed in chapters 9 and 10. In this chapter, we focus on health impacts related to the design, construction, and rehabilitation of homes by grouping risk factors into biological, chemical, and physical agents, how they are identified and remediated, and policies needed to ensure healthy housing for all.

EXPOSURES THAT CONTRIBUTE TO UNHEALTHY HOUSING

Various biological agents, chemical agents, and physical exposures can contribute to unhealthy housing. Structured housing inspections can be used to assess such exposures.

Biological Agents

Biological agents found in homes include allergens and other agents from cockroaches, pets, rodents, dust mites, and fungi (mold). These can trigger allergic and other inflammatory reactions that lead to asthma and allergic rhinitis. Asthma prevalence and morbidity increased from 1980 to 2010 and then reached a plateau in the United States.[17]

Internationally, asthma affects 339 million people and is associated with both premature death and reduced quality of life, in people of all ages. It ranks sixteenth among the leading causes of years lived with disability and twenty-eighth among the leading causes of burden of disease, as measured by **disability-adjusted life years (DALYs)**.[18]

There has been increased exposure to indoor biological agents resulting from changes in home construction methods (such as use of tighter building envelopes associated with reduced ventilation and increased moisture) and from spending increasing amounts of time indoors. Building envelopes are associated with a common housing problem in the form of water leaking from inside and outside into the home's interior (twenty-one million homes in 2017, according to the American Housing Survey). Excessive moisture supports the growth of fungi and provides an environment favorable to dust mites, cockroaches, rodents, and other asthma triggers. Race, income, housing type, presence of smokers, pets, cockroaches, rodents, and mold/moisture-related problems were all independent predictors of both high allergen burden in housing and increased asthma symptoms in the American Healthy Homes Survey.[19]

Dust mite allergens both cause and exacerbate asthma.[20,21] Dust mites are found in bedding, pillows, mattresses, carpets, and upholstered furniture. About 74 percent of homes in the United States have detectable levels of mite allergen in the bedroom, 51 percent have levels associated with sensitization, and 30 percent have levels associated with asthma morbidity.[22]

Cockroach allergens come from the insects' fecal material, saliva, secretions, and body parts. Structural deficiencies in walls, floors, and ceilings allow cockroaches to enter homes, and leaks provide them with water. Cockroach allergens are found in 13 percent of dwellings in the United States,[23] and 5 percent of all dwellings have cockroach allergen levels above the allergic sensitization threshold.[22]

Fungi produce allergens, toxins, and irritants and thereby exacerbate asthma and allergies. They are also markers for damp homes, which are associated with respiratory disease.[24] Up to 21 percent of asthma cases may be associated with dampness and mold,[25] and a systematic review found that children exposed to mold were one and a half times more likely to develop asthma or wheeze.[26] Damp, moldy, and cold indoor conditions may also be associated with anxiety and depression.[27]

Allergen from Alternaria (a type of fungus) is present in 99 percent of US homes, and 56 percent have levels associated with asthma symptoms.[19] Rodent allergens, derived primarily from rodent urine, have been linked to asthma exacerbations.[28] Mouse allergen is found in 41 percent of dwellings in the United States, and 3 percent of homes have levels above the threshold for sensitization.[22]

Higher rates of childhood asthma and asthma exacerbation occur in socioeconomically disadvantaged youth. Risk factors include male gender, parental history of asthma, race, ethnicity, ambient air pollution, and early life exposures to microbes and aeroallergens.[29] Pet dander can also be related to sensitization.

Chemical Agents

Chemicals in the home environment have been associated with neurological toxicity, developmental disorders, asthma and other respiratory illnesses, cancer, and fatalities at high exposures. Chemicals of concern found in homes include lead, volatile organic compounds (VOCs), formaldehyde, asbestos, radon, and also chemicals introduced by building occupants, such as tobacco smoke and pesticides. Deficiencies (such as deteriorating lead-based paint), unvented gas stoves, and introduction of materials that off-gas or otherwise release toxic agents can increase exposure to chemicals. An inadequate supply and poor distribution of fresh air in the building space and deteriorated, hard-to-clean surfaces can allow accumulation of airborne contaminants and pesticide residues, as well as other toxicants. Carpets can be both sources and reservoirs of chemical and biological agents; like other building materials, they are often not tested for contaminants prior to use in construction and housing rehabilitation and can accumulate dust and other harmful agents.[30]

Lead affects the brain, neurodevelopmental processes, and other organ systems.[31] Some of its effects are irreversible, and no safe level of lead exposure has been identified. In the United States, the major source of contemporary lead exposure since the elimination of lead from gasoline and food canning in the 1980s has been ingestion by children of deteriorated lead-based paint in houses built before 1978 and the contaminated dust and soil this paint generates (box 12.2). As of 2012 (the most recent year for which data are available), lead paint hazards still existed in nearly twenty-four million US homes[32] and are more concentrated in

BOX 12.2 LEAD PAINT IN HOMES: A SUCCESS STORY

The success of childhood lead poisoning prevention illustrates the substantial benefits of using scientific evidence to implement healthy homes policies. In the late 1980s, 1.7 million US preschool children had blood lead levels high enough to threaten their neurological development. Much of their lead exposure occurred at home from deteriorated, lead-containing paint. As a result of effective lead prevention policies that have focused on removal of lead from paint and gasoline, this number declined by over 90 percent since the 1970s.[a] The health and monetary benefits associated with controlling residential lead hazards are valued at $84 billion or more for the children born in 2018 alone, with additional benefits for each additional annual birth cohort. Benefits include increased IQ levels in children (which are associated with increased productivity and lifetime earnings), increased market value of homes, and improved energy efficiency of homes.[b]

Such progress was made possible by research demonstrating that much lead poisoning in children results from lead moving from paint to house dust, which children inadvertently ingest through hand-to-mouth contact. This understanding led to expanding lead control efforts from controlling lead paint to eliminating dust and repairing underlying housing conditions that contribute to lead exposure.[c] A public health paradigm focusing on prevention of exposure, not just reacting after children have been poisoned, has emerged.[d] In response to nationwide campaigns, Congress authorized record funding for the Department of Housing and Urban Development in 2021 to address the problem in the millions of US houses that still contain lead hazards.[e]

REFERENCES

a. National Center for Healthy Housing. United States Healthy Housing Fact Sheet. 2019. https://nchh.org/resource-library/fact-sheet_state-healthy-housing_usa.pdf
b. Pew Charitable Trusts and Robert Wood Johnson Foundation. 10 Policies to Prevent and Respond to Childhood Lead Exposure. 2017. https://nchh.org/resource/report_10-policies-to-prevent-and-respond-to-childhood-lead-exposure_english/
c. US Department of Housing and Urban Development (HUD). *HUD Guidelines for the Evaluation and Control of Lead-Based Paint Hazards in Housing.* 2nd ed. HUD LBP-1918. HUD; 2012. https://www.hud.gov/program_offices/healthy_homes/lbp/hudguidelines
d. Residential Lead-Based Paint Hazard Reduction Act. Public Law 102-550; Title X of the 1992 Housing and Community Development Act. 1992. https://www.epa.gov/lead/residential-lead-based-paint-hazard-reduction-act-1992-title-x
e. National Center for Healthy Housing. *Healthcare Financing of Healthy Homes.* National Center for Healthy Housing; 2021. https://nchh.org/tools-and-data/financing-and-funding/healthcare-financing/

low-income housing in the Northeast and Midwest. Much of the world banned the use of lead in residential paint in the 1920s, but the United States did not do so until 1978. Many countries still allow its production despite a global campaign by the United Nations and WHO. Lead may also be present in soil, drinking water, foods, candies, spices, pottery/dishes, cosmetics, toys, jewelry, traditional medicines, painted furniture, other consumer products, and other sources, including exposure to lead associated with certain jobs or hobbies, such as battery plants, automotive repair shops, arts and crafts, and shooting ranges. Approximately one-third of children—up to eight hundred million globally—have blood lead levels at or above the current level established by WHO and the CDC for interventions.[33]

Exposure to high levels of VOCs, such as formaldehyde from building materials, can lead to sensitization to allergens and increase the risk of cancer, respiratory disease, and other problems.[34] Lower levels of VOCs act as respiratory irritants and can cause nausea, headaches, and neurological symptoms. Common household items that release VOCs include paint, varnish, wax, cleaners, cosmetics, particle board and plywood, and so-called air fresheners. Off-gassing of formaldehyde led to concerns about health effects among people living in poorly ventilated Federal Emergency Management Agency's travel trailers used during the Hurricane Katrina response.[35]

Carbon monoxide (CO) exposure causes approximately 450 deaths and more than 15,000 emergency department visits annually in the United States; 64 percent of these exposures occur in the home. From 2010 to 2015 in the United States, a total of 2,244 deaths resulted from unintentional CO poisoning, with the highest numbers of deaths occurring in winter months.[36] Indoor CO sources are poorly functioning furnaces and gas stoves, unvented kerosene and gas space heaters, woodstoves, fireplaces, and automobile exhaust from attached garages. Following power outages associated with hurricanes and other disasters, indoor generator use without adequate ventilation has led to deaths from CO poisoning.[6] Acute exposure to high levels of CO can cause unconsciousness, long-term neurological disabilities, coma, cardiorespiratory failure, and death. Chronic low-level CO exposure can cause viral-like symptoms, such as fatigue, dizziness, headache, and disorientation.

Radon gas is the second leading cause of lung cancer, causing twenty-one thousand deaths annually in the United States.[37,38] It is a colorless, odorless, radioactive gas that occurs naturally in soil and rock throughout the United States. Radon maps have been published by US Environmental Protection Agency (EPA), but they are dated and cannot be used to predict how much radon will be in a particular home.[39] Radon migrates through fractures and porous substrates in building foundations and then enters the breathing zone within buildings via pressure differentials. Some states require disclosure of radon test results on selling a house if radon testing has been conducted; a few communities require radon testing prior to selling a house.

Asbestos is a mineral fiber found in a variety of building construction materials. It was widely used in buildings in the United States until the 1970s as an insulator and fire retardant. When asbestos-containing materials are damaged or disturbed by repair, remodeling, or demolition activities, microscopic fibers become airborne. When inhaled, they can cause lung and other cancers and asbestosis.[40] Globally, asbestos-related lung cancer, mesothelioma, and asbestosis from occupational exposures resulted in 107,000 deaths and 1,523,000 DALYs in 2004.[7,41]

Physical Exposures

Residential injuries, including falls, fire-related inhalation injury, burns and scalds, and drowning, cause thousands of deaths and millions of emergency department visits each year in the United States (chapter 5). Globally, a third of injuries occur in the home, and, in 2016, half of all unintentional injury-related deaths occurred in the home. Although injuries in the home affect people of all ages, home injury rates are highest in the youngest and oldest age groups. Worldwide, about 424,000 individuals die each year from falls, of which the vast majority are in low- and middle-income countries, and more than thirty-seven million falls require medical attention.[7]

Exposure to excessive indoor temperatures caused by hot weather can exacerbate cardiovascular and lung disease and cause death, especially among the poor, the elderly, the socially isolated, and persons living in homes without air conditioning (such as during the Chicago heat wave described in chapter 9). From 2004 to 2018, an average of 702 heat-related deaths (415 with heat as the underlying cause and 287 as a contributing cause) occurred annually in the United States.[42] A heat wave in Ahmedabad, India, in 2010 was associated with 4,462 deaths from all causes, which was 43 percent higher than the deaths during the baseline reference period.[43] An excess of 70,000 people in sixteen countries across Europe died in August 2003 due to a major heat wave. Across Africa, the frequency of extreme heat waves increased to 24.5 observations per year (60.1 percent of land area) between 2006 and 2015, as compared with 12.3 per year (37.3 percent of land area) in the period from 1981 to 2005. People who live in temperate climates are more likely to be affected by high temperatures; the temperature threshold where heat-related deaths begin to increase during a heat wave is lower in cities with cooler climates. Exposure to heat waves earlier in the season has a greater impact on mortality because the population has not had a chance to adapt to higher temperatures.[7] Urban heat islands and residence in poorly insulated buildings also contribute to heat-related morbidity and mortality.

Excess winter deaths due to inadequately heated housing has been estimated at 38,200 per year (12.8/100,000 population) in eleven selected European countries.[12] A study in South Africa showed that informal dwellings were more vulnerable than other types of dwellings to indoor temperature instability, which affected thermal comfort.[7]

Excessive noise in homes may result in sleep disturbances, hypertension, performance reduction, increased annoyance responses, and adverse social behavior (chapter 7). Homes adjacent to airports, railroad yards, and highways and in crowded neighborhoods are exposed to high noise levels. Lack of noise-proofing features such as insulation and double-pane windows is also associated with increased noise exposure. Old single-pane windows have the highest levels of lead paint and dust, so replacing them may simultaneously reduce noise and lead exposure, improve energy efficiency, and increase home market value.[44]

Housing Hazard Assessment

Identification of health and safety hazards in housing is helpful in focusing remediation and prevention. Visual assessment by a trained inspector (either from a local government or community group or property manager) is the first step in detecting health hazards and deficiencies in housing, complemented by resident interviews and, in some cases, by environmental testing. Healthy housing training for community health workers and others is available.[45]

A structured inspection has emerged as the primary assessment tool for most hazards (box 12.3), although some hazards, such as lead or radon, cannot be detected by sight and smell. Assessments should be performed by trained personnel. Several model assessment tools are available.[46] Interviews with residents offer an

---

BOX 12.3 COMMONLY INCLUDED ELEMENTS OF A VISUAL HOME ASSESSMENT

- Site: Pooling of water, damaged fencing (or lack of fencing, especially around swimming pools), erosion, debris and garbage, extensive overgrowth of vegetation, sidewalk cracks, neighborhood quality, nearby pollution sources, and unsafe play area equipment
- Building envelope and exterior: Leaks, gaps in doors and walls that enable pest entry or water incursion, broken or inoperable windows, bulging walls or sagging rooflines, foundation cracks, damaged or missing trim or flashing, and problems with gutters
- Equipment rooms containing HVAC (heating, ventilation, and air conditioning), laundry, electrical, and other systems: Fuel leaks, dirty air filters, misaligned flue vents, the absence of makeup air supplied to replace air exhausted from a space, damaged or frayed electrical wiring or burn marks on fuse or electrical breaker boxes, and faulty fire protection systems
- Living area: Leaks, condensation, water damage, mold, cracks or holes, inadequate ventilation, deteriorated carpeting, scalding water temperature, trip and fall hazards, peeling paint, overuse of extension cords, overloaded circuits, broken electrical sockets, unvented fuel-fired space heaters, inadequate food preparation, storage, and disposal facilities, pests, and inoperable or missing smoke and carbon monoxide alarms

opportunity to educate residents about housing and health[46] and to inform the assessment about the residents' health concerns and perceptions of their home environments.

Environmental sampling of homes can determine levels of harmful substances in air, soil, dust, water, or other media.[46] The results are typically compared either to existing exposure limits or to levels in the outdoor air. Except for lead paint, dust, water, and soil, home environmental exposure standards are lacking for many hazards because Congress has not authorized the EPA to establish them. This makes interpretation of home sampling results difficult. WHO has published indoor air quality guidelines.[47]

IMPROVING HOUSING CONDITIONS SUSTAINABLY THROUGH POLICY

After housing hazards have been identified, policies must be developed to implement interventions to eliminate them. In addition to the conditions found inside homes, the neighborhood in which a home is located affects the health of its occupants. Strategies to promote healthy community design are discussed in chapter 11 and in other chapters.

Planning

Successful implementation of healthy housing requires coordination between national, regional, and local governments; public, private, and civil society actors; architects, urban planners, social housing services, and education; consumer protection agencies; environmental and public health professionals; housing providers; the building industry; and others. Interventions to improve health from poor housing include direct changes to the built environment that require the provision of loans, subsidies, and other investments.[7]

Many interventions yield multiple benefits, and many housing improvements are often combined. For example, eliminating a moisture problem helps prevent mold, dust mites, deteriorated paint, structural rot and degradation, and pest infestation simultaneously. A

Cochrane review showed a decrease in wheezing and rhinitis in adults and reduced acute care visits for children following moisture/mold remediation.[48] These multiple co-benefits enhance the sustainability of healthy housing and buildings because residents are less likely to be faced with high medical bills or eviction; eliminating moisture also improves sustainability through improved durability and reduced need for rehabilitation.[49] Integrating housing development with a health in all policies approach is key to adequate planning.[7]

Box 12.4 presents the results of a review by an expert panel of the effectiveness of a range of housing interventions,[50-53] providing an evidence base to guide healthy housing policy development. WHO published a series of systematic reviews of multifaceted housing interventions, and HUD has funded hundreds of studies since 1999[54] demonstrating the benefits of healthy housing.

Ventilation, Moisture, and Weatherization Policy

Policies that require adequate ventilation, air conditioners, and dehumidifiers decrease humidity levels. Relative humidity between 30 and 65 percent is optimal for health and housing quality and can lower exposure to biological and lead paint hazards, as well as injuries from structural rot. To adequately control humidity, improvements to the ventilation system may be needed, such as changing the source of supply air from a moist basement to a tempered living area or from outside air and dehumidification in some climate zones.

Water intrusion can be eliminated by policies to require structural features, such as proper grading, capillary breaks (small separations between basement floors and walls to avoid "wicking" water from the ground up into the building), water pipe insulation to prevent condensation, exhaust ventilation for kitchens and bathrooms, and high-efficiency windows. If mold contamination is extensive, remediation should be performed in accordance with published mold and moisture remediation guidelines.[55,56]

BOX 12.4 SELECTED HEALTHY HOUSING INTERVENTIONS

- Multifaceted, in-home, tailored interventions for asthma (reduce exposure to triggers)
- Cockroach and other pest control through integrated pest management (reduce allergens)
- Combined elimination of moisture intrusion and leaks and removal of moldy items
- Improved insulation and envelope sealing with ventilation
- Active radon air-mitigation strategies (reduce exposure to radon)
- Exhaust ventilation for cookstoves
- Smoke-free policies (reduce tobacco exposure)
- Residential lead hazard control (reduce lead exposure)
- Portable room high efficiency particulate air (HEPA) filtration
- Heating and cooling system maintenance and installation to maintain indoor temperatures above 18°C (64°F) and less than 25°C to 30°C (77°F to 86°F)
- Reduced crowding to control tuberculosis, diarrhea and other communicable diseases, and stress
- Installed, working smoke and carbon monoxide alarms (reduce fire deaths and injuries)
- Isolation four-sided pool fencing (prevent drowning)
- Preset, safe temperature hot water heaters (prevent scald burns)
- Home modifications such as handrails, grab bars, window guards, improved lighting, and other injury reduction measures
- Temperature-controlled mixer water faucets (burn prevention)
- Home modification to facilitate escape from fires
- A proportion of housing that is accessible to people with functional impairments
- Adequate potable water supply through multiple taps within the home
- Fuel combustion equipment should conform to WHO emission rates and should not include coal or kerosene
- Nighttime outdoor noise should be limited to forty to fifty-five decibels
- Housing rental vouchers (allow moving into healthier housing)
- Moving people from high-poverty to lower-poverty neighborhoods
- Documentation of land ownership

Adequate ventilation to provide fresh outdoor air helps exhaust stale indoor air, control moisture, and dilute contaminants released by building materials and occupants. Standards specifying the amount of fresh air needed and its distribution are available[57] and include kitchen and bathroom exhaust. Policies that require use of ventilation are part of Enterprise Green Communities Criteria and the US Weatherization Assistance Program. Adequate insulation and ventilation are now required in other countries, including the New Zealand Housing Warrant of Fitness and the Healthy Housing Rating System in England. Because the outdoor air must be heated or cooled, a high-efficiency heat recovery system is often installed to reduce energy costs.

If done correctly, increasing energy efficiency improves health[7,58] by reducing drafts, increasing thermal comfort, and controlling excess moisture and mold, as well as mitigating climate change (chapter 17). The US Department of Energy's weatherization assistance program now requires compliance with **ASHRAE** (American Society of Heating, Refrigeration and Air Conditioning Engineers) ventilation standards. A randomized controlled trial showed significant health benefits when weatherization with adequate ventilation occurs,[59] another example of the link between sustainability and healthy housing. **Weatherization** contractors install low-cost energy efficiency measures in low-income housing, thereby bringing such homes closer to green building standards. Such measures include insulation and repair of the building envelope, improvements to heating and cooling systems, electrical system upgrades, and energy-efficient appliances. Many older homes need maintenance, and the repairs address many of the hazards described earlier, such as moisture intrusion, pest entry portals, or inadequate ventilation. Sealing building envelopes without ensuring an adequate fresh air supply will aggravate or create hazards such as mold and dust mites. Early attempts at weatherization following the energy crisis of the 1970s caused **sick building syndrome** due to inadequate attention to ventilation and moisture control.[60]

Tax credits for increasing home energy efficiency have been effective for encouraging homeowners to make improvements.[61] Similar credits for improving ventilation and moisture-proofing homes might create an incentive to add these features.

Radon Mitigation

Radon mitigation involves special ventilation systems (active radon sub-slab depressurization) to eliminate radon gas intrusion by diverting radon from the soil below the foundation away from the home. Foundations can be sealed to reduce radon entry in new construction. Active radon mitigation is effective in reducing exposure.[62] HUD and certain other housing programs now require compliance with radon testing and abatement standards in multifamily housing.[63]

Green Healthy Housing Standards

For homes that require more extensive repairs, green rehabilitation programs play an important role in making housing healthier and preserving affordable housing. One study in Minnesota rehabilitated low-income housing by improving ventilation; reducing moisture, mold, pests, and radon; and incorporating sustainable building products. Adult residents reported improvements in overall health and reductions in chronic bronchitis, hay fever, sinusitis, asthma, and hypertension, while children's overall health improved with decreases in respiratory allergies, ear infections, and eczema. Elevated radon levels fell to below EPA limits in all units following the rehabilitation, and energy use dropped by 45 percent.[64] The evidence of green standards, home repair, and weatherization on improved health is extensive.[65,66]

Approaches to implementing these housing improvement interventions range from educational programs to remediation of existing housing to construction of new housing. Newer programs offer an integrated approach to addressing multiple hazards and seek joint benefits in producing sustainable, green, and healthy housing. Guidelines such as those prepared by the EPA, Enterprise Community Partners, and the US Green Building Council bring together best housing practices and sustainability. For example, the Enterprise Green Communities Criteria include eight elements for housing improvements: Integrative Design; Location + Neighborhood Fabric; Site Improvement; Water; Operating Energy; Materials; Healthy Living Environment; and Operations, Maintenance + Resident Engagement.

Making healthy housing improvements part of the low-income housing improvement process promises to help end the historic separation between housing and health. To operationalize the housing-health connection, Enterprise Community Partners launched the Green Communities Initiative in 2004 with the goal to transform the way affordable homes and apartments for low-income people are designed, located, built, and rehabilitated across the United States.[67] It is the first national standard for green and healthy affordable homes and has been used to create and rehabilitate more than 127,000 green, healthy, affordable homes in almost every state. It is the only national green building criteria and certification program in the United States designed exclusively for affordable low-income housing. Twenty-seven states require or incentivize Enterprise Green Communities as part of their affordable housing finance efforts, often through the

State's Qualified Allocation Plan for low-income housing tax credits. As of 2019, it has leveraged $3.9 billion in the development and preservation of green and affordable homes.

Education

Home visit programs offer support to help residents create healthier homes. Trained staff identify and address common housing issues such as pest infestations, moisture problems, and injury hazards. Focusing on households that include children with asthma, the Seattle–King County Healthy Homes Program sends community health workers to interview residents, assess housing conditions, and develop an action plan to address them.[68] These workers assess progress and provide education during follow-up visits. Clients receive allergen-impermeable bedding encasements for the child's bed, a high-efficiency vacuum, and other resources to keep their homes clean. Healthy homes programs have significantly reduced exposure to hazards and improved asthma-related health outcomes.[52] Other programs have focused on injury prevention through eliminating fall hazards in the homes of seniors or children, installing smoke detectors, and eliminating exposure to toxic chemicals.[69]

When correcting problems in an existing building is not possible or cost effective, the best option is for the resident to move to a better home and demolishing the old home. Some public housing authorities have medical rehousing programs that find more suitable housing for residents whose health conditions require accommodation. Such rehousing provides physical health benefits and reduces anxiety and depression.

One strategy is building new healthy homes, exemplified by the Seattle Breathe Easy Homes project that provided substantial health benefits for children with poorly controlled asthma.[70,71] Such homes include many of the health-promoting features illustrated in figure 12.3.

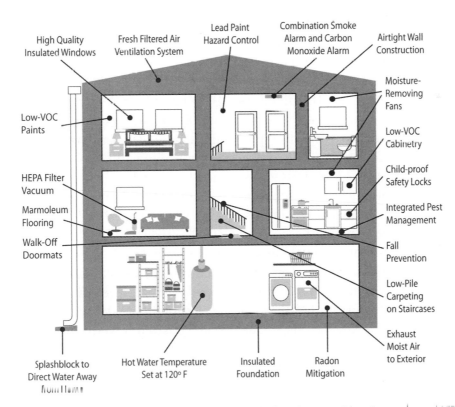

Figure 12.3. Features of a healthy home range from good insulation that provides thermal comfort to moisture control that reduces mold.
Source: Reprinted with permission from Public Health—Seattle & King County

Housing Codes

Housing codes influence the quality of housing by guiding construction permitting and housing inspection programs. Existing codes often do not include important features of healthy homes, such as ventilation and control of radon, lead, and mold. Enforcement occurs only at the local level, largely driven by episodic complaints. In contrast, England and New Zealand have adopted a Housing Health and Safety Rating System and a Housing Warrant of Fitness, respectively, that incorporate many model code provisions related to health and safety.[72,73] Efforts to enhance housing codes that can more effectively protect the health of residents are underway in several US cities, such as Dallas, Texas, and Tukwila, Washington, using the National Healthy Housing Standard, a model code in the United States that explicitly includes health, with annotated scientific evidence support.[74]

Architectural design to improve housing and reduce communicable diseases (such as installation of window screens for malaria, better sanitation, and improved food storage) are underway in several low and middle-income countries.[75] WHO is beginning to implement its housing and health guidelines through support to member states.

A proactive rental housing inspection program is a powerful tool to detect and remediate home health hazards that affect vulnerable populations, such as low-income persons and persons of color living in **substandard housing**. Such programs require periodic scheduled inspection and certification of rental units, rather than identifying hazards based on complaints from tenants who may not recognize hazards or fear retaliation from landlords if they complain. In the Los Angeles inspection program, owners of properties not meeting code standards have thirty days after notification to make repairs or face sanctions. Boston, New Haven, Greensboro, North Carolina, and Portland, Oregon, have similar programs.[76]

A tool to compare local housing codes with national model healthy housing standards is available.[77,78]

HUD requires that most federally assisted housing units receive an annual (proactive) inspection to detect substandard conditions. Otherwise, most inspections occur only because of tenant complaints. Although not currently required in most jurisdictions, regular inspections of all rental units and all privately owned housing at time of sale or lease would greatly increase the number of units inspected, leading to more widespread remediation of hazardous conditions.

Integrated Pest Management (IPM)

IPM controls pests through removing sources of food and moisture, preventing entry, and minimizing use of pesticides.[79] IPM prevents unnecessary chemical exposures and is more effective than the traditional practices of trapping, spraying, and poisoning. A growing number of public housing agencies have adopted policies requiring use of IPM methods, and HUD has issued formal IPM guidance.[80,81]

Smoke-Free Housing Policy

HUD has adopted regulations to ensure that public housing is free of tobacco smoke.[82] These regulations are typically accompanied by counseling and referrals to smoking cessation programs.

Medicaid/Children's Health Insurance Program Financing for Healthy Housing

Some states, such as Michigan, Ohio, Maryland, and Rhode Island, have obtained waivers to help finance lead paint and lead water pipe replacement; Maryland also allows asthma home-based interventions under their waiver. The waivers mark the first time Medicaid funding has been used for physical healthy housing interventions on a wide scale. Some hospitals have also begun to provide financing for healthy home construction.[83]

Cost and Benefit Analysis

Healthy housing intervention policies are informed by cost-benefit analyses, such as those for lead paint abatement[84] and asthma home interventions[85] that show the societal benefits far outweigh the costs, yet the housing market often fails to include occupant health in the price of a home. While homeowners may invest in healthy home improvements to increase both the value of their homes and the health of their families, landlords may have less incentive to make investments to improve the health of their tenants. Even though society may benefit from healthy housing improvements, this market failure means that acquiring the initial investment to implement healthy homes interventions remains challenging for financial institutions and housing providers. Green healthy housing standards may increase the value of the home and therefore the ability to acquire financing. Housing market incentives, subsidies, and enforcement mechanisms are important policy levers to stimulate more investment for healthy housing improvements.

Integrating Healthy Housing and Occupational Health

Increasingly, homes can also be workplaces. Many people spent more time at home in response to the COVID-19 pandemic, including time spent telecommuting. If health hazards are present, the increased time in the home underscores the importance of healthy housing. Research is now underway to determine whether improved ventilation and filtration, reduced crowding, and other building modifications help prevent disease transmission. Early housing regulations were designed to prevent the spread of tuberculosis, typhoid, and cholera. Reestablishing this link is central to the international healthy homes movement. In addition, healthy housing practitioners and occupational safety and health professionals have important opportunities to collaborate[86] because of the growing intersection of home and workplace.

Healthy Housing and Disasters

Although rescue and immediate responses to disasters have improved (chapter 18), integration of health considerations into long-term rebuilding remains problematic. The urge to recover as quickly as possible sometimes means returning to predisaster conditions or using substandard housing such as travel trailers, neither of which are optimal from a health perspective. The Institute of Medicine examined the challenges for disaster recovery, including healthy housing. Well-designed homes can better withstand extreme weather events. HUD requires that rebuilding housing following disasters, which is often financed through Community Development Block Grants (Disaster Recovery), comply with green healthy housing standards if federal funding is used.[87]

CONCLUSION

The connection between housing, health, and sustainability has become a foundational principle for future development. Methods of identifying the linkages among practitioners and of assessing and remediating disparities and hazards in homes have achieved a global scale. Green development, intersectoral planning, and more equitable financing will become more pronounced in future years, achieving gains in physical and mental health and overall economic and social well-being. Evidence-based design and further research to optimize assessment and intervention have never been more important. Increased investment in improved healthier housing and in equitable and sustainable development and enforcement of housing codes and other standards and policies are necessities. Health and housing investments are often the largest investments that we make in our lifetimes, presenting an opportunity for a brighter future.

DISCUSSION QUESTIONS

1. What are the ways in which housing conditions affect health? What health outcomes are most closely linked to housing conditions?
2. What policies are effective for expanding the availability of affordable housing?
3. What interventions are effective for addressing substandard housing conditions?
4. Give an example of a housing program that promotes health and describe how it works.
5. How can investments in healthy housing be financed?

DISCLOSURE OF COMPETING INTERESTS

David E. Jacobs discloses no competing interests.

Amanda Reddy reports being the executive director of the National Center for Healthy Housing; a list of its current and past funders is available on its public website at https://nchh.org/who-we-are/funders-and-sponsors/funders/. She also serves as the acting president and chief executive officer of its subsidiary, Healthy Housing Solutions.

REFERENCES

1. Robert Wood Johnson Foundation Commission to Build a Healthier America. Meet Abang Ojullu. 2011. http://nchharchive.org/LinkClick.aspx?file ticket=nKp4usSEE6U%3D&tabid=144

2. Rybczynski, W. *Home: A Short History of an Idea*. Penguin; 1987.

3. Marcus CC. *House as a Mirror of Self: Exploring the Deeper Meaning of Home*. Conari Press; 1997.

4. US DHHS (US Department of Health and Human Services). *The Surgeon General's Call to Action to Promote Healthy Homes*. US Department of Health and Human Services, Office of the Surgeon General; 2009. https://www.ncbi.nlm.nih.gov/books/NBK44192/

5. King LW. The Code of Hammurabi. 2008. https://avalon.law.yale.edu/ancient/hamframe.asp

6. CDC (Centers for Disease Control and Prevention). Carbon monoxide poisoning after a disaster. US Department of Health and Human Services. Last reviewed August 29, 2017. Accessed November 15, 2021. https://www.cdc.gov/disasters/carbonmonoxide.html

7. WHO. Housing and health guidelines. World Health Organization; 2018. License: CC BY-NC-SA 3.0 IGO. https://www.who.int/publications/i/item/9789241550376

8. US HUD. *Leading Our Nation to Healthier Homes*. US Department of Housing and Urban Development; 2009. https://www.hud.gov/sites/dfiles/HH/documents/hh_strategic_plan.web_posting.pdf

9. Matte TD, Jacobs DE. Housing and health: current issues and implications for research and programs. *Journal of Urban Health*. 2000;77 (1): 7-25.

10. Krieger J, Higgins DL. Housing and health: time again for public health action. *American Journal of Public Health*. 2002;92 (5): 758-768.

11. Sharpe RA, Taylor T, Fleming LE, Morrissey K, Morris G, Wigglesworth R. Making the case for "whole system" approaches: integrating public health and housing. *International Journal of Environmental Research and Public Health*. 2018;15(11):2345. https://doi.org/10.3390/ijerph15112345

12. Braubach M, Jacobs DE, Ormandy D. Environmental burden of disease associated with inadequate housing. World Health Organization; 2011. https://www.euro.who.int/en/publications/abstracts/environmental-burden-of-disease-associated-with-inadequate-housing.-summary-report

13. Jacobs DE. Environmental health disparities in housing. *American Journal of Public Health*. 2011;101(Suppl 1):S115-S122.

14. Lubell J, Crain R, Cohen K. Framing the Issues: The Positive Impacts of Affordable Housing on Health. Center for Housing Policy and Enterprise Community Partners; 2007. http://citeseerx.ist.psu.edu/viewdoc/download?doi=10.1.1.370.4585&rep=rep1&type=pdf

15. Robert Wood Johnson Foundation Commission to Build a Healthier America. Issue Brief 2: Housing and Health. September 2008. http://www.commissiononhealth.org/PDF/e6244e9e-f630-4285-9ad7-16016dd7e493/Issue%20Brief%202%20Sept%2008%20-%20Housing%20and%20Health.pdf

16. National Low Income Housing Coalition. Opportunities to End Homelessness and Housing Poverty. National Low Income Housing Coalition. 2019. https://housingis.org/resource/opportunities-end

17. Akinbami LJ, Simon AE, Rossen LM. Changing trends in asthma prevalence among children. *Pediatrics*. 2016;137(1) e20152354. https://doi.org/10.1542/peds.2015-2354

18. *Global Asthma Report 2018*. Auckland, New Zealand: Global Asthma Network; 2018.

http://globalasthmareport.org/resources/Global_Asthma_Report_2018.pdf

19. Salo, PM, Arbes SJ Jr, Crockett PW, Thorne PS, Cohn RD, Zeldin DC. Exposure to multiple indoor allergens in U.S. homes and its relationship to asthma. *Journal of Allergy and Clinical Immunology*. 2008;121:678-684.

20. Institute of Medicine. *Clearing the Air: Asthma and Indoor Air Exposures*. National Academies Press; 2000.

21. Wilson JM, Platts-Mills TAE. Home environmental interventions for house dust mite. *Journal of Allergy and Clinical Immunology: In Practice*. 2018;6(1):1-7. doi:10.1016/j.jaip.2017.10.003.

22. US HUD. American Healthy Homes Survey Final Report: Allergen and Endotoxin Findings; November 10, 2009.

23. Cohn RD, Arbes SJ Jr, Jaramillo R, Reid LH, Zeldin DC. National prevalence and exposure risk for cockroach allergen in U.S. households. *Environmental Health Perspectives*. 2006;114(4):522-526. doi:10.1289/ehp.8561

24. Institute of Medicine. *Damp Indoor Spaces and Health*. National Academies Press; 2004.

25. Mudarri D, Fisk WJ. Public health and economic impact of dampness and mold. *Indoor Air*. 2007;17(3): 226-235.

26. Castro-Rodriguez JA, Forno E, Rodriguez-Martinez CE, Celedón JC. Risk and protective factors for childhood asthma: what is the evidence? *Journal of Allergy and Clinical Immunology: In Practice*. 2016;4(6):1111-1122. doi:10.1016/j.jaip.2016.05.003

27. Shenassa ED, Daskalakis, C, Liebhaber A, Braubach, Brown MJ. Dampness and mold in the home and depression: an examination of mold-related illness and perceived control of one's home as possible depression pathways. *American Journal of Public Health*. 2007; 97:1893-1899. doi:10.2105/AJPH.2006.093773

28. Phipatanakul, W. 2002. Rodent allergens. *Current Allergy and Asthma Reports*. 2002;2(5): 412-416.

29. Milligan KL, Matsui E, Sharma H. Asthma in urban children: epidemiology, environmental risk factors, and the public health domain. *Current Allergy and Asthma Reports*. 2016;16(4):33. doi:10.1007/s11882-016-0609-6

30. Haines, SR, Siegel, JA, Dannemiller, KC, et al. Modeling microbial growth in carpet dust exposed to diurnal variations in relative humidity using the "Time-of-Wetness" framework. *Indoor Air*. 2020;30: 978-992. https://doi.org/10.1111/ina.12686

31. ATSDR (Agency for Toxic Substances and Disease Registry). *Toxicological Profile for Lead*. Centers for Disease Control and Prevention; August 2020. https://wwwn.cdc.gov/TSP/ToxProfiles/ToxProfiles.aspx?id=96&tid=22

32. DeWalt FG, Cox D, O'Haver R, et al. Prevalence of lead hazards and soil arsenic in U.S. housing. *Journal of Environmental Health*. 2015;78(5)22-29.

33. UNICEF and Pure Earth. The toxic truth: children's exposure to lead pollution undermines a generation of future potential. July 2020. https://www.unicef.org/reports/toxic-truth-childrens-exposure-to-lead-pollution-2020

34. ATSDR. *Toxicological Profile: Formaldehyde Addendum*. Centers for Disease Control and Prevention; 2010. https://www.atsdr.cdc.gov/toxprofiles/formaldehyde_addendum.pdf

35. CDC (Centers for Disease Control and Prevention). Final report on formaldehyde Levels in FEMA-supplied travel trailers, park models, and mobile homes. Centers for Disease Control and Prevention; 2008. Amended December 2010. https://www.cdc.gov/air/trailerstudy/pdfs/femafinalreport.pdf

36. CDC. Number of deaths resulting from unintentional carbon monoxide

poisoning, by month and year—National Vital Statistics System, United States, 2010–2015. *Morbidity and Mortality Weekly Report*. 2017;66(8):234. https://www.hsdl.org/?abstract&did=802862

37. US EPA. *Assessment of Risks from Radon in Homes*. US Environmental Protection Agency, Office of Air and Radiation, Indoor Environments Division; 2003.

38. Lorenzo-González M, Torres-Durán M, Barbosa-Lorenzo R, Provencio-Pulla M, Barros-Dios JM, Ruano-Ravina A. Radon exposure: a major cause of lung cancer. *Expert Review of Respiratory Medicine*. 2019;13:9, 839-850. http://doi.org/10.1080/17476348.2019.1645599

39. US EPA. EPA Map of Radon Zones. 2019. https://www.epa.gov/sites/production/files/2015-07/documents/zonemapcolor.pdf

40. ATSDR. Asbestos and your health. Agency for Toxic Substances and Disease Registry. Accessed October 20, 2021. https://www.atsdr.cdc.gov/asbestos/

41. WHO. Elimination of asbestos-related diseases. 2014. https://www.who.int/publications/i/item/WHO-FWC-PHE-EPE-14.01

42. Vaidyanathan A, Malilay J, Schramm P, Saha S. Heat-related deaths—United States, 2004–2018. *Morbidity and Mortality Weekly Report*. 2020;69:729–734. http://dx.doi.org/10.15585/mmwr.mm6924a1

43. Azhar GS, Mavalankar D, Nori-Sarma A, et al. Heat-related mortality in India: excess all-cause mortality associated with the 2010 Ahmedabad heat wave. *PLOS ONE*. 2018;9(3):e91831.

44. Jacobs DE, Tobin M, Targos L, et al. Replacing windows reduces childhood lead exposure: results from a state-funded program. *Journal of Public Health Management and Practice*. 2016;22(5):482-491. doi:10.1097/PHH.0000000000000389

45. NCHH (National Center for Healthy Housing). NCHH releases new video for NASHP CHW maps training. October 19, 2018. https://nchh.org/2018/10/nchh-releases-new-video-for-nashp-chw-maps-training/

46. CDC and US HUD (Centers for Disease Control and Prevention and US Department of Housing and Urban Development). *Healthy Housing Inspection Manual*. US Department of Health and Human Services; 2008. https://www.cdc.gov/nceh/publications/books/inspectionmanual/default.htm

47. WHO. Guidelines for Indoor Air Quality; Selected Pollutants. 2010. https://www.euro.who.int/__data/assets/pdf_file/0009/128169/e94535.pdf

48. Sauni R, Uitti J, Jauhiainen M, et al. Remediating buildings damaged by dampness and mould for preventing or reducing respiratory tract symptoms, infections and asthma. (Review.) *Evidence-Based Child Health*. 2013;8:3: 944-1000.

49. Wilson J, Jacobs DE, Reddy AL, Tohn E, Cohen J, Jacobsohn E. Home RX: The health benefits of home performance—a review of the current evidence. US Dept of Energy; December 2016. http://tinyurl.com/hu7eu7e

50. DiGuiseppi, C, Jacobs DE, Phelan KJ, Mickalide AD, Ormandy D. Housing interventions and control of injury-related structural deficiencies: a review of the evidence. *Journal of Public Health Management and Practice*. 2010;16(Suppl 5):S32-S41.

51. Jacobs DE, Brown MJ, Baeder A, et al. A systematic review of housing interventions and health: introduction, methods, and summary findings. *Journal of Public Health Management and Practice*. 2010;16(Suppl 5):S3-S8.

52. Krieger J, Jacobs DE, Ashley PJ, et al. Housing interventions and control of asthma-related indoor biologic agents: a review of the evidence. *Journal of Public Health Management and Practice*. 2010;16(Suppl 5):S11-S20.

53. Sandel M, Baeder A, Bradman A, et al. Housing interventions and control of health-related chemical agents: a review of the evidence. *Journal of Public Health Management and Practice*. 2010;16(Suppl 5):S19-S28.

54. US HUD (US Department of Housing and Urban Development). The healthy homes technical studies grant program. HHTS & LTS Grant Program Abstracts FY 2006–2019. 2019. https://www.hud.gov /program_offices/healthy_homes/hhi/hhts

55. National Center for Healthy Housing. A Field Guide for Flooded Home Cleanup. 2019. https://nchh.org/resource-library /a-field-guide-for-flooded-home-cleanup _english.pdf

56. Hung LL, Caulfield SM, Miller JD. *Recognition, Evaluation, and Control of Indoor Mold*. 2nd ed. American Industrial Hygiene Association; January 2020.

57. ASHRAE (American Society of Heating, Refrigeration and Air Conditioning Engineers). Ventilation for Acceptable Indoor Air Quality. Standard 62.1-2019 and 62.2-2019. ASHRAE. 2019.

58. Howden-Chapman P, Pierse N, Nicholls S, et al. Effects of improved home heating on asthma in community dwelling children: randomised controlled trial. *BMJ*. 2008;23(337):a1411.

59. Francisco PW, Jacobs DE, Targos L, et al. Ventilation, indoor air quality, and health in homes undergoing weatherization. *Indoor Air*. 2017; 27(2):463-477. doi:10.1111 /ina.12325.

60. Sundell J, Levin H, Nazaroff WW, et al. Ventilation rates and health: multidisciplinary review of the scientific literature. *Indoor Air*. 2011;21:179-181.

61. US EPA (US Environmental Protection Agency). Federal Income Tax Credits and Other Incentives for Energy Efficiency. 2020. https://www.energystar.gov /about/federal_tax_credits

62. ANSI/AARST (American National Standards Institute and American Association of Radon Scientists and Technologists). Soil gas mitigation standards for existing homes. SGM-SF-2017. 2017. https: //standards.aarst.org/SGM-SF-2017 /index.html

63. US HUD. Office of the Assistant Secretary for Housing. Multifamily Accelerated Processing (MAP) Guide. Chapter 9, Section 9.6.3, 9-32 to 9-36. Revision March 19, 2021. https://www.hud.gov/sites /dfiles/OCHCO/documents/4430GHSGG .pdf

64. Breysse J, Jacobs DE, Weber W, et al. Health outcomes and green renovation of affordable housing. *Public Health Reports*. 2011;126(Suppl 1).

65. Enterprise Green Communities. 2020. https://www.greencommunitiesonline. org/introduction.

66. Wilson J, Jacobs DE, Reddy AL, Tohn E, Cohen J, Jacobsohn E. Home RX: The Health Benefits of Home Performance—A Review of the Current Evidence. US Dept of Energy, December 2016. http://tinyurl .com/hu7eu7e

67. Enterprise Green Communities. 2021. https://www.enterprisecommunity.org /solutions-and-innovation/green -communities

68. King County Department of Community and Human Services. Health Homes Program. https://kingcounty.gov/depts /community-human-services/mental -health-substance-abuse/for-providers /health-home.aspx

69. Phelan KJ, Khoury J, Xu Y, Liddy S, Hornung R, Lanphear BP. A randomized controlled trial of home injury hazard reduction: the HOME injury study. *Archives of Pediatrics and Adolescent Medicine*. 2011;165(4):339-445.

70. Takaro TK, Krieger J, Song L, Sharify D, Beaudet N. The Breathe-Easy Home: the impact of asthma-friendly home construction on clinical outcomes and trigger exposure. *American Journal of Public Health*. 2011;101(1):55-62.

71. Phillips TJ. *High Point: The Inside Story of Seattle's First Green Mixed-Income Neighborhood*. Splash Block Publishing. 2020.

72. Department for Communities and Local Government. *Housing Health and Safety Rating System*. Department for Communities and Local Government (London); 2006. https://assets.publishing .service.gov.uk/government/uploads /system/uploads/attachment_data /file/9425/150940.pdf

73. Barnard LT, Bennett J, Howden-Chapman P, et al. Measuring the effect of housing quality interventions: the case of the New Zealand "Rental Warrant of Fitness." *International Journal of Environmental Research and Public Health*. 2017;4, 1352. doi:10.3390/ijerph14111352

74. APHA/NCHH (American Public Health Association and National Center for Healthy Housing). National Healthy Housing Standard. 2014. https://nchh .org/tools-and-data/housing-code-tools /national-healthy-housing-standard/

75. Architecture for Health. 2020. https: //archiveglobal.org/

76. ChangeLab Solutions. Up to Code: Enforcement Strategies for Healthy Housing. 2015. https://www.changelab solutions.org/sites/default/files /Up to-Code_Enforcement_Guide_FINAL -20150527.pdf

77. National Center for Healthy Housing. Code Comparison Tool. 2020. https: //nchh.org/tools-and-data/housing -code-tools/cct/

78. NCHH 2020. Proactive Rental Housing Codes. 2020. https://nchh.org/resources /policy/proactive-rental-inspections/

79. CDC (Centers for Disease Control and Prevention). *Integrated Pest Management: Conducting Urban Rodent Surveys*. Centers for Disease Control and Prevention; 2006. http://www.cdc.gov/nceh/ehs/Docs /IPM_Manual.pdf

80. US HUD. Office of Public and Indian Housing. NOTICE: PIH-2011-22. April 26, 2011. https://www.hud.gov/sites /documents/PIH-2011-22.PDF

81. US HUD. Healthy Homes Program Guidance Manual. July 19, 2012. https://www .hud.gov/program_offices/healthy _homes/HHPGM

82. US HUD. Instituting Smoke-Free Public Housing. 81 FR 87430, 24CFR 965, 966. December 5, 2016. https://www.federal register.gov/documents/2016/12/05 /2016-28986/instituting-smoke-free -public-housing

83. NCHH. Healthcare Financing of Healthy Homes. 2020. https://nchh.org /tools-and-data/financing-and-funding /healthcare-financing/

84. Pew Charitable Trusts and Robert Wood Johnson Foundation. 10 Policies to Prevent and Respond to Childhood Lead Exposure. 2017. https://nchh.org /resource/report_10-policies-to-prevent -and-respond-to-childhood-lead-exposure _english/

85. Reddy AL, Gomez M, Dixon SL. An evaluation of a state-funded healthy homes intervention on asthma outcomes in adults and children. *Journal of Public Health Management and Practice*. 2017;23(2):219-228.

86. Jacobs DE, Forst L. Occupational safety, health and healthy housing: a review of opportunities and challenges. *Journal of Public Health Management and Practice*. 2017; 23(6):e36-e45.

87. Institute of Medicine 2015. Healthy, Resilient, and Sustainable Communities after Disasters: Strategies, Opportunities, and Planning for Recovery. Committee on Post-Disaster Recovery of a Community's Public Health, Medical, and Social Services; Board on Health Sciences Policy; Institute of Medicine. National Academies Press (US), 2015.

CHAPTER 13

HEALTHY WORKPLACES

Jonathan A. Bach, Paul A. Schulte, L. Casey Chosewood, and Gregory R. Wagner

KEY POINTS

- The design of the work environment contains opportunities to support and promote safety, health, and well-being while contributing to environmental, social, and economic sustainability.
- Work becomes safer through interventions such as reduced use of hazardous chemicals; ergonomically designed tools and workstations; built-in protection from hazards such as falls from heights; tools and equipment designed to be quieter; more effective controls of dust and vapor exposures; and other health-supportive designs, policies, and practices that mitigate risk and reduce stress.
- Improving indoor environmental quality through engineering involving heating and cooling systems, natural daylighting, and outdoor views has beneficial psychological effects on occupants.
- Workplace interventions such as layouts that encourage walking, attractive and well-placed stairwells that encourage use, availability of healthier food options, and an active transportation infrastructure can increase worker health on and off the job and promote sustainability.
- Compliance with occupational safety and health regulations and use of consensus standards, sustainability reporting systems, and third-party building rating systems provide avenues for worker health and safety and environmental performance.

INTRODUCTION

In 2017, a nineteen-year-old "gig economy" bicycle food delivery worker in Massachusetts was killed when he was hit by a truck driver who did not see the cyclist in the truck's blind spot. There was no bicycle lane, and the worker was not wearing protective gear.[1]

In 2017, a twenty-year-old drywall installer in Michigan fell thirty feet to his death when an unguarded skylight he fell onto gave way.[2]

In 2020, a forty-four-year-old farmworker in Kentucky was killed when he entered a grain bin to try to dislodge jammed corn. The corn collapsed on him and smothered him.[3]

In 2015, a sixty-year-old farm caretaker in Michigan was pulling a downed tree when his tractor overturned to the rear and killed him—his tractor did not have a ROPS (Roll Over Protection Structure).[4]

In 2017, a sixty-one-year-old truck driver in Washington State backed her trailer up to a loading dock, walked into the trailer to clean the floor, and was crushed to death when a noisy forklift started loading the truck with a large load that obscured her presence.[5]

In 2018, a sixty-seven-year-old municipal crossing guard in Massachusetts was fatally injured when she was struck by a passing motor vehicle while assisting students in crossing the roadway.[6]

In 2019, a seventy-two-year-old grocery worker in California stocking shelves alone died when he fell from a straight ladder that was wet with rain.[7]

From 2001 to 2007, employees in a large state office building in Connecticut experienced an increased prevalence of asthma, hypersensitivity pneumonitis, and various respiratory symptoms. The building design allowed water intrusion that repeatedly soaked building materials and led to mold. Despite millions of dollars spent on building renovations to try to solve the problem, the state eventually vacated the building and sold it at a loss.[8-10]

In 2020 and 2021, workers in public-facing jobs such as grocery stores and public transit encountered risks of airborne disease transmission during the COVID-19 pandemic.[11]

In all these examples, workers could have been protected by improvements in the design of the workplace environment or in the policies that guide workplace activities.

As part of the Occupational Safety and Health Act of 1970, the US Department of Labor Bureau of Labor Statistics gathers and reports worker injury and illness data.[12] Efforts to reduce nonfatal injuries and illnesses led to a 75 percent reduction in the rate of injuries and illnesses from 1972 through 2019 (figure 13.1). Although the *rate* has greatly decreased, there were still at least 2.8 million workers in the United States who became ill or injured due to work in 2019.

Fatalities from work injuries are less common than nonfatal injuries and illnesses. In the United States, deaths from work injuries decreased 33 percent from 5.2 in 1992 to 3.5 in 2019 per 100,000 full-time equivalent workers[13] (figure 13.2). Despite improvements, at least 5,333 US workers died from workplace injuries in 2019.

Fatalities and nonfatal injuries and illnesses often result from different circumstances[14]

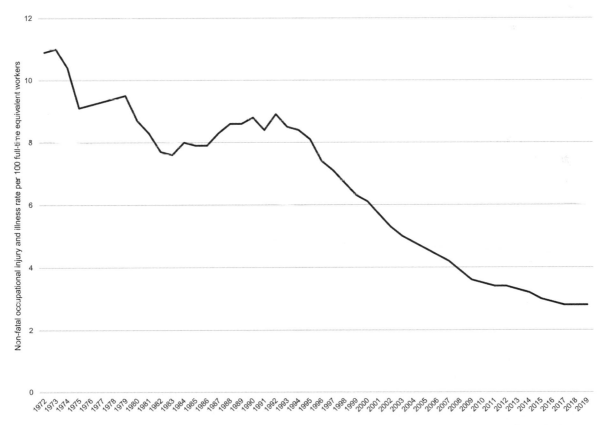

Figure 13.1. Nonfatal occupational injury and illness rate per 100 full-time equivalent workers, private industry, United States, 1972–2019.
Source: Adapted from Jeff Brown, "Nearly 50 years of occupational safety and health data." *Beyond the Numbers: Workplace Injuries* (US Bureau of Labor Statistics). July 2020;9(9). https://www.bls.gov/opub/btn/volume-9 /nearly-50-years-of-occupational-safety-and-health-data.htm

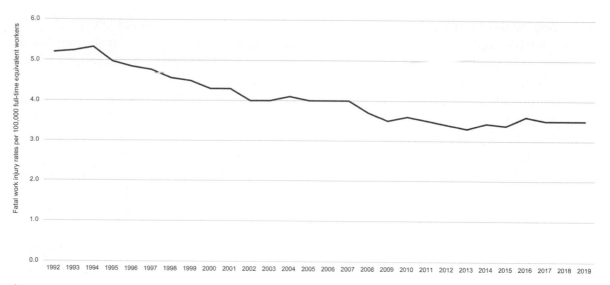

Figure 13.2. Fatal work injury rates per 100,000 full-time equivalent workers, United States, 1992–2019. Sources: Data from US Bureau of Labor Statistics, Census of Fatal Occupational Injuries. 1994 through 2019 rates: News Releases, "Census of fatal occupational injuries," with 1994 through 1999 rates calculated from total fatalities and total employment (rate per 100,000 = 100,000 × fatalities/employment). 1993 rate: Calculated from 1993 fatalities shown in the 1994 news release, plus employment shown on page 20 of The changing character of fatal work injuries (*Monthly Labor Review*, October 1994), Guy Toscano and Janice Windau. 1992 rate: A relative risk analysis of workplace fatalities (*Compensation and Working Conditions*, January 1995), John Ruser.

(figure 13.3). For example, although transportation causes the most fatal injuries, overexertion (such as strains and overuse syndrome) and bodily reactions (such as sprains) cause the most nonfatal injuries. Such data help focus strategies for improved prevention.

Many work-related deaths, injuries, and illnesses can be prevented by better design or by redesign of workplaces and how work is organized and performed. This chapter describes a **design safety review** process to evaluate, reduce, or remove hazards proactively. Since 1994, the United Kingdom has required, by law, a similar process on construction projects, resulting in substantial improvements.[15] The United States and most other nations have no such legal requirement. The design safety review process appears to make a difference: in 2019, the rate of construction fatalities in the United Kingdom was one-sixth that of the United States (1.6 versus 9.7 fatalities per 100,000 full-time equivalent workers, respectively).[16,17]

OCCUPATIONAL HEALTH AND SAFETY

Organized efforts to require safer work often do not gain wide acceptance until major tragedies such as mining collapses, deadly fires, elevator crashes, or industrial explosions occur. One notable case was the 1911 Triangle Shirtwaist Factory incident in New York City, where 146 workers, mostly young women, died in a fire because the factory had locked the exits.[18] As a result, labor organizations were formed that made great strides in improving work safety, with laws and regulations following. Subsequently, standards relevant to worker safety, health, and well-being were developed, such as wage and hour standards, limitations on child labor, and controlled use of toxic substances such as pesticides in agriculture. Mining disasters along with union activism and public pressure contributed to both the Coal Mine Health and Safety Act of 1969 and Mine Safety and Health Act of 1977.[19] A major advance in the United States was the Occupational Safety and Health Act of 1970. The **Occupational Safety and Health Adminis-**

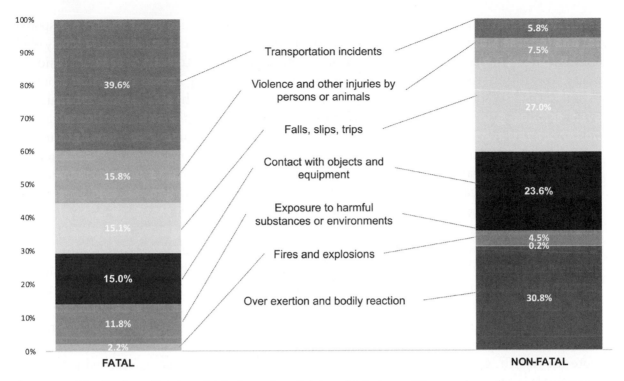

100%

90% — 5.8%

80% — 39.6% — 7.5%

70% — Transportation incidents

60% — Violence and other injuries by persons or animals — 27.0%

50% — 15.8% — Falls, slips, trips

40% — 15.1% — Contact with objects and equipment — 23.6%

30% — Exposure to harmful substances or environments — 4.5%
0.2%

20% — 15.0% — Fires and explosions

10% — 11.8% — Over exertion and bodily reaction — 30.8%

0% — 2.2%

FATAL — **NON-FATAL**

Figure 13.3. Distribution of fatal work injuries and nonfatal work injuries and illnesses by major event category, 2018.
Source: Adapted from Jeff Brown, "Nearly 50 years of occupational safety and health data," *Beyond the Numbers: Workplace Injuries* (US Bureau of Labor Statistics). July 2020;9(9). https://www.bls.gov/opub/btn/volume-9/nearly-50-years-of-occupational-safety-and-health-data.htm

tration (**OSHA**) was created shortly thereafter to develop and enforce workplace health and safety standards for general industry and construction. Other countries experienced similar advances, although worker protections in lower- and middle-income countries, with some exceptions, have progressed more slowly.

Efforts to proactively design out hazards in processes and equipment grew to become the field of **system safety**, especially through efforts in the defense, aerospace, and nuclear industries.[20] A streamlined version of system safety, usable for any business, was advanced by the National Safety Council as "Safety through Design," accompanied by a ten-year effort resulting in a textbook by that name.[21] The **National Institute for Occupational Safety and Health** (**NIOSH**) then continued the effort as **prevention through design**, starting in 2007.[22,23] When a hazard is eliminated by design, worker protection no longer

has to rely on education, perfect compliance with procedures, or flawless use of personal protective equipment. For example, a roof that has railings or parapets at the edge does not require the error-prone use of harnesses and ropes and is a recognized way to eliminate a hazard going back millenia.[24]

Increasing worker involvement in identifying and controlling hazards, followed by management action that makes the work safer and healthier, is a positive trend. OSHA has encouraged such labor-management collaboration for decades,[25] and it is an essential component of the prevention through design consensus standard, ANSI/ASSP Z590.3.[26]

Designing workplaces, as well as work policies and practices, to benefit the safety, health, and well-being of workers is increasingly recognized as important. For example, working overtime is often associated with poorer perceived general health, increased injury rates, more illnesses, or increased mortality.[27] Long hours of work may also increase exposures to chemical and physical hazards in the workplace, and night shifts may expose workers to heightened risk of violence.[28,29] Aging of the workforce also poses new challenges as almost one-fourth of US workers now plan to work until age seventy or more.[30,31] The risks of work are also changing, such as work adjacent to robots and intensification of work due to efficiency in automation. The built environment of the workplace needs to address these newer hazards along with more traditional concerns. The workplace may also be a useful setting for health promotion efforts to maintain worker health. This chapter provides an overview of the elements to consider when designing or modifying a workplace to both protect and promote the health, safety, and well-being of all individuals in its environment.

TYPES OF HAZARDS AND CONTROLS

Although the term *safety* is often used to refer to any workplace hazard, organizations large enough to have dedicated occupational safety and health professionals often assign responsibility for *injury*-causing hazards (typically obvious and sudden) to the "safety" professionals and *illness*-causing hazards (often invisible and cumulative) to the "health" (or "industrial hygiene") professionals. In many organizations, they are combined into Occupational Safety and Health (OSH) or Environmental, Health, and Safety offices. In small organizations, one person may be responsible for all these responsibilities, and that may not even be their main job.

Hazards may be categorized by type: chemical, biological, physical, safety, ergonomic, or psychosocial. By considering the elements in the **hierarchy of controls** in figure 13.4,[32] strategies to control hazards can be identified for each category (table 13.1) This hierarchy provides a useful approach for reducing occupational hazards and is discussed further in a subsequent section.

Continuous Improvement

Central tasks of occupational safety and health professionals are to identify hazards, assess

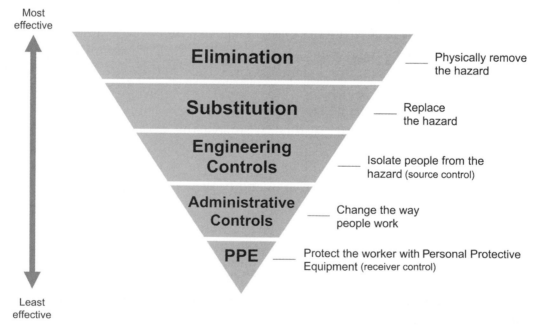

Figure 13.4. Hierarchy of controls for workplace hazards.
Source: Adapted from National Institute for Occupational Safety and Health, US CDC 2020. https://www.cdc.gov/niosh/topics/hierarchy/default.html. Reference to specific commercial products, manufacturers, companies, or trademarks does not constitute its endorsement or recommendation by the U.S. Government, Department of Health and Human Services, or Centers for Disease Control and Prevention.

Table 13.1. Types of occupational hazards with examples of hazards and control strategies.

Hazard Types	Hazard Examples	Control Strategies
Chemical (substance contact)	Solids, liquids, or gases that can damage or be absorbed through skin or eyes; be inhaled to displace oxygen, damage lungs; or be absorbed into body systems Cleaners, solvents, dusts, welding fumes	**Eliminate:** Redesign chemical processes and formulations to eliminate some or all chemicals. Maintain smoke-free workplaces. **Substitute:** Less-toxic chemicals, water, mechanical cleaning **Source control:** Enclosed mixing or reacting areas, local ventilation near the chemical source **Administrative:** Procedures, training, signs **Receiver control:** Personal protective equipment (PPE) such as gloves, respirators, face shields, clothing
Biological (living things contact)	Poor sanitation, contagious disease, mold growth in warm and moist environments, work with bacteria or viruses, medical waste, work with sewage, work with animals, insects, plants (and their venom, poisons, or waste toxins, which are also "chemical" hazards)	**Eliminate:** Work at home when ill, vaccinations **Substitute:** Smaller or less-hazardous lab animals **Source control:** Enclosures, shields/barriers, restraints, ventilation, cloth mask for sneezing/coughing, ultraviolet germicidal irradiation (UVGI) for surfaces, building design and maintenance to avoid water intrusion **Administrative:** Training, sanitation, access control, adequate paid sick leave **Receiver control:** PPE such as gloves, face masks, face shields. General ventilation dilution, filtering, and sterilizing (UVGI lighting in air ducts or across the upper room)
Physical (energy transfer)	Noise; temperature; poor lighting; sunlight; lasers; ultraviolet light; nonionizing radiation (radio, radar); ionizing radiation (x-rays, radioactive materials)	**Eliminate:** Buy quiet tools, move operator controls to safe area, change process to eliminate hazard **Substitute:** Better lighting, quieter tools **Source control:** Shielding, insulating, interlocks that turn off UVGI lights in ducts when opened for maintenance, UV blocking glass in vehicle cabs, shielding for ionizing radiation **Administrative:** Training, procedures, warning signs, alarms, vacating rooms before portable UVGI light use **Receiver control:** PPE such as warm or cool clothing, sunscreen, glasses, and head covering; hearing protection
Safety (forceful contact) *Safety hazards are also "physical" hazards (e.g., electrical energy, thermal energy, and kinetic energy from gravity and moving objects)*	Slips, trips, falls, cuts, crushes, crashes, explosions, electrical shocks, fires	**Eliminate:** Stay at ground level (build modular or prefabricated parts at ground level, to be lifted into place when complete), nonflammable fluids or materials **Substitute:** Slower equipment speeds **Source control:** Nonslip surface, drainage, shields and guard for power tools, explosion-proof electrical fixtures, more electrical outlets to eliminate extension cord use **Administrative:** Training and inspections in housekeeping procedures, warning signs; prohibit work on live circuits **Receiver control:** PPE such as slip-resistant footwear, reflective vests, hard hats

Table 13.1. Continued

Hazard Types	Hazard Examples	Control Strategies
Ergonomic, Human Factors (body stress, cognitive clarity)	Body mechanics, such as reach, force, leverage, repetition, awkward positions; user interface designs (confusing, provoking errors; clear, concise)	**Eliminate:** Use robots to do the most strenuous tasks, automate part of a process to eliminate some worker tasks **Substitute:** Use smaller, lighter parts or product containers, replace confusing labeling or controls with logical, clear ones, tools with more natural grip angles to allow straighter joints **Source control:** Adjustable workstations to position work for each person's most comfortable use, carts with springs that rise higher as product is removed **Administrative:** Training (controls, lifting), warning signs **Receiver control:** PPE such as shock-absorbing gloves, shoes, floor mats, exoskeletons to shift loading to lower body
Work Organization, Psychosocial (harmful stresses)	Work duration, intensity, repetitiveness, environment; work shift, sleep; toxic leadership, criticism, inadequate training, workplace violence	**Eliminate:** Strictly enforce antibullying policies and address violence risks; address toxic leadership **Substitute:** Enhance workplace (light, air, space, clutter, noise, view, proximity to other workers), encourage feedback with fact-finding, not fault-finding, and correct problems found **Source control:** Increase use of collaborative work teams **Administrative:** Use predictable scheduling sensitive to circadian rhythms. Training (deescalation, communication, workplace etiquette, praise in public/ criticize in private) **Receiver control:** Provide employee support, nonpunitive or anonymous reporting channels

risks, and evaluate alternatives. These tasks underlie the most complex system safety efforts in the nuclear, aerospace, and defense industries and the *process safety* efforts in the chemical industry.[33] These principles are also basic to standards for Occupational Health and Safety Management Systems such as the ANSI/ ASSP Z10 or the international ISO 45001.[34,35] To advance worker health and safety, it is useful to summarize a simplified *process* from the prevention through design consensus standard.[26]

The Priority *Is Prevention*

The principles of prevention through design state that preventing occupational injuries and illnesses is best accomplished by eliminating hazards during design, redesign, and operations (see figure 13.4). If hazards cannot be eliminated, consider substituting less-hazardous materials, processes, operations, or equipment. Risks to remaining hazards should be minimized using controls at the source (commonly referred to as engineering controls). Administrative controls such as employee training or warnings or receiver (worker) controls such as personal protective equipment are important but less reliable methods for minimizing occupational injury and illness risks and should not be the first or only choice.

The Process *Is Design*

With the elimination and reduction of hazards as *priority*, it is valuable to have a management *process* to better achieve such improvements. OSHA encourages employee involvement in hazard reduction efforts such as identifying hazards, assessing how severe and how likely the risks might be, and choosing better alternatives.[25] Employees work most closely with the hazards—bringing insights and lessons learned to even the most expert of designers and health and safety professionals. Expression of employee concerns should be encouraged and not penalized. Collaboration with workers can lead to better worker acceptance of solutions since they had a key part in designing them. The tasks of hazard identification, risk assessment, and alternatives assessment are the foundations of system safety, chemical process safety, and the streamlined occupational safety and health process in the ANSI/ASSP Z590.3 Prevention through Design (PtD) standard. When a workgroup forms to carry out this process, the PtD standard refers to it as **design safety review**. This process may be summarized in the following steps:

1. Choose productive players who are experienced in the work tasks, respected by other workers, and can work successfully with management, designers, and health and safety professionals.
2. Come prepared with lessons learned from similar operations.
3. Compile a list of activities and the associated hazards for review.
4. Develop a risk assessment matrix that identifies the likelihood and severity of hazards to help prioritize which hazards to address.
5. Identify and assess alternative strategies to address each high-priority hazard and recommend best strategies.
6. Conduct a review of the workgroup recommendations by the managers responsible for those operations, with acceptance or modification of the recommendations.
7. Make suggested changes with management agreement, train workers, evaluate results, and adjust changes as needed.

PROMOTING HEALTH AND WELL-BEING

The historical focus on preventing bodily harm in the workplace is being enhanced to include a broader opportunity for workplaces to improve worker health and well-being (box 13.1). For example, the *Global Reporting Initiative* (GRI) publishes a sustainability reporting system used by thousands of businesses of all types in more than one hundred countries. GRI has recently enhanced its 403 Occupational Health and Safety standard to measure success in occupational safety and health management, worker harm prevention, and worker wellness.[36] The GRI standards also shift the focus from *trailing indicators*, such as injury rates, to *leading indicators*, such as training levels, audit frequencies, and average time to implement corrective actions.

NIOSH HEALTHY WORK DESIGN AND WORKER WELL-BEING PROGRAMS

The NIOSH Healthy Work Design and Well-Being initiative seeks to protect and advance worker safety, health, and well-being by improving the design of work, management practices, and the physical and psychosocial work environment.[37] The program establishes research goals for the United States around challenging elements of modern work including examining the impact of worker demographics on employer or organizational practices; improving the safety, health, and well-being of workers with nonstandard work arrangements; addressing the safety and health implications of advancing technology; reducing work organization-related chronic health conditions among workers; decreasing the burden of shift work, long hours of work, and sleep deficiency among workers; improving the well-being of workers through healthier work design and better organizational practices; and promoting a sustainable work-nonwork interface, or work-life fit. NIOSH partners with industry, labor, trade associations, professional organizations, and academia to better understand the ways in which the design of work affects overall health

BOX 13.1 PROMOTING WORKER WELL-BEING THROUGH DESIGN

Various guidelines have been developed to encourage features that promote worker health, safety, and well-being through design [a-c] Many of these features are incorporated in the Fitwel and WELL healthy building certification processes (chapter 22). The following are some such features for within and around workplace buildings.

Within Workplace Buildings

- Clearly defined building entrances to encourage common entry points, clarity, safety, and increased social interaction
- Stairwells that are open and inviting, unlocked, temperature controlled, and prominently located to encourage their use (figure 13.5). Point-of-decision prompts may increase levels of stair use among workers.[d]
- Drinking-water stations, refrigerators, and refrigerated vending machines for perishable fruits and vegetables to encourage improved nutrition[e,f]
- Well-maintained break rooms and bathrooms to encourage breaks and rest as needed
- Lactation rooms where new mothers can pump and store milk to encourage breast-feeding and to assist new mothers in returning to work.[g]
- Ergonomically appropriate workstation design to minimize musculoskeletal strain
- Window treatments and skylights that allow natural light while minimizing glare (especially on computer screens) and comfortable artificial lighting to enhance worker well-being[h]
- Rooftop railings and skylight guards to protect maintenance workers

Figure 13.5. Safe and attractive staircases, such as this one in an office building, can promote physical activity and social connections as well as provide flexible working spaces.
Source: Photo courtesy of Perkins&Will

BOX 13.1 CONTINUED

In Areas around Workplace Buildings

- Defined zones for walking, bicycling, and automobiles to increase safety of bicyclists and pedestrians
- Convenient access to public transit to encourage transit use and walking to transit
- Safe and attractive pedestrian paths and trails designed to encourage walking before, during, and after the workday. A worksite walkability audit can assess the safety and attractiveness of the walking routes at a worksite.[i-k]
- Promenades, boardwalks, courtyards, food venues, gardens, and other pedestrian-oriented public spaces to encourage social interaction and increase the livability of office environments[l,m]
- Indoor and outdoor fitness facilities and places to walk to encourage employees to be physically active[n]
- Bicycle infrastructure, including covered bike racks, lockers, showers, and changing rooms to encourage use of active transportation for commuting and during the workday
- Smoking areas, if any, located away from building entrances and air intake vents.[o]

REFERENCES

a. CFAD (Center for Active Design). Publications + Resources. 2021. Accessed March 30, 2021. https://centerfor activedesign.org/resources/
b. NCCOR (National Collaborative on Childhood Obesity Research). Health, Behavioral Design, and the Built Environment White Paper. 2017. https://www.nccor.org/wp-content/uploads/2016/09/nccor-behavioral -design-whitepaper-final.pdf
c. Schulte PA, et al. Considerations for incorporating "well-being" in public policy for workers and workplaces. *American Journal of Public Health*. 2015;105(8):e31-e44. https://doi.org/10.2105/AJPH.2015.302616
d. Soler RE, Leeks KD, Buchanan LR, Brownson RC, Heath GW, Hopkins DH. Point-of-decision prompts to increase stair use: a systematic review update. *American Journal of Preventive Medicine*. 2010;38(Suppl 2):292–300.
e. CDC (Centers for Disease Control and Prevention). *Offering Healthier Options and Physical Activity at Workplace Meetings and Events*. US Department of Health and Human Services, Centers for Disease Control and Prevention, National Center for Chronic Disease Prevention and Health Promotion, Division of Nutrition, Physical Activity, and Obesity; 2014. https://www.cdc.gov/obesity/downloads/tips-for-offering-healthier-options-and-PA-at -workplace-508.pdf (see also https://www.cdc.gov/obesity/resources/strategies-guidelines.html)
f. USDHHS (US Department of Health and Human Services). *Food Service Guidelines for Federal Facilities*. Food Service Guidelines Federal Workgroup; 2017. http://www.cdc.gov/obesity/downloads/guidelines_for_federal _concessions_and_vending_operations.pdf
g. York L. "Lactation Room Design." AIA Best Practices. 2008. http://www.aia.org/aiaucmp/groups/ek_public /documents/pdf/aiap037226.pdf
h. IES (Illuminating Engineering Society). The Lighting Library. Accessed July 14, 2021, https://www.ies.org /lighting-library/
i. Dannenberg AL, Cramer TW, Gibson CJ. Assessing the walkability of the workplace: a new audit tool. *American Journal of Health Promotion*. 2005;20 (1): 39–44.
j. CDC (Centers for Disease Control and Prevention). Worksite Walkability. Healthier Worksite Initiative. 2010. http://www.cdc.gov/nccdphp/dnpao/hwi/toolkits/walkability/index.htm
k. CDC (Centers for Disease Control and Prevention). Physical Activity Resources and Publications. US Department of Health and Human Services; 2021. Accessed March 30, 2021. https://www.cdc.gov/physicalactivity/resources /reports.html
l. CPSTF (Community Preventive Services Task Force). One Pager—Increasing Physical Activity: Built Environment Approaches. 2017. https://www.thecommunityguide.org/sites/default/files/assets/OnePager-Physical-Activity -built-environment.pdf
m. CPSTF (Community Preventive Services Task Force). Combined Built Environment Features Help Communities Get Active. 2021. Accessed March 30, 2021. https://www.thecommunityguide.org/content /combined-built-environment-features-help-communities-get-active
n. CDC (Centers for Disease Control and Prevention). *Physical Activity Breaks for the Workplace: Resource Guide*. October 2019. US Department of Health and Human Services, Centers for Disease Control and Prevention, National Center for Chronic Disease Prevention and Health Promotion; 2019. https://www.cdc.gov/work placehealthpromotion/initiatives/resource-center/pdf/Workplace-Physical-Activity-Break-Guide-508.pdf
n. CDC (Centers for Disease Control and Prevention). *Best Practices for Comprehensive Tobacco Control Programs—2014*. US Department of Health and Human Services, Centers for Disease Control and Prevention, National Center for Chronic Disease Prevention and Health Promotion, Office on Smoking and Health, 2014. www.cdc.gov /tobacco/stateandcommunity/best_practices/index.htm

and well-being and how it can be improved to enable workers to thrive and contribute productively at work, at home, and in society.

Traditional occupational safety and health protection programs have primarily concentrated on ensuring that work is safe and that workers are protected from the harms that arise from work itself. NIOSH's *Total Worker Health* (TWH) research program builds on this approach through the recognition that work is a social determinant of health.[38] Job-related factors such as wages, hours of work, workload and stress levels, interactions with coworkers and supervisors, access to paid leave, and health-promoting workplaces all can have an important impact on the well-being of workers, their families, and their communities.[39-42]

In addition to hazard control and facility design, TWH strategies include interventions supporting healthful communities, fair and adequate compensation and benefits, healthy leadership, organizing work to mitigate stress, health-supporting workplace policies such as paid sick leave and predictable scheduling, prevention of any adverse effects of technology, being responsive to the impact of both traditional and nonstandard work arrangements, and consideration of how people of different ages from different cultural, economic, and educational backgrounds experience work and its hazards.[43,44] The program funds academic Centers of Excellence for *Total Worker Health* that conduct research and develop pilot interventions.[45]

ACCOMMODATING WORKERS WITH DISABILITIES

Design issues related to accommodations for workers with disabilities include accessibility/mobility, hearing, vision, and cognition[46] (chapter 10). For example, a restroom may be modified to meet accessibility requirements, including wider doors and stalls and grab bars suitable for use by persons in wheelchairs. Workplaces must include provisions for emergency evacuation and parking accommodation. Reasonable accommodation may also include modifying an employee's workstation or providing a special chair. Design and policy approaches are both important in providing accommodations for workers with disabilities. The Job Accommodation Network provides a wide range of technical assistance to support the employment of people with disabilities.[47]

COMMUNICABLE DISEASE CONTROL

To reduce the risk of disease transmission through surface contact, there is an increasing use of "no-touch" building controls, such as automatic doors, automatic toilets, soap dispensers, disinfectant dispensers, faucets, and hand dryers. Restrooms can be designed to allow occupants to exit without grasping a pull-door handle. Waste receptacles can be located close to doors for paper towels used for grasping door handles. Workplaces can replace water fountains with no-touch water dispensers to fill employees' individual water bottles. Water or waterless sanitation handwashing should be provided in all types of workplaces, including for outdoor workers such as farmworkers and underground workers such as miners.

Airborne transmission control has been a priority in recent pandemics. To reduce the risks for diseases transmitted via airborne droplets from coughing or sneezing, a six-foot separation distance between workers or between workers and the public is commonly used. For diseases transmitted by aerosols that do not easily settle to the ground, a well-maintained ventilation system with sufficient fresh air and filtration is important.[48] Higher percentages of outside air are helpful, although there are limits based on local climate and system capabilities. Some building sustainability and health certification criteria (see Fitwel and WELL in chapter 22) give added credit when fresh air supplies are increased, which must be balanced with energy-efficiency goals. Many building systems are also able to handle finer filtration media, such as replacing MERV 8 filters with MERV 13 or higher. A source of expert guidance on ventilation is the **American Society of Heating, Refrigerating, and Air-Conditioning Engineers (ASHRAE)**.[49]

Limiting room and building occupancy is another strategy for reducing the concentration of infectious aerosols. Some workplaces have reduced elevator occupancy and changed walking paths to make maintaining distances between people more feasible. Where closer interactions are needed, barriers have been used, often clear glass or plastic, or higher cubicle partitions. In situations such as the COVID-19 pandemic, these strategies appear to be most effective when used in conjunction with requirements for wearing a respirator or other type face mask—provided such masks fit well with minimized leaks, cover both nose and mouth, and do not have exhalation valves. When respirator use is necessary in a workplace, employers should implement a formal program that ensures proper respirator selection and fit, as well as training on the use and limitations of respiratory protection.

Ultraviolet germicidal irradiation (UVGI) can be effective for killing or inactivating contagious particles and may be used in conjunction with other techniques such as dilution or filtration. Because direct UV rays are harmful to the eyes, use in occupied rooms is limited to upper room systems that prevent direct viewing of the bulbs. Other uses include UV lighting inside air ducting and portable UV sterilizing units temporarily placed in an area when no unprotected occupants are present. Combining techniques is an option, such as using MERV 13 or better air filters for primary control and UVGI for high-risk areas such as restrooms or health care common areas. ASHRAE provides guidance on UVGI usage.[50] Also important are workplace policies and education emphasizing such practices as coughing and sneezing etiquette, frequent hand washing, and the importance of staying home when sick. Flexible sick leave policies encourage and enable sick employees to stay home, reducing risk to others at work.

PSYCHOSOCIAL WORKPLACE HEALTH

In seeking to design and manage a pleasant and health-promoting workplace, consideration should be given to the goals and benefits of a psychologically healthy workplace, including the following[51]:

- Civility and respect in the workplace
- Supported and valued employees
- Praise, recognition, acknowledgment, and fairness
- Growth and development opportunities
- Clear leadership and expectations
- Recognition of the need for healthy work-life fit with personal, family, and community demands
- Manageable, reasonably paced workloads, assuring that responsibilities can be accomplished within the time available
- Adequate resources to do the job
- Input/control over work organization
- Consideration of opinions and suggestions of employees—employees participate in decision-making
- Psychological services and supports available to employees when mental health issues occur

Canadian and international voluntary standards including guidance and resources to support psychological health and safety in the workplace are available.[52,53]

WORKPLACE VIOLENCE

In a National Safety Council survey, 22 percent of workers reported being exposed to workplace violence, 12 percent reported that it has caused or contributed to a serious injury in their workplace, and 47 percent reported that their job offered workplace violence training. Additionally, 91 percent of employers said they are prepared to avoid incidents of workplace violence.[54]

Improved psychosocial workplace health may contribute to reductions in violence, and so may the design of the workplace itself. Workplace design should include elements to protect workers from violent acts by members of the public and by other workers. For internal workplace security, secured and monitored entrances and alarmed exits should be considered in workplace designs. More rigorous design elements are needed to protect workers who interact with the public, such as those in convenience stores, gas stations, banks, fast-food restaurants, and post offices, or those in work settings that must protect both workers and their charges, such as health care facilities and schools.[55] Additional security provisions are needed for workplaces such as airports, government installations, chemical plants, and nuclear facilities that may be at risk for terrorist attacks.

Crime prevention through environmental design (CPTED) can reduce violence by thoughtful design and organizational choices (chapter 5). For example, keeping clear lines of sight and visibility from the outside for retail cashier areas, or areas of high-value merchandise, can dissuade thefts and potential violence. Trade-offs may be needed. For example, if a pharmacy is far away from the storefront windows, thefts may be more likely—yet this design may encourage customers to buy more items en route to the pharmacy counter. Guidelines to prevent crime and violence through environmental design can be categorized into four focus areas[56-58]:

- Natural surveillance: Highly visible work areas (well lit, windows not blocked by excessive signage or other objects or plants, hidden areas reduced)
- Natural access control: Removing straight-line access (landscaping, curbing, vehicle and pedestrian pathways, lobby layout designs)
- Territorial reinforcement: Distinguish between legitimate occupants and intruders (entry signs, access control, visitor badging, receptionists clearly see entrances)

- Maintenance: Keeping a workplace maintained, sending the message that people care about and notice what happens in the area

SOCIALLY RESPONSIBLE SUSTAINABILITY

The twin goals of designing and maintaining healthier workplaces and conservation of limited resources are compatible. Dangerous work does not conserve human resources, and newer "green" technologies are not sustainable if they are dangerous. Solar panels, wind turbines, and large storage batteries are environmentally favorable, but operations to build and maintain them come with electrical and falling hazards. Energy-saving efforts like weatherization, renovation, and insulation can result in worker exposure to lead, asbestos, and isocyanate hazards during renovation or installation.

Documenting more sustainable, safer, and healthier business through metrics, levels, or report cards not only indicates success, but can be a competitive advantage. Setting measurable, achievable, time-sensitive goals and milestones is important to achieve sustainable beneficial change. For example, in addition to energy efficiency, key sustainability metrics now often include social aspects such as worker safety, health, and wellness. The US Green Building Council certification program, Leadership in Energy and Environmental Design (LEED), now includes a prevention through design certification credit.[59] This credit expands the consideration of worker health and safety to all occupants during the **facility life cycle**, including early occupants (construction workers) and supporting occupants (operations and maintenance workers). The LEED PtD credit includes a process similar to the *Design Safety Review* process outlined earlier. Since LEED certification is used around the world, requiring use of the LEED PtD credit may be a practical way to include prevention through design collaborative planning and review in new facility designs.

Beyond green buildings, the previously mentioned GRI sustainability reporting standards now include *worker* sustainability metrics.[36] Just as environmental sustainability is improved when complying with such standards, sustainable worker safety and wellness are now benefiting from similar focus as businesses use these standards to compete internationally.

GLOBAL SUSTAINABILITY—FREE TRADE, FAIR TRADE, STANDARDIZATION

The worst of the worker hazards of the Industrial Revolution, whether child labor or grossly unhealthy and unsafe labor, still exist today in some types of work, especially in low- and middle-income nations. Whether garment sweatshops in Asia, deadly mining in Africa, suicides related to intense assembly line pressures,[60] or the dangers to immigrant day laborers working in North America, free trade is not necessarily fair trade at the worker's level. Regulations are crucial to advancing labor protection, as are grassroots efforts such as those promoting "fair trade" goods through labeling and advertising.

Although international commerce and free trade can indirectly give preference to the low initial costs of an unregulated and endangered workforce, they are likely to have unintended consequences. The standardization of international commerce with commitments to international standards and norms—monitored and verified—can improve worker conditions. To sell in a particular nation, a business must meet that nation's standards. If the business wants to market to many of the world's nearly two hundred nations, it is often more practical to comply with a single set of international standards that most nations accept, providing motivation to meet such standards.

Many nations now participate in international standards to enhance their economies. Compliance with such standards is reported in the promotional and financial reports of a business as a sign of stability and corporate responsibility. For example, the International Organization for Standardization (ISO) publishes the ISO 9000 family of standards for quality management and the ISO 14000 family of standards for environmental management that are used by many corporations. Of major importance to workers, especially in developing countries with little national regulation or enforcement, are the newer ISO 45001 standards for occupational health and safety. These standards, developed with the involvement of more than seventy countries, have the potential to improve occupational health and safety management around the world and to promote socially responsible sustainability efforts.[35] The US and international standards are freely available on the web.[25,34,35] Although large corporations may adopt international standards, workplaces in different countries may have different expectations for protecting the health and safety of workers based on their local cultures.[61]

MIGRANT AND UNDOCUMENTED WORKERS

Unauthorized resident status is often accompanied by a degree of worker vulnerability and less consideration by employers for workers' safety. To make a good impression, employees may start working at an unsustainably high pace, which then becomes the expected norm. They may also be constrained from reporting problems at work to supervisors or to government agencies with oversight responsibilities for fear they will be fired or deported. Employers may replace local workers with additional undocumented workers, leading to unsafe expectations across the workforce. Fearing repercussions from hiring undocumented workers, some employers will not request emergency assistance or outside services, such as an ambulance, when needed. Workers' coping strategy may result in disregarding threats to their health and safety to minimize conflicts or legal dangers.[62] Inclusion of migrant health into efforts such as the International Labour Organization (ILO) decent work agenda,[63] the UN agenda for sustainable development,[64] and the UN Global Compact on corporate sustainability[65] could help leverage technical resources, programs, and research to forge partnerships to better understand and improve the health status of the world's migrant workers.[66]

WORK EQUITY

There is increasing recognition that a business without *social equity* is not sustainable. In addition to designing a safe facility, social equity in the workplace should consider such issues as the needs and disparities in the surrounding community, workforce compensation and development, and the supply chain supporting a business.[67]

Some lower-skilled or lower-paid workers, such as meat packers, grocery workers, and crop pickers, sometimes have the most strenuous work. Others, such as sanitation workers and health care workers, may be exposed to higher health hazards. Lower pay should not translate to lower efforts to protect workers, and management is encouraged to protect all workers with equal effort. In fact, the work environments of lower-paid workers frequently need continual attention to assure the workers' safety and health. Socially responsible sustainability can contribute to long-term business success.

THE CHANGING NATURE, OR FUTURE, OF WORK

The nature of work is changing for many people. Influences include changes in technology, demographics, globalization, urbanization, climate, economic conditions, and **telework**. Also changing is the so-called gig or "platform" economy in which, for example, work is accepted on a smartphone app and both the employer and place of work can change daily. Some of these new technologies and work arrangements have the potential for social isolation, loneliness, or frequently changing workplaces, increasing the exposure to novel hazards for which the worker may be ill-prepared.

When applied appropriately, new technologies such as computing, automation, robotics, predictive analytics, and artificial intelligence can assist in ensuring a safer work environment. Such technologies can also enhance human abilities to do new types of work. New jobs for specialists in these technologies are also created. Although technological advances have historically produced more jobs than they have eliminated, some literature suggests this trend may not continue.[68]

Although worker benefits can be many, including improved health and safety, some workers will suffer the anxiety of potential job loss or the stress of unemployment—great health risks in themselves. Successful businesses involve specialists, managers, and experienced workers in collaborative efforts to prepare the workplace and the workforce for changes to come. Workers know the work best, specialists know the changes best, and management knows the financial and market possibilities and limitations best. Such collaboration can reduce anxieties about potential changes. Continuing education and training are often recommended to meet changing business needs and raise morale and reduce anxiety, thus contributing to more successful work teams. Some workers may use their enhanced skills to find a position elsewhere, by choice or necessity, but until that time, their increased skill and motivation benefit both them and their employer.

Some literature suggests that jobs will be fewer with a bifurcation of types of jobs to either high- or low-skill levels as automation replaces jobs of medium skill level. If there are fewer jobs, workers who do not find new jobs will require supportive services and resources that may not be adequately available. Meeting such needs with creative options will require broader societal actions beyond those of individual businesses.[69]

The future of work involves changes to the workplace, work, and workforce in the context of changing national and global political and environmental issues. In 2019, NIOSH launched its Future of Work initiative to investigate emerging occupational safety and health issues.[70,71] Some of its priority topics related to the built environment component of the workplace include emergency preparedness, workspace, automation, robots, and human-machine interfaces.

CONCLUSION

Well-designed workplaces keep workers safe; support engaging, meaningful work; encourage healthy behaviors; and support worker equity as part of planned administrative and supervisory policies, practices, and programs. Worker equity is improved when a design approach is used, as benefits are experienced by both high- and low-paid workers and by workers of all levels of influence within an organization. Considering that the time spent in the workplace is usually second only to the time spent in the home, designing workplaces to both protect and promote the safety, health, and well-being of workers is both a significant opportunity and a critical public health priority.

Disclaimer: The findings and conclusions in this report are those of the authors and do not necessarily represent the official position of the National Institute for Occupational Safety and Health, Centers for Disease Control and Prevention.

DISCUSSION QUESTIONS

1. What workplace design elements might be most effective in protecting workers from injury? Which elements might be most effective in assuring and promoting the overall health of workers? Which elements might affect both worker safety and worker health?
2. What policies and programs can be used in workplaces to maximize worker interaction with the built environment to promote health?
3. What are the limitations of the built environment in protecting and promoting the health and safety of workers?
4. Workers have fewer work-related injuries today as a result of laws, regulations, and enforcement policies than they have in the past. What are the benefits, risks, and barriers to using mandatory interventions to promote the overall health of workers both on and off the job?

DISCLOSURE OF COMPETING INTERESTS

Jonathan A. Bach, Paul Schulte, L. Casey Chosewood, and Gregory R. Wagner disclose no competing interests.

Total Worker Health® is a registered trademark of the US Department of Health and Human Services.

REFERENCES

1. NIOSH (National Institute for Occupational Safety and Health). Fatality Assessment and Control Evaluation (FACE) Program. Massachusetts Case Report 17MA056. 2020. https://www.cdc.gov/niosh/face/stateface/ma/17ma056.html

2. NIOSH. Fatality Assessment and Control Evaluation (FACE) Program. Michigan Case Report 17MI045. 2019a. https://www.cdc.gov/niosh/face/stateface/mi/17mi045.html

3. NIOSH. Kentucky Case Report 20KY006. 2020. https://www.cdc.gov/niosh/face/stateface/ky/20ky006.html

4. NIOSH. Fatality Assessment and Control Evaluation (FACE) Program. Michigan Case Report 15MI104. 2019. https://www.cdc.gov/niosh/face/stateface/mi/15mi104.html

5. WADLI (Washington State Department of Labor and Industries). Truck driver crushed by hay bales. 2020. https://lni.wa.gov/safety-health/safety-research/files/2020/71_197_2020_TruckDriverCrushedByHayBales.pdf

6. Massachusetts State FACE Program. Municipal crossing guard fatally injured when struck by a car—Massachusetts. Report #18MA046. 2020. https://www.cdc.gov/niosh/face/pdfs/18ma046.pdf

7. California Department of Public Health. Two older workers die when they fall from ladders. 2020. https://www.cdph.ca.gov/Programs/CCDPHP/DEODC/OHB/FACE/CDPH%20Document%20Library/OlderFall.pdf

8. Cox-Ganser JM, White SK, Jones R, et al. Respiratory morbidity in office workers in a water-damaged building. *Environmental Health Perspectives*. 2005;113:485-490.

9. Gosselin, KR. Long-vacant state office tower in Hartford—once studied for "sick building" syndrome—has a buyer. *Hartford Courant*. August 15, 2019. https://www.courant.com/business/hc-biz-state-sigourney-street-office-buyer-20190815-u7q35autzjdqnbxh53qtlzgldu-story.html

10. NIOSH. *Health Hazard Evaluation Report: Evaluation of Respiratory Health among Employees in a Water-Damaged Office Building–Connecticut.* US Department of Health and Human Services, Public Health Service, Centers for Disease Control and Prevention, National Institute for Occupational Safety and Health; 2011. NIOSH HETA No. 2001-0445-3141. https://www.cdc.gov/niosh/hhe/reports/pdfs/2001-0445-3141.pdf

11. CDC (Centers for Disease Control and Prevention). Workplaces and Businesses. Accessed October 21, 2021. https://www.cdc.gov/coronavirus/2019-ncov/community/workplaces-businesses/

12. USDOL-BLS (US Department of Labor, Bureau of Labor Statistics). *Survey of Occupational Injuries and Illnesses Data.* US Department of Labor; 2020. https://www.bls.gov/iif/soii-data.htm

13. USDOL-BLS (US Department of Labor, Bureau of Labor Statistics). *Census of Fatal Occupational Injuries.* US Department of Labor; 2020. https://www.bls.gov/iif/oshcfoi1.htm

14. Brown J. Nearly 50 years of occupational safety and health data. *Beyond the Numbers: Workplace Injuries* (US Bureau of Labor Statistics). July 2020;9(9). https://www.bls.gov/opub/btn/volume-9/nearly-50-years-of-occupational-safety-and-health-data.htm

15. OPSI (Office of Public Sector Information). The Construction (Design and Management) Regulations 2007. UK Statutory Instruments No. 320 Health and Safety. 2007. http://www.opsi.gov.uk/si/si2007/uksi_20070320_en_1

16. United Kingdom Health and Safety Executive (HSE). Construction Statistics in

Great Britain. 2019;12. www.hse.gov.uk/construction/resources/statistics.htm

17. USDOL-BLS (US Department of Labor, Bureau of Labor Statistics). The number and rate of fatal work injuries, by industry. 2019. www.bls.gov/charts/census-of-fatal-occupational-injuries/number-and-rate-of-fatal-work-injuries-by-industry.htm

18. Kheel Center, Cornell University. *The 1911 Triangle Factory Fire.* Accessed January 22, 2021. http://trianglefire.ilr.cornell.edu/

19. Wagner GR, Spieler EA. The roles of government in protecting and promoting occupational and environmental health. In: Levy BS, Wegman DL, Rest K, Sokas R, eds. *Occupational and Environmental Health.* 7th ed. Oxford University Press; 2017: 41-58.

20. ISSS (The International System Safety Society). ISSS Resources. Accessed January 22, 2021. https://system-safety.org/page/resources.

21. Christensen WC, Manuele FA. *Safety through Design.* National Safety Council; 1999.

22. Schulte P, Rinehart R, Okun A, Geraci C, Heidel D. National Prevention through Design (PtD) initiative. *Journal of Safety Research.* 2008; 39:115-121.

23. NIOSH. Prevention through Design. 2021. Accessed January 21, 2021. https://www.cdc.gov/niosh/topics/ptd/

24. NIOSH. Workplace Design Solutions: Preventing Falls through the Design of Roof Parapets. 2013. DHHS (NIOSH) Publication 2014-108 https://www.cdc.gov/niosh/docs/2014-108/

25. OSHA (Occupational Safety and Health Administration). Recommended Practices for Safety and Health Programs. 2016. http://www.osha.gov/shpguidelines/

26. ANSI/ASSP (American National Standards Institute/American Society of Safety Professionals). ANSI/ASSP Z590.3-2021 Prevention through Design Guidelines for Addressing Occupational Hazards

and Risks in Design and Redesign Processes. 2021. https://www.assp.org/standards/standards-topics/prevention-through-design-z590-3

27. NIOSH. Overtime and Extended Work Shifts: Recent Findings on Illnesses, Injuries and Health Behaviors. NIOSH Publication 2004-143. 2004. http://www.cdc.gov/niosh/docs/2004-143/

28. NIOSH. Violence in the Workplace. DHHS (NIOSH) Publication 96-100, Current Intelligence Bulletin 57. 1996. https://www.cdc.gov/niosh/docs/96-100/risk.html

29. NIOSH. Work and Fatigue. 2021. Accessed October 25, 2021. https://www.cdc.gov/niosh/topics/fatigue/

30. NIOSH. Productive Aging and Work. 2021. Accessed February 27, 2021. https://www.cdc.gov/niosh/topics/productiveaging/

31. EBRI (Employee Benefit Research Institute). Retirement Confidence Survey. 2003. https://www.ebri.org/retirement/retirement-confidence-survey/2003-survey-results

32. NIOSH. Hierarchy of Controls. 2020. https://www.cdc.gov/niosh/topics/hierarchy/default.html

33. CCPS (Center for Chemical Process Safety), AIChE (American Institute of Chemical Engineering). CCPS Annual Report. Accessed January 22, 2021. https://www.aiche.org/ccps

34. ANSI/ASSP (American National Standards Institute/American Society of Safety Professionals). ANSI/ASSP Z10.0—2019 Occupational Health and Safety Management Systems. 2019. https://www.assp.org/standards/standards-topics/osh-management-z10

35. ISO (International Organization for Standardization). ISO 45001 Occupational Health and Safety. 2018. https://www.iso.org/iso-45001-occupational-health-and-safety.html

36. GRI (The Global Reporting Initiative). GRI 403: Occupational Health and Safety.

2018. https://www.globalreporting.org
/standards/standards-development
/topic-standard-project-for-occupational
-health and-safety/ (standard can be
downloaded for no cost at: https:
//www.globalreporting.org/standards
/media/1910/gri-403-occupational-health
-and-safety-2018.pdf)

37. NIOSH. Healthy Work Design and Well-
Being Program. 2021. Accessed January 21,
2021. https://www.cdc.gov/niosh
/programs/hwd

38. NIOSH. Total Worker Health. What Is Total
Worker Health? 2020. https://www.cdc
.gov/niosh/twh/totalhealth.html

39. Lee MP, Hudson H, Richards R, Chang
CC, Chosewood LC, Schill AL, on behalf
of the NIOSH Office for Total Worker
Health. *Fundamentals of Total Worker Health
Approaches: Essential Elements for Advancing
Worker Safety, Health, and Well-Being.*
US Department of Health and Human
Services, Centers for Disease Control and
Prevention, National Institute for Occu-
pational Safety and Health; 2016. DHHS
(NIOSH) Publication 2017-112.

40. NIOSH. NIOSH Total Worker Health
Program. 2021. Accessed January 21, 2021.
https://www.cdc.gov/niosh/twh

41. Feltner C, Peterson K, Palmieri, et al.
The effectiveness of total worker health
interventions: a systematic review for a
National Institutes of Health Pathways
to Prevention workshop. *Annals of Internal
Medicine.* 2016;165(4):262-269. https://doi
.org/10.7326/M16-0626

42. Anger WK, Elliot DL, Bodner T, et al.
Effectiveness of total worker health
interventions. *Journal of Occupational
Health Psychology.* 2015;20(2):226-247.
https://doi.org/10.1037/a0038340

43. NIOSH. Total Worker Health: Making the
Business Case. How Total Worker Health
Approaches Can Benefit Both Your Workers and Your Organization. 2020. https:
//www.cdc.gov/niosh/twh/business.html

44. NIOSH. Total Worker Health: Priority
Areas and Emerging Issues. 2021. Accessed
January 21, 2021. http://www.cdc.gov
/niosh/twh/priority.html

45. NIOSH. NIOSH Centers of Excellence
for Total Worker Health. 2021. Accessed
March 4, 2021. https://www.cdc.gov
/niosh/twh/centers.html

46. Nevala N, Pehkonen I, Koskela I, Ruusu-
vuori J, Anttila H. Workplace accommodation among persons with disabilities: a
systematic review of its effectiveness and
barriers or facilitators. *Journal of Occupational Rehabilitation.* 2015;25:432-448.
http://doi.org/10.1007/s10926-014-9548-z

47. Job Accommodation Network. A to Z
of Disabilities and Accommodations.
Accessed October 21, 2021. https://askjan
.org/

48. CDC (Centers for Disease Control
and Prevention). Ventilation in
Buildings. Accessed October 21, 2021.
https://www.cdc.gov/coronavirus/2019
-ncov/community/ventilation.html

49. ASHRAE (American Society of Heating,
Ventilating, and Air-Conditioning Engi-
neers). Coronavirus (COVID-19) Response
Resources from ASHRAE and Others.
Accessed October 21, 2021. https://www
.ashrae.org/technical-resources/resources

50. ASHRAE (American Society of Heating,
Ventilating, and Air-Conditioning
Engineers). Search Results for: UVGI. 2021.
Accessed January 22, 2021. https://www
.ashrae.org/search?q=UVGI

51. MSU (Michigan State University). Suicide
in the workplace: prevention opportunities. Hazard Alert Workplace Suicide
Prevention. 2020. https://oem.msu.edu
/images/Alerts/2020/HAZALERTS_Suicide
.pdf

52. CSA (CSAgroup). Psychological Health and
Safety in the Workplace. 2018. CAN/CSA
-Z1003-13/BNQ 9700-803/2013. https:
//www.csagroup.org/article/cancsa
-z1003-13-bnq-9700-803-2013-r2018/

53. BSI (BSIgroup). ISO 45003: The first global standard giving practical guidance on managing psychological health at work. 2021. Accessed January 26, 2021. https://www.bsigroup.com/en-GB/iso-45003/

54. NSC (National Safety Council). Work to Zero: Workplace Violence. 2020. Accessed February 4, 2021. https://www.nsc.org/workplace/safety-topics/work-to-zero/hazardous-situations/workplace-violence

55. Crowe T. *Crime Prevention through Environmental Design*. 2nd ed. Butterworth-Heinemann; 2000.

56. Deutsch, W. Crime Prevention through Environmental Design (CPTED). The Balance Small Business. 2019. https://www.thebalancesmb.com/crime-prevention-through-environmental-design-394571

57. AMFAM (American Family Insurance). Crime Prevention through Environmental Design (CPTED). 2021. Accessed January 26, 2021. https://www.amfam.com/resources/articles/loss-control-resources/crime-prevention-through-environmental-design

58. NCPC (National Crime Prevention Council). Resources: Home & Neighborhood Safety Strategies. 2021. Accessed January 26, 2021. https://www.ncpc.org/resources/home-neighborhood-safety/strategies/

59. USGBC (US Green Building Council) LEED (Leadership in Energy and Environmental Design). Prevention through Design. 2015. https://www.usgbc.org/credits/preventionthroughdesign

60. Chan J, Pun N. Suicide as protest for the new generation of Chinese migrant workers: Foxconn, Global Capital, and the state. *Asia-Pacific Journal*; 2014. Retrieved February 4, 2021. https://apjjf.org/Jenny-Chan/3408/article.html

61. Flynn MA, Castellanos E, Flores-Andrade A. Safety across cultures: understanding the challenges. *Professional Safety*. January 2018. https://blogs.cdc.gov/niosh-science-blog/2018/03/13/safety-across-cultures/

62. Flynn MA, Eggerth DE, Jacobson CJ. Undocumented status as a social determinant of occupational safety and health: the workers' perspective. *American Journal of Industrial Medicine*. 2015;58:1127-1137.

63. ILO (International Labour Organization). *Decent Work for Migrants and Refugees*. ILO; 2016. https://www.ilo.org/global/topics/labour-migration/publications/WCMS_524995/lang--en/index.htm

64. UN (United Nations). *Transforming Our World: The 2030 Agenda for Sustainable Development*. A/RES/70/1. United Nations; 2015. https://www.un.org/development/desa/dspd/2015/08/transforming-our-world-the-2030-agenda-for-sustainable-development/

65. UN (United Nations). United Nations Global Compact. Guide to Corporate Sustainability. 2015. https://www.unglobalcompact.org/library/1151 (also see https://www.unglobalcompact.org/what-is-gc/mission/principles)

66. Flynn MA, Wickramage K. Leveraging the domain of work to improve migrant health. *International Journal of Environmental Research and Public Health*. 2017;14,1248. https://www.ncbi.nlm.nih.gov/pmc/articles/PMC5664749/

67. USGBC (US Green Building Council) LEED (Leadership in Energy and Environmental Design). Social Equity in the Built Environment. 2021. Accessed January 26, 2021. https://www.usgbc.org/resources/social-equity-built-environment

68. Sorensen G, Dennerlein JT, Peters SE, Sabbath EL, Kelly EL, Wagner GR. The future of research on work, safety, health and wellbeing: a guiding conceptual framework. *Social Science & Medicine*. 2021,269.113593. https://doi.org/10.1016/j.socscimed.2020.113593

69. Schulte PA, Streit JMK, Sheriff F, et al. Potential scenarios and hazards in the work of the future: a systematic review of the peer-reviewed and gray literatures. *Annals of Work Exposures and Health.* 2020; 1-31. https://doi.org/10.1093/annweh /wxaa051

70. NIOSH. NIOSH Future of Work Initiative. 2020. Accessed December 19, 2020. https://www.cdc.gov/niosh/topics /future-of-work/default.html

71. Tamers SL, Streit J, Pana-Cryan R, et al. Envisioning the future of work to safeguard the safety, health, and well-being of the workforce: a perspective from the CDC's National Institute for Occupational Safety and Health. *American Journal of Industrial Medicine.* 2020;63:1065-1084. https://pubmed.ncbi.nlm.nih.gov /32926431/.doi:10.1002/ajim.23183

CHAPTER 14

HEALTHY HEALTH CARE SETTINGS

Craig Zimring, Jennifer R. DuBose, and Bea Sennewald

KEY POINTS

- Health care settings represent a unique built environment because their primary function is maintaining and restoring health.
- The impacts of health care facility design on people and the environment are complex and operate at multiple scales from patients, family, and staff in the health care facility to communities and broader society.
- Although health care can be healing, it is costly and can cause harm to patients due to medical errors and infections, and health care facilities use considerable energy and water.
- Health care institutions using evidence-based design can offer direct benefits to patients, families, and staff, such as safety, and indirect benefits by facilitating teamwork and reducing medical errors.
- Health systems are significantly reducing their carbon footprint and resource use by innovative design.
- Principles of health care design apply to both high-income and low- and moderate-income countries by focusing on empowering patients and families, simplifying workflow, and making care safer.
- Health care design impacts communities and society by facilitating access to care and reducing use of energy, water, and other resources.

- Although much investment has been made in hospitals and clinics in the developed world, there is growing focus on providing good-quality, accessible, affordable care in low- and moderate-income countries that recognizes the dignity of all.
- The design of health care facilities ideally optimizes health of the individual, community, and ecosystems while reducing cost.

INTRODUCTION

Joan, age sixty-eight, was the managing partner in a family accounting firm. She had a long history of being physically active and eating healthy. However, she had been experiencing increasing difficulty in organizing her daily tasks at work and home and had become more sedentary.

One afternoon, Joan complained of chest pain and was sent to the hospital by ambulance. She had an extended wait in the noisy and chaotic emergency department after her initial exam. Joan and her husband had difficulty understanding the proposed diagnostic and treatment processes. After additional tests, she was rushed to the cardiac catheterization lab, where she had a stent put in. During her extended recovery in the hospital, she developed a bedsore that became infected by an antibiotic-resistant pathogen that resulted in sepsis, a whole body inflammation, and she was moved to the intensive care unit (ICU).

Fortunately, her ICU was in the new bed-tower, and her quiet single room had space for her husband to spend the night. The room had tunable white lighting that changed color over the course of the day—bluer in the morning to help her wake up and warmer later in the day to help her relax. With her confusion—later diagnosed as mild cognitive impairment—the lighting and settled environment helped her avoid agitation and keep track of day and night, which contributed to her subsequent recovery.

Although health care helps individual patients heal, its impacts are more complex, affecting the people who are treated in and work in health care facilities, the local communities, and the broader society (figure 14.1). In this chapter, we discuss how the design of health care facilities impacts health and experience at multiple scales, both in the developed and developing world. We discuss direct effects, such as the tunable LED lighting in Joan's room and the prevention of infection, as well as how the built environment impacts health care processes. We examine how health care can be improved through better facility design and operations, including evidence-based design and sustainability. Health care is an enormous, complex enterprise—17 percent of the US economy[1]—and numerous innovations are being developed. Approaches such as evidence-based design and sustainability have common themes:

- Adopting systems perspectives that include multiple stakeholders, processes, and physical settings and seeking to reconcile competing incentives
- Paying increased attention to, and seeking to empower, traditionally underrepresented stakeholders such as patients and families, underresourced communities, and those facing chronic disease
- Seeking to create and use evidence in decision-making

As Joan's story shows, although a patient might receive excellent care, the experience is often stressful and difficult to navigate. Health care can be dangerous, with many thousands

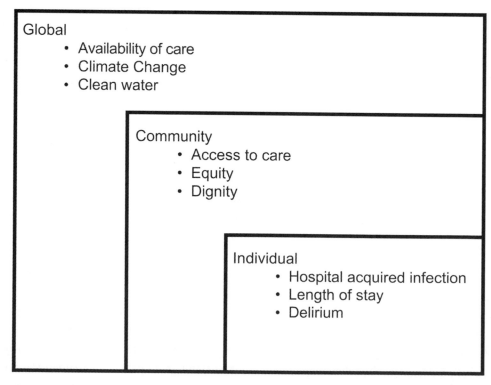

Figure 14.1. Scales of health care impacts: health care influences individual, community, and global health. Source: Jennifer R. DuBose

of people being harmed in US hospitals each year from preventable medical errors or **hospital-associated infections**.[2,3] Although much health care focuses on healing or recovery from an illness, it has an important role in health more generally, providing resources for individuals and communities to be resilient and prevent disease. Global impacts arise from health care's large contribution to carbon emissions; the US health care sector was responsible for more than 6 percent of the US greenhouse gas footprint in 2015.[4]

LINKING HEALTH CARE DESIGN TO OUTCOMES

The history of health care design reflects the evolving understanding of the relationship between design and health.[5] The modern hospital originated in the nineteenth century with the growing realization that light and cleanliness mattered and that design and layout could support the delivery of care. In 1854, the nursing reformer and statistician Florence Nightingale and a group of volunteer women arrived at the converted Turkish barracks at Scutari where there was a death rate of 43 percent in the fetid, smelly military hospital. A nearby hospital, built from small, prefabricated buildings erected on a sloping site to allow drainage and breezes and allowing visibility and supervision, had a death rate of 3 percent.[6] Although before the germ theory of disease—Nightingale thought that disease was airborne—she codified these design principles in 1859 in *Notes on Nursing*,[7] advocating good ventilation, abundant natural light, and healing nature views in what became known as "Nightingale Wards."

This first "evidence-based design" hospital plan held sway in hospital architecture into the twentieth century. Hospitals gradually became larger and more complex, with the growth of specialty care and improvements in building systems such as elevators and mechanical ventilation. The increasing role of industrial engineering methods in hospitals helped use staff time more efficiently, but at the potential cost of treating patients as units of production, rather than as individuals and family members who were partners in improving their own health.[8]

Beginning in the late 1990s, several forces converged to again highlight the relationships between health care design and health. The US Institute of Medicine (IOM) initiated a series of reports, collectively called the Quality Chasm series, documenting that US health care was dangerous for patients. Drawing on studies that analyzed medical records, the IOM argued that as many as one hundred thousand people died each year in US hospitals due to preventable medical errors, and tens of thousands more died from hospital-associated infections.[2,3,9] Subsequent reviews of medical records suggest that the number might be much higher, with estimates of two hundred thousand or more unnecessary deaths annually,[3,10] although some of these persons might have otherwise died from underlying conditions.[11]

In parallel, there was increasing commitment to improving patient experience. Results of patient satisfaction surveys were made public and tied to hospital remuneration.[12] After several decades of lower levels of construction, the United States and subsequently other countries experienced a large program of hospital construction to replace antiquated facilities. Designers of hospital systems looked for new models to differentiate themselves from older, bland, institutional designs and to build market share. They created quiet facilities with private rooms and abundant natural light, often based on hospitality design. These efforts were supported by health care organizations such as the Center for Health Design (https://www.healthdesign.org), the Institute for Healthcare Improvement (http://www.ihi.org), and the Institute for Patient and Family Centered Care (https://www.ipfcc.org).

The IOM Quality Chasm reports revealed the costs and dangers inherent in US medicine. Literature reviews compiled hundreds of articles rigorously linking the physical design of health care facilities to errors, infections, and other safety and quality issues. These reviews concluded that improved design plays a significant role in helping to resolve these problems.[13-17] Health care design can empower patients and families by providing welcoming, culturally appropriate hospitals and clinics with space for families and patient advocates. Ulrich[18] proposed that supportive design of the hospital environment will reduce stress for patients if it fosters perceptions of control, social support, and positive distraction such as views of nature. These dimensions have been supported in subsequent research.[19] Designs that encourage more family involvement, are quieter, have more natural light, and provide more privacy are better rated by patients.[20] More recently, the availability of high-quality, lower-cost LED lighting has allowed electric lights to mimic the color change of daylight, with potential positive impacts on circadian rhythm.[21]

Better design can also support staff. Layouts that allow staff to see other staff and to have informal interactions increase key aspects of medical teamwork such as communication and situational awareness.[22] Health care facility layouts that allow workers to directly see sinks and hand sanitizer stations are associated with better hand hygiene compliance because the direct view encourages increased hand cleaning.[23-25]

These research findings added momentum to the growing field of **evidence-based design**, defined as "the deliberate attempt to base building decisions on the best available research evidence with the goal of improving outcomes and of continuing to monitor the success or failure for subsequent decision-making."[26(p2)] Evidence-based design was adopted by many health care designers and organizations to help achieve patient-centered care[27] and improve patient safety[28] and has been promoted by groups such as the Center for Health Design. In architecture, health and safety concerns were important considerations in revising key guidelines, such as the Facilities Guidelines Institute (FGI) guidelines that are law in thirty-eight states.[29] The 2010 FGI guidelines for the first time required single rooms in almost all new US acute care hospitals because of the risks of cross-infection and impacts on sleep and communication in shared rooms.

Evidence-based design guidelines have been developed for health care facilities overall[30] and for special units such as intensive care units,[31,32] operating rooms,[33] and biocontainment units,[34] as well as to encourage key health care functions such as patient sleep[35] and teamwork.[22] These guidelines have influenced hundreds of hospitals worldwide, such as those of the US Military Health System, Kaiser Permanente, and others. Figure 14.2 shows a recent hospital that incorporates many of these features. Table 14.1 shows several design strategies that have been found to influence health care outcomes.

INFECTION PREVENTION AND INTERRUPTING THE CHAIN OF INFECTION

The IOM Quality Chasm series accelerated attention to preventing hospital-associated infections, with the goal of preventing pathogens from entering health care facilities and moving from infected hosts such as other patients or staff to vulnerable patients or staff.[36] After many years of increasing attention to acute diseases in the developed world,[37] the H1N1, SARS, Ebola, and COVID-19 pandemics focused renewed attention on treating patients with infectious diseases. The "chain of infection model" illustrated in figure 14.3 shows how facilities can help reduce the spread of infections within a hospital by interrupting the path from the source of the infection to a vulnerable patient or staff member.[38] Typically, a pathogen such as a virus is brought into a hospital by a patient or health care worker on their skin or in their system, although it can enter by air (for example,

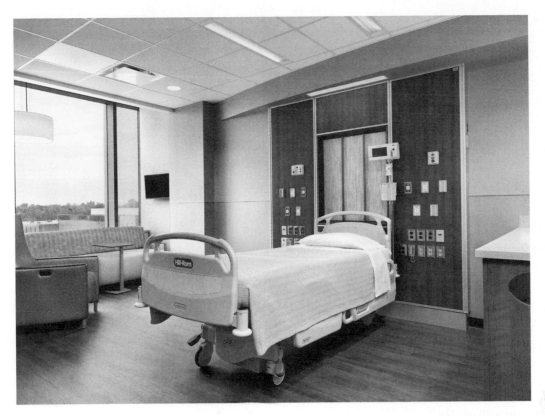

Figure 14.2. New hospital rooms provide comfortable areas for family and visitors, natural light and views, and access to interactive technology for patients and staff. They might also include white lighting adjustable by time of day, which helps patients become alert in the morning and sleep well at night and can change acuity to fit patients' needs. Hand hygiene opportunities are clearly available near the room door.
Source: Alise O'Brien

SARS) or water (for example, Legionella) or be transmitted through contact (for example, Ebola) or droplets (for example, COVID-19).

Design can interrupt the modes of infection directly by isolating people in isolation units or by using air filters and antimicrobial materials, such as coating surfaces with materials like copper or silver that reduce contamination.[39-42] The environment can also help change behavior. For example, moving hand-cleaning opportunities into the line of sight can increase the likelihood of a busy health care worker cleaning their hands between patients.[36] Design of the work area can also support safe doffing of personal protective equipment after treating infectious patients by reminding staff of the key steps and making simpler workflow.[43,44] A lasting lesson from the COVID-19 pandemic is that health care

design needs to be flexible to accommodate unforeseen airborne, waterborne, or contact-transmitted infectious agents.

THE GROWTH OF SUSTAINABLE HEALTH CARE

Simultaneous to the rise of evidence-based design, which has often focused on the effects on individuals as patients or workers in the facility, there has been increased awareness of the role that health care facilities play in community health, as well as the overall global conditions.[45] With their significant use of resources, hospitals and other health care facilities have a substantial impact on the environment and on the health of surrounding communities and an opportunity to contribute to worldwide sustainable development goals.[46] The environmental and public health impacts

Table 14.1. Summary of the relationships between design factors and health care outcomes (relationships with strong evidence are shown with ••; those with growing evidence are shown with •).

Design Strategies or Environmental Interventions

Health Care Outcomes	Single-bed rooms	Access to daylight	Appropriate lighting	Views of nature	Family zone in-patient rooms	Carpeting	Noise-reducing finishes	Ceiling lifts	Nursing floor layout	Decentralized supplies	Acuity-adaptable rooms
Reduced hospital-acquired infections	••										
Reduced medical errors	•		•				•				•
Reduced patient falls	•		•		•	•			•		•
Reduced pain		•	•	••			•				
Improved patient sleep	••	•	•				•				
Reduced patient stress	•	•	•	••			••				
Reduced depression		••	••	•	•						
Reduced length of stay		•	•	•							•
Improved patient privacy and confidentiality	••				•		•				
Improved communication with patients and family members	••				•		•				
Improved social support	•				•	•					
Increased patient satisfaction	••	•	•	•	•	•	•				
Decreased staff injuries								••			•
Decreased staff stress	•	•	•				•				
Increased staff effectiveness	•		•				•		•	•	•
Increased staff satisfaction	•	•	•	•			•				

Source: Adapted from Halawa F, Madathil SC, Gittler A, Khasawneh MT. Advancing evidence-based healthcare facility design: a systematic literature review. *Health Care Management Science.* 2020:1-28; Ulrich RS, Zimring C, Zhu XM, et al. A review of the research literature on evidence-based healthcare design. *HERD: Health Environments Research & Design Journal.* 2008;1(3):61-125.

result from the construction and ongoing facilities operation and management practices that consume clean water, disturb the land, remove vegetation, disrupt habitat, interrupt natural hydrogeological pathways, introduce toxic materials, and require energy to heat and cool, among many other impacts.

There is a growing recognition of the impacts that health care facilities have beyond the individual scale that has been the typical purview of evidence-based design. Sustainable building certification programs such as BREEAM, LEED, WELL Building Standard, and Living Building Challenge have much to offer health care systems on strategies for reducing their negative health and environmental impacts (chapter 22). The health care sector is complex, and to date there has not been wide-

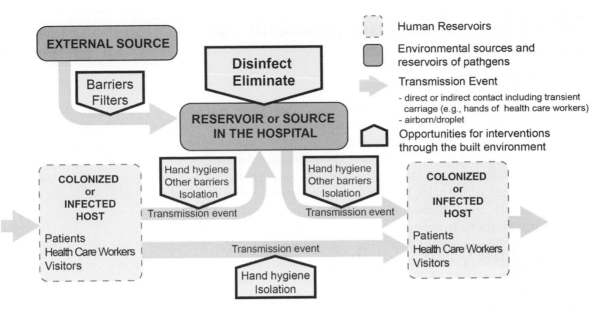

Figure 14.3. Design can help break the chain of infection and the transmission by eliminating pathogens and their movement.
Source: Zimring C, Jacob JT, Denham ME, et al. The role of facility design in preventing the transmission of healthcare-associated infections: background and conceptual framework. *HERD: Health Environments Research & Design Journal*. 2013;7(1_suppl):18-30. doi:10.1177/193758671300701S04

spread adoption of a single, targeted certification program.

Several nongovernmental organizations promote the opportunity that the health care sector has to contribute to sustainability. One is Practice Greenhealth (http://practicegreen health.org), which runs an active program with a network of health care systems encouraging continued progress toward sustainability and sharing best practices for better operations. Another is Health Care Without Harm, which has worked to document the magnitude of health care's contribution to global issues such as climate change.[47]

EQUITY AND ACCESS AS DESIGN ISSUES

The goals of sustainable health care are universal, but the specific challenges with achieving it vary across the world. Even in high-resource settings, such as the United States, there are still large populations who lack access to safe and affordable care. Health care facility design choices play a role in determining who has access to care. Increased distance to health care has been repeatedly found to be associated with worse health care outcomes in the Global North.[48] In lower-income countries, this can be an even larger challenge, with dire consequences, compounded by an inadequate transportation infrastructure (box 14.1).

The location of health care facilities within a community, and the transportation resources of that population, influences who ultimately benefits from those health care services. Equitable access requires expanding the reach of health care, ensuring that the buildings themselves are close to the communities that need them, that people can physically access them because of proximity and connection to the transportation network, and that people can financially access health care through affordable prices or universal insurance.

The design of the facility is an important part of influencing whether people feel welcomed and dignified, regardless of their socioeconomic status, race, nationality, language, value system, gender, and cognitive spectrum, by recognizing and addressing a diverse set of needs and wants. For example, providing gender-inclusive restrooms is an example of a design strategy that creates a welcoming environment.[49] Facilities can also welcome people by honoring

BOX 14.1 CASE STUDY: BRINGING HEALTHY, SUSTAINABLE HEALTH CARE TO THE BUSH

Bea Sennewald

The principles of adopting a systems perspective, empowering patients and families, and using evidence also apply to low- and moderate-income countries where women in the late stages of pregnancy are at increased risk of dying due to long distances to health care facilities. One strategy to improve maternal outcomes has been to build maternal waiting homes close to obstetric facilities where the women in late pregnancy can stay. A study of maternal waiting home patients in Malawi found that perception of the built environment for these homes had a strong influence over patient's overall satisfaction with their experience, especially if they included amenities such as facilities for storing possessions and preparing food.[a]

The Sachibondu Health Centre in Zambia (figure 14.4) was started in 1971 by Ruth Wallis, an English nurse, as part of a Christian mission. Even for Zambia its setting is remote, an hour's drive from the nearest settlement and five hours from the local airport, even in the dry season when the roads are not washed out by floods. The clinic has no permanent doctors; rather, it is staffed by nurses and midwives. It attracts more than three thousand patients per year who travel on foot or by bicycle from as far as 300 kilometers (200 miles) away in Zambia, Angola, and the Democratic Republic of Congo. The most common treatments delivered at Sachibondu are maternity services, including prenatal, delivery, and well-baby clinics; malaria; respiratory illness; and trauma. Outpatient services include HIV treatments and vaccinations.

Figure 14.4. The Sachibondu Health Centre in Zambia is an example of an affordable, safe, and sustainable health care facility in a low-resource setting.
Source: Photo Courtesy of Sachibondu Health Centre. Design and construction by Orkidstudio, Nairobi; medical design and ventilation by Bea Sennewald, London. Solar power installation was by Solar for Sach, Wiltshire, United Kingdom.

When starting the design of the new Sachibondu hospital, the ambition was to create an environment to deliver first-rate health care despite the low-resource setting (figure 14.5). It was to be a place that is safe, calm, and quiet, full of natural light and views of nature—in short, a place that heals and promotes healthy communities. Sachibondu is a community hospital with thirty inpatient beds spread over wards for women (eight beds), men (eight beds), and children (ten beds), plus four individual rooms for patients with infectious diseases. It includes an operating theater and emergency department, a lab, x-ray facilities, and a maternity clinic. Food is cooked in a common kitchen and is served to staff and ambulatory patients on an adjoining terrace. A small compound nearby serves as guest house for expecting mothers and relatives traveling with patients.

BOX 14.1 CONTINUED

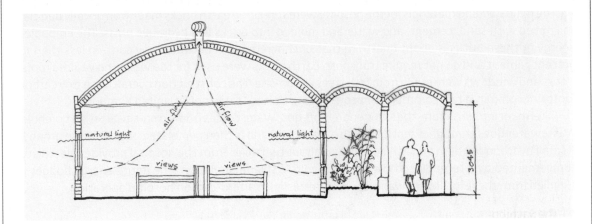

Figure 14.5. Section through patient ward, Sachibondu Hospital, Zambia, highlighting natural lighting and ventilation.
Source: Sketch by Bea Sennewald

The hospital wings are separated by courtyards to give patients and staff views of plants and birds. Each wing is narrow, with windows on both sides to promote natural ventilation (figure 14.6). There are no corridors. All circulation routes are covered outdoor walkways separated from patient rooms with plantings to preserve privacy and quiet for patients. No mechanical cooling is used in the hospital except in the operating theater, where some cooling and filtration are needed for patient safety. Windows on both sides of each wing bring fresh air into the wards, which is then drawn upward and exhausted through small wind-driven ventilators, an effective and inexpensive way to control spread of infection.[b]

Figure 14.6. Sachibondu Hospital floor plan, Zambia, highlighting ventilation and use of space. Tuck shop is the hospital canteen.
Source: Drawing by Bea Sennewald

BOX 14.1 CONTINUED

The main building materials for the hospital were sun-cured earth bricks made from locally dug clay soil mixed with sand, cement, and water and molded into bricks in a hydraulic press. The embodied energy of these bricks is about one-third that of concrete block because they contain less than 10 percent cement and do not require transport. Earth bricks were used for the walls and vaulted roofs. Doors and windows were made from four trees cut on-site. The construction overall has a tiny carbon footprint compared to a community hospital in the United States or the United Kingdom.

In terms of infrastructure, the site is entirely off-grid. Water comes from an on-site artesian borehole. Wastewater goes through a septic tank to a leach field and is then percolated back into the ground. A small hydropower dam on Sachibondu land about two miles from the hospital provides electricity, supplemented by a recently completed photovoltaic solar installation. The entire energy budget is supplied from these local, renewable sources, resulting in a zero-carbon hospital operation.

REFERENCES

a. McIntosh N, Gruits P, Oppel E, Shao A. Built spaces and features associated with user satisfaction in maternity waiting homes in Malawi. *Midwifery*. 2018; 62:96-103.
b. Cox H, Escombe R, McDermid C, et al. Wind-driven roof turbines: a novel way to improve ventilation for TB infection control in health facilities. *PLOS ONE*. 2012; 7(1):e29589.

and respecting the culture of the community, such as the Cherokee Indian Hospital in North Carolina completed in 2015, which incorporated artistic references to culture through an exterior mimicking the tribe's baskets.[50]

Sometimes access to care requires multiple modes of access and different services provided in health centers. Increasingly, health care occurs in a range of settings outside of hospitals and clinics, such as community facilities, wellness centers, and homes. These settings are nearer patients, better attuned to community needs, and less expensive to build and operate. Such facilities can help reduce the carbon footprint for transportation, construction, and operations. For example, while the large US health care provider Kaiser Permanente continues to provide care in hospitals and clinics, it is increasing the range of settings and methods it provides for its patients, including small clinics in shopping areas and one-stop-shopping clinics that provide opportunities for exercise, socializing, and organic markets.[51] COVID-19 significantly increased the use of **telehealth** by as much as 150 percent due to limitations on on-site visits and reduction in regulatory barriers.[52] Telehealth helps move health care from a reliance on care inside a facility and has the potential of reducing carbon footprints related to transportation, construction, and operations, but it also raises equity concerns for patients who do not have access to broadband technology.

HEALTH CARE'S ROLE IN CLIMATE CHANGE

The business of providing health care is resource intensive to varying degrees across the world, leading to a sizable contribution to greenhouse gas emissions. Health care facilities on average are more than twice as energy intensive as the overall building stock. Worldwide, health care was responsible for 4.4 percent of greenhouse gas emissions.[4] The United States boasts the largest absolute total greenhouse gas emissions from health care (27 percent of the global footprint), as well as the highest per capita emissions (1.72 metric tons per capita).[47]

Health care–sector greenhouse gas emissions are divided into three scopes: (1) the direct impacts from clinical procedures that directly generate emissions such as the use of anesthesia and on-site combustion; (2) emissions from energy consumption, which is driven by the design of the health care facilities; and (3) the embodied carbon dioxide from purchased supplies. Emissions from the first two scopes are most influenced by facility design and operations and make up 36 percent of the total health care emissions in the United States, which is a larger percentage than in any other country where it was calculated, pointing to the incredible opportunity the United States has to make a positive difference through the design of the facilities.[47]

Health care systems can reduce their contribution to climate change by improving the design of facilities to reduce energy consumption and by shifting their remaining energy needs to clean, renewable sources. In the US Midwest, the Gundersen Health System has demonstrated leadership in these strategies. Its Sparta, Wisconsin, clinic was designed with LED lighting, occupancy sensors, double-paned windows, and better wall insulation to bring its energy needs down to only half of that for a typical clinic. It met much of their energy needs with on-site photovoltaic arrays and a geothermal system for direct heating and cooling.[53]

The relationship between health care and the changing climate is bidirectional. The massive ecological disturbances from climate change will shift the demands placed on health care (chapter 17). Changes will include the environmental context surrounding health care facilities, such as increases in extreme temperatures, shifts in precipitation patterns, changing coastlines, and more intense and frequent storms.

Hospitals are huge financial investments that are expected to stay in service for fifty years or more, so new hospitals built now need to be designed to withstand a range of future climate scenarios. An iconic example of the impact of the changing climate is Charity Hospital in New Orleans, which was destroyed by Hurricane Katrina in 2005. The replacement hospital was designed to be more resilient, with the exterior fortified to withstand stronger gales and the emergency power supply placed several stories up (unlike the original hospital's generators located in the basement)

to avoid floodwaters.[54] In the 2020 Healthcare Design Showcase, the winning entries highlighted their resilience against one-hundred-year and five-hundred-year floods alongside the design elements that make patient rooms more comfortable and safer.[55]

The impacts of climate change will span all scales of health systems, from threats to individual health, demands on the built infrastructure, changes in community-level disease patterns, and shifts in populations. Health care facilities need to reduce their contribution to climate change and be designed for resilience in the face of the changing climate.

SUMMARY

Hospital systems are increasingly regarding both the impact of design on patient and family safety and empowerment, as well as sustainability as priorities in their new construction and renovation projects. Changing demographics and technologies are influencing health care facilities in multiple ways. For example, as more medical procedures are done on an outpatient basis, the average hospital inpatient tends to be more severely ill than in the past. The medical-surgical patient of today closely resembles the intensive care patient of a few years ago. At the same time, health systems are starting to think beyond their walls about how they promote wellness and health in the community and reduce their environmental impact. They are rethinking their role in the community and want to be a place to which people go when they are healthy. For example, Kaiser Permanente hosts farmers' markets at some of its hospitals to promote healthy eating habits in the community, and many hospitals are providing walking trails and access to wellness activities, becoming a part of the community fabric and connecting to the landscape rather than remaining islands approached through a sea of asphalt. The design of health care facilities is being influenced by this evolving concept of wellness and health both for individuals and for the community and larger world.

DISCUSSION QUESTIONS

1. In what ways can the design of a health care facility affect the health and experience of patients, of staff, and of patients' family members?
2. Why should hospitals be concerned with sustainability?
3. How can evidence-based design be used in built environment settings other than health care facilities, such as schools, office buildings, and community design on a larger scale?
4. What opportunities exist for professionals and staff in health care settings to try to influence the design of the communities in which they work and live?

DISCLOSURE OF COMPETING INTERESTS

Craig Zimring, Jennifer R. DuBose, and Bea Sennewald disclose no competing interests.

REFERENCES

1. Nunn R, Parsons J, Shambaugh J. A dozen facts about the economics of the U.S. health-care system. Brookings Institution. Published March 10, 2020. Accessed November 15, 2021. https://www.brookings.edu/research/a-dozen-facts-about-the-economics-of-the-u-s-health-care-system/

2. Institute of Medicine Committee on Quality of Health Care in America. *Crossing the Quality Chasm: A New Health System for the 21st Century*. National Academies Press; 2001.

3. Makary MA, Daniel M. Medical error—the third leading cause of death in the US. *BMJ*. 2016;353.

4. Lenzen M, Malik A, Li M, et al. The environmental footprint of health care: a global assessment. *The Lancet Planetary Health*. 2020;4(7):e271-e279.

5. Horsburgh CR. Healing by design. *New England Journal of Medicine*. 1995;333(11):735-740.

6. Thompson JD, Goldin G. *The Hospital: A Social and Architectural History*. Vol 20. August 8, 2012 ed. Yale University Press; 1975.

7. Nightingale F. *Notes on Nursing: What It Is, and What It Is Not*. Lippincott Williams & Wilkins; 1992.

8. Lopetegui M, Yen P-Y, Lai A, Jeffries J, Embi P, Payne P. Time motion studies in healthcare: what are we talking about? *Journal of Biomedical Informatics*. 2014;49:292-299.

9. Institute of Medicine Committee on the Work Environment for Nurses and Patient Safety. *Keeping Patients Safe: Transforming the Work Environment of Nurses*. National Academies Press; 2004.

10. Leape LL. Errors in medicine. *Clinica Chimica Acta*. 2009;404(1):2-5.

11. Shojania KG, Dixon-Woods M. Estimating deaths due to medical error: the ongoing controversy and why it matters. *BMJ Quality & Safety*. 2017;26(5):423.

12. Sadler BL, DuBose J, Zimring C. The business case for building better hospitals through evidence-based design. *HERD: Health Environments Research & Design Journal*. 2008;1(3):22-39.

13. Devlin AS, Arneill AB. Health care environments and patient outcomes: a review of the literature. *Environment and Behavior*. 2003;35(5):665-694.

14. Ulrich RS, Zimring C, Zhu XM, et al. A review of the research literature on evidence-based healthcare design. *HERD: Health Environments Research & Design Journal*. 2008;1(3):61-125.

15. MacAllister L, Zimring C, Ryherd E. Exploring the relationships between patient room layout and patient satisfaction. *HERD: Health Environments Research & Design Journal*. 2019;12(1):91-107.

16. Zimring C, Ulrich R, Joseph A, Quan X. The environment's impact on safety. In: Marberry SO, ed. *Improving Healthcare with Better Building Design*. ACHE Management Series/Health Administration Press; 2006:63-79.

17. Halawa F, Madathil SC, Gittler A, Khasawneh MT. Advancing evidence-based healthcare facility design: a systematic literature review. *Health Care Management Science*. 2020:1-28.

18. Ulrich RS. Effects of interior design on wellness: theory and recent scientific research. *Journal of Health Care Interior Design*. 1991; 3:97-109.

19. Andrade CC, Devlin AS. Stress reduction in the hospital room: Applying Ulrich's theory of supportive design. *Journal of Environmental Psychology*. 2015; 41:125-134.

20. MacAllister L, Zimring C, Ryherd E. Environmental variables that influence patient satisfaction: a review of the literature. *HERD: Health Environments Research & Design Journal*. 2016;10(1):155-169.

21. Graves E, Davis RG, DuBose J, Campiglia GC, Wilkerson A, Zimring C. Lighting the

patient room of the future: evaluating different lighting conditions for performing typical nursing tasks. *HERD: Health Environments Research & Design Journal.* 2021;14(2):234-253.

22. Lim L, Moore M, DuBose JR, Obeidat B, Stroebel R, Zimring CM. Spatial influences on team awareness and communication in two outpatient clinics: a multiple methods study. *Journal of General Internal Medicine.* 2020:1-10.

23. Deyneko A, Cordeiro F, Berlin L, Ben-David D, Perna S, Longtin Y. Impact of sink location on hand hygiene compliance after care of patients with Clostridium difficile infection: a cross-sectional study. *BMC Infectious Diseases.* 2016;16(1):203.

24. Nevo I, Fitzpatrick M, Thomas R-E, et al. The efficacy of visual cues to improve hand hygiene compliance. *Simulation in Healthcare.* 2010;5(6):325-331.

25. Cohen B, Saiman L, Cimiotti J, Larson E. Factors associated with hand hygiene practices in two neonatal intensive care units. *Pediatric Infectious Diseases Journal.* 2003;(6):494-499.

26. Malkin J. A visual reference for evidence-based design. Center for Health Design. 2008.

27. Clancy CM, Isaacson S, Henriksen K. Design of the physical environment for changing healthcare needs. *HERD: Health Environments Research & Design Journal.* 2007;1(1):13-14.

28. Henriksen K, Isaacson S, Sadler BL, Zimring CM. The role of the physical environment in crossing the quality chasm. *Joint Commission Journal on Quality and Patient Safety.* 2007;33(Suppl 1):68-80.

29. Facilities Guidelines Institute. *2014 FGI Guidelines for Hospitals and Outpatient Facilities.* Facilities Guidelines Institute; 2014.

30. Malkin J. *Medical and Dental Space Planning: A Comprehensive Guide to Design, Equipment, and Clinical Procedures.* 4th ed. Wiley; 2014.

31. Hamilton DK. Design for critical care. In: Sethumadhavan A, Sasangohar F, eds. *Design for Health: Applications of Human Factors.* Elsevier; 2020:129-145.

32. Thompson DR, Hamilton DK, Cadenhead CD, et al. Guidelines for intensive care unit design. *Critical Care Medicine.* 2012;40(5):1586-1600.

33. Joseph A, Bayramzadeh S, Zamani Z, Rostenberg B. Safety, performance, and satisfaction outcomes in the operating room: a literature review. *HERD: Health Environments Research & Design Journal.* 2018;11(2):137-150.

34. DuBose JR, Matić Z, Sala MFW, et al. Design strategies to improve healthcare worker safety in biocontainment units: learning from Ebola preparedness. *Infection Control & Hospital Epidemiology.* 2018;1-7.

35. DuBose JR, Hadi K. Improving inpatient environments to support patient sleep. *International Journal for Quality in Health Care.* 2016;28(5):540-553.

36. Zimring C, Denham ME, Jacob JT, et al. Evidence-based design of healthcare facilities: opportunities for research and practice in infection prevention. *Infection Control & Hospital Epidemiology.* 2013;34(5):514-516.

37. Mathers CD, Boerma T, Ma Fat D. Global and regional causes of death. *British Medical Bulletin.* 2009;92(1):7-32.

38. Zimring C, Jacob JT, Denham ME, et al. The role of facility design in preventing the transmission of healthcare-associated infections: background and conceptual framework. *HERD: Health Environments Research & Design Journal.* 2013;7:18-30.

39. Zimring CM, Matić Z, Sala MFW, et al. Making the invisible visible: why does design matter for safe doffing of personal protection equipment? *Infection Control & Hospital Epidemiology.* 2018;39(11):1375-1377.

40. Denham ME, Kasali A, Steinberg JP, Cowan DZ, Zimring C, Jacob JT. The role of water in the transmission of healthcare-associated infections: opportunities for intervention

through the environment. *HERD: Health Environments Research & Design Journal*. 2013;7:99-126.

41. Steinberg JP, Denham ME, Zimring C, Kasali A, Hall KK, Jacob JT. The role of the hospital environment in the prevention of healthcare-associated infections by contact transmission. *HERD: Health Environments Research & Design Journal*. 2013;7:46-73.

42. Jacob JT, Kasali A, Steinberg JP, Zimring C, Denham ME. The role of the hospital environment in preventing healthcare-associated infections caused by pathogens transmitted through the air. *HERD: Health Environments Research & Design Journal*. 2013;7:74-98.

43. Wong M, Matić Z, Campiglia G, et al. Design strategies for biocontainment units to reduce risk during doffing of high-level personal protective equipment. *Clinical Infectious Diseases*. 2019;69:S241-S247.

44. Herlihey TA, Gelmi S, Cafazzo JA, Hall TNT. The impact of environmental design on doffing personal protective equipment in a healthcare environment: a formative human factors trial. *Infection Control & Hospital Epidemiology*. 2017;38(6):712-717.

45. Dannenberg AL, Burpee H. Architecture for health is not just for healthcare architects. *HERD: Health Environments Research & Design Journal*. 2018;11(2):8-12.

46. Francis D, Cohen G, Bhatt J, Brask C, Devnani M, Surgenor G. How healthcare can help heal communities and the planet. *BMJ*. 2019;365:l2398.

47. Karliner J, Slotterback S, Boyd R, Ashby B, Steele K. Health care's carbon footprint: how the health sector contributes to the global climate crisis and opportunities for action. In: *Climate-Smart Health Care Series Green Paper Number One*. Health Care without Harm. and Arup; 2019. https://www.arup.com/-/media/arup/files/publications/h/health-cares-climate-footprint.pdf

48. Kelly C, Hulme C, Farragher T, Clarke G. Are differences in travel time or distance to healthcare for adults in global north countries associated with an impact on health outcomes? A systematic review. *BMJ Open*. 2016;6(11):e013059.

49. Torres CG, Renfrew M, Kenst K, Tan-McGrory A, Betancourt JR, López L. Improving transgender health by building safe clinical environments that promote existing resilience: results from a qualitative analysis of providers. *BMC Pediatrics*. 2015;15(1):187.

50. Kovacs Silvis J. Natural beauty: Cherokee Indian Hospital. *Healthcare Design Magazine* website. 2017. https://www.healthcaredesignmagazine.com/projects/ambulatory-care-clinics/natural-beauty-cherokee-indian-hospital/

51. Mohrman SA, Kanter MH. Designing for health: learning from Kaiser Permanente. In: Mohrman SA, Shani AB, eds. *Organizing for Sustainable Health Care*. Emerald Group Publishing, 2012.

52. Koonin LM, Hoots B, Tsang CA, et al. Trends in the use of telehealth during the emergence of the COVID-19 pandemic—United States, January–March 2020. *Morbidity and Mortality Weekly Report*. 2020;69(43):1595-1599. doi:10.15585/mmwr.mm6943a3

53. Sparta Clinic grows Gundersen's sustainable footprint [press release]. Gundersen Health System, June 29, 2018.

54. Catalanello R, Myers B. Look inside the new $1.1 billion University Medical Center, opening Aug. 1. *Times-Picayune* (New Orleans). Published June 18, 2015. Updated July 18, 2019. https://www.nola.com/entertainment_life/health_fitness/article_1ae27fdc-165f-549e-bfe3-0391c2b5b85f.html

55. Healthcare Design Showcase. *Healthcare Design Magazine*. 2020. https://healthcaredesignmagazine.com/trends/welcome-to-the-2020-healthcare-design-showcase

CHAPTER 15

HEALTHY SCHOOLS

Claire L. Barnett and Erika Sita Eitland

KEY POINTS

- School buildings are unique indoor and outdoor environments. They are more densely occupied than offices or nursing homes. They have long hours of use and a multiplicity of indoor activities and functions. In the United States, 95 percent of the occupants are women and children.
- Children in prekindergarten through secondary (pre-K–12) schools are uniquely susceptible to environmental health hazards. Environmental exposures today can affect them for life, they breathe more air per pound of body weight than adults, they cannot recognize hazards, and they are undergoing rapid biological development and educational-social-emotional growth.
- Environmental hazards in and around schools are diverse and not well examined or addressed. Substandard physical conditions and hazards such as poor ventilation and sanitation, lead in paint and water, and asbestos are more prevalent in the poorest schools serving the poorest communities enrolling poor and minority children. Children with developmental and learning disabilities may be even more exposed and more vulnerable to hazards at school than their peers.
- Schools can prevent or control many physical health hazards affecting children's health and learning. For example, they can maintain building systems and grounds and purchase safer products and equipment (often at equivalent prices). They can also take steps to address climate resiliency and mitigation.

INTRODUCTION

It was a cold Monday night in February. The high school auditorium in Providence, Rhode Island, was jammed with politicians, parents, teachers, community organizers, and public health professionals there to discuss how unhealthy schools impacted student health, academic performance, and finances. The forum was planned after the high school students had marched on the state capitol wearing hard hats due to the crumbling state of their schools. Photographs of peeling paint, broken ceiling tiles, and deteriorating bathrooms lined the auditorium, a reminder of the four-year building moratorium for kindergarten through grade 12 (K–12) public schools and years of deferred maintenance that followed the 2008 economic recession. In that time, schools had been left to use plastic tarps for roof repair to prevent leaks, lead paint had peeled off to such a great extent that students were not allowed in certain parts of their building, and classrooms and technology were destroyed when a window latch failed during the winter and caused a pipe to burst, flooding and freezing the classroom. Two and a half years after this February meeting, the state finally confronted these issues head-on, and a $250 million statewide bond was passed with overwhelming support to repair the state's school buildings.

The United Nations Universal Declaration of Human Rights (Article 26) states, "Everyone has the right to education. Education should be free, at least in the elementary and fundamental stages."[1] There are nearly two billion school-aged children globally. With global reports reinforcing the valuable impacts of education on health, employment, poverty reduction, resilience, equity, and greater individual freedoms, there remains a gap between schooling and learning, with the greatest burden faced by low-income countries and communities.[2]

In the United States, where every state has compulsory education laws, fifty-six million children and nearly four million teachers occupy nearly 130,000 public and private K–12 schools.[3] The quality, typology, layout, and maintenance and programs that take place inside these facilities vary greatly. There are no two states exactly alike in how they manage and fund public schools and their facilities, and there are no federal standards for school design or operations, or standardized facility assessment tools, making it challenging to monitor or benchmark the status of K–12 facilities. A 2020 report by the US Government Accountability Office found that more than half of public school districts had multiple building systems in need of updates or replacement (ventilation, for example), with high-poverty districts reporting lower building expenditures and greater reliance on state funding.[4]

The school building can be an active promoter of or an inadvertent barrier to children's health and learning, yet federal efforts to promote healthy physical environments in schools were steeply reduced during the decade prior to 2020—a poor decision given that COVID-19 was found to be an airborne pandemic and US schools have a long history of poor indoor air, ventilation, and sanitation. The Centers for Disease Control and Prevention (CDC) has a Whole School, Whole Community,

Whole Child (WSCC) model (www.cdc.gov /healthyschools/wscc) that addresses critical education and health outcomes, outlines collaborative actions and initiatives to support students, and seeks to engage parents and the community. However, although the WSCC model mentions the physical environment, CDC itself has no program, staff expertise, or funds to address the physical environment in schools.[5] The US Department of Education has an Office of Safe and Healthy Students, which includes "readiness" and "safe and supportive" schools programs, but these programs focus on issues such as bullying and violence rather than on the physical building. The US Environmental Protection Agency (EPA) Indoor Environments Division has twenty-five years of work on school building issues such as indoor air quality, cleaning, and maintenance, but it has been hampered by having only a tiny voluntary grant program to promote its guidance on healthful school buildings and grounds. EPA's Office of Children's Health has provided time-limited grants to states to develop state plans for healthy schools, utilizing EPA guidance. Primary responsibility for safe, healthy school environments falls to a ragged patchwork of state and local school board jurisdictions. This patchwork arrangement was highlighted when COVID mitigation decisions fell to volunteer school boards.

Global efforts to maintain healthy school environments are also uneven. The European Union's Network of Health-Promoting Schools mentions the physical plant, but its emphasis is on traditional school health concerns such as health education, food and nutrition, and exercise. UNICEF's Child-Friendly Schools program promotes both socially and physically healthy learning environments. In a 2009 report, UNICEF stated that more than two-thirds of schools visited in each country provided safe and comfortable learning environments with structurally sound buildings and classrooms and students protected from dangers such as toxic materials, yet teachers and parents acknowledged the ongoing difficulty with security, maintenance, and operation.[6]

This chapter is devoted to healthy learning places, with an emphasis on the physical characteristics of school buildings and sites that have known impacts on the health, development, and learning of all children (figure 15.1). Although the chapter focuses primarily on school-aged children (generally, five to eighteen years old), adult occupants, including teachers, administrative and custodial staff, and paraprofessionals, may occupy failed facilities for years and are also at risk.

This chapter discusses how "children are not just little adults" by explaining their vulnerabilities and how "schools are not just little offices," highlighting several key indoor and outdoor attributes, including density of occupancy, hours of use, air quality, temperature, humidity, lighting, acoustics, and siting. Finally, it describes solutions and strategies for healthier K–12 buildings and grounds.

CHILD VULNERABILITY

Schools are the places in which children spend the most time when not at home. As discussed in chapter 10, school-aged children are in critical windows of rapid physical growth and social development. When students enter school, typically at age five, brain development is about 90 percent complete. Compared to adults, children breathe greater volumes of air and have immature immune systems, ongoing brain and lung development, and higher metabolic rates. These conditions make them more susceptible to extreme temperatures, chemicals in the air and dust, and pathogens in the environment. Children also occupy unique areas in a school, including the floor and playgrounds. School building codes, however, often do not account for these physiological and behavioral differences and may not optimize physical environments for children.

Children cannot always recognize or remove themselves from harm's way, nor articulate their exposures, so they depend on adults to ensure that their environments are safe. There is evidence that children who experience worse health are less likely to finish high school or transition to postsecondary education.[7] The health of school-aged children is a driver of educational attainment with consequences for long-term health and economic success.

About 40 percent of all public school students have chronic health conditions such as asthma, diabetes, and learning disabilities.[8] Moreover, high-poverty schools are disproportionately attended by Black students, Indigenous students, and other students of color.[9]

These students are often eligible for free and reduced meals and attend older and poorly maintained school facilities located in low-income communities,[10] underscoring both social and environmental equity concerns. Low-income families rely on schools for breakfast, lunch, and after-school snacks, representing a substantial part of children's daily food intake. Poor-quality food in schools can play a lasting role in students' knowledge, attitudes, and choices. There is evidence that deliberate efforts to remove unhealthy foods, substitute healthy foods, and nudge healthier choices in schools can positively impact health.[11]

Generally, public schools are major institutional buyers of food and thus could play a larger role in increasing demand for healthier local foods, assuming they have the staff and facilities for preparation and food storage. This can also apply to the food environment surrounding schools, which can impact what students regularly eat inside and outside of home.

PHYSICAL ENVIRONMENTAL FACTORS

It has been well established that school facilities in poor condition adversely impact health and educational outcomes and that the poorest children in the poorest communities typically confront the oldest and worst school facilities.[4,9,11] In the United States, this is due largely to the inability of poor communities to generate ample property tax revenues and the absence of counterbalancing financial aid from the states or the federal government.

(a)

(b)

(c)

Figure 15.1. Varieties of school design. Schools built in the 1920s (a) typically boasted large operable windows and high ceilings, providing plenty of fresh air and daylight. However, hazards such as asbestos and lead pipes were common. Modern schools (b), on the other hand, may have few windows and limited fresh air circulation, problems that are aggravated in modular structures often used as classrooms (c).
Sources: (a) Digital Commonwealth. (b) Google Earth 2021. (c) Wikimedia Commons courtesy of FEMA.

BOX 15.1 CHILD CARE FACILITIES

Many of the findings regarding school indoor air, hazardous materials, noise, and lighting measures in this chapter apply to both schools and child care centers.[a,b] Licensed child care facilities differ from K–12 schools in that they serve much younger children; are subject to some licensing oversight; rely on fee-for-service revenues; have greater staffing ratios; have smaller-scaled furnishings; need diapering and napping areas; and require cleaning and disinfecting of surfaces, toys, and equipment.

In the United States, an estimated twelve million children under the age of five attend child care, with more than one and a half million providers.[c] However, few data are collected on the child care sector by federal and state agencies, and there is little history of robust studies on environmental conditions or impacts on children and staff.

REFERENCES

a. Viet SM, Rogers J, Marker D, et al. Lead, allergen, and pesticide levels in licensed child care centers in the United States. *Journal of Environmental Health*. 2013;76(5):8-14.
b. Quirós-Alcalá L, Wilson S, Witherspoon N, et al. Volatile organic compounds and particulate matter in child care facilities in the District of Columbia: results from a pilot study. *Environmental Research*. 2016;146:116-124.
c. Hashikawa AN, Sells JM, DeJonge PM, Alkon A, Martin ET, Shope TR. Child care in the time of coronavirus disease-19: a period of challenge and opportunity. *Journal of Pediatrics*. 2020;225:239-245.

The age of a school building is a useful marker of the presence of hazards. Persistent, legacy toxics such as lead, asbestos, polychlorinated biphenyls (PCBs), and mercury were placed in school buildings long before the EPA was established and began promulgating applicable regulations. For example, the average age of US public school buildings in 2020 was more than fifty years, predating the Toxic Substances Control Act of 1976, which banned some hazardous chemicals from building materials, and the Lead and Copper Rule of 1991, which regulated lead and copper in drinking water systems. Although toxic substances and hazardous building sites can be avoided during new construction or major renovations, many schools lack the financial resources to purchase the more desirable building sites or fully to remediate legacy hazards. Inadequate maintenance, poor sanitation, and chemical mismanagement can lead to further deterioration and exposures. For example, acidic water will leach lead from water pipes, and failure to maintain roofing or interior ceilings and walls can result in mold growth or release of asbestos and lead paint chips and dust. School decision-makers have little access to information, systematic documentation, or mandatory training on how to identify, prevent, finance, or address environmental hazards common to schools. Without a federal or state tracking and reporting system, including environmental public health services for children with school-based exposures, environmental conditions in schools may go unchecked until there is media coverage of events such as an asthma death, lead poisoning, or a roof or wall collapse.

Expanded federal and state funds and regulations are needed to direct and to assist the oldest and poorest schools and other schools. Needs include not only full remediation of the legacy toxics described below, but also improving lighting, ventilation, and other building systems that are outdated or nonfunctional.

Hazardous Substances

Table 15.1 lists some major hazards found in schools. The list is not exhaustive. Research by the EPA and by the states has revealed that schools have not managed chemical stores safely and that decades of old, mislabeled, and improperly stored flammable, explosive,

Table 15.1. Major hazards found in schools.

Hazards	Possible Exposure Route in Schools	Potential Harmful Effects	Protective Strategies or Policies
Asbestos An insulating fire retardant, it can be found around boilers, in pipes, and in floor tiles.	Exposure occurs by inhalation and by ingestion of dust (through, for example, hand-to-mouth exposure).	Loose (friable) asbestos fibers can be inhaled and lodge deeply in the lungs, increasing the risk of lung cancer, mesothelioma (cancer of the lining of the lungs or abdomen), and other cancers, as well as a scarring disease of the lungs (asbestosis) at high doses.	EPA has not fully banned all asbestos. EPA currently requires schools to inspect, identify, control, and report on all sources of asbestos in schools so that if a renovation project is anticipated, the contractors can remove it or manage it in place.[a]
Flame retardants Polybrominated diphenyl ethers (PBDEs); organophosphate flame retardants (OPFRs); alternative brominated flame retardants.	Used in upholstered and plastic furniture and some electronics to reduce flammability; exposure occurs by ingestion of dust or inhalation.	Neurodevelopmental delays, behavioral problems, reduced IQ, decreased fertility, endocrine disruption, and reduced thyroid function.	PBDEs have been phased out of consumer products but may remain in older products that predate this phase out.
Hazardous chemicals (stored on-site)	Bus garages, custodial closets, science and art labs, pest control products.	Multiple hazards in various products, including explosive and flammable elements.	EPA initiated a school chemical cleanout (SC3) program in 2007; it is currently not funded.
Lead (dust/paint) Layers of old leaded paint can chip or flake off from interior walls, windows, and ceilings and migrate into the indoor dust.	Exposure occurs by ingestion of dust or paint chips, hand-to-mouth exposure, or inhalation.	Lead exposure in children is associated with cognitive deficits, reduced attention span, lower IQ, and more behavioral problems. For students living in older or public housing, there may be a double burden because of remaining lead paint and service lines in housing units that have yet to be remediated.	Lead-based paint was banned in 1978 in the United States, 1992 in the United Kingdom, and 2007 in China, yet evidence suggests that in low- and middle-income countries, lead-based paint may still be used.[b] US EPA's "lead safe renovation rule" applies to all educational facilities where children age six and under are regularly present.
Lead (tap water) Drinking water supply lines and fixtures can contain lead.	Testing at the tap for lead in schools has shown that levels at the tap can be as high as hundreds of parts per million lead. Ingestion and dermal exposure from gym showers can also expose students to high lead levels in schools.[c]		EPA regulates lead in drinking water provided by nontransient community water suppliers, such as schools with their own wells. Schools on municipal water systems are not required by the EPA to test at the tap. In 2016, advocates for clean water began state-by-state campaigns to require testing at the tap in schools. EPA is providing grants for testing in schools, but not for remediation.

Table 15.1. Continued

Hazards	Possible Exposure Route in Schools	Potential Harmful Effects	Protective Strategies or Policies
Mercury Found in older buildings in thermostats, fluorescent bulbs, electrical devices, science labs, and certain polyurethane gym floors as phenyl mercuric acetate, where it was used to help the resin set.	Over time, mercury breaks down and is released as an odorless and toxic vapor at room temperature. It can be inhaled by school occupants.	A neurotoxic chemical that can cause permanent damage. Exposure to vapors is exacerbated in hot, poorly ventilated rooms.	A CDC campaign to eliminate elemental mercury in schools led some states to adopt bans. Several states (New York, Minnesota, and California) have laws banning new installations of synthetic gym floors containing mercury. Short-term, schools are advised to increase ventilation in gyms if mercury vapors are detected. Removal and replacement of all mercury-containing products is another option.
Polychlorinated biphenols (PCBs) In schools built between 1950 and 1979, PCBs are likely present in building caulk and in overhead light ballasts, as well as wall paint and ceiling tiles.[d]	Exposure occurs by ingestion of dust or inhalation.	A persistent compound that is a probable carcinogen and a neurotoxin. The health risks are not only to children but to all female staff of reproductive age because prenatal exposure to PCBs can influence child development.	EPA requires that if PCBs are found, they must be removed and disposed of properly. Testing and disposal are costly.
Pesticides Herbicides, insecticides, fungicides, and disinfectants used to control pests and pathogens indoors and outside.	Exposure occurs by ingestion, inhalation, or absorption.	Pesticides are chemicals designed to kill or deactivate living organisms; their active (and in some cases their inert) ingredients are toxic. This category also includes antimicrobial compounds, also known as disinfectants.	EPA registers pesticides for use but does not ban their use in schools. Many states have enacted laws to reduce the use of pesticides in or around schools and instead promote natural, mechanical, and housekeeping methods to control pests. The COVID pandemic led schools to increase their use of disinfectants, including by broadcast spraying.
Polyvinylchloride (PVC) PVC, a synthetic plastic, is found in furnishings, desks, toys, notebooks, lunch boxes, and flooring.	Inhalation and ingestion.	The vinyl chloride monomer is carcinogenic, and PVC, like many plastics, routinely contains additives such as lead, cadmium, plasticizers, and colorants, which may be neurotoxic, endocrine disrupters, or carcinogens.	Ban or avoid use of PVC flooring and avoid its use for water pipes. PVC was banned in children's toys, but has not been limited in school supplies, furniture, playsets, notebooks, and lunch boxes.

Table 15.1. Continued

Hazards	Possible Exposure Route in Schools	Potential Harmful Effects	Protective Strategies or Policies
Radon Radon is a naturally occurring gas that is present in some geological formations and can seep into buildings.	Inhalation.	Radon is a human carcinogen that could affect all school occupants. Teachers and staff with multiyear exposure in naturally occurring high radon areas may be at higher risk.	US EPA recommends testing for radon in occupied areas at or below ground level. If found, radon gas can be vented to the outside and foundation cracks and crevices sealed.
Wet or contaminated sites Damp buildings.	Inhalation of mold spores.	Dampness and molds are associated with asthma and chronic upper respiratory conditions, but other symptoms such as confusion, blurred vision, and fatigue are also reported.	Water management and maintenance of barriers such as roof and gutter systems.
Contaminated sites Vapor intrusion into buildings.			Postconstruction site remediation is expensive and must be maintained. US EPA issued school siting guidelines in 2011, but made no grants to states and cities to support implementation.

a. US EPA. Asbestos and School Buildings. 2020. Accessed October 23, 2021. https://www.epa.gov/asbestos/asbestos-and-school-buildings

b. UN Environment. Despite bans, most countries still have lead paint. 2018. Accessed October 23, 2021. https://www.unenvironment.org/news-and-stories/story/despite-bans-most-countries-still-have-lead-paint

c. US EPA. Basic Information about Lead in Drinking Water. 2021. Accessed October 23, 2021. https://www.epa.gov/ground-water-and-drinking-water/basic-information-about-lead-drinking-water

d. Herrick RF, Stewart JH, Allen JG Review of PCBs in US schools: a brief history, an estimate of the number of impacted schools, and an approach for evaluating indoor air samples. *Environmental Science and Pollution Research (International)*. 2016,23(3):1975-1985.

corrosive, and other dangerous chemicals sit in US schools, often in science or art lab closets or in basements and bus garages (figure 15.2). There is currently no updated EPA guidance or voluntary grants program to assist state environment or health agencies or schools with the identification of old, mismanaged chemicals or with their safe disposal.

Indoor Air Quality

At the turn of the twentieth century, with the fear of children with tuberculosis coming to school from overcrowded tenements, New York City implemented a new school facility design to promote children's health called "Cathedrals of Learning." At a time when there were no antibiotics, the scheme called for high-ceilinged classrooms with tall windows that opened top and bottom for cross-ventilation and for harvesting natural daylight, and facades that featured great thinkers of Western civilization as a way to facilitate assimilation. In the years after World War II, as suburban sprawl advanced and with the advent of mechanical ventilating systems and air conditioning, tightly sealed school buildings with overhead fluorescent fixtures became the standard in suburban school districts. School

Figure 15.2. Chemical storage in a high school chemistry lab. A surprising amount of hazardous chemicals may be found in schools—not only in labs, but in janitors' closets, in arts and crafts rooms, and elsewhere. Source: United Federation of Teachers (UFT)

districts needed cheap buildings. Architects designed them, and low-bid contractors built them rapidly. Often, these postwar schools were located on inexpensive sites, compromised by prior industrial uses, dampness, or nearby hazards such as busy roads. Today, the United States has a legacy of classic, old "cathedral" schools and somewhat younger schools built on the cheap. Both suffer from lack of maintenance and repair.

What we know today is that everything that goes "right" and "wrong" with a building, from siting to design, construction, maintenance, and products in use, can affect the quality of the indoor air (figure 15.3). The World Health Organization estimates that 93 percent of the world's children under the age of fifteen breathe polluted air, driven by household cooking and ambient air pollution.[12] As discussed in chapter 4, air pollution has multiple impacts on children's health, ranging from asthma and bronchitis to behavioral changes. Similarly, poor indoor air quality in settings such as schools can have many of the same effects—on

respiratory health, cognition, and academic performance.[13-15] In the United States, asthma is the leading cause of student absenteeism due to chronic illness.[16]

Bringing fresh air indoors via natural or mechanical ventilation and filtering indoor air are important strategies for assuring indoor air quality. Fresh air can dilute and flush pollutants found indoors such as allergens, particulate matter, and gaseous released from indoor sources. Carbon dioxide (CO_2) is a proxy measure for ventilation as it is exhaled by humans and builds up in classrooms if not properly vented. Elevated CO_2 levels are associated with wheezing and asthma, poor concentration headaches, poorer test performance and attendance, and fatigue;[17,18] as importantly, they may signal inadequate air exchange and buildup of other air contaminants. The use of building-wide air filtration systems or portable air cleaners can reduce exposure to particulate matter and pathogens. Fresh air intakes should not be placed where they can entrain polluted air from idling vehicles or a dumpster. In the

Figure 15.3. A school athletic facility located near a busy highway. This facility in Cincinnati, Ohio, is located adjacent to busy Interstate 71. Both outside and inside, students using the facility are exposed to vehicle emissions.
Source: Google Earth, 2021

absence of a mechanical ventilation system, schools can open windows, or if windows are sealed for security reasons, schools can install classroom air cleaners. These devices must be maintained, and filters must be changed.

Innovations in sensor technology and building system automation in new buildings can alert school occupants to poor air quality in their classrooms, thus prompting behavioral responses. For example, the triggering of automatic air handling responses such as increasing ventilation rates, or teachers simply opening windows in response to alerts, can alleviate some problems.

Guidance for achieving healthy indoor environments is available. The Indoor Environments Division of US EPA's Office of Air and Radiation issued a voluntary tool kit, *Indoor Air Quality Tools for Schools* (IAQTfS), in the mid-1990s. This resource addresses nearly every aspect of the school environment, from chemical management to pesticide use, cleaning, maintenance, molds, ventilation, and design guidelines.[19] Over the next two decades, webinars and a mobile app educated tens of thousands of school personnel and communities on how to prevent, identify, and remediate indoor air problems. Within a decade, more than three dozen states had adopted regulations to address school indoor air quality based on the IAQTfS program. However, funding for EPA's IAQTfS program was zeroed out in 2013. Without continuous outreach and training, and with high turnover in public school boards and leaders, awareness and capacity to manage air quality issues has diminished.[4]

Gaseous compounds known as volatile organic compounds (VOCs) or semivolatile organic compounds are common indoor air pollutants. In schools, they can be released

BOX 15.2 COVID-19 AND SCHOOLS

In late 2019, the SARS-CoV2 virus that causes COVID-19 appeared and by early 2020 was disrupting all sectors, including education. School building closures around the world forced students to resort to remote learning. But many students lacked critical infrastructure at home, such as reliable electricity and internet access, computers and devices, an adult to supervise, and quiet, private places to study. Learning losses have yet to be measured, but clearly learning suffered for too many.

It also was apparent that in the United States, states did not require local schools to have infection control plans, despite school buildings being more densely occupied than nursing homes and despite about 40 percent of public school children having chronic health conditions. The lack of such policies, when schools have well-established and rehearsed "all-hazard" emergency policies in place, led public health advocates to call for defining and operationalizing such plans. Congress provided COVID relief funds to schools, some of which could be used to address indoor air, but by late 2021, there was no evidence that funds had been used for that purpose.

Emerging evidence suggested that children, especially younger children, were unlikely to spread the virus or to become seriously ill and that schools played little role in transmission.[a,b] However, instances of spread in schools, especially to staff, raised concern, particularly with the emergence of the delta variant in the summer of 2021. School officials, staff, and families had to weigh the COVID risks of reopening schools against the risk of community spread and against the academic, social, physical, and economic risks of prolonged school closures, often without the data needed to inform decisions[c] and often without equitable access to adequate funds to enhance ventilation and sanitation.

In the United States, school closures and reopening plans varied by state and even by town. The absence of coordinated federal leadership, and early disinformation from the White House and other sources, led to confusion and opposition to recommended public health measures. Pre-COVID-19 conditions such as inadequate ventilation and sanitation, overcrowding, and lack of technology exacerbated challenges in reopening schools, especially in high-poverty schools and those serving students of color, low-income students, and students with disabilities. The result was disproportionate drops in attendance and academic performance compared to White, Asian, and more affluent student counterparts.[d] Many schools continued to use their kitchen and support staff to prepare, pack, and deliver meals to needy school families, demonstrating the profound role that schools have in children's lives.

Standard reopening solutions included physical distancing by separating desks; staggered arrival, lunch, and departure times; increased cleaning; and hybrid learning models to lower classroom occupancy. Wealthier public and private schools hired their own consultants, bought and distributed e-learning tools, installed air filtration technologies, and created outdoor learning spaces.

REFERENCES

a. Centers for Disease Control and Prevention. Science Brief: Transmission of SARS-CoV-2 in K–12 Schools and Early Care and Education Programs—Updated. Updated July 9, 2021. Accessed October 23, 2021. https://www.cdc.gov/coronavirus/2019-ncov/science/science-briefs/transmission_k_12_schools.html
b. Li X, Xu W, Dozier M, et al. The role of children in the transmission of SARS-CoV2: updated rapid review. *Journal of Global Health*. 2020;10(2):021101-021101.
c. Oster E. Beyond past due: data to guide US school reopenings. *Nature*. 2021;589(7840):8.
d. Dorn E, Hancock B, Sarakatsannis J, Viruleg E. COVID-19 and student learning in the United States: the hurt could last a lifetime. McKinsey & Company. 2020. Accessed October 21, 2021. https://www.mckinsey.com/industries/public-and-social-sector/our-insights/covid-19-and-student-learning-in-the-united-states-the-hurt-could-last-a-lifetime

BOX 15.3 SUSTAINABILITY AND HIGH-PERFORMANCE, GREEN SCHOOL BUILDING CERTIFICATIONS

In addition to health, environmental sustainability is an important goal for schools. High-performance, green schools—schools designed to promote student success (hence "high performance") and to be environmentally friendly—can provide many benefits: smaller environmental footprints, reduced operating costs, a healthier environment for students and staff, and a platform for promoting students' environmental knowledge, attitudes, and behavior.[a-c] In the United States, there is no federal agency promoting the sustainability of public or private schools, nor any single sustainability or green guide that US schools adopt and follow. However, the US Department of Education issues an annual Green Ribbon recognition award to schools with outstanding efforts to reduce environmental impact and costs, improve health and wellness, and provide environmental education and service learning.

Two well-established certification frameworks address aspects of high-performance green schools:

1. The US Green Building Council (USGBC) was established in 1993 to reduce the impact of the buildings' sector on the environment. Its LEED (Leadership in Energy and Environmental Design; see chapter 22) certification is well recognized nationally and internationally. USGBC issued its first design standard for schools in 2007 and continues this work through its Center for Green Schools (www.centerforgreenschools.org).

2. The Collaborative for High Performance Schools (CHPS; https://chps.net/) criteria are less well known but have an important and greater emphasis on indoor environmental quality features, such as lighting, acoustics, air quality, humidity, and thermal comfort, and require staff training in managing new building systems. The CHPS criteria can be tailored to climate and other regional considerations.

REFERENCES

a. Okcu S, Ryherd E, Bayer C. The role of physical environment on student health and education in green schools. *Reviews on Environmental Health.* 2011;26(3):169-179.
b. Magzamen S, Mayer AP, Barr S, et al. A multidisciplinary research framework on green schools: infrastructure, social environment, occupant health, and performance. *Journal of School Health.* 2017;87(5):376-387.
c. National Research Council. *Green Schools: Attributes for Health and Learning.* National Academies Press; 2007.

from school building materials and classroom supplies, including furnishings, fabrics, cleaning products, adhesives, particle board, pesticides, markers, and more. The presence of VOCs can trigger eye, nose, and throat irritation, headaches, and nausea and can affect the central nervous system. The use of low-emission materials such as unscented cleaning and disinfecting products and water-based markers can minimize these emissions at little or no additional cost.

Overcrowding

School overcrowding occurs when the occupant capacity exceeds what the school was designed and built to accommodate. School crowding has many implications for children's well-being and safety, including access to fire exits and to facilities such as lockers, changing rooms, drinking fountains, lavatories, laboratories, and electrical outlets, as well as adequate fresh air exchanges (ventilation) and space to walk through halls between classes. Overcrowding also stresses facilities, increasing their use and adding more dirt and noise, and increasing the amount of time needed to clean. In some schools, overcrowding is relieved by deploying modular structures ("trailers" or "portable classrooms"). Some research has demonstrated poor air quality in these structures, the result of off-gassed formaldehyde from building components, poor ventilation, moisture intrusion, and other factors. Careful monitoring and management of portable classrooms are necessary to avoid these problems.[20]

Temperature and Humidity

Temperature and humidity are important determinants of indoor air quality satisfaction and are influenced by individual factors and behaviors such as clothing, personal preferences, age, and physical activity. Children are more sensitive to thermal conditions than are adults because they have higher metabolic rates, higher core body temperatures, higher respiratory rates, and a higher body surface area to volume ratio. Studies indicate that student test performance is better at 20°C compared to 25°C (68°F versus 77°F). At temperatures below 10°C (50°F), students begin to experience cold stress.[14]

Increasing global ambient (outdoor) temperatures, especially in midlatitude areas, increases the likelihood of hot days during the school year in areas that typically only had to heat their schools during the twentieth century. Due to the lack of any regular national school building assessments, it is unknown how many schools have a functional air-conditioning system. The lack of air conditioning in US schools has broad implications for children's learning and academic performance. In a study of New York City high school students, taking an exam on a 32°C (90°F) day versus a 24°C (75°F) day was asso-

---

BOX 15.4 GREEN CLEANING AND SAFER PEST CONTROL

Schools are more densely occupied than nursing homes and more intensively used than most offices or people's homes. The use of hazardous and odorous cleaning and disinfecting chemicals can add significantly to schools' indoor air pollution. A movement to promote green cleaning in schools took root in United States in the late 1990s, and within fifteen years, twelve states had adopted policies requiring or promoting the use of independent, third-party-certified green cleaning products in schools (such as Green Seal or EcoLogo certification). Many districts and private schools followed suit. It is important that green cleaning products be assessed for efficacy as well as the health and environmental safety of their chemical ingredients, as even "natural" products can carry risks. For example, some of the many naturally occurring terpene compounds, such as pinene and limonene, may be irritating and sensitizing.[a] However, third-party-certified green cleaning products, used appropriately, are a good example of switching to low-emission, more sustainable, and cost-effective products in schools.

Green cleaning strategies are now recommended by the US Environmental Protection Agency as part of Preventive Maintenance.[b] They may also include regularly cleaning walkways and installing walk-off mats at entries to prevent tracking outdoor dirt inside. Also, training cleaning staff and performing deep cleaning on weekends can lead to sustained healthy environments.

Another compatible effort to reduce the use of toxics indoors is safer pest control (**integrated pest management**), also recommended by the Environmental Protection Agency's Indoor Air Quality Tools for Schools action kit. This approach reduces habitats and food sources for pests and uses mechanical and natural barriers and least-toxic control products with reduced impacts on human health and the environment.[c]

REFERENCES

a. Long DC. Greening of consumer cleaning products. *Green Techniques for Organic Synthesis and Medicinal Chemistry.* 2018:91–115.

b. EPA. Indoor Air Quality Tools for Schools: Preventive Maintenance Guidance. EPA 402-K-18-001. Published 2019. Accessed October 21, 2021. https://www.epa.gov/iaq-schools/indoor-air-quality-tools-schools-preventive -maintenance-guidance-documents#green

c. US EPA. Indoor Air Quality Tools for Schools Action Kit. Published 2020. Accessed October 20, 2021. https: //www.epa.gov/iaq-schools/indoor-air-quality-tools-schools-action-kit

ciated with a 12.3 percent higher likelihood of failing, which is equivalent to the current Black-White achievement gap.[21] Beyond outdoor temperature, increased heat caused by computers in the classroom has been associated with mucosal membrane symptoms, headaches, and fatigue.[22] These problems will intensify with continued climate change, as discussed in chapter 17. Measures to address high ambient heat include increasing the reflective quality of the roof and increasing surrounding trees and other vegetation, which promote indoor thermal comfort and reduce energy consumption for cooling.

Mold, Moisture, and Dampness

There is no such thing as a mold-free building. When buildings are not properly sited, designed, operated, maintained, or ventilated, mold and moisture problems can develop quickly. Breathing mold spores or touching mold can trigger respiratory problems (for example, coughing, wheezing, congestion, and other symptoms, especially in children with asthma or other underlying conditions); neurologic symptoms such as fatigue, irritability, and memory loss have also been reported. At the same time, it is important to realize that growing molds indoors are in fact "digesting" or causing rot in the carbon-based building products: wallboard, shelves, upholstery, books, carpets, desks. Flooded or damp materials should be completely dried out within twenty-four to forty-eight hours or be discarded and replaced. Children should not be directed to clean up mold. Lavatories, kitchens, gyms, and labs should be direct-vented to the outside to control humidity and mold growth indoors and to reduce chemical fumes and other odors from lingering indoors.

Lighting

Schools originally relied upon natural daylight, with tall windows that opened top and bottom. But in the 1970s, the energy crisis led to a shift from fresh air to recirculated air and to the sealing or removal of windows in classrooms to reduce energy loss. Since then, lighting has aimed to balance energy, visual needs, and thermal comfort. New studies, however, have underscored that access to windows and daylighting has positive impacts on building occupants, including better vision acuity, better sleep quality, and reduced symptoms of depression, headache, and nearsightedness.[23,24] Energy-efficient lighting retrofits can result in several bottom-line wins: better lighting, energy savings, elimination of PCBs from older overhead ballasts, and better test scores (figure 15.4).

There are additional considerations for children with cognitive or visual impairments. For students with cortical visual impairments, replacing overhead lighting with up-lighting onto reflective white ceilings can reduce prolonged staring or gazing, a common symptom, and promote student focus.[25] Similarly, lighting that hums, intermittently flashes, or causes glare can distract students from learning. The use of dimmable lights, window coverings, or clerestory windows can reduce glare, avoid overheating from solar gains, and minimize distractions and overstimulation.

Acoustics

Acoustics and noise are critical features in the classroom as children learn to communicate verbally by listening to their teacher and classmates. Background noise, measured in decibels, can interfere with what children need or want to hear. Background noise should not exceed 35 decibels; otherwise, it strains teachers and staff who must speak more loudly to achieve the same speech intelligibility. When noise exceeds 70 decibels, it can lead to adverse effects such as headache, fatigue, and stress. It is recommended that the signal-to-noise ratio be +15 decibels in a classroom to help students developing oral language skills—that is, verbal communication should be at least 15 decibels (roughly threefold) louder than background noise. Sources of background noise include mechanical systems and other classrooms or

Figure 15.4. Classroom lighting. Natural daylighting, especially when accompanied by views of natural outdoor scenes, promotes student well-being and achievement and can reduce school energy use. However, care must be taken to control glare and to manage thermal comfort.
Source: Glamox

BOX 15.5 SAFETY AND SECURITY IN SCHOOLS

Safety and security have become essential features of any school building. In the United States, there were at least ten school shootings with casualties in a public or private school every year from 2000 to 2019, with sixty-six school shootings in 2018–2019 alone.[a] In 2018, the Marjory Stoneham Douglas shooting in Parkland, Florida, left seventeen students and staff dead and seventeen wounded; it ignited a national movement around stricter gun control with #NeverAgain protests across the United States and the March for Our Lives in Washington, DC, a month after the shooting. Common risk-reduction approaches include monitored entrances and exits, internal locks, limiting the number of entries, removing dense foliage around the site where intruders can hide, designing out hidden stairwells, and enhanced security systems. As described in chapter 5, the principles of crime prevention through environmental design may help reduce violence-related behaviors in schools.[b]

Evidence that school hardening and active shooter drills improve student safety and security is mixed.[c] Alternative approaches include an emphasis on developing interpersonal skills, including conflict resolution, robust mental health services, social and emotional supports for students, and programs to prevent bullying and harassment.

REFERENCES

a. National Center for Education Statistics (NCES). Indicator 1: violent deaths at school and away from school. *National Center of Education Statistics.* July 2020. https://nces.ed.gov/programs/crimeindicators/ind_01.asp
b. Vagi KJ, Stevens MR, Simon TR, Basile KC, Carter SP, Carter SL. Crime prevention through environmental design (CPTED) characteristics associated with violence and safety in middle schools. *Journal of School Health.* 2018;88(4):296-305.
c. Price JH, Khubchandani J. School firearm violence prevention practices and policies: functional or folly? *Violence and Gender.* 2019;6(3):154-167.

students. A French study of 586 urban elementary school students found that a 10-decibel (twofold) increase in classroom or home environment noise was associated with reduced mathematics scores. This suggests that daily noise disruptions, like a nearby airport or major highway, can undermine student performance.[26]

Reverberation in a classroom can also be challenging because long reverberation time results in echo-ey spaces that interfere with speech clarity. For younger children, those with auditory impairments, and children with autism spectrum disorder, reverberation can hinder comprehension or be physically uncomfortable. International acoustic standards suggest specific reverberation times for the hearing impaired (0.4 second) and for second-language learners (0.6 second).[27]

SITING AND OUTDOOR ENVIRONMENTS

School siting and planning policies have implications for traffic, active transportation options, community involvement, health outcomes, and environmental justice. Historically, siting decisions have not been regulated by state or federal governments. School districts often purchase or lease substandard facilities or less-desirable land for short-term economic reasons; as a result, schools can end up sited near hazardous facilities, waste dumps, or highways, all with resulting health risks

---

BOX 15.6 DESIGNING SCHOOLS FOR NEURODIVERSITY

Boston's William E. Carter School serves the city's highest-needs students, who have severe or profound cognitive delays, physical handicaps, and complex medical conditions. Ninety percent of students are in wheelchairs. Many suffer from conditions such as cortical visual impairment, cerebral palsy, Down syndrome, and epilepsy that affect their ability to see, hear, move, and think.

The school was designed with **neurodiversity** in mind, integrating students' cognitive, communication, and learning needs and extending to the full sensory experience, including daylighting, layout and scale, patterning, contrast, texture, lighting, acoustics, vibration, and scent. Multiple senses are used simultaneously to overcome individual challenges. For example, color cannot be the only sensory cue to decode information because students are visually impaired, so the design integrates shape, pattern, and position to assist with wayfinding.

Both active and passive design interventions were considered, as illustrated in table 15.2. Active building elements are things the building users might control, such as a light switch and operable walls. Passive things require no human modification, such as south-facing windows and specific colors painted on the wall.

Table 15.2. School design elements for neurodiversity.

Sensory System	Active	Passive
Visual	*Dimmable and tunable lighting systems* to effectively trigger the circadian rhythm and help manage overstimulated students.	*Remove distractions and visual clutter* by reducing the use of pattern and color variation.
Auditory	*Enhanced universal speaker systems* that can play gamma waves to promote motor processing, as well as white noise to mask bursts of impulsive noise.	*Greater use of acoustical dampening* on the ceiling and walls and strategic placement of HVAC and other systems that may "hum."
Proprioception	*Integration of special occupational therapy equipment,* which can be stored and accessed easily by staff.	*Swimming pool* for muscle movement.

---

to school occupants, a particular likelihood in states that provide no funding for school construction and for the poorest urban communities.[28,29] Similar problems have been reported globally, from Great Britain[30] to China.[31] Such decisions have long-term consequences due to the long life span of school buildings (more than fifty years) and property ownership by local public educational agencies. The potential implications are shown in table 15.3. In addition to the control strategies shown in the table, city or state laws can prevent or regulate the reuse of hazardous sites. Other measures could include traffic calming, adding pedestrian and bicycle routes to schools, greenscaping school property, reducing water runoff and flooding, and installing traffic barriers and no-idling zones.

SOLUTIONS

Studies in the United States[4] continue to reveal persistent deficiencies in school facilities. In low-income countries, the situation is even worse, with shortages of such basic infrastructure as sanitary facilities, lighting, and student desks.

Why do these problems persist despite plentiful evidence that better physical environments result in healthier children and staff and better educational outcomes? Several reasons likely operate. In the United States, school leadership turns over frequently, on average more than every five years, meaning that facility problems can be ignored in the short term and left to the next incumbents. School leaders are not required to have any training in environmental or occupational health or in facility management. Competition over scarce funds is another challenge; underpaid professionals such as teachers and their unions argue powerfully for salaries, but less often push for funds for facility repairs. Communities that vote on local school budgets are typically not well informed about the details of facilities and impacts on children and find it easier to understand art and music than new boilers and air conditioning. Schools are knowledge

hierarchies led by highly credentialed education professionals, and facilities directors and head custodians—people who work with their hands—may not command sufficient respect.

Solutions exist for safe, healthy, and sustainable K–12 schools at the federal, state, and local levels.

Federal

- Make pre-K–12 education a federal priority—as critical infrastructure for children's education, health, and development. That would mean, for example, that national pandemic planning efforts would address the functions and staffing required to keep schools open.
- Demand coordination across relevant government agencies (Department of Education, CDC, EPA) and establish a long-term federal strategy to address school safety, health, and sustainability.
- Provide federal funding and regulations to address conditions of public school facilities.
- Establish an environmental public health system for children at risk or with exposures in schools, similar to or parallel to the systems that protect health and safety for school employees (see chapter 13).
- Expand and sustain federal interagency guidance to states and to local districts.

States and Tribal Nations

- Interagency commissions, studies, and interagency coordinated plans at the state or tribal level can be useful tools to advance healthier school facilities.

Local

- Educate others, especially parents, about the impact of school buildings on children's growth, development, and performance. There is a knowledge gap about the environmental health implications of poor building quality. Parents commonly inquire about extracurriculars, student lunches, and teacher quality, but if the

Table 15.3. School siting concerns and implications for health, learning, and equity.

School Siting Concern	Health and Learning Impact	Equity Concerns	Interventions or Policy Responses
Proximity to Roadways *Leads to higher traffic-related air pollution near schools, exposing children, teachers, and staff to higher particulate matter and ozone.*	• Faster biological aging determined by telomere length[a] • Lower attendance rates and test performance[b] • Respiratory health challenges including asthma[c] • Developmental delays[d]	Black and Hispanic students and students eligible for free and reduced lunch disproportionately attend schools in the most polluted areas.[b,e]	EPA's Smart School Siting Guide CDC/ATSDR issued a siting guideline for childcare facilities CDC's Safe Routes to School program
Proximity to Airports *Typically built before communities were residing nearby, airports are a source of frequent and elevated background noise with auditory and nonauditory impacts on school occupants as well as exposure to ultrafine particulate matter.[f]*	• Reduced attention, memory, and problem solving • Reduced comfort and mental health, altered teacher behaviors (e.g., closing windows, limited outdoor activities) • Reduced student performance • Headaches • Airway inflammation, reduced lung function in children and adults with asthma[g]	Low-cost housing can be located by airports; low-income students residing in these areas could have adverse impacts to their sleep and ability to perform well in school.	The U.S. Federal Aviation Administration offers resources through the Airport Improvement Program Grants to abate noise indoors, revises flight paths, and can operate voluntary nighttime restrictions that may impact student sleep.
Distance to Community *Schools can be located far from community centers, preventing active transportation to school and creating safety concerns.*	• Students may not be able to bike or walk to school worsening obesity and weight management. • During an emergency, remoteness may limit responses by critical services (fire, police, emergency medical services).	Rural children are 25% more likely to be overweight than urban children and to have lower physical activity. Rural areas may lack safe sidewalks and intersections, making them prone to car-related injuries. Individuals living in poverty may not have a car, which could lead to educational disruptions.[h]	Safe Routes to School National Partnership, a national nonprofit organization, has developed strategies and programs to help students get to school in a healthy and safe way.[h]
Proximity to Agricultural Areas *Pesticide drift of sprays and dusts (e.g., organophosphates) from nearby farms can be airborne and affect nearby schools and playgrounds, as well as nearby water and soil.*	• Compromised neurodevelopment and respiratory function in children[i] • Increased risk of cancer and endocrine-disruption[j]	Compared to the average adult, children inhale double the amount of aerially sprayed pesticide, and due to their small liver and kidney size, the same amount of chemicals can be ten times more toxic. Children in developing countries experience a higher amount of pesticide exposure.[j]	Regulations limiting agricultural pesticide use within a specific distance (e.g., 0.25 mile or 0.4 kilometer in California)[i] Alternative cropping methods that are less dependent on pesticides or the use of safer formulations[k]

Table 15.3. Continued

School Siting Concern	Health and Learning Impact	Equity Concerns	Interventions or Policy Responses
Proximity to Brownfields *These are previous industrial or commercial sites that may be contaminated and are underutilized to limit exposure. Brownfields tend to be cheap and closer to students in urban settings, making them the only viable locations for new schools.*	Health consequences depend on the pollutant found at the site, such as metals, solvents, polycyclic aromatic hydrocarbons, plasticizers, and insecticides, which all have implications for child health, cognitive function, and academic performance.	Brownfields are typically repurposed to serve the needs of students in poorer communities and low-income communities of color, which may be facing overcrowding. Brownfield-like sites may be found throughout the world where previously contaminated industrial sites are developed to meet community needs.[l]	Brownfields can be cleaned up prior to new school construction. EPA has a Brownfield Remediation Program and specifically the 2018 Brownfields Utilization, Investment and Local Development (BUILD) Act. Early environmental assessments can determine the extent of contamination.[l]
Proximity to Oil and Gas Wells *Industrial drilling and hydraulic fracking near schools expose children to air, water, and soil contamination.*	Increased risk of childhood cancers (acute lymphocytic leukemia, non-Hodgkin's lymphoma).[m]	It is estimated that in nearly 1,400 US schools, approximately 650,000 K–12 students are within one mile of a fracked oil or gas well.[n]	Setback regulations that limit the siting of new wells by schools or new schools by wells, respectively, may reduce exposures, but current research has not determined a safe distance from school to oil and gas wells.

a. Clemente DBP, Vrijheid M, Martens DS, et al. Prenatal and childhood traffic-related air pollution exposure and telomere length in European children: the HELIX project. *Environmental Health Perspectives*. 2019;127(8):87001.

b. Mohai P, Kweon BS, Lee S, Ard K. Air pollution around schools is linked to poorer student health and academic performance. *Health Affairs (Millwood)*. 2011;30(5):852-862.

c. Hauptman M, Gaffin JM, Petty CR, et al. Proximity to major roadways and asthma symptoms in the School Inner-City Asthma Study. *Journal of Allergy and Clinical Immunology*. 2020;145(1):119-126.e114.

d. Ha S, Yeung E, Bell E, et al. Prenatal and early life exposures to ambient air pollution and development. *Environmental Research*. 2019;174:170-175.

e. Wu Y-C, Batterman SA. Proximity of schools in Detroit, Michigan to automobile and truck traffic. *Journal of Exposure Science and Environmental Epidemiology*. 2006;16(5):457-470.

f. Klatte M, Bergstroem K, Lachmann T. Does noise affect learning? A short review on noise effects on cognitive performance in children. *Front Psychology*. 2013;4(578).

g. Habre R, Zhou H, Eckel SP, et al. Short-term effects of airport-associated ultrafine particle exposure on lung function and inflammation in adults with asthma. *Environment International*. 2018;118:48-59.

h. Safe Routes Partnerships. Rural Communities: Best Practices and Promising Approaches for Safe Routes. No date. Accessed July 13, 2021. https://www.saferoutespartnership.org/sites/default/files/resource_files/rural_communities _best_practices_and_promising_approaches_for_safe_routes.pdf

i. Gunier RB, Bradman A, Harley KG, Eskenazi B. Will buffer zones around schools in agricultural areas be adequate to protect children from the potential adverse effects of pesticide exposure? *PLOS Biology*. 2017;15(12):e2004741.

j. UNICEF. Understanding the impacts of pesticides on children: a discussion paper. Published 2018. Updated 2018. Accessed July 13, 2021. https://www.unicef.org/csr/files/Understanding_the_impact_of_pesticides_on_children-_Jan _2018.pdf

k. Damalas CA, Eleftherohorinos IG. Pesticide exposure, safety issues, and risk assessment indicators. *International Journal of Environmental Research and Public Health*. 2011;8(5):1402-1419.

l. Cohen A. Achieving healthy school siting and planning policies: understanding shared concerns of environmental planners, public health professionals, and educators. *New Solutions*. 2010;20(1):49-72.

m. McKenzie LM, Allshouse WB, Byers TE, Bedrick EJ, Serdar B, Adgate JL. Childhood hematologic cancer and residential proximity to oil and gas development. *PLOS ONE*. 2017;12(2):e0170423.

n. Ridlington E, Richardson R, Ferrar K. Dangerous and Close: Fracking Puts the Nation's Most Vulnerable People at Risk. Frontier Group. 2016. Accessed July 13, 2021. https://frontiergroup.org/reports/fg/dangerous-and-close-o

building is preventing children from focusing because of poor air quality and temperature control, student and teacher potential are being squandered.

- Advocate for healthy schools with elected officials, school leaders, and school board members. Urge that environmental assessments be completed, repairs made as needed, and facilities well maintained and operated.

- If building a new school building, carefully consider siting to prevent future unintended adverse health impacts. Work with the design team to ensure that they are building an energy-efficient, green school (Collaborative for High Performance Schools, LEED) that achieves indoor environmental quality credits.

- Support teachers. Efforts such as raising funds for a classroom air purifier or real-time low-cost sensors that measure air pollutants can leverage and reinforce teachers' commitment, promote healthy behaviors, and promote optimal performance and may also serve as a teaching tool for students.

- Engage facility managers. Healthy schools advocates need to understand how pre-K–12 schools are cleaned and maintained and what challenges face custodial staff. During economic recessions, schools defer maintenance, leading to sometimes irreparable building deterioration.

CONCLUSION

Schools are unique environments because they house children and by virtue of their density and the intensity of their use. And children are uniquely vulnerable to a range of environmental hazards. School facilities present extensive environmental challenges to health, well-being, and student and teacher performance, the result of a perfect storm of aging infrastructure, insufficient funding, growing student populations, understaffing, and absence of authoritative guidelines and coordinated oversight—so much so that it has been claimed that in the United States, "public health stops at the schoolhouse door."

However, these problems are increasingly recognized and have given rise to emerging efforts to improve school environments—aiming both for better health and for reduced environmental impact. Success can yield lower student and teacher absenteeism, improved performance, improved health, a more sustainable environment, and reduced costs—a win-win outcome.

DISCUSSION QUESTIONS

1. When was the last time you visited or attended a public school?

2. What do you think are the greatest barriers to fast, responsive investment and policies for healthy school buildings?

3. School budgets are often limited. For existing K–12 facilities, it may be difficult to achieve a holistically healthy school building. If you could invest in one feature of a healthy building, what would it be?

4. Brainstorm and list all the vulnerable populations that should be considered when designing, maintaining, and operating healthy K–12 facilities. Consider children and adults.

5. What public health systems are in place or should be in place to prevent or to investigate and track children's exposures to health hazards in schools?

6. If you were to promote the healthy schools movement, what issue would you advocate for? What would be your strategy for gaining support? Who are your allies in this effort?

7. How would you prepare your local school to stay open during the next pandemic?

DISCLOSURE OF COMPETING INTERESTS

Claire Barnett reports that Healthy Schools Network received no support to write the chapter. Barnett serves a member of the National Coordinating Committee on School Health and Safety (HRSA/MCH), the US EPA Indoor Environments school leadership team, and the NYS

DOH Clean Green and Healthy Schools Steering Committee. She is also a member of the International Society of Indoor Air Quality and Climate and the American Public Health Association; has served on advisory groups for US EPA Office of Children Health and the Council of State and Territorial Epidemiologists; and is a past advisor to the Harvard COVID Collaborative and the Aspen Institute's K–12 Climate Initiative. Healthy Schools Network does not accept contributions from product manufacturers nor does it endorse any products sold to schools.

Barnett also serves on the voluntary national advisory committee of the Collaborative for High Performance Schools (CHPS), a 501(c)(3) not-for-profit organization. In 2021, and pledging no endorsements, Healthy Schools Network accepted and acknowledged national sponsorships for its summit "COVID, Climate, Children, and Schools" from two architectural firms, Green Seal, and the NJ Education Association and in-kind support from CHPS.

Erika Sita Eitland discloses no competing interests.

REFERENCES

1. United Nations General Assembly. The Universal Declaration of Human Rights. Published 1948. Accessed October 23, 2021. https://www.ohchr.org/EN/UDHR/Documents/UDHR_Translations/eng.pdf

2. World Bank. World Development Report 2018: Learning to Realize Education's Promise. 2018. https://www.worldbank.org/en/publication/wdr2018

3. National Center for Education Statistics (NCES). Back to school statistics. Institute for Education Sciences website. 2021. Accessed July 13, 2021. https://nces.ed.gov/fastfacts/display.asp?id=372.

4. US Government Accountability Office. K–12 Education: School Districts Frequently Identified Multiple Building Systems Needing Updates or Replacement. 2020. Accessed October 23, 2021. https://www.gao.gov/assets/710/707374.pdf

5. Rooney LE, Videto DM, Birch DA. Using the whole school, whole community, whole child model: implications for practice. *Journal of School Health*. 2015;85(11):817-823.

6. UNICEF. Child Friendly Schools Programming: Global Evaluation Report. UNICEF. Published 2009. Accessed October 23, 2021. https://www.unicef.org/evaldatabase/files/Global_CFS_Evaluation_Report_Uploaded_Version.pdf

7. Haas SA, Fosse NE. Health and the educational attainment of adolescents: evidence from the NLSY97. *Journal of Health and Social Behavior*. 2008;49(2):178-192.

8. Child and Adolescent Health Measurement Initiative, Data Resource Center for Child & Adolescent Health. 2021. Accessed October 23, 2021. https://www.childhealthdata.org/

9. National Center for Education Statistics (NCES), US Department of Education. The Condition of Education 2020. NCES 2020-144, Concentration of Public School Students Eligible for Free or Reduced-Price Lunch. National Center for Education Statistics. 2020. Accessed July 13, 2021. https://nces.ed.gov/programs/coe/

10. National Center for Education Statistics (NCES). How Old are America's Public Schools? National Center for Education Statistics. 1999. Accessed November 9, 2021. https://nces.ed.gov/surveys/frss/publications/1999048/

11. Marcano-Olivier MI, Horne PJ, Viktor S, Erjavec M. Using nudges to promote healthy food choices in the school dining room: a systematic review of previous investigations. *Journal of School Health*. 2020;90(2):143-157.

12. World Health Organization. More than 90 percent of the world's children breathe toxic air every day. [News release.] World Health Organization. 2018. https://www.who.int/news-room/detail/29-10-2018-more-than-90-of-the-worlds-children-breathe-toxic-air-every-day

13. Annesi-Maesano I, Baiz N, Banerjee S, Rudnai P, Rive S, Sinphonie Group. Indoor air quality and sources in schools and related health effects. *Journal of Toxicology and Environmental Health, Part B*. 2013;16(8):491-550.

14. Wargocki P, Wyon DP. Ten questions concerning thermal and indoor air quality effects on the performance of office work and schoolwork. *Building and Environment*. 2017;112:359-366.

15. Eitland E, Klingensmith L, MacNaughton P, et al. *Schools for Health: Foundations for Student Success*. Harvard TH Chan School of Public Health; 2017.

16. Hsu J, Qin X, Beavers SF, Mirabelli MC. Asthma-related school absenteeism, morbidity, and modifiable factors. *American Journal of Preventive Medicine*. 2016;51(1):23-32.

17. Azuma K, Kagi N, Yanagi U, Osawa H. Effects of low-level inhalation exposure to carbon dioxide in indoor environments: a short review on human health and psychomotor performance. *Environment International*. 2018;121:51-56.

18. Wargocki P, Porras-Salazar JA, Contreras-Espinoza S, Bahnfleth W. The relationships between classroom air quality and children's performance in school. *Building and Environment*. 2020;173:106749.

19. US EPA. Indoor Air Quality Tools for Schools Action Kit. 2020. https://www.epa.gov/iaq-schools/indoor-air-quality-tools-schools-action-kit

20. US EPA. Maintain Portable Classrooms, Part of Indoor Air Quality Design Tools for Schools. No date. Accessed October 23, 2021. https://www.epa.gov/iaq-schools/maintain-portable-classrooms-part-indoor-air-quality-design-tools-schools

21. Park J. Temperature, test scores, and human capital production. Harvard University. February 26, 2017. https://scholar.harvard.edu/files/jisungpark/files/temperature_test_scores_and_human_capital_production_-_j_park_-_2-26-17.pdf

22. Norbäck D, Nordström K. Sick building syndrome in relation to air exchange rate, CO_2, room temperature and relative air humidity in university computer classrooms: an experimental study. *International Archives of Occupational and Environmental Health*. 2008;82(1):21-30.

23. Kocak ED, Sherwin JC. Time spent outdoors and myopia: establishing an evidence base. *Eye Science* 2015;30:143-146.

24. Aries M, Aarts M, van Hoof J. Daylight and health: a review of the evidence and consequences for the built environment. *Lighting Research & Technology*. 2015;47(1):6-27.

25. Roman-Lantzy C. *Cortical Visual Impairment: An Approach to Assessment and Intervention* American Foundation for the Blind; 2007.

26. Pujol S, Levain JP, Houot H, et al. Association between ambient noise exposure and school performance of children living in an urban area: a cross-sectional population-based study. *Journal of Urban Health*. 2014;91(2):256-271.

27. Van Reenen C, Karusseit C. Classroom acoustics as a consideration for inclusive education in South Africa. *South African Journal of Communicable Disorders*. 2017;64(1):e1-e10.

28. Tinney VA, Denton JM, Sciallo-Tyler L, Paulson JA. School siting near industrial chemical facilities: findings from the U.S. Chemical Safety Board's investigation of the West Fertilizer explosion. *Environmental Health Perspectives*. 2016;124(10):1493-1496.

29. Hauptman M, Gaffin JM, Petty CR, et al. Proximity to major roadways and asthma symptoms in the School Inner-City Asthma Study. *Journal of Allergy and Clinical Immunology*. 2020;145(1):119-126.e114.

30. Salvidge R. Toxic waste lies beneath schools in England and Wales, map shows. *The Guardian*. January 15, 2021. Accessed November 9, 2021. https://www.theguardian.com/environment/2021/jan/15/toxic-waste-lies-beneath-schools-and-homes-uk-landfill-map-shows

31. Wong C. China pollution scandal: air, water in school near toxic site normal, say officials. *South China Morning Post*. April 27, 2016. Accessed July 13, 2021. https://www.scmp.com/news/china/policies-politics/article/1938925/china-pollution-scandal-air-water-school-near-toxic

CHAPTER 16

CONTACT WITH NATURE

Howard Frumkin

KEY POINTS

- Nature contact promotes good health, a relationship supported by both theoretical and empirical considerations.
- In the built environment, nature contact may take many forms, such as plants in buildings, views out windows, biophilic building design, community gardens, street trees, and parks and green space.
- The benefits of such nature contact are wide-ranging, from stress reduction to improved birth outcomes, from recovery from illness and surgery to longer life.
- Access to nature is inequitably distributed; in many cities, low-income and minority neighborhoods lack nearby high-quality parks and green space.
- The response to the COVID-19 pandemic highlighted the value of nature contact for managing stress, anxiety, and depression.
- Much remains to be learned about the benefits of nature contact, such as what kinds of nature contact offer the greatest benefit, at what "dose" and frequency, and for which people.
- Providing nature contact may not only improve health but also yield co-benefits such as more disaster resilience, improved access to healthy foods, and conservation of natural resources

INTRODUCTION

Maria and her sister Dolores were as close as two sisters could be. Maria lived with her spouse and children in a high-rise building in Memphis, Tennessee, and Dolores lived with her spouse and children about an hour away, in a small town in northern Mississippi. The families visited regularly; the cousins loved getting together and playing.

As the COVID-19 pandemic spread across the world in early 2020 and travel became more difficult, the two sisters had to replace their regular visits with phone and Zoom calls. Fortunately, both were able to work from home and were financially secure. But as the weeks wore on, it became clear that Maria was growing increasingly anxious and depressed, while Dolores was weathering the challenges better. "How can you stay so upbeat?" Maria asked Dolores. Dolores reminded Maria that their Mississippi home was adjacent to the Holly Springs National Forest and that she and her family could take walks in the forest every day. Maria, in contrast, had many fewer options. There were relatively few parks in Memphis; the city ranked eighty-eighth on the Trust for Public Land ParkScore listing of the largest one hundred US cities, with just 5 percent of the city's land devoted to parks and recreation (compared to a national median of 15 percent). Fewer than half of Memphis residents live within a ten-minute walk of a park. Even when city parks remained open, the roads near them were closed, and there were no convenient transit connections Maria could use to get to a park. Finally, Maria noted that many park visitors were not wearing masks or distancing, so she would not have felt safe there anyway. The bottom line: Dolores had regular opportunities to visit parks, while Maria had none. The sisters concluded that Dolores's "secret sauce," which helped her to cope with the pandemic, was regular walks in nature.

The term *built environment* may conjure images of homes, schools, offices, and streets, but for many people, contact with nature is an integral part of how they experience the built environment—in parks, in backyards, even in the views out their office windows. This chapter reviews the evidence linking nature contact with health, describes how this benefit may be incorporated into healthy community design, and points out accompanying benefits for equity and sustainability.

NATURE CONTACT: A HEALTH BENEFIT?

Many people appreciate a walk in the park, or the sound of a bird's song, or the sight of ocean waves lapping at the seashore. These may be more than aesthetic preferences; they may reflect a deep-seated human connection with the natural world, an impulse to find tranquility, comfort, restoration, even healing, when in contact with nature. Contact with nature could be an important component of our well-being.

From an evolutionary perspective, such a connection with the natural world would come as no surprise. Our species and our immediate predecessors have existed for about two million years, and for more than 99 percent of that time, human lives were embedded in the natural environment. Those who could navigate it well—who could smell the water, identify the plants, follow the animals, recognize the safe havens—likely enjoyed survival advantages. The **biophilia hypothesis** suggests that human beings have an inherent tendency to affiliate with nature.[1] This connection may extend beyond plants and animals to inani-

mate objects such as streams, beaches, and wind. The concepts of the *environment of evolutionary adaptedness* and *adaptively relevant environments* suggest that organisms (including people) thrive best in settings like those in which they evolved over millions of years, giving environmental context to the biophilia hypothesis.

How might nature contact benefit health?[2] One theory emphasizes the importance of *directed attention*, the ability to block distracting stimuli and focus during purposeful activity.[3] According to this theory, excessive concentration can lead to attentional fatigue, resulting in memory loss, diminished ability to focus, and impatience and frustration in interpersonal interactions. Nature contact, accordingly, could be restorative by renewing attention and improving cognitive abilities—a concept known as **attention restoration**. Many studies have supported this hypothesis, linking nature contact with improved attention, cognitive function, and task performance. In one study, for example, student volunteers who took a nature walk substantially improved on a cognitive task that required directed attention, while students who walked in a dense urban setting did not.[4] Other studies found that elementary school children who grew up in green neighborhoods performed better on tests of attention than did children from less green neighborhoods (after controlling for potential confounders),[5] and children with attention deficit hyperactivity disorder (ADHD) who played regularly in green outdoor settings had milder symptoms than children who played in built settings.[6]

Nature contact may also improve health through *stress reduction*. This is an intuitive notion; many people, if they are able, choose vacations in beautiful natural settings, anticipating relief from their stress. Empirical research also supports this notion; in many studies, people exposed to nature scenes (even on video) are more resilient to stressors and recover more quickly than subjects without such contact. For example, in one study, children in homes with high levels of nature contact reacted to stressful life events with significantly less psychological distress than did children in low-nature-contact homes.[7] In a study in Scotland, neighborhood greenness reduced the stress associated with social deprivation.[8] Early studies of nature contact and stress tended to rely on self-reported stress, but more recent studies have used physiological measures such as salivary cortisol levels, strengthening the findings.

Nature contact might be healthy in a third way, by playing a role in healthy *child development*. Psychologists and others[9] have argued that children's ability to develop perceptual and expressive skills, imagination, moral judgments, and other attributes is greatly enhanced by contact with nature (figure 16.1). Research has linked play in natural environments with improved creativity, language and cognitive development, social connections, and independence—not only in childhood, but across the life span into adulthood.[10]

Nature contact may help not only with children's neurobehavioral development, but also with developing immune function. Investigators tested this hypothesis in children in urban day-care centers in the Finnish cities of Lahti and Tampere. The centers initially had little or no green space. Some remained unchanged, whereas in others the outdoor play areas got an intervention: segments of forest floor, sod, planters, and peat blocks for climbing and digging. Children in both the intervention and the comparison settings played outside for an average of ninety minutes each day. After twenty-eight days, the environmental microbiomes in the intervention day-care centers had greater bacterial abundance and diversity, but those in the comparison centers were unchanged. Associated with these microbiome changes, children in the intervention centers had altered skin and gut microbiomes and improved measures of immune function (plasma cytokine levels and regulatory T cell frequencies).[11] Observations such as these have given rise to a movement that aims to reconnect children with nature by greening schoolyards, as described in box 16.1.

Nature contact may benefit health and well-being in still other ways. It may enhance social connections—**prosocial behavior** in children[12] and **social capital** in adults[13] (see

Figure 16.1. Evidence suggests that design that takes advantage of natural features, as in this playground, enhances child development.
Source: Natural Learning Initiative

BOX 16.1 GREEN SCHOOLYARDS

Could children benefit from nature contact at school? A growing body of research suggests that the answer is yes.[a] When schools have nearby trees and natural, vegetated play areas (figure 16.2) and when outdoor time is provided for classes or recess, children's self-regulation and behavior improve, symptoms of attention deficit hyperactivity disorder decline, prosocial behavior increases, academic performance improves, and psychological well-being increases. Perhaps more surprisingly, children in greener schools may be less likely to develop hypertension and obesity. Moreover, if the green schoolyard includes gardens and if children have the opportunity to help cultivate vegetables, they develop a taste for healthy foods.

Green schoolyards, and the nature-based education they facilitate, may advance equity by providing particular benefits for low-income and minority children[b] (perhaps because nature contact is otherwise less available to them) and for girls (by increasing physical activity).[c] They also offer particular benefits for children with emotional, cognitive, and behavioral disabilities.[d]

Is there a downside? Might children in outdoor educational settings be at increased risk of colds or other infections? Not only does contemporary evidence suggest no such risk,[e] but historical evidence from the 1918 flu pandemic suggests that outdoor classrooms, even in cold weather, were highly effective in *controlling* infection—a lesson that might have been helpful if applied during the COVID-19 pandemic.[f]

Figure 16.2. A green schoolyard in Berlin, Germany.
Source: Photo courtesy of Birgit Teichmann

BOX 16.1 CONTINUED

Finally, green schoolyards offer two kinds of benefits beyond children's health and well-being. First, they cultivate proenvironmental attitudes,[g] creating "little conservationists" who go on to make proenvironmental choices that are also healthy choices. (This is seen in adults too: more time in nature predicts more proenvironmental attitudes and behaviors.[h]) Second, green schoolyards do double duty, serving as green amenities for their communities—venues for gardening, recreation, and nature contact after school and on weekends. This practice is known as **joint use**, and it represents a cost-effective way to promote community health.

For these reasons, dozens of environmental, health, design, and educational groups endorsed the concept in 2018 and developed a Green Schoolyards Action Agenda (https://www.childrenandnature. org/schools/greening-schoolyards/). Design concepts, from playgrounds to schoolyard wildlife sanctuaries to schoolyard agriculture, have been published.[i]

REFERENCES

a. Stevenson KT, Moore R, Cosco N, et al. A national research agenda supporting green schoolyard development and equitable access to nature. *Elementa: Science of the Anthropocene.* 2020;8(1).
b. Sprague N, Berrigan D, Ekenga CC. An Analysis of the educational and health-related benefits of nature-based environmental education in low-income Black and Hispanic children. *Health Equity.* 2020;4(1):198-210.
c. Pawlowski CS, Veitch J, Andersen HB, Ridgers ND. Designing activating schoolyards: seen from the girls' viewpoint. *International Journal of Environmental Research and Public Health.* 2019;16(19).
d. Szczytko R, Carrier SJ, Stevenson KT. Impacts of outdoor environmental education on teacher reports of attention, behavior, and learning outcomes for students with emotional, cognitive, and behavioral disabilities. *Frontiers in Education.* 2018;3(46).
e. Frenkel H, Tandon P, Frumkin H, Vander Stoep A. Illnesses and injuries at nature preschools. *Environment and Behavior.* 2018;0(0):0013916518773469.
f. Bellafante G. Schools beat earlier plagues with outdoor classes. We should, too. *New York Times.* July 17, 2020.
g. Olsson D, Gericke N, Boeve-de Pauw J, Berglund T, Chang T. Green schools in Taiwan—effects on student sustainability consciousness. *Global Environmental Change.* 2019;54:184-194.
h. Martin L, White MP, Hunt A, Richardson M, Pahl S, Burt J. Nature contact, nature connectedness and associations with health, wellbeing and pro-environmental behaviours. *Journal of Environmental Psychology.* 2020;68:101389.
i. Danks SG. *Asphalt to Ecosystems: Design Ideas for Schoolyard Transformation.* New Village Press; 2010.

chapter 9). For example, a study in Zurich found that children who regularly played outside in natural areas had more than twice as many playmates as children restricted to indoor play because of heavy nearby traffic,[14] and a study in Guangzhou, China, found that greater neighborhood greenness predicted more regular social interactions among older adults.[15]

Natural settings serve as venues for *physical activity*.[16] They may boost *immune function*, not only in children as described above, but across the life span, perhaps thanks to the phytochemicals released by plants.[17] And natural settings may offer people a respite from noxious exposures by *damping noise*[18] and *reducing air pollution*.[19] Nature contact sometimes triggers the experience of **awe**, a transcendent emotional state associated with health benefits.[20] Finally, nature contact may represent an escape from routine. In all likelihood, the benefits of nature contact flow through more than one of these pathways.

NATURE CONTACT ACROSS THE BUILT ENVIRONMENT

Nature contact occurs at many scales of the built environment. What does the evidence tell us about nature contact at each of these scales?

Buildings

Plants are a long-standing and popular decorative element of buildings. Ancient ruins in Egypt and Pompeii show evidence of ornamental indoor plants.[21] Research findings from offices, schools, and hospitals show that in the presence of plants, people feel subjectively better, report less anxiety and stress, perform better on tasks, take less sick leave, and even heal more quickly, although not all studies have supported these conclusions.[22] Very little exposure is needed; in studies in Japanese, English, and Dutch workplaces, even a single plant on an office worker's desk, or a view of just a couple of plants somewhere in the office, was enough to reduce stress and increase work satisfaction.[23]

It is not only nature *within* the building that offers benefit; it is also what a person can see when *looking out* through the windows. Nature views from buildings are associated with improved health and well-being. In a classic 1984 study, patients recovering from gall bladder surgery were randomly placed either in hospital rooms with views of trees or in rooms whose windows faced a brick wall. Compared to patients with brick-wall views, patients with tree views had significantly shorter hospitalizations (7.96 days compared to 8.70 days), less need for pain medications, and fewer negative comments in the nurses' notes.[24] In another study, at a massive Depression-era state prison in Michigan, prisoners were confined either in cells along the outside wall with a window view of rolling farmland and trees or in cells that faced into the bleak prison courtyard. Cell assignment was random. The prisoners with courtyard views had a 24 percent higher frequency of sick call visits than those with landscape views.[25] In workplaces with window views of nature, workers report lower stress, more job satisfaction, and greater well-being.[26] Even from high in a skyscraper, views of greenery far below are associated with lower stress and improved moods, compared to purely urban views.[27]

In the absence of nature views through windows, a substitute—nature art—may offer benefits. In psychiatric hospitals, images of nature scenes are associated with reduced aggressive behavior compared to abstract art or no art,[28] and in prisons, nature videos are associated with fewer violent infractions.[29]

Of course, nature views do not come in isolation; they come with *daylight*, which is an amenity in its own right. Although the benefits of daylighting are not fully understood, natural daylight is generally found to promote health, well-being, and high-quality sleep.[30] In daylit buildings, students learn better and office workers are happier and more productive.[31] In hospitals, patients in beds near windows have fewer falls and shorter stays compared to patients in beds away from windows.[32] Conversely, poor lighting has negative consequences. Excessively bright lighting can cause squinting and headaches, dim lighting can cause eye strain, and flickering can cause headaches and discomfort. Daylight is also an energy-saving strategy, as it reduces the need for electric lighting. Daylight design strategies may include windows, skylights, louvers, and clerestories (walls with windows above eye level), with electric lighting serving as a backup when needed.

A final way to bring nature into buildings is through **biophilic design**—"an approach that fosters beneficial contact between people and nature in modern buildings and landscapes."[33(p5)] One biophilic design strategy is the use of natural materials such as wood and stone. A related strategy is the use of shapes and forms that evoke beloved elements of nature such as water, sunlight, and plants. For example, **fractal patterns**—complex patterns that repeat at different scales—are found in nature (for example, in geodes, snowflakes, branches, and leaves) and may be used in wallpaper or roof structures. A third biophilic design strategy is place-based or vernacular design that connects to local culture and ecology; this approach could involve geography, history, landscape orientation, or a host of other features. Biophilic design can be seen both at the very small scale of a window planter, a shade sail over a playground, or an artfully designed walkway and at the

Figure 16.3. Biophilic design can be achieved on the small scale of a window planter (*top*), with an artfully designed walkway, or on a larger scale such as Frank Lloyd Wright's Fallingwater house in Pennsylvania (*bottom*).
Sources: (*top*) Wikimedia Commons courtesy Nick. https://creativecommons.org/licenses/by/2.0/deed.en. (*bottom*) Wikimedia Commons courtesy Sxenko. https://creativecommons.org/licenses/by/3.0/

large scale of such iconic buildings as Fallingwater (figure 16.2) or the Sydney Opera House, with its bird and sail-like forms soaring over the waterfront of Sydney Harbor. A challenge is that people's **sense of place** may be largely formed in early childhood (a process called **place attachment**). If the occupants of a single building hail from diverse and varied backgrounds—from deserts to mountains to lakes to oceans to forests—they may resonate with very different natural design elements.

Neighborhoods

Neighborhoods with green surroundings such as tree canopies also offer wide-ranging health benefits. Box 16.2 describes a remarkable series of studies from a public housing project in Chicago. In Indianapolis, children who lived in greener neighborhoods gained less excess weight than did children in neighborhoods with less green space.[34] In a nationwide study in Holland, the greener the neighborhood, the lower the prevalence of sixteen medical conditions, including joint pain, depression, anxiety, headaches, and even coronary heart disease and diabetes.[35] In three Australian cities, people in greener neighborhoods were at lower risk of diabetes, hypertension, and cardiovascular disease (after controlling for risk factors such as low income and education).[36] In London, blocks with more trees had lower rates of antidepressant medication use.[37]

Can these observations be quantified and used to guide policy? A meta-analysis of the relationship between neighborhood greenness and mortality found that each 0.1 unit increase in the NDVI (the normalized difference vegetation index, a commonly used measure of vegetative cover) was associated with a 4 percent reduction in all-cause mortality.[38] When researchers applied this finding to Philadelphia, they calculated that the city would prevent 403 deaths each year if it reached its goal of 30 percent tree canopy in all neighborhoods.[39] Although results of studies vary depending on how vegetation is measured, the distance from people's homes, and other factors, and although the benefits of neighborhood greening can be undermined by gentrification (see chapter 9), the overall pattern is clear: greener neighborhoods are healthier neighborhoods.

Gardens

Long-standing tradition associates gardens with health. In health care settings, this idea takes form in **healing gardens**. Often peaceful oases in otherwise bustling hospitals, these gardens may be used by patients, families, visitors, and staff, who report finding peace and

---

BOX 16.2 NATURE CONTACT IN THE CITY

An important line of research from the University of Illinois Landscape and Human Health Laboratory (formerly the Human Environment Research Laboratory) focused on nature contact in Chicago's inner-city housing projects. One such complex (Robert Taylor Homes) consisted of twenty-eight identical high-rise buildings, arrayed along a three-mile stretch of land bounded by busy roadways and railway lines. Some of the buildings were surrounded by stands of trees, but others opened onto barren stretches of ground. Residents were in effect randomly assigned to a building with one landscape type or the other. Researchers compared residents of the buildings with and without trees, limiting their studies to residents who lived on lower floors to ensure that if trees were nearby, people in the buildings could actually see them.

This research yielded surprising findings. Compared with living in buildings with barren surroundings, living in buildings with trees was associated with the following:

- Higher levels of attention and greater effectiveness in managing major life issues
- Substantially lower levels of aggression and violence
- Higher levels of social connectedness (knowing, greeting, and helping neighbors)
- Lower levels of reported crime
- Higher levels of self-discipline (as measured by tests of concentration, impulse inhibition, and delay of gratification) among girls (but not among boys)

Together, these studies suggest that nature contact in otherwise deprived urban environments—even contact as simple as trees outside an apartment building—offers powerful benefits to the people who live there. (For more information on these studies, see the University of Illinois Landscape and Human Health Laboratory, http://lhhl.illinois.edu/.)

restoration in them.[40] Sometimes hospitals and clinics actively use gardens as venues for **horticultural therapy**, combining environmental and programmatic approaches to treatment. The evidence supporting this therapy is strongest for elders and for people with mental illness,[41] but other benefits may also operate. For example, in one study, horticultural therapy outperformed routine patient education in reducing heart rate and improving mood among cardiac rehabilitation patients.[42]

In the community setting, **community gardens** (called **community allotments** in some countries) are parcels of land, typically publicly owned and community-managed, that are available for gardening. Garden patches are allocated to participating individuals or families, who grow vegetables, fruits, herbs, and flowers and in the process enjoy hands-on contact with soil and plants in outdoor settings. Community gardens are popular in many cities and towns, especially in urban neighborhoods where people otherwise have little or no access to land for cultivation. In Oslo, some community gardens feature small cottages, where gardeners can live during the summer season. Community gardens may provide a number of benefits[43]:

- Building a sense of community among participants (especially in low-income neighborhoods)
- Restoring blighted neighborhoods
- Providing improved access to fresh, nutritious, and affordable food (see chapter 3)
- Building skills (both gardening and interpersonal) among participants
- Improving mental health and well-being
- Promoting physical activity

Although community gardens may be difficult to scale up, few public health interventions offer such a range of benefits at such low cost and with so few downsides.

Parks

Parks have long been prized features of towns and cities. Pioneering urban planners such as Frederick Law Olmsted and municipal officials of the nineteenth and early twentieth centuries considered parks essential oases in cities, allowing urban dwellers of all social classes to connect with nature, enjoy one another's company, breathe fresh air, and pursue recreational activities.

Parks range from small pockets of green space deep within urban canyons to vast reserves of natural land in rural areas (figure 16.4). They offer a range of health benefits. One of the best studied is physical activity; living near a park predicts more physical activity[44] (see chapter 2). Parks also offer mental health benefits, perhaps through stress reduction, both for park visitors and for people who live nearby.[45] In a nationwide study of US children, those who lived near parks reported less screen time and better sleep, were more likely to be physically active, and were less likely to be obese, overweight, or diagnosed with ADHD.[46] Parks also offer indirect health benefits: protecting watersheds, reducing air pollution, and cooling urban heat islands.

The ways in which these benefits operate may vary across populations. Ethnic and racial groups differ in their preferences and in the ways they use parks, as do different age groups. Some groups prefer to use parks for passive recreation such as picnicking, resting, and relaxing, and others tend toward walking, dog walking, and sports. Some like team activities, and others prefer solo activities such as reading or jogging. Among sports enthusiasts, some like baseball, and others prefer soccer. Planners, landscape architects, parks and recreation professionals, and public health professionals need to take these differences into account as they address the needs of diverse populations, through diverse park department leadership, robust community partnerships, co-creation of parks and park programming, community advisory boards, and similar mechanisms, to ensure that parks serve the needs of all.

Not all parks are equal. Research has identified attributes of parks that predict more visits

Figure 16.4. Pioneering urban planners such as Frederick Law Olmsted saw green space and blue space, such as in this park in Atlanta, as essential oases in cities.
Source: Anonymous with permission

and, consequently, greater health benefit.[47] Among these attributes are good maintenance, greenery, the presence of other people, infrastructure such as ballfields and exercise equipment, restrooms, lighting, absence of "incivilities" such as graffiti and litter, and both the perception and reality of safety. Also important are proximity to where people live and ease of access (including transit service). In addition to these physical features (the "hardware"), park use also increases with the right "software"—the engagement of communities in planning activities in and maintaining the parks[48] and, importantly, pro-gramming such as organized and supervised activities.[49]

Many park systems recognize parks' links with health, and some have even adopted health themes in promoting park use. For example, the slogan "Healthy Parks, Healthy People" has been adopted by national, state, and local parks, such as the US National Park Service,[50] Parks Victoria in Australia,[51] and California's East Bay Regional Park District.[52] Public health initiatives have been launched by such parks groups as the National Recreation and Park Association (www.nrpa.org) and the City Parks Alliance (www.cityparksalliance.org).

These groups emphasize not only the health benefits but also the synergistic environmental and economic benefits of parks.

Blue Space

Not all nature contact is "green" (as in vegetation); nature contact can also consist of streams, rivers, lakes, and coastlines—so-called **blue space**. Research in recent years has documented a range of benefits from living near or visiting blue space—similar in many ways to the benefits of green space.[53] In a study in Belgium, people living close to the coast had better general health than those living inland, after controlling for income, green space exposure, and other potential confounders. The association could not be explained by differences in physical activity levels or better air quality.[54] In Barcelona, living near that city's beach was associated with better general health than living inland—an effect that was more pronounced among low-income residents.[55] In Guangzhou, China, a city of thirteen million people, elders who lived near any of the city's waterways (lakes, rivers, or the coast) had better mental health than those who did not.[56] Although research on the benefits of blue space exposure is in its early stages, initial results support the idea that waterfronts, river walks, and beaches should be considered healthy built environment strategies.

BUT IS THE NEWS ALL GOOD?

Although much of the evidence suggests that nature contact is beneficial, it is important to reckon with risks as well.[57] Many trees and plants release pollen, which can aggravate allergies, as well as biogenic compounds, which in certain circumstances contribute to ground-level ozone formation. Street trees in urban "canyons" flanked by tall buildings, if not configured properly, can impede street-level air circulation and increase street-level air pollution exposure. Efforts to increase urban green space and support biodiversity can favor vectors such as ticks or host organisms such as rats, contributing to infectious disease spread. Waterways can serve as habitats for mosquitos and sites of harmful algal blooms. And time outdoors entails sunlight exposure, which is healthy to a point, but hazardous in excess.

Each of these risks can be managed through such strategies as judicious selection of trees and careful planting, preventive treatment for asthmatics during allergy season, vector and rodent control programs, control of organic runoff into waterways, and ultraviolet skin protection during outdoor time. Such risk management tilts the balance of nature contact toward net public health benefit.

NATURE CONTACT AND EQUITY

Not all communities have equal access to nature. In cities the world over, low-income and minority neighborhoods have less access to parks and green space than do affluent and ethnic majority neighborhoods. In South African cities, the disparities in nature access are so striking that they have been dubbed "Green Apartheid."[58] Moreover, when people in disadvantaged neighborhoods do have access to parks and green space, these spaces tend to be less well equipped and maintained, and less safe, than those in affluent neighborhoods.[59] Not surprisingly, then, poor people and people of color are in many cities less likely to visit parks and green spaces[60] and less likely to enjoy the associated health benefits. This is not because of indifference to nature; contrary to some stereotypes, low-income people and members of racial and ethnic minorities when surveyed express strongly positive proenvironmental attitudes.[61] Disparities in nature access contribute to health disparities.

Conversely, contact with nature may deliver relatively greater benefits to low-income than to affluent populations, perhaps because of a larger underlying burden of ill health. For example, a study in Miami showed that people in greener neighborhoods had significantly lower risk of Alzheimer's disease and depression than people in more barren neighborhoods—with the risk reduction nearly twice as great in low-income as in high-income neighborhoods.[62] A nationwide study in England found that in greener neighborhoods, not only was mortality lower, but the health disparity between wealthy and disadvantaged groups was narrowed—what the authors called an **equigenic effect** of nature contact.[63] Targeting public health interventions to populations that will benefit the most is a standard approach, and one that is highly relevant to green space.

Attempted solutions can sometimes worsen inequities—a phenomenon called **green gentrification**. When cities improve parks, tree canopy, and other natural features of a neighborhood, the property values in the neighborhood typically rise, and longtime residents may be priced out. For example, New York City's High Line, a 2.3-kilometer (1.45-mile) elevated park on a former railroad line, triggered a rapid 35 percent increase in the value of adjacent homes.[64] This challenge is further explored in chapter 9.

Another equity concern pertains to disabilities. Some people with disabilities have difficulty accessing and utilizing parks and green space. Park design features can help. For example, wheelchair-accessible trails, water fountains, and restrooms help people with mobility impairments enjoy parks. Well-placed benches enable seniors who are walking to rest when needed. Many park systems provide information on park access for people with disabilities.

GREEN INFRASTRUCTURE

Green infrastructure is a widely used term. In contrast to "gray infrastructure"—constructed, engineered solutions, usually on a large scale—green infrastructure utilizes natural processes to deliver **ecosystem services** such as flood control by coastal mangroves, wastewater treatment by soil bacterial action, and carbon sequestration by forests. According to the European Commission, "Green infrastructure is a strategically planned network of natural and semi-natural areas with other

environmental features designed and managed to deliver a wide range of ecosystem services such as water purification, air quality, space for recreation and climate mitigation and adaptation. This network of green (land) and blue (water) spaces can improve environmental conditions and therefore citizens' health and quality of life. It also supports a green economy, creates job opportunities and enhances biodiversity."[65]

Green infrastructure is often environmentally friendly and often advances sustainability goals. A classic example of green infrastructure is the use of bioswales, retention ponds, and soil percolation to manage stormwater. Such infrastructure is often less expensive to build and operate than highly engineered conventional stormwater systems and can deliver other benefits such as recreational space, water purification, and disaster resilience—particular advantages in informal settlements in the fast-growing cities of the Global South. Another example of green infrastructure is urban forests, which can improve air quality (if the correct species are selected and placed strategically)—at the same time cooling the neighborhoods in which they are planted, reducing power demand during hot weather, and helping with stormwater management. On a smaller scale, vegetated roofs and walls are examples of green infrastructure. These can capture and store stormwater, cool buildings, sequester carbon, and supply food. In each of these cases, green infrastructure offers not just one ecosystem service, but a set of interacting services.

Green infrastructure often benefits health as well. These benefits were on full display during the COVID-19 pandemic (box 16.3). Lowering a city's temperature during a heat wave, or reducing flooding through stormwater management, protects exposed populations. Moreover, many kinds of green infrastructure double as urban green space, which benefits physical and mental health as described above. However, reviews of green infrastructure health benefits have generally found that

BOX 16.3 NATURE CONTACT DURING THE COVID-19 PANDEMIC

As the COVID-19 pandemic erupted in early 2020, people around the world confronted restrictions on their movement, and in many cases full lockdowns. In response to the resulting restlessness, cabin fever, anxiety, and depression, many people sought respite in natural settings such as parks, which was not a surprise given the well-established restorative qualities of nature contact.

However, in many places, parks were closed (figure 16.5). In some cases, park closures were part of more sweeping restrictions. In other cases, parks initially remained open, but authorities found that visitors were congregating in large numbers without physical distancing, and they thus imposed restrictions. Considerable public pushback to park closures arose in many places. Some experts, after balancing risks and benefits, advocated the judicious opening of parks.[a] In some jurisdictions, park restrictions were among the first to be relaxed. In Barcelona, officials compensated for unpopular park restrictions by permitting people out to work in vegetable gardens.

Figure 16.5. Parks, beaches, and other outdoor destinations were closed to minimize the spread of COVID-19, but the inability to access these places was itself a threat to health and well-being.
Source: Wikimedia commons courtesy Famartin. https://creative commons.org/licenses/by-sa/4.0 /deed.en

Meanwhile, evidence of heightened demand for nature contact emerged. In cities across the United States, mobile phone tracking revealed that even as shopping trips fell pursuant to stay-at-home orders, urban park visits continued undiminished.[b] An analysis of Google mobility data showed substantial increases in park visits in eighteen of the twenty-five largest metro areas in the United States during the first few months of the pandemic (although warming weather likely played a role as well).[c] The Cornell Lab of Ornithology reported that downloads of its Merlin Bird ID app had increased by 50 to 100 percent by the third month of the pandemic.[d] There were dramatic year-on-year increases in the issuance of hunting and fishing licenses across the United States.[e] Park visits rose in Stockholm (where parks remained open)[f] and across England (as soon as park restrictions were relaxed).[g] In Hong Kong, people flocked to the scenic Tai Po reservoir every day at levels previously seen only on weekends,[h] and 79 percent of Hong Kong park visitors endorsed the statement that the park environment "helps to improve mental health by relieving my stress and anxiety brought about by the COVID-19 pandemic."[i]

BOX 16.3 CONTINUED

When urban parks were closed, people in Italy increased their visits to nearby small urban gardens, people in Spain and Israel increased their strolling on tree-lined streets, and people in Lithuania and Croatia drove more than usual to green areas outside the city.[j] A detailed study in Oslo, using STRAVA data, Google mobility data, and pedestrian and bicycle counts, revealed a 291 percent year-on-year increase in outdoor activity, which was greatest on the greenest, least urbanized trails.[k]

Nature contact clearly emerged as a highly valued amenity during the pandemic. Accordingly, the pandemic's legacy may include the creation of more parks in urban areas, changes in park design such as wider paths to permit physical distancing, and better maintenance of existing parks.

REFERENCES

a. Slater SJ, Christiana RW, Gustat J. Recommendations for keeping parks and green space accessible for mental and physical health during COVID-19 and other pandemics. *Preventing Chronic Disease.* 2020;17:200204.
b. Hamidi S, Zandiatashbar A. Compact development and adherence to stay-at-home order during the COVID-19 pandemic: a longitudinal investigation in the United States. *Landscape and Urban Planning.* 2021;205:103952.
c. Mainali K, Mills E. Chesapeake Conservancy Studies Park Mobility during COVID 19. Chesapeake Conservancy; July 22, 2020. Accessed October 16, 2021. https://www.chesapeakeconservancy.org/2020/07/22/chesapeake-conservancy-studies-park-mobility-during-covid-19/
d. Cornell Lab of Ornithology. Birdwatchers set world records on Global Big Day. May 15, 2020. Accessed October 16, 2021. https://mailchi.mp/cornell/news-release-birdwatchers-break-records-on-global-big-day-1317584
e. Brown A. The pandemic created new hunters. States need to keep them. Pew Charitable Trusts *Stateline.* December 14, 2020. Accessed October 16, 2021. https://www.pewtrusts.org/en/research-and-analysis/blogs/stateline/2020/12/14/the-pandemic-created-new-hunters-states-need-to-keep-them
f. Barton D, Haase D, Mascarenhas A, et al., Enabling access to greenspace during the COVID-19 pandemic—perspectives from five cities. The Nature of Cities. 2020, May 4, 2020. Accessed July 13, 2021. https://www.thenatureofcities.com/2020/05/04/enabling-access-to-greenspace-during-the-covid-19-pandemic-perspectives-from-five-cities/
g. Day BH. The value of greenspace under pandemic lockdown. *Environmental and Resource Economics.* 2020;76:1161-1185.
h. Tsang D. Coronavirus: Hongkongers flock to barbecue pits at reservoir for fresh air and fun as city grinds to a halt, but how safe is it? *South China Morning Post.* February 22, 2020.
i. Ma ATH, Lam TWL, Cheung LTO, Fok L. Protected areas as a space for pandemic disease adaptation: a case of COVID-19 in Hong Kong. *Landscape and Urban Planning.* 2021;207:103994.
j. Ugolini F, Massetti L, Calaza-Martínez P, et al. Effects of the COVID-19 pandemic on the use and perceptions of urban green space: an international exploratory study. *Urban Forestry & Urban Greening.* 2020;56:126888.
k. Venter ZS, Barton DN, Gundersen V, Figari H, Nowell M. Urban nature in a time of crisis: recreational use of green space increases during the COVID-19 outbreak in Oslo, Norway. *SocArXiv.* 2020.

evidence documenting these benefits is scarce.[66] This will remain an active area of research in coming years.

CONCLUSION

Much remains to be learned about the health benefits of nature contact and about the ways in which these benefits might be designed into the built environment. Some of the outstanding research questions are discussed in chapter 25.

Although there is more to learn, we know enough to act. At the building scale, architects, designers, and decorators should consider incorporating natural elements through the use of plants, gardens, outdoor views, artwork, natural daylighting, and structural elements. At the community scale, trees and other plantings; accessible parks, trails, greenways, and waterfronts; and other natural assets also appear to promote health. Several considerations are important to bear in mind. First, nature contact often yields co-benefits in addition to health promotion—improving air and water quality, reducing energy demand, raising property values, and more. Second, providing green assets is often a partial solution; programming, social marketing, and other approaches complete the health promotion strategy. Third, nature contact is inequitably distributed in most towns and cities; efforts to provide equitable access are essential. Finally, nature contact is likely to benefit different groups differently; it is essential to consider age, race and ethnicity, physical disabilities, and other factors in planning approaches to nature contact that are most likely to promote health and well-being.

DISCUSSION QUESTIONS

1. Can you identify five mechanisms through which nature contact might benefit health?
2. Do you think public health advice ought to include a "recommended daily dose" of nature? What kind of evidence would you want to support such a recommendation?
3. Imagine you are the health advisor to your city's parks commissioner. What advice would you offer to optimize the health benefits of parks?
4. Visit a park close to your home. Systematically describe the park's features, identifying those that promote health and those that do not.

ACKNOWLEDGMENT

Box 16.3, on COVID-19, was adapted from: Frumkin H. 2021. Covid-19, the built environment, and health. *Environmental Health Perspectives*. 2021; 129(7):75001. doi:10.1289/EHP8888

DISCLOSURE OF COMPETING INTERESTS

Howard Frumkin's declarations appear in the preface.

REFERENCES

1. Kellert SR, Wilson EO. *The Biophilia Hypothesis*. Island Press; 1993.

2. Frumkin H, Bratman GN, Breslow SJ, et al. Nature contact and human health: a research agenda. *Environmental Health Perspectives*. 2017.

3. Kaplan S. The restorative benefits of nature: toward an integrative framework. *Journal of Environmental Psychology*. 1995;15(3):169-182.

4. Berman M, Jonides J, Kaplan S. The cognitive benefits of interacting with nature. *Psychological Science*. 2008;19:1207-1212.

5. Dadvand P, Tischer C, Estarlich M, et al. Lifelong residential exposure to green space and attention: a population-based prospective study. *Environmental Health Perspectives*. 2017;125(9):097016.

6. Faber Taylor A, Kuo FEM. Could exposure to everyday green spaces help treat ADHD? Evidence from children's play settings. *Applied Psychology: Health and Well-Being*. 2011;3(3):281-303.

7. Wells NM, Evans GW. Nearby nature: a buffer of life stress among rural children. *Environment and Behavior*. 2003;35(3):311-330.

8. Ward Thompson C, Aspinall P, Roe J, Robertson L, Miller D. Mitigating stress and supporting health in deprived urban communities: the importance of green space and the social environment. *International Journal of Environmental Research and Public Health*. 2016;13(4).

9. Louv R. *Last Child in the Woods: Saving Our Children from Nature-Deficit Disorder*. Algonquin Books; 2005.

10. Snell TL, Simmonds JG, Klein LM. Exploring the impact of contact with nature in childhood on adult personality. *Urban Forestry & Urban Greening*. 2020;55:126864.

11. Roslund MI, Puhakka R, Grönroos M, et al. Biodiversity intervention enhances immune regulation and health-associated commensal microbiota among daycare children. *Science Advances*. 2020;6(42):eaba2578.

12. Putra I, Astell-Burt T, Cliff DP, Vella SA, John EE, Feng X. The relationship between green space and prosocial behaviour among children and adolescents: a systematic review. *Front Psychology*. 2020;11:859.

13. Goldy SP, Piff PK. Toward a social ecology of prosociality: why, when, and where nature enhances social connection. *Current Opinion in Psychology*. 2020;32:27-31.

14. Hüttenmoser M. Children and their living surroundings: empirical investigations into the significance of living surroundings for the everyday life and development of children. *Children's Environments* 1995;12(4):403-13.

15. Zhou Y, Yuan Y, Chen Y, Lai S. Association pathways between neighborhood greenspaces and the physical and mental health of older adults—a cross-sectional study in Guangzhou, China. *Frontiers in Public Health*. 2020;8(539).

16. O'Donoghue G, Perchoux C, Mensah K, et al. A systematic review of correlates of sedentary behaviour in adults aged 18–65 years: a socio-ecological approach. *BMC Public Health*. 2016;16:163.

17. Kuo M. How might contact with nature promote human health? Exploring promising mechanisms and a possible central pathway. *Frontiers in Psychology*. 2015;6.

18. Koprowska K, Łaszkiewicz E, Kronenberg J, Marcińczak S. Subjective perception of noise exposure in relation to urban green space availability. *Urban Forestry & Urban Greening*. 2018;31:93-102.

19. Kumar P, Druckman A, Gallagher J, et al. The nexus between air pollution, green infrastructure and human health. *Environment International*. 2019;133(Pt A):105181.

20. Ballew MT, Omoto AM. Absorption: how nature experiences promote awe and

other positive emotions. *Ecopsychology*. 2018;10(1):26-35.

21. Manaker GH. *Interior Plantscapes: Installation, Maintenance, and Management*. Prentice Hall; 1997.

22. Aydogan A, Cerone R. Review of the effects of plants on indoor environments. *Indoor and Built Environment*. 2020;30(4):442-460. 1420326X19900213.

23. Toyoda M, Yokota Y, Barnes M, Kaneko M. Potential of a small indoor plant on the desk for reducing office workers' stress. *HortTechnology hortte*. 2020;30(1):55-63.

24. Ulrich RS. View through a window may influence recovery from surgery. *Science*. 1984;224:420-421.

25. Moore EO. A prison environment's effect on health care service demands. *Journal of Environmental Systems*. 1981-2;11:17-34.

26. Gilchrist K, Brown C, Montarzino A. Workplace settings and wellbeing: greenspace use and views contribute to employee wellbeing at peri-urban business sites. *Landscape and Urban Planning*. 2015;138:32-40.

27. Elsadek M, Liu B, Xie J. Window view and relaxation: viewing green space from a high-rise estate improves urban dwellers' wellbeing. *Urban Forestry & Urban Greening*. 2020;55:126846.

28. Ulrich RS, Bogren L, Gardiner SK, Lundin S. Psychiatric ward design can reduce aggressive behavior. *Journal of Environmental Psychology*. 2018;57:53-66.

29. Nadkarni NM, Hasbach PH, Thys T, Crockett EG, Schnacker L. Impacts of nature imagery on people in severely nature-deprived environments. *Frontiers in Ecology and the Environment*. 2017;15(7):395-403.

30. Beute F, de Kort YA. Salutogenic effects of the environment: review of health protective effects of nature and daylight. *Applied Psychology: Health and Well-Being*. 2014;6(1):67-95.

31. Konstantzos I, Sadeghi SA, Kim M, Xiong J, Tzempelikos A. The effect of lighting environment on task performance in buildings—a review. *Energy and Buildings*. 2020;226:110394.

32. Iwamoto J, Saeki K, Kobayashi M, et al. Lower incidence of in-hospital falls in patients hospitalized in window beds than nonwindow beds. *Journal of the American Medical Directors Association*. 2020;21(4):476-480.

33. Kellert SR, Heerwagen J, Mador M. *Biophilic Design: The Theory, Science, and Practice of Bringing Buildings to Life*. Wiley; 2008.

34. Bell JF, Wilson JS, Liu GC. Neighborhood greenness and 2-year changes in body mass index of children and youth. *American Journal of Preventive Medicine*. 2008;35(6):547-553.

35. Maas J, Verheij RA, de Vries S, Spreeuwenberg P, Schellevis FG, Groenewegen PP. Morbidity is related to a green living environment. *Journal of Epidemiology and Community Health*. 2009;63(12):967-973.

36. Astell-Burt T, Feng X. Urban green space, tree canopy and prevention of cardiometabolic diseases: a multilevel longitudinal study of 46 786 Australians. *International Journal of Epidemiology*. 2020;49:926-933.

37. Taylor MS, Wheeler BW, White MP, Economou T, Osborne NJ. Research note: Urban street tree density and antidepressant prescription rates—a cross-sectional study in London, UK. *Landscape and Urban Planning*. 2015;136:174-179.

38. Rojas-Rueda D, Nieuwenhuijsen MJ, Gascon M, Perez-Leon D, Mudu P. Green spaces and mortality: a systematic review and meta-analysis of cohort studies. *The Lancet Planetary Health*. 2019;3(11):e469-e477.

39. Kondo MC, Mueller N, Locke DH, et al. Health impact assessment of Philadelphia's 2025 tree canopy cover goals. *The Lancet Planetary Health*. 2020;4(4):e149-e157.

40. Reeve A, Nieberler-Walker K, Desha C. Healing gardens in children's hospitals: reflections on benefits, preferences and

design from visitors' books. *Urban Forestry & Urban Greening*. 2017.

41. Nicholas SO, Giang AT, Yap PLK. The effectiveness of horticultural therapy on older adults: a systematic review. *Journal of the American Medical Directors Association*. 2019;20(10):1351.e1351-1351.e1311.

42. Wichrowski M, Whiteson J, Haas F, Mola A, Rey MJ. Effects of horticultural therapy on mood and heart rate in patients participating in an inpatient cardiopulmonary rehabilitation program. *Journal of Cardiopulmonary Rehabilitation and Prevention*. 2005;25(5):270-274.

43. Soga M, Cox DT, Yamaura Y, Gaston KJ, Kurisu K, Hanaki K. Health benefits of urban allotment gardening: improved physical and psychological well-being and social integration. *International Journal of Environmental Research and Public Health*. 2017;14(1).

44. Bancroft C, Joshi S, Rundle A, et al. Association of proximity and density of parks and objectively measured physical activity in the United States: a systematic review. *Social Science & Medicine*. 2015;138:22-30.

45. Wood L, Hooper P, Foster S, Bull F. Public green spaces and positive mental health—investigating the relationship between access, quantity and types of parks and mental wellbeing. *Health & Place*. 2017;48:63-71.

46. Reuben A, Rutherford GW, James J, Razani N. Association of neighborhood parks with child health in the United States. *Preventive Medicine*. 2020;141:106265.

47. McCormack GR, Rock M, Toohey AM, Hignell D. Characteristics of urban parks associated with park use and physical activity: a review of qualitative research. *Health & Place*. 2010;16(4):712-726.

48. Slater S, Pugach O, Lin W, Bontu A. If you build it will they come? Does involving community groups in playground renovations affect park utilization and physical activity? *Environment and Behavior*. 2016;48(1):246-265.

49. Han B, Cohen DA, Derose KP, Marsh T, Williamson S, Raaen L. How much neighborhood parks contribute to local residents' physical activity in the City of Los Angeles: a meta-analysis. *Preventive Medicine*. 2014;69(Suppl 1):S106-S110.

50. National Park Service. Healthy Parks Healthy People. National Park Service, US Department of the Interior; 2020. Accessed October 16, 2021. https://www.nps.gov/subjects/healthandsafety/health-benefits-of-parks.htm

51. Parks Victoria. Healthy Parks Healthy People. No date. Accessed October 16, 2021. https://www.parks.vic.gov.au/healthy-parks-healthy-people

52. East Bay Regional Park District. Healthy Parks Healthy People. No date. Accessed October 16, 2021. https://www.ebparks.org/about/healthy_parks_healthy_people.htm

53. White MP, Elliott LR, Gascon M, Roberts B, Fleming LE. Blue space, health and well-being: a narrative overview and synthesis of potential benefits. *Environmental Research*. 2020;191:110169.

54. Hooyberg A, Roose H, Grellier J, et al. General health and residential proximity to the coast in Belgium: results from a cross-sectional health survey. *Environmental Research*. 2020;184:109225.

55. Ballesteros-Olza M, Gracia-de-Rentería P, Pérez-Zabaleta A. Effects on general health associated with beach proximity in Barcelona (Spain). *Health Promotion International*. 2020;35(6):1406-1414.

56. Chen Y, Yuan Y. The neighborhood effect of exposure to blue space on elderly individuals' mental health: a case study in Guangzhou, China. *Health & Place*. 2020;63:102348.

57. Lõhmus M, Balbus J. Making green infrastructure healthier infrastructure. *Infection Ecology & Epidemiology*. 2015;5:10.3402/iee.v3405.30082.

58. Venter ZS, Shackleton CM, Van Staden F, Selomane O, Masterson VA. Green Apart-

heid: urban green infrastructure remains unequally distributed across income and race geographies in South Africa. *Landscape and Urban Planning*. 2020;203:103889.

59. Williams TG, Logan TM, Zuo CT, Liberman KD, Guikema SD. Parks and safety: a comparative study of green space access and inequity in five US cities. *Landscape and Urban Planning*. 2020;201:103841.

60. Boyd F, White MP, Bell SL, Burt J. Who doesn't visit natural environments for recreation and why: a population representative analysis of spatial, individual and temporal factors among adults in England. *Landscape and Urban Planning*. 2018;175:102-113.

61. Pearson AR, Schuldt JP, Romero-Canyas R, Ballew MT, Larson-Konar D. Diverse segments of the US public underestimate the environmental concerns of minority and low-income Americans. *Proceedings of the National Academy of Sciences*. 2018;115(49):12429-12434.

62. Brown SC, Perrino T, Lombard J, et al. Health disparities in the relationship of neighborhood greenness to mental health outcomes in 249,405 U.S. Medicare beneficiaries. *International Journal of Environmental Research and Public Health*. 2018;15(3).

63. Mitchell R, Popham F. Effect of exposure to natural environment on health inequalities: an observational population study. *The Lancet*. 2008;372:1655-1660.

64. Black KJ, Richards M. Eco-gentrification and who benefits from urban green amenities: NYC's High Line. *Landscape and Urban Planning*. 2020;204:103900.

65. European Commission. Ecosystem services and green infrastructure. 2020. Accessed October 16, 2021. https://ec .europa.eu/environment/nature /ecosystems/index_en.htm

66. Nieuwenhuijsen MJ. Green Infrastructure and Health. *Annual Review of Public Health*. 2020;42:317-28.

CHAPTER 17

CLIMATE CHANGE, CITIES, AND HEALTH

José G. Siri and Katherine Britt Indvik

KEY POINTS

- Cities are a primary driver of climate change, including through the impacts of their built environments.
- Urban areas experience the most concentrated and extreme impacts of changing climate.
- Climate change affects the health and well-being of people in cities, and impacts will accelerate over time.
- Climate impacts are inequitably distributed, with marginalized and vulnerable populations experiencing the greatest health risks.
- Rethinking and restructuring the urban built environment can play a critical role in mitigating and adapting to climate change while maximizing health co-benefits.
- Creating healthy, sustainable, and equitable urban places in the context of a changing climate requires coordinated action across sectors and scales.

INTRODUCTION

On November 8, 2018, flames tore through Paradise, California, killing at least ninety people and destroying almost twenty thousand buildings. Emergency warning systems and evacuation orders failed due to downed cell phone towers and power lines. Planned evacuation routes were overwhelmed, and critical facilities, including police departments, hospitals, schools, and nursing homes, were consumed by flames (figure 17.1).

The Camp Fire that devastated Paradise was the deadliest and most destructive in California's history, yet just two years later, the 2020 wildfire season broke records again, burning nearly 4.4 million acres—more than 4 percent of the state's land surface. Meanwhile, the 2019–2020 Australian bush fire season engulfed more than forty-six million acres, killing at least thirty-four people and destroying more than thirty-five hundred homes. The economic, social, and ecological losses associated with widespread fire outbreaks are staggering, yet their record-breaking intensity is no coincidence.

Climate change is measurably altering wildfire regimes across the planet. Increasing temperatures and changing precipitation patterns extend fire risks over wider areas for longer periods. In the western United States, the average fire season is now two and half months longer than in the 1970s. Decades of fire suppression policies create dry, fuel-loaded forests that, together with the expansion of the built environment into the "wildland urban interface," increase risk and lead to more damaging fires.

Wildfires affect health and well-being directly and indirectly, and impacts can be far-reaching. Direct harms include injury or death incurred in fighting or escaping fires; respiratory ailments, from acute respiratory distress or failure following smoke inhalation to asthma and other problems related to air quality; and elevated risks of long-term

Figure 17.1. Vehicles destroyed by the Camp Fire, July 2019.
Source: Wikimedia Commons courtesy Frank Schulenburg. https://creativecommons.org/licenses/by-sa/4.0/deed.en

chronic illness such as cancer. Indirect harms include displacement or loss of livelihood; soil and water degradation; economic, food, and health care insecurity; mental health challenges; and cascading impacts on education and other socioeconomic factors.

Reducing fire risks requires long-term action to reduce greenhouse gas emissions and mitigate climate change. Short-term, the built environment can be adapted to reduce vulnerability and increase **resilience** (see chapter 18) through stricter building codes and retrofitting to improve construction techniques and materials, new zoning regulations to restrict construction in fire-prone areas, and community engagement and education. Fire control policies must also recognize the ecological function and systemic causes of fire, moving from a singular focus on suppression toward sustainable management.

Even with many structures built to updated, stricter standards, the Camp Fire destroyed more than 80 percent of homes in Paradise. Newer, fire-resistant houses, when packed together with older, more vulnerable structures, were unable to resist the inferno. Creating healthy and sustainable places in the short and long term requires placing climate change and impacts at the center of strategic and systems-oriented urban planning, design, and decision-making processes.

CLIMATE CHANGE

Climate is defined by the long-term average and volatility of weather variables, including temperature, precipitation, and wind. **Climate change** refers to a persistent shift in the state of the climate system.[1] Although it can result from natural processes, most modern climate change is **anthropogenic**, driven by human activity via **land use change** and the emission of **greenhouse gases (GHGs)** such as carbon dioxide (CO_2) and methane. GHGs trap heat in the atmosphere, a greenhouse effect that amplifies other climate change processes in cascading feedback loops. Atmospheric GHGs, particularly CO_2, have risen steadily for two centuries, accelerating after the middle of the twentieth century with rapidly increasing populations and development. Global average temperature has increased in parallel, by about 1.1°C (about 2°F) since preindustrial times.

Climate is a fundamental system that safeguards life on Earth, one of many threatened by human activity in the current epoch, known as the **Anthropocene**. The interdisciplinary field of **planetary health** aims to understand and address the complex interactions between health, human activity, and environmental change.[2] Globally, the risks, vulnerabilities, and impacts of climate change are increasing and are concentrated in urban areas.[3]

HOW CITIES AFFECT CLIMATE CHANGE

Most people live in cities—about 55 percent in 2018, projected to reach two-thirds by 2050[4]—and the spatial extent of urban areas is projected to triple between 2000 and 2030.[5] Cities concentrate industry and consumer demand and are directly or indirectly responsible for three-fourths of all energy use, related GHG emissions, and most land use change.[6]

Cities cause GHG emissions directly through activities within their boundaries and indirectly through their demand for energy, goods, and services produced elsewhere. Transporting energy and goods into and around urban areas generates further emissions. Multiple approaches exist for measuring these emissions. A **sector-based emissions** framework measures GHGs produced by different sectors of the economy. Most emissions ultimately derive from energy production and use, but individual sectors such as industry, transport, buildings, and agriculture all play critical roles (figure 17.2). Another framework measures **consumption-based emissions**, assigning emissions to the places where goods and services are consumed rather than where they are produced.

Sector-based and consumption-based methods overlap but yield different estimates of total emissions for a given city (figure 17.3).

Large, wealthy cities tend to have higher consumption-based than sector-based emissions because they demand more goods and services from beyond their borders.[7] Apportioning responsibility for emissions equitably among producers and consumers is a core issue in climate policy.

Both total GHG emissions and the relative importance of sources vary widely by city. Transport generates a large fraction of emissions where residents rely heavily on private automobiles. Where buildings and transport are more energy efficient or where meat consumption is high, food may represent a larger proportion of emissions. Cities can undertake GHG inventories to categorize and measure their emissions.

Cities also influence emissions through their impacts on land use. Reckless land use changes can drive deforestation, environmental degradation, and the loss of **carbon sinks** and thus limit the capacity of earth systems to offset anthropogenic GHG emissions. These links can be direct or can reflect cascading feedbacks. For example, cities have typically arisen where agricultural productivity is high. As they expand, productive landscapes are converted to nonproductive uses, soil and water resources are degraded, and microclimates are altered so that increasing amounts of less productive land are needed to feed growing urban populations. This drives deforestation in urban hinterlands, further reducing **carbon sequestration**.

Cities have environmental impacts beyond GHG emissions, including on biodiversity, water, and soil quality. The **ecological footprint** (table 17.1) measures the biologically productive land and water required to produce the resources consumed and to absorb the wastes generated by human activities.[8] The **carbon footprint**—that is, the land area required to counter anthropogenic GHG emissions—is the largest component of the ecological footprint.[9] Together, emissions inventories and carbon and ecological "footprinting" can identify

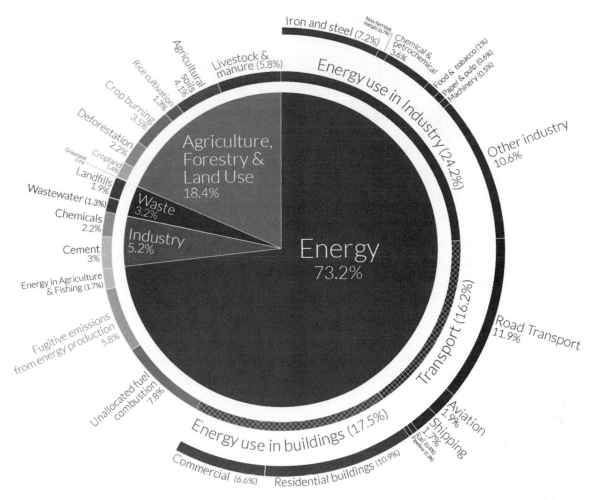

Figure 17.2. Global greenhouse gas emissions by sector, 2016. This figure expands on figure 1.5, emphasizing that energy use accounts for most greenhouse gas emissions and allocating energy use to industry, transport, buildings, and other activities. The built environment includes transport and buildings, but also manifests across this diagram, from cement and steel production (for infrastructure and buildings) to deforestation (a land use change).
Source: Adapted from Climate Watch, the World Resources Institute (2000), via Our World in Data.

those activities and actors with the greatest potential for mitigating climate change and other environmental impacts.

CLIMATE CHANGE AND HEALTH IN CITIES

Climate change affects human health directly (for example, through increasing temperatures or changing weather) and indirectly (through changes to the ecological and environmental systems on which humans depend). Social dynamics (including age, socioeconomic status, and access to public health infrastructure) interact with these effects to determine health impacts (figure 17.4).

City dwellers often face singular **risks** from climate change, especially where **hazards** are increasing in frequency and severity, where urban growth increases **exposure** to such hazards, and/or where rapid urbanization, the expansion of informal settlements, aging populations, or other demographic, economic, and cultural trends increase **vulnerability** (see chapter 18). The social, institutional, physical, and ecological characteristics of cities mediate climate-related health risks, which means that these risks manifest differently in different locations and among different populations. The following sections outline

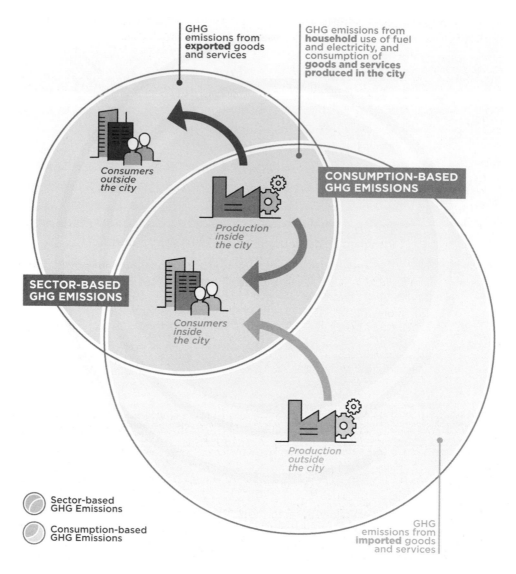

GHG emissions from **exported** goods and services

GHG emissions from **household** use of fuel and electricity, and consumption of **goods and services produced in the city**

Consumers outside the city

CONSUMPTION-BASED GHG EMISSIONS

Production inside the city

SECTOR-BASED GHG EMISSIONS

Consumers inside the city

Production outside the city

Sector-based GHG Emissions

Consumption-based GHG Emissions

GHG emissions from **imported** goods and services

Figure 17.3. Sector-based greenhouse gas emissions (in the upper circle) reflect production in a city, irrespective of where the products are consumed. Consumption-based greenhouse gas emissions (in the lower circle) reflect consumption within the city. The two approaches yield different estimates of a city's emissions. Overlap occurs when products are both produced and consumed within the city.
Source: C40 Cities

some of the main impacts of climate change on urban health.

Heat and Heat Waves

Cities are usually 2°C to 4°C (3.6°F to 7.2°F) warmer than surrounding areas, with nighttime differences sometimes reaching 5°C to 10°C (9°F to 18°F), because urban infrastructure absorbs and retains heat more readily than vegetation and natural surfaces and urban systems (for example, transport, air conditioning, industrial processes) emit waste heat. Cities with larger populations or urban sprawl tend to have more intense **urban heat island** effects (figure 17.5),[10,11] which vary widely in intensity within cities in relation to the layout of their physical, natural, and built environments.

Climate change is increasing the frequency and severity of extreme temperature events, especially heat waves. In some regions (for example, parts of the Middle East and South Asia), rising heat and humidity may exceed the limits of human physiological adaptation, casting doubt on their future habitability.[12]

Table 17.1. The ecological footprint is the biologically productive area (land and water) required to produce the resources consumed and absorb the wastes generated by human activities.

Footprint Component	What It Measures
Grazing land	The demand for grazing land to raise livestock for meat, dairy, leather, and wool products.
Forest product	The demand for forests to provide fuel wood, pulp, and timber products.
Fishing grounds	The demand for marine and inland water ecosystems needed to restock the harvested seafood and support aquaculture.
Cropland	The demand for land for food and fiber, feed for livestock, oil crops, and rubber.
Built-up land	The demand for biologically productive areas covered by infrastructure, including roads, housing, and industrial structures.
Carbon	Carbon emissions from fossil fuel burning and cement production. These emissions are converted into forest areas needed to sequester the emissions not absorbed by oceans. Carbon footprints account for forests' varying rates of carbon sequestration depending on the degree of human management, the type and age of forests, emissions from forest wildfires, and soil buildup and loss.

Source: WWF. *Living Planet Report—2018: Aiming Higher*. Grooten M, Almond REA, eds. WWF; 2018:30.

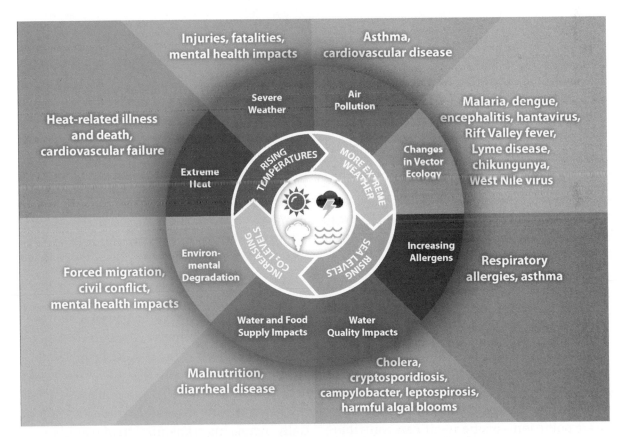

Figure 17.4. Some direct and indirect effects of climate change on health and well-being.
Source: CDC 2021. Reference to specific commercial products, manufacturers, companies, or trademarks does not constitute its endorsement or recommendation by the U.S. Government, Department of Health and Human Services, or Centers for Disease Control and Prevention.

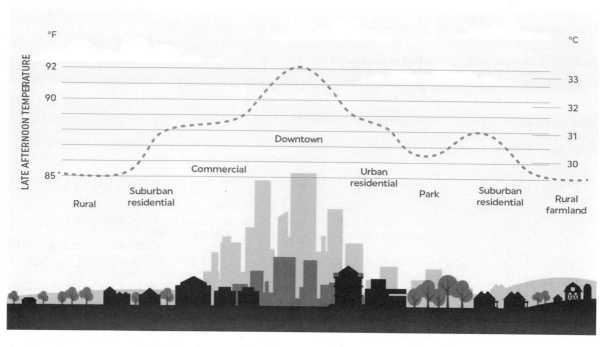

Figure 17.5. Transect of an urban heat island across a city. The city is hotter than the surrounding countryside, with the most intense urban heat island occurring in dense parts of the city, with dark surfaces (such as rooftops and asphalt) and little vegetation.
Source: Courtesy of the Urban Land Institute (Scorched: Extreme Heat and Real Estate); image adapted from data from the Heat Island Group, Lawrence Berkeley National Lab. https://knowledge.uli.org/en/Reports/ResearchReports/2019/Scorched

According to most projections, deaths, injury, and illness associated with extreme cold in cities (for example, hypothermia or worsening of preexisting cardiovascular or respiratory conditions) will decrease—although some regions may become more prone to intense cold events (for example, where polar jet streams become more variable). Overall reductions to cold-related impacts will be more than offset by increasing heat-related impacts.[11]

Heat can trigger acute conditions such as heat stroke, exacerbate underlying cardiovascular or respiratory disease, and contribute to kidney disease. It can also affect mental health and modify social interactions; for example, studies show that violence increases during hot weather.[12] Heat accelerates ozone formation and can worsen the severity and impacts of air pollution—ozone itself can contribute to chronic lung disease (see chapter 4). Heat can also stress critical water resources[13] and create conditions favorable to the spread of vector-borne diseases. Electric grids and water and sanitation systems are more likely to fail during heat waves.

Water Scarcity

An estimated 150 million people live in urban areas affected by chronic water shortages, a number projected to increase to nearly one billion by 2050.[14] Climate change will exacerbate urban water stress through increasingly severe and extended droughts, reductions in the snowpack that supplies water to many cities, and rising sea levels encroaching on freshwater aquifers in others.

Water scarcity and resulting acute and chronic dehydration can trigger a broad range of health problems.[15,16] Scarcity can also undermine personal hygiene and sanitation, potentially increasing transmission of waterborne, foodborne, dermatologic, and other infectious diseases. Variations in rainfall can cause crop and livestock failures, driving economic and food insecurity and under- and malnutrition. Drought can increase concentrations of airborne particles and toxins, posing particular risks to those with chronic underlying respiratory conditions. In combination with heat and built environment factors, drought can increase the risk and impacts of wildfires. Water scarcity can also drive conflict and migration—for example, where rural drought causes agricultural collapse—exacerbating existing social, economic, and environmental challenges.

Sea Level Rise, Precipitation, and Flooding

Many of the world's fastest growing and most populous cities are located on coasts or waterways, and the number of people living in low-elevation coastal zones may double between 2000 and 2060.[17] Meanwhile, average sea levels could rise three feet or more during this century—rendering some areas uninhabitable—and climate change will drive more frequent and severe precipitation events such as hurricanes, increasing the likelihood of floods and landslides.[18]

Increasing storms and floods mean more injuries, exposure-related health conditions, and deaths, as well as longer-term impacts mediated through ecosystems (for example, postdisaster infectious disease outbreaks) or societal systems (for example, mental health issues resulting from loss of livelihoods or assets). Populations displaced in acute events or through managed retreat and relocation processes where remaining is no longer feasible also face broad health and social impacts.[19]

Infectious Diseases

Climate-driven shifts in the distribution of pathogens and vectors and in human behavior can magnify the transmission or severity of disease. For example, changes in temperature or precipitation can extend the range of vector-borne diseases to populations with no immunity or prior knowledge about prevention. Dengue, a prototypical urban infectious disease, has increased thirty-fold since the early 1900s with development patterns and warming temperatures and will continue to expand its range.[20] Climatic change can also affect the survival or transmission of food- and waterborne pathogens, and acute rainfall events (or droughts) can drive outbreaks.

Cities likewise modify the relationships between humans and infectious pathogens. For example, urban **green space** and **blue space**, although often beneficial for health and climate (chapter 16), can foster vector survival. Urban-rural economic and social linkages and globalization foster the geographic spread of disease and expose people during travel. Poor housing, sanitation, and waste management, particularly in crowded, informal peri-urban settlements, can increase transmission risks, and urban deprivation or lack of resources increases vulnerability.

New infectious disease risks can also arise where expanding cities co-opt natural landscapes, amplify resource demands, or promote risky behaviors. Climate change–related environmental disruptions coupled with urban expansion can bring people into contact with new infectious agents, as vectors or reservoir species occupy new habitats, especially where cultural practices increase risk. Viral cross-species **spillover** is commonly associated with encroachment of human activity on wild landscapes and commodification of wild animals, including for dietary consumption—considered the likely origin of the COVID-19 pandemic.[21]

Food Insecurity

Over recent decades, dramatic increases in the use of nitrogen fertilizers and water resources, increasing automation and efficiency of agricultural techniques, and globalized supply chains have increased overall and per capita food supply, supporting growing urban populations. Meanwhile, urban preferences for meat, dairy, and other products have driven increasing emissions from food systems (see figure 17.2).

Food systems are affected by multiple climate factors, including increasing temperatures and CO_2, changing precipitation patterns, freshwater contamination, and increasingly frequent extreme events, which can negatively affect the productivity of pastoral or agricultural systems and the nutritional value of some products. For example, fruits and vegetables, essential to healthy diets, are especially vulnerable to changes in temperature and rainfall. Reduced production, infrastructure impacts, and other climate-driven disruptions are projected to severely affect food security and nutrition among city dwellers. Urban sprawl will displace existing farmland and drive additional land use change.[22]

Food scarcity or nutritional deficits can contribute to undernutrition, malnutrition, and starvation. Longer-term impacts may include wasting and stunting, immunological disruption, and irreversible neurocognitive deficits in children, and even heritable epigenetic changes. Like water scarcity, food insecurity can also drive migration and social unrest, with attendant stress and mental health challenges.

Migration

Climate plays an increasing role in inter- and intrasocietal conflicts and may already have displaced tens of thousands of people, including recent migration from sub-Saharan Africa to Europe and from Central America to the United States. Within this century, climate displacement could affect hundreds of millions of people.[23] Climate disruptions can force individuals or communities to relocate, often from rural to urban areas, increasing pressure on urban systems and services.

Migration can positively impact health by increasing access to resources and services and generating new social bonds and networks. More often, however, climate migrants and refugees face multiple adverse health impacts, both direct (including injury, food and water security, physical or mental stress, and communicable disease) and indirect (including disruptions to social and cultural systems and identity, education and professional development, economic security, and mental health). Furthermore, migrants are often excluded from formal social support and health systems.[24]

CLIMATE CHANGE AND EQUITY

Equity is fundamentally connected to climate change and health in cities. Globally and within cities, exposure, vulnerability, and the health impacts of climate change are inequitably distributed, as determined by economic, social, geographic, demographic, cultural, institutional, governmental, and environmental factors. For example, heat causes greater morbidity and mortality among some groups, such as older adults, pregnant women, homeless people, and outdoor workers.[25] Marginalized or otherwise disadvantaged groups are particularly exposed to and affected by climate-related risks and impacts; for example, poverty is associated with poorer housing conditions and greater exposure to heat, cold, pollution, extreme weather, floods, and infectious disease, in addition to reduced access to services, insurance, and social support.

Urban systems can reflect and sustain historical inequities, as explored in chapter 9; for example, the twentieth-century practice of **redlining** in US cities designated minority areas as financially risky, excluding them from many goods and services. A century later, these areas suffer disproportionately from heat and pollution.[26,27] Additionally, the most severe and immediate impacts of climate change, including health impacts, are concentrated in low- and middle-income countries, especially among people living in **informal settlements**.[28] Tropical and subtropical cities also face elevated risks, as do those on coastlines or floodplains or in arid regions.

The economic and industrial development processes that have driven climate change over time are also inherently inequitable.

Some nations bear enormous responsibility for the unchecked GHG emissions that facilitated their own historical economic development and current prosperity, while developing countries today face pressure to mitigate. Consumption-based emissions patterns reveal the persistence of these inequities, highlighting the extent of wealthier nations' demand for goods and services produced beyond their borders. The nations and regions most vulnerable to climate impacts are generally not those most responsible for climate change; for example, many small island developing states face serious or even total **loss and damage** from sea level rise despite trivial contributions to global emissions. Just as climate equity issues have roots in the past, they also stretch into the future; the greatest climate impacts will be felt by future generations, raising important questions about **intergenerational equity**.

The capacities and resources required to undertake effective mitigation or adaptation—and thereby to limit current and future risks—are also unequally distributed within and across societies.[28] Wealthy, healthy populations have greater adaptive capacity and experience fewer health impacts from climate change, whereas the costs of climate policies can be concentrated among lower-income, vulnerable populations (table 17.2).[29] For example, changes to building codes and housing policies can displace slum dwellers, and congestion taxes can disproportionately affect poorer populations. Recognition that climate risks and impacts are inequitably distributed has led to a focus on **climate justice**, which examines the ethical and political dimensions of climate change from the perspective of human rights.

CLIMATE CHANGE MITIGATION, ADAPTATION, AND CO-BENEFITS

Climate change action generally falls into the categories of **mitigation** and **adaptation**. Mitigation efforts seek to reduce ("mitigate") GHG emissions or to increase the capture of GHGs in carbon sinks and can be implemented by individuals, companies, cities, or countries. Mitigation can involve reductions in consumption, increases in efficiency, reductions in waste, or increases in the capture of CO_2 and other GHGs. Urban areas are key to achieving the cross-sectoral technological, managerial, and behavioral change required to avoid the most significant negative impacts of climate change on human and natural systems.[1]

Adaptation efforts aim to adjust ("adapt") human systems to the changing climate, reducing harmful impacts and capitalizing on beneficial opportunities. Adaptation can involve structural, institutional, ecological, or behavioral measures. Examples include heat wave preparedness plans, seawalls, and stormwater retention ponds. Just as ambitious mitigation will not prevent or reverse all change, adaptation cannot eliminate the long-term risks of climate change, and solutions are not equally accessible to all cities or populations. Nevertheless, effective adaptation measures reduce risks and can improve health. The degree to which cities can adapt to climate change (**adaptive capacity**) depends on the characteristics of their residents, buildings and other infrastructure, and governance, as well as the economic, social, and cultural activities and institutions concentrated within their boundaries.[3]

Many mitigation and adaptation actions directly improve human health. Likewise, health-promoting activities can contribute to climate change mitigation or adaptation. These immediate gains are known as **co-benefits**. For example, climate-driven restrictions on GHG emissions from factories may create improvements to local air quality that improve health (that is, that deliver co-benefits for health). Conversely, vehicles may be regulated to reduce people's exposure to noise and air pollution at the street level, providing co-benefits for climate mitigation. Each intervention benefits both climate and health, despite differences in the underlying motivation.

Table 17.2. Key climate risks and vulnerabilities in eight world cities.

City	Climate Risk	Vulnerabilities
New Orleans, USA	More frequent and severe storms, sea level rise (SLR), land subsidence	City below sea level, dependent on old infrastructure; inadequate housing, evacuation options, and access to services by the poor
Dhaka, Bangladesh	River flooding, waterlogging, SLR, high heat, waterborne disease	Rapid population growth, constrained land supply, large poor population (40% informal), reliance on river embankments
Medellin, Colombia	More frequent and severe precipitation, landslides, mudslides, drought, temperature rise, water supply	Development on slopes without adequate foundations, especially for 280,000 poor households
Metro Manila, Philippines	More frequent and severe storms, storm surge, subsidence, SLR, landslides, high heat	High flood risk, metro produces 40% of national GDP, has density of 18,000 people/km², and 102,000 families living in informal settlements along waterways
Santiago, Chile	Increasing water scarcity, intensifying urban flooding, rising urban heat island effects	Low-income neighborhoods vulnerable to drought, floods, and heat island effects
Jakarta, Indonesia	More frequent and severe storms and flooding, subsidence, SLR	Rapid population growth, projected floods threaten 4.5 million in North Jakarta and informal settlements along the coast and thirteen rivers
Boston, USA	More frequent and severe storms and precipitation, land subsidence, SLR, urban heat	Areas built on landfill, including low-income areas, are flood-prone
Surat, India	More frequent and severe storms, severe river flooding, coastal erosion due to SLR	Rapid urbanization, high rates of informality, floods threaten informal settlements and critical urban industries

Source: Anguelovski I, Shi L, Chu E, et al. Equity impacts of urban land use planning for climate adaptation: critical perspectives from the Global North and South. *Journal of Planning Education and Research.* 2016;36(3): 333-348.

Note: Anguelovski et al. (2016) found that land use planning for climate adaptation can exacerbate place-based social inequalities if interventions negatively affect or displace poor communities or protect and prioritize elite groups at the expense of the urban poor.

Complementary actions across multiple sectors are often key to achieving co-benefits.[30]

Implicitly, climate change mitigation and adaptation seek to safeguard human well-being over the long term, but health co-benefits and costs are rarely explicitly accounted for in climate action or urban planning. Achieving mitigation targets and adapting to climate change requires profound transformations to societies, economies, infrastructure, and public institutions. When the health-related costs of alternative actions or inaction are calculated, co-benefits for health can help motivate difficult but necessary changes.[31]

THE ROLE OF CITIES IN ADDRESSING CLIMATE CHANGE

Urban design and management play a major role in mitigating and adapting to climate change and maximizing co-benefits for health (table 17.3). Local governments are critical to providing infrastructure and services; to estab-

Table 17.3. Cities worldwide taking distinctive action to support climate change mitigation and adaptation while promoting health and well-being.

City	Description
Bristol, United Kingdom Climate emergency plan	In 2018, the city council became the first in the United Kingdom to declare a climate emergency, pledging to become carbon neutral by 2030.
Medellin, Colombia Green corridors	Since 2016, has embraced a network of green corridors along major roads and waterways. These spaces reduce the urban heat island effect, serve as a carbon sink, absorb pollutants, and improve biodiversity.
Chengdu, China Air pollution prevention plan	In 2013, began implementing a plan to reduce air pollution, successfully limiting emergency pollution events, increasing life expectancy, and cutting greenhouse gas emissions by nearly 50%.
Milan, Italy Low-emission zone	From 2019, enacted a low-emission zone, banning circulation of the most polluting vehicles in three-fourths of the city and applying increasingly stringent standards. Expected to reduce congestion, mitigate air pollution and greenhouse gas emissions, and reduce health risks.
Addis Ababa, Ethiopia Light rail system	In 2015, inaugurated the first light rail system in sub-Saharan Africa. The inner-city tram is electric and fueled by the country's almost exclusively renewable-based power grid.

lishing regulatory frameworks within which the choices made by individuals, groups, and companies serve climate goals; and to ensuring that key systems can withstand projected climate conditions and continue to provide essential services (see chapter 18). City action is also critical to ensuring equitable outcomes in the context of climate risks and supporting social capital, which can reduce vulnerability and help drive adaptive collective responses to change.[32] The following sections outline the roles of various urban sectors in responding effectively to climate change.

Land Use Planning and Management and Urban Form

Along with economic, cultural, and physical factors, urban planning and regulatory processes influence the physical form of cities—although not all urban areas are formally planned. Urban form in turn influences resource consumption, GHG emissions, and urban health. For example, **urban sprawl** (as well as **suburban sprawl**) leads to greater reliance on automobiles and more intense

urban heat islands—each of which contributes to greater GHG emissions and poorer health. Responsible urban planning that fosters healthy sustainability is a cornerstone of making healthy places.

Climate impacts and climate-related health risks depend in part on where buildings are sited or more generally on the relationship of urban infrastructure to the physical and natural environment. Zoning laws can promote adaptation and reduce risk, restricting construction where flooding, landslides, fires, or other hazards are likely (that is, accounting for current and future climate risks). Infrastructure location can also modulate environmental factors—providing shade, promoting wind corridors, or regulating microclimate, for example. Managing urban expansion and promoting mixed-use development can also reduce transport and energy needs, promote active transport, improve waste reduction and disposal, and facilitate the efficient and equitable provision of urban services. **Environmental impact assessments** are one tool for guiding development to limit environmental harms and mitigate emissions from land development.

When designed appropriately (for example, with vegetation suitable for future climate), green spaces (for example, parks) and blue spaces (for example, ponds or rivers) are effective tools for mitigating climate change and reducing its health impacts. Natural features mitigate emissions through carbon capture and can reduce cooling-related electricity demands and—where they encourage walking and cycling—transport emissions. Parks can be designed to become flood reservoirs, safeguarding other urban infrastructure; parks and rain gardens likewise absorb stormwater, reducing the burden on sewage and water treatment plants and preventing damage and injuries. Natural spaces reduce urban heat island effects and regulate temperatures, reducing heat stress. They also create opportunities for active transport and other physical activity, reducing obesity and cardiovascular disease while generating mental health benefits from recreation, socialization, and exposure to nature. Not least, natural features in urban hinterlands can provide important adaptation services, as where mangrove forests protect coastal areas from flooding, reduce erosion, and support ecosystem diversity.

Buildings and Energy Efficiency

Buildings contribute to climate change across their life spans, including through the **embodied carbon** in their components (that is, emissions released in securing and transforming their materials and putting them in place) and energy used during their operation and eventual disposal (figure 17.6). Accounting for these factors, buildings may account for around a third of global energy consumption.[1] Local microclimate and accessibility to transit, walking or cycling infrastructure, and other amenities also influence operational emissions from buildings. Critically, decisions about buildings today can lock in long-term costs or benefits.

Building impacts on climate can be reduced by using less-carbon-intensive materials and processes in construction, installation, and maintenance and by designing for energy efficiency—including using renewable energy sources, passive cooling and heating, and improved insulation. Building materials can also reduce climate risks; for example, permeable concrete reduces flooding, and reflective roofing materials reduce building heating. **Nature-based solutions** such as green roofs and walls can provide benefits similar to those of green and blue spaces (see above), such as cooling and reduced energy demand. Water efficiency improvements such as **graywater** recycling can reduce stress on water supplies and limit shortages during drought while improving sanitation access and quality. Features that guard against extreme events such as floods or fires can reduce immediate risks and subsequent needs for maintenance and reconstruction, lessening the risk of displacement and accompanying financial, physical, and mental health impacts. Most of these interventions involve design and construction of new buildings, but **retrofitting** of existing structures is also critical to climate mitigation. Just as for zoning, building design and materials requirements should consider both current and future climate.

With regard to health, higher energy efficiency can improve temperature and humidity regulation and thereby limit exposure to extreme temperatures, mold, and outdoor air pollution[31]—although energy efficiency can also increase exposure to indoor air pollutants absent adequate ventilation.[33] Insulation, passive ventilation, and placement (for example, of walls and windows) can likewise condition indoor temperature and air quality, even during extreme heat and other weather events. Green roofs and walls can limit exposure to heat and pollutants and foster mental health. Traditional and indigenous architecture—developed to manage weather risks without modern technologies—often incorporates

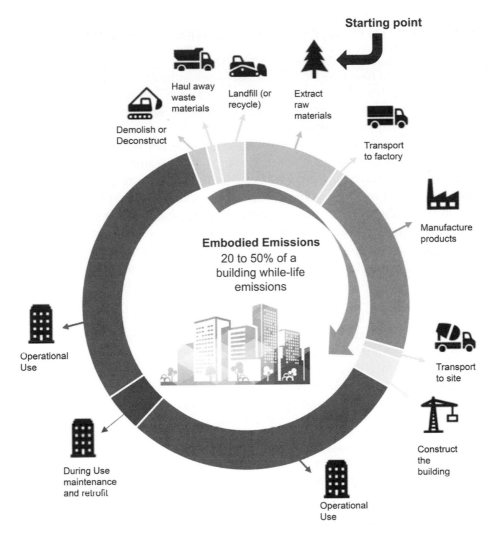

Figure 17.6. A life cycle approach to buildings' embodied emissions. Changes to the construction industry could cut emissions from buildings and industry by up to 44 percent by 2050. Source: C40 Cities

many of these elements and can contribute to solutions today.

Efforts to make buildings more sustainable have resulted in a proliferation of standards, codes, ratings, and certification systems (see chapter 22). The first **green building** rating system, in 1990, was the Building Research Establishment's Environmental Assessment Method (BREEAM). The best known and most widely used is the US Green Building Council's Leadership in Energy and Environmental Design (LEED) rating, but hundreds of programs cater to different contexts and needs.[34] Some systems include variables with implicit connections to health, and some have incorpo-rated health explicitly (see, for example, Taylor and Pineo[35] for a description of health in BREEAM); more often, though, implementation has focused on physical parameters while overlooking human impacts.

Transportation (See Chapter 11)

Transportation is responsible for more than 16 percent of global emissions (see figure 17.2). In urban areas, as much as two-thirds of such emissions could be eliminated by shifting short trips to active transport (for example, walking and bicycling).[31] Electrification of private and public vehicle fleets would yield additional reductions. Permanent, widespread

BOX 17.1 AIR POLLUTION, CLIMATE, AND HEALTH IN CITIES

Many pollutants that negatively impact human health are also greenhouse gases,[a] and efforts to reduce or mitigate air pollution have enormous potential to deliver health co-benefits, especially in urban areas. Globally, fine particulate matter (less than 2.5 microns in diameter, hence $PM_{2.5}$; see chapter 4) pollution from fossil fuel combustion contributed to 8.7 million premature deaths in 2018—one in five of all deaths that year.[b] Climate can affect the distribution, severity, and toxicity of air pollution in cities. Hot, sunny days can increase formation of ground-level ozone, and prolonged droughts can increase levels of suspended particulates such as pollen, smoke, and fluorocarbons, as well as the frequency and severity of forest fires, which in turn diminish air quality.[c] Through their influence on the distribution and growth of plants, molds, and bacteria and on dispersion of pollen, spores, and microorganisms, climate variables also impact the concentration, allergenicity, and timing of indoor and outdoor aeroallergen production, affecting allergic reactions, respiratory conditions such as asthma, and mental health.[d]

Air pollution mitigation efforts focus on reducing fossil fuel consumption and transitioning to clean, renewable energy—for example, in industries and vehicles. Technological solutions (at the household or industrial level) can also improve the efficiency of fuel combustion and reduce resulting pollution—for example, by transitioning to clean cookstoves in domestic settings. In some cases, filters can capture pollution or convert it into less toxic forms (as in the case of catalytic converters). Urban air quality monitoring has played a major role in motivating air pollution control activities and, by extension, climate mitigation. (See also chapter 4.)

REFERENCES

a. Smith KR, Woodward A, Campbell-Lendrum D, et al. Human health: impacts, adaptation, and co-benefits. In: Field CB, Barros VR, Dokken DJ, et al., eds. *Climate Change 2014: Impacts, Adaptation, and Vulnerability. Part A: Global and Sectoral Aspects.* Contribution of Working Group II to the Fifth Assessment Report of the Intergovernmental Panel on Climate Change. Cambridge University Press; 2014:709-754.

b. Vohra K, Vodonos A, Schwartz J, Marais EA, Sulprizio MP, Mickley LJ. Global mortality from outdoor fine particle pollution generated by fossil fuel combustion: results from GEOS-Chem. *Environmental Research.* 2021;195:110754. doi:10.1016/j.envres.2021.110754

c. Yu P, Xu R, Abramson MJ, Li S, Guo Y. Bushfires in Australia: a serious health emergency under climate change. *The Lancet Planetary Health.* 2020;4(1):e7-e8. doi:10.1016/S2542-5196(19)30267-0

d. Barata MML, Kinney PL, Dear K, et al. Urban health. In: *Climate Change and Cities: Second Assessment Report of the Urban Climate Change Research Network.* Cambridge University Press; 2018:363-398.

decarbonization of the transport sector requires compact urban planning and incentivization of active transport, a reduction in travel demand, expansion of public transit, and improved passenger vehicle efficiency and electrification.

Reducing transport emissions results in direct improvements to local air quality (as seen in cities worldwide at the height of COVID-19–related lockdowns), improving health (box 17.1). In adults of all ages, increased use of active transport can improve fitness, reduce risks of cardiovascular disease and cancer, and promote mental health and social connections. A shift to active transport also reduces road traffic accidents in most contexts. Generally, the benefits of active transport outweigh any potential negative consequences, but safety concerns and exposure to air pollution or heat can be significant barriers. Designing cities for shared, safe mobility requires interventions from multiple sectors.[30]

Food Systems (See Chapter 3)

Agriculture accounts for close to a fifth of global GHG emissions and drives significant land use change (see figure 17.2). The highly land-intensive and resource- and energy-inefficient production of red meat generates large quantities of GHGs, including methane. Meat and dairy consumption is driven by increasing incomes and urbanization, with city dwellers consuming significantly more red meat and other animal products than their rural counterparts. Reducing red meat consumption is an enormous opportunity for GHG mitigation and generates health co-benefits, including improved cardiovascular health and reduced diabetes, obesity, and associated risks.[3,36]

Roughly a third of food produced globally for human consumption is lost or wasted, generating massive amounts of avoidable emissions, exploiting land that could be devoted to other productive uses—including for carbon sequestration—and contributing to widespread food insecurity. Food waste also contributes to GHG emissions throughout formal or informal disposal processes and can promote the spread of infectious disease by feeding vermin populations or bringing humans into contact with pathogens or toxins.

Beyond impacts on emissions, the high efficiency and intensity of modern agricultural production systems cause erosion, soil and water degradation, and biodiversity loss. All contribute to conditions that increase vulnerability to climate change and threaten the long-term sustainability of food production.

Although not a replacement for the large-scale shifts in food systems required to address climate change, urban gardening can provide important mental and physical health and social benefits and create carbon sinks. Urban cultivation of crops suitable to local climates can reduce emissions generated in food transport while creating green, permeable spaces with their attendant benefits for mitigation and adaptation. Composting can also limit GHG emissions from food waste, provide natural fertilizer, and preserve soil systems.

Net Zero Commitments

Cities are increasingly pushing to achieve **net zero emissions**—that is, a state in which they contribute no net increase to atmospheric GHGs. Net zero planning is becoming common in specific sectors (for example, buildings, water, and waste), and cities are establishing timelines for achieving full **carbon neutrality**. For example, the World Green Building Council has called for commitments to operationally net zero buildings (that is, buildings that add no net GHGs to the atmosphere through their operation) and to eventually achieve true carbon neutrality over the life course of those buildings.[37]

As of 2020, more than eight hundred cities had committed to achieving net zero by 2050.[38] City-scale net zero requires a radical rethinking of how cities work, including reduced consumption, greater efficiency, shifts to renewable energy and active transport, and offsetting of unavoidable emissions.

GLOBAL RESPONSES AND COMMITMENTS

For decades, scientists have documented accelerating, human-driven changes to the global climate and the increasingly devastating impacts of these changes for current and future generations. A series of international institutions and agreements has emerged in response.

The 1992 Rio Earth Summit led to the United Nations Framework Convention on Climate Change (UNFCCC), an international treaty aiming to stabilize global GHG emissions at safe levels. Since 1995, UNFCCC signatories have met annually to assess progress and negotiate commitments during a Conference of the Parties (COP). As part of the 2015 Paris Agreement, established at the twenty-first COP, countries committed to establishing **nationally determined contributions**, or **NDCs**, toward the global goal of limiting warming to well under 2°C (3.6°F). Meanwhile, the UN **Sustainable Development Goals** (https://sdgs.un.org /goals), adopted in 2015, include a specific goal on climate action, and the 2019 UN Climate Action Summit urged government authorities and leaders of other sectors to present concrete plans for scaling up climate action.

Evidence compiled by the Intergovernmental Panel on Climate Change (IPCC) indicates that limiting average global temperature increase to 1.5°C (2.7°F) above preindustrial

Figure 17.7. Students march in support of global climate action in Australia, among millions worldwide taking part in similar marches before the 2019 UN Climate Action Summit.
Source: Wikimedia Commons courtesy Takver from Australia. https://creativecommons.org/licenses/by-sa/2.0 /deed.en

Table 17.4. Influential networks of cities and local governments involved in climate action.

Network Name	Membership	Description
C40	97 influential cities	Member cities commit to meeting the most ambitious goals of the Paris Agreement.
Global Covenant of Mayors for Climate and Energy (GCoM)	More than 10,000 cities and local governments	Members commit to ambitious, voluntary action to address climate and economic crises through local initiatives, innovative financing, and sustainable infrastructure.
World Organization of United Cities and Local Governments (UCLG)	Local, regional, and metropolitan governments, cities, and associations, representing 70% of the world's population	Advocates for a greater role for local and regional governments in international policy development, implementation, and reporting.
ICLEI-Local Governments for Sustainability	More than 1,750 local and regional governments	Members commit to developing policies and actions aligned with five sustainable urban development pathways: low emission, nature-based, circular, resilient, and equitable.
Cities Alliance	29 networks of local and national governments, nongovernmental organizations, multilateral organizations, private-sector actors, and global foundations	Supports urban programs to reduce poverty and gender inequality, including initiatives to address climate change and promote resilience and sustainability in cities and informal settlements.

levels is necessary to avoid the most significant negative impacts of climate change on human and natural systems,[1] yet despite efforts to mobilize and formalize more ambitious global climate action commitments, emissions have continued to rise at an alarming rate. Preventing irreversible, devastating changes requires rapid, transformative, systemic change—as activists, especially young people, have increasingly called for (figure 17.7).

CITY LEADERSHIP IN CLIMATE ACTION

In the face of insufficiently ambitious commitments to emissions reductions by national governments, cities and local governments have emerged as leaders of climate action. Urban areas can drive political, economic, and social transformations, and climate action at the local scale is significant; for example, the C40 Cities Climate Leadership Group is a network of the world's major cities committed to addressing climate change; its ninety-seven member cities account for one in twelve of all people and 25 percent of global gross domestic product.

Many networks of cities and local governments have committed to common climate goals and priorities (table 17.4). Some are convened and coordinated by philanthropic actors, others by member governments.

CONCLUSION

Climate change presents enormous and urgent challenges to human development. Cities concentrate the impacts of climate change, and these impacts are distributed inequitably across urban spaces and populations. Cities also concentrate the capacity of human systems to mitigate greenhouse gas emissions and adapt to change, and local governments are leading critical climate action in the face of inadequate national commitments. Building healthy urban places requires an understanding of how climate change affects health and how these health impacts are connected to the urban built environment. The most effective responses to climate change will maximize the health co-benefits of mitigation and adaptation actions.

DISCUSSION QUESTIONS

1. What are the most important ways in which cities contribute to climate change?
2. What are some of the direct and indirect impacts of climate change (for example, heat, hurricanes, drought) on urban health?
3. What health equity issue related to urban climate impacts resonates most with you, and why?
4. Give several examples of adaptation and mitigation actions you might take in your city.
5. Describe a health co-benefit climate mitigation or adaptation actions not mentioned in this chapter.

DISCLOSURE OF COMPETING INTERESTS

José G. Siri and Katherine Britt Indvik disclose no competing interests.

REFERENCES

1. Masson-Delmotte V, Zhai P, Pörtner HO, et al., eds. *Global Warming of 1.5° C. An IPCC Special Report on the Impacts of Global Warming of 1.5°C above Pre-Industrial Levels and Related Global Greenhouse Gas Emission Pathways, in the Context of Strengthening the Global Response to the Threat of Climate Change, Sustainable Development, and Efforts to Eradicate Poverty*. Intergovernmental Panel on Climate Change (IPCC) and World Meteorological Organization (WMO); 2018.

2. Myers S, Frumkin H, eds. *Planetary Health: Protecting Nature to Protect Ourselves*. Island Press; 2020.

3. Revi A, Satterthwaite DE, Aragón-Durand F, et al. Urban Areas. In: Field CB, Barros VR, Dokken DJ, et al., eds. *Climate Change 2014: Impacts, Adaptation, and Vulnerability. Part A: Global and Sectoral Aspects. Contribution of Working Group II to the Fifth Assessment Report of the Intergovernmental Panel on Climate Change*. Cambridge University Press; 2014:535-612.

4. United Nations Department of Economic and Social Affairs, Population Division. *World Urbanization Prospects: The 2018 Revision* (ST/ESA/SER.A.420). United Nations; 2019.

5. Seto KC, Güneralp B, Hutyra LR. Global forecasts of urban expansion to 2030 and direct impacts on biodiversity and carbon pools. *Proceeding of the National Academy of Sciences*. 2012;109(40):16083-16088.

6. Coalition for Urban Transitions. *Climate Emergency, Urban Opportunity*. Coalition for Urban Transitions; 2019. Accessed July 13, 2021. https://urbantransitions.global/en/publication/climate-emergency-urban-opportunity/

7. C40 Cities. Consumption-Based GHG Emissions of C40 Cities. C40 Cities. 2018. Accessed December 15, 2021. https://resourcecentre.c40.org/resources/consumption-based-ghg-emissions

8. Grooten M, Almond REA, eds. *Living Planet Report—2018: Aiming Higher*. World Wildlife Fund; 2018.

9. Mancini MS, Galli A, Niccolucci V, et al. Ecological footprint: refining the carbon footprint calculation. *Ecological Indicators*. 2016;61:390-403. doi:10.1016/j.ecolind.2015.09.040

10. Stone B, Hess JJ, Frumkin H. Urban form and extreme heat events: are sprawling cities more vulnerable to climate change than compact cities? *Environmental Health Perspectives*. 2010;118(10):1425-1428.

11. Heaviside C, Macintyre H, Vardoulakis S. The urban heat island: implications for health in a changing environment. *Current Environmental Health Reports*. 2017;4(3):296-305. doi:10.1007/s40572-017-0150-3

12. Raymond C, Matthews T, Horton RM. The emergence of heat and humidity too severe for human tolerance. *Science Advances*. 2020;6(19):eaaw1838. doi:10.1126/sciadv.aaw1838

13. van Staden R. Climate Change: Implications for Cities. Key Findings from the Intergovernmental Panel on Climate Change Fifth Assessment Report. European Climate Foundation, ICLEI—Local Governments for Sustainability, University of Cambridge's Judge Business School and Institute for Sustainability Leadership; 2014.

14. McDonald RI, Green P, Balk D, et al. Urban growth, climate change, and freshwater availability. *Proceedings of the National Academy of Science*. 2011;108(15):6312-6317.

15. Maughan RJ. Hydration, morbidity, and mortality in vulnerable populations. *Nutrition Reviews*. 2012;70(Suppl 2):S152-S155.

16. Frumkin H, Das MB, Negev M, et al. Protecting health in dry cities: considerations for policy makers. *BMJ*. 2020;371:m2936

17. Neumann B, Vafeidis AT, Zimmermann J, Nicholls RJ. Future coastal population growth and exposure to sea-level rise and

coastal flooding—a global assessment. *PLOS ONE.* 2015; 10(3):e0118571. doi:10.1371/journal.pone.0118571

18. Siegert M, Alley RB, Rignot E, Englander J, Corell R. Twenty-first century sea-level rise could exceed IPCC projections for strong-warming futures. *One Earth.* 2020;3(6):691-703.

19. Schwerdtle P, Bowen K, McMichael C. The health impacts of climate-related migration. *BMC Medicine* 2018;16:1.

20. Ebi KL, Nealon J. Dengue in a changing climate. *Environmental Research.* 2016;151: 115-123. doi:10.1016/j.envres.2016.07.026

21. Volpato G, Fontefrancesco MF, Gruppuso P, Zocchi DM, Pieroni A. *Baby Pangolins on My Plate: Possible Lessons to Learn from the COVID-19 Pandemic.* Springer; 2020.

22. Mbow C, Rosenzweig C, Barioni LG, et al. Food security—special report on climate change and land. In: Shukla PR, Skea J, Calvo Buendia E, et al., eds. *Climate Change and Land: An IPCC Special Report on Climate Change, Desertification, Land Degradation, Sustainable Land Management, Food Security, and Greenhouse Gas Fluxes in Terrestrial Ecosystems.* IPCC; 2019.

23. de Sherbinin A. Impacts of Climate Change as Drivers of Migration. migrationpolicy.org. Published October 20, 2020. Accessed February 21, 2021. https://www.migrationpolicy.org/article/impacts-climate-change-drivers-migration

24. Schwerdtle PN, McMichael C, Mank I, Sauerborn R, Danquah I, Bowen KJ. Health and migration in the context of a changing climate: a systematic literature assessment. *Environmental Research Letters.* 2020;15(10):103006.

25. Singh R, Arrighi J, Jjemba E, Strachan K, Spires M, Kadihasanoglu A. *Heatwave Guide for Cities.* Red Cross Red Crescent Climate Centre; 2019.

26. Hoffman JS, Shandas V, Pendleton N. The effects of historical housing policies on resident exposure to intra-urban heat:

a study of 108 US urban areas. *Climate.* 2020;8(1):12. doi:10.3390/cli8010012

27. Nardone A, Casey JA, Morello-Frosch R, Mujahid M, Balmes JR, Thakur N. Associations between historical residential redlining and current age-adjusted rates of emergency department visits due to asthma across eight cities in California: an ecological study. *The Lancet Planetary Health.* 2020;4(1):e24-e31. doi:10.1016/S2542-5196(19)30241-4

28. Smith KR, Woodward A, Campbell-Lendrum D, et al. Human health: impacts, adaptation, and co-benefits. In: Field CB, Barros VR, Dokken DJ, et al., eds. *Climate Change 2014: Impacts, Adaptation, and Vulnerability. Part A: Global and Sectoral Aspects. Contribution of Working Group II to the Fifth Assessment Report of the Intergovernmental Panel on Climate Change.* Cambridge University Press; 2014:709-754.

29. Anguelovski I, Shi L, Chu E, et al. Equity impacts of urban land use planning for climate adaptation: critical perspectives from the Global North and South. *Journal of Planning Education and Research.* 2016;36(3):333-348. doi:10.1177/0739456X16645166

30. Younger M, Morrow-Almeida HR, Vindigni SM, Dannenberg AL. The built environment, climate change, and health: opportunities for co-benefits. *American Journal of Preventive Medicine.* 2008;35(5):517-526. doi:10.1016/j.amepre.2008.08.017

31. United Nations Environment Programme. *Emissions Gap Report 2019.* UNEP; 2019.

32. Kithiia J. Old notion—new relevance: setting the stage for the use of social capital resource in adapting East African coastal cities to climate change. *International Journal of Urban Sustainable Development.* 2010;1(1-2):17-32. doi:10.1080/19463131003607630

33. Milner J, Hamilton I, Woodcock J, et al. Health benefits of policies to reduce carbon emissions. *BMJ.* 2020;368. doi:10.1136/bmj.l6758

34. Vierra S. *Green Building Standards and Certification Systems. Whole Building Design Guide.* National Institute of Building Sciences, 2019. Accessed July 13, 2021. https://www.wbdg.org/resources /green-building-standards-and -certification-systems

35. Taylor T, Pineo H. *Health and Wellbeing in BREEAM.* BRE Global; 2015. Accessed July 13, 2021. https://www.breeam.com /filelibrary/Briefing%20Papers/99427 -BREEAM-Health---Wellbeing-Briefing .pdf

36. Willett W, Rockström J, Loken B, et al. Food in the Anthropocene: The EAT-Lancet Commission on healthy diets from sustainable food systems. *The Lancet.* 2019;393(10170):447-492.

37. World Green Building Council. The Net Zero Carbon Buildings Commitment. World Green Building Council; Published 2018. Accessed December 15, 2021. https: //www.worldgbc.org/

38. Data-Driven EnviroLab and NewClimate Institute. *Accelerating Net Zero: Exploring Cities, Regions, and Companies' Pledges to Decarbonise.* Data-Driven EnviroLab and NewClimate Institute; 2020. Accessed October 26, 2021. https://newclimate .org/2020/09/21/accelerating-net-zero -exploring-cities-regions-and -companies-pledges-to-decarbonise/

CHAPTER 18

COMMUNITY RESILIENCE AND HEALTHY PLACES

José G. Siri, Katherine Britt Indvik, and Kimberley Clare O'Sullivan

KEY POINTS

- Resilience is the capability of a person, structure, or system to withstand shocks or stressors while maintaining or recovering function and continuing to adapt and improve.
- Resilient built environments are critical to safeguarding health and health equity from social, economic, environmental, and other shocks and therefore to long-term health, safety, and sustainability.
- Resilience is multifactorial—it requires integrated actions by different stakeholders across sectors and scales.
- Individual elements or characteristics are not sufficient to predict resilience—it emerges from complex interactions within a socioecological system.
- A structure or system can be resilient to some risks for some people, but not for others—resilience is not always equitably distributed.

INTRODUCTION

On October 2, 2016, Camila and Pablo looked up to the blue sky above Baracoa, Cuba, as their radio issued urgent warnings. Hurricane Matthew, the first Category 5 storm to hit the region in ten years, was headed straight for them.

Later that same day, local civil defense unit volunteers visited to confirm the official evacuation order. Camila finished securing boards over the windows while Pablo phoned his elderly parents in Havana to confirm that they were ready to evacuate if necessary. Soon, the couple headed to a local shelter to wait out the storm with their neighbors.

Matthew made landfall on the evening of October 4, and the wind, rain, waves, and storm surge wreaked havoc. The next day, residents emerged to massive destruction. In Baracoa alone, more than 24,000 of 27,000 dwellings were destroyed or severely damaged. Similar devastation was seen across the region.

There was, however, one notable difference: in Haiti, more than five hundred people were killed; across the southern United States, forty-seven had perished. In Cuba, the site of Matthew's strongest blow, not one person died as a direct result of the hurricane. How did one of the poorest countries in the Western hemisphere escape the severest human costs of this extreme event?

Cuba has repeatedly demonstrated **resilience** in the face of natural disasters, while nearby territories, including the United States, have suffered substantial loss of life and property during the same events.[1] Eight major hurricanes in Cuba from 1996 to 2005 resulted in only seventeen deaths.

Cuba's resilience and disaster risk reduction strategies are rooted in **preparedness** and

Figure 18.1. A man inspecting the wreckage of Hurricane Matthew in Baracoa, Cuba, which made landfall in October 2016. When the hurricane hit the eastern tip of Cuba, nearly 380,000 people were evacuated and thousands of homes damaged, but there were no reports of deaths.
Source: RealyEasyStar/Daniele Bellucci/Alamy Stock Photo

trust (figure 18.1).[2] National disaster management systems have invested in institutional, health, and educational measures to develop social capital, knowledge, and physical infrastructure. From childhood, all Cubans learn how to prepare for and respond to hurricanes and other disasters. In addition to school and community education programs, lists of elderly, disabled, and other vulnerable individuals are maintained so that evacuation and relief efforts can focus on those most in need. Cubans trust that shelters are safe and respect and comply with evacuation orders.

Cuba's 2017 climate change action plan, *Tarea Vida* (Project Life), aims to improve the resilience of the built environment.[3] It includes measures related to land use, location, and building standards, among others. Not all these actions are uncontroversial, and important questions about the economic, social, and cultural implications of relocation, in particular, persist. Nevertheless,

lessons from Cuba and elsewhere show that more resources do not automatically generate more resilience. Instead, building resilient places requires an understanding of social, economic, and environmental systems and their interconnections.

Resilience in the places we live, work, and play is increasingly important to our health as climate change, urbanization, and other global trends pose novel challenges to our societies and welfare. The following sections explore resilience as a critical component of making healthy places.

THE HISTORY OF RESILIENCE THINKING

Throughout history, societies have worked to limit risks, safeguard human lives, and learn from disasters. The Great Fire that scorched Rome in 64 AD, for example, led to wider streets and new firefighting measures.[4] Design considerations to extend useful life, duplicate critical structural elements (**redundancy**), and allow for remediation of damage (**reparability**) have likewise been part of tacit knowledge for enhancing building resilience for centuries.[5]

For just as long, however, communities have faced barriers to implementing resilience strategies: after London's Great Fire in 1666, politics, property rights, and financing concerns limited the extent of reforms.[6] Moreover, risks evolve constantly—in London, despite greater awareness, fire remained a serious risk for centuries in the face of emerging economic and development trends.[7]

The concept of resilience emerged formally within engineering and physical sciences in the 1850s and has evolved in parallel across multiple disciplines, including ecology, psychology, and disaster risk reduction and response.[8] Although alternate definitions share common elements (box 18.1), each applies a distinct viewpoint. For example:

- Engineering and physical sciences use resilience to describe the ability of a material, structure, or system to "bend without breaking" and return to a state of equilibrium.[9]
- In ecology, resilience refers to the capacity of an ecosystem to absorb change and persist under evolving conditions.[9]
- Psychology and social sciences characterize resilience among people and communities by their capacity to withstand, respond, and recover from trauma or stresses.[9]
- In disaster risk reduction and response, resilience is the ability of a community or society to preserve and restore essential functions and services in the face of acute shocks.[10]

RESILIENCE TODAY: SUSTAINABLE DEVELOPMENT, CLIMATE CHANGE, AND DISASTER RISK REDUCTION

In recent decades, resilience thinking has increasingly been applied to the study of complex **social ecological systems**, which involve interconnected interactions between human activities and the natural environment.[11] Along with an expanding recognition of human environmental impacts, the integration of resilience thinking within development and planning processes has contributed to a new focus on **sustainable development**, or development that "meets the needs of the present without compromising the ability of future generations to meet their own needs."[12(p37)]

Resilience and **sustainability** are closely related. A system, structure, or process is sustainable if it can maintain function over time without depleting or damaging the inputs on which it depends or generating hazards faster than they can be remediated. To do so, it must also withstand challenges and adapt to new needs—that is, it must be resilient. Sustainability always depends on resilience over the long term, but resilience becomes more critical as the frequency and severity of challenges increases.

Risk is the product of **hazard**, **exposure**, and **vulnerability**. A hazard is a shock or a stressor that can cause loss of function. Exposure is the probability that an individual, structure, community, or system will encounter a hazard. Vulnerability is the likelihood of loss of function given exposure to a hazard. For example, heavy rainfall events are hazards that impact many cities. Within a particular city, some residents will be more exposed than others—for example, those living in low-lying areas prone to flooding. Of those exposed residents who experience a flood, some will be more vulnerable than others—for example, those who cannot afford flood-resilient housing or who are mobility impaired. Resilient systems reduce exposure and vulnerability and avoid contributing to the worsening of existing hazards or the emergence of new ones.

In the context of **climate change** (see chapter 17), resilience refers to the ability of social-ecological systems to withstand and adapt to climate hazards, including extreme events (for example, droughts or hurricanes) and more gradual changes (for example, sea level or temperature rise). **Adaptation**—anticipating future climate and responding in a way

BOX 18.1 RESILIENCE: DEFINITIONS AND FEATURES

At its core, resilience refers to the properties or capabilities that determine how and to what extent an individual, structure, community, society, or system responds, recovers, and persists when faced with shocks or changes (figure 18.2). Often, resilience also refers to the capacity to adapt, evolve, and improve to reduce the impacts of future shocks. The properties that determine resilience can be physical, mental, institutional, economic, or social, among others; and a shock or change can be acute, repeated, or chronic, originating from natural or societal causes.

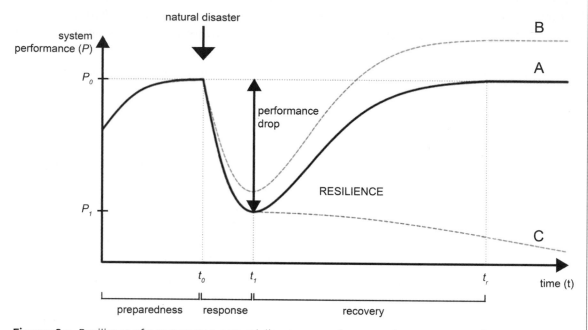

Figure 18.2. Resilience of a system to a natural disaster, mapping several recovery scenarios. A system with a given level of performance (P_o) experiences a disaster at time t_o, during which performance declines to P_f. The time of most significant system failure is designated by t_f, whereas the time to recover to the original state of performance (in scenario A) is designated by t_r. Note that the system may recover to its original state (A), improve to a higher state (B), or lose function altogether (C). Resilience can be characterized by the speed and depth of the performance drop, the speed and extent of recovery, and the extent of improvement over the initial state of performance. Often, a more resilient system will experience a smaller performance drop, quicker recovery, and greater adaptation, as shown here for scenario B. Although resilience operates during and after a shock—in this case, a natural disaster—it is determined by actions taken throughout preparedness, response, and recovery.
Source: Adapted from Rus K, Kilar V, Koren D. Resilience assessment of complex urban systems to natural disasters: a new literature review. *International Journal of Disaster Risk Reduction*. 2018; 31:311-330. With permission from Elsevier.

Resilience depends on place-specific interactions between people and their environments and presents unique challenges in different contexts. Nevertheless, certain features shape the resilience of diverse systems to a wide range of shocks and disruptions (table 18.1).

BOX 18.1 CONTINUED

Table 18.1. Key features of resilient, healthy places.

Feature	Description
Adaptation	Recovering from shocks in ways that account for changing context and continually diminish future risk.
Anticipation	Predicting and assessing future risks and planning for all scenarios, including failure of one or more system components. Implementing early warning systems.
Collaboration	Fostering improved understanding and cooperation among individuals, organizations, and systems.
Communication	Providing for timely, effective information flows among all stakeholders before, during, and after shocks.
Diversity	Making use of a wide variety of resources, strategies, and stakeholders to explore and test different potential strategies and solutions and building on identified strengths.
Equity	Ensuring that everyone is protected from shocks and included in recovery and adaptation.
Flexibility	Creating decision-making structures and response systems able to react and adapt quickly and creatively to unexpected stressors.
Learning	Documenting and analyzing successes and failures to reduce future risks and ensuring that mechanisms are in place to support these processes.
Participation	Engaging individuals broadly and applying their diverse knowledge, experience, cultural perspectives, needs, and priorities in planning and decision-making.
Polycentricity	Vesting decision-making power in more than one place, to better respond to local needs and avoid bottlenecks or system failures during crises.
Redundancy	Duplicating functions, so one failing element does not lead to system failure. Including elements that fulfill multiple environmental, social, and economic functions.
Social capital	Promoting civil society structures and interpersonal relationships to facilitate productive, concerted action before, during, and after shocks.

Note: These are a few of many features that contribute to resilience in healthy places. For more information, see:

Norris FH, Stevens SP, Pfefferbaum B, Wyche KF, Pfefferbaum RL. Community resilience as a metaphor, theory, set of capacities, and strategy for disaster readiness. *American Journal of Community Psychology*. 2008;41(1–2):127-150.

Bahadur Aditya V, Ibrahim M, Tanner T. Characterising resilience: unpacking the concept for tackling climate change and development. *Climate and Development*. 2013;5(1):55-65.

Hassler U, Kohler N. Resilience in the built environment. *Building Research & Information*. 2014;42(2): 119-129.

Schipper L, Langston L. A comparative overview of resilience measurement frameworks: analysing indicators and approaches. Working Paper 422. Overseas Development Institute, 2015. https://www.odi.org/publications/9632-comparative-overview-resilience-measurement-frameworks-analysing-indicators-and-approaches

Sharifi A, Yamagata Y. Resilience-oriented urban planning. In: Yamagata Y, Sharifi A, eds. *Resilience-Oriented Urban Planning: Theoretical and Empirical Insights*. Springer International; 2018: 3-27. https://doi.org/10.1007/978-3-319-75798-8_1

that reduces harm or increases benefits (see chapter 17)—is an essential component of resilience thinking.

Resilience thinking is prominent in **disaster risk reduction**, which seeks to prevent new disaster risks, reduce existing risks, and manage residual risks to safeguard lives and livelihoods. Disasters cause destruction of the built and natural environment, direct health impacts and loss of life, immediate economic losses, and long-term disruption of lives and livelihoods. These impacts are usually worst among vulnerable populations that already face other risks, particularly in informal urban settings.[13,14]

Resilience provides a conceptual framework for developing policies and strategies to reduce disaster risks (box 18.2), prepare for the unavoidable, and support response and **recovery**, exemplified by the slogan "**Build Back Better**," with a focus on sustainability and equity. Effective resilience building encompasses the built environment, including buildings, spaces, and places, as well as the individuals, communities, and other systems that use and depend on them. In the context of increasing complexity, uncertainty, and change, our well-being and that of the natural systems on which we rely depend on designing and creating healthy, resilient places.

BOX 18.2 THE SENDAI FRAMEWORK FOR DISASTER RISK REDUCTION

Resilience increasingly features in international agreements and national and subnational policies, programs, and plans, including those supporting disaster risk reduction and emergency management and response.[a] Many key features of resilience overlap with emergency management and response, including anticipation, collaboration, communication, learning, and redundancy (see table 18.1 in box 18.1).

The Sendai Framework for Disaster Risk Reduction 2015–2030[b] was developed by the United Nations Office for Disaster Risk Reduction. Adopted in 2015, it recognizes the need to prioritize physical and mental health and well-being. It sets targets to assess progress and support ambitious disaster risk-reduction goals and emphasizes improving understanding of disaster risk; strengthening disaster risk governance; investing in disaster risk reduction; and enhancing preparedness for more effective disaster response, recovery, rehabilitation, and reconstruction (table 18.2).

Table 18.2. The seven targets of the Sendai Framework for Disaster Risk Reduction 2015–2030.

Substantially reduce …	Substantially increase …
A. Global disaster mortality	E. Number of countries with national and local disaster risk reduction strategies by 2020
B. Number of affected people	
C. Economic loss in relation to gross domestic product	F. International cooperation to developing countries
D. Damage to critical infrastructure and services disruption	G. Availability and access to early warning systems and disaster risk reduction information

Source: United Nations Office for Disaster Risk Reduction. preventionweb.com

REFERENCES

a. Djalante R, Thomalla F, Sinapoy MS, Carnegie M. Building resilience to natural hazards in Indonesia: progress and challenges in implementing the Hyogo Framework for Action. *Natural Hazards*. 2012;62(3):779–803. https://doi.org/10.1007/s11069-012-0106-8

b. United Nations Office for Disaster Risk Reduction (UNISDR). Sendai Framework for Disaster Risk Reduction 2015–2030. UNISDR; 2015. http://www.unisdr.org/we/coordinate/sendai-framework

WHAT IS A RESILIENT, HEALTHY PLACE?

A resilient, healthy place is one where infrastructure, behavior, and policy interact to safeguard health during shocks or change and where mechanisms are in place to recover, adapt, and transform in ways that reduce future risk and improve health. Such places afford health to all, recognizing that vulnerabilities and exposures are unequally distributed and that risk varies by socioeconomic status, class, caste, sex and gender, ethnicity, disability, migration status, and other characteristics.

Critically, resilient, healthy places not only anticipate risks, but also plan for failure, assessing and minimizing health impacts and inequalities should one or more system components break down. For example, flood management systems may be designed so that excess runoff is directed to uninhabited areas. Buildings may be designed to support health even if water, fuel, heat, or power are lost for extended periods (**passive survivability**). Disaster response efforts may be concentrated in areas of high vulnerability and deprivation.

Ideally, healthy places are resilient to a range of shocks and changes. Some characteristics of individuals and systems support key features of resilient, healthy places across diverse contexts, scales, and hazards (see table 18.1), such as healthy, educated populations; social equity, social capital, and civic trust; efficient, transparent, accountable governments; and surge capacity in critical systems. Other characteristics are specific to place-based risks and stressors, including recurring hazards like floods, or unique events such as sudden, large-scale in-migration.

The resilience of healthy places is an **emergent property**. It emerges from the interactions between infrastructure, behavior, and policy and cannot be evaluated with reference to any individual factor or element. In a sense, infrastructure can be thought of as the "hardware" and behavior and policy as the "software" of resilience—both are essential. For example, a city's resilience to drought depends not only on appropriate infrastructure (for example, reservoirs), but on how people behave when water is scarce, on resource management plans, and on how effectively such plans are implemented (figure 18.3). Similarly, a city full of resilient individuals may not be resilient if supporting elements such as networks, policies, and infrastructure are absent or inadequate.

Healthy Resilience Across Scales

Resilient, healthy places require action at different scales and cross-scale coordination. Consider measures to reduce the health impacts of a heat wave:

- *Individuals* can choose and time activities to reduce their heat exposure, identify the location of cooling centers, and check on vulnerable contacts.
- *Communities* can maintain cooling centers and deploy health workers to high-risk areas.
- *Cities* can create parks and water features, use light surfaces to lower temperatures, and develop heat action plans clarifying responsibilities and thresholds for action.
- *Countries* can upgrade electric grids and decentralize electricity generation to better meet demand during extreme heat events, while conducting long-term risk assessments and designating resources for healthy, heat-sensitive development.
- *Globally*, treaties and other agreements can reduce emissions to mitigate the intensity and frequency of heat waves.

Coordinating actions across scales requires good governance, effective communication and collaboration, and robust social networks. Action at each level can depend on action and embedded inequities at other levels. For example, without well-designed city-level action plans, communities may lack legal authority or capacity to deploy resources to the populations most in need during crises. Moreover, higher-scale interventions and resource allocation may be critical to redressing historical imbalances affecting particularly vulnerable or exposed populations, which otherwise may be self-perpetuating—this can be especially

Figure 18.3. Since 2015, water levels at the Theewaterskloof dam that supplies Cape Town, South Africa, have repeatedly dropped to critical levels, contributing to fears of reaching a "Day Zero" when the city would effectively run out of water. This image, from February 2018, shows the reservoir at well below 30 percent capacity. Building a resilient water provision system in the face of more frequent and intense climate change–induced droughts will require a combination of actions across sectors and scales. Individual and collective measures to reduce use and improve efficiency, government initiatives to enforce restrictions and diversify water sources and dependency, and environmental management for watershed restoration have so far allowed the city to avert crisis. (Edmond C. "Cape Town almost ran out of water. Here's how it averted the crisis." *World Economic Forum*. August 23, 2019.)
Source: Wikimedia Commons courtesy of Antti Lipponen. https://creativecommons.org/licenses/by/2.0/deed.en

important in the context of informal settlements that lack the financing or institutions to implement needed measures. Effective resilience building reduces existing disparities across populations.

Healthy Resilience Across Sectors

Resilient, healthy places also rely on coordinated actions across a variety of sectors. For example, different sectors can jointly reduce health risks from earthquakes:

- The *building sector* can adopt strict seismic codes for building design, materials, and location.

- *Transportation systems* can identify and strengthen weak points (for example, aging bridges) and develop plans for effective routing of emergency vehicles and other traffic and for timely restoration of mobility.
- *Public spaces* can be designed to support short-term response (for example, as designated meeting or shelter areas).
- *Utilities* can build in systemic redundancy, facilitate access to critical machinery, and safeguard networks by identifying and avoiding fault lines or liquefaction areas.

- *Public health* systems can develop response plans, maintain surge capacity, and ensure that hospitals and clinics are earthquake-resistant.
- *Information and communications technology (ICT) providers* can disseminate alerts and instructions through complementary systems (for example, internet, Wi-Fi, radio), and wireless sensor technology can provide early warnings.[15]

PROMOTING HEALTHY RESILIENCE

Achieving healthy resilience requires specific technical and design solutions across sectors. These solutions, in turn, rely on the implementation of rules, regulations, and policies by governments and other institutions, as well as education, training, and capacity building to expand skills and experience. Resilience also requires effective communication across sectors and scales.

Technical and Design Solutions

Although technical solutions alone cannot guarantee resilience, in many contexts they are essential to planning for specific hazards. For example:
- *Flood* solutions include elevating buildings and critical infrastructure (like hospital generators) above projected water levels, designing landscape features to capture and retain excess water, and restricting construction in floodplains.
- *Drought* risks can be reduced by establishing excess water storage capacity, planting drought-tolerant vegetation, installing water-efficient plumbing, and maintaining water distribution systems to minimize leakage.
- *Heat waves* can be countered by planting shade trees, using light surfaces on roads and rooftops and green vegetation on roofs and walls, incorporating passive cooling principles in architectural design, and creating cooling centers.
- Buried utility lines, wind-resistant window coverings, and other storm-proofing architectural elements can protect against *severe weather events*, as can refuge centers stocked with emergency supplies and well-marked evacuation routes.

Unusual or unanticipated hazards often require flexibility in the design and management of the built environment, as illustrated by the experience of COVID-19 (box 18.3).

In emergency management and response, a **multihazard** or **all-hazards approach** embeds essential elements of resilience (see table 18.1) within the fabric of the built environment. Design features across sectors contribute to healthy multihazard resilience:
- Well-designed *public and green spaces* can increase the resilience of energy, health, water, food, and biodiversity systems by improving water and heat management, fostering social capital, and hosting urban agriculture, temporary shelter, or other functions[16] (see chapter 16).
- *Transportation* influences access to food, education, work, health care, and other resources and can improve health by minimizing pollution and encouraging active transport. Resilient transportation systems are diverse, flexible, and equitable, providing alternate routes and modes; they are also less vulnerable to disruptions from congestion, accidents, weather, and disasters[17] (see chapter 11).
- Resilient *buildings* maintain structural integrity and essential functions during shocks and use resources efficiently, reducing stress during moments of high demand.[18] Building design, construction, and operation can safeguard the resilience of ecological systems. Buildings can provide critical services during crises (for example, sporting venues converted to temporary shelters or hospitals).
- *Utilities*, including energy, gas, water, and sewerage, are key to healthy resilience. Failures can cause serious health risks through service disruptions (for example, the interruption of electricity in Puerto Rico following Hurricane María in 2017, lasting nearly a year in some areas) or

BOX 18.3 COVID-19 AND THE BUILT ENVIRONMENT: A NATURAL EXPERIMENT IN RESILIENCE

The COVID-19 pandemic that emerged in 2020 illustrates how important resilient places, spaces, and systems can be for health and health equity. Public health responses to COVID-19 included business and school closures, quarantines, masking, and social distancing measures and, in many cases, partial or full societal lockdowns,[a] with massive social and economic consequences (see chapter 26).

The built environment shaped local responses, and some localities were able to flexibly repurpose particular elements to support reductions in transmission. Examples include:

- Reallocation of street space for cycling and walking or for economic activities such as outdoor dining or retail
- Designation or creation of health facilities (for example, quarantine in hotels, erection of temporary hospitals)
- Large-scale transition to home work and schooling and remote evaluation (for example, telemedicine)
- Limitations on capacity or user flow in retail and service infrastructure (for example, supermarkets, health centers)

Whether localities were able to implement these and other responses depended in general on the strength of their existing urban planning and governance—for example, many potential actions are infeasible in informal settlements.

The impacts of these measures varied widely, depending on interactions with other categories of response. Some countries and communities were able to lower transmission and limit economic damage by communicating clearly; developing innovative information and communications technology-based surveillance systems; reimagining work, education, and care arrangements; providing equitable support (for example, unemployment, social, business, and health care support); and taking rapid, effective public health action. Others fared much worse, and the true extent of health impacts continues to evolve. In general, successful responses incorporated core elements of resilience (see table 18.1), highlighting the relevance of communication, collaboration, equity, and social capital and the critical role of the built environment.

REFERENCE

a.   Han E, Tan MMJ, Turk E, et al. 2020. Lessons learnt from easing COVID-19 restrictions: an analysis of countries and regions in Asia Pacific and Europe. *The Lancet*. 2020. https://doi.org/10.1016/S0140-6736(20)32007-9

environmental hazards (for example, the Fukushima nuclear disaster following the 2011 Tohoku earthquake and tsunami). Utility systems require massive, long-term investment, and it can be challenging to balance resilience, affordability, and quality, which makes regulatory oversight particularly important.[19] Decentralized systems can increase resilience by diminishing reliance on traditional utilities.

- *Health systems* can incorporate redundancy and multifunctionality and expand surge capacity; create and socialize emergency plans; coordinate effectively with other sectors in disaster risk mitigation, preparation, response, and recovery; invest in surveillance and contribute to analyses of health impacts following shocks; and build trust within communities to increase social capital.

- *Information and communication technology (ICT)* infrastructure enables early warning systems and informs disaster response and recovery through maintenance of registries and databases, including backup systems for critical data (for example, medical records, financial data), mapping and spatial coordination, publication of response efforts, and facilitation of payments.[20] ICT can also bolster information sharing, social capital, and collaboration during crises.

Many of these solutions fall within the remit of urban planning, which plays a critical role in building resilience and promoting health and well-being across sectors.[21] More broadly, good governance is essential to the effective coordination and communication that underpins healthy resilience. Careful planning is critical, as actions to improve resilience can exacerbate vulnerability and exposure gaps. For example, restrictions on construction in floodplains may, in some contexts, push poor or vulnerable populations into more isolated areas with reduced access to urban services, including emergency response.

Rules

Among the most basic ways to promote resilience is through rules. These include *standards and codes* for the built environment, formal *laws and regulations* governing the actions of individuals or organizations (see chapter 20), and softer, informal *norms* that establish desirable patterns of behavior (see chapter 19).

A standard consists of "technical definitions, procedures, or guidelines that specify minimum requirements or instructions for manufacturers, installers, and users of equipment" or infrastructure; it *standardizes* a class of object or a process. A code is "a standard that has been enacted into law by a local, regional, or national authority."[22]

Many standards and codes have been developed to promote resilience in the built environment (see chapter 20). Often focused on sustainability, they may or may not address health. Some are specific to resilient design, such as the US Green Building Council Resilient Design for a Changing World standards, geared toward assessing, planning for, and mitigating acute hazards and ensuring passive survivability. Other emerging standards focus

on resilience beyond infrastructural elements. For example, the International Organization for Standardization recently published a standard for Sustainable Cities and Communities, including indicators for resilient cities.

Resilience-oriented laws and regulations may target individuals, businesses, or government institutions. For example, some laws prohibit wasteful water use by private citizens during droughts; others require small businesses to cover liabilities with insurance; still others mandate that public agencies review specific decisions on a predefined schedule. Laws can establish new government bodies, clarify roles and responsibilities, obligate the creation of plans and strategies, mandate the implementation of actions or interventions, or allocate funding.[23]

Beyond formal rules and regulations, norms that set social and cultural expectations around behavior can also promote healthy resilience. For example, in some contexts, extended family structures provide natural social safety nets during crises. During the COVID-19 pandemic, some countries rapidly adopted new norms around social distancing and mask-wearing, enforced as much by communal expectations as by formal penalties. Norms are more effective where social capital is high.

Education, Training, and Capacity Building

Effective education and training are critical to establishing and maintaining healthy, resilient places, as recognized in major disaster risk reduction and other policy documents,[21] yet resilience thinking has not been universally adopted across the fields where it would be of greatest benefit. Civil, transport, and energy engineering, as well as urban planning, architecture, emergency management, public health, and public policy, would all benefit from a resilience focus. Resilience training encompasses a **transdisciplinary** perspective, teaching professionals to engage effectively across sectors and with governments and the public. Academic and professional programs to address these needs are emerging worldwide (see chapter 23).

Beyond formal training, healthy resilience depends on building individual, community, and societal capabilities to prevent, anticipate, respond to, and recover from shocks and to continually adapt to and reduce risk. Effective resilience-based planning incorporates **people-oriented design**, promoting participatory co-design, co-production, and co-implementation, catalyzing communal action and self-organization, and thereby diminishing community dependence on external support.[21]

Several programs have built capacity or created tool kits and training materials for cross-sectoral resilience thinking in cities. For example, the *Making Cities Sustainable and Resilient* program led by the UN Office for Disaster Risk Reduction aimed to promote local-level resilience through improved understanding of disaster risk and increased response capacity. Intended to accelerate implementation of the **Sendai Framework for Disaster Risk Reduction** (see box 18.2) in more than two hundred cities, it trained public officials to understand, assess, and identify options for building local resilience. Similarly, the Rockefeller Foundation's *100 Resilient Cities* initiative provided financial and technical assistance to participating cities to increase resilience to physical, social, and economic challenges. Chief resilience officers helped develop and implement resilience road maps, establishing partnerships with public, private, and nonprofit actors. Health and well-being were among the program's core dimensions.

Communication

Accurate, timely, and effective communication is another essential component of resilient places, requiring anticipation, flexibility, and redundancy across messaging systems and among those responsible for coordinating emergency warning systems and alerts. One effective example is Cuba's civil defense model, which assigns emergency response coordination responsibilities to actors at national, provincial, and municipal levels, including institutional networks that cross multiple sectors. Emergency alerts are issued in four phases (information, alert, alarm, and recovery) and broadcast on public media, with backup radio communication systems in case of power outages.[1] In the United States, the National Response Framework guides cross-sectoral disaster and emergency action, with a focus on promoting scalable, flexible, and adaptable preparation, response, and recovery.

ICT is an increasingly important component of emergency response systems. It can supplement traditional early warning systems with real-time updates communicated to local officials and community members via smartphone applications, email, or other platforms. ICT technologies can also monitor the performance of specific systems under stress, informing resilience building efforts. Although such systems have enormous potential, increasing complexity also creates potential challenges. ICT monitoring and communication systems are vulnerable to instrument failure, programming glitches, power losses and battery requirements and raise cyber- and physical security issues.[20]

ASSESSING HEALTHY RESILIENCE: MEASUREMENT AND MODELING FRAMEWORKS

Assessing the resilience of a structure, community, society, or system is not straightforward, and there is little consensus on best practices.[24] Resilience is highly dependent on place-specific interactions, which may not be broadly generalizable. Assessment also depends on the conceptual entry point—a system resilient from a disaster risk reduction perspective may not be through an ecological lens. Efforts to assess systemic resilience may include measuring whether specific elements meet standardized criteria, simulating how a system might react to a specified shock, or analyzing the performance of a system after a shock.

Efforts to measure or monitor resilience range from issue-specific indicators and scales to broader systems designed to capture fundamental features of resilience (see table 18.1). Most straightforwardly, the resilience of individual elements to specific risks can be assessed. One might measure the proportion of buildings that meet standards for earthquake safety—or identify which have unreinforced masonry and what proportion have plans for retrofitting. Such indicators and regulations are not limited to the built environment—the proportion of financial institutions carrying insurance or how often fire trucks are serviced are relevant resilience indicators. Because resilience is an emergent system property and these measures relate to individual elements, they are insufficient on their own to describe whether a place is resilient. For example, compliance with seismic standards may not prevent serious health and safety risks during and after an earthquake if backup utility systems are lacking or if distribution of essential supplies is disrupted.

Resilience can also be assessed in relation to interactions among individuals or infrastructural elements and with governance structures. For example, one might document mechanisms to protect key infrastructure and health during floods, identify cities with extreme heat action plans, or assess the level of investment in infectious disease surveillance or hurricane early warning systems. More broadly, one can register whether communities have plans in place to rapidly assess needs (for example, for food, water, shelter) in a postdisaster period. Such measures move toward a recognition of the systemic nature of resilience.

More broadly, some monitoring efforts attempt to capture resilience as an intrinsic property of systems or communities, such as by assessing the extent to which decision-making is equitable and participatory or the degree of hierarchy versus decentralization in governance. Many monitoring frameworks and indicators have been proposed to examine whether systems are designed to learn and adapt, whether they incorporate diverse options for dealing with risk, and to what extent they are able to respond flexibly to unpredictable events.[24]

Simulation or Modeling

A more active way to assess system resilience is through simulation or computer modeling. Models can highlight important feedback relationships and potential unintended consequences in complex systems. For example, they can help identify classes of individuals at high risk, bottlenecks in vaccine supply chains, data processing, emergency communications systems, or other important information. Models can also uncover patterns of collective behavior that contribute to risk during a shock, suggesting appropriate policy responses; for example, clear, well-communicated emergency evacuation plans can limit injuries during an acute crisis and ease access for responders.

In some cases, participatory play-acting of scenarios (for example, "war-gaming") can help assess how human actors or institutions are likely to behave in the face of a shock, suggesting opportunities to improve resilience. Such simulations have been used to assess readiness for pandemics, financial crises, earthquakes, and other shocks. Emergency preparedness drills (for example, for earthquakes, fires, or tsunamis) can fulfill similar objectives.

Retrospective Analysis

Effective postdisaster assessment, or retrospective analysis, is critical to assessing resilience, learning, and "building back better."[25] Retrospective analysis can reveal unrecognized flaws in existing systems, highlight inequitable exposures and vulnerability, and uncover regulatory violations. Such assessments should engage key stakeholders across all levels of a system, including decision-makers, implementers, and end users.

Retrospective analysis can provide insight to drive new policies and practices for resilience. For example, the 2011 Tohoku earthquake and tsunami and the subsequent Fukushima nuclear disaster led to improved tsunami information and early warning systems, more tsunami-conscious design and planning of coastal built environments, and a variety of safety improvements in nuclear power plants worldwide. The 2003 SARS epidemic in Asia generated on-the-ground experience and motivated extensive pandemic planning, in some countries leading to a more effective COVID-19 response.

CONCLUSION

In recent years, resilience has gained traction as an organizing principle for development and has been formally incorporated within international frameworks and standards focused on sustainable development, climate change, disaster risk reduction, and humanitarian issues.[26] Although it represents a critical dimension of resilience, health is not always included within traditional definitions. Ensuring healthy resilience in the places we live, work, and play is critical to creating healthy places for all in a rapidly changing world.

DISCUSSION QUESTIONS

1. Can a system or structure be sustainable but not resilient? Resilient but not sustainable? Why or why not?
2. Describe one significant failure of resilience in the built environment and one significant success.
3. How did the COVID-19 crisis highlight resilience or a lack of resilience relevant to making healthy places?

4. What are some concrete actions your city or community could take to improve healthy resilience?
5. What are some ways that the built environment itself can promote community resilience?

DISCLOSURE OF COMPETING INTERESTS

José G. Siri and Katherine Britt Indvik disclose no competing interests.

Kimberley Clare O'Sullivan was supported during the preparation of this chapter by the following research grants: Health Research Council of New Zealand: Research to maximise the health and well-being gains from housing (Programme); University of Otago Research Grant: Exploring the impact of COVID-19 restrictions on household energy use; Endeavour Fund (Ministry of Business, Innovation, and Employment): Public housing and urban regeneration: maximising wellbeing (Programme); and Marsden Fund (Royal Society of New Zealand): 20-UOO-243 Heating up, cooling off: managing summer heat flows in New Zealand homes. She is co-National Expert for New Zealand on the International Energy Agency Users Technology Collaboration Programme on Hard-to-Reach Energy Users and is a collaborating investigator on the on the Canadian Institutes of Health Research (CIHR) Project Grant PA: Healthy Cities Research Initiative (HCRI) Data Analysis Grants 2021/4–2022/4 Research Title: Energy poverty in Canada (EPIC): what are the implications for the health and well-being of Canadians?

REFERENCES

1. Lizarralde G, Valladares A, Olivera A, Bornstein L, Gould K, Barenstein JD. A systems approach to resilience in the built environment: the case of Cuba. *Disasters*. 2015;39(s1):s76-s95.

2. Coates R. Cuba, Irma, and ongoing exceptionalism in the Caribbean. *Alternautas*. 2018;5 (2):56-65.

3. Stone R. Cuba's 100-year plan for climate change. *Science*. 2018;359:144-145.

4. Desmond MM. *Fires in Rome: The Ancient City as a Fire Regime*. Thesis, Trinity College Dublin. School of Histories and Humanities. Discipline of Classics. 2019. http://www.tara.tcd.ie/handle/2262/86169

5. Hassler U, Kohler N. Resilience in the built environment. *Building Research & Information*. 2014;42(2):119-129. https://doi.org/10.1080/09613218.2014.873593

6. Forrest A. How London might have looked: five masterplans after the Great Fire. *The Guardian*. January 25, 2016. http://www.theguardian.com/cities/2016/jan/25/how-london-might-have-looked-five-masterplans-after-great-fire-1666

7. Garrioch D. 1666 and London's fire history: a re-evaluation. *Historical Journal*. 2016;59(2):319-338.

8. Alexander DE. 2013. Resilience and disaster risk reduction: an etymological journey. *Natural Hazards and Earth System Sciences*. 2013;13(11):2707-2716.

9. Norris FH, Stevens SP, Pfefferbaum B, Wyche KF, Pfefferbaum RL. Community resilience as a metaphor, theory, set of capacities, and strategy for disaster readiness. *American Journal of Community Psychology*. 2008;41(1-2): 27-50. https://doi.org/10.1007/s10464-007-9156-6

10. United Nations. *New Urban Agenda*. United Nations. 2016. http://habitat3.org/wp-content/uploads/NUA-English.pdf

11. Folke C. Resilience (Republished). *Ecology and Society*. 2016;21(4). https://doi.org/10.5751/ES-09088-210444

12. World Commission on Environment and Development. *Our Common Future*. Oxford University Press; 1987.

13. Haigh R, Amaratunga D. An integrative review of the built environment discipline's role in the development of society's resilience to disasters. *International Journal of Disaster Resilience in the Built Environment*. 2010;1(1):11-24.

14. Revi A, Satterthwaite DE, Aragón-Durand F, et al. Urban areas. In: Field CB, Barros VR, Dokken DJ, et al., eds. *Climate Change 2014: Impacts, Adaptation, and Vulnerability. Part A: Global and Sectoral Aspects*. Contribution of Working Group II to the Fifth Assessment Report of the Intergovernmental Panel on Climate Change. Cambridge University Press; 2014;535-612.

15. Rahman MU, Rahman S, Mansoor S, Deep V, Aashkaar M. Implementation of ICT and Wireless sensor networks for earthquake alert and disaster management in earthquake prone areas. *Procedia Computer Science, International Conference on Computational Modelling and Security (CMS 2016)*. 2016;85(January):92-99. https://doi.org/10.1016/j.procs.2016.05.184

16. Mukherjee M, Takara K. Urban green space as a countermeasure to increasing urban risk and the UGS-3CC resilience framework. *International Journal of Disaster Risk Reduction*. 2018;28(June):854-861. https://doi.org/10.1016/j.ijdrr.2018.01.027

17. Ganin AA, Kitsak M, Marchese D, Keisler JM, Seager T, Linkov I. Resilience and efficiency in transportation networks. *Science Advances*. 2017;3(12):e1701079. https://doi.org/10.1126/sciadv.1701079

18. Hasik V, Chhabra JPS, Warn GP, Bilec MM. Investigation of the sustainability and resilience characteristics of buildings including existing and potential assessment metrics. *AEI 2017*.

April 6, 2017;1019-1033. https://doi
.org/10.1061/9780784480502.085

19. Decker C. 2018. Utility and regulatory decision-making under conditions of uncertainty: balancing resilience and affordability. *Utilities Policy.* 2018;51(April):51-60. https://doi.org/10.1016/j.jup.2018.01.007

20. Samarajiva R, Zuhyle S. 2013. *The Resilience of ICT Infrastructure and Its Role During Disasters.* Economic and Social Commission for Asia and the Pacific; 2013.

21. Sharifi A, Yamagata Y. 2018. Resilience-oriented urban planning. In *Resilience-Oriented Urban Planning: Theoretical and Empirical Insights.* Lecture Notes in Energy 65. Yamagata Y, Sharifi A, eds. Springer International; 2018:3-27. https://doi.org/10.1007/978-3-319-75798-8_1

22. Heinsdorf M. Code or standard? *Consulting—Specifying Engineer.* July 1, 2015. https://www.csemag.com/articles/code-or-standard/

23. Mehryar S, Surminski S. *The Role of National Laws in Managing Flood Risk and Increasing Future Flood Resilience.* Grantham Research Institute on Climate Change and the Environment; 2020. https://www.lse.ac.uk/granthaminstitute/publication/the-role-of-national-laws-in-managing-flood-risk-and-increasing-future-flood-resilience/

24. Schipper L, Langston L. A Comparative Overview of Resilience Measurement Frameworks: Analysing Indicators and Approaches. Working Paper 422. Overseas Development Institute (London); 2015. https://www.odi.org/publications/9632-comparative-overview-resilience-measurement-frameworks-analysing-indicators-and-approaches

25. PwC. Rebuilding for Resilience: Fortifying Infrastructure to Withstand Disaster. PricewaterhouseCoopers. 2013. https://www.preventionweb.net/publications/view/34786

26. Peters K, Langston L, Tanner T, Bahadur A. Resilience across the Post-2015 Frameworks: Towards Coherence. ODI Briefing Paper. Overseas Development Institute; 2016. https://www.odi.org/publications/10598-resilience-across-post-2015-frameworks-towards-coherence

PART III

STRATEGIES FOR HEALTHY PLACES: A TOOL KIT

CHAPTER 19

HEALTHY BEHAVIORAL CHOICES AND THE BUILT ENVIRONMENT

Christopher Coutts and Patrice C. Williams

KEY POINTS

- The design and conditions of the built environment can directly and indirectly affect health by influencing behavioral choices.
- The built environment acts together with other external factors—including historical and political context, economy, and social cues—to influence behavior.
- Current social trends include behavioral choices aimed at health (such as walking for physical activity) and behavioral choices aimed at environmental sustainability (such as driving less). The built environment can foster choices that advance both health and sustainability.

INTRODUCTION

Antonio lives in the sprawling suburbs of Dallas, Texas. He spends two hours commuting to and from work each day. He often gets fast food for lunch and picks up a pizza or a bucket of fried chicken on the way home for dinner. These are the easy choices in a built environment where the distance between home and work is great, the road network for automobiles is vast, there are few public transportation options, and fast-food outlets are prevalent. He and his wife alternate driving the kids to school, so a few days a week his commute is even longer. On the weekends, he and his wife spend hours driving the kids to and from

various activities. He has a gym membership, but seldom has time to drive to the gym to use it. He knows that this lifestyle is leading him to join the 35 percent of adults in Dallas who get no leisure time physical activity and the 35 percent of adults in Dallas who are obese.[1] Antonio moved to Dallas from Seattle, Washington, where only 15 percent of adults get no leisure time physical activity and 21 percent of adults are obese.[1] In Seattle, he recalls walking to accessible public transit, visiting the numerous public parks, and shopping at local markets for fresh food. He rode his bike to work a few days a week using the ample bike lanes. These were relatively easy choices in an environment that supported these behaviors. He would like to practice some of these same behaviors in Dallas, but the environment makes these choices difficult if not dangerous. His lifestyle in Seattle was not only healthier for him as an individual, but it was also more sustainable. By driving less and purchasing locally produced food, his impact on the environment was greatly reduced.

This anecdote illustrates some of the principles covered in this chapter. First, promoting personal behaviors that enhance individual health requires attention to both the context within which these behaviors occur and factors at the individual and community levels that lead people to choose one course of action over another. Second, the design of the built environment has implications for personal behavior related to individual health, community health, and environmental sustainability. The factors that determine health behaviors are interrelated and complex, as illustrated in the array of theories applied to health behaviors.

THEORIES OF HEALTH BEHAVIOR

There are many theories of human behavior that have been refined with decades of research to better understand the determinants of health behavior. Most of these theories focus on the psychological and sociological determinants of health behaviors at the expense of the built or physical environment, but these theories can be adapted to create a renewed appreciation for the fundamental importance of the built environment in determining health behaviors. Some of the greatest historic gains in public health were achieved by constructing sanitation infrastructure that removed waste and delivered clean water, improving housing conditions, and creating public parks (chapter 1).[2-4] These environmental improvements were necessary to support improved sanitary behaviors and create opportunities for recreation behaviors in crowded cities. Even today, as new threats to health emerge, the design of the environment influences the choices people are likely to make.[5] Models of human behavior that ignore the contexts within which behavioral choices are made overlook a significant determinant of health behavior.[6] There is substantial overlap between the theories presented here, and no single theory is likely to provide a complete picture of the multifaceted and highly complex forces that determine human behavior. Nonetheless, the application, empirical testing, and refinement of theory are steps in an iterative process that systematically advances our scientific understanding of health behaviors.

Health behaviors are determined by the interaction between one's environment and individual and social factors. The influence and interaction of these factors are portrayed in a *social ecological model* of health. The socio-ecological model includes characteristics of the individual (race or ethnicity, age, sex, and heredity), lifestyle, the immediate social and physical environments (including both natural and planned features), and the larger social and physical contexts (political and economic factors, geography, and culture). The socioecological approach recognizes the many external influences, beyond just individual biological factors, that both directly and indirectly determine health and health behaviors. A health map, illustrating a socioecological approach to health, is one such model (figure 19.1).[7] Individual factors are at the center of this model, but individual factors are nested within many other larger spheres of influence on health and health behaviors. Among these larger spheres are social factors that are nested within the built and natural environments.

The theory of planned behavior (TPB) posits individual attitudes and perceived social normative perceptions as determinants of behavior.[8] TPB is distinguished from its earlier iteration, the theory of reasoned action (TRA), for its addition of the **construct** of perceived behavioral control.[9] Neither the TRA nor the TPB explicitly recognizes the physical environment as a determinant of behavior, but the physical environment could interact with the TPB constructs of individual attitudes, perceived social norms, and perceptions of behavioral control that all lead to the intention to perform a given behavior. A study that applied TPB to examine exercise behavior in France found that there were significant interactions between intentions to perform physical activity, making plans to perform physical activity, and the perceived built environment supports for physical activity (for example, walking and biking paths).[10] The integrated behavioral model (IBM) builds on the constructs from TPB, as well as other theories, to create a more accurately complex socioecological portrait of behavior where "a particular behavior is most likely to occur when a person has a strong intention to perform it and the knowledge and skill to do so, no serious

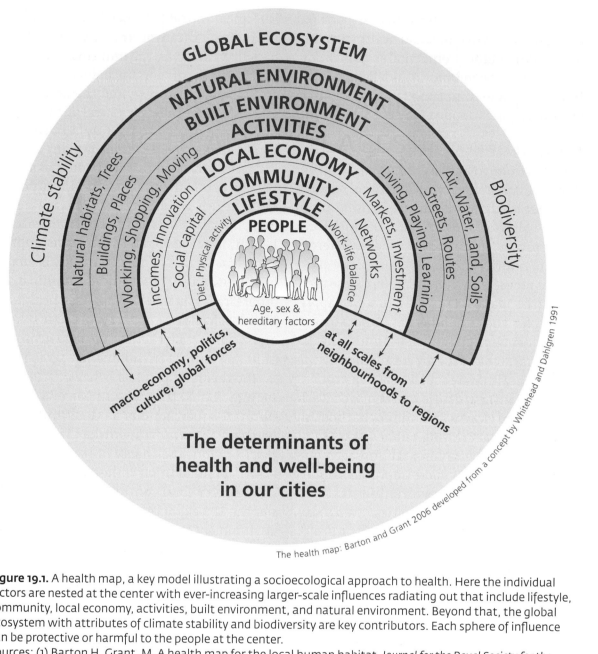

The determinants of health and well-being in our cities

The health map: Barton and Grant 2006 developed from a concept by Whitehead and Dahlgren 1991

Figure 19.1. A health map, a key model illustrating a socioecological approach to health. Here the individual factors are nested at the center with ever-increasing larger-scale influences radiating out that include lifestyle, community, local economy, activities, built environment, and natural environment. Beyond that, the global ecosystem with attributes of climate stability and biodiversity are key contributors. Each sphere of influence can be protective or harmful to the people at the center.
Sources: (1) Barton H, Grant, M. A health map for the local human habitat. *Journal for the Royal Society for the Promotion of Health*. 2006;126(6):252-253. (2) Dahlgren G, Whitehead M (1991). "The main determinants of health" model. In: Dahlgren G, Whitehead M. *European Strategies for Tackling Social Inequities in Health: Levelling Up*. Part 2. WHO Regional Office for Europe; 2007. http://www.euro.who.int/__data/assets/pdf_file/0018/103824/E89384 .pdf

environmental constraints prevent behavioral performance, the behavior is salient, and the person has performed the behavior previously."[11(p105)] This theory does include *environmental constraints* as directly influencing behavior.[11]

The social cognitive theory (SCT) highlights the interactions between the individual, the environment, and behavior.[12] The environment construct in the SCT is typically interpreted as the social environment, but it can also include the physical environment and surroundings. A study that applied SCT to examine physical activity in older women residing in the midwestern United States found that street connectivity emerged as a significant independent factor related to physical activity.[13]

Street connectivity is associated with walking, a common form of physical activity among older adults (chapter 10). SCT also includes the concept of *reciprocal determinism*, where a person is both an agent of change and a responder to change (figure 19.2). In the case of the built environment, people have the power to change the environment through advocacy for better urban and regional planning. Their belief in their ability to change the environment may be influenced by personal factors such as knowledge, expectations, and attitudes, and these factors are reciprocally influenced by the environment. Changes to the environment will support changes in behavior, and the behavioral response to these changes could then have a reciprocal influence on more environmental refinements.

Unlike the previous theories presented in this chapter, the health belief model (HBM) was one of the first theories devoted exclusively to understanding health behaviors. Similar to other theories, HBM focuses on psychological and social factors as determining health behavior, but there are at least two constructs in the model that could account for the influence of built environment. *Perceived barriers* could be hindrances in the physical environment that prevent one from performing a behavior. A stark example of this could be a fence that prevents pedestrians from reaching a desired destination, but more subtle and potentially cumulative barriers could be unmaintained sidewalks, a lack of well-designated pedestrian crosswalks, and long distances between a given origin and des-

tination. *Cues to action* could be the signals one receives from the environment that reinforce certain behaviors. These have typically been interpreted as media cues that reinforce or discourage certain behaviors, but the built environment also provides cues to action. Readily accessible, safe, and efficient public transportation infrastructure—and witnessing others using it—provides environmental cues that using public transportation is a viable option. There are a number of examples of the HBM being applied to the study of environmentally friendly behavior and healthy consumption behavior in the built environment.[14,15] As we saw in the health map socioecological model, protecting the natural environment with more sustainable behaviors lays the foundation for health, as discussed further below.

Similar to the theories previously presented, a *behavioral economics* approach draws on psychology to understand individual-level factors (for example, values, preferences) that influence the choices people make.[16] This approach has been typically applied to health interventions that focus on consumptive behaviors such as weight control and substance abuse, but it can also be applied to understand how changes to the environment can encourage healthy choices. Behavioral economics differs from microeconomic (for example, zoning) or macroeconomic (for example, taxation) because of its focus on individual-level factors and its recognition of the nonmonetary costs to interpersonal relationships or social activities that may suffer due to unhealthy behavior. In a typical microeconomic scenario, zoning

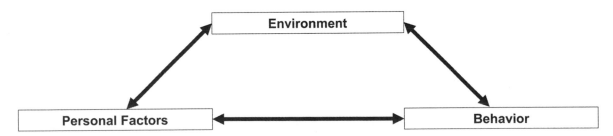

Figure 19.2. In the social cognitive theory, behaviors influence and are influenced by personal factors and the environment.
Source: Christopher Coutts and Patrice Williams

can influence community health behaviors by facilitating or restricting access to certain consumables. It has been shown that the odds of having a healthy diet decrease in relation to a greater neighborhood density of fast-food outlets, and the negative consequences of alcohol abuse decrease by reducing the density of alcohol outlets.[17,18]

Rezoning is a warranted public health intervention in some communities, but behavioral economics provides lessons on how people can be more subtly nudged into making healthier choices. *Nudge theory* posits that changing the *choice architecture*, or the design by which choices are presented, can encourage people to make healthier choices.[19] Nudging does not rely on legislation or enforcement to forbid, punish, or restrict unhealthy behaviors. A nudge allows freedom of choice and is easy to avoid. That said, nudges are not a substitute for, but rather a complement to, regulatory and legislative tools.[20] Nudging simply makes the healthy choice the easy choice. For example, placing healthy food options at eye level in grocery stores and redesigning stairways can make healthy choices easier and more attractive than unhealthy alternatives. Piano staircases, where steps are transformed to resemble piano keys, have been installed in a number of cities around the world. Some step "keyboards" make actual music, whereas other "keys" are just painted onto steps. Research is very limited, but the installation of a piano staircase in Sweden was reported to increase stair usage by 66 percent.[21] These types of nudges also make the healthy choice fun, which is an essential characteristic of effective social marketing (discussed later).

The process people undergo to make behavior changes is captured in the transtheoretical model.[22] Part of this model outlines the stages of change one goes through in adopting a behavior, beginning with no consideration of changing behavior (*precontemplation*) to eventually adopting a behavior for a sustained period of time (*maintenance*) until it becomes the norm (*termination*) (table 19.1). Using car-sharing programs as an example, marketing, incentivizing, and knowing others who participate in car-sharing may move some from precontemplation to contemplating participation. Preparing to practice car-sharing may involve going online to enroll in a car-sharing program before the eventual action of using a car-share vehicle for the first time. Maintenance is more likely when the benefits in cost savings and reduced stress and air pollution are realized.

There is a growing recognition of the role of the built environment in determining health behaviors, but when considering the role of the built environment, we need to be wary of **environmental determinism**. Changes to the environment alone may not initially alter behavior in large segments of the population. The theories and models presented in this chapter reveal that the environment is one among many factors determining health behaviors. These factors interact with one

Table 19.1. Stages of change.

Constructs	Description
Precontemplation	No intention to take action within the next six months
Contemplation	Intends to take action within the next six months
Preparation	Intends to take action within the next thirty days and has taken some behavioral steps in this direction
Action	Changed overt behavior for less than six months
Maintenance	Changed overt behavior for more than six months
Termination	No temptation to relapse and 100% confidence

another in complex ways and ultimately determine if health innovations will be adopted or resisted in a population.

The diffusion of innovations (DI) theory[23] can aid our understanding of the rate and proportion by which health behaviors are adopted or resisted within a population. No matter how conducive the built environment is to promoting health, there will still be *laggards* who delay or avoid making healthy choices (figure 19.3).

For example, imagine a neighborhood with pedestrian crosswalks, connected and extensive sidewalks and bike lanes, little automobile traffic traveling at slow speeds, shade trees, shopping opportunities for fresh food, public parks within a short distance of home, and safety and security for all people regardless of race, gender identity, or sexual orientation. Even in this environment, there will be those who choose not to walk or bike and will instead drive to the fast-food outlet daily. Conversely, no matter how *unconducive* the built environment is to promoting health, there will be *innovators* and *early adopters* who overcome environmental barriers to make healthy choices. Public health typically aims for the greatest public benefit by designing interventions that can be adopted by and benefit the majority of the population, the *early majority* and *late majority* in the case of DI. Making the healthy choice the easy choice through environmental interventions could have a great impact on large segments of the population. Promoting healthy behaviors—such as educating people about healthy diets, recreating in nature, and using public transportation—in an environment that does not support such behaviors will have much less impact. The *health impact pyramid* demonstrates that changing the environmental context in which health behavior decisions are made would have a high impact on the majority of the population with a low level of individual effort (figure 19.4).

This environmental probabilism (not determinism) is evident in *behavior settings* that set the space for specific behaviors.[24] People assess their environment to determine what behaviors are feasible and appropriate in a given context, be it the home, neighborhood, workplace, or school. The access to and specific characteristics of various behavior settings have been examined for their role in promoting active living.[25] For example, parks and trails create the behavior setting for recreational physical activity, and neighborhoods with sidewalks and bike lanes create the behavior setting for physical activity gained for both recreation and transportation.

Many of the theories applied to health behaviors teach us that the adoption of health behaviors is partly influenced by the social cues we receive from witnessing others' behavior. When the built environment supports healthier choices, those making healthy choices

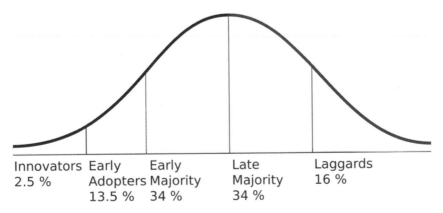

| Innovators 2.5 % | Early Adopters 13.5 % | Early Majority 34 % | Late Majority 34 % | Laggards 16 % |

Figure 19.3. This curve explains how new ideas, products, and practices spread within a society, from the innovators and early adopters to the early majority, followed by the late majority and laggards
Source: Adapted from Wikimedia Commons courtesy of Rogers Everett (public domain). Based on Rogers E. *Diffusion of Innovations*. Free Press; 1962.

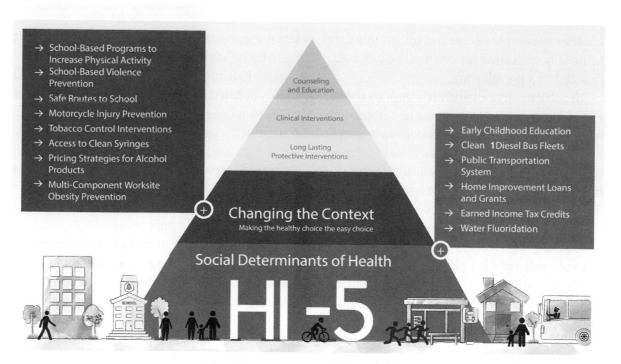

Figure 19.4. This model is based on the health impact pyramid, which has the social determinants of health and changing the context at the base of the pyramid where there is great population impact. The context changes are where built environment changes have the power of "making the healthy choice the easy choice." The higher you go up the pyramid, the greater the individual effort and smaller the societal impact. The Center for Disease Control and Prevention's Health Impacts in 5 Years (HI-5) initiative proposes noted nonclinical community-wide approaches to realize positive health outcomes in five years from initiations that are cost-effective. Source: CDC, Office of the Associate Director for Policy and Strategy. https://www.cdc.gov/policy/hst/hi5/index .html. Reference to specific commercial products, manufacturers, companies, or trademarks does not constitute its endorsement or recommendation by the U.S. Government, Department of Health and Human Services, or Centers for Disease Control and Prevention.

create examples for others to follow. When most people then adopt a health behavior, it becomes the norm and, if sustained long enough, the culture, which is constantly changing over time. These behaviors are not only beneficial to the individual performing them, but also for society at large. *Social marketing* is a method adopted in health promotion that emphasizes the social good of health interventions. Beginning in the 1970s, community-based health promotion interventions attempted to harness the marketing strategies typically employed by profit-seeking companies to encourage specific behavioral choices. To distinguish their efforts from commercial promotions, marketing strategies applied for social good have come to be known as social marketing. The social environment constructs in health behavior theories can aid us in designing more effective health inter-

vention strategies that harness the power of social marketing and social media to improve public health and the environment.[26] The most effective efforts at social marketing make the marketed behavior easy and fun so that it then becomes popular.[27] The ciclovía movement is an example of how "open streets" make outdoor activity easy, fun, and popular (chapter 2). Open streets is the practice of temporarily (and sometime permanently) closing city streets to automobile traffic for exclusive bike and pedestrian use. This makes recreational activity easy where cars otherwise make it dangerous and fun in what is typically a festive atmosphere. In Colombia, credited with beginning the movement in the 1970s, more than 30 percent of the population participates weekly in the program, branded as ciclovías (see chapter 2), and it has been adopted by cities around the world.

The explosion of social media platforms has made it much easier to be aware of others' choices. Although social media provides an abundance of examples not to follow, public health has used social media to provide positive examples that may lead others to practice similar health-promoting behaviors.[28] Another technological advancement is the growing availability of devices that provide feedback on our health behaviors and allow us to share information in our social environments. Accelerometers (for example, Fitbit) are one such example.

Results from a pilot study have shown that people who live and commute in urban environments burn more calories compared to those who live and commute in suburban or rural settings.[29] Even though distances between origins and destinations are shorter in urban environments, trips are more likely to involve walking and biking modes of transport that fold activity into our daily lives. The form of the built environment makes these behaviors the easy choice.

COMMUNICABLE AND CHRONIC DISEASE BEHAVIORS

Today, many low-income countries still lack the basic physical infrastructure to support health behaviors that can reduce infectious (communicable) disease transmission.[30] Public health must continue to promote protection from infectious agents through behaviors such as hand washing, but this not a reasonable expectation in places that lack the basic physical infrastructure (environmental support) that removes and isolates waste and provides clean water to wash one's hands. Even in high-income countries where potable water and waste removal systems are taken for granted, we see evolving environmental supports such as no-touch faucets and paper towel dispensers aimed at reducing infectious disease transmission. The introduction of these environmental supports influences behavior immediately, and, after time, they become the default choice.

In 2020, the COVID-19 pandemic became a stark reminder of how behavior can dramatically affect infectious disease transmission. Hand washing, sanitizing objects, and wearing a protective mask were recommended preventive practices to reduce the transmission of the SARS-CoV-2 virus, but these behaviors depend on the availability of physical provisions (for example, clean water, cleaning agents, hand sanitizer, masks) in our environment. These provisions soon became in short supply, as did the availability of COVID-19 tests and hospital equipment. Even if one were motivated to follow the recommended behaviors aimed at controlling the spread of the SARS-CoV-2 virus, it was difficult without environmental support. The physical environment also played a role in the prescribed social distancing measures. Retail outlets, if not shut completely, encouraged social distancing behavior by controlling movement through entrances and exits, the flow of persons through shopping aisles, and demarcating six-foot distances in checkout lines. Places where people typically congregate (for example, parks, restaurants) were closed as options in one's built environment. The pandemic was a reminder of our global connectedness and the influence that physical provisions and the environment play in infectious disease transmission. The pandemic also instigated some vocal resistance to mandates on personal behaviors perceived as infringing on personal freedoms (box 19.1). Even when provisions such as masks became available, some people, such as members of some conservative groups, among others, chose not to use them. This behavior was reinforced by social cues from political and religious leaders and misinformation spread through conspiracy-perpetuating social media and news outlets.

Infectious diseases will continue to threaten health, but most of the world has undergone an **epidemiological transition**. The world has transitioned from communicable to chronic diseases as the leading causes of morbidity and mortality. Infectious diseases (for example, lower respiratory infections) still account for a significant portion of deaths globally, but most of the leading causes of deaths globally (for example, heart disease, cancer, stroke, chronic obstructive pulmonary disease, diabetes) are all associated with personal behaviors,[31] including physical activity (chapter 2) and dietary practices (chapter 3). This is evident in the combination of sedentary lifestyles and poor diets that have contributed to an epidemic of obesity in the United States and many other countries.[32]

Although susceptibility to chronic diseases is influenced by an individual's socioeconomic status, behaviors, and cultural factors, some populations within the US context are at greater risk due to structural racism.[33-35] From 2015 to 2018, non-Hispanic Black and Hispanic adults had a significantly higher prevalence of physical inactivity compared to non-Hispanic Whites.[36] In addition, non-Hispanic Black and Hispanic adults have a higher prevalence of obesity than non-Hispanic Whites.[37] It should come as no surprise, then, that Black, Brown, and Indigenous residents are more likely to live in neighborhoods that have limited access to environmental amenities, such as parks and trails[38,39] and healthy food choices.[40,41] Public health cannot address these disparities and inequities in health outcomes and behaviors unless it considers the impact of structural racism on health outcomes (chapter 9;

box 19.2). And as we focus on dismantling structures that inhibit creating healthier, more equitable communities conducive to healthy behaviors for *all* populations, we are at the same time providing co-benefits to the global community.

LINKS WITH SUSTAINABILITY

Sustainability often refers to patterns of consumption or development that have a community-level impact and are environmentally sound. Sustainable development "meets the needs of the present without compromising the ability of future generations to meet their own needs."[42] The concept of sustainability is typically not applied when considering behaviors undertaken by individuals for their own personal benefit. However, the built environment and the behaviors it may encourage link the concepts of individual benefit (including health) with the broader concept of sustainability. A built environment that supports more sustainable choices may improve individual health and help communities at multiple scales achieve environmental sustainability.

A *sustainable lifestyle* can be described as one that enhances individual health and well-being while simultaneously supporting the long-term viability of the human and natural community within which the individual resides. This community could be localized in the form of a neighborhood, village, or city, but it could also extend to the global community. Despite the critical role of the natural environment as a determinant of health, nature is still considered "with ambivalence" in public health research and practice.[43] Fortunately, there are a number of built environment interventions that can encourage more sustainable lifestyles that simultaneously benefit the health of individuals, communities, and the natural environment and biosphere.

A shift to active travel (walking or bicycling) and increased use of public or multimodal transit not only promotes physical activity, but also improves air quality and reduces greenhouse gas emissions. More energy-efficient homes built with sustainable materials reduce the degradation of forests and greenhouse gas emissions. A shift from eating meat products to eating locally grown produce reduces a person's risk of cardiovascular disease and obesity while also benefiting local economies, reducing greenhouse gas emissions, and reducing pollution caused by concentrated animal-feeding operations. The question is, then, how do we motivate people to practice these more healthy and sustainable behaviors? The concepts presented in this chapter can aid in addressing this question.

Research has succeeded in identifying behaviors, such as the ones described here, that improve health and environmental quality. We know what we *should* do. Progress has also been made on uncovering the factors (attitudes, values, beliefs) associated with these behaviors. We are now tasked with designing interventions that instill these factors and create the context for healthy and sustainable behaviors to occur.[44] For example, research has found that natural place attachment (that is, connectedness to the local natural environment) is one factor predictive of pro-environmental behaviors.[45] So how do we design interventions that instill factors such as natural place attachment to encourage healthy and sustainable lifestyles? The theories, models, and practices presented in this chapter demonstrate that the personal factors (knowledge, expectations, and attitudes) can be influenced by the physical and social environment. Environmental interventions, such as community gardens, neighborhood greening, and creating greater access to natural areas, may all instill greater natural place attachment,[46] but so too might smaller nudges, such as storm drain labeling that makes people aware of where their waste goes, installing signs along roads marking watershed boundaries, green footprints painted on sidewalks leading to natural features, having local food items marked as "seasonal" available in markets, and outdoor education programs for children folded into school curricula. Innovators and early adopters

BOX 19.2 DISMANTLING STRUCTURAL RACISM IN PURSUIT OF HEALTHY PLACES

Structural racism "refers to the totality of ways in which societies foster racial discrimination, through mutually reinforcing inequitable systems (in housing, education, employment, earnings, benefits, credit, media, health care, criminal justice, and so on) that in turn reinforce discriminatory beliefs, values, and distributions of resources, which together affect the risk of adverse health outcomes."[a(p1454)] American society consists of a racialized system that reinforces and reconstitutes the conditions necessary to ensure social, environmental, and economic inequities between different racial and ethnic groups. Structural changes to our social institutions are therefore a critical component in addressing unhealthy and unsustainable behaviors inequitably encouraged by the built environment.[b] Situating health behaviors within the context of a broader social structure reveals how factors such as racism, sexism, and ableism create and perpetuate hierarchies of power and reduce access to resources with harmful implications for socially vulnerable groups. For example, residential segregation not only disproportionally exposes residents who are Black, Indigenous, and people of color to environmental hazards and pollutants[c-e]; it also reduces access to the resources necessary to support healthy behaviors by concentrating poverty and producing unequal access to city services.[f] Health behaviors among these populations are also influenced by greater densities of tobacco advertisements and alcohol and fast-food outlets.[g-i]

Making environmental improvements in marginalized and vulnerable neighborhoods can also do harm if not done right, however. Removing environmental pollutants, introducing healthier food options, and creating and restoring parks and green spaces through greenspace redevelopment could incite or enable green gentrification,[j] a process that creates or restores environmental amenities, increases property values, and has the potential to displace socially vulnerable populations. Black residents of historically Black neighborhoods undergoing greenspace redevelopment contend with feelings of being "pushed out," excluded from the benefits of neighborhood improvements. They report a heightened awareness of their surroundings and the need to be cautious within their neighborhood due to racial profiling by their new White neighbors under the guise of preventing crime and protecting the neighborhood.[k] These sentiments reflect common experiences of harassment and mistreatment within predominantly White spaces, which could explain why the level of physical activity among Black men decreases significantly in neighborhoods perceived to be predominately White compared to racially diverse or predominately Black neighborhoods.[l] Racial crimes, such as the 2020 murder of Ahmaud Arbery, instill and perpetuate a justified fear. Reducing disparities in health behaviors will require comprehensive structural interventions that engage a range of community-informed strategies focused on confronting the structural, social, and institutional mechanisms through which factors such as racism operate.

REFERENCES

a. Bailey ZD, Krieger N, Agénor M, Graves J, Linos N, Bassett MT. Structural racism and health inequities in the USA: evidence and interventions. *The Lancet*. 2017;389(10077):1453-1463. doi:10.1016/S0140-6736(17)30569-X

b. Brownson RC, Seiler R, Eyler AA. Measuring the impact of public health policy. *Preventing Chronic Disease*. 2010;7(4):1-7.

c. Brulle RJ, Pellow DN. Environmental justice: human health and environmental inequalities. *Annual Review of Public Health*. 2006;27(1):103-124. doi:10.1146/annurev.publhealth.27.021405.102124

d. Bell ML, Ebisu K. Environmental inequality in exposures to airborne particulate matter components in the United States. *Environmental Health Perspective*. 2012;120(12):1699-1704. doi:10.1289/ehp.1205201

e. Mikati I, Benson AF, Luben TJ, Sacks JD, Richmond-Bryant J. Disparities in distribution of particulate matter emission sources by race and poverty status. *American Journal of Public Health*. 2018;108(4):480-485. doi:10.2105/AJPH.2017.304297

f. Williams DR, Collins C. Racial residential segregation: a fundamental cause of racial disparities in health. *Public Health Reports*. 2001;116(5):404-416. doi:10.1016/S0033-3549(04)50068-7

g. Berke EM, Tanski SE, Demidenko E, Alford-Teaster J, Shi X, Sargent JD. Alcohol retail density and demographic predictors of health disparities: a geographic analysis. *American Journal of Public Health*. 2010;100(10):1967-1971. doi:10.2105/AJPH.2009.170464

h. Kwate NOA. Fried chicken and fresh apples: racial segregation as a fundamental cause of fast food density in black neighborhoods. *Health & Place*. 2008;14(1):32-44. https://doi.org/10.1016/j.healthplace.2007.04.001

i. LaVeist TA, Wallace JM. Health risk and inequitable distribution of liquor stores in African American neighborhood. *Social Science & Medicine*. 2000;51(4):613-617. doi:https://doi.org/10.1016/S0277-9536(00)00004-6

j. Gould KA, Lewis TL. *Green Gentrification: Urban Sustainability and the Struggle for Environmental Justice*. Routledge; 2017.

k. Williams PC, Alhasan DM, Krafty R, Coutts C, Miles-Richardson S, Jackson CL. A mixed methods approach to understand the impact of greenspace redevelopment on objective- and subjective-measures of sleep health among Black adults in Southwest Atlanta. (Under review.)

l. Ray R. Black people don't exercise in my neighborhood: perceived racial composition and leisure-time physical activity among middle class blacks and whites. *Social Science Research*. 2017;66:42-57. doi:10.1016/j.ssresearch.2017.03.008

of these innovations then create social cues for others to follow and slowly make these sustainable behaviors and a sustainable culture the norm. Although global environmental challenges, such as climate change (chapter 17), might seem insurmountable for any single person to remedy, individual sustainable lifestyles can lead to healthier individuals and, cumulatively, to healthy communities and a healthy planet (chapter 24).

CONCLUSION

Health behaviors are determined by the interaction between individual, social, and environmental factors. Although many of the theories commonly applied to health behavior do not explicitly include the built environment, they can all be adapted to include the contribution of the built environment in determining health behaviors. Changing the environmental context in which health behavior decisions are made could have a high impact at the population level with a low level of individual effort. The world has transitioned from communicable to noncommunicable diseases as the leading causes of morbidity and mortality. Although susceptibility to noncommunicable diseases is influenced by an individual's socioeconomic status, behaviors, and cultural factors, some populations within the US context are at greater risk due to structural racism. Although we slowly adapt our environments

to being more conducive to healthy behaviors for all, we are at the same time providing co-benefits to the global community. Built environment interventions that encourage behaviors such as driving less and eating less meat benefit the health of individuals, communities, the natural environment, and the biosphere.

DISCUSSION QUESTIONS

1. Name three behaviors in which individuals may engage that are beneficial both to the individual and to the community. How might these beneficial behaviors be encouraged through modifications to the built environment? How might an individual's characteristics facilitate or impede these behaviors?

2. Explain whether obesity is a communicable disease or a chronic disease based on the social ecological model, the theory of planner behavior, the integrated behavioral model, social cognitive theory, the health belief model, or behavioral economics.

3. Outline strategies that, when implemented at each level of the health impact pyramid, can support sustained health improvements in urban, suburban, and rural communities.

4. Identify a specific current community issue in a low- to moderate-income coun-

try and explain how social marketing could be used to address that issue and achieve change.

5. How is structural racism related to health behaviors and health outcomes? What strategies are most opportune to reduce racial and ethnic disparities and address structural racism?

DISCLOSURE OF COMPETING INTERESTS

Christopher Coutts discloses no competing interests.

Patrice C. Williams discloses the receipt of grant funding from the Robert Wood Johnson Foundation Health Policy Research Scholars Program.

REFERENCES

1. Centers for Disease Control and Prevention. 500 Cities Project Data. Published 2016. Accessed May 6, 2020. https://www.cdc.gov/500cities

2. Ashton J, Ubido B. The healthy city and the ecologic idea. *Journal of the Society for the Social History of Medicine*. 1991;41:173-180.

3. Coutts C. *Green Infrastructure and Public Health*. Routledge; 2016. doi:10.4324/9781315647623

4. Kochtitzky CS, Frumkin H, Rodriguez R, et al. Urban planning and public health at CDC. *Morbidity and Mortality Weekly Report*. 2006;55(Suppl 2):34-38.

5. Stulberg B. The key to changing individual health behaviors: change the environments that give rise to them. *Harvard Public Health Review*. 2014;2.

6. Schneider M, Stokols D. Multi-level theories of behavior change: social ecological theory. In: Shumaker J, Ockene K, Riekert K, eds. *Handbook of Health Behavior Change*. 3rd ed. Springer; 2009:85-106.

7. Barton H, Grant M. A health map for the local human habitat. *Journal for the Royal Society for the Promotion of Health*. 2006;126(6):252-253. doi:10.1177/1466424006070466

8. Ajzen I. From intentions to actions: a theory of planned behavior. In: Kuhl J, Beckmann J, eds. *Action Control: From Cognition to Behavior*. Springer-Verlag; 1985:11-39.

9. Fishbein M, Ajzen I. *Belief, Attitude, Intention and Behavior: An Introduction to Theory and Research*. Addison-Wesley; 1975.

10. Gourlan M, Bord A, Cousson-Gélie F. From intentions formation to their translation into behavior: an extended model of theory of planned behavior in the exercise domain. *Sport, Exercise, and Performance Psychology*. 2019;8(3):317-333. doi:10.1037/spy0000158

11. Glanz K, Viswanath K, Rimer B, eds. *Health Behavior: Theory, Research and Practice*. 5th ed. Jossey-Bass; 2015.

12. Bandura A. *Social Foundations of Thought and Action: A Social Cognitive Theory*. Prentice Hall; 1986.

13. Morris KS, McAuley E, Motl RW. Self-efficacy and environmental correlates of physical activity among older women and women with multiple sclerosis. *Health Education Research*. 2008;23(4):744-752. doi:10.1093/her/cym067

14. Kwon HJ, Ahn M. Boomers' intention to choose healthy housing materials: an application of the Health Belief Model. *Sustainability*. 2019;11(18):1-13. doi:10.3390/su11184869

15. Yoon HJ, Kim YJ. Understanding green advertising attitude and behavioral intention: an application of the health belief model. *Journal of Promotion Management*. 2016;22(1):49-70. doi:10.1080/10496491.2015.1107006

16. DiClemente RJ, Salazar LF, Crosby RA. *Health Behavior Theory for Public Health*. Jones & Bartlett; 2013.

17. Moore L V., Diez Roux A V., Nettleton JA, Jacobs DR, Franco M. Fast-food consumption, diet quality, and neighborhood exposure to fast food. *American Journal of Epidemiology*. 2009;170(1):29-36. doi:10.1093/aje/kwp090

18. Holder HD, Gruenewald PJ, Ponicki WR, et al. Effect of community-based interventions on high-risk drinking and alcohol-related injuries. *JAMA*. 2000;284(18):2341-2347. doi:10.1001/jama.284.18.2341

19. Thaler R, Sunstein C. *Nudge: Improving Decisions about Health, Wealth, and Happiness*. Yale University Press; 2008.

20. Lehner M, Mont O, Heiskanen E. Nudging—a promising tool for sustainable consumption behaviour? *Journal of Cleaner Production*. 2016;134:166-177. doi:10.1016/j.jclepro.2015.11.086

21. Shipman H. Smart art for smart cities. In: Mateev M, Poutziouris P, eds. *Creative Business and Social Innovations for a Sustainable Future*. Springer International; 2019:251 253.

22. Prochaska JO, DiClemente CC. Transtheoretical therapy: toward a more integrative model of change. *Psychotherapy: Theory, Research & Practice*. 1982;19:276-288.

23. Rogers EM. *Diffusion of Innovations*. Free Press of Glencoe; 1962.

24. Barker RG. *Ecological Psychology: Concepts and Methods for Studying the Environment of Human Behavior*. Stanford University Press; 1968.

25. Sallis JF, Cervero RB, Ascher W, Henderson KA, Kraft MK, Kerr J. An ecological approach to creating active living communities. *Annual Review of Public Health*. 2006;27(1):297-322. doi:10.1146/annurev.publhealth.27.021405.102100

26. Lefebvre RC. *Social Marketing and Social Change: Strategies and Tools for Health, Well-Being, and the Environment*. Jossey-Bass; 2013.

27. Maibach E. Increasing public awareness and facilitating behavior change: two guiding heuristics. In: Hannah L, Lovejoy T, eds. *Biodiversity and Climate Change*. Yale University Press; 2019:336-346.

28. Thackeray R, Neiger BL, Smith AK, Van Wagenen SB. Adoption and use of social media among public health departments. *BMC Public Health*. 2012;12(1):242. doi:10.1186/1471-2458-12-242

29. Austin J. Retro-"fitbit"ing the built environment: evaluating the pace of urban, suburban and rural conditions. In: *Proceedings of the Association of Collegiate Schools of Architecture/Association of Schools and Programs of Public Health Conference*. 2016;148-153.

30. Pattanayak SK, Pfaff A. Behavior, environment, and health in developing countries: evaluation and valuation. *Annual Review of Resource Economics*. 2009;1(1):183-217. doi:10.1146/annurev.resource.050708.144053

31. World Health Organization. The top 10 causes of death. Published 2018. Accessed May 6, 2020. https://www.who.int/news-room/fact-sheets/detail/the-top-10-causes-of-death

32. Blüher M. Obesity: Global epidemiology and pathogenesis. *Nature Reviews Endocrinology*. 2019;15(5):288-298. doi:10.1038/s41574-019-0176-8

33. Gee GC, Payne-Sturges DC. Environmental health disparities: a framework integrating psychosocial and environmental concepts. *Environmental Health Perspectives*. 2004;112(17):1645-1653. doi:10.1289/ehp.7074

34. Adler NE, Boyce T, Chesney MA, et al. Socioeconomic status and health: the challenge of the gradient. *American Psychologist*. 1994;49(1):15-24. doi:10.1037/0003-066X.49.1.15

35. Shim JK. Constructing "race" across the science-lay divide: racial formation in the epidemiology and experience of cardiovascular disease. *Social Studies of Science*. 2005;35(3):405-436. doi:10.1177/0306312705052105

36. Centers for Disease Control and Prevention. Adult Physical Inactivity Prevalence Maps by Race/Ethnicity. Published 2020. Accessed May 6, 2020. https://www.cdc.gov/physicalactivity/data/inactivity-prevalence-maps/index.html

37. Hales CM, Carroll MD, Fryar CD, Ogden CL. Prevalence of obesity and severe obesity among adults: United States, 2017–2018. NCHS Data Brief, no 360. National Center for Health Statistics. 2020. https://www.cdc.gov/nchs/products/databriefs/db360.htm

38. Rigolon A. A complex landscape of inequity in access to urban parks: a literature review. *Landscape and Urban Planning*. 2016;153:160-169. doi:10.1016/j.landurbplan.2016.05.017

39. Wolch JR, Byrne J, Newell JP. Urban green space, public health, and environmental justice: the challenge of making cities

"just green enough." *Landscape and Urban Planning*. 2014;125:234-244. doi:10.1016/j.landurbplan.2014.01.017

40. Harvard School of Public Health. Toxic food environment: how our surroundings influence what we eat. https://www.hsph.harvard.edu/obesity-prevention-source/obesity-causes/food-environment-and-obesity/

41. Raja S, Ma C, Yadav P. Beyond food deserts: measuring and mapping racial disparities in neighborhood food environments. *Journal of Planning Education and Research*. 2008;27(4):469-482. doi:10.1177/0739456X08317461

42. United Nations General Assembly. Report of the World Commission on Environment and Development: Our Common Future; 1987.

43. Hartig T, Mitchell R, de Vries S, Frumkin H. Nature and health. *Annual Review of Public Health*. 2014;35:21.1-21.22. doi:10.1146/annurev-publhealth-032013-182443

44. Steg L, Vlek C. Encouraging pro-environmental behaviour: an integrative review and research agenda. *Journal of Environmental Psychology*. 2009;29(3):309-317. doi:10.1016/j.jenvp.2008.10.004

45. Scannell L, Gifford R. The relations between natural and civic place attachment and pro-environmental behavior. *Journal of Environmental Psychology*. 2010;30(3):289-297. doi:10.1016/j.jenvp.2010.01.010

46. Scannell L, Gifford R. The psychology of place attachment. In: Gifford R, ed. *Environmental Psychology: Principles and Practice*. 5th ed. Optimal Books; 2014:272-300.

CHAPTER 20

LEGISLATION, POLICY, AND GOVERNANCE FOR HEALTHY PLACES

Eugenie L. Birch

KEY POINTS

- The public and private sectors, civil society, and professional organizations and residents individually and collectively create the built environment.
- The public sector plays a critical role in determining the form and contents of the built environment by establishing policies (statements that guide the courses of action for decision-makers to achieve desired goals) and legislating the rules and laws to realize policies.
- From the colonial period to the mid-twentieth century, local governments managed health issues within the built environment; thereafter, the federal government began to take responsibility for addressing certain concerns including environmental pollution but shared implementation with state and local governments.
- The United States Constitution outlines the form, roles, and responsibilities of the public sector, delegating specific powers for the national government and reserving those not delegated or prohibited in the Constitution to the states, and states through statutory provisions create local governments.
- As sprawling, automobile-dependent settlement patterns have contributed to physical inactivity, injuries, and air pol-

lution, some localities have added health-supporting policies to their management of the built environment.

INTRODUCTION

After three years of intense community engagement, the City of Minneapolis adopted a new comprehensive plan, Minneapolis 2040, that took effect January 1, 2020. To implement the plan, the city has developed new policies, ordinances, and programs that will have dramatic effects on the city's built environment and contribute to the physical and mental health of its citizens over the next twenty years. In this plan, the city declares that its first goal, among fourteen, is to eliminate disparities. Its policies include increasing the amount of affordable housing, banning single-family units, permitting the construction of clusters of tiny houses with common amenities, and supporting public and active transportation. Although this plan will have a strong impact on the city's built environment and may ameliorate some of the housing and transportation related outcomes of racial and income disparities, it will not solve the city's underlying social issues.

In the United States, places strive to be healthy through the actions of the public and private sectors, professional and civil society organizations, and their residents. These groups play important roles individually and collectively in shaping the **built environment**—homes, buildings, streets, open space, and infrastructure. They have done so for decades and have contributed to the dramatic improvement in life expectancy that increased from forty-seven in 1900 to seventy-nine years in 2019.

This chapter focuses on the role of the US public sector in determining the extent, contents, and form of the built environment based on its power to craft legislation, implement policies, make capital investments in place-shaping infrastructure, and adjudicate disputes and decisions that arise in these processes. It acknowledges that the private sector constructs the majority of the built environment, but it does so in adherence to public-sector directives. It incorporates international legislation, policy, or governance examples that highlight notable issues or best practices from around the world (table 20.1). This chapter holds that when operating under good governance practices, *public-sector policies* (statements that guide specific courses of action for decision-makers to achieve desired goals) that get interpreted through *legislation* (the exercise of the power of making rules or laws) and budget allocations are the product of inputs from a range of stakeholders. Finally, it maintains that integrated approaches to planning and development undertaken by different spheres of government are instrumental in producing healthy places. An underlying theme in the discussion is that recognizing and addressing inequities is an essential component of the effective use of legislation, policy, and governance in this work.

THE PUBLIC SECTOR, THE BUILT ENVIRONMENT AND HEALTH: ISSUES OVER TIME

Although the US public sector has long been interested in addressing health-threatening conditions emanating from the built environment, the types of problems, as well as the unit and level of government to deal with them, have varied since the founding of the United States of America. The earliest efforts to protect health through managing the built environment took place in cities at the local level. During the twentieth century, the federal government began to assume responsibility for problems that were too large and widespread to be managed locally.

Local Government: Seventeenth to Mid-Twentieth Centuries

From the seventeenth to the early to mid-twentieth centuries, the public sector has been primarily concerned with avoiding and

Table 20.1. What is a policy?

Not Policy	Policy
Program: A local government creates a program that offers incentives to convenience stores that voluntarily sell fruits and vegetables.	A city council adopts a resolution offering funds to convenience stores in the community that sell a minimum amount of fruits and vegetables.
Education: A business puts up signs encouraging employees to walk more.	A business makes a policy that provides up to 2 hours of paid time per week for employees to exercise.
Education: A school includes information about the harms of smoking in its health class curriculum.	A school board adopts a policy requiring all schools to be tobacco-free, both indoors and outdoors.
Practice: A church pastor promises the mayor that the church playground will be open to the community	A church board adopts an open-use policy that allows the public to use the church playground.

Source: ChangeLab Solutions. What is policy? No date. Accessed November 11, 2021. https://www.changelabsolutions.org/product/what-policy

controlling communicable disease (for example, epidemics of smallpox, yellow fever, diphtheria, malaria), the segregation of nuisance uses with harmful elements (for example, tanneries, slaughterhouses), sanitation (for example, privies, ventilation), the protection of food, the control of animals, and the reduction of fires. Local governments fashioned home-grown solutions. To address disease, they passed quarantine laws and built pest-houses and lazarettos to isolate the ill. To deal with odors and refuse, they restricted nuisance industries to locations distant from residences. To manage sanitation, they encouraged or required the construction of privies. To deal with food security, they monitored the quality of bread, the population's most important dietary staple. To control animals, they prohibited hogs from running freely through the streets and designated burial places for dead horses and cows. To prevent fire, they disallowed thatch roofs and other flammable material.[1]

In the nineteenth century, as places grew in number and size, rapid urbanization and associated industrialization magnified the earlier problems, especially epidemics, calling for large-scale solutions. Public-sector decision-makers supported the construction of municipal water and sanitation systems that in the forty years after the Civil War grew in number from 136 to 3,000.[1] They passed **tenement house** laws establishing maximum lot coverage for buildings and requiring windows for light and air, water and toilets in every dwelling unit, and the provision of fire escapes. The 1901 Tenement House Law of New York City and its successors were replicated widely.[2] By 1914, twenty-four states and eighty-two cities had such regulations.[3(pp12-16)] Later, they developed **zoning codes** to manage overall **land use** and modernized **building codes** to determine construction standards.

Again, New York City led the nation in adopting the first *comprehensive zoning code* in 1916.[4] To ensure light and air, the law governed building heights and segregated industry in special districts to control noise, pollution,

and dangerous traffic. The Supreme Court would uphold the constitutionality of the tenement house and zoning laws, using health to justify their decisions in the 1904 *Tenement House Department v. Moeschen* (203 US 583) and 1916 *Euclid v. Ambler* (272 US 365) decisions, defending zoning (see chapter 1).

Through the twentieth century, public-sector leaders worked to adapt building codes to accommodate advances in engineering and construction, meet the needs of the insurance industry, and promote health as advocated by the American Public Health Association and others. The building codes covered structural standards, occupancy rates, parking requirements, fire and natural disaster considerations, and plumbing and electrical systems.[5]

The resulting laws—tenement house regulations, zoning ordinances, and building codes—determined the character of the individual buildings that compose the built environment. In so doing, they codify basic health standards included in each law.

Mid-Twentieth Century to the Present

By the mid-twentieth century, as threats of communicable disease diminished, a new set of issues arose that would be deemed national: the growth of disease-ridden slums and the increase in environmental pollution. Congress responded with the 1937 Housing Act, the 1949 Housing and Slum Clearance Act (and amendments through 1974), and a battery of environmental laws starting with the Clean Air Act in 1970. With these laws, the national government increased its role in contributing to healthy places but did so in partnership with state and local governments.

In the late twentieth century, chronic diseases, often associated with obesity (for example, diabetes, cardiovascular disease, and some forms of cancer), surfaced as leading causes of illness and death. Health professionals associated these conditions with two problems: a built environment that discouraged physical activity and an American lifestyle that encouraged a high-caloric, fat- and sugar-saturated diet. Added to these, drug dependency, especially among low-income populations, rose dramatically. This led to the emergence of solutions based on tri-level partnerships among the federal, state, and local governments and the development of regional alliances.

By the last decade of the twentieth century, the health impacts of climate change rose in importance, publicized by five extensive reports issued by the *Intergovernmental Panel on Climate Change (IPCC)*. Taken together, the IPCC reports highlight increased vector-borne disease, temperature, and precipitation extremes (for example, floods, drought, food insecurity). Public-sector responses to these threats ranged from the global (2015 Paris Agreement) to the local (sustainability plans).

THE LEGAL BASIS FOR REGULATING THE BUILT ENVIRONMENT

In the United States, the public sector or government, encompassing national to the local levels, affects the built environment in varying ways in shaping its spatial and social arrangements, many of which affect health. The United States is a federal system, one that has a high degree of decentralization or distribution of powers from the central to the local governments. Other governments in the world operate under a unitary system, one that concentrates power at the national level (France and the United Kingdom), or as authoritarian states, where a single individual or small group governs and holds all political power (Cuba, North Korea, Iran).

The US Federal System and the Division of Power between National and Subnational Governments

As a federal system, the United States divides power between national and subnational governments guided by the US Constitution and relevant case law that frame the roles, powers, and responsibilities of each level. The Constitution establishes the national government as having three branches (executive/president, legislative/Congress, and judicial/Supreme Court and associated lower courts) and lists the powers of each. The first provision deals with the legislative branch specifying its organization, its powers, and the process for turning legislation into law. In particular, article 1, section 7, outlines the legislative process, with legislation originating in either the House of Representatives or the Senate, passing both houses, before being sent to the executive for signed approval that turns it into law. If not approved or vetoed, Congress can override a veto with a two-thirds vote in each house. Article 1, section 8, enumerates the areas in which Congress can act: to collect taxes, borrow and coin money, regulate commerce, determine citizenship, declare war, establish post offices and post roads, protect inventions, create courts, regulate behavior on the high seas, maintain an army and navy, and pass laws that are necessary and proper to carry out the listed function.[6] In this capacity, the national government can affect the built environment by offering models for desirable outcomes (for example, bike and pedestrian safety), set and regulate standards (clean air), and allocate budgets (transportation, housing).

The Constitution discusses the other two branches in articles 2 and 3. The president is commander-in-chief of the US military and can enter into treaties with the consent of the Senate; offer pardons; appoint ambassadors, Supreme Court judges, and public ministers; seek the advice of executive departments; give a state of the union report to Congress; and "take care that the Laws be faithfully executed" (US Constitution, article 2, section 3). The judicial branch has jurisdiction over constitutional issues, US laws, and treaties.

As discussed earlier, Congress has developed legislation affecting the built environment that may have not been envisioned by the original framers of the Constitution and that has come under legal challenge. This phenomenon certainly applies to a number of health-related laws, such as the 1906 Pure Food and Drug Act, which protects consumers from adulterating, adding harmful ingredients, or mislabeling food, and the Clean Air Act, which establishes and regulates disease-preventing air quality standards to be implemented by the states. When upholding the constitutionality of the laws, the courts frequently reference two clauses: regulating commerce and exercising necessary and proper actions.[7]

The Constitution permits the president to sign treaties and agreements only with the consent of the Senate. However, since World War II, presidents have entered into more than fifteen thousand such contracts under a different rubric, article 2, section 3, that mandates that the president take care that nation's laws be faithfully executed. A prime example of the application of this concept is the *Paris Agreement*, which addresses climate change, a phenomenon whose health effects include exposure to extreme weather events (for example, hurricanes, droughts, sea level rise, flooding), increased vector-borne disease, and extreme heat. In 2015, President Barack Obama signed the agreement, acting under two laws: the Global Climate Protection Act (1987) and the Clean Air Act (1970); both allow the president to enter into international agreements to achieve their domestic aims.[8]

Division of Power between States and Localities

In detailing the American brand of federalism, the US Constitution delineates the division of power between the federal and state governments through the Tenth Amendment that declares: "powers not delegated to the United States by the Constitution, nor prohibited by it to the States, are reserved to the States respectively, or to the people." In pursuing their constitutionally designated roles, state governments have replicated the three branches (executive/governor, legislative, and judicial) and, in turn, have defined their relationship with localities within their boundaries. Here, a state delegates powers to localities either through legislated statutes that permit local or municipal governments to govern themselves as they wish, popularly known as *home rule*, or take the form of a city charter or statutes that list specific functions, establishing what is

known as *Dillon's rule*, thereby limiting the powers of a locality to those expressly granted by the state. As of 2020, there were three times as many Dillon's rule states as home rule states.

The implications of one versus the other are quite different. In the former instance, a city has broad government authority and can act without state authorization. In the latter circumstance, a locality has more narrow government authority and must seek permission from the state legislature if it wants to undertake new functions. For example, the New York City Charter, enacted in 1898 and last amended in 1989, has several provisions that affect health beyond the creation of a department of health; these include powers related to city planning, environmental protection, sanitation, parks, transportation, aging, and budget.[9] This charter has allowed New York City to pass and implement a great number of laws that affect the built environment, many with provisions that affect health. These range from development regulations that shape the built environment (for example, zoning governing the use and intensity of use of land, building codes, establishing standards for buildings and nonbuilding structures) to health laws that can affect the built environment (for example, regulating conditions related to communicable diseases, monitoring water, sewer and solid waste services). If New York State were governed by Dillon's rule, these policies would all be void unless the state granted the local governments authority to adopt them.

Another legal doctrine concerning the various powers between different levels of government is **preemption**, which permits the power of lower levels of government to be limited or eliminated by higher levels. Preemption can still override local laws in home rule states. Preemption plays a role in a plethora of equity-related issues, such as minimum wage standards, paid sick leave, and regulation of tobacco and alcohol products, and it is defined by three different subcategories: (1) *floor preemption*, which sets minimum standards by higher-level government that prohibits lower-level governments from enacting laws that are less protective; (2) *ceiling preemption*, which prohibits lower-level governments from enacting more protective regulations than higher-level laws; and (3) *vacuum or null preemption*, which prohibits a lower-level government from enacting any regulations on a specific topic.[10] Although preemption can be detrimental to the general well-being and public health of populations when it is ambiguous, is restrictive, or results in unregulated subject matters at the local level, it can also be used a tool that furthers health equity by creating protections for vulnerable populations. For example, the Affordable Care Act of 2010 required restaurants and retail food establishments with twenty or more locations to add calorie and nutrition food labels to their menus. This created a national baseline for improved communication to consumers about their food choices and is intended to reduce caloric intake from these establishments, thereby reducing obesity in the United States.

WHAT THE FEDERAL GOVERNMENT DOES TO PROMOTE HEALTH IN THE BUILT ENVIRONMENT

Today, the federal government promotes health in the built environment. This is done through its powers to develop models, set and regulate standards, and allocate budget to specific programs. These approaches are outlined below with examples from transportation and housing.

Develops Models

Ever since the US Department of Commerce published the *Standard State Zoning Enabling Act* (1924) and the *Standard City Planning Enabling Act* (1927), the various executive departments have provided technical assistance and models for promoting policies and programs to enhance safety, health, and general welfare.[11,12] For example, with 20 percent of the US population having disabilities and in anticipation of aging, the US Department of Transportation is sponsoring a "complete trip" demonstration to accessible transportation for a person with disabilities to go from home to a destination with breaks in the travel chain.[13]

Sets and Regulates Standards

As mentioned earlier, by the mid-twentieth century, local law alone would not guarantee protection from multiple unhealthy environmental conditions experienced in the United States related to water, air, and hazardous waste pollution. The various campaigns by civil society and professional organizations, supported by scientific and popular writing on the subject that publicized the problem, pushed Congress to respond. In quick succession, Congress passed the Clean Air Act Extension of 1970, 1977, 1990 (Clean Air Act), the Federal Water Pollution Control Act Amendments of 1972 (Clean Water Act), the Safe Drinking Water Act of 1974, and the Comprehensive Environmental Response and Liability Act of 1980 (Superfund). This legislation established scientifically based minimum standards, supported cleanup programs, and strengthened enforcement tools for violations. For example, the Clean Air Act established the National Ambient Air Quality Standards and mandated that the states develop implementation plans to meet them. The Clean Water Act established the National Pollution Discharge Elimination System that regulates and monitors the amount of pollutants discharged from a single point into water bodies by any entity. Cities, for instance must conform to it with their sewage and wastewater disposal programs.

The federal environmental laws have not been perfect, but they created much healthier places while, despite some concerns to the contrary, the economy has flourished. In 2017, two former US Environmental Protection Agency (EPA) officials noted that "since the inception of the EPA 46 years ago, the United States has enjoyed significant progress in reducing public health effects from exposure to pollution, and our gross domestic product has tripled."[14] Among the positive results is that water and air pollution from point sources (for example, sewer discharges into water bodies; particulate matter from incineration) has been reduced dramatically. When the Clean Water Act was passed in the early 1970s, only 29 percent of the US population lived in jurisdictions where sewage met the higher secondary treatment standards; by 2020, the figure had risen to 94 percent.[15] Today, 90 percent of the US population served by the more than 150,000 public water systems meet the national standards; in the 1970s, no common standards existed.[16] Between 1970 and 2019, air pollution in the US declined 77 percent.[17]

Internationally, the creation of legally binding treaties and agreements that support collaboration and solidarity between countries has resulted in effective efforts of tackling complex environmental and health threats. Examples are the 1997 Kyoto Protocol and the 2015 Paris Agreement, which both set international standards for addressing global climate change and greenhouse gas emissions.[18]

In setting standards and regulations, three other areas serve as examples of how the federal government can affect the built environment indirectly: smoking, the Corporate Average Fuel Economy (CAFE) standards, and consumer product safety. With regard to smoking, the publication of *Smoking and Health, Report of the Advisory Committee of the Surgeon General of the US Public Health Service* by the US Department of Health, Education and Welfare in 1964 definitively diagnosed smoking as being the cause of several lethal diseases, leading Congress to pass the *Federal Labeling and Advertising Act of 1965*, with its warnings about the dangers of smoking. These actions stimulated four decades of federal (and local legislation) prohibiting smoking in indoor places, public parks, public transportation, and other public facilities. CAFE standards first passed by Congress in 1975 and administered by the US Department of Transportation are fuel efficiency rules that regulate how far a vehicle must travel on one gallon of fuel and thus control carbon emissions. CAFE standards were reduced during the Trump administration and are likely to be increased during the Biden administration as part of the response to global warming.[19] Finally, the EPA established rules to reduce harmful exposures to formaldehyde emitted into the air from certain composite wood products, an action that affects building construction materials.

The process of setting standards and regulations generally involves substantial public input. These processes may be complicated by varying degrees of public support and competing interests between stakeholders that sometimes undermine or resist certain laws.[20] Although public participation is an important aspect of policy change initiatives, individual support is usually influenced by opinions from a personal perspective, considering consequences to the extent that they are personally "effective, fair, and unintrusive."[21(p649)] In addition, other factors such as partisan identity and polarization often drive levels of support and opposition, and disagreements between political parties on issues such as climate change and environmental policy can result in efforts by opposing parties at high levels to limit, slow, or block implementation of certain regulations.[22]

Allocates Budget

Through its budget allocations, the federal government has had a significant impact on the built environment in cities and suburbs, especially in the realms of transportation and housing. Most such projects involve federal funds awarded (often through states and cities) to private contractors to do the actual construction. It has been funding these areas since the New Deal period, but it has increased its authorizations dramatically from the second half of the twentieth century to the present.

Transportation

From 1956 to 2015, Congress authorized seven major transportation acts. The initial effort, the Federal Highway Act of 1956 and its 1962 amendment, resulted in the construction of the nation's forty-one-thousand-mile inter-state highway system and mandated the creation of metropolitan planning organizations (MPOs), now numbering more than four hundred, for urban areas. Over time, the MPOs have advanced regional planning. Between 1991 and 2012, Congress passed five more transportation acts that went beyond highway construction to support more than a trillion dollars' worth of multimodal solutions, including mass transit, active transportation (walking and biking) through rails to trails, mandating alignment with the Clean Air Act, and other planning efforts.

This transportation spending has had multiple outcomes related to health. The early highway acts contributed to the sprawling settlement patterns of the United States and associated auto dependency for all aspects of life. Although only a small percentage of the nation's 2.3 billion acres, one indicator of sprawl is that urban land consumption outpaced population growth. According to the US Department of Agriculture's major land use estimates, urban land more than tripled between 1949 and 2012, while population increase only doubled.[23] Later highway acts were more health-supporting because they allocated funding for active transportation and public transit that in both instances would reduce greenhouse gases while encouraging more healthy behaviors like walking and biking.

Housing

Federal involvement in housing dates to the New Deal period with Congress approving the 1937 Housing Act that supported the construction of public housing and its renewal in the 1949 Housing and Slum Clearance Act, which together resulted in the construction of a million units by 1974 when President Richard Nixon terminated the program. Although the design of the resulting projects—large-scale development of high-density units—has come under extreme criticism recently, the program provided a healthy alternative to available housing at the time and an escape from slums. In an effort to improve deteriorated public housing projects, Congress authorized the HOPE VI program in the 1990s, allocating more than $6 billion for the reconstruction of high-density units into mixed-income developments. From 1949 to 1974, Congress authorized a series of urban renewal programs that had a dramatic effect on the built environment of the nation's cities. Again, these efforts had considerable weaknesses, but they too transformed downtowns and whole neighborhoods according to the standards of the day. After 1974, the federal government provided block grants to localities to undertake self-defined community development initiatives and established a voucher program for low-income families to rent housing from the private sector. It also crafted the low-income housing tax credit—not a budget allocation, but a reduction of government revenues—to encourage the construction of affordable housing, a program that has yielded 3.2 million housing units in mixed-income buildings.

WHAT LOCAL GOVERNMENT DOES TO PROMOTE HEALTH IN THE BUILT ENVIRONMENT: CURRENT INNOVATIONS

Local government activities that shape the built environment and therefore can affect health encompass four areas: complying with federal mandates, engaging in comprehensive planning, crafting and implementing development regulations, and changing priorities in capital and operating budgets. In recent years, local governments have been innovating in each of these areas in an effort to meet multiple goals and reap co-benefits by improving the quality of life and health of their residents while addressing inequality and responding to climate change. The following sections offer examples of these innovations.

Complying with Federal Mandates

As discussed above, when the federal government established standard setting and regulatory frameworks for policies related to the environment, transportation, and housing, it delegated implementation to the states and local governments but maintained some degree of oversight in monitoring local programs and outcomes. This has led some localities to develop innovative solutions that they often have to negotiate with the higher level of government. The city of Philadelphia's *Clean Waters Green City* plan (2011) is a prime example. In violation of the Clean Water Act, which traditionally had been remedied through such hard infrastructure solutions as investing in pipes, concrete channels, and mechanized cleaning systems, the city presented a green infrastructure approach, a twenty-five-year, $1.2 billion commitment to invest in such nature-based solutions (see chapter 16). These efforts include constructing water gardens and bioswales, incentivizing permeable paving in large parking lots and roof gardens, restoring rivers and streams, investing in open space at different scales, and other methods to collect and filter stormwater that would otherwise run into the Delaware and Schuylkill Rivers at the boundary of the city. By 2020, the plan had produced 178 public projects, 48 percent related to increasing open space and 65 percent in low- and moderate-income census blocks. An economic analysis of the effects of the plan includes a $50 million cost savings in health-related costs and $23 million in aggregate household benefits related to increased physical activities stimulated by open space projects.[24] The plan is on target to meet its ten-year goals.

Engaging in Comprehensive Planning: Integrating Health

Around the turn of the twenty-first century, the incorporation of health and wellness into design and built environment practices became more present in public-sector discussions, stimulated by professional organizations including the American Public Health Association, Urban Land Institute, Congress for New Urbanism, Transportation Research Board, American Society of Landscape Architects, and American Planning Association (APA). For example, the APA, the professional organization for forty-thousand US practicing planners and planning officials, picked up the trend, identifying localities that were beginning to place health on an equal standing with land use, transportation, housing, open space, and the environment in their comprehensive, sustainability, and sectoral plans.

To provide information to its members, the APA began a multipronged research, education, and advocacy initiative that continues to this day. Included in its efforts were a Planning Advisory Service study, *Integrating Planning and Public Health: Tools and Strategies to Create Healthy Places* (2006), that offered a list of the appropriate areas of concern: water and air quality, obesity and inactivity, crime, pedestrian safety, hazardous waste sites, and mental health. Six years later, the APA research division, in conjunction with the US Centers for Disease Control and Prevention, would produce *Healthy Planning* (2012) and *Healthy Plan Making* (2013), which assessed the emergence of health in comprehensive and sustainability plans in nearly nine hundred localities. Notably, these publications outlined the range of concerns related the built environment that health planning would encompass: active living, reduction of environmental exposures, emergency preparedness, food security, and mental health protection. Through twenty-two in-depth case studies of plans dating from 1996 to 2011, the APA assessed how and why communities were including these areas and then identified areas needing improvement. The findings emphasized the need to create better sources of data and mapping, improve implementation language, and coordinate programs and funding across city agencies. They also led to a greater focus on the planners' key policy instrument, comprehensive planning, and its means of implementation (zoning, capital improvements) to address its contributions to the nation's obesity epidemic.

Building on the healthy planning research from the first decade of the twenty-first century, the APA gave attention to improving diagnostic and data gaps, illustrating, adapting, and advocating new tools like health impact assessments. In 2016, it published *Health Impact Assessment Can Inform Planning to Promote Public Health*, a review of 134 health impact assessments undertaken across the United States between 2004 and 2014 (see chapter 22 for more on health impact assessments). The report supported their use, arguing that the technique not only gauged the effects of projects, plans, and policies at various scales—street to region—but also would further assist in decision-making through improved issue framing, increased data analysis, citizen involvement, and cross-sector collaboration. Advocates also underlined its use in identifying and correcting inequities in the planning and development of the built environment.[25]

In the ensuing years, an increasing number of localities have included health elements in their comprehensive plans. Two examples are illustrative: the *Los Angeles General Plan* (2015), covering a ten-year period, and the more recent *Minneapolis 2040* (2020); the first plan covers the city of Los Angeles alone, and the Minneapolis plan is part of a long-standing regional strategy. No evaluation is available to document the impacts of these plans on health; however, they do offer guidance on where to target specific health-promoting policy, systems, and environmental change to improve well-being, quality, and length of life across all zip codes.

Plan for a Healthy Los Angeles

The state of California mandates that every city and county produce a comprehensive plan having seven elements (land use, open space, conservation, housing, circulation, noise, and safety), and other elements incorporated at the will of the city or county, every ten years. In 2012, when revising its general plan, the Los Angeles Planning Department added a health and wellness element, Plan for a Healthy Los

Angeles.[26] Here, the city articulates its vision for a healthy city:

A healthy city has neighborhoods where *health-promoting goods and services are abundant and accessible*, so that the healthy choice is the easy choice for all residents. Health is further supported by *safe multi-modal corridors* that offer active transportation alternatives, *access to a diverse housing stock* that offers options for all ages and incomes, *ample opportunities for recreation*, *healthy food options*, and a vibrant economy that offers *quality employment opportunities*.[27(p34)] (emphasis added)

To achieve this vision, the element calls for repurposing vacant spaces for health services; adding basic amenities (water fountains, restrooms, trash cans); building fifty new parks and thirty fully accessible playgrounds in underserved communities; transforming the channelized Los Angeles River into a greenway; siting grocery stores, farmers' markets, and community gardens in areas experiencing inequitable food access and limited healthy food options; and increasing landscape buffers around highways and other noxious activities to reduce pollution. The new element incorporates an innovative *Health Atlas*, a living document that uses performance metrics to track improvements to extensive baseline data on the concentration of high rates of obesity, diabetes, coronary heart disease, and respiratory illnesses as mapped in low-income communities.[27]

Minneapolis 2040

In adopting Minneapolis 2040, the city, along with several other municipalities in the seven-county Twins Cities region, is conforming to the state's Metropolitan Land Planning Act (1977). This law requires the localities to produce plans aligned with the area's regional development plan that covers a number of boundary-transcending systems: water, wastewater, transportation, housing, and open space. In addition to addressing these issues, the city and other municipalities elected to add health to its regional plan. Unlike the Los Angeles plan, it does not have separate chapters on the elements but instead offers a three-part document encompassing goals (fourteen, of which one directly addresses health), topics (eleven short discussions, of which one is on public health), and plan policies (a list of one hundred). In addition to the complete list of policies in the third part, the authors of the plan weave the policies throughout all the sections, and the two sections directly labeled health demonstrate the full range of policies that apply. The point is to show that the plan's parts are synergistic—that many policies apply to more than one goal.

Although the plan's presentation is innovative, the overall content is even more groundbreaking as the plan's new directions aim to create a dense, transit-oriented city while undoing significant racial disparities. In so doing, it not only views racial discrimination as a social and economic issue, but also a health concern. It interprets this belief in the many policies that affect the built environment. For example, to achieve density, it eliminated single-family zoning citywide, thereby automatically permitting duplex and triplex developments on previously single-family lots. To offer more housing choices, it increased housing density and mandates affordable units in multifamily apartments, removes several restrictions on the size and form of dwellings and parking requirements, and permits cluster developments of tiny dwellings with shared common areas. It refines the mixed-use concept, differentiating among categories of land use, ranging from neighborhoods to commercial corridors. In addition, it promotes public transit and active transportation to increase access to affordable transportation. Although these policies are common in many comprehensive plans, what differentiates Minneapolis 2040 is its intentional use to eliminate economic and racial disparities throughout the city.[28]

Crafting and Implementing Development Regulations

As the adoption of zoning swept the United States in the twentieth century, its framers first innovated by providing alternatives for how a building might fit on a lot, then moved to loosen single-use designations, and more recently advocated new devices to promote health. This work, taking place since the 1950s, emanated from changing definitions of what constituted "good" urban life with ideas drawn from scholarly studies in the social and physical sciences, as well as changes in the US economy.[29-31]

Providing Alternatives for Building Design and Land Uses

One of the earliest innovations was the invention of the **floor area ratio** (**FAR**), a figure based on the size of a lot and specific setback requirements to determine the permitted size of a building while providing light and air and, ultimately, determining the number of occupants.[4] Favored by architects, the FAR approach offered more design liberties while allowing municipal decision-makers to have closer controls on density, a key means to affect the health aspects of the built environment.

A second innovation developed around loosening of the laws' single-use orientation to allow mixed-use, walkable neighborhoods. This effort dates from the 1980s, when two groups, urban designers and environmentalists, offered solutions to address US sprawl-induced settlement patterns that the public sector adopted. The first group, which designers labeled **New Urbanists** and led by Miami architects Andres Duany and Elizabeth Plater-Zyberk, crafted traditional neighborhood design principles, based on walkability, mixed use, and a variety of housing sizes, that they then translated into **form-based zoning** codes. These codes determined the location and shapes of buildings, not their use. Since their invention, 387 municipalities have incorporated the ideas into their zoning codes, and 300 more have them under consideration.[32] In

2009, Miami, Florida, replaced its entire traditional zoning ordinance with a form-based code.[32,33]

Although the New Urbanists were primarily focused on offering romanticized historical small-town architectural characteristics to the American landscape as a replacement for the dominant pattern of sprawling, low-density, auto-dependent suburbs, they did have a public health dimension to their arguments. Their explanation of the effects of walkability illustrates this point:

> It's not that walkable neighborhoods make you thin, but they provide an environment where everyday activity is facilitated. That means that some people are going to get more exercise than they would otherwise. Those people are likely to end up healthier.[34(p3)]

The second group, the environmentalists, have many outlets and campaigns. Smart Growth America, an association founded in 2000, provides an example of their contributions. This group's website communicates their vision of the United States as a place "where no matter where you live, or who you are, you can enjoy living in a place that is healthy, prosperous, and resilient," a goal that it pursues by offering research, technical advice, and public education on mixed-use, walkable neighborhoods, transit-oriented development, and urban growth limits, all of which can be instituted through zoning.

Prioritizing Health in Operating and Capital Budgets

By the turn of the twenty-first century, as health became more a prominent topic, public-sector decision-makers crafted a number of responses beyond the planning and zoning changes discussed above. They rethought the design of streets and promoted better nutrition through allowing urban agriculture and siting grocery stores and farmers' markets in areas designated as food deserts. In so doing,

they developed and paid for the emerging innovative ideas through allocations in the operating and capital budgets. The complete streets program is an example of this type of effort.

Municipal agencies, including departments of city planning, transportation, and parks, would soon support what would become known as **complete streets**, an engineering and design approach that incorporates all modes of transportation, from walking to bike to transit to car, so as to enable all people regardless of age or ability to use streets safely. The idea was to reduce pedestrian fatalities (between 2008 and 2017 in the United States, drivers killed more than forty-nine thousand pedestrians) and address obesity (ninety-three million Americans are obese, and many have no or limited access to safe active living amenities due to poor planning in cities and suburbs). These conditions disproportionately affect populations living in low-income census tracts.[35] By 2018, places of all sizes—nearly fifteen hundred communities in fifty states, Puerto Rico, and the District of Columbia—had passed complete streets policies, although the extent of local implementation varies widely.[35]

A recent iteration of many of these ideas is the **fifteen-minute city**, conceived by Carlos Moreno of the Sorbonne University and Paris mayor Anne Hidalgo's special envoy for smart cities. The concept calls for all residents to meet their residential, occupational, recreational, and health needs within a fifteen-minute walk or bicycle ride. City leaders in Barcelona, Detroit, London, Melbourne, Milan, and Portland, Oregon, are working to invest in this goal.[36] It is a challenge to move the fifteen-minute city idea from concept to implementation in Paris's twenty arrondissements, or administrative districts, because of the resulting fragmentation in citywide governance. This issue exists around the globe, in large and small cities, challenging citywide planning, regulating, and implementing (box 20.1).

BOX 20.1 THE NEW URBAN AGENDA

Adopted in 2016 at the United Nations Conference on Housing and Sustainable Development Goals and available in more than thirty languages, the New Urban Agenda serves as a call to action and global guide for sustainable and equitable future urbanization. A tool based on the United Nation's Sustainable Development Goal 11, the New Urban Agenda offers resources and frameworks for various stakeholders on principles of urban development and the links between sustainability and the complex facets of urban life across various contexts. Although the agenda serves as a global resource, special attention is called to the unique emerging challenges of "developing countries…, least developed countries, landlocked developing countries and small island developing States…, middle-income countries…, countries in situations of conflict, as well as countries and territories under foreign occupation, post-conflict countries and countries affected by natural and human-made disasters."[a]

Complementary to the New Urban Agenda are resources such as the following[a]:

- **Subject Index**, referencing key concepts and their corresponding locations
- **Glossary** of terms and definitions
- **Implementing Branding Kit**, which provides graphic support and guidelines
- **New Urban Agenda Illustrated Handbook**, which serves as a user-friendly device for effective planning and implementation by providing definitions and practical applications; the handbook is subdivided into three main chapters of (1) Core Dimensions, (2) Means of Implementation and (3) Governance, Follow-up, and Review

Figure 20.1. The core dimensions and means of implementation of the New Urban Agenda, which serves as a guide for equitable and sustainable urbanization across the world. Source: UN Habitat. *New Urban Agenda Illustrated Handbook.* 2020. https://unhabitat.org/sites/default/files/2020/12/nua_handbook_14dec2020_2.pdf. The content of this publication has not been approved by the United Nations and does not reflect the views of the United Nations or its officials or Member States.

REFERENCE

a.   UN Habitat. New Urban Agenda. United Nations Conference on Housing and Sustainable Urban Development (Habitat 111). United Nations; 2016. https://habitat3.org/the-new-urban-agenda/

CONCLUSION

In United States and around the globe, policy, legislation, and governance have played important roles in the past and will continue to do so in the future in promoting places that ensure health-supporting built environments. Initially in the United States, local governments assumed responsibility for health matters related to sanitation, noxious land uses, fire, and food. Later, the federal government took on responses to issues related to environmental pollution, affordable housing, transportation, and climate change.

Overall, the public sector is instrumental in shaping the built environment. The US Constitution defines the roles of the US tripartite federal system. In general, the federal government sets and regulates standards, allocates budget, and adjudicates disputes related to the built environment. It delegates implementation powers to states and localities to manage the form and character of the built environment through their plans, regulations, and budget allocations.

In the late twentieth century, the association of poor health—especially with the rise of chronic diseases associated with obesity and poor community design—raised planning and public health as a topic equal to transportation, housing, environmental protection. City and regional planners working through the APA, along with other professional and civil society organizations, convinced public-sector decision-makers to institute innovative approaches to managing the built environment. In the first decades of the twenty-first century, they integrated health elements in comprehensive plans, revised their thinking about zoning, developed new diagnostic tools, and refashioned programs in transportation, housing, and alleviating food insecurity.

The damage wrought by the COVID-19 pandemic underlined the importance of raising public health considerations in the policy, legislation, and governance approaches of localities and the other spheres of government to their built environments in the United States and elsewhere. It especially brought a greater understanding of the inequities in many current efforts (see chapter 9). Improvements in problem identification, solutions, and implementation will remain in the forefront of public actions to promote health-supporting built environments in the decades to come.

DISCUSSION QUESTIONS

1. What are the ways in which policy and legislation are different?
2. How might approaches to affecting change differ at the different levels of government?
3. What are complete streets, and why should communities have policies that favor them?
4. What are some actions local governments can take to promote health through the built environment?
5. In what ways could the New Urban Agenda be used to promote health in low-to-middle-income countries?

DISCLOSURE OF COMPETING INTERESTS

Eugenie L. Birch discloses no competing interests.

REFERENCES

1. Duffy J. *The Sanitarians: A History of American Public Health*. University of Illinois Press, 1992.

2. Gilbert JA. Tenements and takings: Tenement House Department of New York v. Moeschen as a counterpoint to Lochner v. New York. *Fordham Urban Law Journal*. 1991;18:3. https://ir.lawnet.fordham.edu /ulj/vol18/iss3/1/

3. DeForest RW. A brief history of the housing movement in America. *Annals of the American Academy of Political and Social Science*. 1914;51(1):8-16. https://www.jstor .org/stable/pdf/1012239.pdf

4. Ellis JG. *Urban Design The Legacy of the New York 1916 Zoning Ordinance*. SPURS; 2017. https://www.spur.org/sites/default/files /events_pdfs/2017.02.22%20Zoning%20 at%20100%20-%20A%20Look%20Back. pdf

5. Listokin D, Hattis DB. Building Codes and housing. *Cityscape*. 2005;8(1):21-67. http: //www.jstor.org/stable/20868571

6. Library of Congress. US Constitution Annotated. 2021. https://constitution .congress.gov/constitution/

7. Lawyers Name Redacted. *Federalism, State Sovereignty, and the Constitution: Basis and Limits of Congressional Power*. Congressional Research Service; 2013. https:// www.everycrsreport.com/files/20130923 _RL30315_c88ad63abd55d1e4900df514f2 c16f709b598ff4.pdf

8. Bundy K, Cummings B, Pardee V, Siegel K. Yes, he can: President Obama's power to make an international climate commitment without waiting for Congress. Center for Biological Diversity Climate Law Institute. December 2009. https: //www.biologicaldiversity.org/programs /climate_law_institute/pdfs/Yes_He_Can _120809.pdf

9. New York City. The NYC Charter. 2006. https://law.justia.com/codes/new-york /2006/new-york-city-charter

10. ChangeLab Solutions. Fundamentals of Preemption. 2019. https://www .changelabsolutions.org/sites/default /files/2020-06/Fundamentals_of _Preemption_FINAL_Accessible-PDF -for-Screen_20200608_0.pdf

11. US Department of Commerce. A Standard State Zoning Enabling Act. US Government Printing Office; 1926. https: //planning-org-uploaded-media.s3 .amazonaws.com/legacy_resources /growingsmart/pdf/SZEnablingAct1926.pdf

12. US Department of Commerce. A Standard City Planning Enabling Act. US Government Printing Office; 1928. https: //planning-org-uploaded-media.s3 .amazonaws.com/legacy_resources /growingsmart/pdf/CPEnabling%20 Act1928.pdf

13. US Department of Transportation. Accessible Transportation Technologies Research Initiative (ATTRI): Complete Trip. 2021. https://www.its.dot.gov /research_archives/attri/index.htm

14. McCarthy G, Burke T. We need a strong Environmental Protection Agency. It's about public health! *American Journal of Public Health*. 2017;107(5). https: //www.ncbi.nlm.nih.gov/pmc/articles /PMC5388973/

15. EPA Alumni Association. Water Quality, A Half Century of Progress. April 2020. https://8aa2f37f-9df5-499a-a6c0 -5423f9491992.filesusr.com/ugd/e7c323 _8d01123b7f274907808fea76e19a20ec.pdf

16. EPA Alumni Association. Drinking Water, A Half Century of Progress. April 2020. https://www.epaalumni.org/hcp /drinkingwater.pdf

17. US Environmental Protection Agency. Our Nation's Air. 2020. https://gispub.epa.gov /air/trendsreport/2020/documentation /AirTrends_Flyer.pdf

18. Hunter D. International environmental law: international treaties and principles protect the environment and guard against climate change. *American Bar Association Journal*. 2021;19:1. https://www.americanbar.org/groups/public_education/publications/insights-on-law-and-society/volume-19/insights-vol--19---issue-1/international-environmental-law/

19. Biden J. Remarks by President Biden Before Signing Executive Actions on Tackling Climate Change, Creating Jobs, and Restoring Scientific Integrity. January 27, 2021. https://www.whitehouse.gov/briefing-room/speeches-remarks/2021/01/27/remarks-by-president-biden-before-signing-executive-actions-on-tackling-climate-change-creating-jobs-and-restoring-scientific-integrity/

20. Drews S, Van den Bergh JC. What explains public support for climate policies? A review of empirical and experimental studies. *Climate Policy*. 2016:16(7):855-876.

21. Huber RA, Wicki ML, Bernauer T. Public support for environmental policy depends on beliefs concerning effectiveness, intrusiveness, and fairness. *Environmental Politics*. 2020;29(4):649-673. doi:10.1080/09644016.2019.1629171

22. Dunlap RE, McCright AM, Yarosh JH. The political divide on climate change: partisan polarization widens in the US. *Environment: Science and Policy for Sustainable Development*. 2016;58(5):4-23.

23. Bigelow DP, Borchers A. 2017. Major Uses of Land in the United States, 2012, EIB-178, US Department of Agriculture, Economic Research Service; August 2017. https://www.ers.usda.gov/webdocs/publications/84880/eib-178.pdf?v=9466.7

24. Neukrug, H. Personal communication with the author. January 18, 2021.

25. WHO. Health Impact Assessment. No date. Accessed January 17, 2021. https://www.who.int/health-topics/health-impact-assessment#tab=tab_1

26. Los Angeles Department of City Planning. Plan for a Healthy Los Angeles. 2015. https://planning.lacity.org/odocument/7f065983-ff10-4e76-81e5-e166c9b78a9e/Plan_for_a_Healthy_Los_Angeles.pdf

27. Los Angeles Department of City Planning. Health Atlas for the City of Los Angeles. 2013. https://planning.lacity.org/odocument/7f065983-ff10-4e76-81e5-e166c9b78a9e/Plan_for_a_Healthy_Los_Angeles.pdf

28. Minneapolis 2040—The City's Comprehensive Plan. City of Minneapolis Department of Community Planning and Economic Development. 2020. https://minneapolis2040.com/media/1488/pdf_minneapolis2040.pdf

29. Frumkin H. Sprawl and public health. *Public Health Reports*. 2002;May-June. https://www.ncbi.nlm.nih.gov/pmc/articles/PMC1497432/pdf/12432132.pdf

30. Sloane DC. Longer View: from congestion to sprawl: planning and health in historical context. *Journal of the American Planning Association*. 2006;72:1. https://www.tandfonline.com/doi/pdf/10.1080/01944360608976720

31. Sanchez T. The most frequently cited topics in urban planning scholarship. *Urban Science*. 2020;4:4 https://www.mdpi.com/2413-8851/4/1/4

32. Tagtachian DA, Barefoot NN, Harreveld A. Building by right: social equity implications of transitioning to form-based code. *Journal of Affordable Housing and Community Development Law*. 2019;28:1. https://repository.law.miami.edu/cgi/viewcontent.cgi?article=1735&context=fac_articles.

33. Steuteville R, Langdon P. *New Urbanism: Best Practices Guide*. 4th ed. New Urbanism News Publications; 2009. https://www.cnu.org/sites/default/files/BestPracticesGuideRed.pdf

34. Lewyn M. The New Urbanist zoning for dummies. George Washington University Law School Public Law and Legal Theory Working Paper No 183. 2006. https://papers.ssrn.com/sol3/papers.cfm?abstract_id=873903

35. The Best Complete Streets Policies of 2018. Smart Growth America. May 2019. https://smartgrowthamerica.org/wp-content/uploads/2019/05/Best-Complete-Streets-Policies-of-2018.pdf

36. O'Sullivan F, Bliss L. The 15 minute city—no cars required—is urban planning's new utopia. *Bloomberg Business Week*. November 12, 2020. https://www.bloomberg.com/news/features/2020-11-12/paris-s-15-minute-city-could-be-coming-to-an-urban-area-near-you

CHAPTER 21

COMMUNITY ENGAGEMENT FOR HEALTH, EQUITY, AND SUSTAINABILITY

Manal J. Aboelata and Jasneet K. Bains

KEY POINTS

- Community engagement entails relationship building, communication, and decision-making involving residents, the people most likely to be impacted by neighborhood change.
- Community engagement efforts employ a range of techniques to enable community members to participate in shaping strategies, processes, and outcomes. This chapter focuses on the land use, design, and built environment arenas, particularly as they pertain to health, equity, safety, and environmental sustainability.
- Community engagement should go beyond "usual suspects" to enlist the perspectives of diverse individuals who have typically been excluded from influencing neighborhood design, land use, and environmental decisions.
- Land use planning in the built environment is highly political, technical, and complicated; therefore, effective community engagement requires commitment to building knowledge, capacity, and relationships based on trust and shared understanding of historical and present-day factors impacting neighborhood health, equity, safety, and sustainability.

INTRODUCTION

In 2018, a group of twenty youth leaders from the BUILD Health L.A. Initiative—a program of the National Health Foundation funded by the deBeaumont Foundation and others—conducted a comparative assessment of park conditions in multiple communities in the Los Angeles region, including their own South Central Los Angeles neighborhood. One of those youth leaders, Naomi Humphrey (figure 21.1), describes her experience:

My peers and I conducted park assessments on all fourteen parks in our district using an audit tool that evaluates parks based on amenities, the condition of facilities, and accessibility. To see if our parks fared any differently from a neighborhood similar in size and population density, we used the same audit tool to assess parks in Santa Monica (California). We assigned each park a letter grade, with "A" as the highest score and "F" being the lowest. Santa Monica parks averaged a "C" grade (72 percent), while parks in Historic South Central averaged an "F" (59 percent) on our audit tool. Several conditions contributed to the low park grades in my community including: graffiti, damaged equipment and old playground sets, broken lights, unkempt bathrooms, and limited amenities like volleyball and tennis courts. In addition, historic South Central has fewer park acres (84 to Santa Monica's 134) despite having a larger population (138,000 to Santa Monica's 93,000). While seeing the low park grades for my community was disheartening, the truth is, the results were not surprising. Graffiti, broken lights, indecent facilities ... these are all things I have heard about and seen in my parks. Like many of my peers, this was something we had accepted as fact: parks have always been this way, and they probably always will be. However, this information better informed my peers and I about the institutional structures that set the stage for park inequity in my community.[1]

Humphrey and her peers shared their findings with community stakeholders and made recommendations to local decision-makers. Along with others, these youth leaders successfully advocated for equity provisions in a countywide funding measure, winning millions of dollars for communities in dire need of parks and open space. Now an alumna of the program and an undergraduate at University of California, Los Angeles, Humphrey continues to be an outspoken advocate for park equity, advising on community-based research and speaking publicly on issues of park and health equity.

The idea that all people affected by an issue—including young people—have a right and responsibility to participate in decision-making related to civic life is a cornerstone of democracy. Humphrey's story shows us that engaged residents hold the power to inform

Figure 21.1. Naomi Humphrey (far left) and other youth leaders from the BUILD Health L.A. Initiative. These youth conducted a comparative assessment of park conditions in multiple communities in the Los Angeles region to see if their local parks fared any differently from neighborhoods similar in size and population density. Their parks scored worse than other parks for several reasons. Their work provided them with clarity on the systemic differences and potential ways to overcome them.
Source: Photo taken by Juan Alaniz—Genesis Productions

decisions and improve the health, safety, and sustainability of their neighborhoods. This chapter provides a broad overview of community engagement in land use, planning, and design to support the health, safety, and sustainability of neighborhoods.

Whether planning for a park or living with a landfill, the active participation of residents is essential for deliberating, illuminating trade-offs, tallying costs and benefits to public health and human safety, and informing what physical structures—from affordable housing to safe sidewalks—do or do not come to fruition in local communities. With decades of scholarship on the topic, community engagement remains a broad and fluid concept, encompassing a wide range of strategies for enlisting the perspectives of residents and ensuring that their voices shape anything and everything, from climate vulnerability assessments to resource allocation and from community plans to land use regulations and zoning codes.

WHAT IS COMMUNITY ENGAGEMENT?

There is no singular, universal, accepted definition of the term *community engagement*. Community engagement literature comes from a wide range of disciplines. Terms such as civic engagement, community participation, civic participation, community involvement, and stakeholder engagement, among others, are often used synonymously or interchangeably with community engagement (box 21.1; figure 21.2).

BOX 21.1 WHAT IS COMMUNITY ENGAGEMENT?

Community engagement …

… is a process through which community members are empowered to own the change they want to see and involves communication, problem-solving, governance, and decision-making skills and strategies. [It] is not just a set of activities and methods confined to a particular project, policy, or process. Rather, it is a way of communication, decision making, and governance that gives community members the power to own the change they want to see, leading to equitable outcomes.[a]

… can take many forms, and partners can include organized groups, agencies, institutions, or individuals … . [It] can also be seen as a continuum of community involvement. Over time, a specific collaboration is likely to move … toward greater community involvement, and … it frequently involves—and often evolves into—long-term partnerships that move from the traditional focus on a single health issue to address a range of social, economic, political, and environmental factors that affect health.[b]

… [is] collaborating with local community-based organizations to enhance the breadth and depth of participation by community residents in local decision-making … many local agencies use a strategy of nurturing relationships with community-based organizations (CBO) to better reach and engage a broader cross section of residents.[c]

REFERENCES

a. Bergstom D, Rose K, Olinger J, Holley K. The community engagement guide for sustainable communities. *Policy Link*. 2012.

b. Clinical and Translational Science Awards (CTSA) Consortium, Community Engagement Key Function Committee Task Force. *Principles of Community Engagement*. 2nd ed. US Department of Health and Human Services; 2011. NIH publication 11-7782. Accessed November 11, 2021. https://www.atsdr.cdc.gov/communityengagement/pdf/PCE_Report_508_FINAL.pdf

c. Institute for Local Government. Partnering with Community-Based Organizations for More Broad-Based Public Engagement. 2015. https://www.ca-ilg.org/sites/main/files/file-attachments/partnering_with_comm_based_orgs_final.pdf

Figure 21.2. Community leaders testifying to advance park equity at 2018 LA County Board of Supervisors meeting. The third speaker from the left and a majority of audience members show their support by wearing matching "PARK EQUITY NOW" shirts.
Source: Photo courtesy of Executive Office of the Los Angeles County Board of Supervisors

Recognizing that there is a great deal of definitional and procedural variability in what community engagement entails, this chapter acknowledges a range of approaches while emphasizing the importance of community-centered approaches designed to develop durable and enduring relationships that reinforce—rather than erode—residents' trust in the systems, institutions, and policies with which they are engaged. In this view, entities committed to community engagement are expected to take seriously both the process and results of community engagement efforts. They move away from "check the box," or episodic, transactions designed to extract input from community residents toward constructive, consistent, and honest dialogue where all parties walk away from experiences feeling heard and respected, even when tensions and challenges inevitably arise. When residents are called on for their input, issues of transparency, accountability, and reciprocity between those engaging residents and those being engaged are elevated and honored before, during, and after the engagement.

WHO "DOES" COMMUNITY ENGAGEMENT?

For the purposes of this chapter, all residents in a community, including young people and seniors, can be primary actors in community engagement. The term *community*, like *community engagement*, is broadly defined. Sometimes community refers to a group of people united by common interest or identity. In other instances, community pertains to those who share natural resources or physical space, for example, a water supply, a zip code, a neighborhood, or a housing development. Community residents are fully capable of organizing themselves to weigh in on critical land use, built environment and sustainability issues—and they frequently do.

In many situations, governments, private developers, conservancies, and for-profit and not-for-profit organizations may endeavor to engage community residents to meet legal or regulatory requirements because they are genuinely desirous of community input and buy-in. These entities may undertake engagement activities themselves or enlist the support of foundations, private consultants, or other intermediary partners to facilitate community engagement efforts. Funders provide resources and in-kind support, offering up comfortable meeting space, providing resources that public dollars may not be used for, such as child care or refreshments, or funding technical assistance. Private consultants and nonprofit partners may bring a range of technical and topical expertise to community engagement. Land use and built environment interventions can be complex, so intermediary groups with expertise to educate and inform residents in ways that meet their needs (for example, linguistic, educational, cultural) can play important roles.[2] This expertise can range from topical knowledge such as setting up a conversation about the projected health and environmental impacts of a new transit line running through a neighborhood, or it can come in the form of high-quality group facilitation, conflict resolution, or synthesis of qualitative and quantitative data generated through community participation.

When initiating a community engagement process, governments may also find it useful to engage one or more community-based, faith-based, youth-serving, or grassroots organizations—sometimes as paid contractors—to generate participation and build capacity among their group members. This strategy can be particularly useful for establishing new ties between government and resident groups where lack of familiarity or mistrust may impede a direct interaction between residents and government. Governments have found that compensating grassroots organizations support these entities for the invaluable community connections that they bring to the table, they invest in their capacity, and they help facilitate the flow of information to maintain continuity between engagement efforts.

Youth are often pointed to as having important perspectives, but literature and practice suggest that they are infrequently engaged, and when they are, their roles tend to be ill-defined or loosely structured.[3] As future community stewards and prospective decision-makers, youth engagement can serve to build knowledge, skills, and confidence of young people, strengthening their sense of **efficacy** or belief in their sense to take actions to address situations with which they are presented. **Collective efficacy** is the belief that one's community can improve the conditions that impact them. Botchwey et al. provide an excellent review of the literature, analyze three case examples involving youth engagement, and suggest a modification to add three rungs to Sherry Arnstein's Ladder of Citizen Participation: consent, advocacy, and incorporation.[3]

Finally, just as the opening story focused attention on the glaring park inequities Naomi Humphrey and her peers documented between more White and affluent Santa Monica and South Central Los Angeles, a disproportionately Black and Latino portion of Los Angeles County, it is important to think critically *and creatively* about engaging historically excluded, underrepresented, and marginalized groups—including young people of color—in defining problems, articulating narratives (for example, stories that reveal how people understand the issues they are weighing in on vis-à-vis their own histories, cultures, and experiences), and elevating solutions rooted in their own knowledge, experiences, and voices. Doing so creates innovative, and maybe even fairer and more just, possibilities for how decisions affecting land use, health, safety, and sustainability will be made.

WHAT IS THE "POINT" OF COMMUNITY ENGAGEMENT?

In 1969, Arnstein wrote an article titled "Ladder of Citizen Participation" for the *Journal of the American Planning Association*, and her document remains a seminal touchstone in the fields of planning and community engagement. Arnstein's ladder depicts a hierarchy of engagement—from manipulation to tokenism to citizen control—in land use decision-making. For Arnstein and many others since her, the purpose of community engagement is to locate the power over important community decisions with residents of a community. By necessity, centering decision-making power with residents means that residents are actively involved in decisions and their wishes are honored and, ideally, adhered to.[4]

"Community" is not a monolith. Within any defined community, there will be differences in knowledge, skill, capacity, history, and culture. All these attributes and more, including age, socioeconomic status, language, political orientation, and access to political structures, will influence opinions as well as how those opinions are received by people in decision-making power—whether a mall developer, a regional planner, or a political leader. Therefore, people in positions of power must be highly aware of their own limitations, biases, and attributes. This is particularly true when engaging with the public to guard against exclusion of people, voices, and perspectives that may bring perceived or unwanted conflict to an engagement effort or may necessitate slowing down a process to ensure higher-quality participation of people who have been historically marginalized and disempowered from influencing decisions that affect their community.

In the decades since Arnstein's writing, the field has witnessed both neighborhood and issue-based organizations that sustain attention to environmental justice and equitable development concerns to help organize, mobilize, and elevate historically marginalized resident voices in land use decisions. Many of these organizations utilize organizing and analytical capacity to push back on projects and policies deemed undesirable by resident groups and to work with community residents over time to envision, accelerate, and advocate for health, safety, and sustainability-promoting innovations in the field. After all, the point of community engagement is to enable a deeper form of participation and democracy to inform neighborhood conditions. The point should never be checking the community engagement box on the road to getting stakes in the ground.

HOW DOES COMMUNITY ENGAGEMENT RELATE TO SOCIAL CAPITAL?

As an overarching strategy for generating input from community members on matters pertinent to health, safety, and the built environment, community engagement is distinct from, but related to, the concept of social capital. (For a deeper discussion of the relational pathways between social capital and health, see chapter 8.) The concept of **participatory democracy** encourages self-determination and enables community members to make decisions about how they will be governed, for example, through voting.[5] When linked to the concept of participatory democracy, community engagement could relate to social capital in at least two important ways. First, community engagement endeavors can foster social capital by creating experiential opportunities for members of a group with shared or divergent identities to come together to build ties, share perspectives, gather information, learn together, and establish trust, norms, and networks. To the extent that community engagement builds collective efficacy and enhances trust, it may build social capital and thus contribute to health. When community engagement is constructed as a continuous effort at building durable ties and reinforcing trust, accountability, and transparency between government and residents, it is more likely to build social capital. The second potential pathway between community engagement and social capital may occur when residents influence the creation of spaces, such as a community center or a plaza, that in turn helps people get to know their neighbors and in that way reinforces the building of social capital.

PRINCIPLES OF COMMUNITY ENGAGEMENT FOR MAKING HEALTHY PLACES

Community engagement can be a mechanism to increase community power and agency to solve issues. Agency is the community's ability to find solutions to the issues it faces.[6] To guide an equitable community engagement environment and ensure inclusion of underrepresented perspectives, the Ohio State University Kirwan Institute for the Study of Race and Ethnicity outlines six principles, shown in box 21.2. The Kirwan Institute for the Study of Race and Ethnicity is a research institute that uses research, engagement, and communication to "create a just and inclusive society where all people and communities have opportunity to succeed."[7]

Principles form the bedrock for the strategies and tactics that will be deployed to engage residents. The following section explores tactical aspects of community engagement: how to engage residents. The procedures that are used should serve as a reflection and an extension of the underlying principles for the engagement. This is why community-rooted organizations driving community change frequently utilize strategies that are deeply guided by principles like those described in box 21.2.

LINKING COMMUNITY ENGAGEMENT PRINCIPLES TO STRATEGIES AND TACTICS

The International Association of Public Participation (IAP2) developed a *public participation spectrum* (table 21.1) that presents a spectrum of increasing public involvement and impact on decision-making, from "inform" to "empower."[8] In the third row of the table, it offers the technique or method that aligns with an array of public participation goals. As evidenced throughout the chapter, there are numerous techniques for engaging community residents. This chapter advances the notion that "form follows function" with respect to selected techniques. Grounded in a vision for equitable and inclusive neighbor-

hoods, principles for inclusive development should be made explicit, and only then should a set of strategies and techniques be selected that embody those principles.

Like Arnstein's ladder, IAP2's spectrum suggests a continuum that moves from lesser to greater levels of engagement. Arnstein's ladder, however, is clearer on the value that it places on each rung of the ladder. For Arnstein, the lower rungs of the ladder are, in fact, forms of nonparticipation. IAP2's spectrum appears to be more agnostic on the underlying values associated with each stage of the spectrum. Further, IAP2's spectrum is more of an institutionally oriented framework, which seems to presuppose that the "engager" is an institution.

For people and organizations focused on community-level change, their understanding, frameworks, and tactics may overlap with those used in institutionally driven engagement. They may, however, take on a broader context (for example, what is your vision for this community), longer time horizons (what would you like to see in this community seven generations from now), and bigger aims for community leadership and power building (how can we invest in resident capacity to act on their own behalf).

As indicated in table 21.1, each public participation technique or method is differentially suited to meet different purposes vis-à-vis the community and the public participation goal. Although there are no hard-and-fast rules about which techniques best achieve which aims, the purpose of table 21.1 is to emphasize that there are a variety of mechanisms that can work in service to the overarching aim of deepening democratic participation of residents in public plans, projects, and policies. It is important to keep in mind, however, that although strategies and tactics may overlap, the vision, intent, and desired goals of institutionally driven frameworks may be very different from those designed to advance and develop community-level change and transformation.

BOX 21.2 SIX PRINCIPLES FOR EQUITABLE AND INCLUSIVE CIVIC ENGAGEMENT

The following are the Kirwan Institute for the Study of Race and Ethnicity's six principles for equitable and inclusive civic engagement.[a]

1. **Embracing the Gifts of Diversity:** The gifts that people bring to their communities represent the brick and mortar of communities. The abilities, competencies, and experiences that community members share with each other often form the bedrock of that community and give them the tools to meet the many challenges in our society. When those gifts are diverse, the community itself benefits by being able to apply them to the many needs within the community. By embracing the power of the diverse gifts of all of our community members, we not only give ourselves and our neighbors more tools to confront our shared difficulties, but we help empower each other and help one another uplift our strengths.

2. **Realizing the Role of Race, Power, and Injustice:** The effects of historical and present economic and social marginalization play a crucial role in shaping our community dialogues and in forming our public places and policies. In many cities, the neglect and isolation of entire communities of people is written into the fabric of the built environment, from informally segregated spaces, to crumbling infrastructure, to a lack of basic amenities for child health and safety. In order to have a truly inclusive, equitable community environment, we must acknowledge the realities of these continuing divides, and the real challenges of power dynamics and multiple, often contrasting, truths and goals.

3. **Radical Hospitality: Invitation and Listening:** Engaging with the entire community starts by truly inviting everyone into the community and valuing their input and leadership. It requires a commitment to everyone belonging and to receiving input from all community members. Starting from values of openness, belonging, and listening can lend outreach efforts much of their energy and longevity. When more people are invited to make community decisions our communities grow stronger and provide opportunities for a wider range of people to grow and succeed.

4. **Trust-Building and Commitment:** Solving long-term community problems requires community members who are willing to build long-lasting partnerships. Trust is the glue that holds these bonds together. Communities across the country have shown us that trust begins with honoring a commitment and keeping a promise. Communities where people work together for common goals start with person-to-person commitments. Residents can widen the circle of inclusion, so that more people and families can recognize and give gifts that make their neighborhoods stronger and healthier for all.

5. **Honoring Dissent and Embracing Protest:** The strength of the diversity in our communities relies upon our ability to accept and respect our differences. In strong communities, voices of disagreement have the potential to strengthen the civic engagement environment by offering alternatives and raising tough questions. Solutions to difficult challenges are rarely realized without entering into conflict. By truly honoring dissent, we can create a civic engagement environment where our diverse bank of ideas and knowledge can be brought together to build communities that are more than the sum of their parts.

6. **Adaptability to Community Change:** Communities, like jazz music, are not static compositions. Much like the people within them, they change over time and with different circumstances. By focusing on values and principles rather than tactics and activities, we can create just the right amount of order needed for a wide variety of dialogues and relationships, without being tied to limiting ideas. In order to tap into this flexibility, we must allow for the long-term adjustments, and the personal transformations, that are necessitated by change.

REFERENCE

a. Kirwan Institute for the Study of Race and Ethnicity. The Principles for Equitable and Inclusive Civic Engagement. Ohio State University. Published 2016. http://kirwaninstitute.osu.edu/wp-content/uploads/2016/05/ki-civic-engagement.pdf

Table 21.1. IAP2 Public Participation Spectrum.

Increasing Level of Public Impact on Decision-Making →

	Inform	Consult	Involve	Collaborate	Empower
Public Participation Goal	To provide the public with balanced and objective information to assist them in understanding the problem, alternatives, opportunities, and/or solutions.	To obtain public feedback on analysis, alternatives, or decisions.	To work directly with the public throughout the process to ensure that public concerns and aspirations are consistently understood and considered.	To partner with the public in each aspect of the decision, including the development of alternatives and the identification of the preferred solution.	To place final decision-making in the hands of the public.
Promise to the Public	We will keep you informed.	We will keep you informed, listen to and acknowledge concerns and aspirations, and provide feedback on how public input influenced the decision.	We will work with you to ensure that your concerns and aspirations are directly reflected in the alternatives developed and provide feedback on how public input influenced the decision.	We will look to you for advice and innovation in formulating solutions and incorporate your advice and recommendations into the decisions to the maximum extent possible.	We will implement what you decide.
Technique/ Method	Open houses Fact sheets Websites	Public comment/ Testimony Focus groups Surveys Public meetings Community interviews	Community forums Public workshops Charrettes **Deliberate polling** Walkability assessments, corner-store assessments, park audits Community/ asset mapping Health impact assessment	Advisory meetings Promotoras	**Participatory budgeting** Ballots Resident participation on commissions, boards, councils **Citizen jury**

Source: Adapted from International Association for Public Participation (IAP2). IAP2 Spectrum of Public Participation. 2018. Accessed November 11, 2021. https://cdn.ymaws.com/www.iap2.org/resource/resmgr /pillars/Spectrum_8.5x11_Print.pdf

THE INCREASING ROLE OF TECHNOLOGY IN COMMUNITY ENGAGEMENT

Technology serves an important role in community engagement and will likely continue to do so into the future. Assistive technology enhances participation for community members who require simultaneous language translation or interpretation and residents who are hard of hearing. As the field of community engagement continues to evolve to further encompass technological solutions—ideally with an eye toward maximizing their benefits while minimizing their downsides—it is probable that some combination of face-to-face and online strategies will optimize desired results. Technological solutions have begun to prove valuable not only in overcoming barriers such as those presented by physical distancing, as seen with the response to COVID-19 pandemic (box 21.3), but also those caused by the spatial and temporal challenges that arise when people cannot, for instance, attend a weeknight meeting or travel long distances to participate in face-to-face engagement.

Technology may also prove useful for addressing group dynamics that commonly challenge community engagement efforts. For instance, when only the most vocal attendees with the strongest opinions speak up at meetings, technology could create a mechanism for other invested residents to share their perspectives. Another way technology could support effective engagement is by helping residents visualize alternative models. Virtual reality and digital models can help residents to explore scenarios—for instance, increased density, reduced parking, more street trees, or the addition of a bike lane—that can often be unfamiliar or worrisome to some stakeholders. For example, the Map Room Project from St. Louis, Missouri, and Savannah, Georgia, uses video projection to dynamically engage people to understand and recast the narratives about their lives and communities.

BOX 21.3 COMMUNITY ENGAGEMENT ADAPTATIONS DURING THE COVID-19 PANDEMIC

In 2020, when the global COVID-19 pandemic resulted in government orders to "shelter in place," most forms of face-to-face community engagement came to a halt. Groups with a history and preference for doing face-to-face engagement suddenly found themselves needing to adapt to online platforms to maintain, expand, or establish new connections with residents. In the Central Coast region of California, an organization known as Community Water Center pivoted to hosting virtual community meetings known as *platicas* with their community partners to continue to connect, engage, and advocate with residents for access to clean and affordable drinking water.[a] Similarly, in the spring of 2020, city planners and consultants designed a virtual charrette to continue their ongoing community visioning effort for a community master plan in Missoula, Montana.[b] They were pleased, and surprised, when community participation increased and generated new participation from members of the Indigenous communities whose tribal land is far from Missoula. Specific outcomes of this digital engagement process are still unknown, reflecting, in part, the reality that there is frequently a long time horizon between actual changes to the physical environment and community engagement. Mandarano et al. provides an overview of additional digital civic engagement examples in city and regional planning.[c]

REFERENCES

a. Community Water Center. Central Coast platicas go virtual. Published 2020. https://www.communitywatercenter .org/enew-english/april2020enews?rq=platicas

b. Smart Growth America. Charrettes go virtual: Missoula, Montana hosts an online charrette to advance a community vision [Webinar]. Smart Growth America. 2020. https://smartgrowthamerica.org /webinar-recap-charrettes-go-virtual/

c. Mandarano L, Meenar M, Steins C. Building social capital in the digital age of civic engagement. *Journal of Planning Literature*. 2010;25(2):123-135.

The contribution of technology to effective community engagement deserves further exploration. The literature demonstrating effectiveness and relative advantages of online engagement is still in its early stages.[9] In whatever ways technology is adopted and integrated in future community engagement, it should be done in ways that adhere to the fundamental principles of engagement discussed earlier. Technology should be viewed as a tool to facilitate deeper exchanges with residents rather than as a technique to check the box for the number of engaged residents. In his article "Designing Effective Public Participation," Luigi Bobbio offers a brief discussion of online versus on-site engagement, noting that "online participation works better when it is aimed at gathering information or at receiving inputs (such as suggestions, proposals, ideas) from citizens."[10]

Until equitable access to technology is achieved, the inherent bias that reliance on technological solutions raises should be factored into technology-based engagement strategies. Although great strides in expanding access to technology have been made, profound concerns such as the persistent digital divide, distrust of government, and fears of sharing information online remain. Thus, although technology and online innovations are certainly tools in the tool kit for community engagement, they do not side-step the need to grapple with hard issues that impede inclusive engagement strategies. Some common barriers to effective engagement are presented in the following section.

OVERCOMING BARRIERS TO EFFECTIVE COMMUNITY ENGAGEMENT

Community engagement efforts can falter for a number of reasons, including biased processes of institutions, mismatched time horizons (for example, short-term project versus long-term community change), lack of resources to support public participation, and divergent expectations of the engagement process. A number of factors can also contribute to successful engagement processes that go beyond the use of "good techniques," such as adhering to the principles for community engagement and using each opportunity to build trust and reinforce durable, honest, and authentic exchanges with those being engaged. Community engagement on issues pertaining to land use, community design, and the built environment require special effort and attention if they are to be inclusive of, and effective among, groups who have typically not received attention, respect, or offers for inclusion on these matters. Table 21.2 outlines common barriers to effective community engagement and solutions for overcoming them.

COMMUNITY ENGAGEMENT TO ADDRESS BUILT ENVIRONMENT INEQUITIES AND SOCIAL EXCLUSION

The goal of every community engagement effort should be to extend the opportunity for residents to participate in constructive processes to impact decisions that affect their lives through, for example, participatory budgeting in Medellin, Colombia (box 21.4), or community involvement in Portland, Oregon (box 21.5). For a range of historical and contemporary reasons, the benefits of democracy and public participation have not been equally distributed across society. From its earliest days, the United States did not include women, African Americans, and Indigenous people, for instance, in the voting franchise. Thus, the term *disenfranchised* was coined. As an extension of participatory democracy, community engagement must aim to overcome the barriers that have cut off opportunities for full inclusion for people who have been marginalized, underrepresented or excluded.

COMMUNITY ENGAGEMENT FOR SAFE, HEALTHY, AND SUSTAINABLE NEIGHBORHOODS: IT'S POLITICAL

A 2017 editorial in the *Los Angeles Times* proclaimed that "land-use rules are outdated and routinely ignored. Every new project is a political negotiation and a fight over height,

Table 21.2. Common barriers and solutions to effective community engagement.

Barriers	Solutions
Highly technical, complex, and long-term decision-making processes create challenges for community engagement. Decisions about land use, zoning, siting, and financing are complicated, involving environmental, regulatory, and legal information. It can take decades to realize a new plan and years for projects to come to fruition. Under these circumstances, capturing and sustaining public participation can be challenging.	Support community-based organizations to undertake effective community engagement on technical issues and stay engaged throughout these processes, including providing technical assistance and expertise. Redesign bureaucratic processes—clarifying and simplifying where possible—to support innovation in public agencies' community engagement efforts. Invest in grassroots, youth-serving, and faith-based organizations to develop knowledge and capacity on land use, built environment, and community development issues.
The tension between time-limited, project-specific feedback and ongoing engagement When government agencies face pressure to deliver results efficiently on a specific project, they run the risk of rushing the process and skipping over the aim of "good community engagement"—to build trust and durable relationships with residents. Communities may experience this as extractive, rather than reflecting genuine interest in community perspectives.	Investment in relationship-building and development of trust through accountability and transparency. Shift the priority of community engagement efforts from getting information to building deep ties. Stop structuring community engagement in ways that are transactional, episodic, and unidirectional—this squanders whatever trust may exist and sets back future efforts.
Lack of sustained funding for resident engagement Community engagement takes time, resources, and intention, yet resources for community engagement are limited, sporadic, and frequently tied to a specific project or outcome.	Earmark government resources for sustained engagement. Draw on academia and the philanthropic community to furnish resources to build relationships for longer-term engagement activities.
Reliance on outdated or ineffective methods for community engagement Government agency staff are typically not experts in community engagement and may rely on engagement techniques that fail to "meet residents where they are"—either literally or figuratively—or that don't acknowledge or address imbalances in political and economic power, thus leading to poor experiences, erosion of trust and credibility, and undesirable outcomes.	Enlist and develop expertise in community engagement and combine it with deep knowledge and understanding of the historical, political, social, racial, and economic climate in which engagement will be taking place.
The siloed nature of government agencies working at the community level Government agencies are typically divided in ways that are inconsistent with how residents perceive their neighborhoods. Residents can become overburdened by requests to engage on a host of separate issues—parks one day, sidewalks the next, when in fact, residents experience their neighborhoods more or less as a coherent, integrated, though complex, entity.	Government agencies need to coordinate their engagement efforts and pool resources together to facilitate sustained, rather than episodic, engagement. Government agencies must find ways to receive and make use of resident input even when they perceive it as "out of their purview." When residents elevate legitimate concerns, every effort should be made to integrate those perspectives and narratives to gain a deeper insight into the resident experience, even when it feels beyond the confines of a government silo.

Table 21.2. Continued

Barriers	Solutions
Unequal access to the microphone A variety of group dynamics can result in exclusion or marginalization that prevents people from active participation in engagement and decision-making processes. Women may be shut down by men (mansplaining); people of color may be silenced (intentionally or implicitly) by White people; young people may not be taken seriously by older, entrenched leaders; or certain individuals may dominate the microphone, crowding out time and space for other perspectives.	Create spaces to amplify diverse community voices, especially those who are traditionally left out. Establish ground rules or group agreements that set standards for participation (e.g., share the mic, step up/step back). People leading community engagement efforts must commit to being watchful for these dynamics, asking, "Who's not speaking up?" and "What practices can I do to invite participation from those who haven't spoken up?" and implementing practices that may be more aligned with people based on their age, preferred language, cultural heritage, and so on. This may mean utilizing other forms of communication than the mic, such as online polls, write-in ballots, or artistic expression to spark dialogue.

density and community impact, making housing construction a high-stakes gamble and turning residents reflexively into NIMBYs."[11] It would be complicated enough if creating safe, healthy, and sustainable neighborhoods were only about developing deeper, more democratic exchanges so that residents can weigh in on the conditions impacting their communities, but, in reality, land use and planning decisions that impact neighborhoods are highly politicized. In many contexts, it would be generous to say that the path from planning to implementation is opaque. Scholars have argued that politicians and bureaucrats too frequently ignore the will and input of "the people" in favor of the monied interests that build and underwrite both political campaigns and major projects in the built environment.[12,13] This phenomena is not just true in an urban megalopolis like Los Angeles; it can be equally relevant in rural and less developed areas, where powerful interests may have an outsized impact on government decision-making, including incentives and land giveaways. For these reasons, the news media is filled with references to a broken system for land use planning and development.

Perhaps the biggest challenges to community engagement for creating safe, healthy, and sustainable neighborhoods are structural. Land use is political and highly contested.

Large-scale corporations, such as multinational construction and development firms, use their considerable resources and political clout to influence political actors who are also too frequently gatekeepers for planning, land use, and land management. Arrangements between politicians and developers routinely override the will of the people as expressed in general or community-specific plans. They negotiate for waivers, compromise with term-limited community benefit agreements, and secure incentives and subsidies to build projects, frequently outside of, parallel to, or in opposition to due public process.

Despite these considerable political and financial hurdles, residents working together have managed to overcome these seemingly intractable power dynamics, resulting in significant outcomes for neighborhood change, as seen in the victory for equitable park funding in Los Angeles County that opened this chapter and Medellín's participatory budgeting and integrated urban projects that heavily relied on community engagement (see box 21.4). The key to achieving effective change in the land use and built environment arenas is understanding that these are politically charged issues. Therefore, a politically informed strategy that recognizes and analyzes where power lies and what is needed to align community assets to realize the will of the residents is vital to

BOX 21.4 INCREASING CITIZEN PARTICIPATION THROUGH PARTICIPATORY BUDGETING: MEDELLIN, COLOMBIA

Medellin, Colombia, is one of the largest cities, globally, to successfully apply participatory budgeting (PB). PB is one mechanism for involving citizens in policy-making. According to the Participatory Budget Project, PB, "is a democratic process in which community members decide how to spend part of a public budget."[a] In Medellin, about 5 percent of the city's budget is set aside for PB. By vote of citizen councils, resources have funded community centers, music and arts organizations, local parks and other community-identified priorities. From LATINNO, an online resource cataloging democratic innovations in Latin America:

> The Participatory Budget of Medellín emerged in 2004 looking for a solution to situations of violence and citizens' lack of trust in its institutions, and later made official with an Agreement of the Municipal Council in 2007.... Citizens first meet in neighborhood assemblies and neighborhoods to identify problems, generate a diagnosis of Local Development Plans and select delegates; then delegates are trained and accredited so that in the next phase they can prioritize options and allocate resources. In the next phase, the decisions taken by the delegates are endorsed by the Local Action Board of each comuna and village for the Municipal Administration to include in the Annual Plan that is finally approved by the City Council to be executed the following year. Finally, the process is evaluated and the communities are accountable for the execution of the prioritized resources. The Participatory Budget of Medellín has achieved wide participation from the citizens of its neighborhoods and communes, and has changed the perceptions and behaviors of citizens in terms of appropriation of public and citizen culture and has allowed a greater incidence of civic responsibility in the definition and implementation of solutions to the problems that affect them.[b]

Consistent with much of the literature on community engagement, the story of PB in Medellin suggests challenges and benefits for both participants and the local government. The literature that has examined PB suggests that it can foster inclusion by demonstrating openness to residents, build and develop leadership skills among participants, enhance the legitimacy of decisions, and enable thoughtful deliberation among stakeholders grappling with alternative proposals.

REFERENCES

a. Participatory Budgeting Project. What is PB? Accessed November 11, 2021. https://www.participatorybudgeting.org/what-is-pb/

b. LATINNO Innovations for Democracy in Latin America. Participatory Budget of Medellín. LATINNO Innovations for Democracy in Latin America. Published 2017. https://www.latinno.net/en/case/5185/

---

translating the efforts of community engagement into the outcomes and results that reflect resident desires for health, safety, and environmental well-being.

CONCLUSION

Community engagement is an overarching strategy for deepening inclusion of residents with the aim of developing durable community ties and advancing resident priorities. It is grounded in principles of democracy, which recognize that people are endowed with the right and responsibility to participate in decisions that impact their lives. Community engagement is challenging for a number of reasons: there is no universally accepted definition, making it difficult to measure; there are contradictory opinions about the benefits of community engagement; and the people who are intended to engage may mistrust government (or the entities seeking to engage them), may lack knowledge and skills to effectively engage, and may be hard to reach from the perspective of the engaging entities because of geographic and linguistic isolation or other barriers such as historical marginal-

BOX 21.5 CITY OF PORTLAND, OREGON'S EFFORTS TO PRACTICE MEANINGFUL AND INCLUSIVE ENGAGEMENT

Starting in 2005, the City of Portland, Oregon, conducted a comprehensive review of its thirty-five-year-old neighborhood association system with the goal of facilitating public participation, especially among communities that have been historically excluded, such as people of color, immigrants, and refugees. This process resulted in an ordinance establishing the Office of Neighborhood Involvement to facilitate public involvement in civic affairs. In 2010, the city adopted a set of public involvement principles to guide government officials and staff in establishing consistent, effective, and high-quality public involvement across Portland's city government.[a] The Office of Neighborhood Involvement was renamed the Office of Community and Civic Life in 2018 to better describe the programming and services provided and the way Portlanders participate in civic culture. The office has three long-term goals: inclusive structures, adaptive governance, and fulfilled and empowered Portland residents.

In addition, the Bureau of Planning and Sustainability set a series of community involvement goals and policies as part of Portland's 2035 Comprehensive Plan to enable community involvement in the planning and investment decision-making process.[b] The 2035 Comprehensive Plan directs the city to do the following:

- Maintain a community involvement program.
- Create and implement a community engagement manual.[c]
- Establish a community involvement committee to advise city planning staff on the design, implementation, evaluation, and improvement of community involvement practices.
- Share methods, tools, and technologies while utilizing best practices for engagement.

These policies apply to legislative land use and transportation projects initiated by the City of Portland and are meant to provide guidance on how both the city and community members learn, adapt, and refine practices for meaningful and inclusive engagement. Equity, environmental justice, and transparency are the immediate priorities for action for the community involvement program. The program also sets aside resources, including staff time, to implement the goals and policies of the comprehensive plan. The *Community Engagement Manual* guides city staff on how to design and evaluate projects on community involvement. Portland recognizes that community engagement is essential for equitable land use systems and infrastructure improvements.

REFERENCES

a.   City of Portland, Oregon. Public Involvement Principles; 2010.
b.   City of Portland, Oregon. 2035 Comprehensive Plan; 2018.
c   City of Portland, Oregon, Bureau of Planning and Sustainability. *Community Engagement Manual*; 2018.

ization and disenfranchisement. Community engagement is also challenging to do well—it takes time, resources, and commitment, which may be constrained because of external factors, like the pressure to complete projects, limited grant funds, or uncertainty about the value of community engagement. Despite the difficulties, community engagement is worthwhile when it provides venues for impacted and excluded groups to participate and influence decisions that affect their lives and their neighborhoods. When married with political strategy, community engagement efforts have the ability to overcome entrenched politics and power dynamics (that often serve to override the will of residents) to result in projects and achieve outcomes that support the health, safety, and sustainability of residents, especially those in underresourced communities.

DISCUSSION QUESTIONS

1. What are the challenges to successful community engagement in creating healthy, equitable, and sustainable neighborhoods? How can these be overcome?

2. In what way are the challenges and strategies different in disenfranchised communities? Do you think it is important to engage residents from disenfranchised, marginalized, or underrepresented groups? Why?

3. What lessons do the examples demonstrate about the factors that contribute to successful community engagement projects? To ineffective processes?

4. What policies, tools, or strategies can be used to counteract potentially inequitable and negative impacts of changes to the built environment?

5. How do power dynamics in communities impact participation?

DISCLOSURE OF COMPETING INTERESTS

Manal J. Aboelata and Jasneet K. Bains disclose no competing interests.

REFERENCES

1. Humphrey N. Unveiling the root causes of park inequity in South Los Angeles. Prevention Institute. Published 2019. https://www.preventioninstitute.org /blog/unveiling-root-causes-park-inequity -south-los-angeles

2. Head BW. Community engagement: participation on whose terms? *Australian Journal of Political Science*. 2007;42(3):441-454.

3. Botchwey ND, Johnson N, O'Connell LK, Kim AJ. Including youth in the ladder of citizen participation. *Journal of the American Planning Association*. 2019;85(3):255-270.

4. Arnstein SR. A ladder of citizen partici- pation. *Journal of the American Institute of Planners*. 1969;35(4):216-224.

5. Bevir M, ed. Key *Concepts in Governance*. SAGE Publications; 2009.

6. Schlosser M. Agency. Stanford Encyclo- pedia of Philosphy. Published August 10, 2015. Revised October 28, 2019. https: //plato.stanford.edu/entries/agency/

7. Kirwan Institute for the Study of Race and Ethnicity. The Principles for Equitable and Inclusive Civic Engagement. Ohio State University. Published 2016. http: //kirwaninstitute.osu.edu/wp-content /uploads/2016/05/ki-civic-engagement .pdf

8. International Association for Public Participation (IAP2). The Spectrum of Public Participation. 2018. https://cdn .ymaws.com/www.iap2.org/resource /resmgr/pillars/Spectrum_8.5x11_Print.pdf

9. Mandarano L, Meenar M, Steins C. Building social capital in the digital age of civic engagement. *Journal of Planning Literature*. 2010;25(2):123-135.

10. Bobbio L. Designing effective public participation. *Policy and Society*. 2019;38(1):41-57.

11. The Times Editorial Board. Editorial: It's time for a new conversation about L.A.'s future. *Los Angeles Times*. March 20, 2017. https://www.latimes.com/opinion /editorials/la-ed-measure-s-growth -20170319-story.html

12. Fulton W. *The Reluctant Metropolis: The Politics of Urban Growth in Los Angeles*. Johns Hopkins University Press; 2001.

13. Davis M. *City of Quartz: Excavating the Future in Los Angeles*. Verso Books; 2018.

CHAPTER 22

MEASURING, ASSESSING, AND CERTIFYING HEALTHY PLACES

Carolyn A. Fan and Andrew L. Dannenberg

KEY POINTS

- Measurement, assessment, and certification are key processes for evaluating health-promoting attributes of the built environment.
- Metrics, data, and tools are used to measure and assess the healthfulness of populations, places, and buildings.
- Tools such as health impact assessments can be used to assess the potential health outcomes of proposed projects and policies and to provide recommendations to promote healthy aspects and mitigate adverse aspects of proposals.
- Certification of buildings and communities facilitate improving designs to favor health and sustainability but may be subject to equity issues.
- Measurements, assessments, and certifications are conveyed to key decision-makers and community stakeholders to be translated into action through policies and projects.

INTRODUCTION

In 2013, the California legislature passed SB 743 to replace motor vehicle Level of Service (LOS) with reduced vehicle miles traveled (VMT) as a required metric under the California Environmental Quality Act (CEQA). For decades, the state used the LOS measurement to evaluate the environmental impacts of development plans and projects. LOS measures the flow of traffic during weekday rush hours and is intended to reduce traffic congestion. However, the use of this metric led to the state unintentionally prioritizing the movement of cars and the widening of roadways. Under the use of LOS in CEQA, pedestrians and bikers were considered hinderances to cars, thereby demoting projects focused on accessibility, sustainability, and active transportation. Widening streets often induces more driving, worsening traffic, and increasing greenhouse gas emissions.

The new recommended measure, reduction of VMT, correlated more directly with factors of negative environmental consequence, such as greenhouse gas emissions and urban sprawl. Analyses suggested that moving toward reduced VMT as the standard measurement for CEQA would significantly impact land use, multimodal transportation, and sustainability. These improvements in planning and development would also have corresponding health benefits, such as increased physical activity, greater community connectivity, and decreased exposure to pollutants.[1-3]

Most people would prefer to live, work, and play in healthy places, but how can one know if a place is healthy? Data and evidence—in the form of measurements, assessments, and certifications—are needed at different decision-making stages of the community design and implementation processes.

- **Measurement** is the process of obtaining quantitative metrics of specific activities and conditions. Measurements form the foundation of both assessment and certification.
- **Tools**, such as walkability checklists, are instruments that enable us to measure or assess built environment characteristics.
- **Assessments** provide a systematic framework for the collection and analysis of qualitative and quantitative data, often to inform decision-making. For instance, **health impact assessments (HIAs)** allow us to predict the potential health outcomes of proposed projects and policies.
- **Certification** is the action or process of assessing and communicating a level of standard or achievement. Leadership in Energy and Environmental Design (LEED) is a well-known example of certification for energy-efficient buildings and communities.

Improvements in measurement, assessment, and certification tools contribute to better observations of the relationships between health and the built environment, the creation and redevelopment of healthy places, and the evaluation of these actions through a health equity lens. For example, better measures of pedestrian and bicyclist usage of paths allow better estimates of demand for future paths. Better assessment of the health impacts of a new affordable housing project can empower the voices of marginalized community members to improve health for all. Better healthy and sustainable building certifications offer residents and consumers greater knowledge and choice in where they live and work. Such actions facilitate the consideration of health impacts and health disparities in decisions about community design.

MEASURING HEALTH AND BUILT ENVIRONMENTS

Surveillance of diseases and injuries, defined as the ongoing systematic collection, analysis, and interpretation of data, is a routine component of public health practice (chapter 1). Reports of the number of cases of infectious diseases such as influenza are used to identify outbreaks and initiate appropriate interventions. For instance, data collected during the surveillance of the COVID-19 pandemic allowed health officials to identify hot spot areas, increase testing, conduct contact tracing, and support stay-at-home policies to control its continued spread. An analogous system exists in transportation through the tracking of motor vehicle–induced injuries, vehicle miles traveled ratings, and motor vehicle traffic demand modeling.

But surveillance is rarely conducted on the built environment factors that contribute to chronic disease, environmental vulnerability, or health equity. Even when relevant data are collected, they are seldom synthesized and disseminated to the public or decision-makers in land use planning, housing, transportation, and public health. For example, few local health officers can identify the sites in their communities where more residents would walk if provided safe pedestrian facilities or where local residents have little access to fresh fruits and vegetables. However, in recent years, cities have begun measuring pedestrian and bicyclist use of key paths, bridges, and roadways, results of which can be used to support improvements in pedestrian and bicyclist infrastructure. For instance, Arlington, Virginia, has thirty-seven permanent bike and pedestrian counters located across the city.[4] Such surveillance is important because routine collection at multiple points allows evaluation of change over time.[5] The measurement and surveillance of bicycle trips in Portland, Oregon, yielded evidence that building new miles of bikeways resulted in a proportionally larger increase in bicycle trips made (figure 22.1).

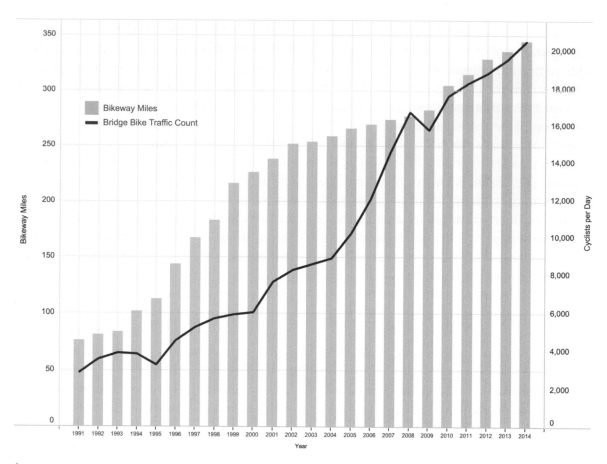

Figure 22.1. Measurement of bicycle use in Portland, Oregon, provided documentation that a fourfold increase in the number of bikeway miles led to a sevenfold increase in the number of bicycle trips over a twenty-four-year period.
Source: Figure by Olivia E. Chatman. Adapted from the Portland Bicycle Count Report 2013-2014. https://www.portlandoregon.gov/transportation/article/545858

These metrics provide a foundation of evidence that can inform future action and policy.

Some metrics quantify features *of the natural and built environment*, whereas others measure *human behavior within and in relation to the environment*. For instance, if researchers were interested in green space and health, they may determine the normalized difference vegetation index (NDVI) of a city. NDVI is a measurement of visible and near-infrared light reflected by plants that allows researchers to determine the density of vegetation and hence the amount of greenspace in an area.[6] A city council member who wants to advocate for more parks in their district might want to measure human behavior, such as number of people visiting city parks per week or proportion of residents within a ten-minute walk of a park.

Other categories of metrics, such as demographics, health outcomes, and sustainability measures, are also important to both public health practitioners and planners. Demographic factors, such as race and ethnicity, gender, and socioeconomic status, are crucial for identifying disparities and inequities. Health metrics allow us to make connections between the built environment and health. For instance, key health outcomes such as obesity, diabetes, and mortality can be compared in neighborhoods with and without zoning regulations for fast-food establishments while controlling for other factors. Finally, measures such as carbon footprint and building energy efficiency are important for crafting a more sustainable built environment that will ultimately promote health and cause less harm to the natural environment (chapter 17).

Table 22.1 provides examples of measures relevant to public health and the built environment. Some measures are routinely collected, whereas other seemingly simple measures may be difficult to collect. For instance, measuring park usage may necessitate the use of a tool like SOPARC by field volunteers if there are no entrance gates or existing visitor counters. The reliability of measurements may be influenced by time of day, season, or weather, as well as financial, resource, labor, or time constraints of the data collectors.

Walkability Measures

As discussed in previous chapters, places that are walkable offer many health benefits, including increased physical activity and social capital as well as decreased injuries and air pollution. Numerous measures of walkability have been studied, such as residential density, proximity to stores and facilities, street connectivity, and perceptions of safety.[7] Some walkability measures can be calculated using data in a geographic information system (such as intersection density), some require field observations of individual streets (street auditing), and others involve surveys of local residents (walkability checklist). A neighborhood that is technically walkable does not necessarily provide the same experience for all residents, especially for persons with disabilities and others concerned about personal safety and security (figure 22.2). Measurement with an equity focus is important to shed light on inequities in the built environment.

A tool called a **walkability checklist** (or **walkability audit**) can be used by community members to measure neighborhood walkability. The following checklist, adapted from the US Department of Transportation, is one example of a simple walkability checklist. It includes five questions easily answered by an adult or by a child with adult supervision[8].

1. Did you have room to walk?
2. Was it easy to cross streets?
3. Did drivers behave well?
4. Was it easy to follow safety rules (could you and your child cross at crosswalks, walk on a sidewalk, cross at lights, and so forth)?
5. Was your walk pleasant?

Each answer to these questions is scored on a six-point Likert scale and summed, with a final score ranging from 5 ("It's a disaster for walking") to 30 ("Celebrate! You have a great neighborhood for walking"). In addition, the checklist contains recommendations for both immediate and community-based action for improvements, as well as a quick health check for users. This nationally developed measurement tool has also been used on a local level, such as in the South Dakota Department of Health's Community Walkability Toolkit for residents.[9] Other walkability checklists and audits may be more complex[10] or be tailored to specific populations, such as the Pedestrians First tool, which measures walkability with an emphasis on babies, toddlers, and caregivers.[11]

In general, a place with sidewalks and safe street crossings, attractive surroundings, low vehicle traffic, a feeling of safety, numerous pedestrians, and multiple desirable destinations nearby is more walkable than a place missing one or several of those elements. Pedestrians present on the street may be considered an *indicator species* for a healthy community, just as the presence of certain types of fish in a lake may indicate clean water.

Another example of a walkability measure is **Walk Score**[12] (figure 22.3). For addresses in the United States, Canada, Australia, and New Zealand, and to a limited extent in other countries, Walk Score applies an algorithm based on several data sources to calculate a walkability score between 0 and 100 that is a function of the number of and distance to desirable destinations such as stores, restaurants, parks, and public transit. The score also incorporates pedestrian friendliness by examining population density, block length, and **intersection density**. Areas with low scores are considered car-dependent, whereas areas with high scores

Table 22.1. Selected built environment and public health measures.

Domain	Subdomain	Examples of Metrics
Active Living	Active Transportation	• Ratio of sidewalk and bicycle lanes to roadway miles • Percentage of population living within one-half mile of frequent-service transit stops • Annual rates of fatal and serious pedestrian and cyclist injuries
	Active Play	• Percentage of population living within one-half mile by network distance (shortest practical path) to park entrances and other usable public open spaces • Acres of park land per 1,000 people • Playgrounds per 1,000 population
Healthy Food System	Access	• Percentage of low-income population living in urban areas not within walking distance of a full-service grocery store • Density of fast-food restaurants • Prevalence of racially targeted unhealthy food and beverage street advertising
	Production	• Acres of urban area currently in use or that have potential for community gardens or urban agriculture
Environmental Exposures	Air	• Number of housing units, schools, and play areas serving vulnerable populations within 500 feet of a high-traffic roadway
	Water	• Percentage of stormwater investment spent on green infrastructure or low-impact development practices (green stormwater) • Percentage of impermeable surface area • Wetness index, relating to runoff and flood risk
	Soil	• Acres of brownfields that are not remediated • Proximity of contaminated regions to residential areas
	Infectious Disease	• Number of waterborne-disease outbreaks • Number of violations of drinking water standards
Emergency Preparedness	Natural Hazards	• Percentage of population living within 100-year and 500-year floodplains • Percentage of homes in wildland-urban interface, where there is increased risk for forest fires • Percentage of population living in storm surge areas
Housing and Community	Housing and Community Development	• Jobs to housing ratio • Percentage of households paying more than 30% of monthly household income toward housing costs
	Public Safety	• Number and proportion of street miles without streetlighting • Percentage of population living in areas with high density of liquor stores
Sustainability	Green Infrastructure	• Percentage of land covered by tree canopy • Number and volume of combined sewer overflows
	Climate Change	• Area with climate responsive building standards • Percentage of building energy use from renewable sources • Per capita water footprint
Equity	Racial Equity	• Dissimilarity index, which measures segregation between the minority and White residents across a geographic area • Percentage of minority residents living in redlined areas that were historically disenfranchised from home ownership and loans • Percentage of low-income and minority residents in a geographic area who are displaced by rising prices
	Universal Design	• Number of public bathrooms per 1,000 population • Availability of gender-neutral bathrooms in work and public spaces • Availability of lactation rooms in work and public spaces • Number of ADA accessible trails in a county • Percentage of buildings with ADA accessible entrances

Source: Adapted from Ricklin A, Shah S. *Metrics for Planning Healthy Communities*. Table 1. American Planning Association; 2017:26. Accessed February 4, 2021. https://planning-org-uploaded-media.s3.amazonaws.com/document/Metrics-Planning-Healthy-Communities.pdf

Figure 22.2. Walkability audits can identify sites with poor pedestrian infrastructure, such as this street, which presents difficulties to pedestrians with limited mobility.
Source: www.ped-bikeimages.org/Dan Burden

266 West Alexander Street

Armour Square, Chicago, 60616

Commute to **Downtown Chicago** 🖉

🚗 8 min   🚌 14 min   🚲 12 min   🚶 41 min

♡ Favorite	🏮 Map

🔍 Nearby Apartments

More about 266 West Alexander Street 🖉

Walk Score
96
Walker's Paradise
Daily errands do not require a car.

Transit Score
79
Excellent Transit
Transit is convenient for most trips.

Bike Score
89
Very Bikeable
Flat as a pancake, excellent bike lanes.

About your score

Add scores to your site

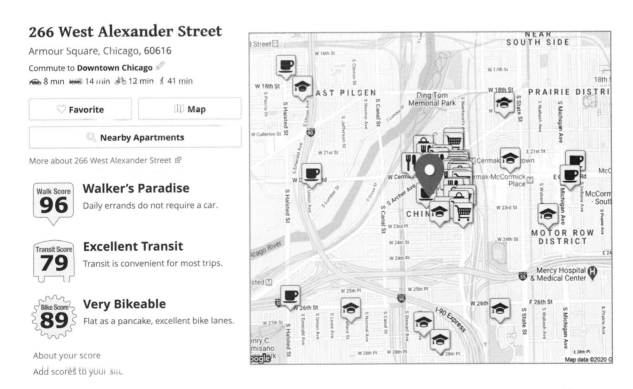

Figure 22.3. The measurement tools Walk Score, Transit Score, and Bike Score allow users to see an address's walkability, proximity to public transit, and bike infrastructure on a 0 to 100 scale.
Source: www.walkscore.com, 2021

have numerous destinations nearby, allowing a resident to walk as part of many daily activities. Walk Score has been validated by academic studies and has been utilized in research on public health and the built environment.[12,13] Using this tool, researchers have explored the association between walkability and various health measures, such as body mass index, physical activity, and diabetes. Walk Score has been incorporated into real estate listings to allow customers to consider walkability and its health implications as a factor in their home-buying and renting decisions. The team behind Walk Score has also developed Transit Score and Bike Score that measure how well a location is served by public transit and bike infrastructure, respectively. Walk Score has limitations, such as not incorporating route directness, sidewalk completeness, and speed limits, and may be better used in research in conjunction with other walkability measures.[13] Micro- and mesoscales, such as the Microscale Audit of Pedestrian Streetscapes, are emerging and provide greater accuracy than Walk Score (chapter 24).

ASSESSING HEALTHY PLACES

Healthy places do not develop spontaneously. Most exist because of numerous decisions over time to build or not build highways, transit systems, sidewalks, housing, commercial and industrial areas, schools, parks, and other features. Most of these decisions are made by planners, architects, zoning boards, city councils, developers, and others who seldom have experience or training in public health. A major message of this book is the need for better communication between public health professionals and those who make decisions about the design of the built environment. One of the most important tools for conveying such information is the health impact assessment.

Health Impact Assessment

A health impact assessment (HIA) is defined as "a systematic process that uses an array of data sources and analytic methods and considers input from stakeholders to determine the potential effects of a proposed policy, plan, program, or project on the health of a population and the distribution of those effects within the population. HIA provides recommendations on monitoring and managing those effects."[14(p5)] In practice, an HIA may be a desktop review of a proposal by a health officer in a few hours or a three-hundred-page report that required a year to write and cost more than $100,000. HIAs are used to examine the health effects of specific built environment projects and of policies that affect the built environment and can be used to assess other economic and social issues.[15]

Conducting an HIA usually involves six steps[14]:

1. *Screening* to establish the need and value of an HIA
2. *Scoping* to identify impacted populations, health effects, research questions, and data and methods
3. *Assessment* to describe the baseline health status of affected populations and predicted effects on health and its determinants
4. *Recommendations* to suggest alternatives or actions to promote health or mitigate adverse health effects
5. *Reporting* of findings and recommendations to decision-makers, the public, and other stakeholders
6. *Monitoring and evaluation* of the adoption, implementation, process, or outcomes of the HIA

HIAs follow five guiding principles[16]:

1. *Democracy*, by authentically engaging the public in decision-making
2. *Equity*, by incorporating equity into the formal decision-making process
3. *Ethical use of evidence*, by utilizing the best available evidence and documenting all processes
4. *Sustainable development*, by promoting short- and long-term improvements to health

5. *Comprehensive view of health,* by bringing together public health practitioners and other sectors to promote health in all policies

Unlike many HIAs in Europe and elsewhere, most HIAs in the United States are conducted voluntarily[15] (box 22.1). Voluntary HIAs are simpler and less expensive than regulatory HIAs, unlikely to attract litigation, and more acceptable in political environments that resist new regulatory burdens. However, voluntary HIAs are less likely to be used in settings where a focus on health impacts may be contrary to the financial interests of a project proponent (for example, a coal mining company). When HIAs are required by law, they are likely to be more complex and expensive and to attract litigation about the content of their assessments or recommendations. But as with an **environmental impact assessment (EIA)**, a required HIA may be more likely than a voluntary HIA to make a difference in mitigating the adverse health impacts of a proposed project or policy.

The National Environmental Policy Act (NEPA) of 1969,[17] and corresponding laws in some states, requires EIAs for many projects to protect air, water, and other aspects of the environment. NEPA regulations allow, and arguably require, an assessment of health impacts, but in practice, health receives little attention in most EIAs. For example, many EIAs will estimate the change in air quality (an environmental impact) resulting from a proposed project but will not estimate the change in asthma rates (a health impact) that could be expected from that change in air quality. Most EIAs focus on mitigating environmental hazards and seldom discuss the health-promoting features of a project (such as new walking trails and parks). A few HIAs have been integrated into the EIA process, such as in the Lake Oswego to Portland Transit Project in Oregon and for oil and gas leasing in the National Petroleum Reserve in Alaska's North Slope Borough.[15]

HIAs may include both qualitative and quantitative measures of health impacts. It is often easy to determine the direction of a health impact in a proposed project or policy but difficult to predict the magnitude of the impact that is needed for cost-benefit analyses. For example, one can predict that more people will walk when a new sidewalk or trail is built, but few existing models predict the likely number of users because usage is affected by numerous factors, such as nearby destinations, perceived safety, and attractiveness. For some projects, data from similar projects in other locations can be used to estimate health impacts. In general, recommendations from HIAs based on qualitative information would be unlikely to change substantially if quantitative data were available. However, quantitative data are needed to conduct cost-benefit analyses that are a component of many project and policy decisions.

Engaging community stakeholders is an important part of the HIA process, especially in the scoping, assessment, and recommendations phases. Input from affected residents may increase community buy-in for a project and help identify relevant social and health issues (chapter 21). Research has shown that HIAs can be a powerful tool for strengthening relationships between communities and government institutions.[18] HIAs may lead to more equitable access to health resources and lessen disparities rooted in environmental harm.[18] Comprehensive HIAs usually have the time and resources needed to incorporate community involvement; rapid desktop HIAs are unlikely to do so.

Do HIAs make a difference? Reviews evaluating HIAs across the globe have examined the process, impact, and outcomes of HIAs.[19,20] A *process* evaluation examines whether the steps of the HIA were conducted. An *impact* evaluation assesses whether the HIA influenced changes in the project or policy. An *outcome* evaluation compares the predicted health impacts of the project or policy to what actually happened in the months or years after the project was completed or the policy went into effect. Impact evaluations have found that HIAs often directly

BOX 22.1 EXAMPLE OF A HEALTH IMPACT ASSESSMENT AND ITS IMPACTS: CITY HEIGHTS SKATEPARK (SAN DIEGO, CALIFORNIA)

The Problem: City Heights, a community of lower-income, predominantly Latino neighborhoods, had an estimated eighteen hundred youth who enjoy the sport of skateboarding. But City Heights had far less park space than the rest of San Diego County, and the closest dedicated public skatepark was more than four miles away. As a result, youth often skate unsafely on streets, sidewalks, and other public property.

What Was Done: The Mid-City Community Advocacy Network (CAN) Youth Council and the nonprofit organization Human Impact Partners worked together to conduct a Health Impact Assessment of the health effects of building a skatepark on a vacant lot near a public park, a soon-to-be-vacant YMCA, and an elementary school, using state grant funds.

What Was Found: A new public skatepark in City Heights would provide hundreds of youth with more opportunity for exercise, social connection, and development, all of which lead to better health and well-being. It would also mean safer streets, less crime, and fewer injuries compared to other sports such as football and basketball.

The Impact: Mid-City CAN used the HIA to make the case to the city council, local residents, and news media for the benefits of the proposed skatepark and to dispel myths about the sport's safety and reputation. The city council approved the idea, the state awarded funding, and design plans moved forward. The skatepark began construction in 2016 and opened in January 2018 (Figure 22.4).[a] The San Diego Section of the American Planning Association selected the Youth Council for an award to recognize their participation in the HIA and civic engagement efforts to create communities of lasting value. As one City Heights skater described the project, "It shows that we have a voice, that we can accomplish anything we want in our community as long as we put the effort to it. It's good for the youth knowing that adults aren't just making the decisions, that youth have a say as well."[b]

Figure 22.4. Park de la Cruz Skate Park in San Diego, created with input from youth community members.
Source: The Skatepark Project (https://skatepark.org/)

(Adapted from Human Impact Partners[b] and Pew Charitable Trusts.[c])

REFERENCES

a. City of San Diego. Park de la Cruz Skate Park. The City of San Diego, Parks & Recreation. Accessed March 31, 2021. https://www.sandiego.gov/park-and-recreation/centers/skateparks/parkdelacruz
b. Human Impact Partners. An HIA of a Skatepark in City Heights, San Diego (Case Story). Human Impact Partners. Accessed February 4, 2021. https://humanimpact.org/hipprojects/skatepark-hia/
c. The Pew Charitable Trusts. City Heights Skatepark. Pew. Accessed February 4, 2021. https://pew.org/2Ki1zbB

impact decision-making, increase awareness of health issues in non-health-related sectors, and give community members a stronger voice in decisions.[19,20] HIAs have also been used to set priorities during major planning and policy processes. Outcome evaluations are seldom conducted due to the difficulty in estimating the health outcomes that may have occurred in the absence of the HIA.

The use of HIAs in the United States has grown over the past two decades, with more than 440 HIAs completed or in progress as of 2021.[21] Hundreds of HIAs have been conducted in Europe, Oceania, and many low- and middle-income countries.[20,22] HIAs are also described as paving the way for **Health in All Policies (HiAP)**, which encourage the consideration of health in all decision-making, especially public policy. HIAs are considered a key tool for incorporating a HiAP approach.[23]

HIAs will continue to evolve as they are utilized by more decision-makers and community members.

Equity Mapping

Equity mapping is an assessment of the "geography of opportunity" (box 22.2). It utilizes **geographic information systems (GIS)** to compare areas where marginalized communities live to where areas of opportunity exist.[24] The visual impact of GIS mapping data allows for equity mapping to be an effective tool in policymaking and advocacy for many stakeholder groups and equity issues. For instance, equity mapping can be used to visually represent indicators related to the built environment and health, such as poverty, employment, housing, access to health care, transportation, land use, zoning, and infrastructure (figure 22.5).

BOX 22.2 EXAMPLE OF EQUITY MAPPING FOR SHADE EQUITY (LOS ANGELES, CALIFORNIA)

Shade is an equity issue. The historical legacy of redlining in Los Angeles and other cities has led to a disparate number of trees and subsequent lack of shade in communities of color and low-income communities.[a] This lack of shade contributes to urban heat islands, exposing residents to extreme heat and exacerbating preexisting medical conditions.

Students at California State University, Los Angeles were paired with local nonprofit organizations for paid internships using skills from courses taken in geographic information system (GIS) mapping and big data. In one such pairing, students partnered with City Plants, a nonprofit group with a mission to create equitable urban tree cover throughout Los Angeles. Students use equity mapping to take data from spreadsheets to create a visualization of where City Plants had planted thirty thousand trees throughout the city over the previous five years. Through the map, the organization was able to identify where they tended to deliver the most trees and where more trees should still be planted.

Subsequently, City Plants was able to support the Los Angeles mayor's Green New Deal goals to plant ninety thousand new trees by 2021 and increase tree canopy in targeted areas by 2028. Equity mapping was also used to help track the plan's tree canopy goals and identify viable locations for tree planting in low-canopy areas. GIS data were used to focus specifically on equity, finding locations in low-income communities that are most impacted by heat.

(Adapted from Wright.[b])

REFERENCES

a. Locke DH, Hall B, Grove JM, et al. Residential housing segregation and urban tree canopy in 37 US cities. *Urban Sustainability*. 2021;1:15. https://doi.org/10.1038/s42949-021-00022-0
b. Wright D. Student-led mapping locates areas in Los Angeles in need of shade equity. Esri blog. Published August 11, 2020. Accessed February 4, 2021. https://www.esri.com/about/newsroom/blog/los-angeles-shade-equity/

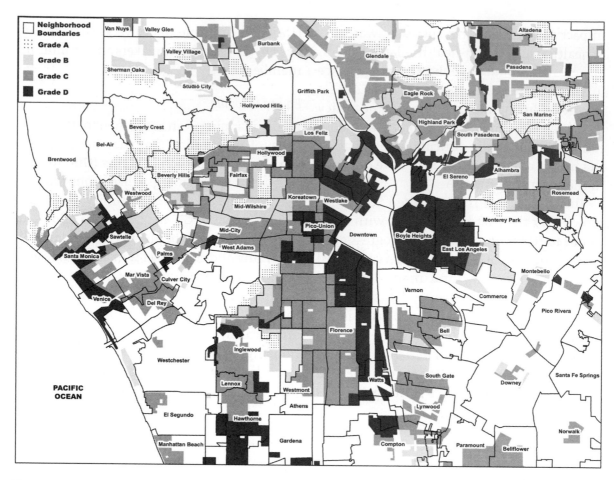

Figure 22.5. Compared to high-income neighborhoods in Los Angeles such as Beverly Hills, redlined neighborhoods such as Boyle Heights continue to have low median incomes, high surface temperatures, and low amounts of green space many decades after federal Home Owners' Loan Corporation mortgage policies contributed to inequities. These disparities are more clearly delineated on color maps (see Hoffman JS, Shandas V, Pendleton N. The effects of historical housing policies on resident exposure to intra-urban heat: a study of 108 US urban areas. *Climate.* 2020;8(1):12. https://doi.org/10.3390/cli8010012).
Source: Map by Olivia E. Chatman
Data Layer Sources: (1) Los Angeles Times. *Mapping LA.* 2021. http://maps.latimes.com/about/#the-data. (2) Nelson RK, Winling L, Marciano R, et al. Mapping inequality. In: Nelson RK, Ayers EL, eds. *American Panorama.* Accessed July 1, 2021. https://dsl.richmond.edu/panorama/redlining/#loc=10/34.005/-118.464&city=los-angeles-ca

TOOLS AND DATA SOURCES

Tools are instruments that allow us to measure or assess characteristics of the built environment. Tools might take the form of a measure or index that compiles existing data to make knowledge available in a new format. A tool could be a website that allows researchers, policymakers, advocacy groups, community leaders, and others to more easily access or visualize important information. Or, a tool could be a standardized instrument, such as a checklist or model, that allows users to collect data in a purposeful way.

Researchers and decision-makers measure or assess built environment characteristics using one or a combination of tools. Tools allow us to access and build upon the knowledge and expertise of others. Table 22.2 includes a selection of existing tools that can assist stakeholders in measuring or assessing health and the built environment. These tools provide ways to measure topics such as food access, transportation, accessibility, livability, and equity.

Publicly available existing data sources are plentiful in domestic and global settings (table 22.3). These data sources are often rigorous,

Table 22.2. Examples of existing tools on health and built environment.

Tool	Description	Example of Use
Walk Score, Transit Score, Bike Score http://walkscore.com/	Tool that determines a score between 0 and 100 for the walkability, public transit service, and bikeability of a given address	Twardzik et al.[a] found that levels of daily moderate to vigorous physical activity were positively associated with higher Walk Score categories
Nutritional Environment Measures Survey (NEMS Tools) https://nems-upenn.org/	Set of tools that assess community and consumer nutrition environments in stores, corner stores and restaurants	Whelan et al.[b] used NEMS to evaluate the food environment of a rural Australian community to inform future interventions to improve food store access
AARP Livability Index https://livabilityindex.aarp.org/	Tool that assesses community livability for all ages, combining data on housing, neighborhood, transportation, environment, health, engagement, and opportunity characteristics	Zhang et al.[c] used the AARP Livability Index to find that built environment had the largest impact on community health across county types
County Health Rankings https://www.countyhealth rankings.org/	Tool that assesses the nature and size of health differences by county. Includes physical environment measures such as traffic volume, severe housing problems, and commutes by car.	In California, San Bernardino County[d] implemented a Healthy City Initiative in many of its jurisdictions after it was ranked 50th out of 56 counties by County Health Rankings (2012)
USDA Food Access Research Atlas https://www.ers.usda.gov /data-products/food-access -research-atlas/	Mapping tool that assesses census-tract-level data on food access using measures such as supermarket, restaurant, and fast-food accessibility.	Briggs et al.[e] paired this tool with the Behavioral Risk Factor Surveillance System (BRFSS). They found that built environment factors were associated with obesity and cardiovascular health in Maine, such as high convenience store density and low full-service restaurant density.
Transportation and Health Tool https://www.transportation .gov/transportation-health-tool	Tool for use by transportation professionals that assesses the transportation environment impacts on safety, active transportation, air quality, and connectivity to destinations	Oh et al.[f] used the tool to evaluate the association between transportation infrastructure and health in Michigan at the county level
WHO Health Economic Assessment Tool (HEAT) for Walking and Cycling https://heatwalkingcycling.org/	Tool that conducts economic assessment of the health benefits of walking or cycling by estimating the value of reduced mortality that results from specified amounts of walking or cycling.	Skayannis et al.[g] applied HEAT to assess how increased bicycle use in Trikala, Greece, could increase life expectancy and reduce health care costs
System for Observing Play and Recreation in Communities (SOPARC) https://activelivingresearch org/soparc-system-observing -play-and-recreation- communities	Validated direct observation tool that assesses park and recreation areas, including park users' physical activity levels, gender, activity modes/types, and estimated age and ethnicity	Evenson et al.[h] conducted a systematic review of studies using SOPARC and found that, generally, men visited parks more than women and that youth and younger children were more active in parks than adults

Table 22.2. Continued

Tool	Description	Example of Use
Microscale Audit of Pedestrian Streetscapes (MAPS) https://activelivingresearch.org/microscale-audit-pedestrian-streetscapes	Tool used to collect audit data on microscale factors of the pedestrian environment and walkability in neighborhoods. Microscale factors include details about streets, sidewalks, intersections, and design characteristics (e.g., road crossing features, presence of trees, bicycle lanes, curbs), as well as characteristics of the social environment (e.g., stray dogs, graffiti, trash). Comes in mini, abbreviated, and full forms.	Thornton et al.[i] assessed streetscapes in San Diego, Seattle, and Baltimore and found neighborhoods with a high proportion of racial/ethnic minorities were more likely to have poorer aesthetics and social elements in the MAPS tool. However, high-income and less-diverse neighborhoods also tended to have worse or absent pedestrian amenities.

a. Twardzik E, Judd S, Bennett A, et al. Walk Score and objectively measured physical activity within a national cohort. *Journal of Epidemiology and Community Health*. 2019;73(6):549-556. doi:10.1136/jech-2017-210245

b. Whelan J, Millar L, Bell C, et al. You can't find healthy food in the bush: poor accessibility, availability and adequacy of food in rural Australia. *International Journal of Environmental Research and Public Health*. 2018;15(10). doi:10.3390/ijerph15102316

c. Zhang X, Warner ME, Wethington E. Can age-friendly planning promote equity in community health across the rural-urban divide in the US? *International Journal of Environmental Research and Public Health*. 2020;17(4). doi:10.3390/ijerph17041275

d. County Health Rankings. In San Bernardino, CA, county health department takes lead to improve area's poor health ranking. County Health Rankings & Roadmaps. April 4, 2012. Accessed February 4, 2021. https://www.countyhealthrankings.org/learn-from-others/stories/in-san-bernardino-ca-county-health-department-takes-lead-to-improve-area%E2%80%99s-poor-health-ranking

e. Briggs AC, Black AW, Lucas FL, Siewers AE, Fairfield KM. Association between the food and physical activity environment, obesity, and cardiovascular health across Maine counties. *BMC Public Health*. 2019;19(1):374. doi:10.1186/s12889-019-6684-6

f. Oh J-S, Kwigizile V, Zahid F, Alzuhairi AHH. Transportation system and its association with human health—a review and modeling approach. Transportation Research Center; 2016. TRCLC 14-03. Accessed February 4, 2021. https://rosap.ntl.bts.gov/view/dot/34374

g. Skayannis P, Goudas M, Crone D, Cavill N, Kahlmeier S, Mitsiadi V. Health related benefits of non-motorised transport: an application of the Health Economic Assessment Tool of the World Health Organisation to the Case of Trikala, Greece. In: Nathanail EG, Karakikes ID, eds. *Data Analytics: Paving the Way to Sustainable Urban Mobility. Advances in Intelligent Systems and Computing*. Springer International; 2019:789-796. doi:10.1007/978-3-030-02305-8_95

h. Evenson KR, Jones SA, Holliday KM, Cohen DA, McKenzie TL. Park characteristics, use, and physical activity: a review of studies using SOPARC (System for Observing Play and Recreation in Communities). *Preventive Medicine*. 2016;86:153-166. doi:10.1016/j.ypmed.2016.02.029

i. Thornton CM, Conway TL, Cain KL, et al. Disparities in pedestrian streetscape environments by income and race/ethnicity. *SSM—Population Health*. 2016;2:206-216. doi:10.1016/j.ssmph.2016.03.004

representative of their target population, and collected repeatedly over years or decades. These characteristics offer many benefits to the validity and reliability of these data. When researchers do not have to collect new data, the process is more efficient and avoids overburdening research participants. Some centers house compilations of vast amounts of publicly available data, such as the Inter-University Consortium for Political and Social Research at the University of Michigan (http://icpsr.umich.edu), the IPUMS databases at the University of Minnesota (http://ipums.org), and the Global Health Data Exchange at the Univer-

Table 22.3. Examples of public data sources that include health and built environment data.

Name	Description
US Census https://data.census.gov/	A count of each resident of the country, collected every decade. Includes basic US demographic and geographical data for research and can also help determine funding and scope of built environment policy like mass transit (1902–present).
City Health Dashboard https://www.cityhealth dashboard.com/	Includes 37 measures of health, the factors that shape health, and drivers of health equity to guide local solutions for the 500 largest US cities (2018–present).
PLACES Project https://www.cdc.gov/places/	Includes model-based estimates of health-related outcomes for multiple levels of geographic analysis in the United States: counties, incorporated and census designated places, census tracts, and zip code tabulation areas (2020–present). Successor to the 500 Cities Project (2016-2019).
Behavioral Risk Factor Surveillance System (BRFSS) https://www.cdc.gov/brfss/	Telephone survey that collects health data on US residents. Includes data on health-related risk behaviors, chronic health conditions, and use of preventive services (1984–present). Can be paired with built environment data sets to conduct research (see table 22.2). Selected Metropolitan/Micropolitan Area Risk Trends (SMART) BRFSS also provides localized health information for cities and surrounding counties.
American Community Survey https://www.census.gov/programs-surveys/acs	Survey of detailed population and housing information of US residents. Includes data on commuting mode and time that help determine transportation and infrastructure planning (2005-present).
Benchmarking Report on Bicycling and Walking in the United States https://bikeleague.org/benchmarking-report	Guide to publicly available data on bicycling and walking. Includes data on health impacts, as well as public policy related to bicycling and walking in the United States (2007–present).
National Health Interview Survey (NHIS) https://www.cdc.gov/nchs/nhis/	Yearly household interview survey that is the primary source of information on the health of civilians in the United States (1957–present).
National Health and Nutritional Examination Survey (NHANES) https://www.cdc.gov/nchs/nhanes/	Study designed to assess the health and nutritional status of adults and children in the United States. Includes interviews and physical examinations (current version 1999–present; previous versions 1960–1998).
Health and Retirement Study, University of Michigan https://hrs.isr.umich.edu/	Longitudinal panel study that surveys a representative sample of approximately 20,000 people in the United States. Includes data on the challenges and opportunities of aging (1990–present).
Office of National Statistics (United Kingdom) https://www.ons.gov.uk/	Collection of national data of the United Kingdom. Includes data on health, social care, well-being, housing, and neighborhoods (1996–present).
Eurostat (European Union) https://ec.europa.eu/eurostat	Data from the official statistical office of the European Union. Includes measures on areas such as transportation, policy, health status, living and housing conditions, quality of life, and sustainable development (1953–present).
Association of Southeast Asian Nations (ASEAN) Stats Data Portal https://data.aseanstats.org/	Statistical database comprising data from 10 countries in Southeast Asia. Includes data on relevant built environment and health measures include length of paved roads, number of public buses, and number of traffic accident casualties (2018–present).

Table 22.3. Continued

Name	Description
Pacific Community Statistics for Development Division https://sdd.spc.int/	Collection of data from more than 20 Pacific Island countries. Includes measures on health and well-being, sanitation, slum neighborhoods, infrastructure, and sustainability (2010–present).
Australian Bureau of Statistics (ABS) https://www.abs.gov.au/statistics	Database of surveys and measures from Australia. Includes data on transportation, population demographics, crime, housing, health, and environmental management. Data can also be viewed by region (1911–present).
Stats New Zealand http://nzdotstat.stats.govt.nz/	Database of measures from New Zealand. Includes data on health, housing, injury, crime, and census data (2001– present).

sity of Washington (http://ghdx.healthdata.org). The linking of data sets can provide even greater insight. For instance, health data from nationally representative, longitudinal surveys that typically do not focus on built environment factors, such as the Behavioral Risk Factor Surveillance System, can be linked with spatial data to measurements of the built environment.

There are disadvantages to using existing tools or data sources. It may be difficult to get the exact measurements desired. For instance, US Census data is organized on the census-tract level. However, locally collected data might only be found by zip code areas, which are larger and may not correspond to census tracts. It may be difficult to find one's targeted population, such as a specific town or neighborhood. Additionally, some racial or ethnic groups—such as those of South Asian or Middle East/North African descent—are not disaggregated from their larger racial groups in most national data sets, which masks existing health disparities. Finally, when using previously collected data sets, researchers must ask who is not represented—for instance, surveys or interviews conducted only in English may not represent the experiences of those who primarily speak other languages. Segments of the population such as unhoused individuals and undocumented immigrants may not be reached by these surveys, or they may fear for the safety and confidentiality of their responses.

Newer methodologies using Google Street View, machine learning, image recognition, and artificial intelligence open new opportunities for measurement and assessment (chapter 24). As the movements for open-source data and reproducible research become the norm, decision-makers and the public will have more equitable access to more information, although such increased access may raise increased concerns about privacy issues.

CERTIFYING HEALTHY PLACES

Certification is a process to document that a building or neighborhood has achieved a high standard of design (table 22.4). Certification processes can help encourage all places toward higher goals of health, sustainability, and economic benefit. Certifications communicate these elements to the public, reducing information asymmetry and helping people choose healthy and sustainable places in which to live and work.

A well-known example of building certification is **Leadership in Energy and Environmental Design (LEED)**. Established in 1998 by the US Green Building Council, it has gradually set a standard for sustainability. LEED use today is widespread—44 percent of spaces seeking LEED certification are outside the United States, including in China, Singapore, the United Arab Emirates, Brazil, and India. LEED certification is obtained when a builder or owner of a building applies for certification by documenting specific building attributes

Table 22.4. Selected certifications for health-promoting buildings and communities.

Certification	Description	Selected Health-Related Criteria
Health-focused certifications		
Fitwel https://Fitwel.org/	Certification for building healthy buildings or neighborhoods.	Database of building emergency equipment, public transit distance, adequate outdoor lighting, on-site sale of produce.
WELL Building Standard https://wellcertified.com/	Standard for places implementing and validating features that support and advance human health and wellness.	Water treatment, health education, mold control, bicycle maintenance tools, natural daylight.
Sustainability-focused certifications		
LEED https://usgbc.org/leed/	Most widely used green building system. Provides framework and ratings for healthy, efficient, and cost-saving new buildings. Can also be applied to interiors, existing buildings, neighborhood development, and cities and communities.	Surrounding density, access to quality transit, bicycle facilities, construction activity pollution prevention, reduced parking footprint.
Living Building Challenge https://living-future.org/	Design buildings that generate more energy than they use, capture and treat all water on-site, and use healthy materials.	Landscape is a source of local and organic food production, universal access, indoor air quality, biophilic design.
SITES https://sustainablesites.org/	Certifies regenerative and environmentally beneficially landscapes. Aligns land development and management with sustainable design.	Redevelopment of degraded sites, limited pesticide use, creating ecologically resilient land that connects people to nature.
Building Research Establishment Environmental Assessment Method (BREEAM) https://breeam.com/	Certification of a building's environmental performance, impact, and innovation across its life cycle. Developed in the United Kingdom.	Acoustic performance, use of materials with low emissions of volatile organic compounds.
Comprehensive Assessment System for Building Environmental Efficiency (CASBEE) https://www.ibec.or.jp/CASBEE/english/	Certification of environmental quality and performance of a building. Developed in Japan.	Renewable energy production, air quality and ventilation, indoor pollutants, seismic aspects.
Institute for Transparency of Contracts and Environmental Compatibility (ITACA) https://www.regione.marche.it/Regione-Utile/Energia/Protocollo-ITACA	Protocol for labeling a building's environmental sustainability across its life cycle. Can be adapted for local regions. Developed in Italy.	Water recycling systems, sustainable transport and mobility, pollutant emissions.
Green Star https://new.qbca.org.au/	Certification of the environmental design and achievements of new and existing buildings. Developed in Australia.	Eco-friendly materials use, construction waste management, heat island effect, light pollution

and pays a fee. The applications are reviewed by the Green Building Council and approved or denied (http://www.usgbc.org).

LEED certification has created a cultural shift such that most new buildings are now designed with energy efficiency as a goal, even when formal certification by LEED is not sought.[25] Standards that are energy efficient generally also promote health. For instance, sustainable design choices that reduce the emission of pollutants will improve the health of residents. Beyond buildings, certifications can also be awarded to neighborhoods and building sites. For instance, LEED for Cities and Communities provides a framework for local leaders and planners to make sustainable plans for natural systems, energy, water, waste, and transportation in their communities. More than one hundred cities and communities use the certification globally.

There are critiques of LEED's certification process, which awards points based on how much the building should save if features are implemented rather than tracking metrics of energy use after the building is constructed.[26] Although there are limited data on how LEED buildings perform on sustainability and carbon emissions after completion,[26] there is a growing movement to collect such measurements in **postoccupancy evaluations** and in recertification processes. Another potential difficulty of certifications such as LEED is the lack of distinction between *initial design* and subsequent *operational management*. For instance, smoke-free buildings are a matter of ongoing monitoring and signage rather than a building design choice. The motivation to optimize sustainability and health may be different when the builder, owner, and user are the same (for example, a university building) compared to when they are different (for example, a commercial office building). Finally, there are equity concerns tied to LEED. One study found an association between LEED-ND (LEED for Neighborhood Development) certification and indicators of gentrification, such as median rent and racial diversity.[27] LEED certification is

beginning to pilot the use of social equity and health promotion credits in its rating system,[28] but more development in the area of equity certifications is needed.

Buildings can also achieve certifications that prioritize a focus on promoting health and equity for their inhabitants. Two examples are Fitwel and the WELL Building Standard, both of which use evidence-based design features to facilitate environments favorable to health. Fitwel, created by the US Centers for Disease Control and Prevention and the US General Services Administration, certifies buildings and communities based on seven health impact categories: community health, morbidity and absenteeism, social equity for vulnerable populations, well-being, access to healthy foods, occupant safety, and physical activity.[29] Features include public transit within one-half mile, on-site sale of fresh produce, natural daylight, fitness rooms, and designs that promote stair use.[29] As of 2020, Fitwel had been used by at least 980 projects in more than 180 countries, potentially impacting more than 820,000 individuals.[29,30] The WELL v2 Building Standard certifies building projects based on concepts of air, water, nourishment, light, movement, thermal comfort, sound, materials, mind, community, and innovation.[31] Design features include mold control, air quality monitoring, food labeling for allergies and nutrition, and bicycle maintenance tools. As of 2020, more than 4,200 projects had been WELL registered in 88 countries, with 301 achieving certification. Table 22.4 provides an overview of selected certifications focused primarily on both health and sustainability and includes international examples.[32]

Overall, most certifications are more focused on sustainability rather than direct impacts on health (box 22.3). One systematic review examined the body of literature on architecture health indices, or measures used to evaluate the healthiness of architectural design.[33] This review found that few indicators focused on mental and social health, and none addressed chronic diseases.[33] Attention

BOX 22.3 THE LIVING BUILDING CHALLENGE: GEORGIA INSTITUTE OF TECHNOLOGY KENDEDA BUILDING

The Living Building Challenge, developed by the International Living Future Institute, is an ambitious sustainable building certification. It requires buildings to be self-sufficient and have net positive energy, water, and waste use—meaning that the buildings produce more energy and water than they use and that they reuse waste beneficially. Other standards of the Living Building Challenge include equity, beauty, safe materials, and health and happiness.

The Kendeda Building for Innovative Sustainable Design, located on the Georgia Institute of Technology campus in Atlanta, is one of a handful of buildings globally designed to achieve the Living Building Challenge Certification (figure 22.6). Completed in 2019, the building achieved this certification in 2021 after one year of full occupancy. The building contains 46,848 gross square feet of usable space, with a total construction cost of $18.6 million.

To achieve the standard of a net positive facility, the building's energy use is expected to be 72 percent more efficient than the average building of the same size. An array of solar panels harnesses more energy than the building consumes. These panels also provide shade to mitigate the urban heat island effect. Each year, 460,000 gallons of rainwater are collected in a 50,000-gallon cistern, processed by rainwater treatment equipment on-site. A rooftop garden also serves to help manage stormwater runoff.

The building is used by students of various departments. It contains classrooms, laboratories, a makerspace, and an auditorium. In addition, an outdoor learning space contains a rooftop garden with a honeybee apiary, pollinator garden, and blueberry orchard. Other spaces include bike storage, a porch area, and roof deck. The building includes signage describing its key features and thus helps educate its users on sustainability.

Figure 22.6. The Kendeda Building for Innovative Sustainable Design in Atlanta is designed to be certified by the Living Building Challenge.
Source: Photos courtesy of Olivia E. Chatman

(Adapted from Georgia Institute of Technology Kendeda Building Fact Sheet and website.[a,b])

REFERENCES

a. Georgia Tech. The Kendeda Building for Innovative Sustainable Design. Georgia Tech. Accessed February 4, 2021. https://livingbuilding.gatech.edu/
b. Georgia Tech. The Kendeda Building for Innovative Sustainable Design Fact Sheet. Georgia Tech. Accessed February 4, 2021. http://livingbuilding.gatech.edu/sites/default/files/documents/kendeda_bldg_fact_sheet_fall_2019.pdf

to health and disease may change with the emergence of more health-focused certifications. For example, the Center for Active Design created the Viral Response Module in 2020 in response to the COVID-19 pandemic.[34] Over time, the availability of these certifications may influence the design and health of buildings and communities even if formal certification is not obtained. Just as LEED brought sustainability into the mainstream,[26] health-focused certification systems may raise awareness of the importance of promoting healthy behaviors and reducing health risks in a variety of places through evidence-based design strategies.

CONCLUSION

An old maxim states, "What gets counted, counts." For example, when motor vehicle traffic volumes and delays are routinely measured, roads receive a large share of all transportation dollars. Pedestrian and bicycling traffic are not routinely measured; therefore, sidewalks and bike paths seldom receive a share of funding proportional to their potential usage. Measurements, assessments, and certifications allow us to evaluate various aspects of human behavior, buildings, and communities; advocate for healthy places; and document the relationships between health and community design. Results from such measurements can assist decision-makers in allocating resources for improvements in community design to promote health.

Although ideal measurements are not available for all built environment components for which they could be useful, without them researchers, policymakers, and planners would be at a loss for where to direct their efforts or make change. Investments and decisions would instead be decided by individual preference, anecdote, or monetary influence.

A greater quantity and quality of measurements, assessments, and certifications that are rooted in equity and community voices can facilitate better decision-making for the health of our communities.

DISCUSSION QUESTIONS

1. What are some types of measures of health-related components of the built environment in a community? Why is it difficult to obtain ideal measures?
2. How do certification standards such as LEED, Fitwel, and WELL promote healthy community design and healthy buildings?
3. Identify five different walkability or park audit tools available at https://active livingresearch.org/toolsandresources/all. How do the tools differ in content and emphasis?
4. In what kinds of settings are health impact assessments (HIAs) particularly useful for assessing the likely effects of proposed projects and policies on people's health?
5. What barriers may prevent an HIA from influencing a decision about a proposed project or policy?

DISCLOSURE OF COMPETING INTERESTS

Carolyn Fan was supported by grant number T32HS013853 from the Agency for Healthcare Research and Quality during the writing of this chapter. The content is solely the responsibility of the authors and does not necessarily represent the official views of the Agency for Healthcare Research and Quality. At the time of writing, she was also a part-time research consultant contracted with Human Impact Partners.

Andrew L. Dannenberg's declarations appear in the preface.

REFERENCES

1. Barbour E, Chatman D, Doggett S, Yip S, Santana M. SB 743 *Implementation: Challenges and Opportunities*. University of California Center for Economic Competitiveness in Transportation; 2019:1-113. Accessed February 4, 2021. https://escholarship.org/uc/item/4gj3n2n3

2. Tyner P, Shepard A. Shifting from LOS to VMT as the Measure of Transportation Impact Assessment: Senate Bill 743 Implementation: Challenges and Opportunities. Caltrans Division of Research, Innovation and System Information; 2019:4. Accessed February 4, 2021. https://dot.ca.gov/-/media/dot-media/programs/research-innovation-system-information/documents/research-results/2886-rr-a11y.pdf

3. Karlin-Resnick J. Why California Accidentally Encouraged Driving, and How That's About to Change. SPUR (The San Francisco Bay Area Planning and Urban Research Association). Published June 30, 2016. Accessed February 4, 2021. https://www.spur.org/news/2016-06-30/why-california-accidentally-encouraged-driving-and-how-thats-about-change

4. Arlington County Commuter Services. Counter Data. Bike Arlington. Published February 4, 2021. Accessed February 4, 2021. http://www.bikearlington.com/counter-data/

5. Ricklin A, Shah S. *Metrics for Planning Healthy Communities*. American Planning Association; 2017:26. Accessed February 4, 2021. https://planning-org-uploaded-media.s3.amazonaws.com/document/Metrics-Planning-Healthy-Communities.pdf

6. Gascon M, Cirach M, Martínez D, et al. Normalized difference vegetation index (NDVI) as a marker of surrounding greenness in epidemiological studies: the case of Barcelona city. *Urban Forestry & Urban Greening*. 2016; 19:88-94. https://doi.org/10.1016/j.ufug.2016.07.001

7. Chiang Y-C, Sullivan W, Larsen L. Measuring neighborhood walkable environments: a comparison of three approaches. *International Journal of Environmental Research and Public Health*. 2017;14(6). doi:10.3390/ijerph14060593

8. US Department of Transportation, Partnership for a Walkable America, Pedestrian and Bicycle Information Center. Walkability Checklist. US Department of Transportation; 2016:4. Accessed February 4, 2021. https://www.nhtsa.gov/sites/nhtsa.dot.gov/files/walkingchecklist.pdf

9. South Dakota Department of Health. Walk! Health South Dakota Community Walkability Toolkit. South Dakota Department of Health. Published 2016. Accessed February 4, 2021. http://healthysd.gov/wp-content/uploads/2016/02/hsd-walkingtoolkit-final.pdf

10. AARP Livable Communities. AARP Walk Audit Tool Kit. AARP Community, State and National Affairs; 2016:16. Accessed February 4, 2021. https://www.aarp.org/content/dam/aarp/livable-communities/livable-documents/documents-2016/Walk-Audit-Tool-Kit/AARP-Walk-Audit-Tool-Kit-100416.pdf

11. Institute for Transportation and Development Policy. Pedestrians First: Tools for a Walkable City. Pedestrians First. 2020. Accessed February 4, 2021. https://pedestriansfirst.itdp.org

12. Walk Score. Walk Score Methodology. Walk Score. Accessed February 4, 2021. https://www.walkscore.com/methodology.shtml

13. Hall CM, Ram Y. Walk Score® and its potential contribution to the study of active transport and walkability: a critical and systematic review. *Transportation Research Part D: Transport and Environment* 2018;61:310-324. doi:10.1016/j.trd.2017.12.018

14. National Research Council (US) Committee on Health Impact Assessment. *Improving Health in the United States: The Role of Health Impact Assessment.* National Academies Press; 2011. Accessed February 4, 2021. https://www.ncbi.nlm.nih.gov/books/NBK83533/

15. Dannenberg AL. A brief history of health impact assessment in the United States. *Chronicles of Health Impact Assessment.* 2016;1(1). http://doi.org/10.18060/21348

16. American Public Health Association (APHA). Promoting Health Impact Assessment to Achieve Health in All Policies. APHA. Published October 30, 2012. Accessed February 4, 2021. https://www.apha.org/policies-and-advocacy/public-health-policy-statements/policy-database/2014/07/11/16/51/promoting-health-impact-assessment-to-achieve-health-in-all-policies

17. United States Environmental Protection Agency (EPA). Summary of the National Environmental Policy Act. 42 USC §4321 et seq. (1969). US EPA. Published February 22, 2013. Accessed February 4, 2021. https://www.epa.gov/laws-regulations/summary-national-environmental-policy-act

18. Sohn EK, Stein LJ, Wolpoff A, et al. Avenues of influence: The relationship between health impact assessment and determinants of health and health equity. *Journal of Urban Health.* 2018;95(5):754-764. doi:10.1007/s11524-018-0263-5

19. Dannenberg AL. Effectiveness of health impact assessments: a synthesis of data from five impact evaluation reports. *Preventing Chronic Disease.* 2016;1(1). doi:10.18060/21348

20. Thondoo M, Rojas-Rueda D, Gupta J, de Vries DH, Nieuwenhuijsen MJ. Systematic literature review of health impact assessments in low and middle-income countries. *International Journal of Environmental Research and Public Health.* 2019;16(11). doi:10.3390/ijerph16112018

21. Pew Charitable Trusts. Health Impact Project. Accessed July 15, 2021. https://www.pewtrusts.org/en/projects/health-impact-project/health-impact-assessment

22. Winkler MS, Furu P, Viliani F, et al. Current global health impact assessment practice. *International Journal of Environmental Research and Public Health.* 2020;17(9):2988. doi:10.3390/ijerph17092988

23. Wyss K, Dolan K, Goff N. Health in All Policies: A Framework for State Health Leadership. Association of State and Territorial Health Officials (ASTHO). Accessed February 4, 2021. https://www.astho.org/HiAP/Framework/

24. US Department of Housing and Urban Development. Equity Mapping and the Geography of Opportunity. HUD User. Accessed February 4, 2021. https://www.huduser.gov/portal/pdredge/pdr_edge_featd_article_042114.html

25. MacNaughton P, Cao X, Buonocore J, et al. Energy savings, emission reductions, and health co-benefits of the green building movement. *Journal of Exposure Science and Environmental Epidemiology.* 2018;28(4):307-318. doi:10.1038/s41370-017-0014-9

26. Barth B. Is LEED tough enough for the climate-change era? *Bloomberg CityLab.* Published June 5, 2018. Accessed February 4, 2021. https://www.citylab.com/environment/2018/06/is-leed-tough-enough-for-the-climate-change-era/559478/

27. Benson EM, Bereitschaft B. Are LEED-ND developments catalysts of neighborhood gentrification? *International Journal of Urban Sustainable Development.* 2020;12(1):73-88. doi:10.1080/19463138.2019.1658588

28. Melton P. USGBC and Social Equity: What's Available and What's Missing. LEEDuser. Published September 14, 2020. Accessed February 4, 2021. https://leeduser.buildinggreen.com/blog/usgbc-and-social-equity-what-s-available-and-what-s-missing

29. Fitwel. What is the Fitwel Standard? Fitwel. Accessed February 4, 2021. https://www.fitwel.org/standard/

30. Chau S. 20 Firms Receive Prestigious Recognition for Advancing the Healthy Building Movement with Fitwel®. Fitwel and Center for Active Design; 2020:4. Accessed February 4, 2021. https://assets.ctfassets.net/fuo6knzstk5a/1X2ZVaoY7eYYbzIYyOWsBp/7a9o6 3a28b88a0277cee27762b710829/20 _Firms_Receive_Prestigious_Recognition _for_Advancing_the_Healthy_Building _Movement_with_Fitwel_Feb4_2020.pdf

31. International Well Building Institute. WELL Certification. WELL. Accessed February 4, 2021. https://www.wellcertified.com/

32. Mattoni B, Guattari C, Evangelisti L, Bisegna F, Gori P, Asdrubali F. Critical review and methodological approach to evaluate the differences among international green building rating tools. *Renewable and Sustainable Energy Reviews*. 2018;82:950-960. doi:10.1016/j.rser.2017.09.105

33. Rice L, Drane M. Indicators of healthy architecture—a systematic literature review. *Journal of Urban Health*. 2020;97(6):899-911. doi:10.1007/s11524-020-00469-z

34. Center for Active Design. Viral Response Module. 2021. https://centerforactivedesign.org/viral-response-module

PART IV

LOOKING FORWARD, TAKING ACTION

CHAPTER 23

TRAINING THE NEXT GENERATION OF HEALTHY PLACEMAKERS

Nisha Botchwey, Olivia E. Chatman, Matthew J. Trowbridge, and Yakut Gazi

KEY POINTS

- Educating a new generation of healthy placemakers requires interdisciplinary training focused on team-based application of public health and design expertise.
- Academic training programs focused on the built environment and public health, ranging from cross-listed courses to dual-degree programs in planning and public health, are increasingly available.
- Better integration of public health and built environment competencies in interdisciplinary courses will be critical going forward and may require targeted offerings beyond the typical semester or quarter.
- The majority of professional education programs focus on understanding and communicating links between health and the built environment. However, there is growing demand for more applied built environment and health training tailored to specific disciplines (for example, public health, architecture, landscape architecture, urban planning, transportation engineering), as well as postgraduate professionals, particularly in the wake of more frequent natural disasters from climate change and the COVID-19 global pandemic.

- More work is needed to (1) define interdisciplinary competencies for healthy placemaking as the basis for better integrated training curricula; (2) produce and deliver accessible online training modules; (3) develop opportunities for collaboration between practitioners and academics across disciplines and diverse communities; and (4) expand funding support for multidisciplinary research, training, and practice.

INTRODUCTION

"I was in my final semester of my graduate urban planning program when my familial homeland Haiti experienced a 7.0 earthquake in January 2010. I simply could not make sense of the aftermath where up to 300,000 people perished in just 35 seconds due to decades of hypercentralization in the capital metropolitan region, unenforced and, in many instances, nonexistent land use regulations, and other human-induced causes," said Dr. Vanessa L. Deane, master of urban planning, assistant clinical professor of urban planning and public service, and director of the Urban Planning Program at New York University Robert F. Wagner Graduate School of Public Service (figure 23.1). "A few months after the quake, Haiti also suffered a public health crisis resulting from a deadly cholera outbreak involving geopolitical dynamics with the United Nations

Figure 23.1. In response to the rebuilding efforts following the 2010 earthquake in Haiti, Dr. Vanessa L. Deane and her team, in partnership with the nonprofit service organization Community2Community, lead the remote, quake-affected, mountainside community in Petit Goâve in an interactive mapping project. These local residents are being trained in the use of geolocation devices to establish neighborhood boundaries on Google Earth.
Source: Courtesy of Vanessa L. Deane

and the practical reality of poor sewage management infrastructure, thereby creating a situation of cascading calamities for an already struggling nation. My training as a built environment professional taught me to think holistically about the interconnected political, economic, and social systems that come to bear on people's livelihoods while also finding ways to concertedly address them, starting at the most basic local neighborhood level through to overall national and, at times, international considerations."

An integrated approach to practice in public health and the built environment is essential to realizing the goal of healthy and sustainable places—buildings, neighborhoods, communities, cities, and regions. Since the early 2000s, explicit efforts have been made to reestablish this vital connection between the two fields (chapter 1). As a result, specialized training

programs are increasingly available, but an expansion of education and training strategies focused on the *application of* team-based public health and design expertise is needed for elementary and secondary students, postsecondary students, and professionals.

NEXT STEPS IN THE DEVELOPMENT OF HEALTH AND BUILT ENVIRONMENT TRAINING

In interdisciplinary education, issues are examined from various disciplinary fields to expand knowledge, skills, and perspectives (see chapter 1). The majority of interdisciplinary education programs focused on healthy placemaking, often called built environment and health, focus on the evidence base for the associations between community design and diseases or behaviors. Programs focused more directly on educating an integrated healthy placemaking "workforce" are growing in universities and professional organizations but are not yet well established. Most programs remain field-specific, both in terms of pedagogy and certifications for built environment and public health practitioners. Moreover, the education programs are predominantly formal academic courses. There are limited continuing education and other training opportunities for existing professionals.

Training programs for the next generation of healthy placemakers should focus on (1) defining competencies for interdisciplinary healthy placemaking, (2) increasing in-person and remote access to training resources to academic and professional audiences, (3) expanding opportunities for collaboration between practitioners, academics, and community members from a variety of ages, functions, and racial and ethnic groups, and (4) diversifying research and funding opportunities at multiple scales.[1]

Establishing a core set of shared learning objectives for healthy place professionals will require adaptation and, at times, expansion of existing competencies in both built environment and public health education. For example, built environment students (for example urban planning, architecture, landscape architecture, civil engineering) are taught to think about data and behavioral patterns of a population from a spatial or geographic perspective, to use policy to incentivize desired development patterns, and to navigate land use decision-making frameworks at a variety of government levels. These are critical skills for promoting healthy places. However, these types of built environment courses frequently lack training in applying a comprehensive public health perspective and approach. The result is that health implications of projects are frequently considered narrowly in built environment curricula, and opportunities to apply measurement, analysis, and evaluation tools available from public health specialties, such as epidemiology and surveillance, are missed. In contrast, public health students

receive training in analytical and strategic approaches, such as evaluating the health impact of environmental exposures, but are generally not trained to consider the geographic and social contexts related to disease processes. It is also difficult for most public health professionals to engage in built environment interventions given their lack of exposure to design theory and the intricacies of laws and policies related to the built environment. Integration of these approaches will be critical going forward and may require targeted offerings beyond the typical semester or quarter academic offering.

BUILDING BALANCED HEALTHY PLACES CURRICULA

Developing integrated healthy placemaking learning experiences can feel daunting, particularly for educators with more expertise in one domain than others. However, a growing library of open-use resources is now available. For example, sample syllabi from interdisciplinary healthy places university courses are available for download at the Built Environment and Public Health Clearinghouse website, a professional education and teaching resource built on a learning-centered approach designed to address the challenges of interdisciplinary teaching, learning, and retooling the current workforce.[2]

The COVID-19 pandemic forced translation of traditional face-to-face content and teaching approaches for online use. Educational institutions across the world had to quickly generate resources to support faculty to teach remotely. For example, Georgia Tech made its Remote and Hybrid Teaching Academy publicly available. Although difficult and time-consuming to develop and deliver quality and engaging content, this mass experimentation in online learning is yielding both new resources and best practices that can help educators jump-start their healthy placemaking educational offerings. The recommendations can be summarized in the following three key steps.

Step 1. Orient and structure courses around "backward design," where instruction focuses on desired learning and targeted skill outcomes.

- What *skills* do students need to make healthy places? What healthy place-making skills are key to bridging the built environment and health disciplines that students should practice or are absent from the students' prior experience?
- What *assessments* will confirm that the students learned how to make healthy places?
- In what *activities and content* should they be engaged in to be skillful healthy place-makers? What assignments or projects provide practice in healthy placemaking? What theories, terminology, history, and other topics are critical for students to build on for this interdisciplinary curriculum?
- What *tools and technologies* can be integrated in the physical or virtual classroom to augment student learning and healthy placemaking?

Step 2. Map out a balance of student inter-actions and other types of engagement for student satisfaction and success.

- Student-content: Lectures, readings, videos, people and place resources. (Videos are six to fifteen minutes long and interactive with embedded self-tests.)
- Student-instructor: Instructor interaction with students in a predictable and scheduled manner, through direct instruction and in one of the following ways: assessing or providing feedback on a student's coursework, providing information or responding to questions about the content course or competency, or facilitating a group discussion regarding the content of a course or competency.
- Student-student: A learning community built from the opportunities for student-student interaction and collaboration either through synchronous means (for example, breakout sessions, student pre-

sentations, group work) or asynchronous means (for example, discussion boards for content-related and social connections).

Step 3. Design authentic assessments of knowledge and application that mirror the expectations from students after graduation. This assessment design both reduces test-taking anxiety and instances of academic dishonesty and reinforces learning and retention.

- Include more frequent quizzes, tests, assignments, and projects or a class-long project that is broken into distinct cumulative units rather than one or two high-stakes exams.
- Incorporate instructor feedback in these more frequent assessments that build on one another as a feedback-corrective loop for enhancing learning.

EXPANDING DIVERSITY IN BUILT ENVIRONMENT AND PUBLIC HEALTH EDUCATION

Increasing and diversifying the population of students interested in built environment and public health will be critical to the goal of building healthy places that are accessible for everyone. Summer programs—like Youth Engagement and Action for Health (YEAH!),[3] iPlan Healthy Communities,[4] and UN-Habitat's use of information communication technology with Minecraft for Youth Participation in Urban Design and Governance[5]—are available for kindergarten through twelfth-grade students. At the undergraduate and graduate levels, students can find this field through guest lectures in introductory sustainability, planning, architecture, landscape architecture, transportation and public health classes, individual course offerings, formal specializations, certificates, and minors. Additionally, applied research opportunities and available joint degree programs in the built environment and public health offer great promise for higher levels of training within university training (table 23.1). When considering the continued development of joint degree programs and interdisciplinary curriculum, efforts should

Table 23.1. Real-world examples of built environment and public health training.

	Example 1	Example 2
Tier 1: Colleges and universities that have faculty members with a health and built environment specialization or research interest.	At the University of Cape Town in South Africa, the *African Centre for Cities* facilitates research and policy discourse related to the many urban issues related to sustainability and health that arise as a result of rapid urbanization, especially in the developing world. (Website: https://www.africancentreforcities.net/)	The Healthy Places Research Group (HPRG) at Georgia Institute of Technology's Center for Quality Growth and Regional Development is a collaboration between individuals interested in the intersection of health and the built environment. HPRG hosts publicly accessible monthly meetings to explore research and information related to health policy, impacts, and the built environment. (Website: https://cqgrd.gatech.edu/hprg)
Tier 2: Schools that offer a course that connects built environment and public health disciplinary topics, which may be cross-listed in the field's course offerings.	*Healthy Communities* is an elective course exploring public health issues, risk factors, and interventions and their relationship to the built environment for students obtaining a master of environments or master of public health at the University of Melbourne. (Website: https://handbook.unimelb.edu.au/2020/subjects/abpl90022)	*Health, Environment, and Planning* is a cross-listed course in the planning, health, and geography departments at the University of Waterloo that examines the determinants of health, health care systems, and health conditions, as well as the role of urban planners in creating healthier environments. (Website: https://uwaterloo.ca/geography-environmental-management/sites/ca.geography-environmental-management/files/uploads/files/geog_432_outline_w2017.pdf)
Tier 3: Schools that offer opportunities for students to complete a specialization, concentration, certificate, or specialized degree at this intersection.	The University of Michigan offers a *Certificate in Healthy Cities* to graduate students interested in gaining the skills and knowledge necessary to work in the cross-disciplinary field of urban health. (Website: https://taubmancollege.umich.edu/urbanplanning/degrees/graduate-certificate-healthy-cities)	Within the Bartlett, a department of built environment faculty and programs at University College of London, there are many specialized programs highlighting health and the built environment, such as the Health in Urban Development MSc, the Healthcare Facilities MSc, and the Health, Wellbeing and Sustainable Buildings MSc. (Website: https://www.ucl.ac.uk/bartlett/)
Tier 4: Programs that offer an opportunity for students to earn a joint degree in a built environment discipline and public health.	The University of Washington offers a three-year concurrent master of public health/master of urban planning degree program through its School of Public Health and the Department of Urban Design and Planning in the College of Built Environments. (Website: https://urbdp.be.uw.edu/programs/mup-graduate-degree/concurrent-degrees/)	Through the Department of Urban and Regional Planning and the Public Health Program, Florida State University offers a master of science in planning/master of public health joint degree. (Website: https://registrar.fsu.edu/bulletin/graduate/departments/public_health/)

be taken to increase student diversity, student funding, applied research, and internship opportunities with relevant partners on the local, national, and international stages.

Specifically, targeting efforts to increase the racial and ethnic diversity of the healthy places workforce is critical, especially today as the world struggles to correct the systemic inequal-

Table 23.2. Number of degrees/certificates awarded at postsecondary US institutions, by race/ethnicity and Classification of Instructional Programs (CIP) code, 2018–2019.

Race/Ethnicity	Total	CIP Code						
		Natural Resources and Conservation	Architecture and Related Services	Engineering	Parks and Recreation, Leisure, and Fitness Studies	Public Administration and Social Service Professions	Social Sciences	Health Professions and Related Programs
Total	1,543,043	28,599	17,526	197,457	70,926	96,827	185,644	946,064
American Indian or Alaska Native	9,591	232	50	451	367	721	746	7,024
Asian	105,305	1,069	1,201	19,550	3,346	3,024	13,628	63,487
Native Hawaiian or Pacific Islander	3,961	44	22	199	180	219	425	2,872
Black or African America	177,355	718	891	6,822	8,637	18,923	16,344	125,020
Hispanic or Latino	224,447	2,738	2,638	18,107	10,888	15,625	35,665	138,786
White	823,332	20,227	7,922	94,496	40,909	47,917	88,664	523,197
Two or more races	47,349	1,145	492	5,649	2,832	2,990	7,389	26,852
Race/ethnicity unknown	63,276	1,052	437	5,142	1,927	3,921	5,425	45,372
Nonresident	88,427	1,374	3,873	47,041	1,840	3,487	17,358	13,454

Source: IPEDS: Integrated Postsecondary Education Data System. IPEDS Trend Generator. 2019. Accessed August 27, 2020. https://nces.ed.gov/ipeds/TrendGenerator/app/build-table/4/24?rid=35&ridv=1%7C3%7C4%7C5%7C6%7C7%7C8%7C9%7C10&cid=71&cidv=03%7C04%7C14%7C31%7C44%7C51%7C45

ities that affect marginalized communities. Increasing the diversity of the workforce begins with growing a pipeline of student populations in the built environment and public health–related programs to thoroughly reflect the communities with which professionals work (table 23.2).[6] Without a concerted effort to recruit, train, and retain a diverse workforce, the professionals who work to make healthy places will be limited in essential skills and perspectives necessary to effectively create health promoting places that are equitable to all community members.

LOOKING BEYOND THE CLASSROOM TO PRACTICE, PROFESSIONAL EDUCATION, AND REAL-WORLD EXAMPLES

Recognition of the necessity of postsecondary training and professional education in built environment and public health is growing rap-idly (as are online resources related to training). In the 2013 Urban Land Institute report titled "Intersections of Health and the Built Environment," 95 percent of Urban Land Institute members either agreed or strongly agreed that human health and the built environment are inextricably linked.[7] In 2017, the Planning Accreditation Board updated its accreditation standards and criteria to incorporate health and built environment into the required course curriculum for accredited planning schools.[8] The National Council of Architectural Registration Boards has a long-standing requirement of facilitating the licensure and credentialing of architects to "protect the health, safety, and welfare of the public."[9] In 2019, the Transportation Research Board of the National Academies of Sciences, Engineering, and Medicine released its report, "A Research Roadmap for Transportation and Public Health," which serves as an important guide for both students and current practitioners involved in research related to transportation projects and public health.[10]

A variety of health and built environment courses and programs have been initiated in universities across the globe, and more are being developed each year. Existing integrative courses and programs in the built environment fields and public health vary substantially in their levels of interdisciplinary content, engagement, and availability in different countries (see table 23.1). Ontario Public Health Association's Public Health and Planning 101 Introductory Course was developed by the Ontario Professional Planners Institute and the Public Health Agency of Canada after identifying barriers to collaboration between the two fields.[11] The online course is available free of charge to anyone working in the public health or planning fields in Ontario or enrolled as a student in one of the fields there. APA Learn offers more than six hundred virtual courses with sixty-nine intersecting with

public health, pandemics, and food systems in an accessible online platform for self-directed continuing planning education.[12]

New leaders in the promotion of healthy places need to be prepared with skills that extend beyond their own disciplines. Examination of current leaders in the promotion of healthy places reveals a diversity of backgrounds. However, even more important is a demonstrated ability to collaborate with diverse partners, communicate and think geographically, and adapt to whatever conditions and needs may be specific to each job, community setting, or project. Leaders in health and built environment issues may have received formal training in public health, planning, or both. (The experience of some leaders is highlighted in boxes 23.1 through 23.5.) Increasingly, positions are available that require or prefer knowledge and experience in both public health and planning. Further, recent graduates in public health or planning who take positions in their field may be seen as stronger applicants if they bring skills from the other field and

---

BOX 23.1 LEADER SPOTLIGHT: SARAH SKENAZY, MCP, MPH

Following completion of her bachelor's degree and a few years of work at the intersection of design, social services, and environmental sustainability, Sarah Skenazy attended the University of California, Berkeley's concurrent master of city planning/master of public health program. During her academic training, she found that the most useful skill she developed applicable to a career at the intersection of the built environment and public health fields—in addition to understanding the relevancy of various geographic and conceptual scales, value systems, methods of research, program planning, and evaluation—was being able to translate across vocabularies. This necessary cross-collaboration between fields emphasizes the importance of developing concurrent degree programs that align the techniques and curriculum of the encompassed professions in a way that allows for effective teamwork between individuals.

Currently, Ms. Skenazy is a research fellow at the Green Health Partnership and a Public Health + District Design consultant on the Design Performance Team in Google's Real Estate + Workplace Services group. Her work falls into three main categories: (1) research and evaluation guidance on understanding the upstream drivers of health and well-being and longitudinal measurements of impact and meaning of physical and social projects; (2) design guidance and scenario testing, which involve exploring how to maximize equitable health benefits in design and infrastructure proposals and projects; and (3) partnership strategy, which investigates building coalitions in support of public health promoting physical and social infrastructure projects across leadership levels within a company, within consultant groups, and with external stakeholders.

BOX 23.2 LEADER SPOTLIGHT: CAILIN HENLEY, MPH

Cailin Henley is a planner at Alta Planning + Design, an active transportation firm in Seattle, Washington, that specializes in Transportation Demand Management/Safe Routes to Schools programming. During her time as a master of public health student at the University of Washington, Ms. Henley enrolled in the Department of Environmental and Occupational Health Sciences and Department of Urban Design and Planning cross-listed Public Health and Built Environment course after becoming interested in assessing the upstream determinants of health beyond clinical and medical care.

While on a site visit for the class, Ms. Henley was paired with an urban design student, and what ensued was a robust conversation about the health correlates unearthed due to their discipline-specific observations of the same subject. Ms. Henley's biggest takeaway from her time in this course was the necessity of public health professionals to address the disproportionate burden of disease on racial minorities by collaborating with and contribution to planning, design, engineering, architecture, and other built environment projects.

"Public health professionals, especially those who come to public health from—or develop a passion for—community organizing and undoing institutional racism, have a role to continuously push the planning and design professions towards equitable solutions, developed in partnership with community. We can make this case through using a health equity lens. I've found that many transportation professionals better understand racism and oppression through seeing the correlates between disease burden with their level of service maps. With a shared understanding of how local transportation and planning decisions affect health outcomes, interdisciplinary groups can then work to understand community-led solutions to that elevate health equity and work towards mobility justice."

BOX 23.3 LEADER SPOTLIGHT: LESLIE MEEHAN, MPA, AICP

Leslie Meehan is the director of the office of primary prevention at the Tennessee Department of Health. She received a master of public administration degree from Tennessee State University. Her interest in the built environment began when volunteering with and subsequently working for Park Pride, an Atlanta-based nonprofit organization focused on creating safe and accessible parks. During this time, she realized that access to parks and recreation space is integral for the social fabric and physical, mental, and environmental health of communities. From there, she began working as a land use planner with the Metro Nashville Planning Department, where she focused on policy and programs supporting active transportation. She subsequently became the director of healthy communities at the Nashville Area Metropolitan Planning Organization, a transportation agency programming $7 billion of infrastructure and programs. There, she worked to transform the policy, scoring criteria, prioritization methodology, data collection, modeling, and allocation of fiscal resources to prioritize health, equity, and complete streets programs. She works at the Tennessee Department of Health cultivating grants, staff, and cross-sector partnerships that support improving population health through the built environment. In her current role, Ms. Meehan works on supporting the built environment through grants, a team of built environment specialists, and programs. She also oversees the Tennessee Livability Collaborative, one of the only-voluntary Health in All Policy efforts at the state level. The collaborative comprises seventeen state agencies, departments, and commissions with a mission of improving the prosperity, quality of life, and health of Tennesseans through state department collaboration in the areas of policy, funding, and programming. She seeks to bring prevention to the more than 120 health department clinics through programs such as Healthy Parks, Healthy Person, which provides incentives for physical activity in parks, and Exercise Is Medicine, a clinical professional training program aimed as assessing and prescribing physical activity.

BOX 23.4 LEADER SPOTLIGHT: TINA YUEN, MCP, MPH

Tina Yuen is currently a senior planner and the co-leader of the Healthy Neighborhoods Team at ChangeLab Solutions, where she oversees projects related to transportation, housing, long-range planning, and land use controls. ChangeLab Solutions is a national organization that advances equitable laws and policies to ensure healthy lives for all. She received dual master of city planning/master of public health degrees from the University of California, Berkeley, which provided her with a solid, interdisciplinary background at the intersection of planning and public health. She encourages current students to use their time in the academic setting as an opportunity to learn tools, including Google Earth, GIS, and Health Impact Assessments, and to explore coursework highlighting topics such as epidemiology and legal policy frameworks.

"I was personally interested in environmental health inequities and environmental justice, and how land use controls impacted the siting and intensity of hazardous land uses in predominantly Black and Brown communities—all of which [have] huge implications for health equity. Being at UC Berkeley gave me an opportunity to explore this topic and understand the factors and considerations that go into land use decisions and how to potentially infuse health into the equation. My educational experience was good at introducing me to core topics in both disciplines. In public health, I learned about key public health topics and skills, such as biostatistics and epidemiology. In planning, I was taught to understand the fundamentals of planning practice and history, like demography, GIS mapping, and planning law. I was also able to take coursework and work with professors who were experts in healthy communities and healthy cities in order to understand more fully how urban and regional planning, place, and the built environment impact health outcomes and health equity.... I would say that even after graduate school ended, my education continues to this day. The intersection of public health and planning is a dynamic and ever-changing landscape that requires a curious and open mind, eager to learn and apply new tools and resources."

BOX 23.5 LEADER SPOTLIGHT: DR. ANDREW IBRAHIM, MD, MSC

Dr. Andrew Ibrahim is an assistant professor of surgery, architecture, and urban planning at the University of Michigan, where he directs the Health and Design Fellowship. In addition, he is a senior principal, chief medical officer at HOK, an international architecture, design, engineering, and planning firm. His academic background includes multiple degrees spanning from a bachelor's in architecture to a doctor of medicine. Dr. Ibrahim sees the connection between health and the built environment in three distinct ways. "First, as a surgeon, I see patients in clinic from all walks of life. As I hear their stories, it is impossible to ignore that their ability to get care and recover from an operation is impacted by the places where they live and spend their time. This has become more apparent in the COVID era where so many visits are virtual and I get a window into their lives at home. Second, as a formally trained health researcher, I am inspired that we are continuing make more data-driven connections to understand the impact of the built environment on health. Finally, as someone in architecture practice, the decisions are becoming more clear. If a client wants to prioritize health in their next design, we now have a better design tool kit to make that happen. It's full of trade-offs, and far from perfect, but it's a real and viable option." Dr. Ibrahim's advice to students is to find various mentors of diverse backgrounds from which different skills and principles can be learned, to explore the work environments of cross-sector careers— including government, nonprofit, and private—so as to understand various problem-solving methods, and to be ambitious in creating a bold and refined vision for one's career.

may be able to evolve their position into one that crosses both fields if they have skills from both disciplines.

CONCLUSION

Achieving the goal of healthy places requires public health and built environment leaders equipped to integrate skills, theory, and tools from both fields. Much of the previous activity in the study of the built environment and health has focused on establishing an evidence base for links or associations between community design and disease states or behaviors. There is increasing recognition that similar innovation is needed in the practice of healthy design and the training of practicing professionals and community leaders that will increase the reach and availability of education and opportunities in the field.

DISCUSSION QUESTIONS

1. What are some examples of vocabulary and communication constructs (for example, acronyms) that are used in urban planning or in public health that frequently need "translation" in the course of interdisciplinary collaboration to promote healthy places?
2. What are the tangible benefits of multidisciplinary research and practice collaboration? What are some strategies for organizing and supporting collaborative projects in academic or practice environments?
3. What are the core competencies that should be acquired by university students and professionals engaged in promoting healthy places? What critical interdisciplinary healthy places skills are most challenging to learn and develop in online learning environments?
4. What are some examples of successful collaborations to promote healthy places in your community? What populations, professionals, and collaborative processes made these projects successful?
5. How are the goals for planners and public health officials similar, and how are they different? What are some examples of jobs or projects that would benefit from cross-trained staff?

DISCLOSURE OF COMPETING INTERESTS

Nisha Botchwey's declarations appear in the preface.

Olivia E. Chatman discloses no competing interests.

Matthew J. Trowbridge reports serving as Chief Medical Officer of the International WELL Building Institute (IWBI).

Yakut Gazi reports serving as a Quality Matters Academic Advisory Council Member from July 2016 to present.

REFERENCES

1. Dyjack DT, Botchwey N, Marziale E. Cross-sectoral workforce development: examining the intersection of public health and community design. *Journal of Public Health Management and Practice*. 2013;19(1):97-99.
2. Built Environment and Public Health Clearinghouse. Georgia Institute of Technology. Accessed October 25, 2021. bephclearinghouse.wordpress.com
3. Botchwey ND, Johnson N, O'Connell LK, Kim AJ. Including youth in the ladder of citizen participation. *Journal of the American Planning Association*. 2019;85(3):255-270.
4. American Planning Association. Update: Kids iPlan Camp. American Planning Association. 2015. https://planning.org/content/content/9101342/
5. Westerberg P, Von Heland F. *Using Minecraft for Youth Participation in Urban Design and Governance*. United Nation Human Settlements Programme; 2015.
6. IPEDS: Integrated Postsecondary Education Data System. IPEDS Trend Generator. 2019. Accessed August 27, 2020. https://nces.ed.gov/ipeds/TrendGenerator/app/build-table/4/24?rid=35&ridv=1%7C3%7C4%7C5%7C6%7C7%7C8%7C9%7C10&cid=71&cidv=03%7C04%7C14%7C31%7C44%7C51%7C45
7. McCormick K, MacCleery R, Hammerschmidt S. Intersections: health and the built environment. Urban Land Institute, Building Healthy Places Initiative. 2013. https://uli.org/wp-content/uploads/ULI-Documents/Intersections-Health-and-the-Built-Environment.pdf
8. Planning Accreditation Board. PAB Accreditation Standards and Criteria. 2017. https://www.planningaccreditationboard.org/pab-accreditation-standards-and-criteria/
9. National Council of Architectural Registration Boards. Education Guidelines. 2019. https://www.ncarb.org/sites/default/files/Main%20Website/Data%20&%20Resources/Guidelines/Education Guidelines.pdf
10. National Academies of Sciences, Engineering, and Medicine. *A Research Roadmap for Transportation and Public Health*. National Academies Press; 2019. https://doi.org/10.17226/25644
11. Mahendra A, Vo T, Einstoss C, et al. Status report, The Public Health and Planning 101 project: strengthening collaborations between the public health and planning professions. *Health Promotion and Chronic Disease Prevention in Canada*. 2017;37(1):24029. doi:10.24095/hpcdp.37.1.02.
12. American Planning Association. APA Learn. American Planning Association. Accessed August, 2020. https://www.planning.org/apalearn/

CHAPTER 24

INNOVATIVE TECHNOLOGIES FOR HEALTHY PLACES

J. Aaron Hipp, Mariela Alfonzo, and Sonia Sequeira

KEY POINTS

- The use of technologies in urban spaces as related to the advancement of public health crosses scales and fields and is dynamic and continually expanding.
- The Smart Cities movement is one effort to capture the variety and use of technology across urban areas. The term *Smart Cities* might be better called *Smart Places*.
- Technologies produce the five V's of *big data*: volume, velocity, veracity, variety, and value.
- The digital divide describes inequities in access to hardware (smartphones, laptop computers) and internet access (5G, fiber, broadband).
- Technological innovations for health challenge those developing and employing the technologies to ensure equity in the value of technology and data, as well as accessibility to visualizations and vernacular.

INTRODUCTION

Today's technology has served to advance both research and practice using big data, gamification, **sensors**, real-time data capture, augmented and virtual reality, **predictive analytics**, machine learning, and artificial intelligence to enhance urban planning, mobility, health prevention and promotion,

participatory planning, and community engagement. This chapter will explore how and if technology is leveraged as part of the *Smart City* agenda to facilitate the creation and evaluation of health-promoting built environments and to address structural and spatial inequities. Additionally, this chapter will explore ethical considerations tied to these technological advances, as well as identify research and practice gaps that can be addressed by emerging technologies.

In his essay "What Is Technology?" Jon Agar begins with a definition of technology as "designed, material means to an end," but adds that technologies must also intervene between scales.[1] For example, a ride-sharing app begins with the scale of an individual person and smartphone, but the app connects the individual to the internet and to hundreds of local drivers, selects the closest one, and offers transportation across the scale of a city. Here we consider technology to be designed, to be a material means to an end, and to cross scales. Specific to *technological innovations for urban health*, we will explore the design and means of technologies related to our built environment, at the scale of individuals and communities, as well as technologies related to urban health, primarily through the behavior of individuals and communities.

WHAT IS THE SMART CITY?

The term **Smart City** is a nebulous one, one whose origins are disputed, one that lacks a standard definition, and one that elicits both negative and positive connotations. Upon reviewing several definitions, it is clear, however, that most definitions include four components: a geographical area of analysis, a description of the technologies involved (both inputs and outputs), a proposed use of that technology, and a statement of the benefits that can be derived therein. Let us analyze each of these components separately, with the aim of arriving at a Smart City definition befitting the theme of this chapter.

Geography: Most Smart City definitions refer to its eponymous target—the city—as one might expect. Others offer broader geographical terms, such as *urban area* or *municipality*. Of note, there are no references to suburbs, exurbs, towns, or rural areas among leading Smart City definitions.[2,3] Accordingly, the popular definition—and indeed the mere term *Smart City*—is limiting and threatens to widen the existing digital divide between urban and rural areas in particular. Rural areas could stand to benefit the most from "Smart" processes, approaches, and technologies, as at least 14.5 million rural residents in 2020 in the United States were without broadband internet access, according to the US Federal Communications Commission.[4] The wide range speaks to the difficulty in tracking and improving access. Future definitions should consider a more inclusive geographical term, such as *place*, *community*, or *area*.

Technology (Inputs): Smart City definitions refer to myriad types of existing and emerging technologies. Notably, most definitions specify the **Internet of Things** (**IoT**; all the devices connected to the internet, including computers, streetlights, cars, and kitchen ovens) and sensor technology as fundamental to the Smart City, as they enable the capture and exchange of so-called big data. Others use broader terms, such as *information and communication technologies* (ICT) or just *digital technologies*.

Less commonly referred to within Smart City definitions is technology—namely hardware—related to energy, utilities, or materials.

Technology (Processing and Outputs): In addition to the technologies used to collect data and information, Smart City definitions also discuss various technologies used to process that big data. These include predictive analytics, machine learning, artificial intelligence, quantum computing, cloud-based software, and geographic information systems.

Functionality: In addition to referencing specific "Smart" technologies, most definitions also discuss how those technologies are utilized, including using insights derived from technology outputs to manage assets, resources, and services efficiently; inform decisions; optimize city operations; share data; and generally solve city problems. Some definitions include more specific use cases, such as the monitoring of traffic and transportation systems, utilities, crime, waste, water supplies, energy, schools, libraries, hospitals, or other community services.

Mission: Some Smart City definitions reference the benefits to be derived from smart technologies. For example, most refer to the enhancement of economic development and quality of life as integral to the goals of the Smart City movement. Others also mention sustainability, resiliency, and inclusivity. Very few, if any, address issues of representation in big data, structural equity, or **spatial injustices** as primary aims—nor is the topic of health specifically called out within prevailing definitions.

For the purposes of this chapter, we offer the following definition of Smart Cities—and suggest replacing the term with the more inclusive "Smart *Places*":

> A governed place that leverages technology to equitably enhance the quality of life and well-being of its residents and increase value across the quadruple bottom line—economic, social, health, and environmental value. Smart Places capitalize on advances in technology,

such as connected devices (IoT), 5G, machine learning, visual machine learning, and other emerging artificial intelligence mechanisms to extract data on a variety of public functions and behaviors, identify patterns in the data, and recommend solutions that increase the efficiency and effectiveness of public infrastructure, programs, and policies. Further, Smart Places utilize technology in a way that promotes transparency, accountability, and public participation and engagement.

THE STATE OF SMART PLACES

There is a risk that the Smart Place movement's primary motivator is to promote high-tech advancements for their own sake. Some critics have noted that many Smart Place proponents or companies have developed shiny solutions in search of a problem to solve.[5] Others have noted that many Smart Place technologies stop short of providing solutions and instead produce loads of data that highlight problems, such as traffic, air pollution, or even health disparities, but fail to leverage that technology to help identify and prioritize approaches that would most effectively and cost-efficiently address and mitigate those problems. This is akin to creating a technological "solution" that helps predict your risk of getting a terminal disease, but stops short of providing insights into steps you could take to mitigate that risk and potentially prevent said disease, or giving guidance as to what measures you could take to increase the likelihood of survival if you do contract said disease. Providing decision-makers—public and private sector alike—with more data without a clear road map for how to analyze, interpret, and translate that data into actionable solutions that equitably enhance quality of life is not only ineffective, it is an inefficient use of time and resources, effectuating yet another problem—what to do with all that data.

To ensure that Smart Place technology is utilized as a means to enhancing quality of life and not an end in itself, there is a move-ment to evolve from a Smart Place that is technology-centric toward one that is human-centric. This shift from a top-down, expert-driven, efficiency-focused approach toward a bottom-up, community-led, effectiveness-focused one, known as Smart City 2.0, aims to create a more inclusive, participatory process that first identifies community issues and challenges from the residents' perspective and then looks to how technology can be utilized to solve those problems.[6] This new, people-focused paradigm for Smart Places lends itself to one that can and should adopt a more holistic approach to understanding and solving "city" problems that focuses on fundamental systemic and structural issues underlying the problems technology is being called upon to address.

SMART PLACES, HEALTH, AND EQUITY

Although the mission behind building a Smart Place is to leverage the power of technology to improve people's quality of life, pre-COVID-19 most Smart Place initiatives were not designed explicitly around public health goals. As part of a 2019 systematic review of the Smart Place literature, only 0.3 percent (19 of 5,454) of the articles identified were related to public health, and few of those included a focus on built environment components of health.[7] Health technology advocates have pointed out that an opportunity exists to expand the Smart Place agenda to understand the nexus between technology, health, equity, and the built environment overall and, in particular, with respect to social determinants of health.[8] Currently, technology is mostly being used to tackle disparate parts of the Venn diagram in figure 24.1 that makes up the "Smart Healthy City." Efforts seem to be focused on the overlap between technology and the built environment and technology and health, with fewer focused on how equity folds into these connections. Next, we will highlight opportunities between technology and the built environment, as well as present examples that stretch into Smart City Health.

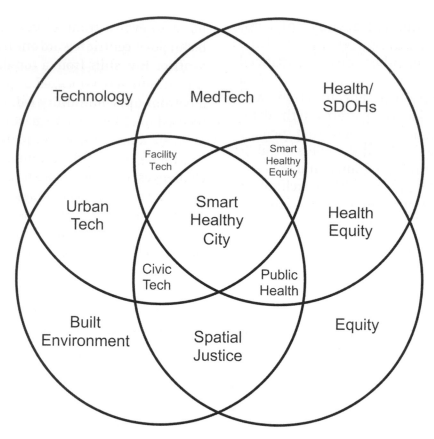

Figure 24.1. Smart Healthy City Framework. Creating smart, healthy cities is inherently transdisciplinary, and its implementation requires holistic approaches that reflect the complex relationships between technology, health, and the built environment. (SDOH = social determinants of health.)
Source: Mariela Alfonzo

TECHNOLOGY AND THE BUILT ENVIRONMENT

Urban tech companies—those that leverage technology to improve "urban" functions, including transportation, waste, utilities, infrastructure, logistics, and overall "city living"—have proliferated recently, aiming to improve various aspects of quality of life. With respect to the built environment, most urban tech companies tend to focus on the individual-level scale, the building scale, or the urban realm scale (macro and regional built environment features), and only a few of them explicitly focus on health or equity.

At the individual scale, although food delivery companies such as Uber Eats and Instacart, which focus on improving logistics and providing more ready access to goods and services, helped many people reduce exposure risk during the COVID-19 pandemic, they have not intentionally integrated a health focus. Most of these companies make no effort to use their technologies in a way that promotes ordering healthier food options. Separately, other urban tech companies focused on the individual scale, including ride-hailing companies, such as Uber or Lyft, face issues of inequity in implementation. For example, research has shown that people of color, in particular Black males, face higher rates of ride cancellations, and many companies have yet to fully address these issues.[9]

At the building scale, some companies—such as Uhoo(R), which monitors indoor air quality—specifically focus on using technology to enhance both the efficiency and quality of life inside buildings, including health. In the wake of COVID-19, some companies that previously focused solely on building efficiency itself—such as Sapient, which offers a "Smart" outlet system meant to reduce needless energy consumption—have broadened their focus to include health, for example, as it pertains to ensuring social distancing. For example, Sapient now offers monitoring and controlling the energy use and availability within certain workspaces to ensure adherence to social distancing.

At the urban realm scale, companies such as UrbanFootprint utilize geospatial systems, open data capture, and simulation models to analyze how regional-level urban planning processes, such as land use, zoning, or transportation measures, might impact traffic, environmental quality, and energy usage. UrbanFootprint is currently working to expand its models to also include public health outcomes. However, UrbanFootprint, like many other urban tech companies, does not focus on the "microscale" built environment features (for example, street-level and neighborhood-level urban design) that have been tied to health outcomes by research.

The most well known urban tech advancements have to do with autonomous vehicles, from individual automobiles to last-mile solutions to buses, technologies that cut across scales. A number of key thresholds remain for these technologies to be mainstreamed, not the least of which is assuring equitable access to autonomous vehicles by residents of disadvantaged communities.[10] Other hardware tech companies have focused more on micromobility. Many companies now offer **e-bikes** and e-scooters, or electric-assisted, including some offered via the **shared economy** system, that address not just mobility, but health equity and access, enabling people to more readily use micromobility options. None of these companies intentionally incorporate the built environment in which these technologies will be used or explicitly address population health. Scooter companies have failed to work directly with cities and regulatory systems to ensure the safety and feasibility of their use and have in some cases inadvertently hindered health access for peo-

ple with disabilities (for example, littering or parking of scooters on sidewalks). A challenge is the development of technology that solves some problem, but frequently does not attempt to solve the problem across a variety of built environment experiences or scales, a diversity of people, or with health as a stated goal.

A small number of urban tech companies focus on data and analysis situated at the nexus of urban health and technological innovations. For example, companies such as Numina are using sensors and visual machine learning to extract data around pedestrian, bicyclist, micromobility, and vehicle behavior in addition to some street features, such as curbs and streetlights, to give cities insights into how their streets are being utilized and get a better understanding of transportation mode-split in real time. Others, such as State of Place (founded by one of the chapter authors), use visual machine learning to extract microscale built environment data, including sidewalks, benches, outdoor dining, street trees, and land uses from digital imagery. State of Place then applies algorithms to derive an indexed score that measures overall quality of place and provides assessments of ten urban design dimensions empirically tied to walkability and predictive analytics. These analytics are used to produce forecast models tying better urban design to higher quality of life, including not just economic development, but also various aspects of health (for example, vehicle/pedestrian collision rates, chronic disease, vehicle miles traveled). Additionally, Remix, a transit planning Software-as-a-Service (see below) company, has helped more than three hundred transportation agencies throughout the United States use data to better model and test their plans to increase transit sheds, or service areas, and efficiency of delivery. Although increasing the efficiency and access of public transportation has clear health benefits, these are not called out as an explicit focus by transportation-focused urban technology companies.

HEALTH AND TECHNOLOGY

The health and medical technology space has grown significantly recently. Most well-known companies in this space tend to be focused on using technology to improve individual health outcomes. For example, companies such as Noom, Peloton, and Fitbit leverage technology to promote healthier lifestyles. However, new advancements in artificial intelligence and predictive analytics have enabled the emergence of new technologies and companies focused on broader population or public health outcomes. For example, companies such as Pivotal have created sophisticated predictive analytics models around the social determinants of health and delivery and access of health care. Additionally, the post-COVID world will continue to see an increased application of telehealth technologies and companies.

Although myriad studies have shown the links between the built environment and health, few companies within the health technology space integrate the role of urban design and planning on health into their technologies. A number of companies that are typically considered urban technology companies do have direct health implications. For example, some companies now offer "smart" bicycle and scooter helmet designs, such as those that are foldable and collapsible, that allow users to safely listen to music, provide them with lighting, and even offer augmented reality navigation.

CHALLENGES AND EQUITY IN SMART PLACES

A number of challenges must be addressed to advance the use of technology to improve public health within the Smart Place agenda. First, regulatory issues in health and health delivery make it difficult to create and implement scalable, recurring models. In the United States, health care has been politicized in a way that creates a significant barrier to advancing public health using technology. Trigger terms such as "socialist medicine" make for divisive rather than productive conversations around

how to improve public health and equity. Second, one of the most pervasive challenges inherent to using technology to advance not just health, but health equity and access, is around the **digital divide**, both with respect to digital access and digital comfort. The digital divide is the inequity in access to smart mobile devices, computers, 5G wireless, or internet. Companies must be more intentional about **inclusive design** and creating just and equitable environments to ensure that the benefits of technological advances are not only accessible to all, but explicitly uplift those who have historically been most marginalized. Other barriers to creating a Smart Healthy City include data-sharing and privacy concerns and profit-based health care models. Finally, the traditionally siloed nature of research and practice with respect to health is a barrier to using technology to truly create a Smart Healthy City; a transdisciplinary framework is needed to address the intersections of health, technology, the built environment, and equity.

The COVID-19 pandemic may have served to accelerate the movement toward Smart Healthy Cities, integrating the use of technology to address a specific set of public health needs, focused intently on the built environment and people's use of the public realm (Chapter 26). The pandemic magnified existing spatial inequities and structural racism that directly contributed to the comorbidities that made vulnerable communities more susceptible to both transmission and severity of the disease. As of September 2020, 3.4 times more Black people and 3.3 times more Latinx people died from COVID-19 than White people.[11] Additionally, these same communities tend to lack access to the kinds of built environment features that promote and facilitate healthy behaviors and outcomes.[12,13]

As we move to promote the use of technology at the nexus of the built environment and health, it is increasingly critical to center this work around inclusion, equity, and justice. When applying technology toward understanding the links between the built environment and population health, the core aim should be to identify, address, and prioritize spatial inequities leading to health disparities within historically marginalized and vulnerable communities, including Black people, Indigenous people, people of color, and those with disabilities. When focusing on technology to advance individual health, it is imperative that intentional efforts be made to ensure that the digital divide—both in terms of physical access and comfort—be overcome, whether by explicit funding efforts or community-led engagement, so that benefits are equitably accessible. The use of emerging technologies in evaluation and surveillance of health behaviors in urban environments holds the opportunity for better, more precise measurements, measurement practices, open data, and analysis. Technology and open data provide the potential to give the power of data back to the people.

Despite the challenges tied to using technology to address the nexus of public health, the built environment, and equity across scales, there are opportunities upon which to capitalize that translate into a strong, robust, and investable market for urban health technology. First, autonomous vehicles aside, much of the technology highlighted earlier is not sophisticated technology. Simple apps such as Noom, Meetup, Lyft, and the like power much of the advancements noted earlier. Second, as the United States shifts to value-based health care, there is more of an emphasis on the social determinants of health and a rethinking of hospitals as core community partners. This opens up the opportunity to incorporate technological advancements to address the nexus between the built environment and public health as it creates an investable market opportunity. The trend in impact investments (investments made to yield social or environmental benefits, as well as financial benefits) has solidified into a formidable movement, enabling the kind of patient capital (that is, start-up funding) sometimes needed at the intersection of technology, the built environment, health, and equity given the complexity of the systemic issues being tackled. Finally, the spatial integration of health data provides an opportunity to advance predictive analytics that inform built environment strategies to promote social determinants of health.[14,15]

TECHNOLOGY, URBAN HEALTH, AND BIG DATA

Smart Places and the technologies therein lead to, or run on, **big data**, or large data sets that are analyzed and mined for patterns and information. Big data is often framed with five characteristics, or the five V's of big data, which also hold importance for technologies and urban health: volume, velocity, veracity, variety, and value.[16]

Volume

The amount of data that are collected constitutes the *volume* of big data related to technology and urban health. For example, Twitter users produce more than half a billion tweets each day. Researchers captured more than sixty thousand tweets using the hashtag #smartcity during one month in 2018 and found examples and opportunities for news alerts, public opinion mining, participatory democracy, sentiment analysis, and culture related to Smart Cities.[17] Twitter and other social media are being used to estimate park visitation[18] and by public health departments for surveillance, disease tracking, and forecasting.[19]

Across several scales, a variety of apps, hardware technology, and **Software-as-a-Service (SaaS)**, software hosted online and provided to multiple users such as Google Docs and Sheets, have been applied to enhance health access, promotion, and delivery. For example, multiple competing apps provide real-time data on location and capacity of public buses, subways, and light rail. Other transportation apps highlight routes between points A and B with information per transit mode on time to destination, calories burned during commute, and carbon emissions saved or spent based on selected mode. There are also for-profit businesses that purchase, repackage, and sell smartphone location data. Each app we engage with that has global positioning satellite (GPS) on in the background or during app use collects this location data, and many then sell this location data to third parties. Researchers or businesses can then purchase aggregated data to understand use of spaces and marketing such as use of a park, attendance to an event, and traffic associated with a new market. Urban health researchers are also creating apps that take advantage of GPS through location-based ecological momentary assessment. When a study participant enters a restaurant, as designated by GPS, the participant will receive a very brief text or app survey to respond to researcher-defined questions, such as are you dining alone or with others or was caloric information available on menu? See box 24.1.

Velocity

Velocity refers to the speed of new data generation, but it can also refer to the speed of new technologies and the rate of analysis and action taken. Continuing with examples from the transportation sector, the velocities of new data generation, technologies, analyses, and action are each present in the automobile industry as personal and commercial vehicles move toward self-driving or autonomous vehicles. To support the development of autonomous vehicles, related software, and transportation infrastructure, most new vehicles now have numerous sensors and cameras located across their body. These data, generally images and LiDAR (Light Detecting And Ranging), are stored in vehicles until the vehicles are parked and can be connected to a home or businesses Wi-Fi (IoT) and uploaded to the various manufacturers such

---

BOX 24.1 MOBILITY-AS-A-SERVICE

The rise of ride-sharing and micromobility (scooter and bike platforms such as Lime, Gotcha, and Bird), in addition to traditional public transit, has given urban residents many mobility options. Mobility-as-a-Service (MaaS), an offshoot of Software-as-a-Service, or SaaS, is an integrated mobility platform (IMP) that combines each of these possible mobility options into a single service, moving mobility options from multiple platforms (for example, Lyft, Lime, local transit app, Google Maps) to a single app focused on access to efficient mobility, and offers the individual user the option to customize payment methods and subscriptions. Jittrapirom et al. provide nine core characteristics of MaaS[a]:

1. The integration of multiple modes of transit into one application.
2. Tariff option or how a resident pays for the service provided by the MaaS. This usually means one subscription to MaaS and not individual accounts with each mode.
3. Single digital platform.
4. Multiple actors, including each of the transportation networks (private and public), the platform, and users.
5. Use of technologies, including 4G, 5G, and GPS, and e-ticketing and payment systems.
6. Demand orientation that is responsive to local transit demands and opportunities.
7. Registration requirement for each individual user usually as a subscription.
8. Personalization that includes past transit behaviors, preferences, and social connectivity.
9. Customization that allows users to demarcate transit preferences.

In the end, MaaS applications are meant to streamline transit options by offering all mobility options to a single user, as with an IMP, and based on their stated preferences and needs, circumvent the need to check multiple apps for the most efficient and inexpensive option to travel from point A to B.

REFERENCE

a. Jittrapirom P, Caiati V, Feneri AM, Ebrahimigharehbaghi S, Alonso González M, Narayan J. Mobility as a service: a critical review of definitions, assessments of schemes, and key challenges. *Urban Planning*. 2017;2,13.

as Ford (https://avdata.ford.com/) and Tesla (https://www.tesla.com/autopilot). Some manufacturers make images, LiDAR, and associated data available to others for analyses.

A nontransportation-sector example of the velocity of technologies and urban health is the 2020 launch of the US Center for Disease Control and Prevention's National Wastewater Surveillance System. Wastewater, or sewage, is tested for the RNA presence of COVID-19 as an early surveillance system for outbreaks. Untreated wastewater can be analyzed near real time for trends and spikes in the presence of SARS-CoV-2, the underlying virus causing COVID-19. In one early study, the authors found that 2.1 billion people could be monitored for presence of COVID-19 from more than 100,000 sewage treatment plants, saving time and money in the detection of the disease.[20]

Veracity

The *veracity*, or validity and accuracy, of data in technology and urban health is not to be overlooked. Technologies have provided improvements in urban health from irrigation, water transmission (for example, aqueducts), and waste removal for thousands of years. The addition of data and computing, and importantly **machine learning** and **artificial intelligence**, brings with it determinations and cause-and-effect scenarios that are programmed into computations and analyses by humans or deduced by machines based on probability and decision trees. Machine learning and artificial intelligence mirror human intelligence, learning, and decisions. An example is taking known information provided by thousands of ground-truth data—such as photos that do and do not include a streetlight—and applying a network of decision trees to determine whether a new image includes a streetlight. The teams behind programming codes and challenges often lack public health professionals, social scientists, and ethicists, as well as gender, racial, and ethnic diversity.

Although facial recognition technology has become very advanced, including unlocking our smartphone, the artificial intelligence has still been found to be flawed especially with non-White skin tones. A different example of veracity are US Environmental Protection Agency (EPA) efforts to report on the validity of personal and small-scale air monitoring devices.[21] Here the EPA tests commercially available air quality monitoring devices against known standards and under controlled conditions. Ideally, the veracity of emerging technologies is part of the development phase, such as the following community-engaged example.

CommunitAR

CommunitAR is the main component of a novel participatory platform that integrates mobile augmented reality (MAR) technology in assessing the built environment.[22] Augmented reality (AR) enhances visual, tactile, and auditory perceptions of users by superimposing virtual computer-generated content on the real world. MAR combines AR with wireless communication and location-based services in smartphones and enables users to interact with the real environment by pointing their mobile device to objects and letting the device augment the scene with three-dimensional digital data. As an AR mobile application, CommunitAR enables users to go into the field and virtually add an array of microscale street features that they believe encourage walking, such as a sidewalk or a bike lane, to their surrounding area. The app also visualizes walkable design alternatives virtually overlaid onto the street environment. After placing street features or the future walkable design in the environment, users can take images of the scene and share them on social media platforms or manually upload them to the cloud database (figure 24.2). CommunitAR is connected to a web mapping service that displays geotagged photos captured by users to public or internal audiences in real time. In the fall of 2020, the app was tested by volunteer residents of eight predominantly minority racial/ethnic neighborhoods in Charlotte, North

Figure 24.2. An example of a feature overlaid on the street environment and ready to be captured by pressing the camera icon. GPS and time information will be shown on the top-left corner of the screen.
Source: Photo Courtesy of Saeed Ahmadi Oloonabadi

Carolina. CommunitAR and its participatory platform contribute to the growing literature of using technology in subjective measuring of microscale built environment factors that influence walking.

Variety

In urban technologies there is great *variety* in the data created and mechanisms through which the data are generated. For example, technology and data may be related to digital inclusion, transportation and mobility, unmanned aerial vehicles (UAVs), artificial intelligence and machine learning, connectivity and IoT, connected communities, pandemic (COVID-19) response, geographic information systems, hot spot policing, and traffic and body cameras. Blockchain is a technology just beginning to relate to healthy places. Blockchain, often thought of with cryptocurrencies such as Bitcoin, includes a distributive element, meaning that many computers hold the code and data, so changes to information have a record with multiple entries across the world.

Encryption, and thus privacy, is another key to blockchain technology. The third key is immutability, which generally means unchangeable, but with blockchain refers to nondeletion of data and previous versions. This can be likened to using a Google Doc for writing and always having access to earlier versions and who made any edit, deletion, or addition. Blockchain technology becomes essential when combining the data of protected health information with other technologies such as evaluating Smart Places. Blockchain technology is also key to protecting the veracity of IoT data collected throughout Smart Places, keeping a chain of command and ledger of edits, and ensuring encryption maintains privacy.[23]

Variety also appears in scale and scope of technologies and urban health. The *Atlanta City Studio* is a pop-up urban design studio within the City of Atlanta's Department of City Planning. Since its inception in 2017, the studio has moved to different physical locations throughout the city to make its work publicly accessible so that residents have an opportunity to play a direct role in the design of their city. The studio operates with a storefront model that is open for the public to visit and staffed by designers who can answer questions on project work. During COVID-19, all city operations moved remote, and the studio transferred all engagement to digital, a process likely to continue as a way to further engage communities. Examples of digital strategies include:

- Virtual community meetings with interactive components, such as a Google Jamboard, that allow viewers to interact with design elements on a street (figure 24.3)
- Map-based community outreach software, such as Social Pinpoint and Wikimap, that allows residents to geotag what they would like to see changed in a master plan
- Leveraging social media for project feedback
- An augmented reality community meeting where community members, via avatars, can talk about and give feedback to projects

New V's of Technology and Urban Health

When considering technology and urban health, there are other V's as well. There is *value*, literal value as mentioned above with Smart Places, but also community value. In late 2019, the ride-sharing apps Uber and Lyft were valued at more than $90 billion, combined. Community value of technologies extends across many areas of urban life, including community services as highlighted in the Atlanta and Charlotte examples above. There is also benefit and value related to mobility, such as **Mobility-as-a-Service (MaaS)** opportunities offered by Uber and Lyft, last-mile help through bike- and scooter-share programs (docked and undocked), and the variety of apps and websites that allow individuals to plan their commutes and routes via public transit, walking, or cycling as on **integrated mobility platforms**. Mobility data are increasingly important for cities to use in infrastructure planning. More than fifty cities participate in the Open Mobility Foundation, an open-source software platform that uses **application programming interfaces** focused on dockless

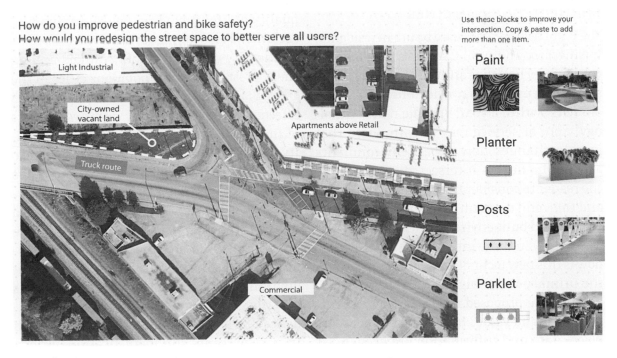

Figure 24.3. Google Jamboard example from a virtual community meeting.
Source: Atlanta City Studio

e-scooters, bicycles, mopeds, and car-share to provide real-time traffic management and inform policy decisions.

Visualization is another new V of technology and urban health, as the use of data visualization can help overcome digital literacy challenges. Platforms and dashboards that display data and allow for data manipulation, mapping, and comparisons are key for the use of technology and data in improving the health of communities. With the variety of communication that occurs with data across technology platforms, it is necessary that *vernacular* does not get in the way of understanding. Collaborations between computer science and public health necessitate shared understanding of terms, and this understanding extends to communities. Finally, *vulnerable* communities and populations often are not included in algorithms, big data, or the development of technologies. Privacy of personal data is always a concern. Inclusion and representation are required to ensure the greatest health benefit of technologies and place.

IMPROVED EFFICIENCY AND CONNECTEDNESS IN CITIES

The V's of technologies used by urban residents, businesses, and public services as related to community health is an ever-expanding landscape. The examples provided herein may be obsolete within a year, or some new technology, app, or service may be introduced that greatly changes how urban environments and public health intersect. We encourage the reader to consider the lens of Smart Places and the Venn diagram of technology, health, equity, and built environments. Where is the technology in these intersecting circles? Also, how is this new technology addressing not only the primary V's of big data and technology, but also the proposed new V's including vulnerability and value? In a connected or Smart Place, data and information are exchanged in many different ways, usually involving at least one of the following scales creating the data and another using the data: individuals, communities, public services, private enterprise, and municipalities. Below we highlight ongoing work improving the connections of urban technology, data, and community health.

Addressing Health Disparities with Predictive Analytics in Philadelphia

Vulnerable communities face myriad structural inequities in access to livable, sustainable places that promote quality of life. At the core of these spatial injustices are poor-quality, community-level, microscale built environments and mobility infrastructure (for example, street trees, parks, crosswalks, bike lanes, sidewalks). For example, disproportionately higher morbidity and mortality from COVID-19 among Black, Latinx, and Indigenous communities stem from disproportionately higher rates of chronic disease in these vulnerable populations, which in turn are tied to exposure to unsafe, unhealthy built environments created by community-level disinvestment. The lack of access to quality urban design results in multiple disparities across many facets of quality of life, including health, economic, social, and environmental outcomes.

The City of Philadelphia, ranked among the poorest of the most populous cities in the United States, is testament to the deleterious effects of the exponentially negative impacts of inequitable built environment and mobility infrastructure investments that lead to multiple disparities, including higher rates of environmental hazards, health behaviors and outcomes, crime and violence, and unemployment. Although the city is aware of the scale and significance of this problem, it lacks data around microscale built environment and mobility features—thus contributing to these spatial injustices evidenced by quality-of-life disparities—which in part prevents the identification, prioritization, and implementation of effective urban design and mobility improvements needed to create more equitable, resilient places.

Given the spatial injustices and structural inequities laid bare by COVID-19 and amplified by the Black Lives Matter protests in 2020, the City of Philadelphia engaged State of Place to conduct an analysis of the spatial relationships between urban design, health disparities, COVID-19 rates, the occurrence and frequency of natural disasters, and equity. State of Place deployed its machine learning–based data collection technology to automatically extract more than 150 microscale urban design features (such as street trees, sidewalks, curb cuts, land uses, and seating) at the street level, block by block, for seventeen zip codes throughout the city, focusing on neighborhoods that reflected disparities in income, race, ethnicity, the quality and access to the public realm, and natural disaster incidence. State of Place also gathered health, demographic, and accessibility data for each of the zip codes. Leveraging advances in predictive analytics, the analysis led to the creation of a forecasting model that ties urban design to health and safety outcomes. Guided by these evidence-based models, the city can now identify and prioritize areas of need (with high levels of spatial injustices) and allocate investment toward built environment features most likely to have the biggest impact on quality of life and health. Providing city makers such as the City of Philadelphia with a predictive analytics tool will help them develop an evidence-based microscale infrastructure investment strategy, leading to more effective and cost-efficient outcomes, while providing the necessary data to ensure a more streamlined community and stakeholder engagement process that builds trust and consensus needed to create more livable, equitable, healthy, and sustainable communities.

CONCLUSION

Urban technologies and Smart Places continue to expand and affect community health across scales. There are innumerable opportunities for technologies, and their collected data, to benefit the well-being of populations across urban spaces. Public health and urban design professionals of the future must work together to ensure the collective veracity and value of these efforts. There are further equity and ethical considerations with urban technologies and healthy places. The variety, velocity, and volume of data and technologies can further the gulf of the digital divide by leaving people behind who do not have the opportunity to gain or increase their digital literacy. This can leave the data, and importantly the decisions with the data, in the hands of the privileged. The veracity of data and technology is also key to ensure truth in measurement and understanding. Value—for funders, investors, and private enterprise—is important for innovation, but value for communities is essential for building trust and empowering communities with their own data. Then we will truly have achieved Smart Places.

DISCUSSION QUESTIONS

1. Make a compelling argument for the use of the term *Smart Place* over *Smart City*.
2. Identify at least one example of a Smart Place technology near your school, home, or work. How does this technology support health, and who within the space is supported?
3. Provide an additional example of urban health big data with examples of each of the five V's: volume, velocity, veracity, variety, and value.
4. New urban health technologies that support Smart Places are developed each day. Describe one new technology and how it improves health, efficiencies, and inequities.

DISCLOSURE OF COMPETING INTERESTS

J. Aaron Hipp reports owning stock in several augmented reality and computing corporations. He has served on his local parks and recreation board and on unpaid committees related to technology and physical activity sponsored by the National Academies of Sciences, Engineering, and Medicine and the National Coalition on Childhood Obesity Research. He has received funding from the Centers for Disease Control, National Institutes of Health, US Department of Agriculture, and Robert Wood Johnson Foundation.

Mariela Alfonzo is the founder and chief executive officer of State of Place, which is also mentioned in the chapter.

Sonia Sequeira serves as an unpaid board member for Concrete Jungle, an Atlanta-based nonprofit organization, was the chair of Global Shapers–Atlanta, and was a previous board member for Community Bucket. She is employed by the City of Atlanta's Department of City Planning, which houses the Atlanta City Studio described in this chapter.

REFERENCES

1. Agar J. What is technology? *Annals of Science.* 2020;77(3):377-382. doi:10.1080/00 033790.2019.1672788

2. Hosseini S, Frank L, Fridgen G, Heger S. Do not forget about smart towns. *Business & Information Systems Engineering.* 2018;60(3):243-257. https://doi.org/10.1007 /s12599-018-0536-2

3. Remington T, Ellis T. *We* need to stop talking about smart cities and start building smart regions. *Forbes.* October 19, 2019. https://www.forbes.com/sites/ ellistalton/2018/10/19/we-need-to -stop-talking-about-smart-cities-and -start-building-smart-regions/?sh =41343891668c

4. Federal Communication Commission. *Fourteenth Broadband Deployment Report.* 2021.

5. Kummitha RKR, Crutzen N. How do we understand smart cities? An evolutionary perspective. *Cities.* 2017;67:43-52. doi:https://doi.org/10.1016/j.cities.2017.04 .010

6. Barns S. Smart cities and urban data platforms: designing interfaces for smart governance. *City, Culture and Society.* 2018;12:5-12.

7. Rocha, NP, Dias A, Santinha G, Rodrigues M, Queirós A, Rodrigues C. Smart cities and public health: a systematic review. *Procedia Computer Science.* 2019;164:516-523. doi:https://doi.org/10.1016/j.procs .2019.12.214

8. Bibri SE. The sciences underlying smart sustainable urbanism: unprecedented paradigmatic and scholarly shifts in light of big data science and analytics. *Smart Cities.* 2019;2:179-213.

9. Ge Y, Knittel CR, MacKenzie D, Zoepf S. Racial and gender discrimination in transportation network companies. *Working Paper 22776.* National Bureau of Economic Research; 2016. https://www .nber.org/papers/w22776

10. Wu X, Cao J, Douma, F. The impact of vehicle automation on transport-disadvantaged people. *Transportation Research Interdisciplinary Perspectives.* 2021;11:100447

11. APM Research Lab. The color of coronavirus: COVID-19 deaths by race and ethnicity in the US. APM Research Lab. March 5, 2021. https://www.apmresearchlab.org /covid/deaths-by-race

12. Price JH, Khubchandani J, McKinney M, Braun R. Racial/ethnic disparities in chronic diseases of youths and access to health care in the United States. *BioMed Research International.* 2013;787616-787616. doi:https://doi.org/10.1155/2013/787616

13. Slater, SJ, Christiana RW, Gustat J. Recommendations for keeping parks and green space accessible for mental and physical health during COVID-19 and other pandemics. *Preventing Chronic Disease.* 2020;17:E59. doi:10.5888/pcd17.200204

14. Corburn J. Urban place and health equity: critical issues and practices. *International Journal of Environmental Research and Public Health.* 2017;14(2):117.

15. Huang B, Wang J. Big spatial data for urban and environmental sustainability. *Geo-spatial Information Science.* 2020;23(2):125-140. doi:10.1080/10095020 .2020.1754138

16. Erl T, Khattak W, Buhler P. *Big Data Fundamentals: Concepts, Drivers, and Techniques.* Prentice Hall; 2016.

17. Alkhammash EH, Jussila J, Lytras MD, Visvizi A. Annotation of smart cities Twitter micro-contents for enhanced citizen's engagement. *IEEE Access.* 2019;7: 116267-116276. doi:10.1109/ACCESS.2019.2935186

18. Wood, SA, Winder SG, Lia EH, White EM, Crowley CSL, Milnor AA. Next-generation visitation models using social media to estimate recreation on public lands. *Scientific Reports.* 2020;10(1):15419. doi:10.1038 /s41598-020-70829-x

19. Edo-Osagie O, De La Iglesia, B, Lake I, Edeghere O. A scoping review of the use of Twitter for public health research. *Computers in Biology and Medicine*. 2020;122:103770. doi:https://doi.org/10.1016/j.compbiomed.2020.103770

20. Hart OE, Halden RU. Computational analysis of SARS-CoV-2/COVID-19 surveillance by wastewater-based epidemiology locally and globally: feasibility, economy, opportunities and challenges. *Science of the Total Environment*. 2020;730:138875. doi:https://doi.org/10.1016/j.scitotenv.2020.138875

21. EPA. Evaluation of Emerging Air Sensor Performance. Air Sensor Toolbox. 2021. https://www.epa.gov/air-sensor-toolbox/evaluation-emerging-air-sensor-performance

22 Oloonabadi SA, Baran PK. Evaluating the usability of a participatory mobile augmented reality app: engaging residents digitally in assessing neighborhood walkability. Poster presented at: Environmental Design Research Association, Transform: Socially Embedded Collaborations; April 4, 2020; Tempe, AZ.

23. Kamel Boulos MN, Wilson JT, Clauson KA. Geospatial blockchain: promises, challenges, and scenarios in health and health care. *International Journal of Health Geographics*. 2018;17(1):25. doi:10.1186/s12942-018-0144-x

CHAPTER 25

HEALTHY PLACES RESEARCH: EMERGING OPPORTUNITIES

Andrew L. Dannenberg, Nisha Botchwey, and Howard Frumkin

KEY POINTS

- Empirical research provides a solid foundation for designing and building healthy places. Such research has not always been used in the design professions.
- Research performed to date can guide many health-promoting design choices now, although further research is needed to answer remaining questions.
- Many remaining questions concern equity, sustainability, and applications in low- and moderate-income countries.
- Numerous research opportunities are available for students, researchers, and practitioners in public health, planning, architecture, and other fields to advance the evidence base for creating healthy places.
- Data collected for purposes unrelated to health, including "big data," can sometimes be used creatively to document links between health and the built environment.
- Natural experiments are a valuable approach to documenting the links between health and the built environment, especially because randomized controlled trials are rarely possible in community settings
- Case studies of healthy and unhealthy places can be helpful for identifying areas in which further research would be useful.

INTRODUCTION

Scene: Weekly meeting of the city council in a southern city.

Councilwoman Susan Walker (who bikes daily for transportation): "Given our city's high level of pedestrian- and bicycle-related injuries, I want to do something to make our streets safer for pedestrians and cyclists and to encourage physical activity in our children and adults. Based on advice from our health officer, today I am introducing a bill to adopt a complete streets policy for our city. This policy means that every road being built or renovated in our city will be designed to safely accommodate the needs of pedestrians and bicyclists as well as the potential expansion of public transit. I heard they passed a law like this in a city in California five years ago, and now they report fewer pedestrian and cyclist injuries and deaths."

Councilman Bill Driver (whose family owns an automobile dealership): "That sounds like a terrible idea. Crashes may be a problem, but people simply should be more careful when they walk and bike in our city. I want our transportation money used to reduce traffic congestion by widening roads. I got delayed in a bad traffic jam today while driving to this meeting. I want all the potholes and bottlenecks fixed on our roads before wasting money on sidewalks and bike lanes for the few people who walk and bike here now. Also, you said this idea worked in California—what makes you think it would work here?"

Councilwoman Walker [as an aside to her assistant]: "If we are to have any chance of getting this bill passed, we need to provide good evidence on the costs and health benefits of a complete streets policy, and we also need to know the weaknesses in our arguments due to research gaps. Can you help me find this information?"

In recent years, numerous research studies have focused on the impacts of the built environment on health. For example, based on a rigorous literature review, the *Guide to Community Preventive Services*[1] recommended "with sufficient evidence" built environment strategies that combine one or more interventions to improve pedestrian or bicycle transportation systems with one or more land use and environmental design interventions to increase physical activity. The guide also describes other strategies to promote physical activity for which there is "insufficient evidence" and for which further epidemiological, social, interventional, and policy research is needed. In the scenario in the chapter opening, the councilwoman needs to find reliable evidence that a complete streets policy will reduce pedestrian and cyclist injuries and encourage physical activity. She also needs to identify the co-benefits and unintended consequences of implementing such a policy.

Political decisions are often made with incomplete information about potential consequences. Stronger evidence increases the likelihood that health-promoting decisions will be made. Although gaps in knowledge should not impede decision-makers from acting now to improve the built environment, continued research is essential to ensure that decisions

affecting community design incorporate evidence-based and cost-effective strategies. This chapter reviews some current research needs and possible approaches to addressing these needs.

Although in the ideal world all decisions are fully supported by high-quality evidence, human behavior and political considerations influence decisions in the real world. So beyond assembling robust evidence, it is at least as important to communicate that evidence in ways that connect with audiences—often with stories or other narratives alongside the numbers. Many academics now prepare summaries of their research for lay audiences and use social media such as blogs or Twitter to further communicate their findings. Such messaging needs to include the "why" the research is important along with the "how" and the "what" of the work. The messaging should also include an indication of the study's limitations so that policymakers and the public have realistic expectations of what science can tell us—and a tolerance for the inevitable uncertainty.

CONSIDERATIONS FOR RESEARCH ON HEALTH, EQUITY, AND THE BUILT ENVIRONMENT

Research on health, equity, and built environment issues is generally interdisciplinary and can be addressed by academics or practitioners across many fields. For example, an obesity researcher may examine transportation policies, a nutritionist may address access to healthy foods, a climate change expert may study community resilience in relation to the built environment, a planner may look at health elements in comprehensive plans, and a transportation researcher may create tools to measure walking and bicycling. Funding for such work often comes from other fields because there are few funding sources focused specifically on supporting health and equity in built environment research. The Robert Wood Johnson Foundation (https://www.rwjf.org/en/our-focus-areas/topics/built

environment-and-health.html) and other members of the Convergence Partnership (https://www.convergencepartnership.org/) have played an important role in funding research in the field.

Several issues should be considered in conducting healthy places research. First, communities can help frame research questions and carry out research in collaboration with investigators. In this approach, known as *community-based participatory research*, academic researchers partner with community members to answer questions like "What do we wish we knew about healthy places?" and "What are the big questions we need to address for our community to be healthy?" Second, built environment questions involve social justice, so every research project should consider equity by examining how the possible solutions would lead to the distribution of resources, opportunities, and privileges across communities, especially the impact on disadvantaged populations. Third, built environment interventions have multiple impacts on health and equity, so outcome analyses should examine both short-term and long-term benefits, as well as unintended consequences. Most decisions in the built environment involve trade-offs, so decision-making should compare various options and be informed by evidence about the risks, benefits, and costs of each. For example, is it better to use available transit funds to build a few miles of light rail, a larger network of bus rapid transit lines, or an even larger network of bicycle trails?

Fourth, decisions about the built environment have long-term implications, so research should consider both short- and long-term outcomes. A building may stand for decades, and a street network may persist for centuries. The trees we plant today will mature in fifty or one hundred years when climate conditions may be different, perhaps favoring different species that now thrive. Fifth, measuring exposure is often difficult; for example, how does one measure a "dose" of exposure to access to a park? Sixth, establishing an association between health and a built environment component requires replication of a study in multiple settings because no single study is definitive.

Seventh, consideration of research ethics is essential; studies involving human subjects require approval by an institutional review board to protect privacy and other rights of individuals. Eighth, inclusion of healthy places research in low- to moderate-income countries is critical to provide a more complete picture of opportunities to improve health in those settings. Finally, although local decisions have a major impact on behavior, national and global influences shape outcomes in varying ways, so research should consider built environment issues on multiple scales as described below.

Looking forward, research in health and the built environment should address key societal issues that shape future cities and health outcomes among global populations, including climate change (chapter 17), obesity (chapter 2), aging (chapter 10), urbanization (chapters 11 and 12), and the food/water/energy nexus (chapters 3, 6, and 17). Health, sustainability, and equity and their intersections with community design exist at multiple spatial scales, and addressing them requires cross-sector interventions. Research gaps in these areas include questions such as the unique impacts of built environment interventions designed to address these issues for historically vulnerable groups, including youth, the elderly, low-income, and racial and ethnic minorities. Other topics include the complex relationship between displacement and infrastructure investments, in addition to exploring innovative ways to measure the effectiveness and outcomes of interventions at multiple scales. The relationship between community design and major societal issues can be broken into discrete questions that can be addressed by designing and funding specific research projects.

Research in health and the built environment can be conducted at multiple geographic scales.[2] The *microscale* level includes fine-grained design details of the environment, such as building design, pedestrian facade, and benches at bus stops. This is also considered the overlay of the structural form of built environments.[3] Automatic measures of this scale are challenging.[4] The *mesoscale* level includes streetscapes or the size and arrangement of large objects such as buildings and trees.[3] The *macroscale* or neighborhood level includes residential density, land use diversity/mix, distance to destinations, and street connectivity.[5,6] These are sometimes referred to as the "D" variables of development: density, diversity, design, destination accessibility, and distance to transit. These variables are often measured on the census-tract level using geographic information system data, US Census data, and other readily available tools.

APPROACHES FOR RESEARCH ON HEALTH AND THE BUILT ENVIRONMENT

Although randomized controlled trials are seldom possible when studying community designs, several types of research are particularly useful in examining health and built environment issues. The first is **natural experiments**, research in which investigators can examine health impacts in settings where change has occurred that is unrelated to investigator efforts. For example, in one natural experiment, investigators examined the relationship of changes in body mass index to the completion of a light rail transit line in Salt Lake City, Utah.[7] In Europe, investigators documented the increase in number of miles bicycled and associated health benefits after numerous pop-up cycle lanes were installed by redistributing street space in response to the COVID-19 pandemic.[8] Other examples of natural experiments include changes in physical activity, body mass index, or diet related to occurrences such as a public transit strike, refurbishing a park, or opening a new healthy food outlet.[9] Methods may include pre- and postassessments of the exposed population with or without similar measurements in an unexposed comparison group. To take advantage of natural experiments, investigators need to be alert to events that provide a potentially measurable change and to be prepared to initiate such research promptly.

A second research approach is to conduct creative *analyses of data collected for reasons other than an investigation into health*. For example, researchers have used data collected for transportation purposes in the National Household Travel Survey to examine the amount of walking associated with using public transit[10] and the relationship between social capital and commute time.[11]

A third approach is **policy research**, in which investigators examine types of built environment policies passed in various jurisdictions, ideally in conjunction with measures of health in those localities. One such survey examined the prevalence of complete streets policies in US municipalities.[12] Another report examined factors that influenced municipal officials' involvement in transportation policies supportive of walking and bicycling.[13] In Australia, investigators examined the longitudinal health impacts of the Liveable Neighbourhoods policy.[14]

Fourth, large **cohort studies** developed for purposes other than built environment research may offer an opportunity for examining cross-sectional[15,16] and longitudinal[17-20] impacts of the built environment on health. Many of these studies were designed to study cardiovascular disease risk factors and included measures of the built environment in either initial or later data collection.

A fifth type of research focuses on **cost-benefit analysis** and **cost-effectiveness analysis** of built environment interventions, such as pedestrian and bicycle infrastructure improvements to increase physical activity.[21-25] Policymakers often request results of such studies.

A sixth approach to obtain new insights is *analyses of big data* that may contain millions or billions of data points. Examples of such extremely large data sets include information collected by remote sensing of vegetation or air pollution, geographic movement of cell phones to measure traffic flow, physical activity sensors worn by individuals, frequency of searches of specific words on the internet, frequency of specific words used on social media, and records of the use of public transit farecards. For example, community mobility during the COVID-19 pandemic was estimated by the proportion of cell phones recorded during the day as being more than 150 meters (492 feet) from their usual nighttime location.[26] The creativity of investigators in formulating suitable research questions enhances the value of such analyses as methods for analyzing extremely large data sets continue to develop.

Locally conducted research often carries the most weight in decisions made by city council members and state legislators. Although local planners and public health practitioners who implement small-scale infrastructure policies may have little capacity for conducting rigorous research, they can contribute to the evidence base by conducting **evaluations** of policies or projects, often using before and after or comparison group methods. An evaluation can provide information about whether a policy or other intervention is effective, has unintended consequences, can be improved, or should be continued and replicated elsewhere. A simple survey of users of a new multiuse trail can provide insight into what works and can help justify similar projects elsewhere. Some interventions are likely to be more effective than others in certain locales because of weather, topography, or subpopulations. For example, installing a soccer field rather than a baseball diamond in a park will promote more physical activity if local residents prefer to play soccer. Detailed *case studies* can be used to document the experience of specific communities in creating a healthy built environment. For example, one case study documented the creation and use of a jogging trail around a cemetery in a low-income area in Los Angeles.[27]

Related to evaluations, **implementation research** can be conducted to promote the systematic uptake of research findings and other evidence-based practices into routine practice.[28] For example, one study examined stakeholder perceptions of the successes and failures of built environment interventions in four Canadian cities.[29]

TARGETING RESEARCH GAPS

One goal of healthy places research is to establish a causal link between an exposure and a health outcome. As described in chapter 1, Hill's criteria provide a framework for both establishing causality and identifying research gaps. For example, applying the criteria to sidewalks and physical activity, the exposure to sidewalks would occur prior to increases in physical activity, the relationship would be statistically strong, and increasing the number of sidewalks would lead to increasing amounts of physical activity in a dose-response relationship. Additionally, the relationship between sidewalks and physical activity would be consistent among different populations and in different geographic settings, and there would be a plausible basis that sidewalks might help increase physical activity. Alternative explanations should be ruled out, and the relationship between sidewalks and physical activity could be altered by changing selected variables in experimental settings. To target further research efforts, an investigator could examine the existing literature and determine which of these criteria are missing.

Connections between the built environment and health are complicated by the long causal pathway between the component of the built environment and the health outcome. Figure 25.1 provides a simplified example of the links between citywide adoption of a complete streets policy and public health outcomes. A more complete figure would show many more pathways to various health outcomes, as well as interactions among variables. Each link, such as the connection between adoption of a complete streets policy and implementation of that policy, needs to be supported by evidence. Gaps in the evidence are areas for future research. A single intervention such as a complete streets policy is insufficient to lead to a

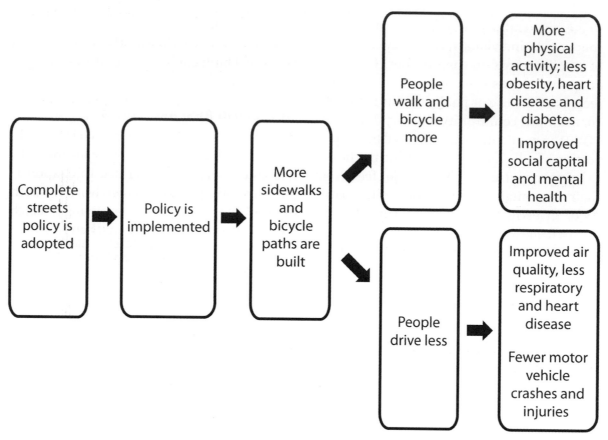

Figure 25.1. A simplified causal chain of the health impacts of a complete streets policy.
Source: Andrew Dannenberg

major change in health outcomes such as obesity. For complex health issues with numerous causes, multiple interventions are needed. An example of a more complete causal chain, also known as a logic model, includes inputs, strategies, outputs, and short-, medium-, and long-term outcomes, as well as cross-cutting contextual factors.[30]

Research gaps related to healthy community design continue to evolve, and each new research finding is likely to raise additional questions. Many research reports conclude with a specific mention of further research that is needed. Existing compilations of evidence, such as the *Guide to Community Preventive Services* (http://www.thecommunityguide.org) and Cochrane reviews (http://www.cochrane.org), often indicate where evidence for various interventions is insufficient, thereby suggesting research opportunities.

Health impact assessments (chapter 22) can also be used to identify research gaps. Such assessments typically review existing literature and may mention where the literature is insufficient to document a link between a health impact and a proposed policy or project. Groups outside of public health, such as the National Cooperative Highway Research Program, have published lists of research needs relevant to health and the built environment.[31] In addition, annual professional conferences, such as those of planning, transportation, architecture, and public health investigators, are opportunities for experts to share their work and discuss areas needing further research.

Developed from a variety of sources, table 25.1 presents a list of many current research gaps related to designing healthy communities. Although such a list cannot be complete,

Table 25.1. Research questions and possible study designs related to the impact on health of community design and transportation choices.

Research Question	Possible Study Design
1. Physical activity	
What community policies are best correlated with increased physical activity?	Select sets of communities with high levels and with low levels of physical activity and examine which policies are present or absent in each set.
What are best practices in designing and building trails along water, sewer, electrical system, and gas utility rights-of-way and along active rail corridors to promote physical activity?	Identify case studies in which trails have been built in utility and rail corridors and conduct local interviews to assess benefits and challenges.
How do per capita levels of pedestrian and bicycle infrastructure funding relate to physical activity levels, equity, and injury rates?	Compare pedestrian and bicycle infrastructure funding in multiple cities or states in relation to physical activity levels, demographic characteristics, and injury rates.
2. Food environment	
What types of policies and incentives and disincentives can encourage more supermarkets, grocery stores, and farmers' markets and fewer convenience stores and fast-food outlets?	Gather and analyze case studies of communities that have used policies, incentives, and disincentives to improve their local food environment.
What are the impacts of farmers' markets and other healthy food outlets in building social connections, support, and cohesion? What are their impacts on levels of walking and bicycling?	Gather and analyze case studies of communities that have introduced farmers' markets and other healthy food outlets.
What are the nutritional health effects of school vegetable gardens on children?	Measure student diets in a set of schools before and after implementing school vegetable gardens.
3. Injuries	
What practices are used in states to report nonfatal crashes? What recommendations can be developed for collecting nationally comparable data on nonfatal injuries sustained by pedestrians and bicyclists that may or may not involve motor vehicles?	Survey state and metropolitan transportation agencies to determine how they collect, store, and analyze nonfatal crash data, particularly cases involving pedestrians, bicyclists, and micromobility users. Identify existing nonfatal injury surveillance programs that could be adapted for a new crash-related injury reporting system.
Are older teenagers better drivers if they gained road experience by riding bicycles in their younger teen years?	Survey a group of teens age 17 to 18 about their bicycling experience at age 12 to 14 and compare that experience to their recent driving records, or gather bicycling and driving information while following a cohort of teens from age 12 to 18.
Considering crime prevention through environmental design (CPTED) approaches, do specific design elements focused on public safety have secondary public health consequences related to physical activity, injury, social capital, mental health, or social equity? Do "eyes on the street" lead to racial profiling?	Collect qualitative data from focus groups of residents and service providers in communities where CPTED-related interventions have been implemented. Examine before and after health indicators associated with the specific types of CPTED-related changes.

Table 25.1. Continued

Research Question	Possible Study Design
4. Air and water quality	
In rural and urban areas at risk of poor air quality due to wildfires, what are best practices to minimize health risks from smoke exposure that extends over many days?	Document smoke-related health impacts and assess policies and practices used to reduce smoke exposure during wildfires in multiple locations in recent years.
What are the health and air pollution reduction benefits of community gardens, rooftop gardens, greenways, and other types of increased vegetation? Do greener communities have lower air pollution levels and better health than less green cities after controlling for other factors?	Compare air pollution and health status indicators in communities with and without major proportions of land invested in gardens and green space.
How have communities that recycle wastewater into drinking water convinced their residents about water safety?	Conduct focus groups in communities that have successfully conveyed such water safety messages.
What are the health impacts of residential septic systems versus municipal sewage systems? Should planners prefer increased use of municipal systems for health reasons?	Compare rates of diarrhea and of water-related disease outbreaks in communities with various levels of residential septic systems and municipal sewage systems. Conduct cost-benefit analyses of installing municipal sewage systems.
5. Mental health and social capital	
What specific types of activities, design elements, and programming in parks and other public spaces contribute most to attracting diverse users and to increasing social interaction and social capital among and within diverse populations?	Gather and analyze case studies of communities in which their parks and other public spaces have attracted diverse users. Conduct focus groups with some of those users to identify attractive features and with nonusers to identify barriers to use.
Which factors of placemaking projects lead to a greater sense of community and place attachment?	Conduct focus groups of users of selected placemaking projects that are considered successful.
To what extent is the design of the built environment less important for promoting social capital when people are communicating by social media, texting, and other new technologies?	In various built environments, compare social capital among persons with high and low levels of use of social media and other technologies.
What are the mental health benefits and unintended consequences of daylighting and other types of lighting in workspaces and living spaces?	Compare indicators of mental health and productivity in settings with and without daylighting, or before and after introduction of daylighting into workspaces and living spaces.
6. Environmental justice, social equity, and gentrification	
What policies and interventions can protect low-income and other disadvantaged communities at risk of gentrification and displacement by projects designed to promote healthy sustainable communities?	Identify, analyze, and disseminate case studies of places where low-income persons were appropriately accommodated rather than displaced in redevelopment settings that followed Smart Growth principles.
What guidelines and policies are needed so that community and building designs are more inclusive for all people and routinely exceed the minimum standards set by the Americans with Disabilities Act?	Conduct focus groups with disability advocacy organizations. Develop case studies of communities and buildings that successfully facilitate inclusivity.

Table 25.1. Continued

Research Question	Possible Study Design
6. Environmental justice, social equity, and gentrification (continued)	
How could paratransit providers better coordinate with other services such as visiting nurses or food delivery to optimize meeting the essential needs of the elderly and persons with disabilities, especially during a pandemic or other times of disrupted transport services?	Develop and evaluate a pilot program that coordinates paratransit and other services for the elderly and persons with disabilities.
Which tools are most useful to assess whether public funds are being spent equitably on transportation, parks, schools, and other public infrastructure? To what extent do 311 nonemergency hotlines help get sidewalk defects, potholes, and other infrastructure problems fixed faster and more equitably?	Analyze GIS data to compare the locations of public funds expenditures to neighborhood income levels. Analyze GIS data to compare the median time to resolution for 311 call complaints to neighborhood income levels.
Compared with areas having a narrow range of housing values, what are the effects of mixed-income neighborhoods on public safety and public health, such as crime rates, rates of chronic disease, and social cohesion?	Examine before and after crime victimization rates, health measures, and social capital in communities where mixed-income urban redevelopment is planned, controlling for confounders. Conduct a survey of residents' perceived risk compared with true risk.
To what extent are Safe Routes to School investments made to promote equity in disadvantaged populations?	Analyze a statewide or national inventory of Safe Routes to School programs to examine the demographic characteristics of populations who benefit from such programs.
How does involvement of youth in advocating for healthy, equitable, and resilient places improve the overall well-being of low-income youth?	Review pre- and postindividual and group measurements of youth participating in advocacy curricula in promotion of healthy places.
In informal settlements in low-income countries, what spending priorities, such as sanitation, electricity, or schools, most effectively promote community health, well-being, and economic development?	Conduct a retrospective analysis of spending and economic, social, and health outcomes of population groups in informal settlements in low-income countries.
What are the mental health implications of trail development on nearby low-income residents subject to displacement pressures?	Interview residents in target neighborhoods subject to displacement from infrastructure improvements before, during, and after the trail development.
How much can be done to improve the community before such changes increase the risk for gentrification and displacement? For example, displacement risk is unlikely to increase from adding a small pocket park but is likely to increase from adding a light rail station.	Select a sample of 100 communities with various-sized improvements and a comparison group of 100 similar communities without improvements and assess which improvements were and were not associated with subsequent property value increases and displacement.
7. Land use and transportation	
Which transportation agencies now include explicit health indicators in their project prioritization criteria? How were these indicators selected? How have these health indicators influenced agency decisions?	Document case studies of where transportation agencies have incorporated health indicators into their project prioritization processes and subsequent impacts on agency decisions.

Table 25.1. Continued

Research Question	Possible Study Design
7. Land use and transportation (continued)	
What are the best methods for monitoring mode share? Does increasing the use of pedestrian/bicycle counters help get more equitable funding for pedestrian/bicycle infrastructure?	Examine information from communities that have used different methods of gathering mode share data. Examine distribution of pedestrian/bicycle counters and infrastructure funding from an equity viewpoint.
Do public bicycle-sharing programs increase physical activity and reduce automobile use?	Examine trips taken, miles traveled, and physical activity levels in a defined population in cities before and after introducing regular and e-bike bicycle-sharing programs.
Do communities where local government pays for sidewalks have better sidewalk infrastructure and maintenance than places where homeowners pay for sidewalks?	Compare the quantity and quality of sidewalks in communities where local government pays with that in communities where homeowners pay for sidewalks.
What rigorous economic evaluations have been done to assess the short-term and long-term health impacts of transportation capital projects and programs? What data and new methods are needed for such economic evaluations?	Conduct literature searches on types of cost-benefit and cost-effectiveness analyses now performed for transportation projects and on similar analyses involving health impacts in other sectors, such as energy and housing. Conduct an economic evaluation from a health perspective to compare an investment in a large-scale transit project to a similar investment in a large-scale highway project.
What are the most useful tools and metrics for measuring the economic impacts of improved walkability and bikeability in communities?	Conduct a literature review of studies of the economic impacts of walkability and bikeability in communities.
How can the health benefits of public transit implementation be translated into metrics for health outcome improvements and health care cost savings?	Examine metrics used in other types of health outcome studies and adapt these metrics for use in quantifying the health benefits of transit.
How prevalent is *hazard busing* (busing students short distances where walking is too hazardous), and how do planners decide where it is needed?	Survey school districts on policies for hazard busing and on economic and health implications of such policies.
8. Nature contact	
Through what mechanisms does nature contact benefit health?	Conduct experimental studies that measure changes in stress markers and/or immune markers.
What forms of nature contact provide the greatest benefit for health?	Conduct experimental or natural experiment observations comparing different types of nature contact.
What "dose" of nature contact provides the greatest benefit for health?	Conduct experimental studies comparing different durations and/or intensities of exposure.
What measures of nature contact best predict human health benefit?	Examine associations between different metrics and health outcomes.
How does optimal park design vary by cultural, ethnic, and other demographic factors?	Conduct survey research and studies of park use patterns in settings with various demographics.

Table 25.1. Continued

Research Question	Possible Study Design
9. Research tools and methods	
What existing and emerging technologies (such as mobile device tracking through Bluetooth and global positioning systems) can be used and validated to better measure physical activity and travel behaviors? How can pedestrian and bicycle counts be derived from such technologies?	Identify and validate new measuring technologies in laboratory and in real-world settings. Conduct studies to validate mobile device trackers with calibrated bicycle and pedestrian counters and identify and adjust for sources of bias such as underrepresented groups.
How can remote sensing of environmental factors such as air pollution, housing, light emissions, and vegetation be combined longitudinally with health measures to better understand their relationships?	Convene a workshop of remote sensing experts and public health researchers to explore how these tools might be best used to examine healthy community questions.
How are communities using online mapping or data visualization platforms, as well as other innovative experiential ways of community involvement such as temporary pop-ups and virtual reality? What are the impacts on health of using such tools?	Document how various data visualization tools are being used in other fields for community engagement. Explore how such tools are being used in urban planning and transportation (e.g., NC Vision Zero[k]).
What are the best level of service indicators for bicycle and pedestrian infrastructure?	Review the literature on level of service indicators (e.g., Asadi-Shekari[l]). Survey transportation agencies to assess how these indicators are being used in practice.
What are the best ways to perform *all cost accounting*, including the cost of health impacts in community design decisions?	Develop case studies in which estimates of costs of health impacts are added to other financial estimates as part of community design decisions.
10. Public policy and other cross-cutting issues	
What types of zoning codes, building codes, parking regulations, and incentive and disincentive programs promote health or lead to adverse health outcomes?	Review the planning literature to identify codes that promote or discourage healthy activities. Compare health outcomes and political circumstances in communities that have and have not adopted model codes and incentives.
When buildings or communities are designed and certified as health-promoting, how can such outcomes be documented?	Compare before and after health indicators of persons who move into buildings or communities certified and advertised as health-promoting.
How can incentives such as density bonuses and disincentives such as impact fees be used to encourage community designs that promote health for groups with diverse race/ethnicity, income, life stage, and disability status?	Conduct interviews and cross-sectional surveys with policymakers, regional planners, developers, and bankers in a variety of communities.
For specific physical design interventions to have the desired health outcomes, what catalysts or other conditions must exist simultaneously, such as active neighborhood groups, cohesiveness, high degrees of social capital, or health-promotion services?	In multiple communities, compare the implementation of selected interventions, such as building sidewalks or transit systems, to assess factors that influenced the health impacts of those interventions.

Table 25.1. Continued

Research Question	Possible Study Design
10. Public policy and other cross-cutting issues (continued)	
What barriers, such as lack of knowledge or interest, prevent planners from considering public health impacts in their decisions? What barriers prevent public health officials from becoming more involved in the planning process?	Conduct focus groups with planners and public health practitioners to identify these barriers, and then develop partnerships to work on addressing these barriers.
What community health benefits and unintended consequences occur when there is shared use of school facilities by community residents after school hours and on weekends?	Examine health indicators in communities before and after implementation of shared use agreements.
How can benchmarking data such as https://www.countyhealthrankings.org/ and http://bikeleague.org/benchmarking-report be used to influence choices that favor health-promoting policies?	Gather and analyze success stories from cities, counties, and states that have used data from health and physical activity benchmarking reports.
What are the health benefits and political challenges in implementing complete streets policies? What are the best metrics to assess the degree of implementation of complete streets policies? How do these metric values differ based on density?	Review the literature on complete streets (e.g., Zhao[m]). Interview transportation officials who have tried to implement complete streets policies, including those who were unsuccessful.
What tools and methods are needed in rural areas to promote healthy community design that are different from those used in more urban and suburban areas?	Conduct focus groups with planners from rural, suburban, and urban settings in which they can interactively discuss their successes and challenges in promoting healthy community design.
What policy interventions related to community design are most impactful in improving health outcomes in rural communities?	Evaluate similar policies implemented in urban, suburban, and rural communities for intended population behavior change and health outcomes.
11. Sustainability	
What are the potential health, equity, and sustainability benefits of building codes beyond injury prevention?	Review the literature on building codes (e.g., Edwards[n]). Identify case studies of communities in which building codes are being used to provide multiple benefits.
Which types of sustainable green practices have positive impacts on health, and which ones have few impacts or adverse impacts on health?	Review and analyze a range of current, sustainable green practices to identify links between green practices and health impacts.
What are best practices for local and state task forces that focus on designing sustainable and resilient communities, and how can health considerations be incorporated into their work?	Interview members of such local and state task forces about the opportunities and challenges in addressing sustainability, resilience, and health in their work.
What urban strategies have been most effective in shifting travel patterns, in decarbonizing buildings, in vegetating cities, in conserving water, and in providing beloved public spaces?	Compare the impacts of urban strategies on these outcomes in leading cities such as those in the C40 Network (https://www.c40.org/).
What specific transportation strategies simultaneously optimize reduced carbon emissions, reduced air pollution, reduced noise, and improved safety?	Develop models with metrics of various approaches such as low-emission zones, taxes, improved pedestrian/bicycle infrastructure, bike-share programs, and improved transit.

Table 25.1. Continued

Research Question	Possible Study Design
12. Resilience	
What social approaches best encourage neighborhood networking and mutual aid in the event of a disaster?	Conduct experiments to explore various means of neighborhood support such as block captains, drills, and neighborhood parties.
What heat wave preparedness plans most effectively protect communities from the health effects of extreme heat?	Study existing plans in multiple cities and how they functioned after extreme heat events.
For a selected city, what are the city's greatest vulnerabilities in the event of a disaster and what are the best approaches to reduce them?	Conduct modeling and table-top exercises in that city to assess electrical, water, communications, transportation, and other essential infrastructure.
13. Pandemic preparedness and response	
How can streets and public spaces best be adapted to facilitate increased biking and walking during a pandemic? How do physical activity levels and mode share change when streets are closed to through traffic?	Develop case studies of the experiences of various cities in increasing places for walking and biking during the COVID-19 pandemic.
What is the role of transit systems in the spread of infectious diseases? How can they be redesigned to reduce such risks? What are the safest and most practical transportation options for essential workers during pandemics?	Develop case studies of the experiences of various transit systems during the COVID-19 pandemic.
How do concerns about disease transmission influence the willingness of users to share ride-hailing vehicles, micromobility modes, and autonomous vehicles? How can those concerns be addressed?	Conduct knowledge, attitude, and practice surveys of users and nonusers of ride-hailing services and micromobility modes during and after the COVID-19 pandemic.
How can policies be designed to support transportation systems that are resilient to the short-term and long-term health effects of pandemics?	Develop case studies of the experiences of transportation systems in multiple cities during the COVID-19 pandemic focused on successes and challenges.
What is the role of land use density in relation to the incidence of infection during pandemics? What are the implications of this role for long-term land use planning and policy?	Review the emerging literature on pandemics and land use density (e.g., Hamidi[o]). Conduct focus groups with practicing city planners to examine various scenarios.
14. Emerging technologies	
How can trail and road designs be improved to better accommodate new technologies, especially e-bikes and e-scooters, that often travel at speeds too fast for many trails and too slow for many roads?	Examine case studies of communities that have best accommodated a broad mixture of travel modes.
What are the estimated changes in sedentary behaviors and health and equity outcomes that may result from the predicted widespread use of autonomous vehicles and associated changes in vehicle miles traveled, modal split, and land use?	Use existing published reviews to guide modeling of potential health outcomes of autonomous vehicles. Examine case studies in settings where autonomous vehicles have been introduced.

Table 25.1. Continued

Research Question	Possible Study Design
14. Emerging technologies (continued)	
What are the potential health impacts for low-income and marginalized populations if they have inequitable access to autonomous vehicles?	Develop scenarios of settings in which low-income populations do and do not have equitable access to autonomous vehicles and estimate associated health impacts. Identify options to improve equitable access.

Source: Adapted from a-j and other sources.

a. Dannenberg AL, Jackson RJ, Frumkin H, et al. The impact of community design and land-use choices on public health: a scientific research agenda. *American Journal of Public Health.* 2003:93:1500-1508. http://doi.org/10.2105/ajph.93.9.1500

b. Dannenberg AL, Rodriguez DA, Sandt LS. Advancing research in transportation and public health: a selection of twenty project ideas from a U.S. research roadmap. *Journal of Transport and Health.* 2021;21:101021. https://doi.org/10.1016/j.jth.2021.101021

c. Frumkin H, Bratman GN, Breslow SJ, et al. Nature contact and human health: a research agenda. *Environmental Health Perspectives.* 2017:125(7):075001. https://doi.org/10.1289/EHP1663

d. National Academies of Sciences, Engineering, and Medicine (NASEM). *A Research Roadmap for Transportation and Public Health.* NCHRP Research Report No. 932. National Academies Press; 2019. https://doi.org/10.17226/25644

e. Project for Public Spaces. *The Case for Healthy Places: Improving Health Outcomes Through Placemaking.* Project for Public Spaces; 2016. http://bit.ly/33iyXFm

f. Sohrabi S, Khreis H, Lor D. Impacts of autonomous vehicles on public health: a conceptual model and policy recommendations. *Sustainable Cities and Society.* 2020;63:102457. https://doi.org/10.1016/j.scs.2020.102457

g. Tonne C, Adair L, Adlakha D, et al. Defining pathways to healthy sustainable urban development. *Environment International.* 2021;146:106236. https://doi.org/10.1016/j.envint.2020.106236

h. Transportation Research Board. Conference on Health and Active Transportation. Washington, DC. December 11–12, 2019. TRB Circular E-C264. 2020. http://onlinepubs.trb.org/onlinepubs/circulars/ec264.pdf

i. Transportation Research Board. Summary of Transportation Research Needs Related to COVID-19. TRB Circular E-C267. 2020. http://onlinepubs.trb.org/onlinepubs/circulars/ec267.pdf

j. Transportation Research Board. Opportunities for Research on Transportation and Equity. TRB Circular E-C270. 2020. http://onlinepubs.trb.org/onlinepubs/circulars/ec270.pdf

k. NC Vision Zero. *North Carolina Vision Zero Analytics.* 2020. https://ncvisionzero.org/data-analytics/vision-zero-analytics/

l. Asadi-Shekari Z, Moeinaddini M, Shah MZ. Non-motorised level of service: addressing challenges in pedestrian and bicycle level of service. *Transport Reviews.* 2013;33(2):166-194. http://doi.org/10.1080/01441647.2013.775613

m. Zhao JZ. How do Complete Streets matter for communities? The case of Richfield, Minnesota. Minnesota Department of Transportation; 2020. https://conservancy.umn.edu/handle/11299/216456

n. Edwards N, Chauvin J, Blanchet R. Advocating for improvements to building codes for the population's health. *Canadian Journal of Public Health.* 2019;110:516-519. https://doi.org/10.17269/s41997-019-00191-7

o. Hamidi S, Sabouri S, Ewing R. Does density aggravate the COVID-19 pandemic? *Journal of the American Planning Association.* 2020;86(4):495-509. http://doi.org/10.1080/01944363.2020.1777891

this table includes a wide range of ideas based on published literature, interdisciplinary research workshops, discussions of the chapter authors with colleagues, and other sources. This list and other published research agendas have been and will be useful in identifying research projects for both students and experienced investigators in this field. The research ideas in table 25.1 are also listed online at www.islandpress.org/makinghealthyplaces and on the Built Environment and Public Health Clearinghouse website www.bephc.org. The authors hope that readers will use these websites to provide feedback about the suggested research topics, to add new information as it becomes available about these topics, and to add new research possibilities as they arise. Such ongoing interactions with investigators will move the evidence base for health and built environment interventions forward.

CONCLUSION

Although enough is known about the links between health and built environment to support many health-promoting design choices now, more research is needed to identify new interventions and to further evaluate the health impacts of built environment design choices. Challenges in the field include setting priorities among research opportunities and translating research findings into practical interventions.[14] Multiple approaches are available for conducting health and built environment research.

Although public health recommendations are based primarily on research findings, the work of design professionals often represents an integration of creative thinking, research findings, and engineering possibilities. We encourage planners, architects, and other design professionals to think in research terms and to collaborate with public health colleagues to conduct research on designing healthy places. In addition, identifying the most effective methods for communicating research findings to decision-makers is itself a substantial research question.

DISCUSSION QUESTIONS

1. Why is conclusive proof of a link between a particular built environment design and a specific health impact seldom available?
2. What are the advantages and disadvantages of using *natural experiments* to document links between health and the built environment?
3. How can case studies be used to guide future community design decisions?
4. What are some examples of data collected for purposes other than healthy community design that might be useful for conducting research on links between health and the built environment?
5. Given resources to conduct a research project on one of the emerging opportunities described in this chapter, which topic would you select, and how would you design a research study to provide new information on the subject?

DISCLOSURE OF COMPETING INTERESTS

Andrew L. Dannenberg, Nisha Botchwey, and Howard Frumkin's declarations appear in the preface.

REFERENCES

1. Guide to Community Preventive Services. Physical activity: built environment approaches combining transportation system interventions with land use and environmental design. 2016. https: //www.thecommunityguide.org/findings /physical-activity-built-environment -approaches

2. Garfinkel-Castro A, Kim K, Hamidi S, Ewing R. Obesity and the built environment at different urban scales: examining the literature. *Nutrition Reviews*. 2017;75(Suppl 1):51-61. https: //doi.org/10.1093/nutrit/nuw037

3. Harvey C, Aultman-Hall L. Measuring urban streetscapes for livability: a review of approaches. *Professional Geographer*. 2016;68(1):149-158. https://doi.org/10.1080 /00330124.2015.1065546

4. Harvey C, Aultman-Hall L, Troy A, Hurley SE. Streetscape skeleton measurement and classification. *Environment and Planning B: Urban Analytics and City Science*. 2017;44(4):668-692. https://doi .org/10.1177/0265813515624688

5. Ewing R, Clemente O. *Measuring Urban Design: Metrics for Livable Places*. Island Press; 2013.

6. Sallis JF, Slymen DJ, Conway TL, et al. Income disparities in perceived neighborhood built and social environment attributes. *Health & Place*. 2011;17(6):1274-1283. https://doi.org/10.1016/J .HEALTHPLACE.2011.02.006

7. Brown BB, Smith KR, Jensen WA, Tharp D. Transit rider body mass index before and after completion of street light-rail line in Utah. *American Journal of Public Health*. 2017;107(9):1484-1486. https://doi .org/10.2105/AJPH.2017.303899

8. Kraus S, Hoch N. Provisional COVID-19 infrastructure induces large, rapid increases in cycling. *Proceedings of the National Academy of Sciences*. 2021;118(15):e2024399118. https://doi .org/10.1073/pnas.2024399118

9. Crane M, Bohn-Goldbaum E, Grunsei A, Bauman A. Using natural experiments to improve public health evidence: a review of context and utility for obesity prevention. *Health Research Policy and Systems*. 2020;18(1):48. https://doi.org/10.1186 /s12961-020-00564-2

10. Le VT, Dannenberg AL. Moving toward physical activity targets by walking to transit: National Household Transportation Survey, 2001–2017. *American Journal of Preventive Medicine*. 2020;59(3):e115-e123. https://doi.org/10.1016/j.amepre.2020.02 .023

11. Besser LM, Marcus M, Frumkin H. Commute time and social capital in the U.S. *American Journal of Preventive Medicine*. 2008;34(3):207-211.

12. Carlson SA, Paul P, Kumar G, Watson KB, Atherton E, Fulton JE. Prevalence of Complete Streets policies in U.S. municipalities. *Journal of Transport & Health*. 2017;5:142-150. http://dx.doi.org/10.1016/j .jth.2016.11.003

13. Zwald ML, Eyler AA, Goins KV, Brownson RC, Schmid TL, Lemon SC. Understanding municipal officials' involvement in transportation policies supportive of walking and bicycling. *Journal of Public Health Management and Practice*. 2017;23(4): 348-355. http://doi.org/10.1097 /PHH.0000000000000152

14. Hooper P, Foster S, Giles-Corti B. A case study of a natural experiment bridging the "research into policy" and "evidence-based policy" gap for active-living science. *International Journal of Environmental Research and Public Health*. 2019;16:2448. http://doi.org/10.3390/ijerph16142448

15. Grazuleviciene R, Andrusaityte S, Gražulevičius T, Dėdelė A. Neighborhood social and built environment and disparities in the risk of hypertension: a cross-sectional study. *International Journal of Environmental*

Research and Public Health. 2020;17: 7696. http://doi.org/10.3390/ijerph17207696

16. Gustat J, Anderson CE, Chukwurah QC, Wallace ME, Broyles ST, Bazzano LA. Cross-sectional associations between the neighborhood built environment and physical activity in a rural setting: the Bogalusa Heart Study. *BMC Public Health* 2020;20:1426. https://doi.org/10.1186/s12889-020-09509-4

17. Hirsch JA, Moore KA, Clarke PJ, et al. Changes in the built environment and changes in the amount of walking over time: longitudinal results from the Multi-ethnic Study of Atherosclerosis. *American Journal of Epidemiology.* 2014;180(8):799-809. https://doi.org/10.1093/aje/kwu218

18. Méline J, Chaix B, Pannier B, et al. Neighborhood walk score and selected cardiometabolic factors in the French RECORD cohort study. *BMC Public Health.* 2017;17:960. https://doi.org/10.1186/s12889-017-4962-8

19. Rummo P, Guilkey D, Shikany JM, Reis J, Gordon-Larsen P. How do individual- and neighborhood-level sociodemographics influence residential location behavior in the context of the food and built environment? Findings from 25 years of follow up in the CARDIA Study. *Journal of Epidemiology and Community Health.* 2017;71(3):261-268. http://doi.org/10.1136/jech-2016-207249

20. Astell-Burt T, Navakatikyan MA, Feng X. Urban green space, tree canopy and 11-year risk of dementia in a cohort of 109,688 Australians. *Environment International.* 2020;145:106102. http://doi.org/10.1016/j.envint.2020.106102

21. Gotschi T. Costs and benefits of bicycling investments in Portland, Oregon. *Journal of Physical Activity and Health.* 2011;8 (Suppl 1):S49–S58. https://doi.org/10.1123/jpah.8.s1.s49

22. Gu J, Mohit B, Muennig PA. The cost-effectiveness of bike lanes in New York City. *Injury Prevention.* 2017;23(4): 239-243. https://doi.org/10.1136/injuryprev-2016-042057

23. Knell G, Brown HS, Gabriel KP, et al. Cost-effectiveness of improvements to the built environment intended to increase physical activity, *Journal of Physical Activity and Health.* 2019;16(5):308-317. http://doi.org/10.1123/jpah.2018-0329

24. Anderson CE, Izadi M, Tian G, Gustat J. Economic benefits of changes in active transportation behavior associated with a new urban trail. *Translational Journal of the ACSM.* 2021;6(2). http://doi.org/10.1249/TJX.0000000000000158

25. Whitehurst DGT, DeVries DN, Fuller D, Winters M. An economic analysis of the health-related benefits associated with bicycle infrastructure investment in three Canadian cities. *PLOS ONE.* 2021;16(2):e0246419. https://doi.org/10.1371/journal.pone.0246419

26. Lasry A, Kidder D, Hast M, et al. Timing of community mitigation and changes in reported COVID-19 and community mobility—four U.S. metropolitan areas, February 26–April 1, 2020. *Morbidity and Mortality Weekly Report.* 2020;69:451-457. http://dx.doi.org/10.15585/mmwr.mm6915e2

27. Aboelata M, Mikkelsen L, Cohen L, Fernandes S, Silver M, Parks LF. Evergreen Cemetery Jogging Path. In: *The Built Environment and Health: 11 Profiles of Neighborhood Transformation.* Prevention Institute; 2004:6-9. https://www.preventioninstitute.org/publications/the-built-environment-and-health-11-profiles-of-neighborhood-transformation

28. Hering JG. Implementation science for the environment. *Environmental Science and Technology.* 2018;52(10):5555-5560. http://doi.org/10.1021/acs.est.8b00874

29. Firth CL, Stephens ZP, Cantinotti M, Fuller D, Kestens Y, Winters M. Successes and failures of built environment

interventions: using concept mapping to assess stakeholder perspectives in four Canadian cities. *Social Science & Medicine.* 2021;268,113383. https://doi.org/10.1016/j.socscimed.2020.113383

30. Joly BM, Polyak G, Davis MV, et al. Linking accreditation and public health outcomes: a logic model approach. *Journal of Public Health Management*

and Practice. 2007;13(4):349-356. http://doi.org/10.1097/01.PHH.0000278027.56820.7e

31. National Academies of Sciences, Engineering, and Medicine (NASEM). A Research Roadmap for Transportation and Public Health. NCHRP Research Report No. 932. National Academies Press; 2019. https://doi.org/10.17226/25644

CHAPTER 26

COVID AND THE BUILT ENVIRONMENT

Howard Frumkin

KEY POINTS

- Throughout history, cities have confronted infectious disease outbreaks and have responded with a range of policies, practices, and design strategies. The COVID-19 pandemic that erupted in 2020 is the latest chapter of that history.

- Several features of the built environment increased the risk of COVID-19. They included crowding (as distinct from urban density), spatial patterns associated with poverty and racism, air pollution, and poor indoor air circulation.

- Responses to the pandemic included a range of built environment strategies. They included modifications to building design to permit physical distancing between people; working from home; reallocation of streets from vehicular traffic to walking, cycling, and commerce; a shift from mass transit to other travel modes; enhanced use of parks and green space; and residential relocation from cities to suburban and rural locations.

- The postpandemic recovery presents many opportunities to advance health, equity, and sustainability in the built environment. The long-term impact of COVID-19 on cities is a story yet to be written.

INTRODUCTION

Cities have always confronted outbreaks of disease. Part of the response has played out in changes to the built environment: laza-rettos in Italian cities following the plague in the fifteenth century, water and sewage infrastructure in London following cholera in the nineteenth century, building regulations to assure light and fresh air in New York triggered by tuberculosis in the early twentieth century.

In 2020, as COVID-19 erupted around the world, cities were again hit early. In the most crowded and deprived urban settings, the attack rate was terrifying: a study in Mumbai less than four months after the city's first confirmed case found a seroprevalence of 55 to 61 percent in slum neighborhoods, compared to 12 to 19 percent in nonslum neighborhoods.[1]

But the pandemic was not confined to cities. Small towns and rural areas were largely spared in the early months of the pandemic, but the incidence of COVID in these settings soon climbed. This was partly due to certain crowded settings (nursing homes, multigenerational households, and workplaces such as meatpacking plants), partly due to demographic risk factors (older, sicker, and poorer populations), and partly due to failure to adopt protective behaviors.

Some argued that the risk of infection would permanently undermine the appeal of cities. Urban geographer Joel Kotkin, for instance, predicted that "a globalized world that spreads pandemics quickly will push workers back into their cars and out to the hinterlands."[b] But other commentators disagreed. "Rumors of the impending demise of the city due to fear of pandemic have been

457

greatly exaggerated," wrote ecologists Rob McDonald and Erica Spotswood.[3]

Only time will tell which prediction is more accurate. However, two historical patterns are likely to hold true. First, throughout history, cities have rebounded from pandemics, continuing to attract people with the promise of opportunity, vibrant lives, and prosperity. Second, in the words of two Egyptian commentators, "Epidemics have transformed our built environment because of the fear of infection,"[4(p1)] "Consequently," according to these writers, "architecture and urbanism after the Covid-19 epidemic will never be the same." What features of the built environment play a role in the spread of COVID-19, and what lessons and practices may emerge from the pandemic?

FEATURES OF THE BUILT ENVIRONMENT THAT INCREASE INFECTION RISK

Several features of the built environment increase risk of COVID-19 transmission or possibly of severity of disease. Chief among them are crowding (both indoor and outside, but especially indoor), poverty, poor air circulation (indoor), and air pollution.

Crowding

Close proximity to other people, especially without masks and during activities such as talking, shouting, and singing or while coughing and sneezing, emerged early as a risk factor for disease transmission. Crowded places—prisons, churches, dormitories, restaurants, public markets, nursing homes, buses, and workplaces such as meatpacking plants—were implicated in outbreaks.[5,6] Similarly, crowded home environments—a typical feature of poor neighborhoods in both wealthy and poor countries—were found to increase the risk of COVID-19.[7,8] In some studies, crowded neighborhoods had higher transmission rates than less-crowded neighborhoods[9]—a pressing challenge in the slums of poor cities.[10] Restrictions on the level of occupancy of stores, theaters, sporting events, and places of worship quickly emerged (figure 26.1).

Figure 26.1. As accumulating evidence confirmed airborne spread of SARS-CoV-2, the cause of COVID-19, many jurisdictions limited the number of people who could be in indoor spaces, often to 25 or 50 percent of usual capacity.
Source: SafetySign.com

Some observers equated crowding with urban density and decried the risks of density. However, crowding is not the same as density. As urban planner Brent Toderian pointed out, "Density is generally used as a measure of how many people live and work on how much land, or how much building space is in an area. Crowding is literally how close everyone is to each other at a given time and place. You can have density without crowding, and you can have crowding without density."[11] Studies found that although larger cities initially had higher rates of COVID, density did not independently predict infection incidence, perhaps because city residents were more able or willing to socially distance, wear masks, and otherwise take protective actions.[12,13] Residents of compact neighborhoods reduced their shopping trips more than did residents of suburban and rural areas—perhaps because of greater ability to "trip-stack," greater availability of delivery services, or greater willingness to observe stay-at-home guidelines.[13] When COVID-19 struck, Taipei, Auckland, and Berlin fared far better than New York, London, and Lima, not because they are less dense, but because of more effective policies and behavioral changes to control disease spread.[14] Moreover, density could even be protective, as dense urban neighborhoods can be quite resilient. "Barring supply chain collapse," wrote Ben Holland of the Rocky Mountain Institute, "they far outperform suburban communities in their access to food and other critical needs during crises."[15]

Clearly, although crowded places can be a risk factor for COVID, density is not destiny. Well-designed dense cities, with broad sidewalks, parks, and public spaces, provide enough room to enable people to avoid crowding. Effective leadership and social and behavioral factors play very large roles as well, sometimes eclipsing the effects of density. People will always want to gather, so future design of buildings and communities, mindful that disease outbreaks will recur, will need to incorporate ways to reduce close person-to-person contacts when needed and to facilitate risk reduction through behavioral changes.

Poverty and Racism

Poverty and racism are generally viewed more as social than as environmental factors. But societal and market forces concentrate poor people and people of minority racial and ethnic backgrounds in particular neighborhoods, and these neighborhoods often suffer from poor health—hence the observation that "your zip code determines your health more than your genetic code"[16,17] (see chapter 9). Throughout the COVID-19 pandemic, the risk of infection and the risk of dying were differentially distributed across neighborhoods within cities, and both poverty and racial/ethnic minority status emerged as key determinants of risk. In a study of 158 counties in ten US metropolitan

areas with early COVID-19 surges, the higher the proportion of the non-White population, the higher the incidence and mortality from COVID-19—a gradient that was steeper in poorer counties.[18] A census-tract level study in Louisiana found that people in the most deprived neighborhoods had almost a 40 percent higher risk of contracting COVID-19 than those in the least deprived neighborhoods.[19] Similar results were found almost everywhere neighborhood risk was studied.

What accounts for this geographic variation? Worse baseline health, worse health care access, and fewer available ICU beds in high-risk neighborhoods all likely contributed.[20] More crowded housing, precluding people from distancing from each other, likely played a role.[21] Importantly, high-risk neighborhoods were more likely to be home to frontline and essential workers: delivery workers, grocery store clerks, nursing home aides, and others whose jobs entail contact with the public, who were unable to work from home, and who often had to commute by public transit.[22] The defining characteristics of COVID-19 "hot spot" neighborhoods varied from city to city; in New York City, the concentration of frontline workers was the strongest predictor, whereas in Chicago, the levels of poverty, unemployment, and Black residents were more predictive.[23] But the general pattern of COVID-19 risk disparities by neighborhood, reflecting "upstream" social determinants of health, was a stark reminder that persistent inequities map to the built environment and require wide-ranging political, economic, and social solutions.[24,25]

Poor Air Circulation

If the air in an indoor space is poorly circulated, especially if the space is crowded and if people do not use masks, the risk of exposure to airborne aerosols increases.[26] Accordingly, recommendations from professional societies and governments worldwide include increasing the supply of outdoor air, limiting air recirculation, increasing air filtration, maintaining exhaust ventilation in areas such as kitchens, and using ultraviolet germicidal irradiation in some circumstances.[27,28] Although some measures, such as opening windows, cost little or nothing, major improvements to heating, ventilation, and air-conditioning (HVAC) systems can be quite expensive to install and operate. Moreover, current HVAC systems are designed to manage temperature, humidity, and contaminant levels under nonpandemic conditions; modifying them to deliver very large volumes of clean air could be inefficient, energy-consuming, and costly. As a result, some have suggested that new HVAC paradigms are needed. Examples include supplying personal ventilation directly to people's individual breathing zones (say, at their worksta-

tions) instead of ventilating the entire interior building space (figure 26.2)[29] and using "precision HVAC" based on localized monitoring and artificial intelligence guidance.[30]

Air Pollution

A fourth aspect of the built environment that can increase risk of COVID is air pollution. Within months of the initial outbreak of COVID-19, evidence emerged linking higher ambient levels of fine particular matter and oxides of nitrogen with increased risk of COVID—both of contracting the disease and of disease severity and death.[31] Within cities, neighborhoods near such sources as roadways and waste facilities—where residents are disproportionately poor and members of minor-

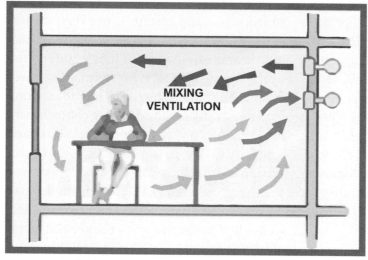

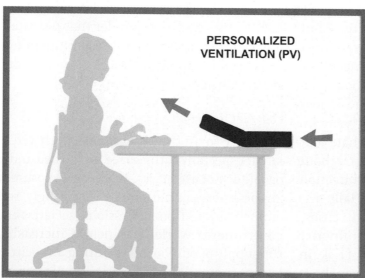

Figure 26.2. Conventional ventilation (top) versus personalized ventilation (bottom). Ventilating an entire room requires more energy, is costlier, and may offer less protection from infection than delivering fresh air directly to people's breathing zones.
Source: From Melikov, AK. COVID-19: Reduction of airborne transmission needs paradigm shift in ventilation. *Building and Environment.* 2020;186:107336. With permission from Elsevier.

ity groups—were at particular risk, helping explain part of the excess risk of COVID-19 seen in these populations. Conversely, the economic slowdown triggered by the pandemic, with drastic reductions in traffic and other pollution sources, delivered some of the cleanest urban air in memory in some of the world's most polluted cities (figure 26.3).[32] People in cities in North India could see the Himalayas for the first time in their lives—an inspiration, for the postpandemic recovery, for people inured to poor air quality. There were already many reasons to reduce ambient air pollution (see chapter 4), but reducing the risk of COVID-19 reinforced this health and environmental mandate.

Figure 26.3. Daytime views of the India Gate in Delhi on October 17, 2019 (top) and on April 8, 2020, during the pandemic (bottom). Air quality improved dramatically in many cities around the world.
Source: Staff/Reuters/Newscom. In: Bourzac K. 2020. COVID-19 lockdowns had strange effects on air pollution across the globe. *Chemical and Engineering News.* September 25, 2020.

POTENTIAL LONG-TERM IMPLICATIONS OF COVID-19 FOR THE BUILT ENVIRONMENT

The COVID-19 pandemic led to a wide range of adaptive changes in the built environment, from the scale of buildings to the scale of entire cities. Although the pandemic was tragic and destructive, some of the responses had great appeal and could be promising models for long-term use: repurposing streets for pedestrians and cyclists, reinforcing the use of parks, improved urban air quality through reduced driving. Other changes, such as relocation from cities to suburbs and rural areas, are more complex and nuanced, and their long-term implications are unclear.

Infection-Safe Buildings

As discussed earlier, building HVAC systems can help provide clean air and reduce the risk of infection. But this is not the only building design strategy that could emerge as a long-term legacy of the COVID-19 pandemic. Building features that permit physical distancing can help reduce airborne transmission and may offer additional health and well-being benefits. One example is wider hallways and staircases: even in nonpandemic times, more attractive stairways can encourage the use of stairs, which promotes physical activity (albeit sometimes at an incremental cost). Similarly, design elements such as personal balconies and shared courtyards allow people to get outside and to socialize while maintaining distance; these can provide nature contact and exemplify "density done right" that is appealing and functional even when there is no pandemic.[33]

Working from Home

COVID-19 brought a large-scale shift to working from home instead of the office, for those whose jobs permitted it. Will this persist? One view holds that employees will want to continue to work in offices, drawn by social interaction, a professional working environment, and the chance to separate home life from work life (figure 26.4). But the pandemic led to a reimagining of the role of the office. Future offices might have fewer people working in them at the same time, with people working from home one or two days per week, but the

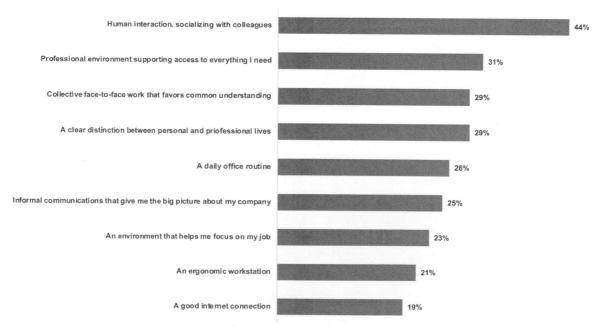

Figure 26.4. What employees miss most about being in the office. Results of a May 2020 survey of 3,000 respondents across North America, Europe, and Asia several months into the COVID-19 pandemic.
Source: JLL Human Performance Survey, May 2020

offices would remain central to work life, perhaps maximizing their appeal and value by offering amenities such as more space per person, learning and development opportunities, entertainment, food, and fitness facilities.[34]

An opposing view holds that companies will emerge from the COVID pandemic realizing that their employees accomplish much when working from home and that the companies can save money by downsizing their offices. Moreover, as one commentator wrote, "People don't really want to get back to the office.... The commute will still be long; there will still be too many meetings and time-sucks; it'll still feel like a mad rush to get out the door in the morning or get dinner on the table at night."[35] There is evidence that many employees would embrace working from home. In a Pew Research Center survey in October 2020 among employees who said that their job responsibilities could be carried out at home, 54 percent said that they would want to work from home after the COVID-19 pandemic had ended.[36] Another survey by the consulting firm PwC, in early June 2020, found that 83 percent of workers wanted to continue working from home after the pandemic at least one day a week, including 32 percent who wanted to do so full-time—responses that remained stable in a follow-up survey in late 2020.[37] Employers may be equally keen to promote teleworking, if employees are just as productive (or more so) and happier when working from home and if the employers can save money by reducing the amount of office space they require. As the pandemic evolved, major employers such as Facebook and Twitter announced plans for large-scale permanent shifts toward teleworking.[38,39] But this was not just a tech sector or a Silicon Valley phenomenon; traditional heartland firms also embraced teleworking. Nationwide Insurance substantially downsized major office hubs in central Ohio, Des Moines, Scottsdale, and San Antonio and permanently closed offices in Gainesville, Raleigh, Richmond, and elsewhere.[40] The demand for office space may fall substantially.[41]

The growth of teleworking, and its impacts, will vary by location, economic sector, and earning level. Higher-paid workers have more flexibility to work from home than those lower on the economic ladder.[36] Increased teleworking may disproportionately burden women, who shoulder substantially more child care responsibilities than do men—a disparity that was on full display during the pandemic.[42] Wealthy and low-income nations also differ, with estimates suggesting that about one in three US workers, but only about one in eight workers in poor countries, are able to work from home.[43-45]

This shift could have far-reaching consequences. Reduced commuting could reduce energy use and air pollution in metro areas, although some of the energy savings are countered by increased home energy use and non-work travel.[46] If more teleworking reduces the daytime population in city business districts, businesses that serve office workers, from restaurants to bookstores to fitness clubs, could suffer. A shift from office-based work to home-based work could drive demand for home office space—through larger homes or through more flexible design.

Working from home also has occupational health implications (see chapter 13). For example, media reports during the early months of COVID-19 noted that when people switched from ergonomic office furniture at work to long hours on laptops on their home sofas, beds, and kitchen counters, complaints of musculoskeletal strain and symptoms rose.[47] The market for safer home office furniture may expand.

Reenvisioned Streets

As COVID-19 exploded during the first half of 2020, travel demand plummeted, and traffic on city streets fell precipitously. Meanwhile, people confined to their homes yearned to get outdoors for relief, seeking fresh air and physical activity. Conventional sidewalks became crowded and were too narrow to permit people to maintain distance from one another. In response, many cities closed streets to traffic and designated them for walking and cycling, outdoor dining, and even classes. Bogotá's ciclovía, a 120-kilometer (75-mile) street network dedicated to cycling one day each week, expanded to seven days per week. Oakland, California, restricted vehicle access on 120 kilometers (75 miles) of its streets, or about 10 percent of its street network. Other cities, from Boston to Seattle to San Antonio, from Athens to Lima to Sydney, took similar steps—some intended to be permanent.[48] These alterations aimed not only to facilitate walking and cycling, but also to create spaces for outdoor dining, markets, and even school classes; to make room for people to queue up when entry to stores was limited; and to permit delivery vehicles to operate.[48]

City officials reported increased pedestrian use of the streets (figure 26.5). In Oakland, one observer wrote, "As if in an earlier era, small children are riding bikes in the middle of the street without their parents needing to worry."[49] In Frankfurt, when an 800-meter- (0.5-mile-) long stretch of the Mainkai riverfront was closed to vehicles, both utilitarian and recreational physical activity rose dramatically: a 45 percent increase in peak hour cycling, a 20 percent increase in peak hour walking, an 1,150 percent increase in children cycling independently, and a 25 percent increase in the presence of people with restricted mobility.[50] It remains to be seen how much such street reallocations find long-term favor with the public, planners, and city officials and how many of the changes outlast the COVID-19 pandemic.

Changing Modes of Travel

The COVID-19 pandemic brought a dramatic reduction in the use of mass transit as people both reduced their travel and shifted to other modes. Fear of infection displaced the usual leading criteria for choosing a travel mode—

Figure 26.5. Bayview Avenue, Toronto, during the COVID-19 pandemic in 2020. Once the street was closed to vehicles, pedestrian and bicycle activity substantially increased.
Source: Robin Pueyo

travel time, convenience, space and privacy, and cost—and became the most important factor.[51] In some transit systems, ridership fell by more than 90 percent.[52] Initially, some cities began running buses and trains at higher frequency while restricting the number of passengers on board. Some cities made transit riding free. Both approaches could have value in the long run, as higher frequency transit greatly increases convenience, and low prices incentivize transit use.

However, as low ridership devastated their revenues, transit systems came under intense financial pressure. Budget shortfalls across US transit systems collectively ran to the tens of billions of dollars. By several months into the pandemic, many transit systems were slashing their services and laying off staff. Reduced service forfeits many of the health and social benefits of transit (see chapter 11). Moreover, poor people and people of color, who account for a large share of transit riders in many cities, are disproportionately impacted.[53] A prolonged contraction of urban mass transit could be catastrophic. As one commentator wrote, "Without reliable public transit, a modern city simply cannot function properly. Students can't get to school, the majority of employees who can't do their job from home can't get to work, and retailers in central business districts are left hawking their merchandise along empty streets."[54]

Fortunately, studies suggest that COVID-19 transmission on buses, subways, and trains during the pandemic was relatively rare. Monitoring in cities such as Paris, Tokyo, and Milan attributed few if any outbreaks to transit use (1 percent of clusters in Paris, none in Tokyo or Milan), likely because riders were compliant with wearing masks. Taipei and Hong Kong, where transit ridership remained relatively high throughout the pandemic, did not suffer outbreaks related to transit use.[55,56] However, the use of transit relates as much to public confidence as to objective data.

As travel recovered after the first wave of COVID-19, automobile traffic increased far faster than transit ridership, in cities from São Paulo to Seattle to Sydney.[57] There was clearly a shift from transit to private automobiles[58]; time will tell whether, and to what extent, this shift persists.

Ride-share services such as Uber and Lyft also saw dramatic reductions in use during the pandemic as people worried about being in close quarters with strangers. Uber's bookings fell by as much as 80 percent compared to a year earlier.[57] However, bicycle use rose. Bike-share services saw substantial increases in use—by 100 percent in Seoul,[59] 150 percent in Beijing,[57] and 67 percent in New York[57]—although these figures fell in many cities during lockdowns. Bicycle purchases in the United States had doubled by April, two months into the pandemic,[57] perhaps portending long-term increases in cycling.

The future of travel after the pandemic is unclear. If transit systems confront residual financial pressure, there could be a "**transit death spiral**" of reduced service, deferred maintenance, and staffing shortfalls leading to decreased ridership. If, on the other hand, transit systems rebound (which will require significant government investments), transit ridership may well return to prepandemic levels. Shifts to walking and cycling during the pandemic may have staying power, especially in cities that make long-term improvements to infrastructure such as dedicated streets.

A New Appreciation for Green Space and Nature
During the pandemic, as activity and mobility were restricted, people around the world were drawn to natural features of the built environment, such as parks and trails—not a surprise, given the well-established restorative qualities of nature contact (chapter 16).[60,61] Although there were some barriers, such as park closures and fear of contacting other people,[62] visits to natural settings increased in many places. If public affinity for such places remains strong, the pandemic's long-lasting impact may include the creation of more parks

in urban areas, changes in park design such as wider paths to permit physical distancing, or better maintenance of existing parks[63] (see chapter 16, box 16.3).

A Shift from Cities to Exurbs and Rural Areas

Throughout history, people of means have fled cities to escape outbreaks of disease. Examples range from the British hill stations in colonial India[64] to the many Philadelphians who decamped to the Pennsylvania countryside during the 1793 yellow fever outbreak.[65] During the COVID-19 pandemic, many people departed cities as well. In mid-March 2020, two weeks after the first case of COVID-19 was confirmed in New York City, the *New York Times* reported a "panicked exodus" of wealthy New Yorkers to their second homes,[66] and by May 1, six weeks later, mobile phone tracking data revealed that hundreds of thousands of New Yorkers were gone; in some wealthy neighborhoods, more than 40 percent of residents had departed, presumably to second homes, to vacation rentals, and to stay with family or friends.[67]

But COVID-19 was different from historic waves of infectious disease. Those who left the city could work remotely thanks to the internet. They could shop using online retailers. They could access health care using telemedicine. They could remain in touch with loved ones, and their children could attend school, using Zoom—or children could attend local schools. Could the shift from cities to exurban and rural areas portend a long-term postpandemic trend?

Some evidence suggested an underlying inclination to depart large cities. A Gallup poll in 2018 asked Americans about their residential preferences. Forty percent lived in cities, but only 29 percent chose a city as their preferred setting; 31 percent lived in a town or a rural area, but 39 percent said they preferred such a setting.[68] In surveys by real estate companies several months into the pandemic, one-half to two-thirds of urban residents indicated that they would move out of the city if they could continue to telework.[69,70] However, evi-

dence was mixed as to whether a substantial migration occurred from cities to suburbs and rural areas; it may have been limited only to certain cities such as New York and San Francisco.[71]

How might the contours of cities change if COVID-19 does drive a shift out of large cities? Economists at the University of Southern California modeled the impact on US cities of large-scale postpandemic teleworking.[72,73] They predicted that many people would remain in cities, attracted by amenities such as restaurants and the arts, but that many others would relocate toward the suburbs and beyond, freed from the need to live near work and attracted by lower housing prices and lifestyle options. On balance, there would be a redistribution away from the urban core toward the periphery—with far-reaching consequences. Large coastal cities would shrink, and smaller cities away from the coasts would grow. Housing prices in large cities would fall, enabling more diverse urban populations. Businesses might distribute smaller satellite offices around a city or region in lieu of a single large headquarters. Traffic congestion would diminish, and commutes would ease. Some commercial real estate in cities, vacated by businesses, might be converted to residential space, easing current housing shortages—as proposed by the Real Estate Board of New York.[74]

After the pandemic, according to many commentators, cities would rebound. "Cities have been the epicenters of infectious disease since the time of Gilgamesh," wrote urbanist Richard Florida, "and they have always bounced back—often stronger than before."[75] *New York Times* columnist Farhad Manjoo pointed out that COVID-19 had in no way diminished the rationale for cities, that cities are "indispensable as engines of economic growth, catalysts of technological and cultural innovation … and … one of the most environmentally sustainable ways we know of for housing lots of people." In fact, Manjoo continued, "Not only are cities worth saving, they are also ripe for rebirth."[76]

CONCLUSION

Indeed, the COVID-19 pandemic unleashed a flood of aspirational proposals for that rebirth—for "built back better" postpandemic buildings, neighborhoods, and cities.[75,77,78] Architects called for innovative building design features to reduce disease transmission[4] and for designing homes with swing space to accommodate both living and working.[79] Conservationists called for more urban parks and green space and for nature-based solutions.[80] Transportation planners called for rethinking streets, trading automobile-centered design for the "complete streets" that had proven their value during the pandemic.[48] Clean air advocates strategized about extending some of the pandemic-related reductions in polluting activities to prolong the air quality benefits.[81]

Social justice advocates called for correcting historical injustices in the built environment that contributed to health inequities. "The post-COVID-19 response," wrote Maimunah Mohd Sharif, executive director of the United Nations Human Settlements Programme, "will require these failures to be addressed and all urban residents provided with basic services—especially health care and housing—to ensure everyone can live with dignity and be prepared for the next global crisis."[75]

Technology enthusiasts pointed to the enormous potential for innovative technologies and data to improve health, service delivery, commerce, and social connectedness in cities.[82] Disaster planners noted the need to build resilience, not only to future pandemics, but to a range of disasters[79] (see chapter 18). They cited some surprising lessons from COVID-19; for example, after home confinement brought a tragic increase in domestic violence,[83] will future building standards require locks on interior doors? Will homes include more capacity to stockpile food and supplies or to deliver diagnostic and treatment services such as cardiac monitoring? Neal Gorenflo, an advocate of "shareable cities," argued that post-COVID cities should become more self-governing (more independent of state and national gov-ernments), more self-sufficient financially and materially, more democratic (with residents more engaged in urban governance), and better at cooperating and sharing resources with each other.[84]

Overall, the pandemic recovery offers a panoply of lessons, which will continue to emerge for years. It also offers a historic opportunity—to ground placemaking firmly in human needs, justice, and environmental sustainability; to adopt indicators and metrics that reflect those priorities; to improve the efficiency and fairness of urban governance; and to harness emerging technology to make healthier, more sustainable, and more resilient places than ever before.[85]

DISCUSSION QUESTIONS

1. How would you distinguish urban density from crowding? How would you explain this distinction to a mayor? A health commissioner? A business owner? A worried parent?

2. Research at the neighborhood level showed a link between a history of redlining and being hard hit by COVID-19. Give at least three reasons that could explain this association.

3. What transportation policies might you recommend that could draw on the COVID-19 experience to promote health, clean air, and other benefits?

4. How did the pandemic affect commercial real estate demand and prices in your city? What follow-on impacts did this have?

5. What are the advantages and disadvantages of working from home? What design strategies, in both offices and homes, can accommodate greater teleworking and optimize the well-being of workers?

6. During a pandemic such as COVID-19, how would you advise the parks commissioner in your city to balance the need for infection control with the demand to be in parks?

ACKNOWLEDGMENT

This chapter was adapted from a published paper: Frumkin H. Covid-19, the built environment, and health. *Environmental Health Perspectives.* 2021;129(7):75001, doi:10.1289/EHP8888.

DISCLOSURE OF COMPETING INTERESTS

Howard Frumkin's declarations appear in the preface.

REFERENCES

1. Malani A, Shah D, Kang G, et al. Sero-prevalence of SARS-CoV-2 in slums versus non-slums in Mumbai, India. *The Lancet Global Health*. 2020.

2. Kotkin J. After the pandemic: how the coronavirus will change our lives for-ever—from music to politics to medicine. Not-so-mass transit. *Washington Post*. March 20, 2020. Accessed October 16, 2021. https://www.washingtonpost.com /outlook/2020/03/20/what-will-have -changed-forever-after-coronavirus-abates

3. McDonald R, Spotswood E. Cities are not to blame for the spread of COVID-19—nor is the demise of cities an appropriate response. In: *The Nature of Cities*. April 14, 2020. Accessed October 16, 2021. https: //www.thenatureofcities.com/2020/04 /14/cities-are-not-to-blame-for-the -spread-of-covid-19-nor-is-the-demise-of -cities-an-appropriate-response/

4. Megahed NA, Ghoneim EM. Antivirus-built environment: lessons learned from Covid-19 pandemic. *Sustainable Cities and Society*. 2020;61:102350.

5. Leclerc QJ, Fuller NM, Knight LE, Funk S, Knight GM. What settings have been linked to SARS-CoV-2 transmission clus-ters? *Wellcome Open Research*. 2020;5:83.

6. Yip TL, Huang Y, Liang C. Built environ-ment and the metropolitan pandemic: analysis of the COVID-19 spread in Hong Kong. *Building and Environment*. 2020;107471.

7. Emeruwa UN, Ona S, Shaman JL, et al. Associations between built environment, neighborhood socioeconomic status, and SARS-CoV-2 infection among preg-nant women in New York City. *JAMA*. 2020;324(4):390-392.

8. von Seidlein L, Alabaster G, Deen J, Knudsen J. Crowding has consequences: prevention and management of COVID-19 in informal urban settlements. *Building and Environment*. 2020:107472.

9. Kadi N, Khelfaoui M. Population density, a factor in the spread of COVID-19 in Algeria: statistic study. *Bulletin of the National Research Centre*. 2020;44(1):138.

10. Lall S, Wahba S. Cities, crowding, and the coronavirus: predicting contagion risk hotspots. In: *World Bank Blogs—Sustainable Cities*. World Bank. Published April 23, 2020. Accessed October 16, 2021. https: //blogs.worldbank.org/sustainablecities /cities-crowding-and-coronavirus -predicting-contagion-risk-hotspots

11. Toderian B. Dear Gov. Cuomo, the problem is crowding, not "density"! In: *StreetsBlog NYC*. Posted April 6, 2020. Accessed October 16, 2021. https://nyc .streetsblog.org/2020/04/06/op-ed-dear -gov-cuomo-the-problem-is-crowding -not-density/

12. Hamidi S, Sabouri S, Ewing R. Does Den-sity Aggravate the COVID-19 Pandemic? *Journal of the American Planning Association*. 2020;86(4):495-509.

13. Hamidi S, Zandiatashbar A. Compact development and adherence to stay-at-home order during the COVID-19 pandemic: a longitudinal investigation in the United States. *Landscape and Urban Planning*. 2021;205:103952.

14. Bai X, Nagendra H, Shi P, Liu H. Cities: build networks and share plans to emerge stronger from COVID-19. *Nature*. 2020;584(7822):517-520.

15. Holland B. Coronavirus and the fragility of auto-centric cities. Rocky Mountain Institute. Published April 13, 2020. Accessed October 16, 2021. https: //rmi.org/coronavirus-and-the-fragility -of-auto-centric-cities/

16. Williams DR, Collins C. Racial residential segregation: a fundamental cause of racial disparities in health. *Public Health Reports*. 2001;116(5):404-416.

17. Diez Roux AV, Mair C. Neighborhoods and health. *Annals of the New York Academy of Sciences.* 2010;1186:125-145.

18. Adhikari S, Pantaleo NP, Feldman JM, Ogedegbe O, Thorpe L, Troxel AB. Assessment of community-level disparities in coronavirus disease 2019 (COVID-19) infections and deaths in large US metropolitan areas. *JAMA Network Open.* 2020;3(7):e2016938.

19. KC M, Oral E, Straif-Bourgeois S, Rung AL, Peters ES. The effect of area deprivation on COVID-19 risk in Louisiana. *PLOS ONE.* 2020;15(12):e0243028.

20. Arasteh K. Prevalence of comorbidities and risks associated with COVID-19 among Black and Hispanic populations in New York City: an examination of the 2018 New York City Community Health Survey. *Journal of Racial and Ethnic Health Disparities.* 2020;1-7.

21. Baidal JW, Wang AY, Zumwalt K, et al. Social determinants of health and COVID-19 among patients in New York City. *Research Square.* 2020;rs.3.rs-70959. doi:10.21203/rs.3.rs-70959/v1

22. Do DP, Frank R. Unequal burdens: assessing the determinants of elevated COVID-19 case and death rates in New York City's racial/ethnic minority neighbourhoods. *Journal of Epidemiology and Community Health.* 2021;75:321-26.

23. Maroko AR, Nash D, Pavilonis BT. COVID-19 and inequity: a comparative spatial analysis of New York City and Chicago hot spots. *Journal of Urban Health.* 2020;97(4):461-470.

24. Naik Y, Baker P, Ismail SA, et al. Going upstream—an umbrella review of the macroeconomic determinants of health and health inequalities. *BMC Public Health.* 2019;19(1):1678.

25. Johnson-Agbakwu CE, Ali NS, Oxford CM, Wingo S, Manin E, Coonrod DV. Racism, COVID-19, and health inequity in the USA: a call to action. *Journal of Racial and Ethnic Health Disparities.* 2020;1-7.

26. Bhagat RK, Davies Wykes MS, Dalziel SB, Linden PF. Effects of ventilation on the indoor spread of COVID-19. *Journal of Fluid Mechanics.* 2020;903.

27. Guo M, Xu P, Xiao T, He R, Dai M, Miller SL. Review and comparison of HVAC operation guidelines in different countries during the COVID-19 pandemic. *Building and Environment.* 2021;187:107368.

28. Morawska L, Tang JW, Bahnfleth W, et al. How can airborne transmission of COVID-19 indoors be minimised? *Environment International.* 2020;142:105832-105832.

29. Melikov AK. COVID-19: Reduction of airborne transmission needs paradigm shift in ventilation. *Building and Environment.* 2020;186:107336-107336.

30. Ding J, Yu CW, Cao S-J. HVAC systems for environmental control to minimize the COVID-19 infection. *Indoor and Built Environment.* 2020;29(9):1195-1201.

31. Copat C, Cristaldi A, Fiore M, et al. The role of air pollution (PM and NO(2)) in COVID-19 spread and lethality: a systematic review. *Environmental Research.* 2020;191:110129.

32. Liu F, Wang M, Zheng M. Effects of COVID-19 lockdown on global air quality and health. *Science of the Total Environment.* 2021;755(Pt 1):142533.

33. Roberts D. How to make a city liveable during lockdown. In: *Vox.* Published April 22, 2020. Accessed October 16, 2021. https://www.vox.com/cities-and-urbanism/2020/4/13/21218759/coronavirus-cities-lockdown-covid-19-brent-toderian

34. Ulbrich C. Why global cities will flourish in a post-COVID future. World Economic Forum. Published August 26 2020. Accessed October 16, 2021. https://www.weforum.org/agenda/2020/08/future-of-cities-covid-19/

35. Petersen AH. Are you sure you want to go back to the office? The future of work is flexibility. *New York Times.* December 23, 2020.

36. Parker K, Horowitz JM, Minkin R. *How the Coronavirus Outbreak Has—and Hasn't—Changed the Way Americans Work.* Pew Research Center. 2020.

37. PwC Research and Insights. US Remote Work Survey. Results published June 25, 2020, and January 12, 2021. Accessed October 16, 2021. https://www.pwc.com/us/en/library/covid-19/us-remote-work-survey.html

38. Conger K. Facebook starts planning for permanent remote workers. *New York Times.* May 21, 2020.

39. Dwoskin E. Americans might never come back to the office, and Twitter is leading the charge. *Washington Post.* October 1, 2020.

40. Smith R. Nationwide announces permanent shift to work-from-home. *Insurance Business.* April 30, 2020. Accessed October 16, 2021. https://www.insurancebusinessmag.com/us/news/breaking-news/nationwide-announces-permanent-shift-to-workfromhome-221148.aspx

41. Fulton W. How the COVID-19 pandemic will change our cities. *Urban Edge.* March 29, 2020. https://kinder.rice.edu/urbanedge/2020/03/30/how-covid-19-pandemic-will-change-our-cities

42. Bateman N, Ross M. Why has COVID-19 been especially harmful for working women? Brookings Institution. Brookings Gender Equality Series website. Published October 2020. Accessed October 16, 2021. https://www.brookings.edu/essay/why-has-covid-19-been-especially-harmful-for-working-women/

43. ILO. *Working from Home: Estimating the Worldwide Potential.* International Labour Organization; 2020.

44. Dingel JI, Neiman B. How many jobs can be done at home? *Journal of Public Economics.* 2020;189:104235-104235.

45. Saltiel F. Who can work from home in developing countries? *Covid Economics.* 2020;7:104-118.

46. Hook A, Court V, Sovacool BK, Sorrell S. A systematic review of the energy and climate impacts of teleworking. *Environmental Research Letters.* 2020;15(9): 093003.

47. Wilser J. The pandemic of work-from-home injuries. *New York Times.* September 4, 2020.

48. National Association of City Transportation Officials (NACTO). *Streets for Pandemic Response & Recovery.* NACTO and Global Designing Cities Initiative; 2020.

49. Bliss L. Drivers not wanted on Oakland's "Slow Streets." *Bloomberg CityLab.* April 17, 2020. Accessed October 16, 2021. https://www.bloomberg.com/news/articles/2020-04-17/how-oakland-made-pedestrian-friendly-slow-streets

50. Pandit L, Fauggier GV, Gu L, Knöll M. How do people use Frankfurt Mainkai riverfront during a road closure experiment? A snapshot of public space usage during the coronavirus lockdown in May 2020. *Cities & Health.* 2020:1-20. doi:10.1080/23748834.2020.1843127

51. McKinsey and Co. Five COVID-19 aftershocks reshaping mobility future. McKinsey Center for Future Mobility. September 17, 2020. Accessed October 16, 2021. https://www.mckinsey.com/industries/automotive-and-assembly/our-insights/five-covid-19-aftershocks-reshaping-mobilitys-future

52. Liu L, Miller HJ, Scheff J. The impacts of COVID-19 pandemic on public transit demand in the United States. *PLOS ONE.* 2020;15(11):e0242476.

53. Clark HM. *Who Rides Public Transportation? Passenger Demographics and Travel.* American Public Transportation Association; 2017.

54. Thompson D. What will happen to cities in 2021. *The Atlantic;* December 9, 2020. Accessed October 16, 2021. https://www.theatlantic.com/ideas/archive/2020/12/the-2021-post-pandemic-prediction-palooza/617332/

55. Sadik-Khan J, Solomonow S. Fear of public transit got ahead of the evidence. *The Atlantic*. June 14, 2020. Accessed October 16, 2021. https://www.theatlantic.com/ideas/archive/2020/06/fear-transit-bad-cities/612979/

56. Joselow M. There is little evidence that mass transit poses a risk of coronavirus outbreaks. *E&E News*; July 28, 2020.

57. Bliss L, Lin JCF, Patino M. Pandemic travel patterns hint at our urban future. *Bloomberg CityLab*. June 18, 2020.

58. Olin A. Public transit has lost its momentum during the pandemic. Can it be regained? *Urban Edge*; August 5, 2020. Accessed October 16, 2021. https://kinder.rice.edu/urbanedge/2020/08/05/coronavirus-pandemic-houston-metro-public-transit-ridership

59. Park S, Kim B, Lee J. Social distancing and outdoor physical activity during the COVID-19 outbreak in South Korea: Implications for physical distancing strategies. *Asia Pacific Journal of Public Health*. 2020; 32(6-7):360-362. doi:10.177/1010539520940929

60. Kleinschroth F, Kowarik I. COVID-19 crisis demonstrates the urgent need for urban green spaces. *Frontiers in Ecology and the Environment*. 2020;18(6):318-319.

61. Slater SJ, Christiana RW, Gustat J. Recommendations for keeping parks and green space accessible for mental and physical health during COVID-19 and other pandemics. *Preventing Chronic Disease*. 2020;17:200204.

62. Payne R. Will the COVID-19 outbreak propel the demand for active spaces or scare the public away? *Cities & Health*. 2020;1-4. doi:10.1080/23748834.2020.1790259

63. Lennon M. Green space and the compact city: planning issues for a "new normal." *Cities & Health*. 2020;1-4.

64. Kennedy D. *The Magic Mountains: Hill Stations and the British Raj*. University of California Press; 1996.

65. Powell JH. *Bring Out Your Dead: The Great Plague of Yellow Fever in Philadelphia in 1793*. University of Pennsylvania Press; 1949.

66. Bellafante G. The rich have a coronavirus cure: escape from New York. *New York Times*. March 14, 2020.

67. Quealy K. The richest neighborhoods emptied out most as coronavirus hit New York City. *New York Times*. May 15, 2020.

68. Americans big on idea of living in the country [press release]. Gallup; December 7, 2018.

69. Redfin. Post-pandemic migration from expensive cities likely as 1 in 4 newly remote employees expect work-from-home to continue [press release]. May 15, 2020. Accessed October 16, 2021. https://www.redfin.com/news/wfh-leaving-new-york-san-francisco/

70. Zillow. A rise in remote work could lead to a new suburban boom [press release]. May 13, 2020. Accessed October 16, 2021. http://zillow.mediaroom.com/2020-05-13-A-Rise-in-Remote-Work-Could-Lead-to-a-New-Suburban-Boom#assets_28775_137595-135

71. Patino M. What we actually know about how Americans are moving during Covid. *Bloomberg CityLab*; 2020.

72. Delventhal MJ, Kwon E, Parkhomenko A. How do cities change when we work from home? *Journal of Urban Economics*. 2021. doi:10.1016/j.jue.2021.103331

73. Delventhal MJ, Parkhomenko A. Spatial implications of telecommuting. Centre for Economic Policy Research, COVID Economics Vetted and Real-Time Papers 61-4. December 2020. Accessed October 16, 2021. https://cepr.org/sites/default/files/CovidEconomics61.pdf

74. Haag M, Rubinstein D. Midtown is reeling. Should its offices become apartments? *New York Times*. December 11, 2020. Accessed October 16, 2021. https://www.nytimes.com/2020/12/11/nyregion/nyc-commercial-real-estate.html

75. Florida R, Glaeser E, Sharif MM, et al. How life in our cities will look after the coronavirus pandemic. *Foreign Policy.* May 1, 2020. Accessed October 16, 2021. https://foreignpolicy.com/2020/05/01/future-of-cities-urban-life-after-coronavirus-pandemic/

76. Manjoo F. Why should we ever return to living and working so close together? *New York Times.* December 20, 2020. Accessed October 16, 2021. https://www.nytimes.com/2020/12/22/opinion/cities-coronavirus.html

77. Bloomberg City Lab. How the coronavirus recovery is changing cities. *Bloomberg City Lab.* June 22, 2020. https://www.bloomberg.com/features/2020-city-in-recovery/

78. Holland O. Our cities may never look the same again after the pandemic. *CNN.* May 9, 2020.

79. Keenan JM. COVID, resilience, and the built environment. *Environment Systems and Decisions.* 2020;40(2):216-221.

80. Allen W. Nature in cities in a post-Covid-19 world: don't blame urban density in a pandemic. *The Nature of Cities.* September 3, 2020. Accessed October 16, 2021. https://www.thenatureofcities.com/2020/09/03/nature-in-cities-in-a-post-covid-19-world-dont-blame-urban-density-in-a-pandemic/

81. De Vito L, Barnes J, Longhurst J, Williams B, Hayes E. The legacy of COVID-19: lessons and challenges for city-scale air quality management in the UK. *Cities & Health.* 2020;1-4. doi:10.1080/23748834.2020.1796422

82. Acuto M. Will COVID-19 make us think of cities differently? *NewCities.* March 20, 2020. Accessed October 16, 2021. https://newcities.org/the-big-picture-will-covid-19-make-us-think-cities-differently

83. Moreira DN, Pinto da Costa M. The impact of the Covid-19 pandemic in the precipitation of intimate partner violence. *International Journal of Law and Psychiatry.* 2020;71:101606.

84. Gorenflo N. What COVID-19 suggests for the future of sharing cities. Shareable website. Published 2020. Updated October 13, 2020. Accessed October 16, 2021. https://www.shareable.net/the-future-of-sharing-cities-post-covid-19/

85. Tompkins S. 4 priorities for a better built environment in the post-COVID city. In: *COVID Action Platform.* World Economic Forum; 2020.

CHAPTER 27

HEALTHY, EQUITABLE, AND SUSTAINABLE BUILT ENVIRONMENTS FOR THE FUTURE

This book has explored a cornucopia of concepts and evidence about the built environment, across scales from buildings to neighborhoods to metropolitan areas. We have emphasized several key themes: how the places in which we live, work, study, and play affect our health through diverse pathways; the fundamental importance of equity and justice; the tightly linked priorities of health and environmental sustainability as we confront the climate emergency; the globalized world we inhabit, with Los Angeles, Lagos, and Lima differing in many respects but converging in many others; the promise and peril of new technologies alongside the wisdom of time-tested, human-centered principles of placemaking.

We want to close with a final theme: hope and aspiration. In today's world, news is often grim and public discourse often caustic. Confidence in public institutions is faltering, the social connections that sustain our society often seem frayed, and many of the places in which we spend time feel soulless. It is easy sometimes for hope to give way to despair.

But hope is essential. Despair breeds apathy and stasis; hope breeds engagement and action. In her book *Hope in the Dark*, writer Rebecca Solnit tells us that "hope is an ax you break down doors with in an emergency, because hope should shove you out the door." "Hope," she continues, "just means another

world might be possible, not promised, not guaranteed. Hope calls for action; action is impossible without hope." Solnit quotes German philosopher Ernst Bloch, whose three-volume *The Principle of Hope* is perhaps the definitive work on the subject: hope "requires people who throw themselves actively into what is becoming, to which they themselves belong."

In this final chapter, we have convened fifteen thinkers and doers at the forefront of making healthy places—people who have "thrown themselves actively into what is becoming." We selected and invited them based on their thought leadership and their diversity in personal backgrounds, expertise, sectors, and locations. They are planners, architects, and physicians. Some focus on housing, others on transportation, others on neighborhoods and parks. Some work with the "hardware" of places, some with the "software." Some work in wealthy settings, others in low-income settings. Together, they weave a tapestry of positive visions for built environments of the future. We hope this "panel discussion" (with the "panelists" appearing in alphabetical order) will inspire you, our reader, with hope and energize you to throw yourself into creating places throughout the world that are healthy, equitable, sustainable, and beautiful.

CALL TO ACTION: SIX CRITICAL DECISION AREAS

Professor Hugh Barton, Dip TP, MPhil, MRTPI, AoU

Emeritus Professor of Planning, Health and Sustainability

WHO Collaborating Centre for Healthy Urban Planning

University of the West of England

Bristol, United Kingdom

The global crises of ecology and climate and the huge disparities in health outcomes, linked to unequal environmental costs, air pollution, physical inactivity, obesity, and mental illness, can only be tackled by shifting dominant economic and spatial trajectories. There are six critical areas where public health and planning must shout from the rooftops, "If you want healthy, equitable, sustainable environments, you must act on these things!"

The first is property; the second is powers; the third, values; the fourth, systems; the fifth, location; and the sixth, place. In terms of *property*, private rights have to be balanced by full recognition of communal rights, especially where new or renewed development is concerned. This plays into the legal and financial *powers* of local authorities to plan integrated settlements, purchasing nonurban and underused land at below-market rates so that social and physical infrastructure can be provided. However, municipalities cannot act alone. Government departments, institutions, developers, financial bodies, and voluntary/community sectors all need to share essential *values* so that decisions are consistent and mutually reinforcing. This is the huge task of public health planning: to persuade everyone that healthy settlements—planning for the needs of rich and poor, old and young, Black and White, fast and slow, human and other species—matter profoundly for society and for Earth.

Healthy environments rely on *systems* thinking: the active recognition that spatial, social, economic, and ecological decisions are not isolated but part of whole system evolution. Natural and human systems are interdependent—urban and rural, transport and land use, green space and social space, pedestrian-priority and viable local facilities, all are linked. And in that context, the most crucial spatial decisions are about *location* and the broader spatial framework. If the location and structure of development are poor, disconnected, and unintegrated, no amount of quality design can compensate. It amounts to shutting the stable door after the horse has bolted. But equivalently, location is not enough. The bottom line is that the *places* where people live, love, work, learn, and play must be functional and attractive for users, inviting varied experience while providing spaces that feel safe.

In overview, what's good for individual health is also good for the planet. The key intervening variable is the human habitat. We need settlements that offer clean earth, air, water, and carbon-neutral energy; spatial and development strategies that provide excellent, equitable access to housing, jobs, food, facilities, and green space and nature; places that orient people toward healthy behavior, active travel, social engagement, and conviviality—places of pleasure and delight!

For further information: Barton H, Grant M, Guise R. *Shaping Neighbourhoods: For Local Health and Global Sustainability*. 3rd ed. Routledge; 2021.

BIOPHILIC CITIES

Timothy Beatley, PhD

Teresa Heinz Professor of Sustainable Communities

Department of Urban and Environmental Planning

University of Virginia School of Architecture

Charlottesville, Virginia

Imagine living in a neighborhood where you are immersed in nature: trees, parks, gardens, and green balconies drench your senses in a daily banquet of delightful sights, sounds, and smells. In this **biophilic city**, rooftops have become meadows, supporting birds, butterflies, and many other forms of life—an abundant and biodiverse urban nature. Even the facades of buildings have become beautiful vertical gardens and living walls. There is food growing nearby on rooftops and in urban orchards. Out your front door, the grocery store, your office, or your child's school are just a few minutes away by foot or bicycle; along the way, you wave to friends and stop to talk with neighbors. The city is sustainable and regenerative; solar panels and wind turbines supply your electricity, and even organic household waste becomes a source of energy for the city. The building you live in is designed to use energy and water sparingly, collecting and reusing rainwater, graywater, and even sewage, which is treated through a natural wetland system and eventually finds its way back to the drinkable water from your tap.

This is a neighborhood in a future that is at once good for you and good for the planet. It may seem a utopian and unrealistic vision. But around the world, cities are embracing just such transformations. From Milan to Bogotá, cities have repurposed streets from automobility toward walking, bicycling, and newer forms of micromobility. San Francisco's famous "parklets" are small green spaces and public seating areas in what used to be two or three on-street parking spaces. Singapore's Park Connectors network, 185 miles (300 kilometers) of pathways, many elevated at tree-canopy level, provides easy access to parks and larger natural areas but also itself offers delightful experiences of outdoor nature. Arlington County, Virginia, is supplementing its trail network with "casual use spaces," where people can bird-watch, stroll, and picnic. Seoul's new "skygarden," a former highway overpass, has been converted into a nearly 1-kilometer-long elevated walking path and arboretum, containing some twenty-four thousand trees and plants. The Sendero Verde housing project in East Harlem will have hundreds of affordable housing units, a school, and community space; in its nearly half-acre (0.2 hectare) green courtyard, crossed by a winding path that traces an old Lenape Indian trail, people will have places to garden, exercise, sit quietly, or perform onstage. These and countless other examples hold out the promise of cities that are at once ecologically restorative and highly livable, that are deeply enjoyable, beautiful, and equitable places to live—cities, in short, designed for human and planetary flourishing.

For further information: Biophilic Cities, https://www.biophiliccities.org/.

A REGENERATIVE AGENDA THAT PROMOTES HEALTH EQUITY FOR ALL

Rachel Hodgdon

President and CEO, International WELL Building Institute

Cochair, Paul Hawken's organization for Regeneration

Washington, DC

The global health crisis of COVID-19 has disrupted our society at every level. But it's also gifted us a rare opportunity to walk a different path: to reform and reframe our relationship with our planet and with each other and to allow us to envisage a world where everyone, everywhere, can enjoy their fair share—not as a function of privilege but as an inarguable human right.

It's a possibility we can't afford to squander. We must enthusiastically embrace the chance to radically reimagine the spaces around us, to acknowledge the significant role that buildings can play in driving health equity, and to invest in bold, regenerative development that enriches and elevates—rather than depletes and destroys—our precious ecosystems.

I believe this to be a goal that is firmly within our purview—but only if we're sufficiently ambitious. With vision and commitment, we can create accessible buildings that are designed and developed in synergy with their environment, that give more than they take, and that offer all who enter an opportunity to live the healthiest version of their lives—where no one is forgotten or forsaken. By focusing on the healthful intersection of people and planet, we can innovate spaces that establish the well-being of both as an urgent priority—spaces that incorporate healthier materials to improve indoor air quality while reducing environmental pollution, that inhale the clean air that enhances human cognition while exhaling air that benefits the atmosphere around us, and that employ daylight-

ing as an effective strategy to conserve energy while boosting performance and supporting restful, regenerative sleep.

It will take time to see the fruits of our labor, and we'll need to recruit fresh allies who not only share our vision, but who already expect more. I'm confident, though, that a second wave of **sustainability natives**—young people who have grown up immersed in the language and practice of sustainability and for whom sustainability comes naturally—is quietly but resolutely emerging: a youthful cohort with the spirit and imagination to change all our futures by demanding people-first places. These young idealists are fluent in the language of sustainability and intuitively make decisions to use what they need, not just take what they can. They understand that health and well-being are inextricably connected. They make an active choice to live in harmony with the planet, not in opposition to it, and they revere the earth that sustains all life, recognizing the abundance that exists for us all.

For further information: International Well Building Institute, https://www.wellcertified.com/.

ACHIEVING HEALTHY URBAN AFRICA: ADDRESSING THE CHALLENGE OF URBAN INFORMAL SETTLEMENTS

Professor Blessing Mberu, PhD

Senior Research Scientist and Head of Urbanization and Wellbeing Unit

African Population and Health Research Center

Nairobi, Kenya

Africa is the least urbanized and the fastest urbanizing region in the world. Urban Africa, with 472 million people, is projected to double its population by 2050. Productive jobs, affordable housing, and efficient infrastructure are urgently needed. However, urban infrastructure development is lagging, and urban poverty is growing along with massive slum settlements. Slum dwellers face interconnected challenges: rapid social, economic, demographic, and epidemiological transitions; multiple intersecting health risks and vulnerabilities; and complex, fluid governance arrangements, often with a near absence of public services and/or neglect from state institutions. These conditions perpetuate socioeconomic, health, and well-being inequities, especially afflicting women, children, older people, migrants, and refugees.

But it is not all grime, gloom, and doom for slums and slum dwellers. Slums are places full of potential, rich in creativity, talent, and entrepreneurship. Slum dwellers are consumers who demand decent and affordable basic services such as housing and sanitation and strive for jobs or businesses that generate income for their families. They are a population ready for change and innovation and easy to be reached with interventions and opportunities. There is great potential for progress.

Evidence generation to guide policy and action must be prioritized. There is a deficit of data and scientific knowledge regarding slum health in Africa. Rigorous evidence is needed in national data systems and official statistics to make the slums visible and inform policies.

Maximizing the potential of slums will also require policies and actions critical to improving health for all. These extend beyond needed improvements in the health system. Success will also need to prioritize key investments in the social determinants of health, which will result ultimately in a built environment that actually improves people's lives. Real progress in achieving an urban Africa without slums will include massive investments in infrastructure, including water, sanitation, waste management, electricity, good roads and sidewalks, parks and green spaces, transit service, and healthy housing.

In addition to these infrastructure investments, social structures and development "software" are needed. These include economic opportunities that tap into local talent, engage youthful populations, utilize local raw materials, and build on abundant innovative spirits. Other precursors to success include good municipal governance, active civil society, social engineering toward gender equity, good school systems with functional curricula, enabling structures to access investment capital, and leveraging technology. These approaches build on the system dynamics modeling approaches of interdisciplinarity, transdisciplinarity, and intersectoral collaborations in addressing urban risks and development challenges. Together they can achieve a healthy urban Africa.

For further information: APHRC, Urbanization and Wellbeing in Africa, https://aphrc.org /runit/urbanization-and-wellbeing-in-africa/.

WE MUST BUILD CITIES FOR TRUST

Charles Montgomery, BSc

Author, *Happy City: Transforming Our Lives through Urban Design*

Vancouver, British Columbia

If you dropped your wallet or purse on the way to work today and a stranger found it, do you think you would get it back?

This may be the most important public health question of all. That's because almost nothing contributes more to the good life than social trust. People who say they trust other people are happier, healthier, and live longer than people who expect the worst in others. High-trust cities are more likely to bounce back from disasters. Ask enough people the lost wallet question, and you get a pretty good picture about the well-being of society as a whole.

Unfortunately, social trust has been strained in recent years. Surveys show that people—Americans in particular—are losing confidence in neighbors, strangers, and institutions. Anxiety and suspicion are on the rise. This crisis of social isolation reached a nadir during the coronavirus lockdowns of 2020. Loneliness spread like a toxic mist, disproportionately infecting elderly and single people.

The personal toll of this trust epidemic has been brutal, but the collective cost may be devastating, because if we don't place faith in the good intentions of others, we won't take the collective actions needed to solve the great challenges of our age.

Cities must be part of the solution, because they actively shape our relationships. Buildings, transportation systems, and public spaces all mediate our ability to experience positive, face-to-face encounters with other people.

We have now learned enough about the dynamics between trust and urban systems to set a course toward more social cities. We know, for example, that car-dominated sprawl steals people's time with family, friends, and neighbors. We know that children who grow up in walkable communities are more likely to climb the socioeconomic ladder, in part because of the chance encounters they have every day. And we are learning that neighbors develop deeper bonds when their homes are clustered in small social pods.

We also know that cities must rebuild trust with groups they have long marginalized. Black Americans, for example, have suffered from decades of planning practices that left their communities isolated and underinvested. This means that the path to the city of trust requires more than social design. It demands sincere co-creation with members of equity-seeking groups. And it demands reparative reinvestment.

The city of trust favors social spaces over iconic buildings by celebrity architects. It privileges complexity over simple solutions. It values lived experience over grand gestures. It nurtures relations rather than status. It acknowledges the simple truth that moments of connection between family, friends, and strangers produce the greatest joy of city life, but they are also the engine of urban resilience. High-trust places are always stronger in hard times.

By investing in social spaces and systems, we can nurture the relationships that keep us all healthy and happy in the long run.

For further information: The Happy City. https://thehappycity.com/.

A PEOPLE-BASED, HEALTHY, EQUITABLE, AND SUSTAINABLE TRANSPORTATION SYSTEM

Toks Omishakin, MURP, PhD

Director, California Department of Transportation (Caltrans)

Sacramento, California

In a world that is often blurred and ambiguous, more often gray than black and white, I know one undeniable exception: our urgent obligation to be stewards of the health and well-being of future generations. There is no gray area here.

I see this as a calling, a privilege we embrace when doing our part. Providing our families today and future generations with an equitable, sustainable, and safe existence rests directly in our hands. Only when this concept is embraced, invested in, and consistently acted upon will we have a society that is acceptable for all. We must create an accessible and equitable civilization designed for all people. To let this opportunity pass us by would be—in no uncertain terms—tragic.

These solutions we are seeking can often be found in the places and systems we create. In the transportation realm, I sum up our calling in three words: Put People First. Not vehicles, not highways, not infrastructure. Humans, flesh and blood, are our why. People are the reason we do anything and everything; their well-being is our purpose. If we start with the best interest of people—all people—as our default basis for transportation planning, the healthier future we envision will take shape.

We, the practitioners of the built environment, must embrace a philosophy encompassing equitable mixed housing, accessible transit, and increased Complete Streets and Slow Streets. Our dependence on vehicles will wane, while our utilization of varying forms of Active Transportation will become second nature. With significantly less money being spent on freeway expansion, the focus of funding should shift to rail, transit, tech-based mobility options, bicycling, and walking. We should increase our focus on improving the maintenance and operations of the existing systems. We know this will result in favorable ripple effects on our health, environment, the economy, and overall quality of life.

California has the largest transportation network in the United States. We are paying attention and shifting accordingly. We continue our fight for equity in all areas related to California's transportation system. Our Department of Transportation released, for the first time in its history, an Equity Statement with a "4Ps" implementation framework: *People* (a diverse workforce), *Programs and Projects* (that engage impacted and underserved communities), *Partnerships* (with minority-owned and disadvantaged businesses), and *Planet*. We created a new office on Race and Equity to ensure that all of our work is done through an aperture of equity. And we redirected $100 million in state highway maintenance funds to improve transit, walking, and biking opportunities while prioritizing underserved communities across the state. I believe our progress is not an aberration but instead a turning point that is benefiting people in our communities today.

We have the next generations in clear view. Our grandchildren are reliant on today's transportation engineers, planners, innovators, and government officials at every level. We must acknowledge and remedy the mistakes of the past and bequeath to our grandchildren a better nation, one that in some ways would look unfamiliar to previous generations.

Does this sound lofty? Yes. But our people deserve it, and we can achieve it.

For further information: Caltrans Sustainability, https://dot.ca.gov/programs/sustainability.

A KAIROS MOMENT FOR HEALTHY SUSTAINABLE CITIES: BECAUSE HEALTH DOES NOT TRICKLE DOWN FROM GOOD INTENTIONS

Tolullah Oni, MMBS, MPH (Epi), MMed, MD (Res)

Public health physician and Urban Epidemiologist

MRC Epidemiology Unit, University of Cambridge

Cambridge, United Kingdom

Research Initiative for Cities Health and Equity (RICHE)

School of Public Health and Family Medicine

University of Cape Town

Cape Town, South Africa

Achieving the Africa Union's Agenda 2063—including health and well-being, inclusive sustainable cities for thriving societies, and sustainable development—requires transformational change in African cities. But health does not trickle down from good intentions. We have a critical window of opportunity to reimagine Africa's fast-growing cities as spaces and places of well-being and sustainability. We need a health foresight approach that places health at the center of sustainable urban development.

My "UrbanBetter" vision is:

- By 2030, every urban development or infrastructure initiative in Africa proactively designs health and sustainability into cities.
- By 2063, youth are driving the revisioning of cities, bending the curve of the rising infectious and noncommunicable diseases burden through climate-resilient, healthy communities.

Operationalizing this vision requires increasing the supply of health from place and increasing the demand for healthy places and spaces ("approach" on the x-axis in figure 27.1), as well as creating research and practice/advocacy platforms as the acupuncture points informing and implementing action ("action platforms" on the y-axis).

Central to achieving this vision is partnership across boundaries of sector, disciplines and cities. Some of this work is well underway. AirQo, a partnership between Makerere University, Kampala City government, and the private sector, is expanding air quality monitoring across Ugandan cities (figure 27.1; box A). The African Development Bank is strongly featuring sustainability in its planning for inclusive health in post-COVID Africa (figure 27.1, box A). UrbanBetter, my learning and advocacy platform (https://urbanbetter.science/), is working to create a groundswell of young people to increase demand for healthy sustainable places (figure 27.1, box B). The Lagos Urban Development Initiative's Linear Park Project is focused on increasing parkland through wetland conservation, promotion of biking and bikeability, and climate-smart agriculture (figure 27.1, box B). African researchers are integrating health into urban policy in Cape Town, South Africa, and Douala, Cameroon, through intersectoral, transdisciplinary research (figure 27.1, box C). In the Ajegunle-Ikorodu community resilience project, the Lagos State Resilience Office, the University of Lagos, and community members are jointly developing a resilience action plan for the community, privileging indigenous knowledge and lived experiences (figure 27.1, box D).

But there is much more to be done. These innovative approaches should be normalized,

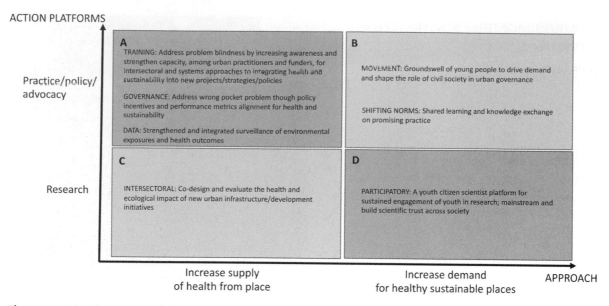

ACTION PLATFORMS

Practice/policy/ advocacy

A
TRAINING: Address problem blindness by increasing awareness and strengthen capacity, among urban practitioners and funders, for intersectoral and systems approaches to integrating health and sustainability into new projects/strategies/policies

GOVERNANCE: Address wrong pocket problem though policy incentives and performance metrics alignment for health and sustainability

DATA: Strengthened and integrated surveillance of environmental exposures and health outcomes

B
MOVEMENT: Groundswell of young people to drive demand and shape the role of civil society in urban governance

SHIFTING NORMS: Shared learning and knowledge exchange on promising practice

Research

C
INTERSECTORAL: Co-design and evaluate the health and ecological impact of new urban infrastructure/development initiatives

D
PARTICIPATORY: A youth citizen scientist platform for sustained engagement of youth in research; mainstream and build scientific trust across society

Increase supply
of health from place

Increase demand
for healthy sustainable places

APPROACH

Figure 27.1. The "UrbanBetter" vision, including increasing healthy place supply and demand, research, and practice/advocacy.
Source: UrbanBetter (https://urbanbetter.science)

coordinated, and implemented across the region. The African Union could champion health and sustainability, beyond just gross domestic product, as measures of successful development. National academies of science and the African Academy of Science could better integrate health and sustainability goals by supporting more intersectoral, transdisciplinary, multistakeholder research.

Change will take time, but not just chronological time. *Kairos*, an ancient Greek notion of time, refers not to a specific quantity of time, but to opportune time for transformative action. Moments of societal disruption offer a unique opportunity for radically particular action. Africa's young population and dynamic cities are well placed to catalyze and accelerate a reimagination of the "Urban," to embrace adaptive systemic change, and to place health at the center of sustainable, inclusive urban development. If only we are brave enough.

For further information: UrbanBetter, https://urbanbetter.science/.

SENSEABLE CITIES FOR HEALTH AND SUSTAINABILITY

Carlo Ratti, PhD

Professor of Urban Technologies and Planning

Director, SENSEable City Lab

Massachusetts Institute of Technology

Cambridge, Massachusetts

Founding Partner, CRA-Carlo Ratti Associati

Turin, Italy

How can we achieve a more *healthy, sustainable, and just built environment of the future?* To answer this question, we have to look closely at one of the most important phenomena going on today, the unprecedented convergence between the natural and artificial worlds—two poles that were long seen as opposite.

This convergence is happening in two ways. On one hand, we can capitalize on the increasing integration of digital technologies into the built environment, from sensors and actuators to artificial intelligence. We are already living in the "ubiquitous computing" scenario that was first foretold by computer scientist Mark Weiser in the mid-1990s, by which digital systems function quietly the background without us even noticing. In this digitized landscape, buildings and cities acquire some characteristics of living beings—above all, responsivity, namely the ability to adapt to the surrounding conditions in real time. Although this paradigm is often called "smart city," I prefer the name "senseable city," which highlights its capacities to sense through the use of digital technologies and be sensible to people and society's needs and desires.

On the other hand, we are seeing more and more projects incorporating natural elements into our cities. This can be done with the use of plants in buildings and the implementation of urban farming or through turning organic elements—from mycelium in fungi to lowly orange peels and coffee grounds—into full-fledged construction materials. In this way, a truly circular architecture is achieved. Buildings are born from the soil and then go back to it once they have run their course, without leaving any trace.

According to the "biophilia hypothesis" proposed by Harvard biologist Edward O. Wilson, humans possess an innate yearning to "affiliate with other forms of life." If we follow the trajectories indicated by the double convergence between the natural and artificial worlds, I believe we truly can pave the way for a senseable city that better responds to our needs for health and sustainability.

For further information: MIT Senseable City Lab, https://senseable.mit.edu/.

FROM COVID-19 TO A HEALTHIER BUILT ENVIRONMENT

Sagar Shah, PhD, AICP

Planning and Community Health Manager

American Planning Association

Chicago, Illinois

Globally, the years 2020–2021 pushed people to think and act differently due to COVID-19. In the United States, in addition to the public health crisis, the social justice movement across the country has raised questions about the existing systems and principles. The one question that has been posed to me several times in the last few months is, "How is the year 2020 going to affect and shape planning, in particular planning for health?" Although there are challenges, I see 2020 as a turning point and an opportunity to engage in much-needed transformation. I am optimistic about the path forward, and my vision of success is rooted in three existing trends.

First, technological advances and COVID-19 have together accelerated the digitization of life. Many employers will make telework a permanent arrangement. This trend would allow for the resulting empty spaces (office, parking, and so forth) to be retrofitted into green areas and affordable housing, thus improving access to these vital social determinants of health for historically overburdened communities.

Second, in light of present and past discriminatory incidents against Black and Indigenous people and people of color, including shootings—many of which happened in public spaces—the fundamental principles of public space design and management will change. The new norms will help create inclusive, healthy places that reflect the local community's culture and needs and promote design principles that invite everyone without being hostile to anyone.

Finally, during the pandemic, community support for infrastructure such as bike lanes and pedestrian-only streets that promote healthy lifestyles, which are often viewed as symbols of displacement, increased. Planners, policymakers, and elected officials will sustain this positive outlook of the community members and implement health-promoting policies and strategies such as an improved built environment without displacing existing residents.

This vision will be made possible by routine cross-sector collaboration between the built environment and health professions, community-based organizations, and elected officials. The pandemic years provided opportunity and momentum to plan for health and equity. We will build on this momentum by transforming our practice, coming together, and fighting health inequalities with everything we have. The good news is that we have done this before, as when we planned for resiliency post Hurricane Katrina, and we will do this again.

For further information: American Planning Association, Planning and Community Health, https://www.planning.org/nationalcenters/health/.

MY HOPE FOR THE FUTURE? PARKS WILL BECOME PART OF OUR HEALTH CARE SYSTEM

Mitchell J. Silver, FAICP, Hon. ASLA, Hon. RTPI, Hon. FPIA, FAcSS

Former commissioner, New York City Department of Parks and Recreation

Principal, Vice President of Urban Planning, McAdams

Raleigh, North Carolina

There is no question that 2020 will be a year for the history books. It was a year of extreme trauma, from a global pandemic that disrupted every social norm we've taken for granted to civil unrest that exposed centuries of racism to political chaos that unmasked domestic terrorism. Through it all, one place in our cities emerged as a sanctuary of sanity—our parks. When every gathering place was closed, our cherished green spaces remained open. I will never forget watching people enter Central Park where I worked as commissioner; I could literally see the stress drip off visitors as they entered the iconic green landscape. Whether people needed a place for physical health or mental well-being, nature was there to embrace them. So it should come as no surprise that as we venture in the next phase of the twenty-first century, parks will not be viewed as just nice amenities, but as vital infrastructure to help keep us sane, as landscapes that makes us feel alive, and as places that bring us joy and happiness. Our parks system should unquestionably be viewed as part of our health care system.

In the years following the 1918 pandemic, the United States experienced a renaissance of new parks and green spaces. But cities in the earlier part of the twentieth century were at the dawn of urbanization. Today, our cities are developed. Land for parks is expensive or targeted for other competing needs. The recent pandemic has awakened us to the value of parks as did the 1918 pandemic, but not everyone has access to a park. Underused elements of the public realm including streets, sidewalks, plazas, and other paved surfaces have come into sharper focus. The new frontier in the twenty-first century will be to reclaim the public realm for the people and to make it more green, accessible, and inclusive.

Parks are also democratic spaces for social cohesion where we welcome everyone regardless of race, ethnicity, income, or gender. The social unrest reminded many Americans of the generational trauma caused by systemic and institutional racism. Our parks and public spaces were reinforced as places to gather, to celebrate, to protest, to reflect, and to recharge. We need these spaces not only for physical health, but also for mental health. Like the theme of the children's book *The Giving Tree* by Shel Silverstein that I read to my daughter when she was a child, I have hope for the future because parks and green spaces will continue to give us what we need and ask for nothing in return—except that we nurture and care for them so that we can mutually co-exist in healthy harmony. We must ensure parks become part of our health care system.

For further information: New York City Department of Parks and Recreation https://www.nycgovparks.org/.

ARMED WITH KNOWLEDGE OF RECENT SUCCESSES, WE CAN REBUILD OUR CITIES FOR HEALTH

Bruce Stiftel, MRP, PhD, FAICP

Professor Emeritus of City and Regional Planning, Georgia Institute of Technology

Chair, Planners for Climate Action research working group, UN-Habitat

Atlanta, Georgia

It is easy to be frightened about the urban prospect in the 2020s. More than a billion people live in slums. A billion lack regular access to potable water. Almost two-and-a-half billion lack basic sanitation facilities. Yet the world will need to make room for two-and-a-half billion new city dwellers by 2050. Lagos, Nigeria, alone will have more than eighty million residents by century's end. Something like two hundred million people will migrate to avoid climate disaster.

Consider, though, how fast our cities can change. Pea soup–thick smog dominated US cities in the late nineteenth century, and a river in Ohio was on fire in the 1970s. Soon after the turn of this century, though, urban air and water in most US cities conformed to quite lofty standards. The same urban avenues that were the domain of horse-drawn carriages in 1910 were dense with automobiles by 1930.

Those who plan and build cities have woken up to the connections between urban design and health. The mayor of Paris has called for neighborhoods in which residents can get to all necessary services within a fifteen-minute walk. New York City has a policy saying that everyone should live within a ten-minute walk of a park. Streets that once choked on car traffic now move thousands of bicycles on safe bikeways in Amsterdam and provide green infrastructure and cooling flow of water in Seoul. City codes that once prohibited agriculture now smile on community gardens and backyard chicken coops.

Fixing unhealthy cities will require hard choices about priorities and enormous investment, but we now have the tools to fix these problems, increasingly we have the political awareness necessary to make it happen, and, with popular support, we have industry recognition that it is good business to do so. In many cities, we rebuild half the built environment every fifty years. With good choices, cities of the mid-twenty-first century can be home to healthy lives at levels never seen before.

For further information: World Cities Report 2016, https://unhabitat.org/world-cities-report.

CREATING PATHWAYS TO HEALTH EQUITY IN URBAN INFORMAL SETTLEMENTS: LESSONS FROM NAIROBI

Alice Sverdlik, PhD

Lecturer in Social Development

Global Development Institute

University of Manchester, United Kingdom

Transformative, bottom-up change is possible when led by residents of informal settlements ("slums"), where more than a billion people globally live in inadequate housing with minimal services and infrastructure. Across hundreds of African and Asian cities, a social movement called Slum Dwellers International (SDI) forms community groups to provide livelihood loans, empower women, foster social cohesion, and advocate for vital interventions in their settlements. SDI affiliates also collect data through enumeration and mapping, helping challenge their invisibility to policymakers and to catalyze future initiatives.

A pioneering example is Mukuru, one of Nairobi's largest slums, with three hundred thousand residents. Novel responses are helping to address the area's complex health risks. For instance, floods are common in Mukuru's riparian areas, with flooding risks exacerbated by minimal drainage and solid waste collection. Elevated levels of air pollution are linked to nearby factories and unclean cooking fuels. Further threats stem from Mukuru's overcrowded rental housing, hazardous electricity, and paltry water and sanitation infrastructure. Schools and health facilities are often inaccessible or of very low quality.

But Mukuru also illustrates the power of community-led transformation via collective organizing, detailed data collection, and equitable partnerships. After years of rigorous action-research and advocacy by Mukuru residents, Nairobi's county government responded. In 2017, the county declared Mukuru a Special Planning Area (SPA), ushering in a highly participatory upgrading process.

Subsequently, the SPA generated holistic upgrading plans with inputs from government, academic, and civil society actors. The Kenyan slum-dweller federation *Muungano wa Wanavijiji*, alongside SDI-Kenya (its technical support nongovernmental organization) and a grassroots fund called Akiba Mashinani Trust, has anchored a participatory planning process grounded in Mukuru residents' priorities. The Mukuru SPA also created an innovative model of eight planning consortia comprised of government, civil society, academic, and private-sector partners. The consortia developed a holistic planning structure simultaneously focusing on (1) housing, infrastructure, and commerce; (2) education, youth affairs, and culture; (3) health services; (4) land and institutional frameworks; (5) water, sanitation, and energy; (6) finance; (7) environment and natural resources; and (8) coordination, community organization, and communication.

Nairobi's government is already improving roads, housing, and water in Mukuru, with future plans to provide additional infrastructure, clinics, schools, and community facilities. The government also committed to replicating this approach in Nairobi's other informal settlements.

The Mukuru SPA demonstrates that marginalized residents, government officials, and other local stakeholders can work collaboratively and scale up solutions to tackle multiple risks. For other fast-growing cities of the Global South, the Mukuru SPA provides a valuable model of how to create community-led change with far-reaching potential.

For further information:
- Slum Dwellers International, https://sdinet.org/.
- Mukuru Special Planning Area, https://www.muungano.net/about-the-mukuru-spa.

- Sverdlik A, Makau J, Kimani J, et al. Achieving scale, social inclusion, and multifaceted shelter solutions: lessons from the Special Planning Area (SPA) in Mukuru, Nairobi. City Briefing, International Institute for Environment and Development. 2020. https://bit.ly/3s2AdIT.

This contribution was reviewed and approved by author Sverdlik's collaborator Jane Wairutu.

LOVE STARTS AT HOME

Katie Swenson, MArch

Architect, MASS Design Group

Boston, Massachusetts

Home is an essential building block of our lives—the place we learn, we love, and from which we launch. Housing is the essential building block of neighborhoods, and neighborhoods are the essential building blocks of cities. Without a home, everything else falls apart. There are nearly forty million people in the United States who are housing insecure, including more than a million who are without homes at all and others who live in fear of eviction or are otherwise on the edge. How will we commit to ensuring a home for everyone?

A mural in the Point neighborhood of Salem, Massachusetts, reads, "Knowing your neighbor will transform love into power." Why does love matter in cities? Love is what makes us commit to solving hard problems, to shelter and protect each other. Love may be the only force powerful enough to ensure that every member of our society has a safe and secure home that is connected to the other necessary amenities of life, including recreation space, healthy food options, and transportation to work, school, and medical care.

I believe that the United States has a future where everyone has a place to call home—not just any place, but a place that promotes health and is environmentally friendly, a place that provides not only shelter, but dignity, identity, and grounding in a community. To do that, we need to commit to a national housing policy that reflects our deepest care for each other. The right to housing is recognized in many countries and in the Universal Declaration of Human Rights. The United States must create a federal housing policy that ensures equitable access to high-quality housing. But as we know, love starts at home, and states and cities must do the policy work to ensure that federal dollars are invested in housing that reflects the cultural and ecological values of diverse communities. Community development corporations are among the place-based organizations that advocate for the well-being of their neighbors and translate their love and concern into dignified, secure, healthful housing in their communities. To make housing home, we need to agree on a vision of a country where every person has a home, and that starts by knowing your neighbor.

BUILDING ON AND MOVING FORWARD WITH KINDNESS AND COMPASSION FOR ALL PEOPLE AND OUR LIFE-SUSTAINING PLANET

Susan Thompson, PhD

Professor of Planning and Head, City Wellbeing Program

City Futures Research Centre

School of Built Environment, Faculty of Arts, Design and Architecture

University of New South Wales, Sydney

Some two decades ago, I was in the right place at the right time to be at the forefront of developing healthy built environments from an urban planning perspective. My geographic focus has been the state of New South Wales, Australia, where I've had the immense privilege to champion urban planners from metropolitan regions to those working in rural towns and remote locations to embrace healthy built environments in locally relevant ways. So, what is my vision for the healthy, sustainable, and just built environment of the future?

First is that we continue to build on the enormous policy and practice gains made since the turn of the twenty-first century. We must not be complacent, taking the progress already made for granted. My aspiration is that all necessary legislative structures will be firmly in place to mandate the provision of health supportive places. There will be no question that health and well-being are central concerns of strategic and statutory planning. It will be commonplace for planning professionals to work respectfully alongside other experts. Together, they will acknowledge that everyone, no matter where they live or their economic position in society, has equal rights to live in a health supportive place on an environmentally sustainable planet that is planned and managed in harmony with all living creatures.

Second, at the heart of my vision is the incorporation of Indigenous knowledge, culture, respect for elders, and practices of caring for country. Aboriginal and Torres Strait Islander first nation peoples are the oldest continuous living culture on Earth, having inhabited the Australian continent for more than sixty thousand years. A healthy, sustainable, and just built environment will celebrate, honor, and build on this legacy.

Considering future generations is the third part of my vision. Children and young adults will be heard in planning consultations, with their concerns, ideas, and aspirations respected and taken seriously. Those in positions of power will responsibly consider the impact of all planning decisions on the generations to follow.

Finally, I hope that my profession of planning can foster the conditions to slow the current pace of daily life, making it easier for all to enjoy their local environments, appreciating the community around them and the beauty of nature. Kindness infuses this vision with a wish for a caring and compassionate approach to others and a deep thoughtfulness about human impact on the environment, especially the implications of today's actions for tomorrow. Planners will create the physical and sociocultural infrastructure to support this vision, safeguarding every inhabitant's right to lead the healthiest and happiest life possible.

For further information: UNSW City Futures Research Centre, https://cityfutures.be.unsw.edu.au/.

COVID IS AN ACCELERANT FOR CHANGE

Jason Vargo, MPH, MCRP, PhD

Former Lead Research Scientist

Climate Change and Health Equity Program

California Department of Public Health

Senior Researcher, Community Development

Federal Reserve Bank of San Francisco

San Francisco, California

As an urban planner who worked at a state health department on the COVID pandemic, I see three areas of potential lasting change: health equity, technology and data, and shared sense of place.

Health equity may at last be better operationalized. The pandemic has exposed injustices along the lines of race and class, and disparities in COVID outcomes have daylighted many of their root causes. In California, we committed to reporting COVID case rates by income, prevalence of crowded housing in a community, and health insurance coverage. We also included a first-of-its-kind health equity (HE) metric in our plan to reopen safely. This blueprint ties the reopening of the economy to lower rates of COVID transmission, and the HE metric ensures that transmission is reduced in the least advantaged parts of counties. Public health is increasingly examining COVID case rates and deaths using the California Healthy Places Index or similar metrics such as the CDC's Social Vulnerability Index or the Area Deprivation Index. We're looking to do the same for sexually transmitted illnesses, maternal and child health, and chronic diseases. Using place-based measures for health reporting and prioritizing investments can strengthen the connections between local placemakers and public health.

The pandemic made health data more available and relevant than ever to the public and professionals from fields other than health. Combined with emerging urban technologies, more localized, transparent, and reliable health data—and health equity indices as mentioned above—are yielding powerful insights for making healthy places. The unprecedented attention to public health is also attracting a new cohort of highly skilled data scientists, engineers, and analysts. This capacity to collect diverse, meaningful data, analyze it skillfully, and deliver information to the public and decision-makers, as we did with COVID, will serve public health for years to come.

The pandemic changed our conception of "where we live." We grew accustomed to new activities, new routes, new destinations. Outdoor public spaces were sought out and created. Roads were reclaimed from automobiles. I loved seeing curbside parking spots turned into parklets overnight and hearing of communities that "closed" streets (although I prefer to think of them as "opened") to give people more room to be safe while physically distanced and active outside. I was motivated by my own trips to a local former landfill that morphed into a thriving public space with activist pop-up art, recreational opportunities, and plenty of benches for contemplative reflection.

Change takes a long time, but once it begins, it happens much faster than you could ever imagine. I see COVID catalyzing immense opportunities for making healthy places—places that are equitable, data-informed, and community-oriented.

For further information: California Department of Public Health, Climate Change and Health Equity Section, https://www.cdph.ca.gov/Programs/OHE/Pages/CCHEP.aspx.

In the foreword to this book, Dr. Richard J. Jackson wrote that "just because it is this way doesn't mean it has to be this way." The authors' voices throughout this chapter reflect that same conviction. They envision a world in which housing, streets, neighborhoods, parks, and cities are healthy places—and not only healthy, but also places that help sustain and restore ecosystems and the planet, places that embody respect, opportunity, and security for all people; places that are resilient to disaster and disruption; and places that are human-scaled, pleasing, and beautiful. Achieving such places requires the work of many professionals, including design professionals such as planners and architects and health professionals such as physicians, nurses, and epidemiologists. It requires robust evidence that makes trade-offs clear, documents what works and what does not, and guides wise decisions. It requires active community engagement, strong leadership, effective public policies, good governance, and innovative technologies. Above all, it requires vision.

We, the editors, hope that the evidence presented in this book, and the visions shared in this final chapter, will inspire students, professionals, and members of the public—empowering them to propel change and to create healthy, equitable, and sustainable places for all people.

GLOSSARY

accessory dwelling unit (ADU): A smaller dwelling unit on the property of a primary house; also called in-law or granny unit.

active intervention: An intervention that requires an action by the host to be effective, such as fastening a seat belt.

active recreation: Physical activity that is done for recreation, enjoyment, sports, hobbies, health, or exercise during leisure time.

active transportation: Physical activity that is done primarily for the purpose of moving from one destination to another, usually by walking or bicycling; also called human-powered transportation or active travel.

adaptation: In the context of climate change, the process of adjustment to current or expected climate and its effects so as to reduce harm or exploit beneficial opportunities.

adaptive behavior: Behavior or response toward new environments, tasks, objects, and people that is beneficial to the individual's well-being and allows them to apply new skills to those new situations.

adaptive capacity: The ability of systems, institutions, humans, and other organisms to adjust to potential damage, to take advantage of opportunities, or to respond to consequences.

affordable housing: Housing that a household can pay for while retaining enough money to pay for other necessities such as food, transportation, and health care; affordable is sometimes defined as not exceeding 30 percent of a household's income.

age-friendly (world, community, city): Places that foster healthy and active aging for all ages, with an emphasis on the needs of older populations.

agency: An individual's or community's ability to find solutions to the issues it faces.

aging in community: Being able to remain and live independently in one's community as one grows older and as one's needs change because of city- or community-level initiatives; community-centric focus.

aging in place: Being able to remain and live independently in one's home and thus community because of building-level retrofits as one grows older and as one's needs change; dwelling-centric focus.

air pollution: Contamination of air by physical, chemical, or biological agents, including solids (particulates), gases (ozone, oxides of nitrogen, and others), and toxins (for example, formaldehyde). May be indoors ("household air pollution") or outdoors ("ambient air pollution").

air quality index (AQI): The US Environmental Protection Agency tool for communicating air pollution levels for each of five individual pollutants—ozone, particulate matter, carbon monoxide, sulfur dioxide, and nitrogen dioxide—and the associated health risks. AQI ranges from 0 to 500, with values below 50 designated "good" and values above 100 increasingly unhealthy.

all-hazards approach: In emergency preparedness, an approach that focuses on building critical capacities for preparing for and managing a full spectrum of natural and human-caused disasters; also called multihazards approach.

American Society of Heating, Refrigeration and Air Conditioning Engineers (ASHRAE): An American professional association of engineers who work on heating, cooling, and ventilation systems.

Anthropocene: A proposed new geological epoch named for the significant human-driven changes to the structure and functioning of planetary systems.

anthropogenic: Resulting from or produced by human activities.

anxiety: A feeling of nervousness or fear in response to an upcoming event, potential danger, or another trigger.

application programming interface: The interface or ability for multiple parties, apps, or end users to interact with data. It is through APIs that an individual can call, or access, data from sites such as Google Maps and Twitter.

architecture: The art and science of designing buildings.

artificial intelligence: The use of computer systems to perform tasks that normally require human intelligence, such as speech recognition and decision making.

assessment: A systematic framework for the collection and analysis of qualitative and quantitative data, often to inform decision-making.

attention restoration: Return of attention and reduction of distraction, irritability, and impatience; thought to be promoted by contact with nature.

augmented reality: The reality as seen through a camera lens is augmented, or changed with digital technologies, such as adding a digital bike lane to a real-time video capture of a streetscape.

awe: A transcendent emotional state that may be triggered by contact with nature and may be associated with health benefits.

bias: In epidemiology, any systematic error (for example, in selection of subjects or collection of data) that results in an incorrect estimate of the association between an exposure and an outcome.

big data: Large amount of data often collected by urban technologies. The five V's of big data are volume, velocity, veracity, variety, and value.

biophilia hypothesis: The theory that humans have an inherent need to affiliate with nature.

biophilic city: *See* biophilic design

biophilic design: A design strategy that fosters beneficial contact between humans and the natural world.

blue space: Visible, outdoor, natural surface waters, including coastlines, riverfronts, and lakeshores, with potential for the promotion of human health and well-being.

body mass index (BMI): A weight-to-height ratio, calculated by dividing a person's weight in kilograms by the square of the person's height in meters, used as a measure of obesity.

bonding social capital: *See* social capital.

bridging social capital: *See* social capital.

broken windows theory: The theory that features of the built environment such as litter and vandalism are demoralizing to residents, can trigger disengagement and further neglect of a place, and can adversely affect mental health, social capital, and well-being.

brownfield: A former industrial or commercial site with residual environmental contamination, typically by toxic chemicals.

Build Back Better: A slogan coined after the 2004 Asian tsunami, invoked after many disasters and most recently used in the context of COVID-19, conveying the aspiration that postdisaster recovery should achieve not a return to predisaster "normal," but improved levels of resilience, equity, environmental performance, healthfulness, and functionality.

building codes: Regulations established by a government agency describing design, building procedures, and construction details for new buildings or those undergoing remodeling, including houses and commercial buildings.

built environment: Settings designed, created, modified, and maintained by people, such as homes, schools, workplaces, neighborhoods, parks, roadways, and transit systems.

bus rapid transit (BRT): A high-quality bus-based transit system that delivers fast, cost-effective services through the provision of dedicated lanes, with busways and stations typically aligned to the center of the road, off-board fare collection, and frequent operation.

carbon footprint: A measure of total carbon emissions attributable to a person, product, place, or system.

carbon neutral: A feature of buildings or communities that entails producing zero net carbon emissions. Carbon emissions are minimized through energy conservation and the use of renewable energy sources, and carbon that is released is balanced by carbon sequestration or offsets.

carbon sequestration: The process of storing carbon in a natural or artificial carbon pool (for example, forests, grasslands, coastal ecosystems; landfills, geological or mineral sequestration).

carbon sink: A reservoir (natural or human, in soil, ocean, and plants) where a greenhouse gas, an aerosol, or a precursor of a greenhouse gas is stored.

case-control study: An epidemiologic study that compares people with a condition of interest to people free of that condition to assess whether certain exposures are associated with the condition.

causation: The creation or production of an effect. In epidemiology, causation is defined in many ways, from deterministic to probabilistic. Causation is often evaluated using formal criteria (Bradford Hill criteria).

certification: The action or process of assessing and communicating a level of standard or achievement.

charrette: A planning workshop at which government staff, community residents, and developers collectively engage in a visioning process regarding a plan, project, or proposal.

chronic diseases: Conditions that persist over time and require ongoing medical attention, limit activities of daily living, or both. Examples include heart disease, cancer, and diabetes, which are leading causes of death and disability. Also called noncommunicable diseases.

citizen jury: A group of community members who deliberate and make recommendations to decision-makers on a particular issue.

City Beautiful movement: A movement in North American architecture and urban planning around the turn of the twentieth century that advocated elite culture and monumental grandeur in cities.

citymaking: Comprehensive approach to designing, managing, and evaluating urban life and public spaces.

civil engineering: The field of engineering focused on the design, construction, and maintenance of built environment elements such as bridges, roads, canals, and dams.

Clean Water Act (CWA): A US federal law enacted in 1972 that establishes the basic structure for regulating discharges of pollutants into water and quality standards for surface waters.

climate change: A change in the state of the climate that can be identified by changes in the mean or the variability of its properties and that persists for an extended period, typically decades or longer.

climate gentrification: Climate-protective investments or decisions that contribute to increased social and ecological vulnerability for working-class, minority, and immigrant communities, either because of concentrated environmental investment in high-income communities or the displacement of marginalized groups to less protected neighborhoods.

climate justice: Justice that links development and human rights to achieve a human-centered approach to addressing climate change, safeguarding the rights of the most vulnerable people and sharing the burdens and benefits of climate change and its impacts equitably and fairly.

co-benefit: The positive effect that a policy or measure aimed at one objective might have on other objectives, thereby increasing the total benefits for society or the environment.

cognitive functioning: The ability to learn, reason, make decisions, solve problems, remember, and, importantly, pay attention.

cohort study: A type of epidemiological study in which a well-defined group of people who have had a common experience or exposure are followed to determine the incidence of health outcomes of interest.

collective efficacy: People's ability to mobilize to undertake collaborative action.

combined sewer overflow: When excess liquid from a combined sewer system is diverted to overflow and discharged into designated water bodies.

combined sewer system: A network of sewer pipes that collects both sewage and stormwater and moves it via gravity to be treated. Used extensively in older cities and now being replaced by separate systems.

community gardens/allotments: Land with allocated patches where individuals and groups can grow food and other plants.

complete streets: Streets designed and operated so that all users, including pedestrians, bicyclists, motorists, and transit riders of all ages and abilities, can safely move along and across the streets.

comprehensive plan: An official document adopted by a local government that serves as a guide for making land use changes, preparing capital improvement programs, and determining the rate, timing, and location of future growth; also called master plan or general plan.

confounding: In epidemiology, a source of systematic error that arises when the association between an exposure and a health outcome is distorted by a third variable (the confounder).

connectivity: The directness or ease of travel on sidewalks, paths, and streets between two points; a facilitator of active transportation.

conservation zoning: Zoning that aims to preserve natural resources by regulating or limiting development in natural areas.

construct: Hypothesized cause of an observed behavior.

consumption-based emissions: Greenhouse gas emissions arising from goods and services consumed by residents of a particular place, whether produced within the boundaries of that place or elsewhere. *See also* sector-based emissions.

cost-benefit analysis: A systematic way of assessing the costs and benefits of various policy options, usually expressing both costs and benefits in monetary terms. Used to assess whether costs outweigh benefits and to inform decisions among different policies.

cost-effectiveness: *See* cost-effectiveness analysis.

cost-effectiveness analysis: A systematic way of assessing the costs and benefits, especially health outcomes, of interventions. Used to compare interventions in terms of the cost of gaining a unit of a health outcome and to inform decisions among different interventions.

crime prevention through environmental design (CPTED): An approach to reducing aggressive and criminal behavior by adjusting characteristics of the built environment.

cross-sectional study: An epidemiologic study design in which data on exposures and health outcomes are collected at the same time.

crowding: A physical phenomenon referring to a high number of people in a space such as an apartment or a classroom (measured by density) and a perceptual phenomenon referring to the felt experience of excess proximity to other people such that one's personal space is violated.

cumulative exposures: The concept that multiple exposures—chemical, physical, psychological, and social—acting over a person's entire life span combine to define a person's level of risk.

decarbonization: The process of eliminating the carbon emissions associated with electricity generation, industry, and transport.

deliberative polling: Polling that engages community members in dialogue on current issues, a proposed project, or policy changes to generate more informed and representative public opinions.

density: The number of people, jobs, or dwellings per unit area.

depression: A common ailment featuring sadness, sleep disturbance, low energy, low self-esteem, reduced feelings of pleasure, and loss of interest in things. Affects most people at some point and may be serious and persistent in some.

desalination: The process of removing salt from seawater.

design: The act of imagining and specifying how things are made.

design safety review: In occupational health, a formal proactive process to evaluate and then reduce or remove workplace hazards.

digital divide: Unequal access to hardware (smartphones, laptop computers) and the internet (5G, fiber, broadband).

disability: a physical or mental impairment that substantially limits one or more major life activities; it is a feature of person-environment fit that results from a mismatch between the goals and abilities of an individual and the demands of both the social and physical environment.

disability-adjusted life year (DALY): A measure of overall disease burden; one DALY is the loss of the equivalent of one year of full health. DALYs for a disease or health condition are the sum of the years of life lost due to premature death and the years lived with a disability due to the disease or health condition.

disaster risk reduction: The process of preventing new and reducing existing disaster risk and managing residual risk, which contributes to strengthening resilience and therefore to the achievement of sustainable development.

dose-response relationship: An association between an exposure and health outcome in which the health outcome increases or decreases directly or inversely as the amount of exposure (dose) increases or decreases.

e-bike: Bicycle with an electrical motor that assists riders in climbing hills, taking longer trips, and overcoming limited mobility.

ecological footprint: A measure of the quantity of biologically productive land area required to produce the resources consumed and absorb the wastes generated by human activities.

ecological gentrification: *See* green gentrification.

ecological study: In epidemiology, a study that assesses the overall frequency of a health outcome in a population in relation to a population exposure, based not on individual data, but on average levels of exposure and health outcome across a population.

ecosystem services: Benefits people obtain from the ecosystem categorized into four major services: provisioning, regulating, cultural, and supporting services.

efficacy: In the context of health, the ability of an intervention (such as a medication or an environmental change) to improve health.

embodied carbon: The greenhouse gas emissions associated with extracting, processing, manufacturing, transporting, and disposing of materials, which represents the climate change impact of materials across their life cycle; also called embodied emissions.

embodied water: The water consumed in producing food or other products, which is typically "hidden" from sight at the point of consumption; also called virtual water, embedded water.

emergent property: A property of a complex system that is meaningful only at the level of the entire system and that can neither be predicted from nor reduced to its component activities or structures. Emergent properties of resilience emerge from the interactions between infrastructure, behavior, and policy.

empirical evidence: The results of experimental or observational research conducted within a rigorous and reproducible scientific study design.

environmental determinism: Behavioral characteristics are largely or completely the result of environmental conditions.

environmental engineering: The field of engineering that focuses on the environmental performance of built environment elements, ranging from buildings to large-scale public works.

environmental health: The field of public health concerned with how human health, disease, and injury are affected by environmental factors, including direct negative (chemical, physical, and biological agents) and positive (nature contact) effects and the health effects of the broad physical and social environments, such as housing, urban development, land use, and transportation.

environmental impact assessment (EIA): The process of evaluating the likely environmental impacts of a proposed project or development, taking into account interrelated socioeconomic, cultural, and human health impacts, both beneficial and adverse.

environmental injustice: Disproportionate exposure to environmental hazards (such as pollution sources) or amenities (such as parks) and unequal distribution of power, political voice, legal protection, and resources needed to secure safe, healthy conditions, typically affecting low-income communities or communities of color; also called environmental inequity. Referred to as environmental racism when directed at racial and ethnic minorities.

environmental justice (EJ): Fair treatment and meaningful involvement of all people, regardless of race, color, national origin, or income, with respect to environmental laws, regulations, policies, and conditions; also a grassroots movement that began in the 1980s and that promotes these goals.

environmental privilege: Disproportionate access to parks and green space, fresh food, healthy housing, transit, legal protection, and other environmental amenities, benefiting wealthier and majority ethnic and racial groups while excluding marginalized groups.

environmental racism: *See* environmental injustice.

epidemiological transition: A change in the patterns of health, accompanying economic development, from communicable to noncommunicable diseases as the primary causes of morbidity and mortality.

epidemiology: The study of the distribution and determinants of health conditions or events among populations and the application of that study to improving health.

equigenic effect: Attenuation of health disparities between social classes by an environmental or social circumstance such as green space.

equity: Fairness or justice in the rights, opportunities, protections, and treatment of different groups of people.

evaluation: A systematic assessment of the effectiveness and consequences of an intervention.

evidence-based design: Design in which decisions about the built environment are based on credible research to achieve the best possible health outcomes.

evidence-based practice: The idea that empirical evidence should be systematically collected, evaluated, and used as the basis for decisions.

evidence synthesis: Systematic efforts to identify and aggregate evidence from different studies to reach robust conclusions.

exposure: In toxicology, contact with a substance by swallowing, breathing, or touching the skin or eyes. May be short term (acute) or long term (chronic). In disaster management, the presence of people; livelihoods; species or ecosystems; environmental functions, services, and resources; infrastructure; or economic, social, or cultural assets in places and settings that could be adversely affected.

facility life cycle: A consideration of workplace hazards throughout the life of a facility, including early occupants (construction workers) and supporting occupants (operations and maintenance workers), as well as subsequent renovation and demolition workers.

fifteen-minute city: A city in which residents have access to the goods and services they need on a regular basis within a short distance of home, close enough for walking or bicycling.

floor area ratio (FAR): The ratio of the gross building area to the parcel's land area. Regulations about FAR influence the shape, size, and mass of a building.

food apartheid: Areas of inequitable food access where limited options exist and the policies and practices, current and historic, come from a place of anti-Blackness.

food desert: A place that has little or no access to the foods needed to maintain a healthy diet and that is served instead by fast-food establishments or convenience stores.

food environment: The availability and selection of foods in a particular setting, such as a school or a neighborhood.

food swamp: A place with abundant calorie-dense, low-quality food options (i.e., fast food).

form-based zoning: Zoning that focuses on required features and performance of buildings rather than on prohibitions and specifications of land uses.

fractal patterns: A common pattern occurring in nature in which each part of an object (such as a snowflake or tree branches) has the same form as the whole.

fresh food access: The ongoing opportunity to procure fresh fruits and vegetables and other nutritious foods within one's community.

Garden City movement: An urban planning approach introduced by Sir Ebenezer Howard in the United Kingdom at the turn of the twentieth century that envisioned cities as planned, self-contained communities with defined mixes of housing, industry, and agriculture and surrounded by "greenbelts."

gentrification: A sociocultural phenomenon in which older, declining neighborhoods are renovated, property taxes rise, and lower-income residents may be displaced because they can no longer afford to live there.

geographic information systems (GIS): A computer system designed for storing, manipulating, analyzing, and displaying data in a geographic context.

graywater: Wastewater generated from domestic activities such as showers and bathtubs and washing dishes and clothes, but not including wastewater from toilets. Graywater is potentially reusable.

Great Acceleration: The dramatic, continuous, and roughly synchronous surge in growth of numerous forms of human activity, beginning with the Industrial Revolution, accelerating in the mid-twentieth century, and continuing to the present.

green building: An approach to designing, building, and operating buildings that emphasizes energy efficiency and environmental performance.

green gentrification: A form of gentrification (see above) triggered by the provision of parks and other green infrastructure—an undesirable outcome of actions that purportedly advance environmental goals and social welfare.

greenhouse gases (GHGs): Naturally and anthropogenically derived gases in the atmosphere that absorb and emit radiant energy, trapping solar energy at the earth's surface ("greenhouse effect"). Includes carbon dioxide, methane, nitrous oxide, fluorinated gases, and others.

green infrastructure: The range of measures that use plant or soil systems, permeable pavement, or other permeable surfaces or substrates, stormwater harvest and reuse, or landscaping to store, infiltrate, or evapotranspirate stormwater and reduce flows to sewer systems or surface waters.

green space: Land that is partly or completely covered with grass, trees, shrubs, or other vegetation, including parks, community gardens, and forests, with the potential to support ecosystem services and human health.

growth management: A combination of techniques used to determine the amount, type, and rate of community growth to be directed to designated areas.

Haddon matrix: An injury prevention model developed by Dr. William Haddon that related the phases of injury prevention (preinjury, injury, postinjury) with the main components of injury mechanisms (host, vehicle/vector, sociocultural environment, and built environment).

happiness: A term that refers to positive emotions, which may be a momentary feeling, a general feeling of well-being, or a positive subjective assessment of one's life.

hazard: A naturally occurring or human-induced situation that poses a threat to life, health, property, or environment.

healing garden: A garden intended to promote recovery and recuperation from illness or injury through either passive use or purposeful activity.

health: "A state of complete physical, mental, and social well-being and not merely the absence of disease or infirmity," according to the World Health Organization. This broad definition goes well beyond a narrowly biomedical view to include many dimensions of thriving, including comfort, happiness, and well-being. However, some people who have adapted to disabilities or limitations (such as a chronic disease or a mobility limitation) object to this definition because they consider themselves to be healthy.

health care: Clinical and preventive services, administered by trained and licensed professionals, that aim to cure or manage diseases and injuries and promote health.

health disparities: Differences among specific population groups in their burden of adverse health conditions and their access to health protective factors.

health equity: A social condition in which everyone has the right, and a fair and just opportunity, to be as healthy as possible.

health impact assessment (HIA): A combination of procedures, methods, and tools that systematically assesses the potential effects of a proposed policy, plan, program, or project on the health of a population and the distribution of those effects within the population; HIA identifies appropriate actions to manage those effects.

Health in All Policies (HiAP): A collaborative approach for integrating and articulating health considerations into policymaking and programming across sectors and levels of government with the goal of improving the health of all communities and people.

health inequity: When individuals and groups of people experience differing levels of disease, disability, death, and medical care because of social position or other socially determined circumstances.

Healthy Cities movement: A movement originating in the 1980s and now led by the World Health Organization that advocates a health-promoting approach to urban governance, environmental design, and service delivery.

Hierarchy of Controls: A sequence of ways to control exposures to workplace hazards that is arranged in order of effectiveness, beginning with the most effective: elimination, substitution, engineering controls, warnings, administrative controls, and personal protective equipment.

horticultural therapy: A treatment approach utilizing plants and horticultural activities to promote healing or to improve peoples' social, educational, psychological, or physical well-being.

hospital-associated infections: Infections acquired by patients in hospitals or other health care facilities while they are receiving health care for another medical condition.

housing codes: Federal, state, or local government ordinances that set minimum standards of safety, sanitation, and habitability for existing residential buildings, as opposed to building codes that govern new construction.

implementation research: The scientific study of methods and strategies to facilitate the uptake of evidence-based practice and research by practitioners and policymakers; also called implementation science.

incidence: The rate of onset of new cases of a disease per unit of time.

incivilities: Unpleasant elements in neighborhoods or streets, such as abandoned buildings, broken windows, trash, litter, and graffiti.

inclusionary zoning: A method of incorporating affordable housing into development projects by requiring the developer to build some affordable units or contribute to a trust fund devoted to affordable housing construction.

inclusive design: Design incorporating all abilities and adaptations.

infill development: Building in existing developed areas on vacant lots and underutilized parcels, thereby increasing density.

informal settlement: An urban settlement that develops outside of the legal systems intended to record land ownership, provide basic services, and regulate planning, land use, buildings, and public health and safety.

injury: Unintentional or intentional damage to the body resulting from acute exposure to kinetic, thermal, mechanical, electrical, or chemical energy or from the absence of such essentials as heat or oxygen.

intentional injury: Injury caused by a person with intent to do harm, such as homicide, assault, child maltreatment, elder abuse, or suicide.

integrated mobility platforms: Information systems with user interfaces (apps) that integrate different modes of transport and facilitate route planning, travel, and payment (for example, Lyft, Lime, local transit apps, Google Maps).

integrated pest management: An approach to pest control that prevents entry of pests into homes; deprives pests of access to shelter, food, and water; and minimizes use of pesticides.

intergenerational equity: In the context of climate change, equity between present and future generations, acknowledging that past and present emissions, vulnerabilities, and policies impose costs and benefits for people in the future and of different age groups.

Internet of Things (IoT): The network of internet-connected devices and technologies.

interpersonal violence: Acts of aggression and assault against children, elders, intimate partners, acquaintances, and strangers.

intersection density: A measure of the number of intersections in an area; higher intersection densities correspond to shorter block lengths and contribute to walkability.

joint use: Formal arrangements between two government entities, such as a school district and a park department, providing for shared use of a venue, such as a schoolyard doubling as a public park.

landscape architecture: The design profession focused on exterior spaces, including interior courtyards, gardens, campuses, public spaces, river corridors, and entire ecological regions.

land use: The totality of arrangements, activities, and inputs in a certain land cover type.

land use change: A change from one land use category to another, such as the conversion of forest to farmland or to urban development.

land use mix: The ways in which different land uses—residential, office, retail/commercial, public space, and others—are commingled.

land use plan: A document that guides the use of land in a county or city, based on local needs and goals.

Leadership in Energy and Environmental Design (LEED): An internationally recognized green building certification system, developed by the US Green Building Council, providing third-party verification that a building or community was designed and built using strategies aimed at improving performance in energy savings, water efficiency, carbon dioxide emissions reduction, indoor environmental quality, and stewardship of resources and sensitivity to their impacts.

legibility: In the context of a building or a neighborhood, the ease with which people can orient to where they are and find their way to where they want to go. Legibility is enhanced by such features as clear signage, recognizable landmarks, and simple layouts and routes.

leisure-time physical activity: Physical activity engaged in by choice by individuals during nonwork time and not required to perform essential activities of daily living.

level of service: The speed, convenience, comfort, and security of transportation facilities and services as experienced by users.

life cycle assessment: A technique for assessing the potential environmental and health impacts associated with a product, process, or system from its origins through production and use to its final disposition.

locally unwanted land use (LULU): A land use with negative consequences for those who live nearby, such as a hazardous waste site or a polluting industry.

loneliness: The subjective experience of feeling disconnected from other people. *See also* social isolation.

loss and damage: Broadly, harm from (observed) impacts and (projected) risks; in the context of the 2013 Warsaw Mechanism on Loss and Damage, harms from climate change.

low-emission zone (LEZ): A defined area within a city from which vehicles that do not meet certain emission standards are barred.

machine learning: A branch of artificial intelligence using data and analysis to automate decisions by identifying patterns.

macroscale pedestrian environment: Characteristics of the urban form related to walkability (see below), typically measured at the level of administrative districts such as census tracts. Examples include residential density, land use diversity, distance to destinations, and street connectivity.

maladaptive behavior: Behavior or response to an environment, policy, or situation that is damaging or counterproductive to the individual and to their health, safety, or quality of life.

measurement: The process of obtaining quantitative metrics of specific activities and conditions.

mental health: A state of well-being in which people realize their own abilities, can cope with the normal stresses of life, work productively, and make contributions to their community.

meta-analysis: The process of synthesizing, using statistical methodologies, research results from similar independent studies that have addressed a shared hypothesis.

metropolitan planning organization (MPO): A federally required organization of local officials and other interested parties that provides oversight to transportation planning on the regional rather than the single-city level in areas with a population more than 50,000.

micromobility: The use of small, lightweight vehicles typically at speeds below 15 miles per hour, including bicycles, e-bikes, electric scooters, and electric skateboards.

microscale pedestrian environment: Elements of urban form at the small scale, such as transit stops, sidewalks, and crossing infrastructure, as well as other aesthetic elements such as street trees, lighting, and building design, that influence walkability (see below).

mitigation: In the context of climate change, a human intervention to reduce emissions or enhance sequestration of greenhouse gases.

Mobility-as-a-Service (MaaS): Platforms that enable users to plan and access multiple types of transportation based on personal travel needs, such as an app that arranges a taxi ride to the train station together with a train journey.

mobility justice: Relates to equitable investment in and access to transportation infrastructure, especially for low-income persons and communities of color; also called transportation justice.

moderate-to-vigorous physical activity: Moving your body fast enough or at a high enough level of intensity to burn off three to six times or more than six times as much energy per minute as you do when you are sitting quietly (3 to 6 or 6+ metabolic equivalents, or METs).

morbidity: Nonfatal illness or injury affecting physical or mental health and well-being.

mortality: Death.

multihazard approach: *See* all-hazards approach.

National Institute for Occupational Safety and Health (NIOSH): US federal agency focused on research on occupational safety and health issues.

nationally determined contributions (NDCs): Under the 2015 Paris Agreement on climate change, a country's plans for reducing its emissions. Some countries' NDCs also address how they will adapt to climate change impacts and what support they need from, or will provide to, other countries to adopt low-carbon pathways and to build climate resilience.

natural experiment: An observational study in which events or interventions affect defined subpopulations but are not under the control of the researcher.

naturally occurring retirement community (NORC): Neighborhood with a majority of older adults who remain in place, but not designed to meet their needs as they continue to live independently in their homes.

nature-based solutions: Solutions to challenges such as stormwater management that are inspired and supported by nature and that are designed to be cost-effective to provide joint environmental, social, and economic benefits and to build resilience.

net zero (emissions): A state of balance between anthropogenic emissions of greenhouse gases and removal of these gases such that there is no net addition of greenhouse gases to the atmosphere.

neurodiversity: The concept that brain function and behavior vary across a population. In the context of the built environment, typically cited to acknowledge that settings such as schools should be designed to accommodate this diversity.

New Urbanism: An urban design movement that promotes walkable neighborhoods, mixed land use, connectivity, and vibrant public spaces and activity centers.

NIMBY: An acronym for "not in my backyard," referring to resistance by local residents to locating a project near their homes based on financial, social, or other reasons.

nitrogen oxide (NO_x): A gas consisting of nitrogen and oxygen formed through combustion of fossil fuels and in other ways and representing an important air pollutant.

nonpoint-source pollution: Pollution coming from widely distributed processes, such as when rainfall over a large area picks up and conveys natural and human-made pollutants into surface waters and groundwater. *See also* point-source pollution.

obesity: Excessive body weight, defined for adults as a body mass index (see above) of 30 to 40 (with a BMI above 40 defined as severe obesity) and defined for children and adolescents (two to nineteen years old) as a BMI at or above the age- and sex-specific ninety-fifth percentile on CDC growth charts.

Occupational Safety and Health Administration (OSHA): US federal agency that regulates workplace safety and health issues.

on-site wastewater treatment systems (OWTSs): An alternative to a municipal sewage system, such as a septic tank, that manages wastewater at the point of generation and typically serves individual houses or a small number of households.

ozone: A highly reactive toxic gas with powerful oxidizing properties, consisting of molecules with three oxygen atoms. In the stratosphere, formed from ultraviolet (UV) action on oxygen molecules and blocks incoming UV radiation (a health benefit). At ground level, formed as a secondary air pollutant from precursors (hydrocarbons and nitrogen oxides), contributing to "smog" and threatening health.

participatory budgeting: A democratic process that enables community members to decide how to spend part of a public budget.

participatory democracy: A concept that emphasizes broad participation of constituents in directing and operating the political systems and decisions impacting their lives.

particulate matter (PM): Small solid or liquid particles (also called aerosols) formed via combustion or friction that remain suspended in the air long enough to affect air quality. Often followed by a subscript number (10 or 2.5) to indicate particle size; smaller particles ("fine PM") have greater health effects.

passive intervention: An intervention designed into the built environment that requires no action by the host to be effective, such as a highway guard rail.

passive survivability: The ability of a building to maintain critical life-support conditions for its occupants if services such as power, heating fuel, and water are lost for an extended period.

people-oriented design: An approach that puts people at the center of planning, emphasizing practices that prioritize people's aspirations and ordinary experiences when imagining and implementing complex systems, services, or products; also called human-centered design.

person-environment fit theory: Explains how a person's individual characteristics influence and are influenced by the social and built environment in which the person lives, works, and plays.

physical activity: Voluntary bodily movement that requires energy expenditure.

place attachment: The emotional bonds that people develop for places that are the sites of positive experiences and memories.

planetary boundaries: The concept, proposed in 2009, that certain Earth systems have limits that, if transgressed, risk tipping the planet into irreversible and potentially catastrophic change.

planetary health: The health of human civilization and the state of the natural systems on which civilization depends.

planned unit development: A preplanned development with subdivision and zoning rules that are applied to the project as a whole rather than to individual lots or areas.

planning commission: A group of citizens, either elected or appointed by the mayor or city or county commissioners, that functions as a fact-finding and advisory board to elected officials in areas of planning and development.

point-source pollution: Any single identifiable source of pollution from which pollutants are discharged, such as a pipe, ditch, ship, or factory smokestack. *See also* nonpoint-source pollution.

policy research: Social scientific research related to policies that may be descriptive or analytical or may deal with causal processes and explanations for policies.

polycentricity: In urban planning, a metropolitan area configuration with multiple centers of commercial and residential activity. In governance, vesting decision-making power in more than one place to better respond to local needs and avoid bottlenecks or system failures during crises.

postoccupancy evaluation: The process of analyzing how functional and comfortable a building is after users have been occupying it for six months or longer.

potable water: Water that is safe to drink.

precautionary principle: "When an activity raises threats of harm to the environment or human health, precautionary measures should be taken even if some cause and effect relationships are not fully established scientifically" (1998 Wingspread Statement).

predictive analytics: Use of data, statistics, and algorithms to predict future outcomes.

preemption: The act of a higher level of government (state or federal), by legislative or regulatory action, eliminating or reducing the authority of a "lower" level over a given issue.

preparedness: A state of readiness, often used in relation to natural or human-induced disasters.

prevalence: The proportion of a population suffering from a condition at a given point in time, defined as the number of cases of disease per unit of population.

prevention, primary: Interventions to stop disease or injury from occurring.

prevention, secondary: Interventions to stop or delay the onset of adverse symptoms or effects once disease has started or an injury is occurring.

prevention, tertiary: Reducing the harm or suffering once a disease has occurred or providing rehabilitation after an injury to minimize long-term health damage.

prevention through design: In occupational health, a design approach aimed at preventing or minimizing risks associated with construction, manufacture, use, maintenance, and disposal of facilities, materials, and equipment.

prior appropriation doctrine: Legal entitlement to water rights based on earliest use of the water ("first in time, first in right"). *See also* riparian rights.

program evaluation: A structured effort to assess the performance and outcomes of a program according to defined criteria.

prosocial behavior: Behavior that benefits other people, either individually or on a societal scale, such as sharing among children and volunteerism among adults.

public health: The science and art of promoting health and preventing disease, injury, and disability in populations.

public water systems (PWS): Systems that provide water through pipes or other conveyances to at least twenty-five people or fifteen service connections for at least sixty days per year.

racial capitalism: Capitalist structures that inequitably exploit particular groups through culturally and socially constructed differences such as race, gender, region, and nationality.

Radiant City: An influential Utopian design concept championed by the French-Swiss architect Le Corbusier in 1930 but never built, featuring linear layout, high-rise housing blocks, and plentiful green space.

rain harvesting: The collection and storage of rainwater.

randomized controlled trial (RCT): In epidemiology, a clinical trial in which people are randomly assigned to different treatment groups (sometimes including a placebo group); commonly used to test new treatments.

reciprocity: The practice of exchanging goods, services, or other assistance with others for mutual benefit.

recovery: In the context of disasters, the regaining of function following a disaster, including restoration of basic services and rebuilding of infrastructure.

recreational physical activity: Physical activity that is done for recreation, enjoyment, sports, hobbies, health, or exercise during leisure time; also called active recreation or leisure-time physical activity. *See also* utilitarian physical activity.

redlining: The practice of designating certain neighborhoods as ineligible for credit based on race or ethnicity. This equates to a denial of financial services (mortgages, insurance, loans), most often to residents of minority neighborhoods.

redundancy: In engineering and disaster planning, the duplication of critical components or functions so that one failing element does not lead to system failure.

regional plan: Planning on a larger spatial scale than a town or city, extending to "any geographic area that possesses a certain unity of climate, soil, vegetation, industry, and culture" (Lewis Mumford). Typically considers land use, infrastructure, ecosystem services, and economic development.

reparability: The capability of a system or structure of being restored to partial or full functionality.

residential density: The number of residential dwelling units per unit of land area.

resilience: The ability of a person, structure, or system to withstand shocks or stressors while maintaining or recovering function and continuing to adapt and improve.

retrofitting: The process of modifying something after it has been created. Retrofitting a building involves changing its systems or structure after its initial construction and occupation, and retrofitting a suburb involves changing land uses, transport infrastructure, and other features.

reverberation: In acoustics, the length of time a sound lingers in a room.

riparian rights: Legal entitlement to water use based on ownership of land that contacts a waterway. *See also* prior appropriation doctrine.

risk: The potential for adverse consequences where something of value is at stake and where the occurrence and degree of an outcome is uncertain. Risk results from the interaction of vulnerability (of the affected system), its exposure over time (to the hazard), and the hazard and the likelihood of its occurrence.

road diet: The narrowing of a road or calming of traffic on a road by various means, including removing traffic lanes, reducing traffic speed, widening sidewalks, and adding bike lanes.

routine activities theory: A theory that suggests that crime and violence occur due to the convergence in space and time of motivated offenders, suitable targets, and absence of capable guardians.

Safe Routes to School: A transportation agency program that supports infrastructure improvements, education, and enforcement efforts to enable and encourage children to walk or bicycle to school.

safety: In general, a low risk of injury or other harm. In the context of health interventions, a low risk of causing adverse effects (such as medication side effects).

sanitary sewer overflow: *See* combined sewer overflow.

sanitary sewer system: An underground pipe or tunnel system for transporting sewage (as opposed to stormwater) from residential and commercial buildings to treatment facilities or disposal.

sanitation: A set of technologies, practices, and policies that promote health through provision of clean water, management of sewage and solid waste, food safety, and rodent control.

sector-based emissions: Greenhouse gas emissions arising within the boundaries of a particular place; also called territorial emissions. *See also* consumption-based emissions.

self-selection: Assignment of oneself to a particular condition, as when people with particular needs or preferences choose to live in places that facilitate their preferred behaviors.

Sendai Framework for Disaster Risk Reduction: A framework adopted by the United Nations in 2015 for actions by member states to reduce disaster risk and losses in lives, livelihoods, and health and in economic, physical, social, cultural, and environmental assets.

sense of belonging: A sense, among members of a group, of solidarity, trust, and attachment toward one another.

sense of place: The way people perceive and relate to a place or the features of a place, often with a sense of belonging and affinity. *See also* place attachment.

sensors: Devices that sense or record a variety of data passing the sensors lens or intake, including pedestrians on a greenway or nitrogen dioxide in the air.

setback: The distance that must be provided between a building and a street or other feature, as specified by a municipal code.

shared economy: Peer-to-peer interaction and sharing of resources such as vehicles (Lyft) and homes (Airbnb).

sick building syndrome: A set of symptoms reported by people with shared exposure through living or working in a building, including irritation of the nose, eyes, and mucous membranes; fatigue; dry skin; and headaches.

site plan: A scale drawing showing proposed uses for a parcel of land reflecting the development program and applicable regulations.

Slow Streets: A program that uses signage and temporary barriers to slow speed and limit vehicle traffic and to promote socially distanced walking, biking, and running activities.

slum: *See* informal settlement.

Smart City: An urban area that features systematic collection and use of data, using Internet of Things sensors and technologies, to manage operations and resources efficiently.

smart growth: An urban planning approach that aims to manage the growth and land use of a community so as to minimize damage to the environment, reduce sprawl, and build livable, walkable, mixed-use communities.

social capital: The networks, relationships, and social trust shared among people that facilitate coordination and cooperation for mutual benefit. Bonding social capital refers to ties between community members who are similar to each other with respect to socioeconomic status, race and ethnicity, religious affiliation, or other dimensions of social identity; bridging social capital refers to ties between community members that cut across these dimensions.

social cohesion: The perception of trust and feelings of solidarity associated with belonging to a group.

social contagion: The social transmission of attitudes, beliefs, or behaviors, propelled by such mechanisms as imitation, conformity, universality, and mimicry.

social-ecological model: A health behavior model that explains the complex and overlapping interplay across individual, relationship, community, societal, and environmental factors that puts people at risk or promotes their health and well-being.

social-ecological system: An integrated system that includes human societies and ecosystems in which humans are viewed as part of nature.

social infrastructure: Institutions and facilities such as schools, libraries, and churches that shape the ways in which people interact.

social isolation: The objective experience of being alone. *See also* loneliness.

Software-as-a-Service (SaaS): The hosting and provision of apps by third parties and individuals across the internet.

spatial injustice: Unequal allocation of socially valued resources (i.e., jobs, political power, social status, income, social services, environmental goods) in space, as well as unequal opportunities to make use of these resources over time.

spatial scale: A concept of geographic extent, ranging from small (such as a room or building) to intermediate (such as a neighborhood or city) to large (such as a region, nation, or planet).

special or conditional use permit: In zoning, a permit issued after public review that allows a previously excluded use or activity in a specific zone.

spillover: The process by which a pathogen is transmitted from a reservoir host species to a recipient host species. Zoonotic spillover is transmission from wildlife or domestic animals to humans.

stormwater: Surface water resulting from heavy falls of rain or snow.

stress: The feeling of not having the resources to meet the demands of the moment. Stress can trigger endocrine and neurologic responses that, if prolonged, may be unhealthy.

structural inequality: A system of privilege created by organizations, institutions, governments, or social networks that advantages some people and marginalizes or disadvantages other people.

structural violence: Acts of neglect or harm by formal or informal institutions, including racism, police violence, and other biases.

subdivision ordinances: Local ordinances that outline specific requirements for the conversion of undivided land into building lots for residential or other purposes.

subdivision regulations: *See* subdivision ordinances.

subjective well-being: A positive assessment of one's circumstances, comprised of affective (emotional) and cognitive (evaluative) components, usually assessed through self-evaluations of satisfaction with work, family and social relations, levels of interest and engagement, and general fulfillment in life.

substandard housing: A house or apartment that does not have a safe, working kitchen, bathroom, or plumbing or electrical service or that lacks an adequate source of heat and that may have leaks, moisture damage, pest portals of entry, and inadequate lighting.

suburban sprawl: The unplanned and often haphazard growth of an urban area across a larger geographic area. *See also* urban sprawl.

Supplemental Nutrition Assistance Program (SNAP): An antihunger program through the US Department of Agriculture Food and Nutrition Service that provides nutrition benefits to supplement the food budget of low-wage working families, low-income seniors, people with disabilities living on fixed incomes, and other households with low incomes.

surveillance: In epidemiology, the ongoing systematic collection, analysis, and interpretation of data essential to the planning, implementation, and evaluation of public health practice.

sustainability: A dynamic process that assures the persistence of natural and human systems in an equitable manner.

sustainability native: Someone who has grown up immersed in the language and practice of sustainability and for whom sustainability comes naturally.

sustainable development: Development that meets the needs of the present without compromising the ability of future generations to meet their own needs and that balances social, economic, and environmental concerns.

Sustainable Development Goals: The seventeen global goals for development for all countries established by the United Nations through a participatory process and elaborated in the 2030 Agenda for Sustainable Development.

systematic review: A structured approach to evidence synthesis that identifies and combines available studies according to formal procedures designed to minimize bias.

system safety: The application of engineering and management principles, criteria, and techniques to achieve acceptable risk within the constraints of operational effectiveness and suitability, schedule, and cost throughout the system's life cycle.

taking: An appropriation of private property by government action, typically through the exercise of eminent domain. The private owner is generally entitled to compensation.

telehealth: The use of information and communications technologies to support remote health care services, health education, public health, and health administration; also called telemedicine.

telework: A work arrangement under which an employee performs work duties from home or another location rather than at the usual workplace; also called telecommuting or working from home.

tenement house: A house or low-rise (five to seven stories) apartment building carved into separate residences and rented to individuals and families in overcrowded US cities in the nineteenth century. Residents experienced cramped quarters, poor lighting and ventilation, and no or limited indoor plumbing conditions.

third place: A social place that is neither home (first place) nor workplace (second place), such as parks, pubs, barbershops, churches, and libraries. Popularized by sociologist Ray Oldenburg, who emphasized the role of third places in civil society and social capital.

tight building: A building designed to minimize the exchange of indoor and outdoor air as an energy-saving strategy but that thereby risks accumulating contaminants in indoor air.

traditional neighborhood design: An approach to planning neighborhoods that features human scale, diversity of land uses, walkability, connectivity, and public spaces, drawing inspiration from historical approaches to city planning.

transdisciplinary: Integrating formal evidence from multiple research disciplines with nonresearch evidence in a way that fosters engagement and creates new knowledge and theory to achieve a common goal. Transdisciplinary approaches contrast with multidisciplinary approaches, in which research disciplines work in parallel while following their individual precepts and ways of working, and with interdisciplinary approaches, in which they integrate to create new knowledge and theory, but without transcending the boundaries of the research community.

transit death spiral: A vicious cycle of reduced public transit use leading to reduced revenues and in turn to reduced service, deferred maintenance, and staffing shortfalls, which lead to further decreased ridership.

transit-oriented development (TOD): A pedestrian-oriented, walkable, high density, high-quality, mixed-use development near a rail or bus station with limited parking, thereby integrating mass transit into land use planning.

transportation planning: The profession and the process that assess transportation needs in a defined geographic area, project future needs, design transportation solutions, and allocate transportation investments.

ultraviolet germicidal irradiation (UVGI): The use of ultraviolet energy to kill viral, bacterial, and fungal organisms in a building or on a surface.

unintentional injury: Inadvertent injury resulting from events such as motor vehicle crashes, falls, drowning, and poisoning.

universal design (UD): The design of products and environments to be usable by all people, to the greatest extent possible, without the need for adaptation or specialized design.

upzoning: The process of increasing the zoning density in a neighborhood, often allowing multifamily units on lots that were previously limited to single-family houses.

urban design: The art and science of designing the physical features of cities and towns.

urban growth boundary: A line drawn around a metropolitan area, designating the limits of allowable growth. Land outside the boundary is protected from new development.

urban heat island: Urban areas that are warmer than surrounding suburban and rural areas due to the concentration of heat-retaining artificial surfaces, the emission of waste heat, and other factors, posing increased risk to residents during hot weather.

urban planning: The profession dedicated to envisioning, planning, and monitoring the development and redevelopment of towns, cities, and entire regions, especially for land use, transportation, and environmental decisions; also called urban and regional planning, town planning.

urban renewal: The process used by local governments to redevelop land deemed blighted, generally in inner cities, to create opportunities for new housing, businesses, and other economic development.

urban sprawl: The unplanned and often haphazard growth of an urban area across a larger geographic area, characterized by low-density land use, low connectivity, and dependence on the automobile for transportation.

utilitarian physical activity: Physical activity that is done for the purpose of work or of moving from one destination to another, usually by walking or bicycling.

vehicle miles traveled (VMT): The total number of miles traveled by motor vehicles in a given geographic area and specific time period.

virtual water: *See* embodied water.

visitability: An affordable, sustainable, and inclusive design approach for integrating basic accessibility features as a routine construction practice into all newly built homes.

vulnerability: The propensity or predisposition to be adversely affected. Vulnerability encompasses a variety of concepts and elements, including sensitivity or susceptibility to harm and lack of capacity to cope and adapt.

walkability: A feature of urban form reflecting the ease and convenience of walking to common destinations; areas with greater walkability have mixed land use, connected streets, sidewalks that are in good condition, features that protect pedestrians from traffic, and pleasant scenery.

walkability audit: *See* walkability checklist.

walkability checklist: A systematic assessment of pedestrian infrastructure in a neighborhood used to identify sites where improvements are needed.

walkable community: A community in which it is easy and safe for all people to walk to get goods and services or for recreation or employment.

Walk Score: An index based on Google Maps that incorporates distances from a specific location to stores, parks, schools, and other destinations to provide a walkability score ranging from 0 (car-dependent) to 100 ("walker's paradise").

wastewater: Water that has been used in the home, in a business, or as part of an industrial process.

water footprint: The amount of freshwater consumed or polluted in the production or supply of goods and services.

water paradox: The complex relationship humankind has with water because it is essential to life and is perceived as abundant and accessible, yet water shortages are increasingly plaguing all nations.

water stress: A situation in which the water resources in a region or country are insufficient for its needs.

weatherization: The process of upgrading features on an older home to improve energy efficiency.

zero-step entrance: A building entrance with no steps, a maximum one-to-twelve slope, and a minimum three-foot door width to facilitate wheelchair access.

zoning: The legal regulation of the allowable use of property and the physical configuration of property development for the protection of public health, safety, and welfare.

zoning code: *See* zoning ordinance.

zoning ordinance: Legislation and regulation that specifies allowable land uses.

ABOUT THE EDITORS

Nisha Botchwey, PhD, MCRP, MPH, is a planning and public health scholar and the dean of the Hubert H. Humphrey School of Public Affairs at the University of Minnesota. Botchwey previously served as associate professor in Georgia Tech's School of City and Regional Planning, adjunct professor of environmental health in Emory University's Rollins School of Public Health, associate dean of academic programs at Georgia Tech Professional Education, and associate professor of urban and environmental planning and public health at the University of Virginia. Botchwey's planning and public health contributions focus on youth advocacy for health equity and healthy planning pedagogy. She co-authored *Health Impact Assessment in the United States* (Springer, 2014) and multiple peer-reviewed publications. Botchwey earned her AB in environmental science and public policy from Harvard, her MCRP and PhD in city and regional planning from the University of Pennsylvania, and her MPH from the University of Virginia.

Andrew L. Dannenberg, MD, MPH, is an affiliate professor in the Department of Environmental and Occupational Health Sciences and the Department of Urban Design and Planning at the University of Washington. Before coming to Seattle, he served as team lead of the Healthy Community Design Initiative at the US Centers for Disease Control and Prevention (CDC). His research and teaching focus on the health aspects of community design, including land use, transportation, urban planning, equity, climate change, and other issues related to the built environment. Previously, he served as director of CDC's public health training division, as preventive medicine residency director and injury prevention epidemiologist at the Johns Hopkins School of Public Health, and as a cardiovascular epidemiologist at the National Institutes of Health. Dannenberg is board-certified in preventive medicine and was previously board-certified in family practice. He served as lead editor of the first edition of this book. He received his AB from Swarthmore, MD from Stanford, and MPH from Johns Hopkins.

Howard Frumkin, MD, MPH, DrPH, is professor emeritus of environmental and occupational health sciences at the University of Washington School of Public Health and senior vice president of the Trust for Public Land. He previously served as head of the "Our Planet, Our Health" initiative at the Wellcome Trust in London, as dean of the University of Washington School of Public Health, as director of the CDC National Center for Environmental Health and Agency for Toxic Substances and Disease Registry (NCEH/ATSDR), and as professor and chair of environmental and occupational health at Emory University's Rollins School of Public Health. His career has focused on health aspects of climate change, the built environment, nature contact, and sustainability. In addition to the first edition of this book, his previous books include *Environmental Health: From Global to Local* (Jossey-Bass, 3rd ed., 2016), *Planetary Health: Protecting Nature to Protect Ourselves* (Island Press, 2020), and *Planetary Health: Safeguarding Human Health and the Environment in the Anthropocene* (Cambridge University Press, 2021). He was educated at Brown (AB), the University of Pennsylvania (MD), and Harvard (MPH and DrPH).

LIST OF CONTRIBUTORS

Manal J. Aboelata, MPH: Deputy executive director, Prevention Institute (chapter 21)

Charisma S. Acey, MPP, PhD: Associate professor of city and regional planning, University of California, Berkeley (chapter 6)

Mariela Alfonzo, PhD: Founder and chief executive officer, State of Place (chapter 24)

Isabelle Anguelovski, PhD: ICREA research professor, Catalan Institution for Research and Advanced Studies; director, Barcelona Lab for Urban Environmental Justice and Sustainability, Autonomous University of Barcelona (chapter 9)

Jonathan A. Bach, PE, CSP, CIH: Prevention through Design coordinator, National Institute for Occupational Safety and Health, US Centers for Disease Control and Prevention (chapter 13)

Jasneet K. Bains, MPH, MURP: Associate program manager, Prevention Institute (chapter 21)

Claire L. Barnett, MBA: Executive director, Healthy Schools Network (chapter 15)

Hugh Barton, DipTP, MPhil, MRTPI, AoU: Emeritus professor of planning, health and sustainability, WHO Collaborating Centre for Healthy Urban Planning, University of the West of England, Bristol

Timothy Beatley, PhD: Teresa Heinz Professor of Sustainable Communities, Department of Urban and Environmental Planning, University of Virginia School of Architecture

Eugenie L. Birch, PhD, FAICP: Lawrence C. Nussdorf Professor of Urban Research and co-director, Penn Institute for Urban Research, Weitzman School of Design, University of Pennsylvania (chapter 20)

Emmanuel Frimpong Boamah, PhD: Assistant professor of urban and regional planning, University at Buffalo (chapter 6)

Carolyn Cannuscio, ScD: Associate professor of family medicine and community health, Perelman School of Medicine, University of Pennsylvania (chapter 3)

Chun-Yen Chang, PhD: Professor of horticulture and landscape architecture, National Taiwan University (chapter 7)

Olivia E. Chatman, MCRP: Program associate—Food Initiatives, Reinvestment Fund (chapter 23)

L. Casey Chosewood, MD, MPH: Director, Office for Total Worker Health, National Institute for Occupational Safety and Health, US Centers for Disease Control and Prevention (chapter 13)

Helen V. S. Cole, DrPH, MPH: Co-coordinator for Urban Environment and Juan de la Cierva Incorporation Fellow, Health and Equity Research, Barcelona Lab for Urban Environmental Justice and Sustainability, Autonomous University of Barcelona (chapter 9)

Christopher Coutts, PhD, MPH: Professor of urban and regional planning, Florida State University (chapter 19)

Priyanka Nadia deSouza, MSc, MBA, PhD: Assistant professor of urban and regional planning, University of Colorado Denver (chapter 4)

Jennifer R. DuBose, MS: Principal research associate, College of Design, Georgia Institute of Technology (chapter 14)

Roxanne Dupuis, MSPH: PhD student, Department of Social and Behavioral Sciences, Harvard T. H. Chan School of Public Health (chapter 3)

Erika Sita Eitland, MPH, ScD: Director, Human Experience (Hx) Lab, Perkins + Will (chapter 15)

Carolyn A. Fan: PhD student, Department of Health Systems and Population Health, University of Washington School of Public Health (chapter 22)

Yakut Gazi, PhD: Associate dean for learning systems, Georgia Tech Professional Education, Georgia Institute of Technology (chapter 23)

Karen Glanz, PhD, MPH: George A. Weiss University Professor, Perelman School of Medicine and School of Nursing, University of Pennsylvania (chapter 3)

Susan Handy, MS, PhD: Distinguished professor, Department of Environmental Science and Policy, University of California, Davis

J. Aaron Hipp, PhD: Associate professor of community health and sustainability, College of Natural Resources, North Carolina State University (chapter 24)

Rachel Hodgdon: President and chief executive officer, International WELL Building Institute (chapter 27)

Katherine Britt Indvik, MSc: Policy engagement specialist, Urban Health Collaborative, Dornsife School of Public Health, Drexel University (chapter 17, 18)

Richard J. Jackson, MD, MPH: Professor emeritus, Fielding School of Public Health, University of California, Los Angeles (foreword)

David E. Jacobs, PhD, CIH: Chief scientist, National Center for Healthy Housing (chapter 12)

Xiangrong Jiang, PhD: Postdoctoral associate, Department of Landscape Architecture, University of Illinois at Urbana-Champaign (chapter 7)

Ichiro Kawachi, MD, PhD: John L. Loeb and Frances Lehman Loeb Professor of Social Epidemiology, Harvard T. H. Chan School of Public Health (chapter 8)

Kasley Killam, MPH: Research affiliate, Harvard T. H. Chan School of Public Health; Founder, Social Health Labs (chapter 8)

Patrick Lott Kinney, ScD: Beverly Brown Professor of Urban Health, Boston University School of Public Health (chapter 4)

Jordana L. Maisel, PhD: Director of research, IDEA Center, University at Buffalo (chapter 10)

Blessing Mberu, PhD: Senior research scientist and head of Urbanization and Wellbeing Unit, African Population and Health Research Center (chapter 27)

Meaghan McSorley, MPH, MURP: PhD student, School of City and Regional Planning, Georgia Institute of Technology (chapter 2)

M. Renée Umstattd Meyer, PhD, MCHES, FAAHB: Associate dean for research and professor of public health, Robbins College of Health and Human Sciences, Baylor University (chapter 2)

Charles Montgomery: Author, *Happy City: Transforming Our Lives through Urban Design* (chapter 27)

Christopher N. Morrison, PhD: Assistant professor of epidemiology, Mailman School of Public Health, Columbia University (chapter 5)

Toks Omishakin, MURP, PhD: Director, California Department of Transportation (Caltrans) (chapter 27)

Tolullah Oni, MMBS, MPH (Epi), MMed, MD (Res): Public health physician and urban epidemiologist, MRC Epidemiology Unit, University of Cambridge; honorary associate professor, Research Initiative for Cities Health and Equity, School of Public Health and Family Medicine, University of Cape Town (chapter 27)

Kimberley Clare O'Sullivan, PhD: Senior research fellow, He Kainga Oranga/Housing and Health Research Programme, and New Zealand Centre for Sustainable Cities; Department of Public Health–Wellington, University of Otago (chapter 18)

Corinne Peek-Asa, PhD, MPH: Vice Chancellor for Research, University of California, San Diego (chapter 5)

Carlo Ratti, PhD: Professor of urban technologies and planning and director, SENSEable City Lab, Massachusetts Institute of Technology; founding partner, CRA-Carlo Ratti Associati (chapter 27)

Amanda Reddy, MS: Executive director, National Center for Healthy Housing (chapter 12)

Paul A. Schulte, PhD: Director, Division of Science Integration, National Institute for Occupational Safety and Health, US Centers for Disease Control and Prevention (chapter 13)

Bea Sennewald, MArch, AIA: Director of projects, Article 25, London, UK (chapter 14)

Sonia Sequeira, MPH, MSW: Community engagement manager, Atlanta City Studio, Department of City Planning, City of Atlanta (chapter 24)

Sagar Shah, PhD, AICP: Planning and community health manager, American Planning Association, Chicago, Illinois

Mitchell J. Silver, FAICP, Hon. ASLA, Hon. RTPI, Hon. FPIA, FAcSS: Former commissioner, New York City Department of Parks and Recreation; principal, vice president of urban planning, McAdams, Raleigh, North Carolina (chapter 27)

José G. Siri, PhD, MPH: Senior science lead for cities, urbanisation, and health; Our Planet, Our Health Priority Area, Wellcome Trust (chapters 17, 18)

Bruce Stiftel, MRP, PhD, FAICP: Professor emeritus of city and regional planning, Georgia Institute of Technology; chair, Planners for Climate Action research working group, UN-Habitat (chapter 27)

William C. Sullivan, PhD: Professor, Department of Landscape Architecture, University of Illinois at Urbana-Champaign (chapter 7)

Alice Sverdlik, PhD: Lecturer in social development, Global Development Institute, University of Manchester (chapter 27)

Katie Swenson, MArch; Architect, MASS Design Group (chapter 27)

Susan Thompson, PhD: Professor of planning and head, City Wellbeing Program, City Futures Research Centre, School of Built Environment, Faculty of Arts, Design and Architecture, University of New South Wales (chapter 27)

Matthew J. Trowbridge, MD, MPH: Associate professor, University of Virginia School of Medicine; chief medical officer, International WELL Building Institute (chapter 23)

Jason Vargo, MPH, MCRP, PhD: Senior researcher, community development, Federal Reserve Bank of San Francisco; former, lead research scientist, Climate Change and Health Equity Program, California Department of Public Health (chapter 27)

Gregory R. Wagner, MD: Adjunct professor, Department of Environmental Health, Harvard T. H. Chan School of Public Health (chapter 13)

Patrice C. Williams, PhD, MPH: Research scientist, Department of Urban Studies and Planning, Massachusetts Institute of Technology (chapter 19)

Nsedu Obot Witherspoon, MPH: Executive director, Children's Environmental Health Network (chapter 10)

Chia-Ching Wu: PhD student, Department of Landscape Architecture, University of Illinois at Urbana-Champaign (chapter 7)

Craig Zimring, PhD: Professor and director, SimTigrate Design Lab, Georgia Institute of Technology (chapter 14)

INDEX

Page numbers followed by "b," "f," and "t" indicate boxes, figures, and tables.

cognitive functioning, 115, 118–119, 169

cohort studies, 12, 442

Coleman, James, 130

collective efficacy, 130, 131, 375

communal living, 135–136, 137t

CommunitAR, 431–432

Community Development Block Grants, 215

community engagement: 371-387; barriers to, 381, 382–383t; COVID-19 pandemic and, 380b; inequity and, 381; Medellin, Colombia and, 384b; overview of, 373–374, 373b, 384–385; people involved with, 374–375; political nature of land use and, 381–384; Portland, Oregon and, 385b; principles for, 377; purpose of, 375–376; social capital and, 376; strategies and tactics for, 377–380; technology and, 380–381

community gardens/allotments, 16, 59, 60f, 138, 289, 392t, 446t

Community Guide, 12, 440, 444

community-based participatory research, 441

compact development, 192–193

compassion, 490

complete streets programs, 40, 155, 175-177,194, 365, 440, 442-444, 450t

comprehensive plans, 190, 362–363

comprehensive zoning codes, 356

confounding, 12

connectivity, 37, 45t, 188, 192, 193f, 340–341, 391, 442

conservation zoning, 17, 18

Constitution (U.S.), 357–358

consumption-based emissions framework, 301, 304f

continuous improvement, 226, 228

Convergence Partnership, 441

cooking, 72–75, 91

cost-benefit analyses, 215, 442

cost-effectiveness, 10, 92–93, 442

COVID-19 pandemic: 457-473; built environment factors increasing risk from, 458-461; climate change and, 307; community engagement and, 380b; equity and, 428; food access and, 62; future and, 484, 491; health decisions and, 345, 346b; loneliness and, 138; long-term implications of, 462–466; mental health and, 123–124; nature contact and, 281–282, 292–294, 293–294b; overview of, 457–458; physical activity and, 46b; resilience and, 330b; schools and, 268b; technology and, 431, 432, 433; telehealth and, 252; training and, 414; transportation and, 197; unequal vulnerability to, 148; use of street spaces and, 194; vulnerable populations and, 173b; water supplies and, 101; workplace safety and, 233

crime prevention through environmental design (CPTED), 88–90, 89f, 120, 234

cross-sectional studies, 11–12

crowding, 119–120, 269–270, 458–459

Cuba, 321–322, 332

Culdesac Tempe project (Phoenix), 191

cumulative exposures, 122

curb ramps, 170f

Curitiba, Brazil, 194–195

cycling: air quality and, 79b; benchmarking 401t; bike sharing and, 194; ciclovía movement and, 36, 40, 41f, 195–196, 344, 344f, 464; civic mobilization and, 155; COVID-19 pandemic and, 465; Davis, California and, 186–187; injuries and, 445t; metrics for, 390f; micromobility and, 194–196

data sources, 401–402t

Davis, California, 186–187

daylight exposure, 118, 286

Deane, Vanessa L., 412, 413, 413f

New Urbanism, 19, 133–134, 192, 364–365, 366b

Nightingale, Florence, 245

nitrogen oxides (NO$_x$), 68t, 70, 71b

noise pollution, 209, 271–272, 285

nonpoint-source pollution, 101

normalized difference vegetation index (NDVI), 390

nudge theory, 342

null preemption, 359

nutrition, 53–58

Nutrition Environment Measures Study (NEMS), 57–58, 399t

Oakland, California, 34–35, 46b

obesity, 53–54

occupational health, 222–242; COVID-19 pandemic and, 463; future of work and, 236–237; health care settings and, 245; healthy housing and, 215; overview of problems in, 222–224, 223f, 224f, 225f. *See also* design safety review process

Occupational Safety and Health Administration (OSHA), 224–225

oil wells, 276t

Ojullu, Abang and Ananaya, 202–203

Oldenberg, Ray, 132

Olmsted, Frederick Law, 14–15, 289–290, 290f

Omishakin, Toks, 480

Oni, Tolullah, 481–482

online shopping, 57

open streets, 36, 40, 41f, 344, 344f, 464

Orchard Village (Maryland), 133–134

Our Common Future report (WCED), 22

overnutrition, 54

ozone, 68t, 70, 71b, 73f, 306

Pandemic Electronic Benefit Transfer (P-EBT) program, 62b

pandemics: food insecurity and, 62b; health care settings and, 245–246; research

suggestions for, 450t; workplace safety and, 232–233. *See also COVID-19 pandemic*

Paradise, California, 300–301, 301f

paratransit, 176

Paris Agreement, 358, 360

parking, 189

parks, 289–291, 485

participatory budgeting, 384b

participatory democracy, 376

particulate matter (PM), 68t, 69–70, 70f, 71t, 72f, 73f, 314b

passive interventions, in injury prevention, 87

passive survivability, in building design, 327

pathogens, 245–246

peer pressure, 131

people-oriented design, 332

person-environment fit theory: children and, 164–168, 168b, 177t; disabled people and, 171–174, 177t; older adults and, 168–171, 177t; overview of, 165, 177–178; solutions to challenges and, 176–177; universal design and, 174–176

pesticides, 264t

Philadelphia, Pennsylvania, 52–53, 53f, 106, 106b, 362, 434–435

physical activity: moderate-to-vigorous, guidelines for, 35; active recreation and, 41–44; active transportation and, 36–41; nature contact and, 285; overview of, 34–36, 44–47; research suggestions for, 445t

place attachment, 115, 287

planetary health, 22–23, 301

planning, 17, 155–156, 210, 211b

platform economy, 236

point-source pollution, 101

policies, 55, 210–215, 355t, 449–450t. *See also* governance

policy research, 442

pollution: *See* air quality, water quality

spillover, 307

standards, 235–236, 331, 359–360

State of Place, 427

Stiftel, Bruce, 486

stores, 55–56, 57–58, 155

storm surges, 106

stormwater management, 106–107, 292

streets, 463–464. *See also* complete streets programs; open streets

stress, 115–118, 131, 228t, 282

stress-buffering effect, 131

structural inequality, 160, 346–347, 348b

structural violence, 88

subdivision ordinances, 190

subjective well-being, 115, 116

suicide, 167

Supplemental Nutrition Assistance Program (SNAP), 56

surveillance, 10–11, 389–390

sustainability: behavioral choices and, 347–349; certification programs for, 403t, 404–406; food environment and, 61b; health care settings and, 247–249; measures of, 390; overview of, 22–24; research suggestions for, 450t; resilience and, 323; schools and, 269b; workplace safety and, 234–235

sustainability natives, 477

Sustainable Development Goals (SDGs), 23–24, 23f, 315

Sverdlik, Alice, 487–488

Swenson, Katie, 489

System for Observing Play and Recreation in Communities (SOPARC), 399t

system safety, 225

systematic reviews, 12

systems thinking, 475

tactical urbanism, 44

takings, 15

Talen, Emily, 17

taxation, 57, 158t

technology: built environment and, 426–428; challenges and equity and, 428–429; community engagement and, 380–381; efficiency, connectedness and, 434–435; health and, 428; overview of, 423; research suggestions for, 450–451t; Smart City and, 426f; Smart Places and, 425; urban health, big data and, 429–434

telehealth, 252

telework, 236

tenement house laws, 356

tertiary prevention, 13

Thackrah, Charles Turner, 7

Theewaterskloof dam (Cape Town, South Africa), 328f

theory of planned behavior, 339

theory of reasoned action, 339

third places, 132

Thompson, Susan, 490

tight buildings, 20

tobacco smoke, 214

tools, 389–390, 398–402, 399–400t

total maximum daily load (TMDL), 107

Total Worker Health research program (NIOSH), 232

Toxic Release Inventory facilities, 146

Toxic Substances Control Act of 1976, 262

toxins, 145–147, 166, 167–168, 205–210

traditional neighborhood design, 192, 193f

traffic calming, 194

trailing indicators, 229

training: building curricula for, 414–415; diversity and, 415–416, 417t; next steps for, 413–414; overview of, 412–413, 421; in real world, 416t, 417–421; resilience and, 331–332

transit, 176, 191, 464–465

transit-oriented development (TOD), 19, 194

TransMilenio system (Bogotá, Colombia), 195, 196f